Natural Products Isolation

METHODS IN BIOTECHNOLOGY™

John M. Walker, SERIES EDITOR

7. **Affinity Biosensors:** *Techniques and Protocols,* edited by *Kim R. Rogers and Ashok Mulchandani, 1998*

6. **Enzyme and Microbial Biosensors:** *Techniques and Protocols,* edited by *Ashok Mulchandani and Kim R. Rogers, 1998*

5. **Biopesticides:** *Use and Delivery,* edited by *Franklin R. Hall and Julius J. Menn, 1998*

4. **Natural Products Isolation,** edited by *Richard J. P. Cannell, 1998*

3. **Recombinant Proteins from Plants:** *Production and Isolation of Clinically Useful Compounds,* edited by *Charles Cunningham and Andrew J. R. Porter, 1998*

2. **Protocols in Bioremediation,** edited by *David Sheehan, 1997*

1. **Immobilization of Enzymes and Cells,** edited by *Gordon F. Bickerstaff, 1997*

METHODS IN BIOTECHNOLOGY™

Natural Products Isolation

Isolation

Edited by

Richard J. P. Cannell

Glaxo Wellcome Research & Development, Stevenage, Herts, UK

Humana Press ✻ Totowa, New Jersey

Library of Congress Cataloging in Publication Data

Main entry under title:

Methods in molecular biology™.

Natural products isolation/edited by Richard J. P. Cannell.
　　p. cm.—(Methods in biotechnology; 4)
　　Includes index.
　　ISBN 0-89603-362-7 (alk. paper)
　　1. Natural products.　2. Extraction (Chemistry).　I. Cannell, Richard J. P.　II. Series: Methods in biotechnology　(Totowa, NJ); 4.
　　QD415.N355　1998
　　547.7—dc21　　　　　　　　　　　　　　　　　　　　　　　98-16651
　　　　　　　　　　　　　　　　　　　　　　　　　　　　　　　　CIP

Preface

Biodiversity is a term commonly used to denote the variety of species and the multiplicity of forms of life. But this variety is deeper than is generally imagined. In addition to the processes of primary metabolism that involve essentially the same chemistry across great swathes of life, there are a myriad of secondary metabolites—natural products—usually confined to a particular group of organisms, or to a single species, or even to a single strain growing under certain conditions. In most cases we do not really know what biological role these compounds play, except that they represent a treasure trove of chemistry that can be of both interest and benefit to us. Tens of thousands of natural products have been described, but in a world where we are not even close to documenting all the extant species, there are almost certainly many more thousands of compounds waiting to be discovered.

The purpose of *Natural Products Isolation* is to give some practical guidance in the process of extraction and isolation of natural products. Literature reports tend to focus on natural products once they have been isolated—on their structural elucidation, or their biological or chemical properties. Extraction details are usually minimal and sometimes nonexistent, except for a mention of the general techniques used. Even when particular conditions of a separation are reported, they assume knowledge of the practical methodology required to carry out the experiment, and of the reasoning behind the conditions used. *Natural Products Isolation* aims to provide the foundation of this knowledge. Following an introduction to the isolation process, there are a series of chapters dealing with the major techniques used, followed by chapters on other aspects of isolation, such as those related to particular sample types, taking short cuts, or making the most of the isolation process. The emphasis is not so much on the isolation of a known natural product for which there may already be reported methods, but on the isolation of compounds of unknown identity.

Every natural product isolation is different and so the process is not really suited to a practical manual that gives detailed recipe-style methods. However, the aim has been to give as much practical direction and advice as possible, together with examples, so that the potential extractor can at least make a reasonable attempt at an isolation.

Natural Products Isolation is aimed mainly at scientists with little experience of natural products extraction, such as research students undertaking natural products-based research, or scientists from other disciplines who find they wish to isolate a small molecule from a biological mixture. However, there may also be something of interest for more experienced natural products scientists who wish to explore other methods of extraction, or use the book as a general reference. In particular, it is hoped that the book will be of value to scientists in less scientifically developed countries, where there is little experience of natural products work, but where there is great biodiversity and, hence, great potential for utilizing and sustaining that biodiversity through the discovery of novel, useful natural products.

Richard J. P. Cannell

Contents

Preface v

Contributors ix

1 How to Approach the Isolation of a Natural Product
   Richard J. P. Cannell 1

2 Initial Extraction and Product Capture
   F. Patrick Gailliot 53

3 Supercritical Fluid Methods
   Ed Venkat and Srinivas Kothandaraman 91

4 Isolation by Low-Pressure Column Chromatography
   Gino M. Salituro and Claude Dufresne 111

5 Isolation by Ion-Exchange Methods
   Claude Dufresne 141

6 Isolation by Preparative HPLC
   Paul Stead 165

7 Isolation by Planar Chromatography
   Simon Gibbons and Alexander I. Gray 209

8 Separation by High-Speed Countercurrent Chromatography
   James McAlpine 247

9 Crystallization and Final Stages of Purification
   Norman Shankland, Alastair J. Florence,
      and Richard J. P. Cannell 261

10 Dereplication and Partial Identification of Natural Products
   Frank VanMiddlesworth and Richard J. P. Cannell 279

11 Purification of Water-Soluble Natural Products
   Yuzuru Shimizu 329

12 Special Problems with the Extraction of Plants
   Gloria L. Silva, Ik-Soo Lee, and A. Douglas Kinghorn 343

13 Isolation of Marine Natural Products
   Amy E. Wright 365

14 Scale-Up of Natural Products Isolation
   Michael S. Verrall and Stephen R. C. Warr 409

15 Follow-Up of Natural Product Isolation
      Richard J. P. Cannell 425

Index 465

Contributors

RICHARD J. P. CANNELL • *Glaxo Wellcome Research & Development, Stevenage, Herts, UK*

CLAUDE DUFRESNE • *Merck Research Laboratories, Rahway, NJ*

ALASTAIR J. FLORENCE • *Department of Pharmaceutical Sciences, University of Strathclyde, Glasgow, UK*

F. PATRICK GAILLIOT • *Merck Research Laboratories, Rahway, NJ*

SIMON GIBBONS • *Department of Natural Products Chemistry, Xenova Ltd., Slough, UK*

ALEXANDER I. GRAY • *Department of Pharmaceutical Sciences, University of Strathclyde, Glasgow, UK*

A. DOUGLAS KINGHORN • *Department of Medicinal Chemistry and Pharmacognosy, College of Pharmacy, University of Illinois at Chicago, IL*

SRINIVAS KOTHANDARAMAN • *Rutgers University, Piscataway, NJ*

IK-SOO LEE • *College of Pharmacy, Chonnam National University, Yongbong-Dong, Kwangju, Korea*

JAMES MCALPINE • *Phytera, Worcester, MA*

GINO M. SALITURO • *Merck Research Laboratories, Rahway, NJ*

NORMAN SHANKLAND • *Department of Pharmaceutical Sciences, University of Strathclyde, Glasgow, UK*

YUZURU SHIMIZU • *Department of Biomedical Sciences, University of Rhode Island, Kingston, RI*

GLORIA L. SILVA • *Universidad Nacional de Cordoba, Facultad de Ciencias Quimicas, Cordoba, Argentina*

PAUL STEAD • *Glaxo Wellcome Research & Development, Stevenage, Herts, UK*

FRANK VANMIDDLESWORTH • *Glaxo Wellcome Inc., Research Triangle Park, NC*

ED VENKAT • *Merck Research Laboratories, Rahway, NJ*

MICHAEL S. VERRALL • *SmithKline Beecham Pharmaceuticals, Brockham Park, Betchworth, Surrey, UK*

STEPHEN R. C. WARR • *SmithKline Beecham Pharmaceuticals, Brockham Park, Betchworth, Surrey, UK*

AMY E. WRIGHT • *Division of Biomedical Marine Research, Harbor Branch Oceanographic Institution, Fort Pierce, FL*

1

How to Approach the Isolation of a Natural Product

Richard J. P. Cannell

1. Introduction

It can seem a formidable task, faced with a liter of fermentation broth–a dark, viscous sludge–knowing that in there is one group of molecules that has to be separated from all the rest. Those molecules possibly represent only about 0.0001%, or 1 ppm of the total biomass and are dispersed throughout the organism, possibly intimately bound up with other molecules. Like the proverbial needle in a haystack, you have to remove lot of hay to be left with just the needle, without knowing what the needle looks like or where in the haystack it is.

1.1. What Are Natural Products?

The term "natural product" is perhaps something of a misnomer. Strictly speaking, any biological molecule is a natural product, but the term is usually reserved for secondary metabolites, small molecules (mol wt < 1500 amu approx) produced by an organism but that are not strictly necessary for the survival of the organism, unlike the more prevalent macromolecules such as proteins, nucleic acids, and polysaccharides that make up the basic machinery for the more fundamental processes of life.

Secondary metabolites are a very broad group of metabolites, with no distinct boundaries, and grouped under no single unifying definition. Concepts of secondary metabolism include products of overflow metabolism as a result of nutrient limitation, or shunt metabolites produced during idiophase, defense mechanisms, regulator molecules, and so on. Perhaps the most cogent theory of secondary metabolism has been put forward by Zähner, who described secondary metabolism as evolutionary "elbow room" *(1)*. If a secondary metabolite has no adverse effect on the producing organism at any of the levels of

From: *Methods in Biotechnology, Vol. 4: Natural Products Isolation*
Edited by: R. J. P. Cannell © Humana Press Inc., Totowa, NJ

differentiation, morphogenesis, transport, regulation, or intermediary metabolism, it may be conserved for a relatively long period during which time it may come to confer a selective advantage. Secondary metabolism therefore provides a kind of testing ground where new metabolites have the opportunity, as it were, to exist without being eliminated, during which time they may find a role that will give an advantage to the producing organism. This is supported by the fact that secondary metabolites are often unique to a particular species or group of organisms and, while many act as antifeedants, sex attractants, or antibiotic agents, many have no apparent biological role. It is likely that all these concepts can play some part in understanding the production of the broad group of compounds that come under the heading of secondary metabolite.

Isolation of natural products differs from that of the more prevalent biological macromolecules because natural products are smaller and chemically more diverse than the relatively homogeneous proteins, nucleic acids and carbohydrates, and isolation methods must take this into account.

1.2. The Aim of the Extraction

The two most fundamental questions that should be asked at the outset of an extraction are:

1. What am I trying to isolate?
   There are a number of possible targets of an isolation:
   a. An unknown compound responsible for a particular biological activity.
   b. A certain compound known to be produced by a particular organism.
   c. A group of compounds within an organism that are all related in some way, such as by a common structural feature.
   d. All of the metabolites produced by one natural product source that are not produced by a different "control" source, e.g., two species of the same genus, or the same organism grown under different conditions.
   e. A chemical "dissection" of an organism, in order to characterize all of its interesting metabolites, usually those secondary metabolites confined to that organism, or group of organisms, and not ubiquitous in all living systems. Such an inventory might be useful for chemical, ecological, or chemotaxonomic reasons, among others.
2. Why am I trying to isolate it?
   The second fundamental question concerns what one is trying ultimately to achieve, for defining the aims can minimize the work required. Reasons for the extraction might be:
   a. To purify sufficient amount of a compound to characterize it partially or fully.
   b. More specifically, to provide sufficient material to allow for confirmation or denial of a proposed structure. As in many cases this does not require mapping out a complete structure from scratch but perhaps simply comparison with a standard of known structure; it may require less material or only par-

tially pure material. There is no point in removing minor impurities if they do not get in the way of ascertaining whether the compound is, or is not, compound X.

c. The generation/production of the maximum amount of a known compound so that it can be used for further work, such as more extensive biological testing. (Alternatively, it may be more efficient to chemically synthesize the compound; any natural product that is of serious interest, i.e., is required in large amounts, will be considered as a target for synthetic chemistry.)

1.3. Purity

With a clear idea of what one is trying to achieve, one can then question the required level of purity. This in turn might give some indication of the approach to be taken and the purification methods to be employed.

For example, if you are attempting to characterize fully a complex natural product that is present at a low concentration in an extract, you will probably want to produce a compound that is suitable for NMR. The purity needed is dependent on the nature of the compound and of the impurities, but to assign fully a complex structure, material of 95–100% purity is generally required. If the compound is present at high concentration in the starting material and there already exists a standard against which to compare it, structure confirmation can be carried out with less pure material and the purification will probably require fewer steps.

The importance of purity in natural products isolation has been highlighted by Ghisalberti *(2)*, who described two papers that appeared at about the same time, both reporting the isolation from plants of *ent*-kauran-3-oxo-16,17-diol. In one paper, the compound has a melting point of 173–174°C and $[\alpha]_D$–39.2°(CHCl$_3$); in the other, no melting point is reported, but the compound has an $[\alpha]_D$–73.1°(CHCl$_3$). Either the compounds are different or one is significantly less pure than the other.

If a natural product is required for biological testing, it is important to know at least the degree of purity and, preferably, the nature of the impurities. It is always possible that the impurities are giving rise to all or part of the biological activities in question. If a compound is to be used to generate pharmacological or pharmacokinetic data, it is usually important that the material be very pure (generally >99% pure), particularly if the impurities are analogs of the main compound and may themselves be biologically active.

In some cases, a sample need only be partially purified prior to obtaining sufficient structural information. For example, it may be possible to detect the absence of a certain structural feature in a crude mixture—perhaps by absence of a particular ultraviolet (UV) maximum—and conclude that the mixture does not contain compound A. In other cases, such as X-ray crystallography studies, material will almost certainly be required in an extremely pure state, generally >99.9% pure.

It is worth bearing in mind that the relationship between the degree of purity achieved in a natural product extraction, and the amount of work required to achieve this, is very approximately exponential. It is often relatively easy to start with a crude, complex mixture and eliminate more than half of what is not wanted, but it can be a painstaking chore to remove the minor impurities that will turn a 99.5% pure sample into one that is 99.9% pure. It is also probably true to say that this exponential relationship also often holds for the degree of purity achieved versus the yield of natural product. In the same way that no chemical reaction results in 100% yield, no extraction step results in 100% recovery of the natural product. Compound will be lost at every stage; in many cases it may be that, to achieve very high levels of purity, it is necessary to sacrifice much of the desired material. In order to remove all the impurities it may be necessary to take only the cleanest "cuts" from a separation, thus losing much of the target material in the process (though these side fractions can often be reprocessed).

These factors may, of course, have some bearing on the level of purity deemed satisfactory, and it is useful to ask at each stage of the extraction, whether the natural product is sufficiently pure to answer the questions that are to be asked of it.

At present, there are two main reasons why scientists extract natural products: to find out what they are and/or to carry out further experimental work using the purified compound. In the future, it may be easy to determine structures of compounds in complex mixtures; indeed, it is already possible to do this under some circumstances, but at present, most cases of structural determination of an unknown compound require that it be essentially pure. Similarly, to obtain valid biological or chemical data on a natural product usually requires that it be free from the other experimental variables present in the surrounding biological matrix.

1.4. Fractionation

All separation processes involve the division of a mixture into a number of discrete fractions. These fractions may be obvious, physically discrete divisions, such as the two phases of a liquid–liquid extraction, or they may be the contiguous eluate from a chromatography column that is artificially divided by the extractor into fractions.

The type of fractionation depends on the individual sample and the aims of the separation. Typically, a column is run and the eluate divided into a manageable number of even-sized fractions, followed by analysis of the fractions to determine which contain the desired compounds. (So, the eluate from a silica column with a bed volume of 10 mL becomes, perhaps, 20 × 5-mL fractions.) Obviously, collecting the eluate as a large number of very small fractions means that each fraction is more likely to contain a pure compound, but it requires more work in analyzing every fraction. This also runs the risk of spreading the target compound over so many fractions that, if originally present in only low concentrations, it may evade detection in any one of the fractions. If the separation process is relatively crude, it is probably more sensible to collect only a few large, relatively crude fractions and quickly home in on those containing the target.

Alternatively, one may monitor "on-line" and fractionate the eluate accordingly. This is generally used at the later stages of separation for separations of less complex mixtures, typically on high-performance liquid chromatography (HPLC) separations monitored by UV, where one can identify and isolate material corresponding to individual peaks.

1.5. Assays

A point that may seem fairly obvious, but worth reiterating, is that, with a complex mixture from which one or a few specific compounds are to be isolated, a means of keeping track of the compound through the extraction process is needed. There are two main ways to follow a compound: (1) physical assay (for example, HPLC, thin-layer chromatography [TLC], liquid chromatography-mass spectometry [LC-MS], and perhaps involving comparison with a standard), or (2) bioactivity assay.

It is not within the scope of this book to discuss at length biological screening and the rapid developments that are being made in this field, but some typical bioactivity screens are listed in **Table 1**.

There are a number of basic points that should be kept in mind when assaying fractions:

1. Samples dissolved or suspended in a solvent different from the original extraction solvent should be filtered or centrifuged to remove any insoluble matter. Assay samples that include a volatile solvent, or different solvents, are usually best dried and redissolved in the original extraction solvent, water, or other solvent in which the compound is known to be soluble. For example, an aliquot of a methanol extract of a broth may be dried, then resuspended and partitioned between water and chloroform. The two phases, or part thereof, can then be redried, redissolved in equal volumes of methanol, and assayed. This may make subsequent assay easier for two reasons:
   a. The test solvent may not be compatible with the assay.
   b. Redissolving the two phases back into the same solvent makes quantitative and qualitative comparisons much easier, particularly if one of the test solvents is very volatile, creating problems with evaporation and differences in concentration.
2. Samples acidified or basified should be readjusted to their original pH to prevent them from interfering with the assay. If volatile acids/bases are present, they may be removed by evaporation.
3. Controls consisting of the solvents and/or buffers, acids, and so on, without sample, should always be carried out to ensure that observed assay results are in

Table 1
Typical Bioactivity Screens

Activity	Common assay form
Antibacterial	Seeded agar diffusion, turbidometric
Antifungal	Seeded agar diffusion, turbidometric
Enzyme inhibitory	UV, colorimetric, radiolabeled, scintillation proximity assay (SPA)
Antitumor	Cell line
Toxicity	Whole organism, e.g., brine shrimp lethality
Antiparasitic	Whole organism, e.g., insect larvae, antihelminth
Receptor binding	Enzyme-linked immunosorbent assay (ELISA), radioimmunoassay (RIA), SPA, chemiluminescence, fluorescence
Transcription-based	Chemiluminescence, fluorescence

fact caused by the natural product. The separation may result in fractions that do not have homogeneous "backgrounds" and this may affect the assay. For example, a gradient chromatography system may well result in fractions with increasing organic solvent concentration that might itself affect the assay. In order to allow for the effect of this discrepancy, either a series of control samples should be tested–in this case, fractions from a blank gradient run with no sample–and these results subtracted from the assay results, or, all of the fraction aliquots must be treated in a way that allows them to be presented to the assay in the same form. This might mean drying the samples and redissolving them in the same solvent. Care must be taken to redissolve in a solvent compatible with the assay (e.g., methanol, dimethylsufoxide [DMSO]), and that will solubilize compounds eluting from both the polar and nonpolar ends of a gradient elution. Additionally, for practical reasons, it is often preferable not to take samples to complete dryness as it is sometimes difficult to resolubilize all the components. Samples can be partially dried by evaporation or vacuum centrifugation, such that the more volatile organic solvent is removed leaving only the residual aqueous extract; then volumes can be adjusted to give the same relative concentration. Alternatively, samples may be adsorbed each on its own solid phase extractant (*see* **Subheading 2.3.2.**) and then eluted in a small volume of suitable solvent. This can serve both to concentrate and to further clean the sample by "desalting"–separating the compounds from more polar materials or inorganic components that may have been introduced into the mobile phase to improve chromatography, which may affect the assay.

4. Ideally, the assay should be at least semiquantitative, and/or samples should be assayed at a series of dilutions in order to determine where the majority of the target compound resides. It may well be that the separation process, e.g., the chromatography column, dilutes the activity in a way such that it is not detectable in the assay without concentration, and so the nonappearance of an active fraction may

not mean that the activity is lost but that the assay is insufficiently sensitive for unconcentrated fractions. For this reason, it is always wise to quantify approximately the recovery of compound at each stage.

Such matters may sound obvious and trivial, but preparing fractionation-samples for assay in a suitable way can be a time-consuming and surprisingly troublesome process, often representing a major portion of the work in a bioassay-guided extraction.

1.5.1. Overlay Assay

Sometimes it is possible to combine more closely the separation and the bioassay, as in the case of TLC overlay assays. In this case, the sample may be separated by TLC, the TLC plate dried to remove traces of solvent, and the assay performed *in situ*, on top of the plate. This usually takes the form of the reactants immobilized in a gel poured or sprayed over the plate and the results visualized. The most commonly used form of this assay is an antimicrobial assay in which the plate is covered with agar seeded with microorganism and then incubated, after which microbial growth is seen throughout the agar except over those regions of the chromatogram that contain the antimicrobial components.

As long as the assay can be visualized, either by obvious microbial growth or by the use of a colored reaction product, this principle can be applied to a wide range of assays, including enzyme and receptor-based assays. This principle of immobilizing, or spotting, a small amount of sample onto a TLC plate is one of the quickest and most convenient means of assaying a large number of samples, and this method of overlay assay is widely used for assaying fractions from all types of separation.

1.6. Quantification

During the isolation of a natural product, it is necessary to track the compound and, if possible, obtain some estimate of the recovery at each stage. This can often be done by routine analytical techniques that may involve the use of a standard.

During the isolation of an unknown bioactive compound, the compound is monitored by following the bioactivity at each stage. It is also useful to quantify, at least approximately, this bioactivity at each stage. Approximate quantification is generally carried out by assaying a set of serial dilutions of each fraction at each stage of the separation. To detect the peaks of activity, it is often necessary to assay fractions at a range of dilutions, which serves to indicate the relative amounts of activity/compound present in each fraction. It can then be seen in which fraction(s) the bulk of the active components lie and also allows for some estimation of the total amount of activity recovered, relative to the starting material. Accounting for all the initial activity can be helpful in avoiding potential problems.

For example, one may produce column fractions that obviously contain active compound but which a quick calculation reveals, represent only approx 5% of the activity that went on to the column. There are many possible explanations for such "disappearance" of activity, but essentially, quantification can act as a warning that there is more to look for. Likely explanations may include:

1. There is more than one active component and the major component has not been eluted.
2. Most of the active component has been degraded or modified by the separation process.
3. The starting sample was not prepared so as to be fully compatible with the mobile phase, so that a large proportion of the active component precipitated when loading on to the top of the column.
4. Most of the active component(s) spread across a wide range of fractions in a concentration too low to be detected by the assay.

Quantification also helps to avoid the temptation to assign all the activity of an extract to a particular peak on a chromatogram, when in fact, much of the activity may be represented by a very minor peak or a potent compound present in very low concentrations almost insignificant apart from its bioactivity. These are often more interesting than abundant compounds as they are more bioactive and are less likely to have been previously described.

For similar reasons, it is prudent to retain a reference sample of the mixture at each stage of the process so that it can be assayed alongside the fractions and serve as a record of material recovered at each stage of the process.

2. Where to Start?

How to begin the isolation of a natural product? First, something about the nature of the compound needs to be known so that the approach to take can be determined.

2.1. Determination of the Nature of the Compound

How much needs to be discovered depends on how much is already known and what our aim is. The general features of a molecule that are useful to ascertain at this early stage might include: solubility (hydrophobicity/hydrophilicity), acid/base properties, charge, stability, and size.

1. If the aim is to isolate all of the secondary metabolites of an organism and not to focus on a specific molecule, this information may be less important but still can be useful in getting an idea of the range of compounds being worked with.
2. If the aim is to isolate a known compound(s), much of this information will already be established, or will probably be apparent from the structure. (It may even be that a physical assay exists for the compound and this may provide the basis for an isolation.)
3. If the target is an unknown molecule, it is probable that little is known about the nature of the compound.

At this early stage, a small portion of the mixture can be examined in a series of small batch-wise experiments.

2.1.1. Hydrophobicity/Hydrophilicity

An indication of the polarity of the compound in question can be determined by drying a portion of the mixture and attempting to redissolve it in a few, perhaps three or four, solvents covering the range of polarities. Suitable solvents include water, methanol, acetonitrile, ethyl acetate, dichloromethane, chloroform, petroleum ether, and hexane.

It is usually fairly obvious if everything redissolves, but if the mixture is a complex one, the sample can be centrifuged or filtered and the supernatant tested to determine solubility of the desired natural product (**Note 1**).

The same information can be obtained by carrying out a range of solvent-partitioning experiments, typically between water and ethyl acetate, chloroform/dichloromethane, or hexane, followed by assay to determine how the compound distributes itself (**Note 2**).

2.1.2. pK$_a$ (Acid/Base Properties)

Further information can be gleaned by carrying out the partitioning experiments mentioned above at a range of pH values–typically 3, 7, and 10. Adjust the aqueous solution/suspension with a drop or two of acid or alkali (or preferably buffer), then add the solvent, mix, and assay the two phases.

$$HA \rightleftharpoons H^+ + A^-$$
Organic Phase   Aqueous Phase

As well as providing information on the pK$_a$ of the target compounds, these tests can also be useful in ascertaining their stability at different pH values (**Note 3**).

2.1.3. Charge

Information about the charge properties of the compound can be obtained by testing under batch conditions, the effect of adding a range of ion-exchangers to the mixture.

To aliquots of the aqueous mixture (ion-exchangers will, of course, only act as such in water), portions of different ion-exchange resins are added. When dealing with an unknown quantity of a compound, it is not possible to know how much to add–if ambiguous results are obtained, e.g., apparent binding to all forms of exchanger, an order of magnitude more or less should be tried. The important thing is that approximately the same amount in terms of binding capacity is added to each to make the results comparable. An approximate starting concentration might be 100 mg resin/1 mL microbial broth.

The supernatant of samples should be tested after mixing with strong and weak anion exchangers and strong and weak cation exchangers, each at a range of pH values, e.g., pH 3.0, 7.0, and 10.0. From this can be deduced whether the compound is a strong or weak acid or base. This may then suggest an extraction approach, perhaps involving ion exchange or adsorption chromatography (**Note 4**). A guide to the various types of ion-exchange resins is given in Chapter 5.

2.1.4. Heat Stability

If a biologically active natural product, or any product from a natural source, is not stable to heat, there is a likelihood that it is a protein. If this is the case, the observed biological activity may be as a result of enzyme activity or simply to nonspecific binding by the protein to components of the biological assay, giving rise to interference or "false" activity. Most natural product chemists, particularly those guided by bioactivity for the purposes of finding potential therapeutic agents or those with chemotaxonomic interests, are generally more interested in small nonprotein secondary metabolites where proteins are an unwanted distraction.

A typical heat-stability test would involve incubation of the sample at 80/90°C for 10 min in a water bath (taking into account loss of volume or any physical changes in the sample, e.g., clotting, aggregation), then assay for the unaffected compound. This is most appropriate for biological assays as it may be difficult to detect breakdown of a compound in a mixture by physical means.

A positive result may mean that the extraction comes to a halt because of lack of further interest or that it can proceed unhindered by the interference of associated protein. However, it should be remembered that heat can also denature or modify other natural products.

Many biological samples prior to assay are extracted with a water-miscible solvent such as methanol. Proteins can be excluded from the extract by ensuring that the samples (and the methanol) are completely dry prior to extraction. Proteins will rarely dissolve in most solvents in the absence of water. This can be carried out by extracting the sample in methanol, drying the extract, then re-extracting the extract with methanol, thus ensuring that no water is carried over into the final extract.

2.1.5. Size

Proteins can also be detected and/or eliminated by the use of ultrafiltration membranes. These come in a variety of forms through which a sample may be passed by pressure, by vacuum, or by centrifugal force in the case of ultrafiltration cones (filters contained in sample tubes that are centrifuged). The filters have a cutoff at a given molecular weight and can be used to separate proteins from small molecules. They are not generally useful for the fractionation of mixtures of small molecules as the lowest cutoff values are approx 2000 amu. Dialysis tubing can be used in the same way; small molecules (less than a few thousand amu) can pass through dialysis tubing into the surrounding medium, whereas proteins will be retained within the tubing.

2.2. Localization of Activity

At the early stages of the extraction, one of the first and the most obvious questions to ask is whether the natural product of interest is localized to one part of the organism.

2.2.1. Microbial Broths–Extracellular or Intracellular?

If the compound is in the free medium, already separated from the bulk of the biomass, this is likely to make the extraction easier, particularly in a liquid culture grown in a minimal medium (such as that generally used for a plant cell or microalgal culture) and which is therefore fairly "clean." If the material is associated solely with the cells, it may be possible to separate immediately the extracellular material and concentrate on extracting the cell mass. In this way, the sample is at least concentrated in a single swift step, virtually free of media constituents. If the material is divided between the cells and the supernatant, it is desirable to shift this balance one way or the other so that the compound is associated entirely with either the cells or the supernatant. This may be possible by altering the pH or by adding surfactants. It may be that the natural product is actually excreted by the cells but remains associated with the cell surface for reasons of hydrophobicity, adsorption, or biological affinity.

2.2.2. Plants

Provided that the whole plant is not already milled to a homogeneous powder, it should be fairly straightforward to determine whether the compounds of interest are localized to certain parts of the plant, e.g., leaves, root, stem, bark, root bark, and so on. If so, this may allow for disposal of perhaps three-quarters of the plant before the actual work even begins, thus rendering the mixture less complex and possibly leading to avoidance of problems brought about by the presence of other parts of the plant.

2.3. Selecting General Separation Conditions

2.3.1. Literature

It obviously makes sense to find out whether the extraction of the natural product has been reported in the literature. However, there is no correct purification method for each natural product and no compulsion to follow such a method. It may be easier to develop a new process, particularly if the biological matrix is different, e.g., the same compound from a different organism or a different medium, or if facilities for the reported separation are not readily available.

In the isolation of unknown compounds, this approach is, of course, not possible, but the literature may be used to facilitate and limit the amount of necessary work. This is discussed further in Chapter 10.

2.3.2. Solid Phase Extraction

This involves sorption of solutes from a liquid medium onto a solid adsorbent (like a flypaper removing flies from a room by retaining them when they land on the sticky paper) by the same mechanisms by which molecules are retained on chromatography stationary phases. These adsorbents, like chromatography media, come in the form of beads or resins that can be used in column or in batch form. They are often used in the commercially available form of syringes packed with medium (typically a few hundred milligrams to a few grams) through which the sample can be gently forced with the plunger or by vacuum. Solid phase extraction media include reverse phase, normal phase, and ion-exchange media.

If an aqueous extract is passed down a column containing reverse phase packing material, everything that is fairly nonpolar will bind, whereas everything polar will pass through. The nonpolar material can then be eluted with a nonpolar solvent to give a sample that has been partially purified.

There are a number of uses of solid phase extraction:

1. Determination of the nature of the unknown compound: Determination of the resins that bind the desired natural product provides information about the nature of the compound. For example, if the compound is retained by a reverse phase medium, it must have some degree of hydrophobicity.
2. Selection of separation conditions: By the same reasoning, it is possible to get some idea of a suitable starting point for a purification. By eluting bound material using a stepwise series of solvents with increasing eluting power, rather than by a single elution step, it may be possible to find chromatographic conditions that selectively bind and elute a particular compound.
3. Dereplication and characterization: The characteristic binding profile of a compound on a number of solid phase extraction resins can be used for comparative and dereplication purposes. Compounds that bind differently to the same media must be different, and if a series of extracts is suspected of containing the same unknown natural product (e.g., all the extracts possess the same biological activity), the fact that they all exhibit the same binding profile might lead to a decision to first isolate the component from one of the extracts, then use that as a standard with which to examine the other extracts.
4. Preparative purification: As well as functioning as a means of developing separation conditions, solid phase extraction is widely used as a purification step in its own right and in this sense can be viewed as a form of two-phase partition. This

is commonly used at the early stages of an extraction as a fairly crude "clean-up" step, to separate the target natural products from the bulk of the contaminants, or at the final stages of a purification to get the isolated natural product in pure, concentrated solution. In both cases, this usually involves the removal of large amounts of polar contaminants (e.g., buffer salts, media components) by extracting target compounds using some form of nonionic binding medium, washing the resin with water to remove nonbinding contaminants, and then eluting the compounds with solvent.

5. Concentration: Compounds at low concentrations in relatively large volumes can be concentrated by extraction onto a solid phase extraction medium and then eluted in a small volume of a strong eluent. This is typically used for concentrating analytes that are present in only trace amounts, such as drug metabolites in serum samples, or environmental contaminants in seawater.

2.3.3. Gradient HPLC

Running a sample of the natural product extract on analytical gradient HPLC (**Fig. 1**) using a mobile phase gradient of wide ranging polarity should serve to separate the mixture and elute all the components. On the basis of retention time, it should be possible to select general chromatographic conditions (either HPLC or low-pressure columns) for further preparative purification.

2.3.4. TLC

TLC separations can also be used to select column chromatography conditions. TLC conditions that give a useful R_f value, i.e., compound separates from the majority of other components without staying at the origin or with the solvent front, can be approximately transferred to column chromatography. Identification of the target compound or on the TLC plate can be carried out by comparison with a standard, by chemical staining, or by an overlay assay carried out on top of the developed plate in the case of an unknown biologically active component, or by scraping off, extracting, and assaying portions of the adsorbent.

However, it is not always straightforward to translate TLC systems to column systems. This is partly because TLC cannot be seen simply as a two-dimensional column. Unlike column chromatography, TLC is a nonequilibrium technique, which means that the conditions of the mobile and stationary phases are not constant throughout the plate but vary during the run and according to the position on the plate. This can lead to difficulties in trying to reproduce TLC separations in a column form. As a general rule, it is advisable to use a slightly less polar mobile phase for normal phase column chromatography (and slightly more polar for reverse phase columns) than that used to obtain a reasonable R_f value on TLC.

Armed with some knowledge of the nature of the compound and some idea of suitable general separation approaches, one can usually establish a successful isolation method much more quickly than if none of these preliminary tests is carried out.

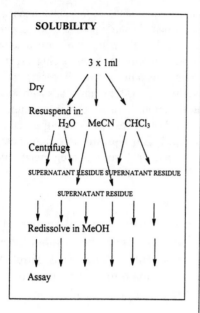

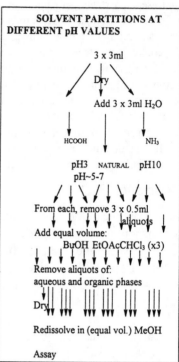

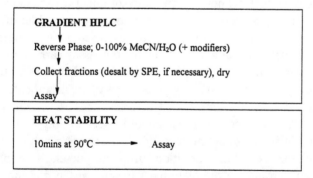

Fig. 1. Example of some simple tests that might be carried out on a crude methanol extract to determine the nature of compound for selection for general separation methods.

3. Chromatography

Many of the separation processes described in later chapters are forms of chromatography. It might therefore be of value to have some understanding of what chromatography is. Chromatography involves the distribution of a compound between two phases–a moving, *mobile phase* that is passed over an immobile *stationary phase*. Separation is based on the characteristic way in which compounds distribute themselves between these two phases.

For Compound X this can be described in terms of its distribution coefficient:

$$K_D = \frac{[X]_{\text{stationary phase}}}{[X]_{\text{mobile phase}}}$$

This is characteristic for a molecule independent of the amount of solute.

So, as one phase carrying the solute passes over the stationary phase, the solutes are in constant, dynamic equilibrium between the two phases. For any given compound, the position of this equilibrium is determined by the strength of interaction of the compound with the stationary phase and the competition for the stationary phase between the compound and the mobile phase. The stationary phase may be a solid or a liquid and the fluid mobile phase may be liquid or gas, to give liquid chromatography and gas chromatography, respectively.

Gas chromatography, particularly gas-liquid chromatography (GLC) is a widely used analytical technique but cannot be used for preparative isolation of natural products and will not be discussed in this book. Liquid chromatography however, is widely used and comes in many different forms.

3.1. Classification of Liquid Chromatography

Chromatography can be classified in a number of ways (**Fig. 2**):

1. Classification on the basis of the physical arrangement of the system. Chromatography can be carried out in the form of a column (column chromatography) (**Fig. 3**) or on a flat surface (planar chromatography). The latter includes various forms of TLC and paper chromatography, amongst others and is the subject of Chapter 7. Countercurrent chromatography involves two liquid phases and is the subject of Chapter 8. Most chromatography is carried out in the form of a column of stationary phase with a moving liquid mobile phase and comprises everything from capillary columns, to HPLC, to large-scale gravity-fed columns.
2. Classification according to the mode of separation. It is perhaps more useful to divide chromatographic forms according to the mode of separation on which each is based. These basic forms of molecular interaction, which determine chromatographic behavior, are listed below but are discussed at greater length in the relevant chapters.

3.1.1. Adsorption

This involves partitioning of molecules between the surface of a solid stationary phase and a liquid mobile phase. The dynamic equilibrium of solutes as they switch between the stationary and mobile phases (the processes of sorption and desorption, respectively) is specific for each molecule and is affected by competition that exists between solutes and solvent for sites on the stationary phase. This is a purely physical process involving the formation of no

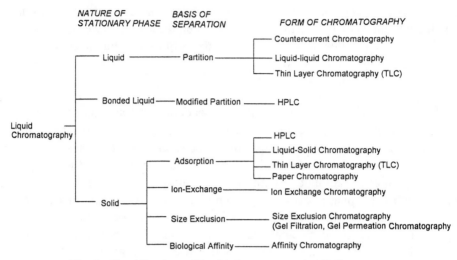

Fig. 2. Classification of liquid chromatography (LC) systems.

chemical bonds, but only the relatively weak forces of hydrogen bonds, Van der Waals forces, and dipole–dipole interactions. For this reason, almost any inert material can in theory be used as an adsorbent, the only proviso being that it does not react either with the sample or the mobile phase and that it is insoluble in the mobile phase. Common examples include silica (as a column or as a TLC stationary phase), cellulose, styrene divinylbenzene, alumina, and carbon.

3.1.2. Partition

Partition chromatography employs the separation principle of liquid–liquid extraction. When one of the liquids is coated onto a solid support, such as a column of cellulose coated with water, or a silica TLC plate coated with adsorbed water, a stationary phase is created on which separation can be carried out with an immiscible/organic mobile phase, employing the principles of liquid–liquid extraction with the advantages of chromatography. However, this method suffers from the disadvantages that the liquid stationary phase tends to be stripped (leached) from the column as a result of shear forces acting on it from the movement of the mobile phase and by the solubility of the liquid stationary phase in the mobile phase. For this reason, partition chromatography in this simplest form is rarely used these days.

More usually, the liquid stationary phase is chemically bound to the inert support to give a "bonded phase." This involves the formation of a (hydrolytically) stable bond, often, for example, between the surface silanol group of a silica support and a chlorosilane. The silane usually carries a hydrocar-

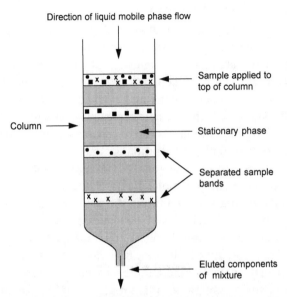

Fig. 3. Much preparative chromatography is carried out as a form of liquid chromatography with a column of solid packing material (stationary phase) over which is passed a liquid (mobile phase) containing the sample.

bon chain (usually of 1, 2, 6, 8, or 18 carbon length) and this is in effect, the liquid stationary phase. Bonded phase chromatography (also known as modified partition chromatography) of this sort is really a combination of partition and adsorption chromatography, and the distinction between these two forms is generally somewhat blurred. A liquid can also act as a stationary phase even when it is not bound to a support, as in the case of countercurrent chromatography.

Normal phase/reverse phase: If the stationary phase is more polar than the mobile phase, this is normal phase chromatography. An example of this is a silica column with its polar silanol groups and a mobile phase of an organic solvent. When the stationary phase is less polar than the mobile phase, this is reverse phase chromatography, exemplified by the hydrocarbons bound to the silica support and a water/acetonitrile mobile phase. Reverse phase chromatography is very widely used as a form of HPLC (*see* Chapter 6) and most natural products have a region of hydrophobicity that leads to their retention to some extent on a reverse phase column.

3.1.3. Charge

Many natural products exist as ionic species or are ionizable at a given pH and this property can be used as a "handle" for isolating these molecules.

3.1.3.1. ION-EXCHANGE CHROMATOGRAPHY

This involves a stationary phase that consists of an insoluble matrix, the surface of which carries a charged group, either negative or positive. These charged groups are associated with a counter-ion of the opposite charge, and as the name suggests, the principle of separation lies in the ability of the sample ions to exchange with the counter-ions and bind to the stationary phase. A system in which the stationary phase carries a negative charge and the counter-ions are positively charged is cation-exchange chromatography; the opposite is anion-exchange chromatography. Separation occurs because of the differences between sample molecules in their degree and strength of interaction with the exchange sites. Once the sample molecules are bound, they can be eluted selectively from the binding site by altering the pH of the mobile phase, thus altering the dissociation characteristics of the charged species, or by increasing the ionic concentration of the mobile phase, thus increasing competition for the exchange sites and forcing off the sample ions. The degree of interaction obviously depends on the nature of the sample ions and of the functional groups on the ion-exchange resin. Sample ions that react strongly with the stationary phase ions are strongly retained and will elute more slowly, whereas weakly binding solute ions will be eluted more rapidly. This process is discussed at greater length in Chapter 5.

3.1.3.2. ION-PAIR CHROMATOGRAPHY/ION-SUPPRESSION CHROMATOGRAPHY

Ions can also be separated on a nonpolar stationary phase such as a reverse-phase modified partition column by altering the pH of the mobile phase to suppress the ionization of a molecule so that it will be retained as a neutral species and hence will interact with the stationary phase. Essentially, the same principle is applied for ion-pair chromatography, in which the mobile phase contains a relatively large organic molecule with an ionizable group and lipophilic region and which acts as a counter-ion to form a reversible ion-pair with a sample ion. This ionic modifier acts either by pairing with the sample ion in free solution to form an uncharged species that can then partition into the stationary phase and/or by interacting with the stationary phase via its lipophilic region to give a stationary phase with charged groups that can form an ion-pair with sample ions. The advantage of this technique is that it allows polar and nonpolar samples to be separated in the same system.

3.1.4. Size

Chromatography based on differences in the size of molecules is somewhat different from other forms of chromatography as there is no direct sorption between sample and stationary phase. Size exclusion chromatography (also known as gel permeation chromatography or gel filtration) is based around a column of packing material formed from beads of a polymer such as poly-acrylamide, agarose, or silica. The degree of polymer crosslinking is controlled and gives rise to beads with a certain porosity. This pore structure is such that the largest solute molecules cannot enter the pores—they are excluded because they are too big, whereas the smaller molecules with a diameter less than that of the pore diameter are able to diffuse into the beads, and the smallest molecules are able to diffuse into the smallest pores. It is these spaces in the cross-linked polymer that act as the stationary phase. The largest molecules will pass rapidly through the column, following the most direct route between the beads. Smaller molecules with a greater diffusible volume accessible to them will take a more circuitous route through the column as they diffuse into the pores and will take a longer time to reach the bottom of the column. The smallest molecules can penetrate the smallest pores, travel further, and hence will be eluted last (**Fig. 4**).

The interstitial spaces of the beads act as eddies where solutes are out of the full flow of the mobile phase, and this serves to increase retention time.

Even though there is no physical interaction between the sample molecules and the stationary phase, it is still possible to describe the behavior of a sample molecule/solute in terms of a distribution coefficient (K_D) where the stationary phase is represented by the interstitial spaces of the polymer bead.

$$K_D = (V_e - V_o)/V_i$$

where V_e is the elution volume of the solute, V_o is the void volume–the elution volume of compounds that are completely excluded from the gel pores, and V_i is the volume of liquid inside the gel pores available to the very smallest solutes.

Although size exclusion chromatography is a very simple and nondestructive technique, it is best suited for the separation of biological molecules over a very wide size range, such as proteins, for which it is frequently used. As most secondary metabolites are fairly small molecules without marked differences in size, size exclusion chromatography is rarely used for the separation of these molecules. The exception to this is Sephadex LH20, which is widely used because of its advantages of being usable in nonaqueous systems and that gel filtration is not the only factor at work in the separation process; adsorption also plays a major role.

3.1.5. Biological Specificity

Affinity chromatography depends on specific interactions of biological molecules such as an antibody–antigen interaction, enzyme-inhibitor interaction, DNA–DNA binding, DNA–protein interaction, or a receptor–agonist/antagonist interaction. The ligand (or receptor) is covalently bound to the packing mate-

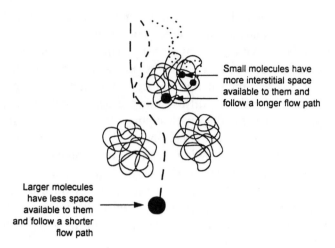

Small molecules have
more interstitial space
available to them and
follow a longer flow path

Larger molecules
have less space
available to them
and follow a shorter
flow path

Fig. 4. Behavior of solutes in a size exclusion chromatography system.

rial and acts as the stationary phase. The mixture is then passed through the column, and those molecules with a specific affinity for the ligand are retained while the remainder pass through. The material might then be eluted by altering the pH and/or the buffer composition in order to weaken the interaction between the samples and the ligand (**Fig. 5**).

As natural product extraction often involves the isolation of compounds with specific biological activity, this might seem the ideal way to isolate such molecules. Indeed, biological specificity is very often the basis by which the natural product is originally detected within the mixture and is the means by which the compounds or fractions can be assayed.

However, the preparative isolation of secondary metabolites is not often carried out by affinity chromatography, mainly because it is often a rather laborious and time-consuming process to obtain sufficient quantities of a suitable ligand and to carry out the reactions necessary to form a stable stationary phase. Also, if the starting mixture is complex, as is often the case with microbial or plant extracts, there are likely to be other components present that interfere and/or disrupt the receptor-ligand interaction or themselves adsorb nonspecifically to the stationary phase. Moreover, recovery of the product depends on the interaction being reversible.

The use of affinity chromatography for the preparative isolation of natural products is not discussed at length in this book though its role may increase in the future (as purified recombinant proteins become more available). However, the use of biological specificity as the basis for screening organism extracts as part of the overall discovery process of bioactive natural products is extremely important and is increasing as the range of biological targets for which a bioactive molecule is aimed, increases.

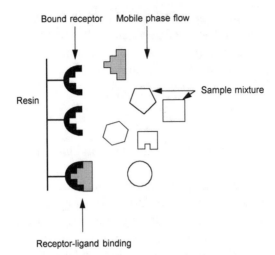

Fig. 5. Principle of affinity chromatography.

3.2. Detection

Chromatography is usually monitored by changes in UV absorbance. As each compound has a characteristic absorption coefficient, this absorbance may be quite different for different compounds, particularly at longer wavelengths. For this reason, monitoring unknown compounds by UV detection is best carried out using short wavelengths, near "end absorbance," typically between 200 and 220 nm. Almost all organic compounds will exhibit some absorbance in this range; wavelengths any shorter tend to cause the absorbance of the mobile phase solvents to interfere. Ideally, a UV diode array detector is used; this measures absorbance over the entire UV wave range so that a UV spectrum can be obtained at any point on the chromatogram. As every compound has a characteristic UV spectrum, this can provide useful information about the compounds in the mixture. Compounds with no significant UV absorption relative to the mobile phase can be monitored by changes in refractive index or by electrochemical detection (rarely used for preparative work).

3.3. Principles of Chromatography

Detailed knowledge of chromatography theory is not necessary in order to perform effective separations, but a knowledge of the principles underlying the chromatographic separation is helpful in understanding how to monitor and improve separations.

As has been described, separation occurs because in the dynamic equilibrium of solute molecules transferring between the two phases, different molecules spend different proportions of time in the mobile and stationary phases. Solute molecules migrate only when they are in the mobile phase (and all solutes in the mobile phase migrate at the same speed). The speed at which a solute moves through the column is directly related to the proportion—the mole fraction—of a particular group of molecules in the mobile phase. If R_x = mole fraction of X in the mobile phase:

$$R_x = \mu x/\mu m$$

or

$$\mu x = \mu m \cdot R_x$$

where μx = rate of movement of solute band and μm = rate of movement of mobile phase.

This is essentially the same as the distribution coefficient and the chromatographic process consists essentially of thousands of dynamic equilibria. However, there is not sufficient time for the sample to reach fully its equilibrium distribution between the two phases. The sample remaining in the mobile phase is carried down to a fresh portion of the column where it moves onto the stationary phase from the mobile phase. As concentration of the solute in the mobile phase from this first portion decreases, solute in this region of the column moves back from stationary phase to mobile phase, in keeping with the distribution coefficient, and is carried down to the second portion of the column where once again equilibrium is (nearly) achieved. This does not take place as a series of discrete steps but as a continuous dynamic process (**Fig. 6**).

3.3.1. Retention

Solutes only move down the column when they are in the mobile phase, moving at the same speed as the mobile phase. The rate of migration of a solute, therefore, is inversely proportional to its distribution coefficient.

The degree of retention of a solute can be described by three retention parameters: retention time (t_R), retention volume (V_R), and capacity factor (k').

The retention time (or elution time) is the time between injection and elution (measured at peak maximum) of a solute. As this is directly related to the mobile phase flow rate, which may vary between systems, it is sometimes more appropriate to express this value in terms of retention volume, V_R.

$$V_R = F \cdot t_R$$

where F = flow rate of mobile phase.

The retention time is the time that a solute spends in the stationary phase plus the time it spends in the mobile phase (t_M). t_M is the same for all solutes and includes time spent in the dead volume of the column, and so it is sometimes preferable to use the adjusted retention time (t'_R), which consists only of the time a solute spends in the stationary phase.

$$t'_R = t_R - t_M$$

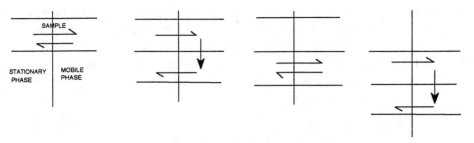

Fig. 6. The sample is continuously exchanging between the mobile and stationary phases as the mobile phase flow carries it down the column.

The phase capacity factor (k') is the net retention time relative to the nonsorbed time (t_0) and is therefore directly related to the distribution coefficient of a solute between two phases:

$$k' = \frac{t_R - t_0}{t_0}$$

or in terms of retention volumes:

$$k' = \frac{V_R - V_M}{V_M}$$

where V_M is the volume of mobile phase in the column.

$$k' = \frac{K \cdot V_S}{V_M}$$

where V_S is the volume of the stationary phase.

The elution time of a nonsorbed compound (t_0) is equal to the column length (L) divided by the mobile-phase velocity (v). Therefore, the retention time of a sorbed compound can be described as:

$$t_R = L/v \, (1 + k')$$

This gives the overall relationship between solute retention, distribution of a solute across stationary and mobile phases, column length, and mobile phase flow rate.

It can be seen from this that doubling the length of the column, for example, will double the retention time. By substituting a term for k' ($k' = [V_R - V_M]/V_M$) into this expression, it can be seen that, aside from column length and flow rate (variables that will be the same for all the solutes of the same chromatographic separation), the important factor affecting the retention time of a solute is K_D, or its distribution between the stationary and mobile phases. This in turn is dependent on the relative volumes of mobile phase and stationary phase (or more correctly, in the case of adsorption chromatography, the adsorbent surface area). Ultimately therefore, it can be seen once again that the relative retention time depends on the distribution coefficient of a particular molecule, and the larger this is, the greater will be the retention time. It is the differences in this value between different molecules, that we can exploit to bring about their separation by chromatography.

3.3.2. Column Efficiency

So, the process of sorption and desorption of solute molecules onto the stationary phase is similar to samples partitioning between two phases in a separating funnel, or it is analogous to a series of steps in fractional distillation, except that the process of a group of solute molecules reaching equilibrium in a particular part of the column is not a series of discrete steps but is a continuous, dynamic process. We can picture the chromatographic system as comprising a number of regions in which equilibrium is assumed to be achieved or, effectively, to be a series of very short transverse columns.

The number of these theoretical transverse slices of column is known as the theoretical plate number (N) and reflects the number of times a solute partitions between the two phases. N is a measure of the efficiency of the column and will determine how broad the chromatogram peaks will be. A column with a high number of theoretical plates will be efficient and will produce narrow peaks.

$$N = (t_R/\sigma)^2$$

where σ^2 is the band variance.

N can be measured from the peak profile (**Fig. 7**). Assuming the peak to be Gaussian, the baseline width of the peak as measured by drawing tangents from the curve to the baseline is equivalent to four standard deviations. Therefore:

$$\sigma = \omega_b/4 \text{ and } N = 16(t_R/w_b)^2$$

In practice, it is often preferable to use the value for the peak width at half-peak height, particularly when the peak is not symmetrical. This results in the expression:

$$N = 5.54 \, (t_1/w_{1/2})^2$$

N calculated this way using t_R is a measure of the efficiency of the whole system that includes the dead volume. In order to calculate and compare efficiencies of columns alone, it is necessary to use t'_R (adjusted retention time) in place of t_R in the above expression, to obtain the effective plate number.

As N is a measure of the number of partitions a solute undergoes, it is directly proportional to column length; i.e., the longer the column length, the greater the separation. It is sometimes more useful to express the column efficiency in

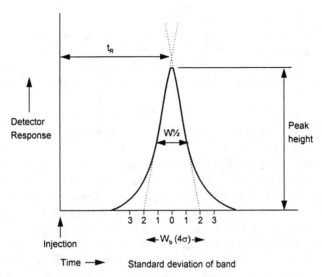

Fig. 7. Profile of a solute peak and measurement of *N*.

terms of the distance a solute travels in the mobile phase when undergoing one partition. This is the height equivalent to a theoretical plate or plate height (*H*).

$$H = L/N$$

where *L* is the column length, and *H* is independent of the column length.

3.3.3. Dispersion

Obviously, the aim is for a chromatographic separation in which peak width is narrow relative to the time of elution (w_t/t_R is minimized), i.e., the number of theoretical plates is maximized. There are three main factors that give rise to band broadening: (1) multiple path effect (eddy diffusion), (2) axial (longitudinal) diffusion, and (3) mass transfer—slow transfer/equilibration between mobile and stationary zones.

1. The multiple path effect refers to the fact that the flow through a packed bed of particulate matter is very tortuous. The total distances traveled, and the velocity at any given time, of individual particles will vary widely due to the heterogeneous and random nature of the flow paths through the bed. As particles can diffuse laterally between two flow paths (a process known as coupling), the overall effects of this Eddy diffusion are not as significant as they would be if every particle remained in its own "individual" flow path, as this lateral diffusion tends to average out the flow paths. The effects of this can be minimized by the use of spherical particles of regular size.

   This effect of Eddy diffusion on the overall plate height can be expressed as the *A* term.

$$A = 2 \lambda d_p$$

where d_p is the particle diameter and λ is a packing constant.

2. Within a column, there will also be *longitudinal* (or *axial*) *diffusion* of solutes. This is most significant at low flow rates when the band is resident in the column for relatively long periods of time. This can be expressed as the B term.

$$B = 2\gamma D_M$$

where D_M is the diffusion coefficient of the solute in the mobile phase and γ is an obstruction factor.

3. Mass transfer relates to the rates at which equilibration of the chromatographic process is achieved, and is governed by the diffusion of the solutes within the mobile phase and a liquid stationary phase, and governed by the kinetics of sorption-desorption. When equilibration between the mobile and stationary phases is slow, band dispersion will be relatively large due to the fact that molecules in the stationary zone get "left behind" as the main band passes over. This dispersion will increase with increase in flow rate (and with increase in equilibration time). The effects of mass transfer can be expressed as two C terms; C_m describes mass transfer in the mobile phase, and C_s describes mass transfer in the stationary phase.

The overall effect of these factors can be combined in the van Deemter Equation, which relates plate height (column efficiency) to flow rate (μ).

$$H = A + B/\mu + C_s\mu + C_m\mu$$

An inverse plot of the van Deemter Equation (**Fig. 8**) illustrates the relationship between column efficiency and flow rate.

Other band-broadening effects derive from the fact that solute species in the same flow path will not all move with the same velocity (those in the center will move faster than those at the edge) and that the particle structure may contain pores or eddies of nonmoving mobile phase out of which solute particles must diffuse in order to return to the main flow of mobile phase.

3.3.4. Sorption Isotherms

Sorption is the general term that refers to the interaction of a solute with the stationary phase, whether that interaction involves adsorption, ion-exchange, or gel permeation (size exclusion). When the relative concentrations of solute in the stationary and mobile phases are the same, independent of concentration (as is normally expected by reference to the K_D of the solute), the peak shape will remain basically the same and will be symmetrical. This relationship, which describes amount of solute sorbed relative to concentration in mobile phase (at constant temperature), is the *sorption isotherm*.

When describing or theorizing about chromatography, the assumption is made that the sample load is a flat-ended plug that, through the processes of

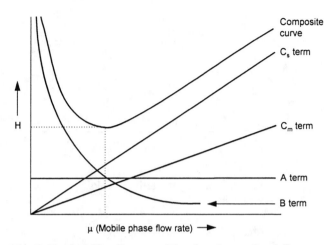

Fig. 8. Typical Van Deemter Plot showing optimal flow rate.

diffusion, soon broadens with a Gaussian distribution. In this case, the sorption isotherm is linear—the value of K_D will be constant across the peak.

However, not all systems exhibit a linear isotherm; when relatively strong interactions exist between solute and stationary phase, and relatively weak interactions exist between solutes themselves, there will initially be rapid sorption of solute onto the stationary phase until the stationary phase is "covered" by solute, at which point the uptake of solute will decrease. This means that the K_D of the solute is not constant across the peak, at low concentrations, K_D will be large and this results in a peak shape that is not symmetrical but that "tails."

Less often, the interactions between solute molecules may be strong relative to those between solute and stationary phase, in which case initial uptake of solute molecules by the stationary phase is slow but increases as the first solute molecules to be adsorbed draw up additional ones. In such a case, the peak has a shallow front and a sharp tail and is said to be a "fronting" peak (**Fig. 9**). Fronting and tailing can be a problem because they tend to lead to overlap of peaks. Dealing with the sorts of problems associated with such phenomena is discussed more fully in Chapter 6.

3.3.5. Separation and Selectivity

The preceding sections should show, if nothing else, that separation of compounds occurs because the compounds have different distribution coefficients. The column shows selectivity toward the compounds or, put another way, the compounds are selectively retained as is shown by their different retention times. This selectivity (α) can be measured by the separation factor and the relative retention and can be described in a number of ways:

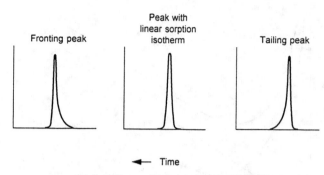

Fig. 9. Fronting and tailing peaks.

$$\alpha = K_B/K_A = k'_B/k'_A = t_R B/t_R A$$

Once again, all of these are expressions simply describing the relative values of the distribution coefficients of A and B, that is, just a measure of the way in which the equilibrium of A lies between the mobile and stationary phases compared to the way in which B is distributed between the two phases. If $\alpha = 1$, A and B will partition between the two phases in exactly the same way and there will be no separation (even on a very efficient column).

3.3.6. Resolution

Figure 10 shows a typical chromatogram. It is clear that the peaks appearing on the chromatogram after a short time are sharp and symmetrical whereas compounds that elute later give rise to broader peaks.

The degree of separation of two compounds, or degree of resolution, is determined by two factors: how far apart the tops of the peaks are and how broad the base of the peaks are. As compounds separate, the individual bands will tend to disperse and broaden, and to obtain the best resolution, peaks should be as narrow as possible. So, two compounds may have very different retention times—they may be well-separated—but if the column gives rise to very broad dispersed bands, they will not be well-resolved. Similarly, two compounds may not be well-separated, but if they move through the system as tight bands, they may be well-resolved.

The resolution (R_s) of two compounds can be defined as the peak separation divided by mean peak width.

$$R_s = \frac{t_R B - t_R A}{1/2(wA + wB)}$$

where $t_R B$ and $t_R A$ are the retention times of compounds B and A respectively and wA and wB are the basal peak widths of peaks A and B.

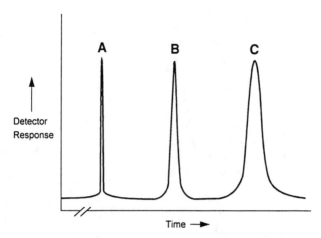

Fig. 10. Peak broadening with time.

Figure 11A demonstrates that when two triangular peaks are just touching on the baseline; i.e., when they are just resolved, $R_s = 1$. However, this assumes that the peaks are triangular, whereas in reality they are Gaussian and as shown in **Fig. 11B**, a value of $R_s = 1$ corresponds to a separation of only approx 94%. In order to achieve baseline resolution (**Fig. 11C**), an R_s value of about 1.5 is required. Strictly speaking, these figures are only valid when the peaks are of equal height.

Certainly, the most important factor in resolution is the selectivity of the system, but it is not the only factor; the efficiency of the column is also important, as this determines the degree of peak broadening.

To describe resolution in terms of experimental variables that can be used to optimize resolutions, the expression is:

$$R_s = 1/4N[\alpha - (1/\alpha)][k'/(k' + 1)]$$

The application of this expression is described in **Subheading 3.5.**

It is rarely necessary to carry out any calculations in the process of purifying materials by chromatography, but making some estimates of resolution can help to give an idea of how pure a sample one can expect to obtain from a given separation. In practice, one rarely finds it necessary even to make estimates but for the purpose of this exercise, applying some R_s values to various peak profiles will help to give an idea of the type of results to be expected from a given separation (**Fig. 12**). This is the kind of information that can usefully be elicited from an analytical chromatogram prior to commiting a large amount of sample onto a large-scale preparative separation.

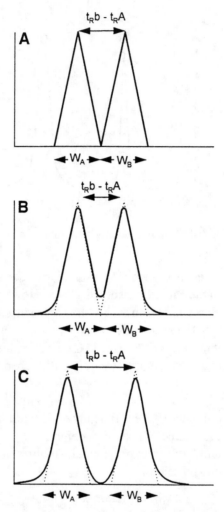

Fig. 11. Measurement of peak resolution. **(A)** $R_s = 1$. **(B)** $R_s = 1$. **(C)** $R_s > 1$.

3.4. How To Use a Chromatogram

Simply by looking at a chromatogram, one can obtain a good deal of information that is useful in the preparative isolation of a natural product.

3.4.1. Identity

The single most useful piece of information that can be obtained from a chromatogram is the retention time (t_R). A compound will always have the same retention time under a given set of conditions, and if two samples have

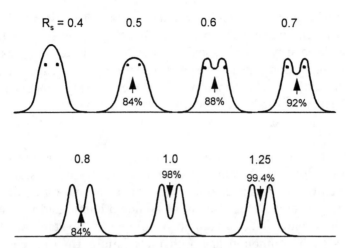

Fig. 12. Retention values for two components of equal peak width with corresponding purity percentages (. represents point of true band center).

the same retention time, they are very possibly the same compound. To be of use, the process requires being able to measure t_R with reasonable accuracy (one of the strengths of HPLC). In practice, other compounds may have the same, or at least indistinguishably similar, retention times, so one should not rely on retention time as a sole means of identifying a peak/compound with absolute certainty.

The surest means of determining whether two samples are the same compound by reference to their retention time is to inject them together in the same sample, thus avoiding problems associated with slight variations in retention times in different runs. If two samples coinjected produce a single peak, then it is probable that they are the same compound (with the degree of certainty dependent on the efficiency of the system and the "quality" of the chromatography). If, however, the two samples give rise to two peaks, it is certain that they cannot be the same compound. The use of diode array detectors also allows for comparison of UV spectra.

The retention time of a sample in a particular chromatographic system also reveals more general information about that compound.

3.4.2. Physical–Chemical Nature

Generally, nonpolar compounds will tend to elute more slowly from a reverse phase system, whereas the more polar a compound, the later it will elute from a normal phase system.

When starting with an unknown compound, a useful generic method for discovering something about the nature of its polarity is to run it on an HPLC (or

TLC) system with gradient elution, followed by some form of assay to determine the compound's chromatographic behavior. By using a gradient mobile phase covering a wide polarity range, it should be possible to ensure that almost every compound is eluted. Some idea of the polarity of the compound and useful starting conditions for the development of a system to separate the compound(s) from the rest of the mixture can be inferred from the time of elution.

3.4.3. Amount

For a given compound, the area under a chromatographic peak is directly proportional to the amount of compound. By using standards of known concentration, it is possible to calibrate a chromatographic system and to use it to establish the amount of a known compound in a sample. Of course, in the isolation of an unknown compound, no standard is available, and as each compound has a characteristic extinction coefficient (absorptivity), the degree of UV absorbance is specific to individual compounds. It is possible to quantify material corresponding to a particular peak only in relative terms.

Means of integration: Most modern HPLC apparatuses have an associated integration system that integrates the peaks on a trace as a set of values or relative percentage values that can then be translated into real values with standards of known concentration. If no built-in integration system is available, the most common practice is to measure the peak height and to use this value as a measure of quantity. On a chromatogram with sharp peaks, the relationship between peak height and concentration bears a close approximation to that of peak area and concentration. Although the relationship between peak height and concentration deviates more for broader peaks, peak height is often sufficient to provide an approximate value of the proportion of natural product recovered at each stage of the purification.

Alternatively, it is possible to calculate peak area by multiplying the peak height by half-peak width at half-height, or even by cutting out peaks from a paper chromatogram and weighing them to get a relative measure of compound concentration. (Measurement of peak area is less convenient than that of peak height and may sometimes even be less accurate due to the practical difficulties of measuring peak width.) Where two or more peaks overlap, the best means of roughly estimating peak area is to draw a line from the bottom of the valley between two peaks to the baseline and calling this the division between the two compounds. However, the accuracy of this method decreases as the difference in size of the peaks increases. However, in the case of overlapping peaks, the center of the chromatographic band is not the same as the top of the peak when the two bands are displaced toward each other (**Fig. 13**). This means that the

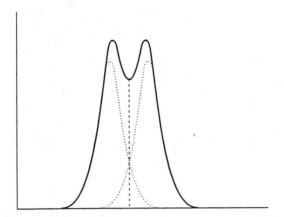

Fig. 13. Apparent and true position of overlapping peaks.

peak-height measurement in such cases is an overestimation of concentration. It also means that apparent retention times are shifted, so that obtaining an accurate t_R value for identification purposes is made much more difficult in cases of incomplete resolution. Ideally, to get both quantitative and retention time data with reasonable accuracy, it is best to have a R_s value in the region of at least 0.8–1.0.

Quantitation is generally more important in analytical chromatography than in preparative isolation work. In natural product extraction, it is generally used to monitor approximate levels of recovery following different stages of extraction, or to get a feel for the amounts of material being examined. However, by examination of peak shape, it is also possible to get a feel for the degree of purity that can be expected.

When collecting fractions from chromatographic separations in which peaks overlap, a judgment has to be made between quality and quantity; that is, taking a cut at A (**Fig. 14**) will result in recovery of the main compound that is purer than that obtained if the cut were taken at B, but will mean a lower recovery.

If the aim is to extract only some material of high purity, it is more sensible to sacrifice some of the compound of interest and take a cut that contains little or none of the peak overlap. If, on the other hand, the emphasis is on isolating the maximum yield, a broader cut should be taken with a view to subsequent purification steps to remove minor contaminants. Additionally, of course, it is often prudent to collect material in a number of fractions so that a majority of compound will be contained in a fairly pure form, and only a small proportion will need to be further purified. (All of these estimations are based on the assumption that both compounds give the same detector response per unit of concentration.)

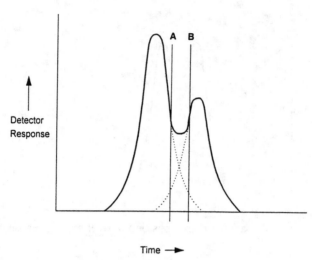

Fig. 14. Overlapping peaks.

3.5. How To Improve a Separation

As described in a previous section, the resolution factor R_s can be expressed as:

$$R_s = 1/4N[\alpha - (1/\alpha)][k'/(k' + 1)]$$

This shows that the resolution of a number of components can be related to three main functions: the capacity factor (k'), number of theoretical plates (N), and selectivity (α).

3.5.1. Capacity Factor (k')

k' is a measure of the number of additional volumes of mobile phase in the system required to elute a solute following the elution of a nonsorbed component and hence is a direct measure of solute retention. In practice, often the easiest way of improving the resolution of a separation is to ensure that a system is used in which the compounds to be separated have a reasonable value of k'. A value of $k' = 0$ means that the solute is not retained at all—it elutes at the solvent "front." In most cases, a useful value of k' is between 1 and 10, and in attempting to resolve two close peaks, it is rarely of any value to increase retention so that $k' > 20$. k' values of greater than 20 represent inordinately long retention times; from the above equation, it can be seen that as k' increases, $k'/k'+1$ tends toward 1, and further increases in k' have little effect in improving resolution.

3.5.1.1. SOLVENT SELECTION:

In practice, the means by which k' is optimized in most chromatographic separations is by the selection of a solvent of suitable polarity, or solvent strength. There are a number of different measures of polarity of a solvent, the most commonly used being the Snyder solvent strength parameter, E^0. This is based on the adsorption energy of the mobile phase on alumina. A list of solvents in order of increasing eluent strength, an eluotropic series, is given in **Table 2**. Descending the table, the values of E^0 increase, resulting in a higher value of k' in a reverse phase system. Generally, increasing solvent strength E^0 by 0.05 will decrease k' by a factor of 2–4 (**Note 5**).

There are a few basic rules of thumb that can usefully be followed in the selection of a suitable mobile phase solvent.

1. The first basic starting point is to find a solvent in which the sample is soluble. However, high solubility in the solvent at the expense of nonsolubility/noninteraction in the stationary phase is not desirable.
2. When using an aqueous-organic solvent mixture for partition/adsorption chromatography, the 10% rule is a good approximate guide. This states that a 10% change in the organic solvent content of the mobile phase results in a two- to threefold change in k'.
3. As most detection is based on UV absorbance, it is usually necessary to use solvents that have low absorbance at fairly low wavelengths so that the absorbance of the solutes is detectable against the background, even at wavelengths as low as 210 nm. This is one of the reasons why methanol, acetonitrile, tetrahydrofuran, and water have become such widely used mobile phases for HPLC.

The selection of particular solvents for individual forms of chromatography is discussed further in later chapters.

3.5.1.2. GRADIENT ELUTION

In circumstances where not all of the components of a mixture are eluted from the column within a reasonable time using a single, unchanging solvent system (isocratic elution), it may be necessary to use a system in which the mobile phase composition changes during the separation (gradient elution). By using two solvents, the proportions of which change during a run, it is possible to separate solutes with widely different retention times. These mobile phase changes may occur at a number of set intervals (step gradient) or continuously throughout the run (continuous gradient). This is commonly used, for example, in reverse phase chromatography, in which the polarity of the mobile phase is gradually decreased (and vice versa in normal phase) or in ion-exchange chromatography, in which the ionic strength of the mobile phase is increased. Gradients also have the advantage that not only do they allow for the separation of components with widely different properties in a single separation, but they often result in better separations of closely eluting solutes because the gradient serves to focus and sharpen the chromatographic bands. The disadvantages lie in the extra apparatus required, as well as the greater inconvenience—repeat

Table 2
Eluotropic Series of Solvents

Solvent	$E^0(Al_2O_3)$	Boiling pt., °C	Viscosity, mN.s.m^{-2}(20°C)	UV Cutoff, nm
Pentane	0	36	0.24	210
Cyclohexane	0.04	69	0.98	210
CCl$_4$	0.18	77	0.97	265
Toluene	0.29	111	0.59	286
Diethyl ether	0.38	35	0.25	218
Chloroform	0.40	62	0.57	245
Dichloromethane	0.42	40	0.44	235
Tetrahydrofuran	0.45	66	0.55	220
2-Butanone	0.51	80	0.32	330
Acetone	0.56	56	0.32	330
1,4-Dioxane	0.56	107	1.44	215
Ethyl acetate	0.58	77	0.45	255
Diethylamine	0.63	115	0.33	275
Acetonitrile	0.65	82	0.37	190
2-Propanol	0.82	82	2.50	210
Ethanol	0.88	78	1.20	210
Methanol	0.95	64	0.59	210
Water	1.00	100	1.0	–

gradient separations are less amenable to automation and generally require more time than the equivalent number of isocratic separations, as it is necessary to equilibrate the column between runs (**Note 6**; **Fig. 15**). Examples of gradient elutions relating to various forms of separation are given in the relevant chapters.

In developing separations of natural products, obtaining a useful value of k' is so fundamental that we generally do it instinctively, and it is obvious that a primary objective is to find stationary and mobile phases that retain the solutes but from which the solutes are eluted within a reasonable time.

3.5.2. Efficiency (N)

Improving the column efficiency, i.e., increasing N, will make the peaks sharper and narrower and hence will reduce the overlap between peaks, but it will not affect the fundamental basis of the separation. The relative retention times of a mixture of components will remain the same. This factor in the above expression involves the square root of N which means that in reality, an increase in N has to be fairly large to make any significant difference. This sort of improvement in separation is seen most dramatically in the difference between classical gravity-fed, large particle columns with plate values of hun-

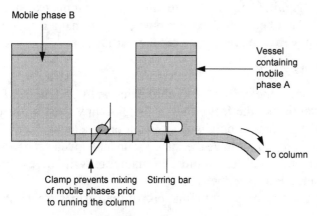

Fig. 15. A simple gradient former (**Note 6**).

dreds or thousands, and HPLC columns with their small regular particles and their typically high plate numbers of tens of thousands. This is why HPLC has become such a valuable technique—the increase in theoretical plates has made it possible to resolve components for which classical columns are just too inefficient.

3.5.2.1. PARTICLE SIZE

In order to increase the number of theoretical plates, it is necessary to increase the opportunity for equilibrium of solutes between the mobile and stationary phases to occur, i.e., it is necessary to maximize the surface area of the stationary phase. This can usually be done by reducing the particle size—at least in the case of a stationary phase in which the chromatography takes place on the surface of the column packing material. This has led to common use of columns consisting of regular particles 5 μm (or even 3 μm) in diameter. This also means that high pressures are required to force mobile phase through such tightly packed material, which is why HPLC columns, pumps, and associated hardware are so widely used.

When discussing column efficiency, it is sometimes more valuable to express this in relation to particle size. This is known as reduced plate height (*h*):

$$h = H/d_p$$

where d_p is the mean particle diameter. This describes the number of particles corresponding to H and is a dimensionless parameter that can be used to directly compare columns of different particle size.

Increasing the column length will increase the number of theoretical plates; but, as has been shown, this will also proportionately increase retention time and, hence, band-broadening. In practice, there is not a great deal that can be done to alter N significantly in order to improve resolution, except by radically changing the form of column used, e.g., switching from open column to HPLC or to a column with a smaller, more regular particle size.

3.5.3. Selectivity (α)

In practice, once the basic type of chromatography and mode of separation have been established, the factor that tends to occupy most of the extractor's time during the process of obtaining a separation is selectivity (α).

Even if two compounds have the same K_D under a given set of conditions, it should be remembered that liquid chromatography involves three sets of molecular interactions (*see* **Fig. 16**)

These interactions are all combinations of the various electrostatic forces, namely:

1. Ionic interactions.
2. Dipole–dipole interactions.
3. Van der Waal's forces.
4. Hydrogen bonding.

By changing the chemical nature of the mobile phase or stationary phase, it is possible to alter the balance of all three sets of interactions. For example, if a strongly nonpolar stationary phase is used with a very polar mobile phase to separate lipids, the principle of "like has an affinity for like" applies and the solutes will tend to spend a much greater proportion of time on the stationary phase and hence will have a very long retention time.

The process of selecting a mobile phase solvent to give a suitable value of k' is mentioned above. However, in order to optimize *relative* retention (α) of solutes, the commonest approach is to modify the mobile phase more subtly. There are a number of basic approaches that can be tried in order to optimize selectivity:

1. In systems involving an organic solvent, whether alone or in an aqueous mixture, changing the solvent to a different one that gives about the same value of k' may lead to changes in selectivity. This may require a slight alteration of the organic solvent concentration.
2. The aqueous content of the mobile phase can be modified by addition of modifiers such as acids (or less commonly, bases) or inorganic buffer salts that can give rise to changes in the overall sets of interactions.

Solvents can be grouped on the basis of their properties as proton donors (acidic), proton acceptors (basic), and dipole interactions. Solvents can be positioned within the Solvent Selectivity Triangle (**Fig. 17**) on the basis of the relative involvement of each of these three factors as parameters of solubility. Mobile phases consisting of a mixture of three solvents can be optimized by

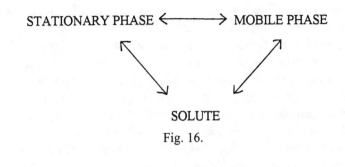

STATIONARY PHASE ←———→ MOBILE PHASE

SOLUTE

Fig. 16.

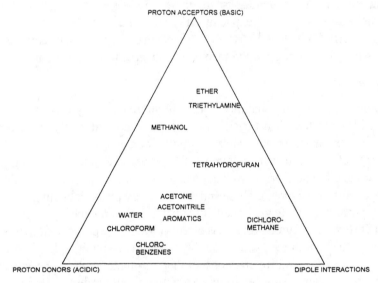

Fig. 17. Solvent selectivity triangle.

selecting solvents from as far as possible from each other in the Solvent Selectivity Triangle (as long as they are miscible). In practice, it is rarely necessary to go to such lengths to obtain a separation, but in problematic cases and as a general underlying model of how to compare solvents, it may be of some use.

The interaction between mobile phase and stationary phase should not be overlooked. For example, many of the very widely used HPLC columns consist of silica particles coated with chemically bonded hydrocarbons to give a nonpolar reverse phase stationary phase. However, there are generally a number of free silanol (-Si-OH) groups that can play a significant role in the adsorption of solutes. The addition of various mobile phase modifiers (e.g., inorganic buffer ions) can lead to interaction with these groups and alter the nature of the solutes' adsorption. This is particularly important in the elution of

basic compounds, which, at the pH values generally used on silica-based columns, tend to interact strongly with silanol groups and in some cases prove very
difficult to elute. This is often the stage at which ion-pair modifiers may be added.
This may take the form of pH adjustment to ensure, for example, that weak acids
are protonated and so are retained satisfactorily on a reverse phase column, or it
may involve the addition of larger counter-ions (e.g., tetrabutylammonium ion as
counter-ions for anionic species, and alkyl sulfonates as counter-ions for cationic
solutes). When separating ionic and nonionic solutes in the same sample, it is
generally best to optimize the separation of the nonionic solutes first and then
add counter-ions to improve the chromatography of the ionic solutes.

In practice, in many separation systems, these processes are at work to some extent
even if the separations are not explicitly characterized as such (e.g., much practical
reverse phase HPLC involves the use of modifiers and pH adjustment that often exploits
the processes of ion-pairing and ion suppression, in order to achieve separations).

3.5.4. Summary

It is worth remembering that most forms of chromatography involve more than
one form of interaction. Most systems tend to be classified neatly as adsorption,
partition, ion-exchange, or other single form of chromatography. In practice, however, a separation mechanism is almost always very complex and multifarious
because of the array of interactions that involve the sample molecules, and the various components of the mobile phase and the stationary phase, including the "inert"
stationary phase material (e.g., the cellulose on which an ion-exchanger may be supported or the free silanol groups of silica coated with a reverse phase stationary phase).

This is perhaps both the beauty and the bane of chromatography. There is an
infinite number of overall interactions so that chromatography is an amazingly
versatile tool that can separate an infinite variety of mixtures, but working out how
this might be done in each individual case is not always easy or straightforward.

These same basic principles apply for all forms of chromatography.
Although at first sight HPLC, centrifugal TLC, countercurrent chromatography, and size exclusion chromatography are physically very different and the
basis of separation may or may not be different, the underlying principles gov-
erning the chromatography are the same in all cases.

4. General Extraction Strategy

The purification of a natural product can often be broken down into three
main stages:

1. Release of compound from intracellular milieu/cell mass and removal of bulk of
   biomass. Most of the bulk of the biomass (plants or microbes) exists as fairly
   inert, insoluble, and often polymeric material, such as the cellulose of plants or
   fungi and the microbial cell wall. The first step of the extraction is to release and

solubilize the smaller secondary metabolites by a thorough solvent or aqueous extraction. This can be done by a series of stepwise extractions, using solvents of varying polarity, which acts as the first fractionation step, or by using a single "all-purpose" solvent such as methanol, which should dissolve most natural products at the same time as enhancing their release from the cellular matrix/cell surface by permeabilizing the physical barrier of the cell walls. The bulk of the insoluble material can then be removed by filtration or centrifugation.

2. Having made the initial extract, one is usually still faced with a pretty complex mixture. Much of this material will be grossly different from the target compound in that much of it may be inorganic or very polar organic material, whereas the target compound is fairly nonpolar, and the aim of the second step is often to try and strip away a large proportion of the unwanted material in a fairly low-resolution separation step. Such a step may involve an open silica column or a series of liquid–liquid extractions, with the aim of a mixture containing all the natural product of interest but comprising only a small proportion of the initial extract, i.e., a relatively small volume of sample that is amenable to the final high-resolution step that will follow.

3. The third general stage is often a high-resolution separation to separate those components still remaining and which must, by reason of still being associated with the target compound after two main fractionation procedures, bear at least some similarity with it. Whereas the second stage might involve a general fractionation with subsequent analysis and work-up of the fractions, this third stage tends to involve preliminary work modifying and altering conditions to achieve the desired separation before preparative work is carried out. This final stage is often, but not always, achieved by HPLC or TLC.

This breakdown of an extraction into three well-defined stages is certainly a simplification. Many purifications do not divide neatly into routine steps, and short cuts are more than welcome. Sometimes the extractor is lucky and a desired compound crystallizes out of a crude broth extract, but unfortunately this does not happen very often!

Schemes 1–5 are typical examples of extractions taken fairly randomly from the *Journal of Antibiotics* and the *Journal of Natural Products*. The general process outlined above is exemplified in the isolation of spirocardins A and B (**Scheme 1**) *(3)*. The compounds were found to be in the broth filtrate, which was extracted twice with ethyl acetate (half volume of supernatant). The ethyl acetate phase containing the compounds was concentrated by evaporation under reduced pressure, then washed with an equal volume of water saturated with sodium chloride to completely remove water and very polar materials, then further reduced to give an oil. This was then redissolved in a minimal volume of ethyl acetate and chromatographed on a silica column developed with hexane containing increasing amounts of acetone. This resulted in two fractions, containing spirocardins A and B, respectively, as the main components. These two fractions were then chromatographed separately again on silica gel (the more polar spirocardin B requiring a more polar eluent). The compounds were finally chromatographed on a reverse phase HPLC system to remove minor impurities.

A similar type of procedure is shown in **Scheme 2** for the isolation of glucopiericidinols from a *Streptomyces* sp. fermentation, the main difference being that this extraction incorporates chromatography on Sephadex LH20. This purification is also notable in that the final stage involved a chiral HPLC separation of two diastereoisomers *(4)*.

The isolation of antifungal and antimolluscicidal saponins from *Serjania salzmanniana* also involved the use of a silica column, but it then followed this with separation by countercurrent chromatography (**Scheme 3**). An interesting feature of the final preparative TLC stage was the use of water as a nondestructive visualization "stain." As these compounds are so hydrophobic, this region of the plate remained white (dry), and the remainder of the plate turned dark (wet) *(5)*.

For the more polar fungal metabolite epipentenomycin I (**Scheme 4**), an aqueous extract of the fungus was purified by two forms of ion-exchange chromatography. A final reverse phase HPLC step was employed, but the very polar mobile phase suggests that the compound was hardly retained by this stationary phase, and that this technique was only just within the limits of its usefulness for such a polar compound *(6)*.

Cispentacin, shown in **Scheme 5**, bears some structural similarity to epipentenomycin and was also isolated using two ion-exchange chromatography systems. The broth supernatant was loaded directly onto the ion-exchange column without any prior treatment, and unlike the epipentenomycin I isolation, the final step employed chromatography on a column of activated charcoal to afford a solid of 96% purity. The compound was then purified even further by recrystallization from acetone-ethanol-water *(7)*.

An unusual extraction procedure is shown in **Scheme 6** for the purification of soraphen $A_{1\alpha}$ from a myxobacterium. An adsorbent resin was added to a large-scale fermentation vessel prior to inoculation so that the metabolite was continuously adsorbed as it was produced. Not only did this simplify the isolation, but it also resulted in increased production of the compound by the organism, possibly because adsorbent effectively removed metabolite from the system, thus reducing any feedback inhibition. The eluate from the resin was sufficiently clean that it required only solvent extraction prior to a crystallization step that yielded reasonably pure soraphen $A_{1\alpha}$ *(8)*.

5. Conclusions

Once some information about the nature of the compound has been established, a strategy for the purification can be planned. There is no "correct way"

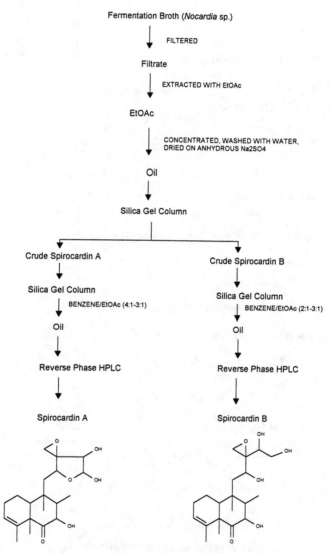

Fermentation Broth (*Nocardia* sp.)

↓ FILTERED

Filtrate

↓ EXTRACTED WITH EtOAc

EtOAc

↓ CONCENTRATED, WASHED WITH WATER, DRIED ON ANHYDROUS Na2SO4

Oil

↓

Silica Gel Column

Crude Spirocardin A

↓

Silica Gel Column

↓ BENZENE/EtOAc (4:1-3:1)

Oil

↓

Reverse Phase HPLC

↓

Spirocardin A

Crude Spirocardin B

↓

Silica Gel Column

↓ BENZENE/EtOAc (2:1-3:1)

Oil

↓

Reverse Phase HPLC

↓

Spirocardin B

Scheme 1. Isolation of Spirocardins A and B.

to extract a natural product; there are a myriad of effective methods. In practice—and quite sensibly—people tend to turn to a method or technique that they are familiar with or that is routinely used in their lab (and the experience that comes with this

Fermentation Broth

EtOAc Extraction of Whole Broth

EtOAc Layer

      CONCENTRATED,
      WASHED WITH METHANOL

Oil

Silica Gel Column

Sephadex LH20 Column

      ELUTE WITH MeOH

Mixture of Glucopiericidinols A1, A2 and Glucopiericidin A

Silica Gel Column

      CHCl$_3$-MeOH (9:1)

Mixture of Glucopiericidinols A1 and A2

Reverse Phase HPLC

Glucopiericidinol A1   GlucopiericidinolA2

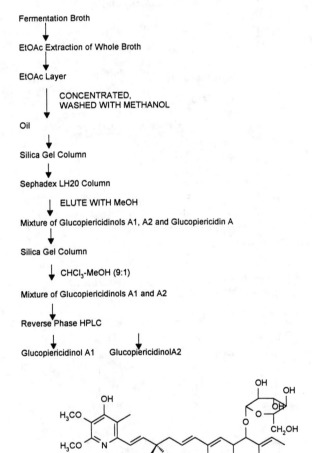

Glucopiericidinol A$_1$, Glucopiericidinol A$_2$ R1, R2 = OH, CH$_3$

Scheme 2. Isolation of Glucopiericidinols.

obviously makes a succesful isolation more likely). There is a danger, however, in becoming blinded or narrow-minded and not considering fully the worth or ease of other techniques or being reluctant to try other approaches because they are unfamiliar.

MeOH Extract of Powdered Stems of *Serjania salzmanniana*

| EVAPORATED TO DRYNESS

MeOH-H$_2$O (1:2) Suspension of Residue Extracted x3 with CHCl$_3$

| COMBINED CHCl$_3$ EXTRACT EVAPORATED TO DRYNESS

Column Chromatography of Residue on Silica Gel

Fractions Monitored by TLC (CHCl3-MeOH-H2O [7:3:1])
Fractions with R$_f$ Values 0.04-0.14 Pooled

Countercurrent Chromatography (CHCl$_3$-MeOH-H$_2$O [7:3:1])

Silica Gel Column Chromatography OR Preparative TLC (EtOAc-MeOH-H$_2$O [18:7:10])
of Fractions Containing Saponins **1-4**

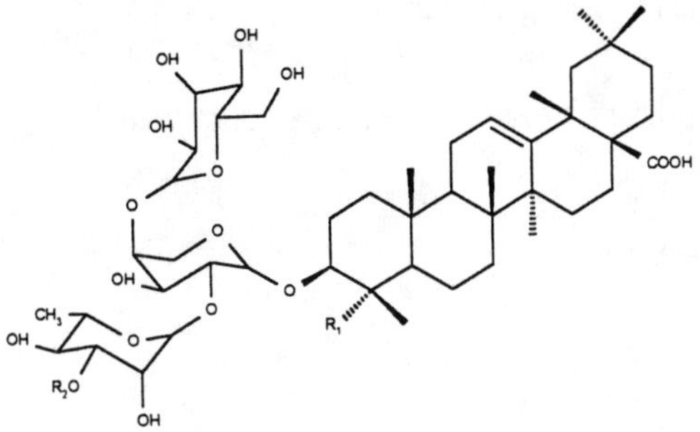

	R1	R2
1	CH$_2$OH	H
2	CH$_3$	H
3	CHO	H
4	CH$_2$OH	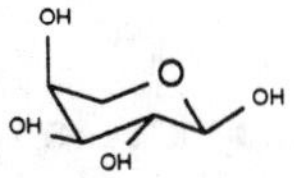 (sugar structure)

Scheme 3. Isolation of Saponins from *Serjania salzmanniana*.

It is perhaps slightly artificial to discuss purification apart from the context of structure determination. We rarely isolate compounds without attempting at

Dried Fungus (*Peziza* sp.)

↓ EXTRACTED x4 WITH H₂O (WITH SONICATION)

Pooled Aqueous Extracts

↓ EVAPORATION
  REDISSOLVED IN SMALL VOLUME OF H₂O
  CENTRIFUGED TO REMOVE PARTICULATES

Aqueous Concentrate

↓

Anion Exchange Column (Sephadex QAE)

↓ H₂O ELUTION

Cation Exchange Column (SPC25)

↓

Reverse Phase HPLC (Mobile Phase: 0.05% AcOH/H2O)

↓

Epipenteneomycin I

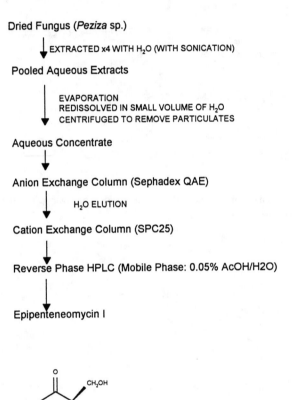

Scheme 4. Isolation of Epipentenomycin I.

some stage to determine exactly what they are. In many instances, the aim of isolating a natural product is to determine its structure and whereas it has generally been the case that in order to elucidate the structure of a natural product, that natural product has first to be isolated, technological developments mean that this necessity is decreasing. Coupled, or "hyphenated," techniques, such as LC-MS and LC-NMR, that unite separation and structural analysis into a

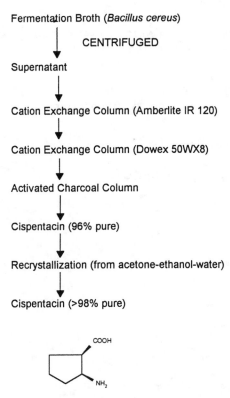

Scheme 5. Isolation of Cispentacin.

single system, mean that structures can be fully or partly determined as a separation is carried out, without first preparing some pure material. Developments in two-dimensional NMR techniques also mean that it is becoming increasingly possible to determine structures of components of complex mixtures such as microbial broths. Additionally, the increasing power of physical methods exemplified by the increasing field strength of NMR spectrometers, and improving ionization techniques of mass spectrometry, mean that now it is

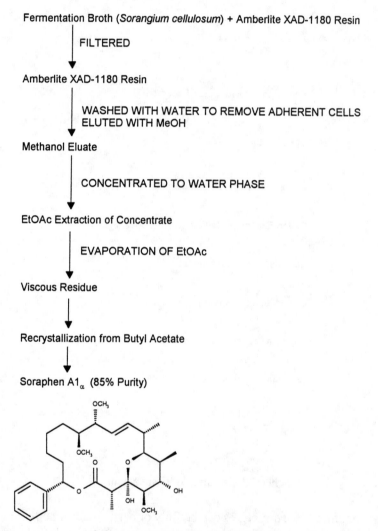

Fermentation Broth (*Sorangium cellulosum*) + Amberlite XAD-1180 Resin

    FILTERED

Amberlite XAD-1180 Resin

    WASHED WITH WATER TO REMOVE ADHERENT CELLS
    ELUTED WITH MeOH

Methanol Eluate

    CONCENTRATED TO WATER PHASE

EtOAc Extraction of Concentrate

    EVAPORATION OF EtOAc

Viscous Residue

Recrystallization from Butyl Acetate

Soraphen A1$_\alpha$ (85% Purity)

Scheme 6. Isolation of Soraphen A1α.

often possible to elucidate structures from very small amounts of material thus adding to the blurring of the boundaries between analytical and
preparative methods.

6. Notes

1. Care should be taken to ensure that the material is fully resuspended. If, for example, the sample is dried for several hours in a heated vacuum centrifuge, it may settle on the bottom of a tube as a hard crust that may be very difficult to fully resuspend. There is also a danger of a soluble compound appearing to be insoluble because it is physically associated with insoluble material and not properly accessible to the solvent. In this case, ultrasonication, or mechanical mixing of samples is useful.

2. If the compound does not appear to be in either phase, check that it does not form part of the insoluble layer, or emulsion, that sometimes forms at the partition interface.

3. These tests, essentially very simple and straightforward, present their own practical problems. If a small portion of what may be a fairly limited sample is being used, one may be forced to work with small volumes, which can lead to errors and problems. It is difficult, for example, to carry out solvent–solvent extractions using very small volumes. A small amount of solvent may easily evaporate in a short time or "creep" up the side of the vessel, and the loss of these small amounts may represent a large proportion of the total volume and may lead to large errors in the results of subsequent assays. With small volumes, the formation of some insoluble material/emulsion at the phase interface can lead to distortions in the relative volumes of the phases, and sampling from, or separating, the phases without significant carryover from the other phase can be tricky. These problems can be countered by using larger volumes where possible.

   Many of the solvents used (particularly water-immiscible solvents) will need to be evaporated before bioassay in aqueous systems. The resulting residue can be redissolved in a more suitable solvent, such as methanol or DMSO, then diluted to an appropriate tolerable level. Similarly, it is sometimes wise to adjust the pH with volatile acids, bases, or buffers so that they can be readily removed if it is necessary to dry a sample prior to assay, thus reducing the chance of interference with the assay or the compound.

4. The importance of testing controls (i.e., resins treated with solvents/solution but containing no sample) should be emphasized, particularly when using bioactivity assays. It is not uncommon for assay-interfering materials to be washed from resins or for traces of contaminants in solvents to be concentrated during the process, giving rise to misleading bioactivity results or even spurious chromatogram peaks.

5. Although adsorption energy on alumina is used as the standard parameter, the values for silica are very similar.

   The other main measures of solvent strength, the Hildebrand solubility parameter (δ) and the solvent polarity parameter (P'), are calculated by addition of the various intermolecular forces and addition of figures related to the solubility of the solvent in ethanol, dioxane, and nitromethane, respectively. They result in similar eluotropic series, though there are significant differences that reflect the fact that there are several properties of the solvent (dipole moment, solvation properties, and so on) that determine the degree of interaction between the solvent and the stationary phase.

6. Stepwise elution has the advantage that it doesn't require complex equipment. However, it is possible to make a simple gradient former suitable for some circumstances, as shown in **Fig. 15.**

References

1. Zähner, H., Drautz, H., and Weber, W. (1982) Novel approaches to metabolite screening, in *Bioactive Secondary Metabolites: Search and Discovery* (Bu'Lock, J. D., Nisbet, L. J., Winstanley, D. J., eds.), Academic, London, pp. 51–70.
2. Ghisalberti, E. L. (1993) Detection and Isolation of Bioactive Natural Products, in *Bioactive Natural Products: Detection, Isolation and Structural Determination* (Colegate, S. M. and Molyneux, R. J., eds.), CRC, Boca Raton, FL.
3. Nakajima, M., Okazaki, T., Iwado, S., Kinoshita, T., and Haneishi, T. (1989) New diterpenoid antibiotics, spirocardins A and B. *J. Antibiot.* **42,** 1741–1748.
4. Funayama, S., Ishibashi, M., Anraku, Y., Miyauchi, M., Mori, H., Komiyama K., and Omura, S. (1989) Novel cytocidal antibiotics, glucopiericidinols A1 and A2. Taxonomy, fermentation, isolation, structure elucidation and biological characteristics. *J. Antibiot.* **42,** 1734–1740.
5. Ekabo, O. A., Farnsworth, N. R., Henderson, T. O., Mao, G., and Mukherjee R. (1996) Antifungal and molluscicidal saponins from *Serjania salzmanniana. J. Nat. Prod.* **59,** 431–435.
6. Bernillon, J., Favre-Bonvin, J., Pommier, M., and Arpin, N. (1989) First isolation of (+)-epipentenomycin I from *Peziza* sp. carpophores. *J. Antibiot.* **42,** 1430–1432.
7. Konishi, M., Nishio, M., Saitoh, K., Miyaki, T., Oki, T., and Kawaguchi, H. (1989) Cispentacin, a new antifungal antibiotic I. Production, isolation, physico-chemical properties and structure. *J. Antibiot.* **42,** 1749–1755.
8. Gerth, K., Bedorf, N., Irschik, H., Hofle, G., and Reichenbach, H. (1994) The soraphens: a family of novel antifungal compounds from *Sorangium cellulosum* (Myxobacteria) I. Soraphen A$_{1\alpha}$: fermentation, isolation, biological properties. *J. Antibiot.* **47,** 23–31.

Selected References

Sewell, P. A. and Clarke, B. (1987) *Chromatographic Separations.* Wiley, Chichester, U.K.
Bristow, P. A. (1976) *LC In Practice.* hetp, Cheshire, UK.
Poole, C. K. and Poole, S. K. (1991) *Chromatography Today.* Elsevier, Amsterdam.
Colegate, S. M. and Molyneux, R. J. (eds.) (1993) *Bioactive Natural Products: Detection, Isolation and Structural Determination.* CRC, Boca Raton, FL.
Weinstein, M. J. and Wagman, G. H. (eds.) (1978) *Antibiotics: Isolation, Separation, Purification,* Journal of Chromatography Library, vol. 15. Elsevier, Amsterdam.
Natori, S., Ikekawa, N., and Suzuki, M. (1981) *Advances in Natural Products Chemistry. Extraction and Isolation of Biologically Active Compounds.* Halstead, Wiley, New York.
Wagman, G. H. and Cooper, R. (eds.) (1989) *Natural Products Isolation: Separation Methods for Antimicrobials, Antiviral and Enzyme Inhibitors,* Journal of Chromatography Library, vol. 43. Elsevier, Amsterdam.
Verrall, M. S. and Hudson, M. J. (eds.) (1987) *Separations for Biotechnology.* Ellis Horwood, Chicester, UK.

Kennedy, J. F. and Cabral, J. M. S. (eds.) (1993) *Recovery Processes for Biological Materials*. Wiley, Chicester, UK.

Marston, A. and Hostettmann, K. (1991) Modern separation methods. *Nat. Prod. Rep.* **8,** 391–413.

Verrall, M. S. (1996) *Downstream Processing of Natural Products*. Wiley, Chichester, U.K.

Ikan, R. (1991) *Natural Products: A Laboratory Guide*. Academic, San Diego, CA.

Belter, P. A., Cussler, E. L., and Hu, W. S. (1988) *Bioseparations*. Wiley, New York.

2

Initial Extraction and Product Capture

F. Patrick Gailliot

A fermentation broth is a complex mixture of components that often contains only trace amounts of a desired product. Microorganisms typically produce a desired product at low concentration (<3% w/v), and in the early stages of research and development, desired compounds may only be present at the few parts per million concentration in fermentation broth, making the initial capture task even more challenging. The primary goals of the initial capture stage are to concentrate the product, separate the product from the biomass, and purify the product from dissimilar impurities. Final purification that separates closely related impurities is typically achieved via preparative chromatography or crystallization. In most situations, initial capture requires a sequence of operations to achieve the goal of a concentrated, sufficiently purified extract suitable for the final purification step, and, as such, it can represent a significant investment of resources.

This chapter has four sections that focus on laboratory-scale capture steps: solids removal, solvent extraction, solid phase adsorption, and expanded bed adsorption. Although these techniques are widely applicable, most of this chapter is aimed at extraction of microbial fermentation broth. Techniques specific to initial extraction of plants and marine organisms can be found in Chapters 12 and 13, respectively. The first section describes laboratory-scale procedures for batch filtration and centrifugation. The second section describes solvent-extraction procedures with either water-miscible or -immiscible solvents. The third section describes using adsorbents for solid-phase extraction. The fourth section describes a technique known as expanded bed adsorption, which is unique in that it enables resin-column recovery of product directly from unclarified fermentation broth.

From: *Methods in Biotechnology, Vol. 4: Natural Products Isolation*
Edited by: R. J. P. Cannell © Humana Press Inc., Totowa, NJ

1. Solid–Liquid Separation

1.1. Introduction

In fermentation work, product recovery from cell or cell debris presents a particularly challenging initial solid/liquid separation step. The solids are often compressible and gelatinous with small density differences compared to the liquid phase. Fermentation broth exhibits a wide range of physical properties because of the different morphologies of solids. Clarification of fermentation broth can be accomplished using either centrifugation or filtration. Although clarification is conducted early in the recovery sequence, it often occurs after the solvent-extraction step. For example, centrifugation of a fermentation broth containing low-density, small particulate solids after solvent addition benefits from the increased specific gravity difference between the solids and the aqueous-solvent liquid phase.

Although many broth properties influence the choice between filtration or centrifugation, the dominating factors are the solid's particle size and the solid–liquid density difference. Centrifugation is more strongly influenced by the particle size than is filtration. For some broth filtration, the filter capacity is only slightly affected by particle sizes over a wide range. As particle size decreases, separation costs via centrifugation increase more rapidly than for filtration. The general size crossover point at which filtration is preferred over centrifugation is in the 1- to 2-μm range, or roughly the size of *Escherichia coli*. Solid–liquid density difference is also an important factor for centrifugation but has negligible influence in filtration. Filtration's disadvantage is that small particles result in significantly low permeation rates, and membrane pores often become fouled by dissolved and insoluble contaminants, further lowering permeation rates.

1.2. Centrifugation

Centrifugation has been used to recover yeast from fermentation broth for nearly 100 yr. Since yeast are approximately an order of magnitude larger than bacteria, centrifugation capacity for yeast is approx 100 times greater than for bacteria. Typical viscosity for a bacterial fermentation broth may be 1–2 cP. Since bacteria are primarily 70–80% water, the bacteria and the medium-composition-density difference is generally low (0.1 g/L or less). Although the density difference is low, the dominant factor that determines the time and *g*-force needed to separate cells from the medium is the particle size. **Table 1** gives some phase characteristics of different solids.

Axelsson *(1)* provides a thorough discussion of centrifugation theory and industrial-scale applications. One of the important design features of modern centrifuges is that they are self-cleaning so that solids are removed without stopping broth feed. General-purpose laboratory centrifuges are not self-

Table 1
Sizes and Specific Gravities of Representative Solids *(8)*

Solids type	Particle size, μm	Solid–liquid density difference, kg · m^{-3}
Cell debris	0.2 × 0.2	0–120[a]
Bacterial cells	1 × 2	70
Yeast cells	7 × 10	90
Mammalian cells	40 × 40	70
Plant cells	100 × 100	50
Fungal Hyphae	1 × 10 (matted)	10
Floccules	100 × 100	—

[a]Cell debris densities vary depending on composition e.g., lipid content.

cleaning and must be completely stopped to remove accumulated solids. In one example *(2)* of the use of a pilot plant disk stack centrifuge (Westfalia Separator SB7) for centrifugation of *E. coli* fermentations, it was calculated that the liquid capacity was approx 275 L/h. In another study *(3)* of a centrifuge (Alfla-Laval BTPX 205), Datar and Rosen describe achieving a 10-fold cell solids concentration factor for *E. coli*. Liquid capacity will decrease sharply when processing cell debris.

For spherical particles and Newtonian fluids, the settling velocity under an applied centrifugal force was described by Hsu *(4)* as:

$$V = d^2 (\delta\rho) \omega r / 18 \, \mu$$

where V is the settling velocity, d is particle diameter, ω is the angular velocity, r is the particle radial position, μ is the liquid viscosity, and $\delta\rho$ is the difference between the particle and liquid specific gravity. While there are often deviations from the ideal case, the equation provides useful guidance for manipulating physical broth properties to improve settling. For example, if the particle density is 1.05 g/L and the liquid density is 1.02, then a small decrease in liquid density to 0.96 (e.g., by methanol addition) could triple the settling velocity. If the methanol also lowers the viscosity, the settling rate would be further increased. Since the settling rate is proportional to the "square" of the particle diameter, simply cutting the particle size in half will quadruple the required settling time. Provided the product is not heat labile, increasing the temperature to lower viscosity also improves the settling rate. The angular velocity and particle radial position are fixed by the laboratory centrifuge dimensions. A typical laboratory centrifuge with 4 × 1-L bottle capacity operates at 3500–6000 rpm and applies 3000–5000*g* centrifugal force.

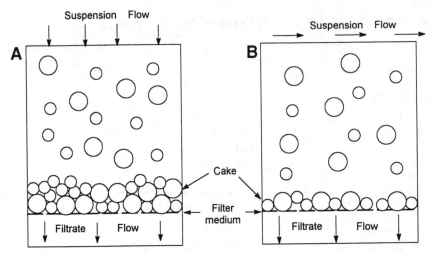

Fig. 1. Basic filtration modes. **(A)** Dead-end filtration. **(B)** Crossflow filtration.

1.3. Filtration

The driving force for filtration is the differential pressure across the membrane surface, and this can be controlled using either vacuum below the membrane or pressure above the liquid. Pressure can provide several advantages. One is that pressure minimizes denaturation of proteins and other biological molecules by reducing foaming downstream of the membrane. Pressure also minimizes evaporation of solvent from the filtrate receiver. Pressure filtration also allows the use of driving forces greater than atmospheric pressure (760 mmHg), but this advantage is often limited by the compressibility of the solids.

There are two basic configurations for filtration: dead-ended and crossflow. **Figure 1** shows the differences between dead-ended and crossflow filtration. In dead-ended filtration, the suspension flow is perpendicular to the membrane surface, and solids accumulate at the membrane surface. In crossflow filtration, the liquid moves parallel to the membrane surface.

1.3.1. Dead-Ended Filtration

Dead-ended filtration of fermentation broth is complicated by the problem of low porosity and compressibility of the accumulated solids, which results in gradually decreasing permeability during the filtration cycle. With compressible solids, an increase in the differential pressure across the membrane can actually lead to a reduced permeation rate. This problem can be reduced by the use of filter aids added to the broth and onto the filter paper as a precoat. The two most widely used filter aids are the diatomaceous earths and the perlites.

Table 2
Typical Properties of Diatomaceous Earths *(9)*

Grade	Density, lb-ft^{-3} Dry	Wet	pH	Water adsorption,%	Relative flow rate
Filter Cel	7.0	15.9	7.0	235	100
Standard Super Cel	8.0	17.9	7.0	255	200
512 Hyflo	8.0	17.9	7.0	250	300
Super Cel	9.0	17.9	10.0	245	500
501	9.5	16.9	10.0	250	750
535	12.0	17.6	10.0	245	1350
545	12.0	18.0	10.01	240	2160

The diatomaceous earths are skeletal remains of tiny aquatic plants deposited centuries ago while the perlites are processed from volcanic rock. Typical properties of the diatomaceous earths manufactured by Johns-Manville are presented in **Table 2**.

A dead-ended laboratory filtration apparatus is relatively simple. It consists of a vacuum rated filter flask, large filter funnel with perforated plate, and a filter paper disk covering the perforations. The filter paper should be wetted and vacuum applied to hold the paper against the funnel while a precoat water slurry of filter aid is applied to the funnel to create a precoat layer of approx 0.5 in. thickness. Additional filter aid should be added to the fermentation broth and well mixed before pouring broth onto the funnel. Amount of filter aid added depends on the broth characteristics, but a typical starting point would be 50 g/L of broth.

1.3.2. Crossflow Filtration

The most common technique used to achieve the movement of liquid parallel to the membrane surface is by pumping the slurry across the membrane surface. This flow induces shear forces on the particles at the surface, which reduces the depth of the solid boundary layer at the membrane surface, thus allowing higher permeation rates. Crossflow filter modules are available in different geometric arrangements: hollow fiber, spiral, plate-frame, and tubular. There is also a wide selection of membrane materials, including some that are solvent-resistant. **Table 3** gives some of the advantages and disadvantages of the various geometric arrangements. Precautions should be taken not to use plate-frame modules equipped with turbulence-enhancing screens, since they quickly become plugged with particulate. The two most widely used pore sizes for solid–liquid separation in biotechnology are microfilters and ultrafilters. Pore sizes of commonly used microfilters range from 0.1 to 0.65 μm. Ultrafilters have pores smaller than microfilters and are rated in terms of their nominal molecular-weight cutoff (NMWC). Commonly used

Table 3
Advantages and Disadvantages
of Crossflow Module Configurations *(10)*

Configuration	Advantages	Disadvantages
Tubular	Wide channels less prone to blockage Crossflow velocity between 2 and 6 m/s Reynolds numbers >10,000 Easy to clean Simple membrane replacement	Low surface area-to-volume ratio High liquid holdup High energy consumption
Hollow fiber	High wall shear rates $(4000–14,000\ s^{-1})$ High surface area-to-volume ratio Low liquid holdup Low energy consumption	Narrow channels more prone to blockage Crossflow velocity between 0.5 and 2.5 m/s Reynolds numbers 500–3000 Max. operating pressure limited to approx 2 bar High membrane replacement cost
Spiral wound	High surface area-to-volume ratio Low capital cost Reasonably economical	Narrow channels more prone to blockage Design prone to collapse Requires clean feed streams
Flat sheet	Simple membrane replacement Visual observation of permeate from each membrane pair Moderate energy consumption	Cannot be backflushed Low surface area-to-volume ratio Relatively high capital cost

ultrafilters range from 10,000 to 500,000 NMWC. After removing particulate via microfiltration, ultrafiltration can also be used to concentrate soluble macromolecules.

For a laboratory crossflow filtration, a basic system consists of a pump, retentate reservoir, permeate reservoir, pressure gages, filter module, connections, and valves. **Figure 2** is an example of a typical setup. The connections are generally flexible tubing, and peristaltic pumps are most commonly used for low-to-moderate pressure applications. Higher pressures or flow rates may require rotary lobe pumps. Procedures for preconditioning, operating conditions (pressure, temperature, circulation flow rate, and so on), cleaning, sanitization, and storage vary with module configuration and manufacturer.

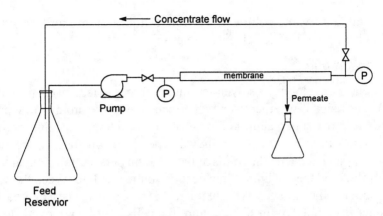

Fig. 2. Crossflow lab setup.

One problem with crossflow membrane devices is the limited ability to handle heavy particulate concentrations (typically >10 vol %) or large particulate. Heavy particulate concentrations or large particulate can cause blockage of the device components, such as tubing, inlet/outlet ports, or the flow channels, rather than the membrane pores. Narrowly spaced flow channels give better shear but increase pressure drop and the possibility of pluggage. To protect against pluggages, broth may require pretreatment to remove particles above 100 μm using vibrating screens or bag filters. The detailed theory of crossflow filtration can be found elsewhere *(5–7)*.

2. Solvent Extraction

2.1. Introduction

Solvent extraction is widely used during early purification of fermentation-derived products and, indeed, of all natural product matrices for initial and intermediate purification prior to final purification by chromatography, crystallization, or precipitation. Solvent extraction provides the ease of liquid handling, the potential for high-throughput operation, and the potential for adaptation to continuous operation. Both water-miscible and immiscible solvents are used for extracting compounds from the biomass. Frequently, multiple approaches can be employed to purify a fermentation-derived product. Wildfeuer *(11)* describes many possible approaches for purification of the antibiotic cephalosporin C.

A number of literature reviews of liquid–liquid extraction of antibiotics *(12)*, small molecules *(13)*, and biopolymers *(14)* have been published. The goal of this section is to give practical instructions for developing solvent extraction for a laboratory-scale process. Several examples of solvent extraction using water-miscible solvents followed by liquid–liquid extraction, or solvent extraction using immiscible solvents, are provided.

2.1.1. Background

Researchers developing a solvent-extraction process face two initial decisions. One decision is whether to extract directly the whole broth or to separate the solids and the supernatant before solvent extraction. Deciding between direct solvent extraction or solids removal depends on whether the product is completely associated with the solids or the medium or is partially contained in both the solids and the medium. If the desired solute is split between the solids and the medium, then direct solvent extraction is probably the best approach. If the product is completely in the medium, the cells may be removed first by centrifugation or filtration and then the product recovered from the medium by either solvent extraction or adsorption. When the product is completely cell-associated, there are two general approaches. One is to extract directly the whole broth with solvent and separate the phases by centrifugation. The other is to centrifuge or filter the whole broth to concentrate the solids and then to extract the solids with water-miscible solvents. Centrifugation or filtration is then used again to separate the solvent from the cells.

The other decision is the choice between water-miscible and water-immiscible solvents. Direct solvent extraction with water-miscible solvent has the disadvantage of resulting in more dilute solute concentration. To offset the dilution effects, the first step after removal of solids is usually concentration by solid phase adsorption or solvent partition. Direct extraction with water-immiscible solvent provides a larger immediate concentration factor but may be accompanied by a more difficult liquid–liquid separation owing to emulsion formation.

2.1.2. Partition Coefficients

The distribution of a solute between two immiscible phases expresses the degree of separation performance. Liquid–liquid extraction relies on the uneven distribution of solutes between the two immiscible phases. It is usually expressed in terms of a partition or distribution coefficient:

$$K = C_a/C_b$$

where C_a, C_b are the solute concentrations at equilibrium in phase a and phase b, respectively. Usually in fermentation broth, the initial extraction phases are culture medium and an immiscible solvent but in subsequent extractions they may be two immiscible solvents (e.g., methanol-hexane, aqueous sodium chloride-tetrahydrofuran). Since the mutual solubility of water and solvents is often not negligible, the phases must be mutually saturated before determination of a partition coefficient.

The primary goals of solvent extraction are solute concentration and purification. When the solute has a strong partition coefficient and impurities have a weak partition coefficient, it is possible to achieve some degree of purification. If the desired solute partitions strongly to the solvent and a low solvent-to-feed ratio is used, a concentration of the solute can also be achieved. In a typical situation, the extraction can eliminate the majority of the dissimilar impurities but extracts many of the close analogs, which must be separated in the final purification steps.

Partition coefficients of solutes are influenced by aqueous-solution properties (pH, ionic strength) and the solvent (hydrophobicity, polarity). Partition coefficients are relatively insensitive to temperature or solute concentrations over the ranges normally used in fermentation-broth processing. Among the aqueous properties, the pH is one of the more important variables (particularly for weak bases and acids). Several primary and secondary metabolites, such as penicillin, are weak acids or bases, and the pH can be used to control and even reverse the distribution coefficient. A list of pharmaceutical products that are weak acids or bases and are extracted with solvent is given in **Table 4**.

2.1.3. Solvent

Successful development of a commercial-scale solvent-extraction process depends to a large degree on selection of the most appropriate solvent. Important criteria for solvent selection include price, toxicological constraints, availability, solute selectivity, recovery difficulties, physical properties (water solubility, specific gravity, viscosity, boiling point), and operational hazards (flammability, volatility). Final choice would likely be a compromise among these criteria.

Commonly used water-immiscible solvents in industrial-scale processes include alcohols (isobutanol, *n*-butanol), ketones (particularly methyl isobutyl ketone), acetates (butyl, ethyl, isopropyl), hydrocarbons (toluene, hexanes), and methylene chloride. These solvents are inexpensive, readily available, and exhibit physical properties of low viscosity and density significantly different from water. Common water-miscible solvents are the alcohols (particularly methanol). For laboratory-scale processes, the selection is greater since selection is not constrained by economics. Craig and Sogn *(16)* have prepared an extensive compilation of such solvents.

At the laboratory scale, the economics, toxicological, or operational hazards of the solvent are usually not determining factors. Key criteria at laboratory scale are typically selectivity and solubility. However, if there is a probability that a laboratory procedure will be scaled up, then other factors (e.g., cost, toxicity, recoverability) should also be considered in the early laboratory development. **Table 5** lists physical properties of solvents commonly used for

Table 4
Solvent Extraction of Antibiotics *(20)*

Product	Medium	Solvent	pH
Actinomycin	Medium-free cells	1 methanol + 2 methylene chloride	2.5
Adrianimycin	Medium-free cells	Acetone	Acidic
Bacitracin	Cell-free medium	*n*-Butyl alcohol	7.0
Chloramphenicol	Cell-free medium	Ethyl acetate	Neutral-alkaline
Clavulanic acid	Cell-free medium	*n*-Butyl alcohol	2.0
Cycloheximide	Cell-free medium	Acetone/chloroform	Acidic
Ethromycin	Cell-free medium	Amyl acetate	Alkaline
Fusidic acid	Cell-free medium	Methyl-isobutyl ketone	6.8
Griseofulvin	Medium-free cells	Butyl acetate	Neutral
Macrolides	Cell-free medium	Methyl-isobutyl ketone, ethyl acetate	Alkaline
Nisin	Cell-free medium	Methylene chloride + secondary octyl Alcohol	4.5
Nisin	Whole broth	Methylene chloride	2.0
Oxytetracycline	Cell-free medium	Butyl alcohol	
Penicillin G	Cell-free medium	Butyl acetate, amyl acetate	2.0
Salomycin	Medium-free cells	Butyl acetate	9.0
Tetracycline	Cell-free medium	Butyl alcohol	
Tylosin	Cell-free medium	Amyl acetate, ethyl acetate	
Virginiamycin	Cell-free medium	Methyl-isobutyl ketone	Acidic

extraction of fermentation products. More complete listings can be found in the solvent handbooks *(16,17)*. Safety information can be found in the Material Safety Data Sheets provided by suppliers.

2.1.4. Equipment

There are several equipment types used in the chemical industry for commercial-scale solvent extraction. The most common is a mixer–settler arrangement consisting of one vessel with agitator for contacting the liquid phases and an unagitated vessel for gravity separation of the phases. To increase yield and reduce solvent use, several mixer-settler units are sometimes operated in countercurrent mode. A number of pilot-plant-scale and manufacturing-scale extractors have been developed to meet various needs. These include pulsed columns, agitated columns (rotating disk, Oldshue-Rushton), sprayed

Table 5
Properties of Common Solvents Used in Fermentation Broth Extraction[a]

Solvent	Polarity index	Refractive index @20°C	UV (nm) cutoff @ 1 AU	Boiling point, °C	Viscosity (cPoise)	Solubility in water, % w/w
Acetic Acid	6.2	1.372	230	118	1.26	100
Acetone	5.1	1.359	330	56	0.32	100
Acetonitrile	5.8	1.344	190	82	0.37	100
Benzene	2.7	1.501	280	80	0.65	0.18
Butyl acetate	4.0	1.394	254	125	0.73	0.43
n-Butanol	3.9	1.399	215	118	2.98	7.81
Carbon tetrachloride	1.6	1.466	263	77	0.97	0.08
Chloroform	4.1	1.446	245	61	0.57	0.815
Cyclohexane	0.2	1.426	200	81	1.00	0.01
1,2-Dichloroethane	3.5	1.444	225	84	0.79	0.81
Dichloromethane	3.1	1.424	235	41	0.44	1.6
Dimethylformamide	6.4	1.431	368	155	0.92	100
Dimethyl sulfoxide	7.2	1.478	268	189	2.00	100
Dioxane	4.8	1.422	215	101	1.54	100
Ethanol	5.2	1.360	210	78	1.20	100
Ethyl acetate	4.4	1.372	260	77	0.45	8.7
di-Ethyl ether	2.8	1.353	220	35	0.32	6.89
Heptane	0.0	1.387	200	98	0.39	0.0003
Hexane	0.0	1.375	200	69	0.33	0.001
Methanol	5.1	1.329	205	65	0.60	100
Methyl-t-butyl-ether	2.5	1.369	210	55	0.27	4.8
Methyl ethyl ketone	4.7	1.379	329	80	0.45	24
Pentane	0.0	1.358	200	36	0.23	0.004
n-Propanol	4.0	1.384	210	92	2.27	100
iso-Propanol	3.9	1.377	210	82	2.30	100
di-iso-Propyl ether	2.2	1.358	220	68	0.37	—
Tetrahydrofuran	4.0	1.407	215	65	0.55	100
Toluene	2.4	1.496	285	111	0.59	0.51
Trichloroethylene	1.0	1.477	273	87	0.57	0.11
Water	9.0	1.333	200	100	1.00	100
Xylene	2.5	1.500	290	139	0.61	0.018

[a]Data are from Phenomenex® analytical HPLC brochure.

towers, packed towers, mixer-settler units, and centrifugal contactors. A discussion of equipment selection can be found in Pratt and Hanson *(18)*. In the pharmaceutical industry, the liquid–liquid separator most frequently used is the centrifugal type such as the Podbeilniak. The latter is used quite extensively in the pharmaceutical and biotechnology industries because of its ability to handle high-throughput operations, the short contact time between phases, and the ability to separate emulsions. There are several laboratory and pilot-plant-scale apparatuses designed for countercurrent extraction *(19)*.

2.2. Methods and Examples

These procedures can be used for initial solvent extraction of hydrophobic solutes from fermentation broth and for a liquid–liquid purification of the solvent extract. These examples use simple laboratory equipment and batchwise agitation and settling stages. Provided the partition coefficient is large enough, only one batchwise extraction is needed. As the partition coefficient becomes less favorable, more than one extraction may be needed to achieve acceptable yields.

Since these examples are for research-laboratory work, economic concerns such as solvent recovery, reuse, or cost are not considered. Solvents such as acetonitrile or tetrahydrofuran have some immiscibility properties that are quite useful in laboratory work. However, economic costs would likely prevent their use in a commercial process. The goal in each example is to end up with a solvent extract that can easily be vacuum-concentrated and used in final purification steps (i.e., crystallization, precipitation, chromatography).

Examples 1 and 2 use acetonitrile for whole-broth solvent extraction. Tetrahydrofuran and isopropanol can also be used in this way. These solvents are completely miscible with water but have partial miscibility with aqueous sodium chloride. They also partition strongly to water-immiscible solvents (i.e., toluene, hexane, methylene chloride). Therefore, after initial extraction of whole broth it is possible to reject water and polar impurities in a subsequent liquid–liquid step. One advantage of this approach is avoidance of emulsions that can be a problem when water-immiscible solvents are used. Another advantage is that the partition coefficient and selectivity can be manipulated during the liquid–liquid step. Liquid phases usually separate with gravity settling owing to large specific gravity differences between phases.

Example 3 uses whole-broth-ethyl acetate extraction with solvent swing by pH adjustment. Solutes must be either weak acids or weak bases that can be extracted in or out of solvent by adjusting pH above or below the pKa of the solute. Since solutes may be unstable at extreme pH values, it is important to determine stability with small samples before using this method. This procedure is the purification method used commercially for many antibiotics, with penicillin being the most widely studied example. **Figure 3** shows the large changes of the distribution coefficient of penicillins and its impurities as a function of pH. Since any water-immiscible solvent can be used in this procedure, and because there are several interdependent parameters involved (partition coefficient, selectivity, emulsion tendency, separation characteristics), solvent

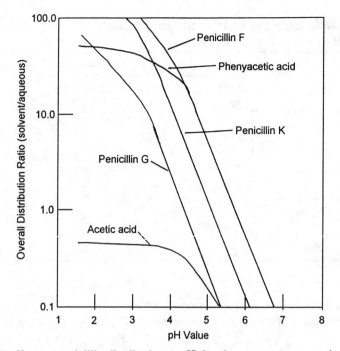

Fig. 3. pH effect on penicillin distribution coefficient between aqueous and solvent *(22)*.

selection is best carried out by trial and error. Time and effort invested in selecting a solvent depends on the individual situation. Ideally, the level of extract purity achieved will be high enough to allow crystallization or precipitation as the next purification step. A procedure for screening solvents is given in **Subheading 2.2.4.**

Example 4 is similar to example 3 except that the solvent swing is designed to be used with hydrophobic, nonionic solutes that are cell-associated. Low-molecular-weight alcohols (methanol, ethanol, propanol) are completely miscible with certain water-immiscible solvents (e.g., toluene, hexane, and so on) but have such strong partition coefficients for water that addition of small amounts creates two immiscible phases. **Table 6** gives the partition coefficient of alcohols between water and hydrocarbons. Advantages of this approach are similar to those cited for examples 1 and 2.

2.2.1. Example 1: Initial Acetonitrile Extraction Followed by Acetonitrile/Aqueous NaCl Purification

To the fermentation broth held in an Erlenmeyer flask containing a magnetic stir bar, add the minimum amount of acetonitrile needed to solubilize solute (**Note 1**). Agitate vigorously until equilibrium has been established (**Note**

Table 6
Partition Coefficients of Alcohols Between Water
and Organic Solvents at 25°C *(21)*

Solvent	Methanol	Ethanol	*n*-Propanol	*n*-Butanol
n-Hexane	0.0024	0.0083	0.03	0.25
n-Octane	0.0024	0.0068	0.03	0.25
Cyclohexane	0.0016	0.0079	0.028	0.13
Benzene	0.013	0.031	0.23	0.66
Toluene	0.007	0.03	0.15	0.50
Chlorobenzene	0.011	0.021	0.18	0.50
Chloroform	0.055	0.14	0.40	2.2
Carbon tetrachloride	0.008	0.018	0.12	0.51
Diethyl ether	0.14	0.32	0.40	4.1
n-Octanol	0.18	0.50	1.8	7.6
tri-*n*-butyl phosphate	0.20	0.54	2.7	14.5

2). After reaching steady state, transfer the whole broth-acetonitrile mixture to centrifuge bottles and centrifuge to separate solids from the supernatant. If maximum yield is desired, the wet solids should be extracted again with more aqueous acetonitrile (the same composition as the initial whole broth-acetonitrile). Combine the supernatants in an Erlenmeyer flask containing a magnetic stir bar, and while mixing, gradually add sodium chloride until the supernatant forms two liquid phases, an acetonitrile-rich phase and an aqueous-rich phase (**Note 3**). Transfer the contents to a graduated separating funnel, and allow the phases to separate by gravity. Note the volume of each and remove a sample of each using a pipet or syringe. Measure the solute concentration in each phase, determine the partition coefficient, and calculate the total amount of solute contained in the upper and lower phases. If solute recovery in the acetonitrile phase is acceptable, discard the lower aqueous phase. If recovery is unacceptable, there are two options to increase recovery. One is simply to back-extract the aqueous phase with more acetonitrile. The other is to simultaneously increase the acetonitrile volume and decrease the aqueous volume. This is done by returning the contents to the Erlenmeyer flask and adding more sodium chloride, mixing well, and then separating the phases.

2.2.2. Example 2: Initial Acetonitrile Extraction Followed by Aqueous Acetonitrile-Toluene Purification

To the fermentation broth held in an Erlenmeyer flask containing a magnetic stir bar, add the minimum amount of acetonitrile needed to solubilize solute (**Note 1**). Agitate vigorously until equilibrium has been established (**Note**

2). After reaching steady state, transfer the whole broth-acetonitrile mixture to centrifuge bottles and centrifuge to separate solids from the supernatant. If maximum yield is desired, the wet solids should be extracted again with more aqueous acetonitrile (the same composition as the initial whole broth-acetonitrile). Combine the supernatants into a Erlenmeyer flask containing a magnetic stir bar, and while mixing, gradually add toluene until the supernatant forms two liquid phases, a toluene-acetonitrile upper phase and an aqueous acetonitrile lower phase (**Note 4**). Transfer the contents to a graduated separating funnel, and allow the phases to separate by gravity. Note the volume of each phase and remove a sample of each using a pipet or syringe. Measure the solute concentration in each phase, determine the partition coefficient, and calculate the total amount of solute contained in the upper and lower phases. If solute recovery in the acetonitrile-toluene phase is acceptable, discard the lower aqueous phase. If recovery is unacceptable, back-extract the aqueous phase with more acetonitrile-toluene (**Note 5**).

2.2.3. Example 3: Ethyl Acetate Extraction Followed by pH Swing Purification

Acidify the whole broth to a pH value below the solute's pKa value. Add 100 mL ethyl acetate to 200 mL acidified whole broth in a 500-mL centrifuge bottle. Place bottle on shaker and agitate vigorously until equilibrium has been established. After reaching steady state, centrifuge in a small laboratory table-top centrifuge equipped with a swinging-bucket rotor in order to separate the liquid phases. Siphon to remove the upper ethyl acetate phase. If the partition coefficient does not strongly favor the ethyl acetate and maximum yield is desired, the aqueous phase should be extracted again with more ethyl acetate. Combine the ethyl acetate extracts in a Erlenmeyer flask containing a magnetic stir bar and add 50 mL water. Adjust the pH to a value above that of the solute's pKa value using base. Mix the solutions for approx 10 min and then transfer to bottles and centrifuge to separate the liquid phases (**Note 6**). Using a pipet, remove the lower aqueous phase containing the solute and transfer to an Erlenmeyer flask. If the partition coefficient does not strongly favor the aqueous phase, or if recovery of aqueous phase is low due to emulsion formation, the ethyl acetate should be extracted again with more water. Transfer the aqueous buffer to an Erlenmeyer flask containing a magnetic stir bar and add 25 mL ethyl acetate. Acidify the mixture to the desired pH using acid. Transfer the contents to a graduated separating funnel and allow phases to separate by gravity (**Note 7**). Note the volume of each phase and remove a sample of each using a pipet or syringe. Measure the solute concentration in each phase, determine the partition coefficient, and calculate the total amount of solute contained in the upper and lower phases. If solute recovery in the ethyl acetate phase is acceptable, discard the lower aqueous phase. If recovery is unacceptable, back-extract the aqueous phase with more ethyl acetate.

2.2.4. Selection of Water-Immiscible Solvents

Solvent-screening experiments can be carried out in 50-mL graduated test tubes. Add equal portions of fermentation broth and solvent to each test tube. Mix thoroughly using a vortex mixer or orbitory shaker until equilibrium is reached. Follow this with centrifugation in a small laboratory table-top centrifuge equipped with a swinging-bucket rotor. The centrifugal force and time required to achieve adequate separation of liquid phases varies with each broth and solvent combination. All samples should be centrifuged under the same conditions (time, speed) to allow comparison of emulsion formation tendencies. Record the volume of both liquid phases, and if there is an emulsion layer, note its size. Remove a sample of each liquid phase. Measure the product concentration and determine the partition coefficient. Take another sample of the solvent phase and evaporate to dryness in a air-circulation oven in order to measure the weight of other impurities coextracted with the product. Select the solvent based on yield and purity.

2.2.5. Example 4: Initial Methanol Extraction Followed by Aqueous Methanol-Toluene Purification

Fill centrifuge bottles half-full with whole broth, centrifuge solids, and discard the supernatant. Add methanol (about 5–10 mL/g of wet solids) to bottles. Place bottle on shaker and agitate vigorously until equilibrium has been established. After reaching equilibrium, centrifuge in a small laboratory table-top centrifuge equipped with a swinging-bucket rotor to separate the solid–liquid phases. Extract solids a second time with methanol to ensure complete extraction of solute from the solids. Combine the methanol extracts in a Erlenmeyer flask containing a magnetic stir bar and add an equal volume of toluene. After mixing for approx 5 min, allow settling, and sample both liquid phases. If the solute has not partitioned sufficiently into the toluene phase, mix and gradually add more water to force the solute into the toluene phase. Transfer the contents to a graduated separating funnel and allow the phases to separate by gravity (centrifugation may be necessary). Cut and discard the lower aqueous methanol phase. Add an equal volume of 90% methanol/water (v/v) to the toluene phase in a separating funnel and mix well. After mixing for approx 5 min, allow settling for sufficient time to take samples of both liquid phases. If the solute has not partitioned sufficiently back into the methanol phase, mix and gradually add hexane to force the solute back into the methanol phase.

3. Solid Phase Extraction

3.1. Introduction

Solid phase extraction utilizes adsorbents for sample cleanup, trace enrichment, and fractionation of desired products in crude solvent extracts from fermentation broth. Solid phase extraction avoids the emulsion problems often encountered in liquid–liquid extraction and achieves significant simultaneous concentration and purification factors. When used for sample cleanup, the cartridge either retains the desired solutes while passing undesired components or passes the desired solutes while retaining interfering components. Trace enrichment allows concentration of components that are present below normal detection limits. Fractionation uses a step gradient to elute components of differing polarities.

3.2. Background

Solid phase extraction exploits the same product/sorbent interactions used in high-performance liquid chromatography. Separation efficiency is largely a function of the sample application flow rate and the sample/adsorbent volume ratio. As with any chromatographic method, there is a direct relationship between flow rate and separation efficiency, but an inverse relationship between flow rate and time required for separation. Lower flow rates improve separations but increase assay sample time. When flow rates are too high, the product may not have sufficient contact with the adsorbent. Consequences of excessive flow rate during loading may include:

- Peak resolution loss.
- Premature product breakthrough.
- Low product recovery.

Overloading the sample can lead to variable recovery or loss of resolution. Factors that determine the volume ratio include:

- Concentration of the products.
- Concentration of compounds related to interfering peaks.
- Capacity factor of products and interfering peak material.

When 100% recovery of multiple products from a sample matrix is required, the sample loading is limited by the product with the lowest capacity factor. If 100% recovery of one product is required, the sample loading should continue until just before breakthrough occurs for that product. Adjustment of the solvent composition of the sample can be used to increase the difference between capacity factors for products and materials related to interfering peaks.

3.3. Materials and Equipment

There are three general adsorbent classes used most often in solid phase extraction applications: polar, ion-exchange, and nonpolar. Each class exhibits unique properties of retention and selectivity based on interactive properties of the products and the adsorbent surface. If the chemical structure and functional groups of desired products are known, this information can be used in choosing the initial type of column for evaluation. **Table 7** lists some general selection guidelines. Resin particles are typically 40-μm-diameter particles with either 60- or 300-Å pores. The adsorbent's retention capacity is approx 5% of the adsorbent's weight. If a sample matrix is complex, the capacity for the desired product may be much less so. Most companies that sell analytical HPLC columns also market the prepacked solid phase extraction columns.

Solid phase extraction columns are disposable cartridges containing the prepacked adsorbent as shown in **Fig. 4**. The housing is constructed of polypropylene with a sample reservoir space above the adsorbent. The column outlet end has a Luer tip for attachment to multiple sample manifolds, robotics systems, or for single-sample processing. **Figure 5** is an example of a simple vacuum, or pressure, setup using a syringe. When sample throughput is not the critical factor, liquid may be passed through the cartridge simply by using gravity. Adsorbent is held in place between two 20-μm polyethylene fritted disks. The amount of adsorbent per cartridge generally ranges from 50 mg to as much as 10 g. Larger columns are used for greater retention capacity or for large volume samples.

3.4. Methods

3.4.1. Crude-Extract Preparation

The method of preparation of the crude extract prior to loading on the solid phase extraction column will depend on the compatibility of the column and the solvent. For example, if an aqueous methanol extract is loaded onto a normal phase column (e.g., silica gel, diol, or alumina), the sample must first be evaporated to dryness to remove water, which is incompatible with normal phase adsorbents, and then the residue must be dissolved in a nonpolar solvent such as ethyl acetate, toluene, or hexane that has limited solubility for the product. Conversely, if a toluene extract is loaded onto a reverse phase column (e.g., C8, C18), the sample should be evaporated to dryness and the residue dissolved in a minimal volume of solvent compatible with the mobile phase.

Even when the solvent is compatible with the column, preparation may still be needed depending on whether the product is to be adsorbed or passed through the column as interfering impurities are adsorbed. In some cases, the polarity of extract may be such that the product and/or impurities pass through the solid phase extraction column unretained. To achieve binding, the polarity must be altered either by addition of a weaker solvent (e.g., hexane to ethyl acetate extract for polar extraction, or water to acetonitrile extract for nonpolar extraction) or by partial removal of a solvent by vacuum rotary evaporation.

Simple dilution has the advantages of taking very little time and of being less likely to lead to precipitation of product because of over concentration. Its disadvantages are that sample loading time increases and the dilution may reduce the

Table 7
Adsorbent Selection Guide[a]

	Adsorbent	Analyte functional groups	Mode	Matrix	Typical solvents
Nonpolar extraction	C18-octadecyl	Strong nonpolar	Hydrophobic groups	Aqueous:Water	Methanol
	C8-octyl	Moderate nonpolar	Aromatic rings	Acetonitrile	
	C2- ethyl	Weak nonpolar	Alkyl chains	Buffers	Ethyl acetate
	CH-cyclohexyl	Weak nonpolar		Biological	Chloroform
	PH-phenyl	Moderate nonpolar		fluids	Acidic methanol
	CN-end capped	Moderate nonpolar			Hexane
	cyanopropyl	Moderate nonpolar/ polar			
Polar extraction	CN-cyanopropyl	Moderate nonpolar/ polar	Hydrophilic groups: Hydroxyls	Nonpolar	Methanol
			Amines	Hexanes	Isopropanol
	2OH-diol	Polar	Heteroatoms	Oils	Acetone
	Si-silica	Polar	(S, O, N)	Chloroform	
	NH$_2$-aminopropyl	Polar		Lipids	
Cation exchange extraction	SCX-benzenesulfonic acid	Strong cation	Cations:	Aqueous:	Alkaline buffer
	PRS-propylsulfonic acid	Strong cation	Amines	Water	High ionic
	CBA-carboxylic acid	Weak cation	Pyrimidines	Acidic buffers	strength buffer
				Biological fluids	
Anion exchange extraction	SAX-quaternary amine	Strong anion	Anions:	Aqueous:	Acidic buffer
	PSA-primary/ secondary amine	Weak anion/polar	Carboxylic acids	Water	High ionic
			Sulfonic acids	Acidic buffers	strength buffer
	NH$_2$-aminopropyl	Weak anion/polar	Phosphates	Alkaline buffers	
	DEA- diethylaminopropyl	Weak anion/polar		Biological fluids	

(continued)

Table 7 (continued)

	Adsorbent	Analyte functional groups	Mode	Matrix	Typical solvents
Covalent extraction	PBA-phenyl boronic acid	Covalent	Vicinal diols	Aqueous Alkaline buffer Biological fluids	Acidic buffer Acidic methanol

[a]Data taken from Varian Sample Preparation Products catalog (Harbor City, CA).

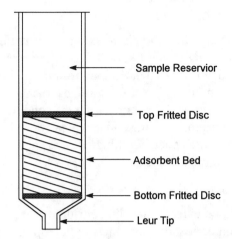

Fig. 4. Typical solid phase extraction cartridge.

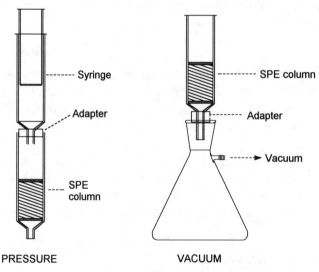

Fig. 5. Typical SPE cartridge setup.

adsorption capacity. Vacuum concentration has the advantages of shorter loading times and higher adsorption capacity because of the increased product concentration. Its disadvantages are the extra equipment needed and the time required for the concentration. Any gross contaminants or particulate matter that appear during the dilution or concentration steps should be removed with a 20-μ prefilter.

3.4.2. Column Preconditioning

Prior to sample loading, the solid phase extraction cartridge column should be prewashed with a strong eluant (**Note 8**). After the prewash the cartridge must be equilibrated with 6–10 holdup volumes (a holdup volume is approximately equivalent to 1 mL per 0.5 g of adsorbent) of eluant of similar polarity to the sample solution. Flow rate during the conditioning is not critical in the way that it is for sample loading and is typically carried out at 5–10 mL/min. Once the adsorbent has been equilibrated, it is important to prevent the adsorbent drying out before sample application.

3.4.3. Sample Loading

The sample should be loaded onto the cartridge at less than 5 mL/min to achieve a narrow band of adsorbed products at the top of the cartridge (**Note 9**). When one of the objectives is to achieve trace component or maximum product concentration factor, the sample volume load should be just less than the maximum capacity of the adsorbent. This value may be determined experimentally (**Note 10**).

3.4.4. Wash

After loading, the cartridge should be washed with at least two holdup volumes of eluant of the same polarity as the sample feed. Collect the wash separately from the spent feed in case there is any product breakthrough.

3.4.5. Elution

Pipet the desired amount of solvent into the reservoir space above the adsorbent. Draw the solvent through very slowly. Minimum elution volume is two holdup volumes. The amount and strength of the elution solvent must be determined experimentally and depends on the objectives of the solid phase extraction (**Note 11**).

4. Expanded-Bed Adsorption

4.1. Introduction

There is always a need for streamlining the initial purification steps of products that are derived from fermentation. Recent advances in a technique called expanded-bed adsorption have shown the ability to eliminate the solid–liquid separation step and thereby increase product yield and reduce processing time. Expanded-bed adsorption is not a new concept, since there are reported applications for streptomycin (23) in the 1950s and novobiocin (24) in the 1970s. However, these applications used adsorbents that were not specifically designed for expanded-bed-adsorption procedures and often required complicated column equipment. Recent commercial availability of adsorbents specifically designed for expanded-bed-adsorption procedures has led to a renewed interest in the technology.

Adsorbents used in an expanded bed can lead to both concentration and purification of desirable natural products whereas the particulate pass through the column unretained. Expanded-bed adsorption differs from conventional column adsorption in the packing of the adsorbent. Conventional columns have adsorbent held rigidly in place between the supporting inlet and outlet distributors. This results in high efficiency of adsorption, but it requires a particulate-free feed solution. Expanded-bed columns have liquid space above the adsorbent that allows adsorbent movement and a larger void space between adsorbent particles when liquid flows upward. The void space between adsorbent particles is less efficient for adsorption but allows particulate solids to pass through the column. One of the difficulties of expanded-bed-adsorption columns is the control of the uniformity of the bed expansion to prevent liquid bypassing the adsorbent. This is known as channeling, and it results in insufficient contact for adsorption to occur between adsorbent and broth.

4.1.1. Background

In an expanded-bed column, the upward flow of liquid causes a drag force on the settled adsorbent beads and, if unrestrained by a top screen, the bed will begin to expand when the minimum fluidization liquid velocity is reached. As liquid flow rate continues to increase, the bed expands further, resulting in a larger void space between the adsorbent beads. If the liquid velocity continues to increase, the terminal velocity will eventually be reached, and the adsorbent will flow out of the column. Terminal velocity is determined by the column length and the physical properties of the adsorbent and the liquid. As long as the flow rate is between the minimum and terminal velocity, the adsorbent bed will remain in an stable expanded state as determined by the equilibrium between the downward gravitational force and the upward drag force. Expanded beds of this type have been described by Zaki and Richardson *(25)* and Lewis and Bowerman *(26)*. If the liquid contains particulate with a terminal velocity less than the operating flow rate, the particulate will simply pass through the void space between the adsorbent and be completely unretained in the column. Through appropriate design of the adsorbent physical properties (e.g., density, particle-size distribution), it is possible for the liquid flow in an expanded bed to closely approach ideal plug flow. Frontal analysis of breakthrough curves of Q-Sepharose and S-Sepharose Fast Flow (Pharmacia LKB Biotechnology AB, Uppsala, Sweden) using bovine serum albumin showed that the absorption performance of the expanded bed was similar to the packed bed *(27)*. This helps to maximize the equilibrium stages (theoretical plates) in the column and results in good adsorption.

Although there are variations, most expanded-bed-adsorption procedures generally consist of five basic steps as shown in **Fig. 6**. First, the packed bed of adsorbent is converted to an expanded bed using a particulate-free liquid. Second, the sample feed (e.g., a broth) containing particulate matter is fed through the column until the adsorbent is saturated with product. Third, the column is upwashed to remove particulate remaining in the voids of the bed. Fourth, the expanded bed is converted back to a packed bed by gravity settling or reversed flow and the product is eluted from the adsorbent. Fifth, the adsorbent is cleaned to remove strongly bound impurities and then re-equilibrated before the next batch.

Prior to the late 1980s, there were no adsorbents specifically designed for expanded-bed procedures, and this was a major obstacle to the implementation of this technology both at the laboratory and the industrial scale. Adsorbents must have both the physical properties for fluidization as well as the binding capacity and selectivity for the product. During the past several years, several adsorbents and columns specifically tailored for expanded-bed adsorption have been introduced.

Most reported applications have been for protein purification *(28–30)*. One example *(31)* was for direct recovery of Annexin V, an intracellular recombinant protein, from *E. coli* homogenate, using the Streamline™ DEAE adsorbent (Pharmacia). The procedure was developed in a laboratory-scale column (50 mm diameter by 1000 mm length) and then successfully scaled to a pilot-plant column (200 mm diameter by 950 mm length). The yield was 95% for both laboratory and pilot-plant runs and achieved a threefold reduction in volume compared to the homogenate.

Reported applications for small molecules have remained relatively limited. One application *(32)* using whole-broth solvent in an expanded-bed-adsorption application was for the capture of immunomycin using Sepabeads™ adsorbent (Mitsubushi Kasei, Tokyo, Japan). Immunomycin is a small molecule (mol wt <900) that has no ionic functionality, and therefore methanol was added to a fermentation broth to solubilize the immunomycin before passing the broth through the expanded-bed-adsorption column. The process was scaled up from a 1-in. lab column to a 30-in.-diameter pilot-plant column. Yields of immunomycin exceeded 95% and resulted in more than a 30-fold reduction in volume. In another example *(33)*, an expanded-bed adsorption was used for the discovery and isolation of pneumocandins from *Zalerion arboricola*. Again, this application used methanol as the solubilizing solvent and Sepabeads as the adsorbent, but include precentrifugation to remove large particulate solids. In this example, the centrifugation flow rate was significantly enhanced, since removal of fine particulate was not required.

This section is not an exhaustive study but is meant to provide practical considerations and illustrate basic methods in the development of an expanded-

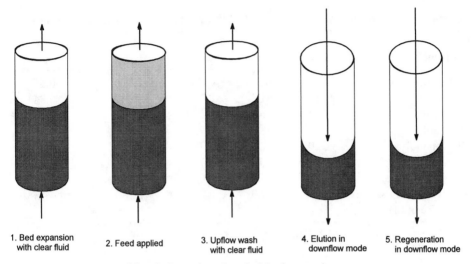

1. Bed expansion with clear fluid 2. Feed applied 3. Upflow wash with clear fluid 4. Elution in downflow mode 5. Regeneration in downflow mode

Fig. 6. Steps in expanded-bed operation.

bed-adsorption procedure. It has been written for a hydrophobic, nonionic product that requires addition of a solvent to the broth. The general approach described is similar to that used for proteins using buffer solutions and ionic products using pH shifts. It is hoped that this section will bring expanded-bed adsorption to the attention of researchers in natural products isolation and allow them to benefit from this powerful technique.

4.1.2. Materials: Solvents and Adsorbents

In order to use expanded-bed adsorption for nonpolar, water-insoluble products in a fermentation broth, it is necessary to add a water-miscible solvent initially to solubilize the product. Some common solvents used to solubilize nonpolar products are shown in **Table 8**. When solvents are used to solubilize a nonpolar product, it is essential to use the minimum volume of solvent required, as addition of excess solvent decreases the capacity of the adsorbent. This decrease in adsorptive capacity occurs for two reasons. The resin adsorption isotherm for the product is decreased owing to the excess solvent. Also, excess solvent decreases the product concentration in the liquid phase, and when operating in the linear range of the adsorption isotherm, this lower product concentration leads to a proportional decrease in the resin capacity. Operation in the linear range is the usual situation for the dilute-product solution encountered in fermentation broth in the early stages of research and development. However, the solvent addition does have an important beneficial side effect that increases procedure productivity. Solvent added to whole broth decreases both the specific gravity and the

Table 8
Common Water-Miscible Solvent for Solubilizing Nonpolar Compounds *(35)*

Solvent	UV[a] cutoff	B.P., °C	Density, g/cc	Refractive index	Viscosity, cP
Methanol	205	64.5	0.786	1.326	0.551
Acetonitrile	190	81.6	0.776	1.342	0.341
Acetone	330	56.1	0.784	1.356	0.303
Ethanol	210	78.3	0.785	1.359	1.08
2-propanol	205	82.2	0.781	1.375	2.04
1-propanol	240	97.2	0.799	1.384	1.94
Tetrahydrofuran	212	65.9	0.888	1.405	0.460
2-Methyl-2-Propanol (*t*-Butanol)		82.3	0.781	1.385	4.438

[a]Approximate wavelength below which solvent has low UV absorbance *(36)*.

viscosity of the liquid phase, which leads to increased terminal velocity of the adsorbent and results in shorter adsorption time cycles. The solvent has no effect on the relative difference in the terminal velocity between the adsorbent and the particulate in the whole broth.

A partial listing of available resins is given in **Table 9**. The Sepabeads adsorbents were introduced commercially in the mid 1980s (Mitsubushi Kasei) and were designed with a density of approx 1.2 g/L, achieved by bromination of the styrene divinyl benzene copolymer base matrix. A beneficial side effect of the bromination was that the surface hydrophobicity was increased relative to the naked polymer. In the case of β-lactam antibiotics such as cephalosporin C, the capacity was more than doubled from 25–50 g/L for the HP series (Mitsubushi Kasei Corp.) to 90–120g/L for Sepabeads. The Streamline adsorbents for proteins were introduced in 1993 (Pharmacia) and also feature a well-defined density of 1.2 g/L achieved by inclusion of an inert core material in the matrix.

4.1.3. Laboratory Equipment

A typical laboratory setup includes a column, fraction collector, and peristaltic pump connected with flexible tubing. In some cases an on-line spectrophotometer may be useful, but generally the large number of UV-absorbing compounds in the feed results in data that has a weak, or no, correlation with product adsorbance. The standard practice is to collect the column-effluent fractions and perform analysis by methods such as HPLC to determine product concentration in the effluent.

One of the differences between conventional packed bed and expanded-bed adsorption involves the selection of column length. A longer column length

Table 9
Adsorbents for Expanded Bed Adsorption[a]

Property	Streamline SP	Streamline DEAE
Type of ion exchanger	Strong cation	Weak anion
Functional group	Sulfopropyl (SP)	Diethylaminoethyl, DEAE
	$-O\text{-}CH_2CHOHCH_2O(CH_2)_3SO_3$	$-O\text{-}CH_2CH_2N(C_2H_5)_2H$
Ionic capacity per milliliter adsorbent	0.17–0.24 mmol/mL	0.13–0.21 mmol/mL
Matrix structure	Macroporous, crosslinked agarose, 6% containing a crystalline quartz core	Macroporous, crosslinked agarose, 6% containing a crystalline quartz core
Mean particle size (range)	200 μm (100–300 μm)	200 μm (100–300 mm)
Particle density	Approx 1.2 g/mL	Approx 1.2 g/mL
Degree of expansion at 300 cm/h	2–3	2–3
Binding capacity, mg/mL adsorbent	Approx 70 mg Lysozyme	Approx 55 mg BSA

Property	Sepabead SP205	Sepabead SP206	Sepabead SP207
Surface area (m²/g dry)	507	556	627
Pore volume (mL/g)	1.04	0.94	0.79
Pore size diameter (angstroms)	Broad	200–800	100–300
Particle density (g/mL)	1.17	1.19	1.18
Particle size range (μm)	250/4500	250/600	250/600
Adsorption capacity			
Cephalosporin-C	91	101	118
α-Lactoalbumin (mw 14000)	30	30	19
Albumin (mw 66000)	30	26	5
γ-Globulin (mw120000)	25	15	2

[a]Data for Streamline obtained from Pharmacia Biotech '95 product catalog (Piscataway). Data for Sepabeads obtained from Mitsubishi Kasei Catalogs (Tokyo, Japan).

than is generally used for a conventional column is required because adsorbent-particle diameters are larger than conventional packed adsorbent, and there is more interstitial space between the adsorbent beads; thus the mass-transfer zone is longer. The simulated breakthrough curve of cephalosporin C with XAD-16™ (Rohm & Haas, Philadelphia, PA) adsorbent shown in **Fig. 7** illustrates the impact of bed depth on mass transfer for a specific particle size. According to the model, the large beads (310-μm diameter) required a minimum column length of 75 cm to achieve a sharp breakthrough curve. This was actually a study of packed beds; these beds have less interstitial space than found in an expanded bed and therefore represent slightly better conditions than achievable in

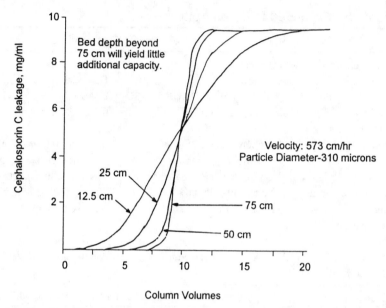

Fig. 7. Simulated breakthrough of Cephalosporin C effect of column length *(34)*.

an expanded bed. A typical expanded-bed-adsorption laboratory column may be 2–5 cm diameter by 50–100 cm length. Since pressure drop is extremely low, there is no upper limit for the column length.

Even more important than general dimensions are the bottom (feed inlet) and top (effluent outlet) liquid distributors. The bottom (feed inlet) distributor must allow free passage of the particulate, uniformly distribute the feed over the cross section of the column, and retain the resin when the flow is stopped or in the downflow direction. The top (effluent outlet) connection should be movable so that it can be raised during the upflow loading cycle to just above the expanded bed and then lowered during the downflow elution cycle to just above the packed-bed height. Since the top connection must allow passage of particulate but does not have to retain resin during downflow, it can be used without any screen. A screen may be useful as protection against accidental resin loss during the expanded-bed loading cycle or if upflow packed-bed wash or elution is desired. Two simple schematic designs of distributors are shown in **Fig. 8**. In Design A, the feed flows through the resin support screen that has openings slightly less than the adsorbent diameter, typically 200–600 μm. This design requires screening or other whole-broth pretreatment to ensure that none of the feed particulates are larger than the screen opening. In Design B, the feed is introduced above and then deflected off the bottom screen to diffuse the inlet jet-nozzle effect and to provide relatively uniform distribution across the cross-

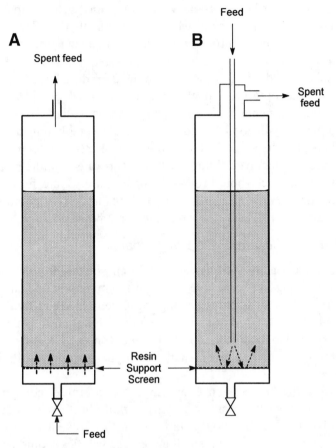

Fig. 8. Expanded-bed feed arrangements. (**A**) Feed passes through adsorbent support. (**B**) Feed enters above adsorbent support screen.

section of the column. An advantage of this design is that it will not plug if traces of particulate in the feed are larger than the screen openings.

4.2. Method

4.2.1. Whole-Broth Preparation

Some fermentation broths are immediately suitable for expanded-bed-adsorption procedures, but others may require adjustment before processing. As previously discussed, one requirement is that the particulate solids must have lower terminal velocity than the adsorbent in order to permit passage of the particulate whereas the adsorbent is retained. Some broths may form filamentous mycelia or clumps that can accumulate and block the openings of the inlet distributor screen or have sufficiently high terminal velocity to accumulate in the column. There are various techniques to handle these larger solids. One is to pass the whole broth through a simple mesh screen before application to the column. If the product is intracellular, the screening should be carried out after the solvent addition in order to minimize product losses in the discarded solids. Another option is to declump the solids via a high-shear pump or homogenizer. If the fermentation broth has high viscosity, the terminal velocity of the adsorbent may be too low and result in unacceptably long adsorption cycle times. This problem could be countered by an increase in temperature if the product is not heat-labile or dilution with solvent-water mixture having the same composition as the whole-broth-solvent mixture. Some fermentation broths may contain too much biomass and not flow through the column without entrapping adsorbent. These may be diluted or subdivided.

4.2.2. Whole-Broth–Solvent Ratio Determination

Solvent determination involves screening different solvents for product solubility and then titrating the best solvent to find the minimum solvent:whole-broth ratio. One method for screening a range of solvents is to add 1 vol of each solvent to 2 vol of whole broth. Samples are mixed for at least 1 h and then centrifuged or filtered to remove the solids. Product concentration in the supernatant is measured, and the solvent with the highest product solubility is selected (**Note 12**).

After choosing the best solvent, determine the minimum concentration required of that solvent by titrating 1 vol of whole broth with increasing amounts of solvent. Titration should start with a low solvent concentration such as 10% (v/v) and proceed with small increases. Samples should be mixed for at least 60 min and then centrifuged or filtered to remove the solids. Product concentration in the supernatant is measured, and the total quantity of product in the liquid phase is determined by multiplying liquid volume and product concentration. A solvent concentration is selected that is slightly less than that required for maximum product extraction (**Note 13**).

4.2.3. Formation of the Expanded Bed

Before the whole-broth–solvent stream can be fed to the column, the packed bed must be converted to an expanded bed. This is done by pumping a solids-free liquid through the column in an upflow direction and gradually increasing flow until the expanded bed is 1.5–3 times the packed-bed height and has stabilized. This liquid can be water or a water-solvent solution at the same ratio as the whole-broth-solvent feed. When forming an expanded bed in small-lab-scale columns, precautions should be taken to avoid accidentally introducing air into the bottom of the column since an air bubble may form across the cross-section of the column and cause the resin to move up the column as a packed plug (**Note 14**).

4.2.4. Product Adsorption

Once the bed has expanded and stabilized, the whole-broth–solvent mixture containing particulate can be pumped into the column. Since the physical properties (i.e., density, temperature, viscosity) of the whole-broth–solvent solution will be different from the liquid used to form the expanded bed, an adjustment of the pumping rate will be necessary to maintain the same level of bed expansion. Usually, the flow rate must be reduced (**Note 15**). In some situations, the whole-broth–solvent feed properties are so different from the liquid used to form the expanded bed that severe channeling through the bed occurs, causing feed to bypass the adsorbent (**Note 16**). Typical volumetric flow rates through a column are 3–10 packed-bed volumes per hour. As whole-broth–solvent is pumped through the expanded-bed column, the effluent should be collected using a fraction collector and each fraction assayed by an analytical method such as HPLC to measure product breakthrough. The whole-broth–solvent should be pumped onto the column until product concentration in the effluent reaches a predetermined percentage of the inlet-feed concentration.

4.2.5. Washing

In an expanded-bed-adsorption procedure, the wash following the adsorption step serves the primary function of removing the residual whole-broth–solvent containing particulate from the column and the secondary function of removing the weakly bound impurities. Since the whole-broth–solvent feed contains particulate, the initial stage must be done in the expanded-bed mode. Physical properties of the wash solution should be chosen carefully to avoid unnecessary product loss and long wash cycles (**Note 17**). After the particulate have been removed, washing may be continued in order to remove adsorbed impurities and any residual whole-broth–solvent liquid phase. This wash may be continued in either the packed or expanded-bed modes. The adsorbent is returned to a packed bed by stopping the flow and allowing gravity settling. If an adjustable top outlet is used, it should be lowered to the packed adsorbent height. A packed bed at this stage has advantages over the expanded bed; the limits of flow rate imposed by fluidization are eliminated and flow rates can be chosen at will. Interstitial space between adsorbent beads is smaller so that the bed volume is reduced and less wash volume is needed.

4.2.6. Elution and Cleaning

For the same reasons that the final washing is carried out in the packed-bed mode, the elution is invariably also carried out in a packed-bed mode. The elution can be carried out in either the same direction as the adsorption or in the reversed direction. The elution solvent may be anything, and the choice is not constrained to the solvent used to solubilize the product. If the capacity of the adsorbent was not fully utilized, then much of the product will be near the bottom of the column, and the reverse direction is preferable if a weak gradient elution is employed. The choice of the elution protocol can be made using general chromatographic selection criteria. After product elution, it is necessary to remove any adsorbed impurities that are more nonpolar than the product of interest. This can be accomplished by washing the column with more bed volumes of the elution solvent or by washing with a more nonpolar solvent (**Note 18**).

4.2.7. Scale-Up Considerations

The procedure for the scale-up of an expanded-bed-adsorption process is relatively straightforward and the principles are similar to those used for a packed-bed process. It is important that the length of the laboratory column be equal to the pilot-plant column. If the pilot-plant equipment is not specifically designed for expanded-bed-adsorption procedures, it should be modified as described in the previous section on laboratory equipment. To verify that the expanded-bed flow patterns are similar for the lab and pilot-plant columns, pulse tests using NaCl solution should be carried out. The adsorbent used, whole-broth–solvent ratio, bed height, and linear velocity, should not be changed on scale-up. The volumetric flow should be increased in proportion to the increase in the cross-sectional area of the two columns. Thus, the superficial velocity will be maintained and the adsorption and the fluidization properties will be constant.

4.3. Conclusions

Although the expanded-bed-adsorption procedure is in the relatively early stages of its redevelopment, it has already shown considerable promise for streamlining the isolation of products from unclarified fermentation broth. In a single, simple step, the product is concentrated, purified, and clarified without the need for centrifuges or filters. The applications could expand even further as resin manufacturers customize the high-density adsorbents by attaching ligands that are both robust and highly selective for a desired product.

5. Notes

1. To determine a minimum solvent–whole-broth ratio, take four 50-mL test tubes and add 10 mL whole broth to each test tube. Add 5, 10, 15, and 20 mL acetonitrile to the test tubes, respectively. Mix all samples for the same length of time (at least 1 h), then centrifuge solids and determine solute concentration by an appropriate assay. Calculate the total solute contained in the supernatant by multiply-

ing liquid volume and solute concentration. Use the lowest solvent–whole-broth ratio that contains the maximum amount of product.

2. The time needed to reach equilibrium can be a few minutes to several hours. With water-miscible solvents such as acetonitrile, equilibrium is generally reached in less than 60 min. Determine equilibrium time by preparing a 25-mL sample in a 50-mL test tube with acetonitrile–whole-broth ratio as determined in **Note 1**. Continuously shake test tube and take 2-mL samples at 10-min intervals. Immediately centrifuge a 2-mL sample to separate supernatant from solids and determine solute concentration in the supernatant. When the solute concentration of consecutive samples is the same, equilibrium has been reached.

3. Sodium chloride decreases the miscibility of water and acetonitrile. A minimum of approx 20 g sodium chloride added to 1 L of 50% aqueous acetonitrile solution will cause the formation of two liquid phases, a small upper acetonitrile-rich phase and a large lower aqueous-rich phase. Continued addition of sodium chloride increases the size of the acetonitrile-rich phase as more acetonitrile is forced out of the aqueous phase. The increasing salt and decreasing solvent content of the lower phase gradually increases the partition coefficient of hydrophobic solutes for the acetonitrile-rich phase.

4. Acetonitrile has a strong partition coefficient for toluene such that a two-liquid-phase mixture readily occurs when the toluene is added. A minimum of ~25 mL of toluene added to 1 L of 50% aqueous acetonitrile solution will cause the formation of two liquid phases, a small (200-mL) upper acetonitrile-rich phase and a large (825-mL) lower aqueous-rich phase. Continued addition of toluene increases the size of the acetonitrile-toluene phase as more acetonitrile is partitioned to the toluene phase. The amount of toluene added alters both the size of the upper toluene-acetonitrile phase and the hydrophobicity of the upper phase.

5. The acetonitrile-toluene composition can be approximated since the toluene does not partition into the lower phase. The difference in volume between the toluene added and the total upper-phase volume is owing to acetonitrile.

6. It is not uncommon for the high pH step to produce emulsions that are difficult to separate even by centrifugation. The use of additives is sometimes helpful in separating the emulsion phases.

7. The low pH separation can usually be carried out with gravity settling and has few problems with emulsions.

8. Reverse phase cartridges should be washed with 6–10 holdup vol of acetonitrile or methanol. Ion-exchange cartridges should be washed with 6–10 vol of methanol (optional). Normal phase columns do not require a wash step.

9. As a general guideline, cartridges containing less than 300 mg adsorbent should be loaded at 0.2–1.0 mL/min while cartridges containing more than 300 mg may be loaded at 2–5 mL/min. While low flow rates give better recovery and selectivity, an excessively low flow rate reduces sample throughput and should also be avoided. To measure the effects of flow rate, a series of loading experiments can be carried out as follows:
   a. Load sample at a conservatively low flow, collect effluent fractions, and assay for product concentration.

   b. Continue feeding sample until product concentration in the spent reaches approx 10% of sample feed.

   c. Perform the appropriate elution procedure and measure quantity and purity of product.

   d. Load a new cartridge at double or triple the initial flow rate. Continue to increase flow rate until either capacity or purity becomes unacceptable.

10. Capacity is a function of several factors: total concentration of all components in the sample, sample-solvent polarity, and the affinity of the components for the adsorbents. Overloading the adsorbent can result in poor or variable product recovery. If retention of the desired product is too low, the sample-solvent polarity may be too high or the adsorbent may be too weak. For example, if material in a 50% methanol extract of a fermentation broth does not bind sufficiently to a C8 reverse phase cartridge, the methanol concentration should be reduced (e.g., by dilution with water or by evaporation of methanol), or the adsorbent should be changed to C18 (more hydrophobic).

11. The elution-solvent strength depends on whether the aim is for a concentrated sample containing all of products or for fractionation of components. For concentrated products in a minimum elution volume, a strong elution solvent should be used immediately. For example, a reverse phase cartridge may be eluted with methanol, isopropanol, or tetrahydrofuran. If fractionation of adsorbed products is needed, the elution-solvent strength should be increased in gradual increments and fractions collected for analysis. For example, a reverse phase cartridge loaded with a sample in 40% methanol could be eluted with two holdup volumes of methanol increasing in 10% increments.

12. It can be misleading to select a solvent based on product solubility in pure solvents, since the solubility of some products changes dramatically in the presence of water. For example, solubility data for immunomycin in methanol as a function of the percentage water indicates there is a decrease in solubility from 400 g/L to 40 g/L as the water content increases from 0 to 25%.

13. Any significant change in the broth (e.g., higher product content, change in media ingredients, pH) may change the optimum solvent concentration and necessitate new tests.

14. If this happens and there is a top screen, the flow should be increased to attempt to force the air out the column. If there is no top screen, flow should be reversed and increased to attempt to force the air out the bottom. After removing the air, flow should be reversed to establish the expanded bed. Another approach would be to remove the top of the column and insert a thin rod to stir the resin to release the air bubble.

15. If the adsorbent has high capacity and feed contains many adsorbed components in addition to the product, there is the possibility that effective adsorbent density will increase during an extended adsorption cycle. In this case, the flow rate must be increased if constant bed height is required or, if constant flow rate is desired, the expanded bed height will decrease.

16. This problem can be corrected by establishing the expanded bed using an aliquot of whole-broth–solvent that has been clarified by centrifugation or filtration.

17. If the capacity of the adsorbent is fully utilized, the concentration of the product in the feed and in the adsorbent in the lower portion of the column will reach equilibrium. Thus, washing with an aqueous solvent that has the same composition as the whole-broth–solvent feed will result in some desorption of product. To avoid this loss, the wash solution should have a lower solvent content than the feed. To minimize the volume of wash needed to displace the particulate from the column, viscous wash solutions may be helpful in achieving more plug flow-like behavior. There is some suggestion in the literature of protein purification that more viscous wash solutions are more effective.

18. As the adsorbent has contacted a crude stream that contains many unknown components, the use of HPLC may not be the best indicator that all impurities have been removed. A useful assay method is the measurement of the total dissolved solids in the column effluent. In addition to strong solvents, 1 M NaOH or 1 M H_2SO_4 can also be used to remove strongly adsorbed impurities.

References

1. Axelsson, H. A. C. (1985) Centrifugation, *in Comprehensive Biotechnology,* vol. II (Cooney, C. C. and Humphrey, H. E., eds.), Pergamon, New York, pp. 325–347.
2. Brunner, K. H. (1983) Separators in biotechnology. *Chem. Tech.* **4,** 39–45.
3. Datar, R. and Rosen, C. G. (1987) Centrifugal separation in the recovery of intracellular protein from E. coli. *J. Chem. Eng.* **34,** 49–56.
4. Hsu, H. W. (1981) *Separations by Centrifugal Phenomena.* Wiley, New York.
5. Gabler, F. R. (1985) Cell processing using tangential flow filtration, in *Comprehensive Biotechnology,* vol. II (Cooney, C. C. and Humphrey, H. E., eds.), Pergamon, New York, pp. 351–367.
6. Fischer, E. and Raasch, J. (1985) Cross-flow filtration. *Ger. Chem. Eng.* **8,** 211–216.
7. Beaton, C. P. (1980) The application of ultrafiltration to fermentation products, in *Polymer Science and Technology,* vol. 13 (Cooper, A. R., ed.), Plenum, New York. pp. 373–405.
8. Datar, R. V. (1984) Centrifugal and membrane filtration methods in biochemical separation, *Filtr. Sep.* Nov./Dec., p. 402.
9. Belter, P. A. (1985) Filtration, in *Comprehensive Biotechnology,* vol. II (Cooney, C. C. and Humphrey, H. E., eds.), Pergamon, New York, pp. 347–350.
10. Datar, R. V. and Rosen, C. G. (1993) Cell and cell debris removal: centrifugation and crossflow filtration, in *Biotechnology,* vol. 3 (Stephanopoulos, G., ed.), VCH, New York, pp. 472–502.
11. Wildfeuer, M. E. (1985) Approaches to Cephalosporin C purification from fermentation broth, in *Purification of Fermentation Products* (Le Roith, D., Shiloach, J., and Leahy, T. J., eds.), ACS Symposium Series 271, American Chemical Series, Washington, DC, pp. 155–174.
12. Hatton, T. A. (1985) Liquid-Liquid Extraction of Antibiotics, in *Comprehensive Biotechnology,* vol. II (Cooney, C. C. and Humphrey, H. E., eds.), Pergamon, New York, pp. 439–449.
13. Schugerl, K. (1993) Liquid-liquid extraction (small molecules), in *Biotechnology,* vol. 3 (Stephanopoulos, G., ed.), VCH, New York, pp. 558–589.

14. Kulla, M. R. (1985) Liquid–Liquid Extraction of Biopolymers, in *Comprehensive Biotechnology*, vol. II (Cooney, C. C. and Humphrey, H. E., eds.), Pergamon, New York, pp. 451–471.

15. Craig, L. C. and Sogn, J. (1975) Isolation of antibiotics by countercurrent distribution, in *Methods in Enzymology*, vol. XLIII (Hash, J. H., ed.), Academic, New York pp. 320–346.

16. Flick, E. W. (ed.) (1991) Industrial Solvents Handbook, 4th ed., Noyes Data Corp., New Jersey.

17. Berdy, J. (ed.) (1987) CRC Handbook of Antibiotic Compounds, CRC, pp. 1980–1987.

18. Pratt, H. R. C. and Hanson, C. (1983) Selection, pilot testing, and scale-up of commercial extractors, in *Handbook of Solvent Extraction* (Lo, T. C., Baird, M. I. H., and Hanson, C., eds.), Wiley, New York, pp. 475–495.

19. Baird, M. H. I. and Lo, T. C. General laboratory scale and pilot plant extractors, in *Handbook of Solvent Extraction* (Lo, T. C., Baird, M. I. H., and Hanson, C., eds.), Wiley, New York, pp. 497–506.

20. Schugerl, K., Mattiasson, B., and Hatton, A. (1992) Extraction in biotechnology. Springer-Verlag, Heidelberg, Germany.

21. Kertes, A. S. and King, C. J. (1986) Extraction chemistry of fermentation product carboxylic acids. *Biotechnol. Bioeng.* **28**, 269–282.

22. Queener, S. and Swartz, R. (1986) Penicillins: biosynthetic and semisynthetic, in *Economic Microbiology*, vol. 3 (Rose, A. H., ed.), Academic, New York, pp. 35–112.

23. Bartels, C. R., Klieman, G., Korzun, N., and Irish, D. B. (1958) A novel ion exchange method for the isolation of streptomycin. *Chem. Eng. Prog.* **54**, 49–52.

24. Belter, P. A., Cunningham, F. L., and Chen, J. W. (1973) Development of a recovery process for novobiocin. *Biotechnol. Bioeng.* **15**, 533–549.

25. Richardson, J. F. and Zaki, W. N. (1954) Sedimentation and Fluidisation: part 1 *Trans. Inst. Chem. Eng.*, **32**, 35–53.

26. Lewis, E. W. and Bowerman, E. W. (1952) Fluidization of solid particles in liquids. *Chem. Eng. Prog.* **48**, 603–609.

27. Chase, H. A. and Draeger, N. M. (1984) Expanded-bed adsorption of proteins using ion-exchangers. *Sep. Sci. Technol.* **27**, 2021–2039.

28. Chase, H. A. and Draeger, N. M. (1992) Affinity purification of proteins using expanded beds. *J. Chromatogr.* **597**, 129–145.

29. Hansson, M., Ståhl, S., Hjorth, R., Uhlén, M., and Moks, T. (1994) Single step recovery of a secreted recombinant protein by expanded bed adsorption. *Biotechnol.* **12**, 285–288.

30. Chase, H. A. (1994) Purification of proteins by adsorption chromatography in expanded beds. *Trends Biotechnol.* **12**, 296–303.

31. Barnfield Frej, A. K., Hjorth, R., and Hammarström, A. (1994) Pilot scale recovery of recombinant annexin V from unclarified *Escherichia coli* homogenate using expanded bed adsorption. *Biotechnol. Bioeng.* **44**, 922–929.

32. Gailliot, F. P., Gleason, C., Wilson, J. A., and Zwarich, J. (1990) Fluidized bed adsorption for whole broth extraction. *Biotechnol. Prog.* **6**, 370–375.

33. Schwartz, R. E., Sesin, D. F., Joshua, H., Wilson, K. E., Kempf, A. J., Göklen, K. A., Kuehner, D., Gailliot, P., Gleason, C., White, R., Inamine, E., Bills, G.,

Salmon, P., and Zitano, L. (1992) Pneunocandins from *Zalerion Arboricola*: I. Discovery and Isolation. *J. Antibiotics* **45**, 1853–1866.

34. Cartier, P. G., Maikner, J., Deissler, K. C., and Firouztale, E. (1993) Purification of fermentation products with polymeric media. presented at 205th Amer. Chem. Soc. Nat. Mtg., Denver, CO, March 28–April 2.

35. Ruddick, J. A., Bunger, W. M., and Sakano, T. K. (1986) Organic Solvents: Physical Properties and Methods of Purification. Wiley.

36. Snyder, L. R. and Kirkland, J. J. (1979) Introduction to Modern Liquid Chromatography. Wiley.

3

Supercritical Fluid Methods

Ed Venkat and Srinivas Kothandaraman

1. Introduction

Natural products from plants and microorganisms have been of great interest and importance for many years. They are the source of many pharmaceutical compounds, flavors, fragrances, spices, oils, and food and beverage ingredients. The use of supercritical fluid extraction (SFE) as a general extraction strategy for a wide range of "active ingredients" or "analytes" from plant and microbial samples is of particular importance in the extraction of "unknown" natural products or for preparing whole-organism extracts for chemical analysis, bioassay, or screening programs. SFE offers many advantages: it leads to lower solvent usage, controllable selectivity, cleaner extracts, and less thermal degradation as compared to conventional solvent-extraction and steam-distillation methods. There has been a spurt of activity in the use of supercritical fluids for extraction purposes; SFE is emerging as an attractive alternative to conventional solvent extraction and steam distillation. Also, strict environmental regulations concerning the use of common industrial solvents, most of which are hazardous to human health, are indirectly contributing to the explosive growth of SFE technology.

The critical point of a pure substance is defined as the highest temperature and pressure at which the substance can exist in vapor–liquid equilibrium. At temperatures and pressures above this point, a single homogeneous fluid is formed and is said to be supercritical. Supercritical fluids can dissolve a wide variety of organic compounds and their solvent power can be varied near their critical points by small pressure and temperature changes. **Figure 1** illustrates the pressure–temperature relationship of a pure substance. Supercritical fluids possess superior mass transfer properties by virtue of their low viscosities and high solute diffusivities, along with the ability to penetrate microporous mate-

From: *Methods in Biotechnology, Vol. 4: Natural Products Isolation*
Edited by: R. J. P. Cannell © Humana Press Inc., Totowa, NJ

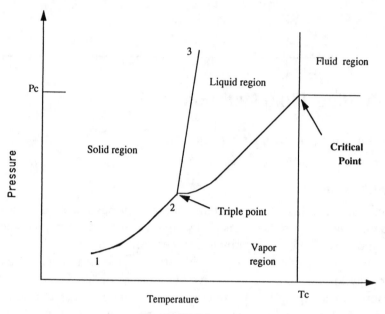

Fig. 1. PT Diagram.

rials. Supercritical carbon dioxide (SCO_2)—with its particularly attractive properties such as nontoxicity, nonflammability, noncorrosiveness, chemical inertness, low critical temperature (304°K), moderately low critical pressure (73 atm)—easy availability, cost-effectiveness, and environmental acceptability, is the preferred solvent for many supercritical extractions.

Cagniard de la Tour discovered the critical point in 1822. Hannay and Hogarth reported on the ability of a supercritical fluid to dissolve low vapor pressure solid materials *(1)*. Since then, a spectrum of solids have been studied in a variety of supercritical fluids. Naphthalene is the most extensively studied solute, and carbon dioxide the most popular supercritical fluid. Over the last decade, a large number of books have been published on SFE *(2–17)*. Most of these are proceedings of conferences. McHugh and Krukonis present a good historical review of the research and process applications in this field *(8)*. Bruno and Ely review the theory and practical applications of SFE *(3)*.

2. General Introduction to SFE

2.1. Solubility of Solids in Supercritical Fluids

For solutes of low volatility, absolute solubility depends greatly on choice of solvent, since solubility always increases with temperature at constant density. The effect of solute properties on solubility is essentially twofold: solubility depends on solute volatility or vapor pressure and on the strength of solute-solvent intermolecular forces. To compare the latter effects, a dimensionless enhancement factor *(E)* is used; this factor is defined as the ratio of solute partial pressure (mole fraction × total pressure) in the solvent phase (y_2P) to ideal gas partial pressure or vapor pressure (P_2^{sat}) (**Eq. 1**):

$$E = \frac{y_2P}{P_2^{sat}} \qquad (1)$$

By factoring out solute volatility, the enhancement factor allows comparison of solvent and secondary solute effects. Empirically, there is a linear relationship between the log of the enhancement factor and solvent density. For nonpolar and polar solutes in supercritical carbon dioxide, plots of enhancement factor coincide, indicating that differences in solubility are primarily due to vapor-pressure differences. Nonlinear behavior is noted in the case of high solubilities. The enhancement in pure fluids is relatively independent of solute structure but is sensitive to solvent polarity and density.

Cosolvents, entrainers, or modifiers are added to enhance solubilities and solute selectivities. They are normally used at low concentrations, i.e., 1–5 mole %. Methanol is a good example. For nonpolar solutes containing no functional groups, cosolvent-induced solubility enhancement is quite similar for all cosolvents and depends only on cosolvent concentration. This kind of enhancement results from alteration of the solvent properties rather than specific interactions. In the case of polar or heterocyclic solutes, the nature of the cosolvent becomes an important limit on the magnitude of the enhancement factor, e.g., hydrogen bonding or dipole–dipole interactions with the solute. It is these types of specific interactions that make it possible to tailor a solvent/cosolvent mixture to enhance the solubility of a particular solute *(18)*.

Brennecke and Eckert *(19)* and McHugh and Krukonis *(8)* provide excellent reviews of solubility in supercritical fluid. Mention must be made of Francis who, during the 1940s, obtained solubility information on about 250 compounds with liquid carbon dioxide just below its critical point. He found that liquid carbon dioxide is an excellent solvent for organic materials and many of the compounds studied were completely miscible *(20)*. Bartle et al. compiled solubility data for a variety of solids and liquids of low volatility in supercritical carbon dioxide *(21)*.

2.1.1. Experimental Techniques for Measurement of Solubilities in Supercritical Fluids

There are a number of approaches to the measurement of solubilities in pure and mixed supercritical fluids; an excellent review can be found in Bruno and Ely *(3)*. These fall into four major categories: dynamic or flow methods, static or equilibrium methods, chromatographic methods, and spectroscopic methods.

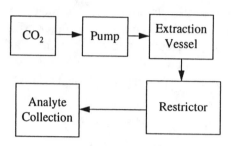

Fig. 2. Typical SFE System.

The flow method is the simplest and the most straightforward. In the flow method, the solvent fluid is supplied to a compressor by a pressure cylinder. At the desired pressure, the fluid passes into the thermostatted extractor cell that contains the solute present in appropriate matrix (e.g., multiple layer of glass wool). The fluid dissolves the solute in the extractor and, on expansion through a heated metering valve, precipitates solute into a series of collection vessels to be measured gravimetrically. The volume of the decompressed fluid is totaled by a wet or dry gas test meter. Static or equilibrium solubility measurement methods are used to eliminate the need to sample the supercritical fluid solution. A high-pressure flow cell is placed in the flow circuit to monitor the dissolution process by spectrophotometry.

2.2. General Outline of a Typical SCO₂ System

2.2.1. Solvent

As shown in **Fig. 2**, the essential parts of a typical SFE system include a carbon dioxide source, a pump, an extraction vessel, and an analyte-collection device—normally a vessel. Although an SFE system can be constructed with separate pieces of hardware, most users prefer to buy complete commercial units. A number of vendor companies sell SFE systems and accessories in this increasingly competitive market. A partial listing is provided in **Table 1**.

Supercritical carbon dioxide (SCO_2), with its particularly attractive properties, is the preferred solvent for many supercritical extractions. The quality of carbon dioxide is very important. Generally, cryogenic-grade carbon dioxide is not pure enough for most SFE applications; high-purity carbon dioxide is required. The carbon dioxide must be free of water, hydrocarbons, and halocarbons. Because the analyte is usually collected over a period of time in SFE, impurities in the supercritical fluid—especially those with high boiling points—may also be collected and concentrated. The carbon dioxide purity is more important for certain detectors used in the analytical step. SFE-grade carbon dioxide is available from several vendors.

Table 1
Vendors for SFE Systems and Accessories

Applied Separations
CDS Analytical
Chrompack International BV
Hewlett-Packard
Isco
JASCO
LINC Quantum Analytics
Microtech Scientific
Perkin-Elmer
Supelco
Suprex

2.2.2. Pressure System

To bring the carbon dioxide to supercritical state, a pump must be used for pressurizing. The pump used in SFE must generate high pressure, deliver reproducible volumes, and supply a constant flow rate. Generally, it should be able to pump liquid carbon dioxide and other fluids at the high pressures required for the supercritical state. Because the retention times of separated analytes are being measured, a constant flow rate is highly desirable. In SFE, the analyte is collected for a finite time before it is analyzed further. Therefore, the total volume of supercritical fluid passed through the extraction chamber is of importance.

Two types of pumps have been used for SFE: reciprocating and syringe pumps. Both pumps meet the flow and pressure requirements of SFE. The pumps must be modified to handle supercritical fluids since the compressibility of these fluids is different from the liquids that were designed for the pumps. Reciprocating pumps, most often used in HPLC, have an "infinite" reservoir and supply a continuous flow of supercritical fluid. Modifiers can be added by using doped cylinders or a second pump with proportioning valves. The major disadvantage of a reciprocating pump is that the pump head must be cooled to pump the liquid carbon dioxide. Low-cost cryogenic-grade carbon dioxide most often is used to cool the pump head.

Syringe pumps can provide pulseless flow and can be easily filled with liquid carbon dioxide. Syringe pumps do not have to be cooled because the carbon dioxide is liquefied by pressure, not temperature. However, because the pumps have limited volume, the syringe must be filled and repressurized when the pump cylinder is emptied. Also, when changing modifiers, the pump head must be thoroughly flushed to prevent carryover. The pump should be able to deliver fluid at 0.5–4 mL/min flow rates. Faster flow rates enable extraction times to be reduced.

2.2.3. Sample Preparation

An extraction vessel is required to hold the matrix to be extracted. The matrix could be plant material, fermentation broth, and so on. To develop an SFE method, the matrix's physical form must be considered. If the matrix is in bulk form, some preliminary sample preparation—such as grinding, sieving, drying, mixing, or even wetting—may be required. For nonporous or semiporous solids, a smaller particle size allows faster extraction. In some cases, a pH adjustment or the addition of solvent into the extraction cell may aid the SFE process. If the sample is a semisolid, gel, or liquid, it must be immobilized on a solid support, since SFE is generally unsuitable for liquid samples because of difficulties in handling two phases under pressure. Application of the sample to a piece of filter paper, to a solid support such as diatomaceous earth, or to a drying agent can facilitate the extraction and prevent the matrix from being swept out of the extraction cell. Particularly wet matrices may require water removal for good recovery and reproducibility of analyte extraction. Adding sodium sulfate and diatomaceous earth with thorough mixing to make a free-flowing powder has been reported to give excellent results. The extraction cell can be as simple as a stainless steel tube with compression endfittings or as complex as automatic sealing thimbles. The cell must withstand the pressure generated by the pump and must also be inert. Most SFE samples have masses <10 g, a compromise between a sample mass requiring a large volume of supercritical fluid for quantitative extraction and the amount needed for a representative sample or for trace analysis. The size of commercial analytical SFE extraction cells ranges from 100 µL to 50 mL. The amount of supercritical fluid needed to conduct a typical extraction is dependent on many parameters; generally, at least three extraction-cell volumes are required. The extraction cell is usually in an oven to control the temperature. Since the temperature affects the supercritical fluid density, any fluctuation in the temperature would cause a change in the density and hence the solvent strength. In addition, higher temperatures will increase the solubility of an added modifier and cause equilibria complications.

2.2.4. Extraction

Extractions can be performed in static, dynamic, or recirculating modes. In the static mode, the extraction cell is pressurized with supercritical fluid and allowed to equilibrate before the analyte is removed for collection. In the dynamic mode, the supercritical fluid is passed through the extraction cell and the analyte is collected continuously. In the recirculating mode, the same fluid is pumped through the sample; then, after some time, it is repeatedly pumped to the collection device. No systematic studies have compared these approaches, but the dynamic method appears preferable because fresh supercritical fluid continuously passes through the sample.

The importance of adding modifier to the supercritical fluid was discussed earlier. The modifier is added using a pump or a doped carbon dioxide cylinder. Adding the modifier to the extraction cell with the sample is an easy and effective way to introduce the modifier into the supercritical fluid. This procedure works in the static and recirculating modes, and it is not much different from adding modifier through the pump.

A technique for maintaining the extraction cell under pressure is required for the system to reach the supercritical state. This pressurization often is accomplished by using a fixed or variable restrictor. Fixed restrictors are used more frequently and usually consist of a piece of capillary tubing whose internal diameter and length can provide the appropriate back pressure. Pressure and, therefore, supercritical fluid density are changed by varying the flow rate through the restrictor. Because of the complex relationship between temperature, pressure, density, and flow rate, the restrictor must be replaced to vary the system pressure to change the density at constant flow rate.

Thus, in SFE, several restrictors typically are used with the instrument. During method development, fixed restrictors must be changed between extractions. Fixed restrictors come in several varieties: linear, tapered, integral, and those designed with frits. Variable restrictors are designed to regulate pressure independent of flow rate by mechanically regulating the size of a small opening. Variable restrictors are more complex than fixed restrictors but do not have to be changed during method development or during any given method. They allow the "decoupling" of flow and pressure.

2.2.5. Sample Collection / Trapping

As the supercritical carbon dioxide passes through the restrictor, the change in pressure in the restrictor causes the pressure of the supercritical fluid to decrease, and eventually gaseous carbon dioxide may form. This step is called depressurization. The analyte is then swept into an on- or off-line collection device.

In on-line collection, the analytical instrument is usually coupled to the extraction experiment. The analyte is trapped at the head of a GC, SFC, or HPLC column, and then analyzed. Thus, an advantage of the on-line approach is good sensitivity because the analyte is concentrated; a disadvantage is that all of the analyte is directed into the analytical instrument and none can be analyzed by other techniques without performing another extraction. On-line extraction can also deposit many contaminant(s) onto the column head. There is a risk of overloading the column. The on-line approach minimizes operator intervention.

In off-line collection, the effluent is depressurized, and the analyte is collected in a solvent, an open container, or an analyte trap packed with a solid support. Off-line collection is simpler, and the collected sample can be analyzed by several methods. Thus, the SFE instrument is decoupled from the analytical instruments. Other advantages of the off-line approach are accommodation of larger sample sizes, feasibility of multiple analyses from a single extraction, and accommodation of a wider range of analyte concentrations. In the analyte trap approach, the use of different solvents for elution can serve as an additional experimental parameter for increased selectivity and cleanup. In the open-container collection approach, aerosol may form because depressurization of the supercritical fluid produces a high flow rate of gaseous carbon dioxide.

2.3. Description of a Supercritical Apparatus

Figure 3 is a schematic diagram of the experimental apparatus designed and constructed by Dr. Arthur T. Andrews, of Merck & Co., Rutgers University, Piscataway, NJ *(22)*. The extraction/circulation/sampling system is located in a GCA Precision Model 18EM forced convection oven (46 × 33 × 48 cm), modified by the installation of a PID temperature controller. Thus, isothermal operation (±0.2°C) is assured. The primary circulation loop consists of a modified Milton Roy extraction vessel, a magnetically coupled gear pump, and a sampling/monitoring system parallel to the main flow loop. All primary components are constructed of stainless steel (SS). Tubing (0.64 cm OD) in the main loop is rated for a pressure of 10,000 psi. The sample loop is constructed of 0.16- and 0.32-cm steel tubing to minimize volume. Valves and fittings are manufactured by Autoclave Engineers and Crawford (SWAGELOK™). Overall limits on operating temperatures and pressure are 25–100°C and 4000 psig, respectively.

Liquid CO_2, from an eductor-equipped cylinder, passes through a 7-μm filter and is delivered to a Milton Roy Model 396-89 piston pump. During continuous flow desorption runs, the pump head may be cooled via an external cooling bath to prevent cavitation. Pump overpressurization is prevented by an adjustable pressure control valve (PCV) (Haskel Model 53379-4) and a safety rupture disk (10,000 psig rated). The basic unit, consisting of the body, the O-ring sealed cap, and the lock ring, was obtained from an original Milton Roy screening apparatus. A 0.16-cm SS sheath thermocouple, type K, was inserted into the vessel for measuring bed temperature. The primary O-ring is made of Buna N synthetic rubber, which is compatible with high-pressure CO_2.

Circulation of the SCO_2 is driven by a magnetically coupled gear pump, Micropump Model 183HP-346, specially modified by the manufacturer for operation up to 5000 psi. A 40-μm filter (FI) is installed upstream of the pump, and a 2-μm sintered metal filter is located downstream to prevent solids from entering the sample valve. A safety rupture disk (PSE), rated at 4300 psi, protects

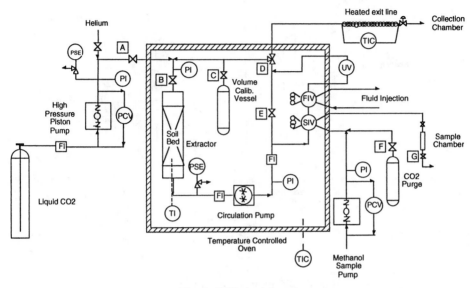

Fig. 3. SCF Apparatus.

the pump from overpressurization. The 24 V DC pump motor is controlled by a Cole Parmer Model 2630 speed controller. The pump body is constructed of stainless steel, and the gears are of RYTON, a hard polymer. RYTON is compatible with high pressure CO_2. The pump flow is rated at 100 mL/min at 10 psi pressure drop. During circulation under supercritical conditions, a flow rate of approx 140 mL/min was achieved at a midrange pump speed.

A fraction of the main recirculating flow is diverted through a parallel sample path that contains, in series: a 6-port sample valve (SIV) (Rheodyne Model 7010, with a 142-µL loop); a 6-port injection valve (FIV) (Rheodyne 7010, 1040-µL loop). Flow rate through this sample path is controlled by throttling the diversion valve in the main flow circuit to achieve a ΔP of 10 psi between the pump outlet and the extractor inlet. Flow rate in the parallel sample path is estimated at approx 1 mL/min, based on tests with methanol. A larger volume (142 µL) of pressurized sample is injected into a flowing stream of methanol, which is collected in a closed 2-mL chamber. The methanol/CO_2/analyte mixture is carefully discharged into a tared vial, and the sample loop and chamber flushed with additional methanol and purged with CO_2 from an external reservoir. In this manner, CO_2 is allowed to disengage from the sample. Based on the solubility of CO_2 in methanol, approx 80% of the gas flashes off, and the remaining methanol solution contains less than 1% CO_2. A

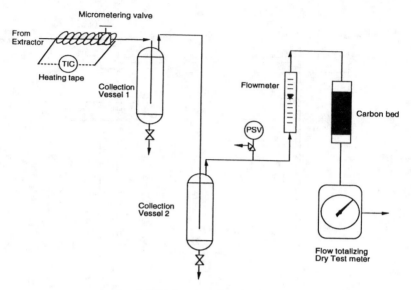

Fig. 4. Discharge collection system.

fluid injection valve with a 1040-μL loop is used during system calibration and for injection of cosolvents.

Temperatures are measured at two points within the system. As noted previously, a thermocouple (TI) inside the extractor measures the bed temperature. Another type-K thermocouple is located inside the oven near the sample valves. Output from these thermocouples are read from an Omega Model DP-462 digital thermometer. Accuracy of the thermocouple system was verified to be within ±0.2°C. Pressures are measured at two points–at the inlet of the extractor and at the discharge of the gear pump. Omega Model PX425-6KGV pressure transducers, with accuracies of ±0.2% full scale (0–6000 psi), are calibrated with an external test gage. Output from the transducers is converted by Omega Model DP-280 digital pressure indicators (PI). Periodic calibration checks of the transducers found the pressure to be within 1% of the reading.

Figure 4 describes the discharge collection system used during flow studies. The CO_2 flashes through a heated metering valve (Autoclave Engineers Model 30 VRMM) into two 150-mL stainless steel collection chambers (Hoke) in series. Flow rates are measured by a Matheson Model 603 glass rotometer, protected from overpressurization by a 5-psi safety relief valve. After passing through a 15-cm bed of activated carbon to remove residual organic matter, the final CO_2 gas flow is totaled in a Singer DTM-115 dry test meter, which was externally calibrated with CO_2 flow. Exit gas from the meter exhausts to a fume hood.

3. Factors to be Considered in SFE Method Development

3.1. Solubility of Target Compound

Before proceeding to develop a method for SFE of a natural product, the feasibility has to be ascertained. To determine the feasibility of SFE as a potential extraction technique, the solubility of the target compound in supercritical carbon dioxide or other supercritical fluid of choice (e.g., butane) has to be determined. If the compound is poorly soluble in supercritical fluid(s), SFE is probably not the preferred extraction method. Solubility experiments to determine the effect of temperature and pressure (which in turn control the density) on the solubility of the target compound in the supercritical fluid have to be performed.

3.2. Cosolvents

The effect of cosolvents on the solubility of the analyte of interest would have to be determined next. Based on the information obtained, a suitable cosolvent can be chosen and used for the extraction. The above information is often available in the literature for most compounds of commercial interest. However, in the absence of literature data, especially for those new research-based novel molecular entities of unknown identity, solubility experiments have to be performed.

3.3. Matrix

While the consideration of parameters such as flow, temperature, density, time, and modifiers may be fairly straightforward, perhaps the least predictable factor is that of matrix effects. The matrix either has the analyte lying on its surface (adsorbed), or the analyte is entrained in the matrix (absorbed). In the case of adsorption, the extraction can be accomplished with milder conditions. If the analyte is absorbed into the matrix, stronger extraction conditions and longer extraction times may be necessary. The matrix also carries its own modifiers in the form of water, and/or fats, and/or oils. If the desired analyte is of a polar nature, the water content of the matrix will facilitate the extraction. If the desired analyte is nonpolar, the water will inhibit the extraction. The opposite effects are evident with oils/fats in the matrix. If significant variations of the matrix are expected, an extraction scheme must be developed with these extremes in mind. (The importance of matrix effects is exemplified in the extraction of cyclosporine, as discussed below.)

The extraction of the immunosuppressant drug cyclosporine from the fungal cell mass of *Beauvaria nivea* provides a classic example of matrix effects *(23)*. The method of pretreatment of the fungal mycelia exhibits a profound effect on the yields and rates of cyclosporine extraction. The extraction of cyclosporine was carried out on different samples of the fungal mycelia subjected to varying degrees of air- and oven-drying. When the mycelia were oven-dried, the lowest yields were obtained. Scanning electron microscopy (SEM) examination revealed that this oven-dried material had a completely solid nonporous surface. However, the air-dried material which was quite open and had many broken mycelia was more amenable to extraction. The best yielding material, however, was found to be the minimally air-dried mycelia having a moisture content of 29.5%, but it also exhibited one of the poorest extraction rates.

The explanation for the observed results, as interpreted by the author, are as follows. Several factors may be interacting to restrict the removal of some of the cyclosporine from the mycelia microstructure. In the fully oven-dried material, all the cell structures have collapsed together, forming a dense, virtually impermeable matrix that might prevent the supercritical fluid from reaching the cyclosporine sites and/or the removal of the cyclosporine from the mycelial microstructure–a mass transport restriction. The air-dried material, on the other hand, has only partially collapsed together, and the individual mycelia were not packed together. This means that more surface area for supercritical fluid penetration to the cyclosporine sites was available. However, the collapse of internal structures interfered with complete removal of cyclosporine. When air-dried material was more finely ground, resulting in more broken and open mycelia, better extraction yields and rates were achieved. SEM pictures of the air-dried mycelia showed few natural pores in the dried mycelial hyphae. The moist mycelia were closer to their natural state, and thus all the internal structures were basically intact. The supercritical fluid was thus able to enter more areas of the mycelial hyphae than it could with fully dried material. However, the presence of water decreased the rate of extraction appreciably due to the hydrophobic nature of the cyclosporine molecule.

3.4. Density

Density is an important parameter since the solvating power of the supercritical fluid is proportional to its density. The higher the density, the more the analyte is able to be extracted from the matrix. Temperature control is necessary because the density of a supercritical fluid is directly tied to the temperature for any given pressure.

3.5. Flow

Flow is an important consideration because of the partitioning coefficient of the analyte between carbon dioxide and the matrix. Higher flows (or long extraction times) may be necessary to sweep all the analyte out of the extraction chamber. Low flows may be necessary if the kinetics of the system are slow. For most SFE separations, extraction takes 20–30 min.

3.6. Modifiers

Modifiers can be added to the extraction chamber, or to the supercritical fluid, to increase the polarity range for extraction. Pure carbon dioxide is useful for nonpolar to slightly polar compounds. A modifier must be used to extract moderately polar compounds. Common modifiers are methanol, methylene chloride, and hexane. Little work has been done using modified carbon dioxide systems for highly polar analytes.

4. Applications of SFE to Natural Products

4.1. Introduction

In this section, SFE is compared with conventional extraction strategies such as solvent extraction and steam distillation. Conventional solvent extraction has quite a few disadvantages:

1. Long time (reflecting difficulty penetrating matrix).
2. Large solvent volume.
3. Labor-intensive.
4. Use of more powerful solvents for complete and fast extractions, resulting in large amounts of unwanted tarry residue.
5. Low specificity and extraction efficiency.
6. Environmentally unfriendly.

Steam distillation has the following disadvantages:

1. Long time.
2. Needs relatively large amount of sample.
3. Energy-intensive.
4. Not suitable for thermally unstable compounds.

SFE has the following advantages:

1. Higher diffusion rates than liquid solvents.
2. Lower viscosities than liquid solvents.
3. Higher vapor pressure than liquid solvents.
4. Higher densities compared to gases, higher solvating power.
5. Solubility and (to some extent) selectivity can be controlled by modification of parameters.
6. Low polarity of carbon dioxide can be modified with cosolvents.
7. Suitable for heat-sensitive compounds.

Many of the above-mentioned advantages also apply to liquids that have been raised to near-supercritical (but subcritical) regions *(20)*. These properties are exploited in "accelerated solvent extraction" that employs high pressure at elevated temperatures. The increased temperature also increases the volatility of the analytes and their solubility in the solvent. Thus SFE may be appropriate for solid or powdered matrices where conventional solvents diffuse very slowly under normal conditions. However, supercritical fluids face the same problem as conventional solvents with impervious matrices, such as solid polymers, and are generally unsuitable for liquid samples (because of problem of handling two phases under pressure) unless they can be absorbed onto porous support.

The disadvantages of SFE are:

1. Carbon dioxide, which is the most commonly used solvent, has low polarity and hence cannot extract polar compounds.
2. Presence of water may cause problems.
3. Unpredictability of matrix effect.
4. Need for specialized/expensive equipment.

4.2. Applications

SFE has been used for a relatively long time on a large industrial scale and only recently on a smaller, laboratory scale. There are excellent reviews that cover the entire gamut of SFE applications *(3,8)*. The often cited example is decaffeination of coffee. Other examples of natural products' extraction in the food industry include extraction of hops, spices, flavors, and vegetable oils. **Table 2** lists selected companies that are involved in supercritical fluid processes for natural products *(24)*.

Bevan and Marshall *(25)* and Castioni et al. *(26)* have reviewed the applications of SFE in the extraction of natural products. Applications in the pharmaceutical industry include extraction from plant materials, extraction from fermentation broths, and crystallization from supercritical fluid solutions. Good reviews are available in the literature *(27,28)*. Stahl et al., among others, describe the extraction of chamomile and chrysanthemum flowers as well as calamus, turmeric, and valerian roots for pharmaceutically active components *(16)*.

Monocrotaline, a pyrrolizidine alkaloid of chemotherapeutic interest, has been extracted from the seeds of *Crotalaria spectabilis* using supercritical carbon dioxide and carbon dioxide–ethanol mixtures *(29)*. Other alkaloids that have been extracted using SFE include nicotine and caffeine. Environmental applications of supercritical fluids include regeneration of activated carbon, extraction of organic contaminants like polynuclear aromatic hydrocarbons and polychlorinated biphenyls from water and soils, and the newly emerging field of supercritical water oxidation.

Some more specific examples are described below.

4.2.1. SFE of Plant and Microbial Metabolites—General

The use of SFE as a general extraction strategy for plant/microbial biomass is of particular importance in the extraction of "unknown" natural products, or

Table 2
Commercial Applications of SFE of Natural Products

Natural product	Location	Start-up year	Company
Various	United States	1979	Phasex
Coffee	Germany	1979	HAG-General Foods
Hops	Australia	1982	Carlton & United
Hops, Spices	Germany	1982	SKW Chemicals
Hops, Spices	England	1983	English Hops
Hops	United States	1984	Pfizer
Hops	Germany	1985, 1988	Barth
Tea	Germany	1986	SKW Chemicals
Coffee	United States	1988	General Foods

for preparing whole-organism extracts for chemical analysis, bioassay, or screening programs. Several plant materials were tested for possible extraction of antineoplastic agents in an exploratory survey *(8)*. The extractions were performed in a flow apparatus and the extracts were analyzed for active components by bioassay or cytotoxicity tests. Cocks and others compared SFE with other organic solvents such as methanol and dichloromethane for the extraction of biologically active compounds from the biomass of microbial fermentations *(33)*. The conditions of the SFE were chosen with the objective of obtaining a range of extracts rather than of selectivity. The SFE resulted in a wide range of structural types including some polar metabolites. It was observed that the extraction strength of supercritical carbon dioxide alone was lower than that of dichloromethane. However, all of the components of interest that were extractable with methanol and dichloromethane were also extractable with the addition of methanol as a cosolvent to carbon dioxide.

4.2.1.1. SFE OF PARTHENOLIDE FROM FEVERFEW PLANT

Many plants, used as spices or flavor ingredients, are preserved by drying and are ideal matrices for SFE. Once ground to a powder, they have a large surface area and are highly permeable, leading to rapid and efficient extractions. Interest in SFE of plants has principally been for the isolation of essential oils, but recently SFE has also been used to obtain pharmaceutically active compounds. The extraction of the sesquiterpene lactone parthenolide (**Fig. 5**) from feverfew plants has been described by Smith *(30)* and Smith and Burford *(31)*. SFE was compared with steam distillation and solvent extraction. While SFE extracted the less-volatile lactones and parthenolide, the steam distillation extracted the volatile terpenes. SFE resulted in incomplete extraction compared

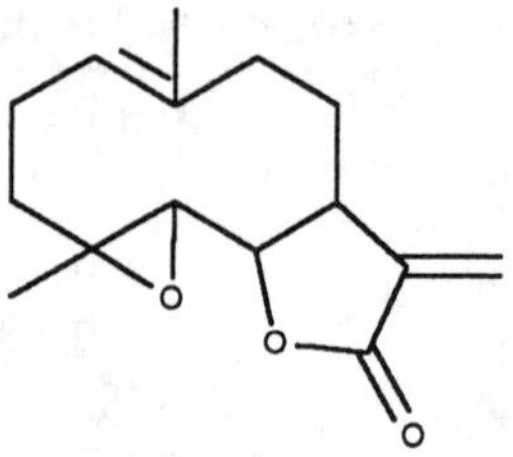

Fig. 5. Parthenolide.

to solvent extraction. The addition of 4% methanol resulted in complete extraction but with a loss in selectivity because of the co-extraction of chlorophyll and other poorly volatilized components. So SFE is no more selective than solvent extraction, but it is easier to manipulate the extraction power by adjusting the pressure or temperature.

Smith and Burford *(31)* exploited the relatively weak eluent strength of unmodified CO_2 in a small-scale preparative extraction. Dried feverfew was extracted with CO_2 and the extract passed through a short silica column, which retained the slightly polar sesquiterpene lactones and allowed the volatile essential oils through to the collection vessel. The extraction vessel was then switched out of the flow of supercritical fluid and 10% methanol was added to the CO_2 flow to the column, which eluted a lactone fraction containing 80% parthenolide. A simple thin-layer chromatography clean up yielded pure parthenolide. Although the extraction of parthenolide from the plant material was incomplete, the time required to obtain milligrams of a pure sample was reduced to a few hours compared to the days or weeks required when using traditional solvent-extraction methods and purification stages.

4.2.1.2. SFE of Taxol from Pacific Yew Tree

Taxol (Fig. 5 in Chapter 7), a complex diterpene plant metabolite, has been found to be an effective drug in the treatment of ovarian and lung cancer. The extraction of taxol from the bark of the Pacific yew tree was the subject of investigation by a group from Georgia Tech (Athens, GA) *(32)*. They found that 50% of the taxol present could be extracted using a CO_2-ethanol mixture as opposed to 25% extraction with SCO_2 alone. The supercritical extraction of taxol was also found to be more selective than a conventional liquid ethanol extraction. Several investigators are evaluating the extraction of taxol from the needles of ornamental yews.

4.2.1.3. SFE of Cyclosporine from *Beauvaria nivea*

Although they are almost more important than plants as a source of novel pharmaceuticals, relatively few studies have explored the SFE of natural products from microorganisms. Cyclosporine (Fig. 7 in Chapter 15), an immuno-suppressant drug occurring as an intracellular product of the fungus *Beauvaria nivea*, has been extracted with SCO_2 *(23)*. The methods of pretreatment of the fungal mycelia affected the yields and rates of cyclosporine extraction as described in **Subheading 3.3.** on matrix effects.

5. Conclusions

Supercritical fluid extraction (SFE) is emerging as an attractive alternative to conventional solvent-extraction technologies for a number of important reasons. SFE is a "one-step" and "less-harsh" purification method, obviating the need for several extraction steps and the range of precautions that are practiced conventionally. Also, natural products are mainly used as active ingredients for use in food and beverages, pharmaceuticals, and flavors that demand high purity, stability, and yields. Also, SFE is an environmentally friendly technology. In a world of increasing environmental awareness, regulations and cost, SFE offers several advantages over conventional solvent extraction and distillation methods. Supercritical carbon dioxide (SCO_2), with its particularly attractive properties, is the preferred solvent for many supercritical extractions. For plant/microbial extractions, SFE gives extracts that are cleaner, contain less insoluble polar material and uses milder conditions than conventional solvent extraction. However, some solutes/matrices may not be amenable to SFE. Also, aqueous solutions can cause problems. Since SFE burst into prominence only recently, there is a dearth of published information on the "how-to"-type "recipe." This must not discourage an aspiring scientist from exploring and evaluating the applicability of SFE technology. The authors have attempted to provide practical guidance and information to scientists with little experience in supercritical extraction.

6. Notes

1. A major portion of the information provided here has been excerpted from two good review papers *(34,35)*. It must be made clear that SFE has only recently come into prominence. Therefore, there is a dearth of published information on the "how-to"-type details of SFE method development. No recipe of SFE methods is currently available.

References

1. Hannay, J. B. and Hogarth, J. (1879) On the solubility of solids in gases. *Proc. R. Soc. London* **30**, 324.
2. Bright, F. V. and McNally, M. E. P. (1992) *Supercritical Fluid Technology: Theoretical and Applied Approaches to Analytical Chemistry.* American Chemical Society, Washington, DC.
3. Bruno, T. J. and Ely, J. F. (1991) *Supercritical Fluid Technology: Reviews in Modern Theory and Applications.* CRC, Boca Raton, FL.

4. Charpentier, B. A. and Sevenants, M. R. (1988) *Supercritical Fluid Extraction and Chromatography.* American Chemical Society, Washington, DC.
5. Johnston, K. P. and Penninger, J. M. L. (1989) *Supercritical Fluid Science and Technology.* American Chemical Society, Washington, DC.
6. Kiran, E. and Brennecke, J. F. (1993) *Supercritical Fluid Engineering Science.* American Chemical Society, Washington, DC.
7. McHugh, M. A. (1991) *Proc. 2nd Int. Symp. Supercritical Fluids.* Boston, MA.
8. McHugh, M. A. and Krukonis, V. J. (1994) *Supercritical Fluid Extraction, Principles and Practice.* Butterworth, Boston, MA.
9. Paul, P. F. M. and Wise, W. S. (1971) *The Principles of Gas Extraction.* Mills & Boon Limited, London, UK.
10. Paulaitis, M. E., Penninger, J. M. L., Ralph D., Gray, J., and Davidson, P. (1983) *Chemical Engineering at Supercritical Fluid Conditions.* Ann Arbor Science: The Butterworth Group, Ann Arbor, MI.
11. Penninger, J. M. L., Radosz, M., McHugh, M. A., and Krukonis, V. J. (1985) *Supercritical Fluid Technology.* Elsevier, Amsterdam, The Netherlands.
12. Perrut, M. (1988) *Proc. 1st Int. Symp. Supercritical Fluids.* Nice, France.
13. Rizvi, S. S. H. (1994) *Supercritical Fluid Processing of Food and Biomaterials.* Blackie Academic and Professional, Glasgow, UK.
14. Smith, R. M. (1989) *Supercritical Fluid Chromatography.* The Royal Society of Chemistry, London, UK.
15. Squires, T. G. and Paulaitis, M. E. (1987) *Supercritical Fluids: Chemical and Engineering Principles and Applications.* American Chemical Society, Washington, DC.
16. Stahl, E., Quirin, K. W., and Gerard, D. (1988) *Dense Gases for Extraction and Refining.* Springer-Verlag, Berlin.
17. Wenclawiak, B. (1992) *Analysis with Supercritical Fluids: Extraction and Chromatography.* Springer-Verlag, Berlin.
18. Tomasko, D. L., Hay, K. J., Leman, G. W., and Eckert, C. A. (1993) Pilot scale study and design of a granular activated carbon regeneration process using supercritical fluids. *Environ. Progress* **12,** 208–217.
19. Brennecke, J. F. and Eckert, C. A. (1989) Phase equilibria for supercritical fluid process design. *AIChE J.* **35,** 1409–1427.
20. Francis, A. W. (1954) Ternary systems of liquid carbon dioxide. *J. Phys. Chem.* **58,** 1099–1114.
21. Bartle, K. D., Clifford, A. A., Jafar, S. A., and Shilstone, G. F. (1991) Solubilities of solids and liquids of low volatility in supercritical carbon dioxide. *J. Phys. Chem. Ref. Data* **20,** 713–756.
22. Andrews, A. T. (1990) *Supercritical Carbon Dioxide Extraction of Polycyclic Aromatic Hydrocarbons from Contaminated Soil.* Ph.D. thesis, Rutgers, The State University of New Jersey, Piscataway, NJ.
23. te Bokkel (1990) *Supercritical Carbon Dioxide Extraction of Cyclosporine from the Fungus* Beauvaria nivea. Ph.D. thesis, The University of Western Ontario, Canada.
24. Yalpani, M. (1992) New separation tools offer opportunities for food/beverage products. *Genet. Eng. News* **2,** 10–12.

25. Bevan, C. D. and Marshall, P. S. (1994) *Natural Products Rep.* 451–466.
26. Castioni, P., Christen, P., and Veuthey, J. L. (1995) Analusis **23,** 95–106.
27. Larson, K. A. and King, M. L. (1986) Evaluation of supercritical fluid extraction in the pharmaceutical industry. *Biotech. Progress* **2,** 73–82.
28. King, M. B. and Bott, T. R. (1994) *Extraction of Natural Products Using Near-Critical Solvents.* Blackie A & P, Glasgow, UK.
29. Schaeffer, S. T., Zalkow, L. H., and Teja, A. S. (1988) Supercritical extraction of *Crotalaria spectabilis* in the cross-over region. *AIChE J.* **34,** 1740–1742.
30. Smith, R. M. (1996) Supercritical fluid extraction of natural products. *LC-GC Int.* Jan, 8–15.
31. Smith, R. M. and Burford, M. D. (1992) *J. Chromatog.* **627,** 255–261.
32. Jennings, D. W., Deutsch, H. M., Zalkow, L. H., and Teja, A. S. (1992) Supercritical extraction of taxol from the bark of *Taxus brevifolia. J. Supercritical Fluids* **5,** 1–6.
33. Cocks, S. et al. (1995) High-performance liquid chromatography comparison of supercritical-fluid extraction and solvent extraction of microbial fermentation products. *J. Chromatog.* **A697,** 115–122.
34. Majors, R. E. (1991) Supercritical fluid extraction—an introduction. *LC-GC* **9,** 78–86.
35. Pipkin, W. (1990) Practical considerations for supercritical fluid extraction. *Amer. Lab.* November, 40D–40S.

4

Isolation by Low-Pressure Column Chromatography

Gino M. Salituro and Claude Dufresne

1. Introduction

In the 90 yr since the discovery of chromatography, tremendous advances have been realized. It is not the scope of this chapter to review the history or theory of liquid chromatography. The reference section lists a number of good books to that effect *(1–6)*. The goal of this chapter is to illustrate the technique of liquid chromatography as it applies to the isolation of natural products. A brief review of the theoretical basis for the various applicable separation mechanisms and column packings will be presented, followed by practical recommendations and examples of natural products isolations.

In low-pressure column chromatography, as in high-performance liquid chromatography (HPLC), the chromatographic packing material consists of a densely packed adsorbent through which a mobile phase is "flowed." Depending on the choice of the packing material and mobile phase, several separation mechanisms are available. This chapter will deal with low-pressure (usually open-column) chromatography in the sense of a liquid mobile phase used with a solid packing material. Separate chapters cover this application under the form of HPLC and ion-exchange chromatography. We will concentrate on the most widely used techniques that are applicable to the isolation of natural products. Packing materials such as silica gel, both normal and modified, as well as synthetic and carbohydrate polymeric materials will be covered. Useful applications for the isolation of natural products will be described.

2. Retention Mechanisms

In liquid chromatography, separation of components of a mixture, or solutes, occurs by selectively distributing the various components between a

From: *Methods in Biotechnology, Vol. 4: Natural Products Isolation*
Edited by: R. J. P. Cannell © Humana Press Inc., Totowa, NJ

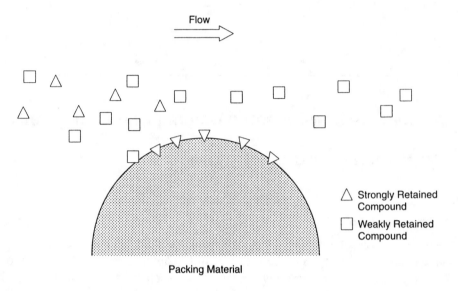

Fig. 1. Illustrated adsorption separation mechanism.

mobile phase and a stationary phase. A number of factors are involved in determining the distribution coefficients of solutes between a mobile and a stationary phase. These revolve around the chemical and physical nature of both phases. For any combination of phase characteristics, a number of interactions between the solutes and the two phases are also possible.

Since solutes must interact with the stationary phase to be adsorbed, the greater the surface area offered by the stationary phase, the greater the number of possible interactions. Thus, adsorbents that offer a high ratio of surface area to packing volume give rise to better separations. The equilibrium that exists between the tendency of solute molecules to bind preferentially to the stationary phase or remain in solution in the mobile phase is reflected by a chromatographic parameter termed the distribution constant. This constant is entirely dependent on the chemical nature of the system. The various factors involving solute/phase interactions will be discussed by briefly reviewing separation mechanisms and stationary phase compositions.

2.1. Adsorption

Adsorption chromatography is based on the ability of solute molecules to interact with the stationary phase. As shown in **Fig. 1,** these interactions in turn slow the movement of solutes through the packed column. The nature of the interactions between solutes and stationary or mobile phases can be hydrogen bonding, van der Waal type, dipole–dipole, Coulombic, acid-base, complex-

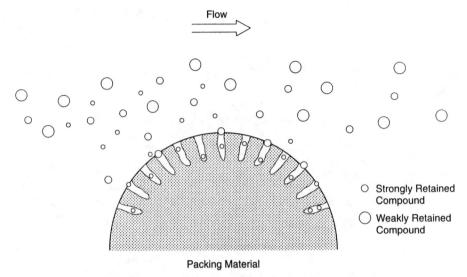

Fig. 2. Illustrated size exclusion separation mechanism.

ation, or charge transfer. The observed retention is most often the result of a combination of several of these types of interactions. Desired interactions are reversible processes. Inappropriate choices of stationary phases can lead to irreversible adsorption of solutes onto the packing material, or at least very poor recovery.

2.2. Size Exclusion

Size-exclusion chromatography (gel permeation chromatography; gel filtration) is based on the ability of molecules to penetrate chromatography particles (5). As illustrated in **Fig. 2**, large molecules in the liquid phase cannot penetrate the pores on the surface of the beads and are thus unretained by the column. Small molecules can easily penetrate the pores, and this exchange will retard their movement with the liquid phase. In the absence of other interactions, as determined by the choice of a fairly inert stationary phase, this mode of separation predominates. As a result of this mechanism, molecules elute in order of decreasing molecular weight. Since packing materials used for this type of chromatography are fairly inert, sample recovery from this type of column is usually very good.

2.3. Partition

Partition chromatography is based on the ability of solutes to distribute between two liquid phases. In open-column chromatography, one of the liquid

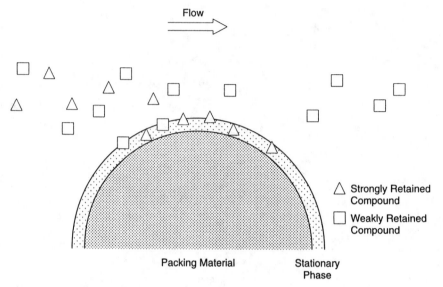

Fig. 3. Illustrated partitioning separation mechanism.

phases is immobilized in the packing material (*see* **Fig. 3**). The mobile phase, of different composition to the stationary liquid phase, is then passed through the column. The solid support used to immobilize the liquid stationary phase should be inert or rendered inert. Sephadex LH-20 and silica gel are often used for this purpose. In general, the stationary liquid phase is aqueous, whereas the mobile phase consists of relatively nonpolar organic solvents.

3. Types of Stationary Phases

Packing adsorbents are available in a wide variety of materials *(6)*. A number of physical structures with various chemicl traits are manufactured. A description of the physical nature of the packing consists of the particle size, shape, porosity, and surface area. Average particle diameters in open-column chromatography can range from approx 10 to 200 μm. Smaller particle sizes (2–8 μm) are generally only reserved for HPLC as they give rise to substantial back pressure when a mobile phase is passed through. The particles can also range from irregularly shaped to absolutely spherical. The porosity of a particle reflects the ratio of the volume of surface pores to the total volume of the particle. In totally porous particles, pores throughout the whole particle are accessible. Pore sizes can vary tremendously from approx 50 nm to macroscopic size. In any given commercial packing, parameters of size, shape, and porosity can be either spread over a wide range or controlled within a very narrow range. In choosing a stationary phase, it is necessary to realize that nominally identical adsorbents may differ tremendously from manufacturer to manufacturer.

3.1. Silica

Silica gel is perhaps the most widely used stationary phase for the separation of natural products. It is a three-dimentional polymer of tetrahedral units of silicon oxide, chemically represented by $SiO_2 \cdot H_2O$. Being a porous material, it offers very large surface areas, typically in the range of 100–800 m^2/g. The average particle size of silica gels used in open-column chromatography is usually in the 40- to 200-μm range with pore sizes in the 40- to 300-Å range. Smaller particle sizes give rise to impractically high back pressure and are usually reserved for HPLC columns.

The chemical nature of the surface of silica gel consists of exposed silanol groups. These hydroxyl groups are the active centers and potentially can form strong hydrogen bonds with compounds being chromatographed. Thus, in general, the stronger the hydrogen-bonding potential of a compound, the stronger it will be retained by silica gel. For example, polar compounds containing carboxylic acids, amines, or amides are strongly adsorbed on silica gel. Nonpolar compounds, such as terpenes or other compounds lacking polar functional groups contain few hydrogen-bonding sites and are thus poorly to nonretained on silica gel.

How strongly a given compound is retained depends equally on the polarity of the mobile phase. The stronger the hydrogen-bonding potential of a solvent, the better it is as an eluant to elute polar compounds adsorbed on a silica gel column. Similarly, very nonpolar solvents would be used to chromatograph nonpolar compounds. Examples of nonpolar solvents useful for silica gel chromatography include hexane and dichloromethane, while polar solvents would include ethyl acetate and methanol. Column development usually involves increasing the percentage of the polar solvent during a chromatography run. Small percentages of water can be used to recover strongly bound compounds. Note that as the water or methanol content of the mobile phase is increased, small amounts of the silica gel packing will dissolve and contaminate the eluates. Water use with silica gel is limited to pH values of less than 7.0. At higher pH values, silica gel readily dissolves.

3.2. Bonded Phase Silica

Silica gel may be chemically modified in a number of ways that alter both its chromatographic and physical properties. As shown in **Fig. 4**, the reactive silanol groups of silica gel may be blocked with a variety of silylchlorides to produce a nonpolar (reverse phase) or polar (bonded normal phase) chromatography support. The most commonly employed bonded phase silica gels are the reverse phase class although the use of bonded normal phase silica has increased with improved materials.

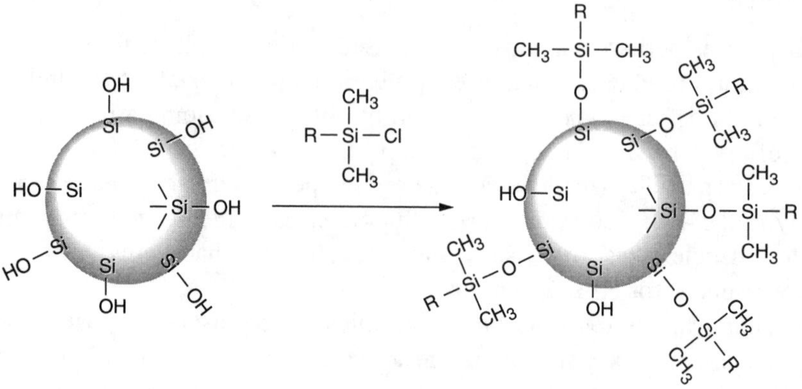

$R = -CH_2(CH_2)_nCH_3$ $n = 0$ to 16
$= $ Phenyl, etc...

Fig. 4. Preparation of bonded silica gel

Treatment of chromatographic grade silica gel with chlorodimethyl-alkylsilanes or chloroalkoxysilanes transforms the polar stationary phase into a nonpolar surface. The use of monochlorosilanes ensures monomolecular surface coverage with a high degree of reproducibility in packing material performance. End-capping of the remaining accessible silanols by a second silanization reaction using a small silating reagent such as chlorotrimethylsilane prevents the often undesired effect of exposed silanols. Indeed, exposed silanol groups would impart a normal phase nature to the adsorbent, giving rise to broad or tailing peaks. Alkyl chain lengths of C-2, C-4, C-6, C-8, and C-18 can be prepared; however, the C-8 and C-18 materials are the most frequently used.

Since the degree of adsorption to reverse phase silica gel is proportional to the lipophilicity of the compounds being chromatographed, mobile phases used are usually aqueous. An organic modifier such as methanol, acetonitrile, or tetrahydrofuran is used and its concentration increased during the development process. The pH of the aqueous phase can also be controlled. A common application involves the use of a small percentage of trifluoroacetic acid (TFA), usually in the 0.01–0.1% range.

Bonded normal phase silica is prepared in a manner analogous to the production of reverse phase supports, as shown in **Fig. 5**. Rather than straight-chain alkyl or phenyl silanes, short-chain, functionalized silanes are attached to the silica gel matrix. Amino-, diol-, and cyano-based bonded normal phases are commonly encountered. The main advantage of bonded normal phase supports over unmodified silica gel is the increased stability to polar solvents, including water, which allows the separation of very polar compounds that

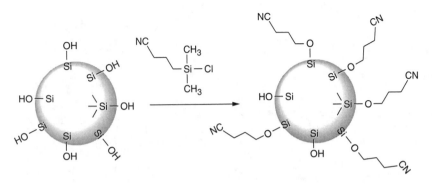

Fig. 5. Normal phase bonded silica gel.

would be too highly retained on silica gel. These silica phases can be used with a wide range of solvents, nonpolar to polar, including water.

Due to the higher cost of production, bonded phase silica chromatography supports are considerably more expensive than silica gel. Therefore, these materials are most frequently used for HPLC columns. Nevertheless, the high resolution and unique selectivities of these media do make them appropriate for use in open-column chromatography.

3.3. Polyacrylamide

Synthetic polymers can be formed as spherical beads for chromatography. A gel based on the copolymerization of N,N'-methylene-*bis*-acrylamide and acrylamide (*see* **Fig. 6**) is Bio-Gel® (Bio-Rad, Hercules, CA). The particle sizes of these gels range from less than 45 to 180 µm.

As with carbohydrate packings, these gels are fairly inert and free of charge and are thus well-suited to the chromatography of labile compounds. These gels are also extremely hydrophilic. They swell in water (*see* **Table 1**) and are almost always used with water as the mobile phase. Up to 20% (v/v) of lower alcohols can be used to improve the solubility of the sample. The nature of the chromatographic interactions revolve around hydrogen bonding. They are thus well-suited for the chromatography of carbohydrates, peptides, and tannins.

An added benefit of these columns is that they are resistant to bacterial attack upon prolonged storage.

3.4. Carbohydrates

Some of the most useful materials for the chromatography of labile natural products are the fairly inert polymers of carbohydrates. Polysaccharides can be crosslinked to produce three-dimensional networks (*see* **Fig. 7**). These polymeric materials can then be formed into beads.

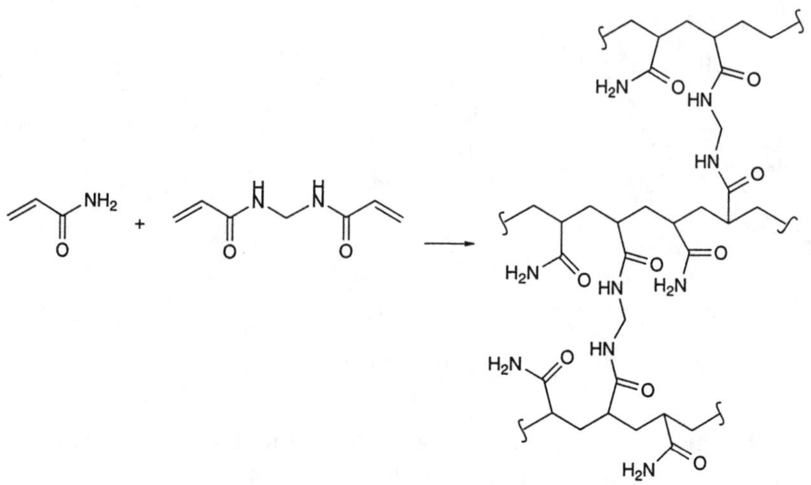

Fig. 6. Polyacrylamide gels.

Table 1
Fractionation Range of Bio-Gel Gels

Gell type	Useful fractionation range, mol wt	Approx swollen volume in water, mL/g dry beads
P-2	100–2000	3
P-4	800–4000	4
P-6	1000–6000	6.5
P-10	1500–20,000	7.5

Sephadex® (Pharmacia, Uppsala, Sweden) is such a gel, manufactured from the crosslinking of otherwise water-soluble dextran with epichlorohydrin. The resulting water-insoluble polymer has glycerin-ether bonds as the crosslinker. Because this gel is so hydrophilic, it swells in water. The swollen beads can chromatograph compounds based on their molecular sizes. The degree of swelling has a big impact on the chromatographic properties of the gel. The denser the gel, the lower the useful molecular-weight fractionation range.

In the Sephadex G series, the number represents the amount of water picked up by the dry beads upon swelling. For example, Sephadex G-15 picks up 1.5 mL/g of dry beads, whereas the G-100 picks up 10 mL/g. The G-15 is thus denser than the G-100 and is used for smaller compounds as shown in **Table 2**.

The highly crosslinked G-10 and G-15 are well-suited to the separation of natural products. In addition to water, the beads can be swollen in DMF,

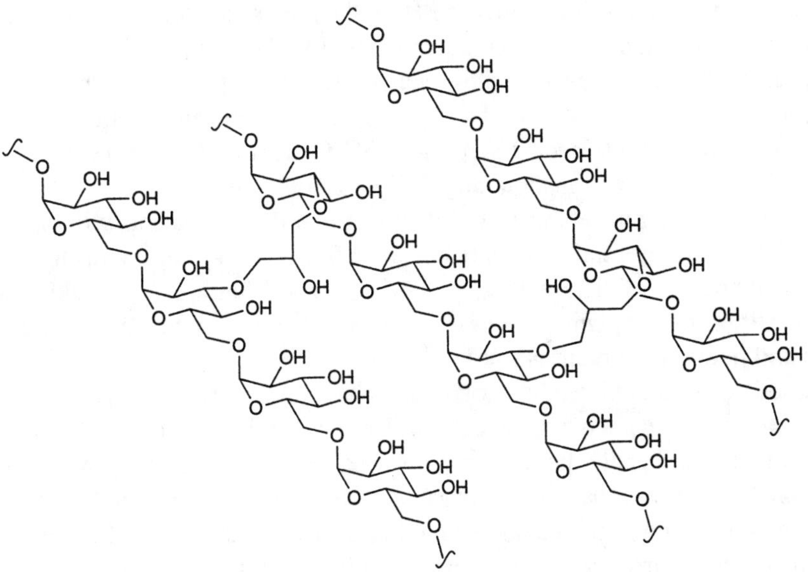

Fig. 7. Crosslinked Dextran.

Table 2
Fractionation Range of Sephadex G-Series

Sephadex type	Useful fractionation range, mol wt	Approx swollen volume in water, mL/g dry beads
G–10	0–700	2.5
G–15	0–1500	3
G–25	100–5000	5
G–50	500–10,000	10
G–100	1000–100,000	15

DMSO, ethylene glycol, and aqueous methanol. Such gels are very well suited for the fractionation of water-soluble natural products such as carbohydrates and small peptides. Even though the major mode of separation is that of gel filtration, (i.e., molecules are separated based on their relative abilities to penetrate small bead pores), additional adsorption mechanisms exist, such as hydrogen bonding, giving rise to good fractionations.

Sephadex LH-20 is a hydroxypropylated Sephadex G-25. This derivatization adds lipophilicity to the gel, at the same time retaining its hydrophilicity. The gel swells in polar solvents, such as water, methanol, and THF, to about four times its dry volume. The added lipophilicity that allows this gel to swell adequately in organic solvents makes LH-20 the preferred gel in this class for the fractionation of organic-soluble natural products. In gel filtration mode, compounds are separated based on their size. This separation mode is operational when a single solvent is used for the separation. Thus, compounds of molecular weight of approx 4000 are usually not retained by Sephadex LH-20 and would thus elute in the void volume. The useful fractionation range is approx 100–4000.

When a solvent mixture is used, the more polar of the solvents will be taken up by the gel preferentially. This results in a two-phase system with stationary and mobile phases of different compositions. Chromatography now takes place by a partition mechanism. The best results are obtained when a mixture of a polar and nonpolar solvent is used.

An additional separation mode exists for Sephadex gels. It was found that phenolic and heteroaromatic compounds have unusual affinity for this type of gel. These compounds are thus generally more strongly retained than would otherwise be expected based on their size, especially when lower alcohols are used as eluting solvents.

These polysaccharide gels are stable in all solvents except for strong acids, which would hydrolyze the glycosidic linkages. Furthermore, since these materials are fairly inert, rarely does irreversible adsorption take place. The net result is that biological activity is almost always fully recovered. An additional benefit is that the column can be used for several experiments without the need for regeneration. One drawback of carbohydrate columns is that they can be attacked by microorganisms.

3.5. Polystyrene

Styrene-divinylbenzene polymers (*see* **Fig. 8**) are often used as backbones for ion-exchange resins; however, in the absence of ionizing groups, the polymer can form a gel resin useful for reverse phase chromatography.

The most commonly used resins are the HP and SP series from Mitsubishi Chemicals and the XAD family from Bio-Rad. The Mitsubishi SP200 series differs from the HP20 series in that the polymer is brominated. This results in SP resins being more retentive. Equally important is the increased density that facilitates upflow operations. These materials are often encountered as relatively large particle-size beads (250–600 μm) which do not provide high-resolution chromatographic separations, but are very useful for desalting and adsorption-elution of natural products from fermentation broths. Chromatographic grades of polystyrene resins such as MCI Gel CHP20p and SEPABEADS SP20ms are available in particle sizes useful for open-column chromatography (37–150 μm) as well as for HPLC columns (10 μm).

Polymeric resins have several advantages over the commonly used silicagel based reverse phase materials. The cost of polystyrene-based resins is considerably less than bonded phase silica gel adsorbents. Also, the potential

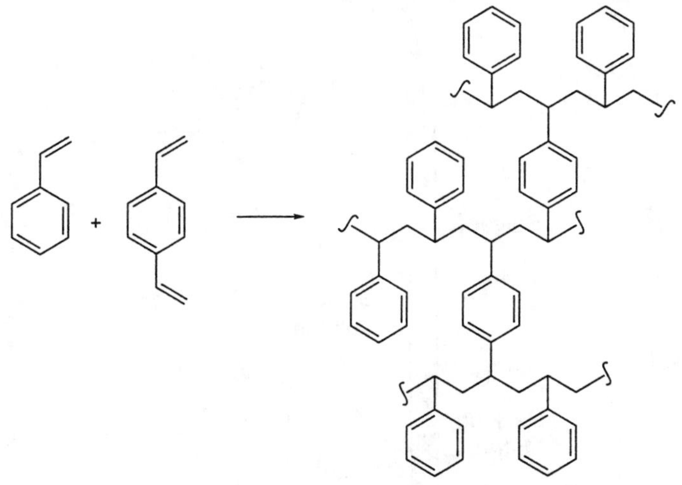

Fig. 8. Polystyrene–DVB polymers.

problems caused by exposed silanols in silica-based materials is avoided. Compounds such as tannins, which can give poor separation and recovery on silica-based columns, often are easily purified on polystyrene adsorbents.

3.6. Alumina

Alumina is a porous polymer of aluminium oxide (Al_2O_3). Alumina can be produced with an acidic, basic, or neutral surface, based on the pH of the final wash of the synthetic absorbent. Its reactivity can also be controlled by varying the moisture content of the sample in a manner analogous to the control of silica gel activity.

An aqueous slurry of acidic alumina will have a pH of approx 4.0 and is most useful for the separation of acidic compounds such as carboxylic acids. Basic alumina (pH approx 10.0) is useful for the separation of such basic compounds as alkaloids. Neutral alumina (pH approx 7.0) is most often used for the separation of relatively nonpolar compounds such as steroids.

Alumina is no longer a commonly used adsorbent due to its ability to catalyze a variety of reactions. Base-labile compounds are particularly prone to degradation upon chromatographic separation on alumina. Because of this reactivity, it is essential that small trial chromatographic separations be performed in order to elucidate proper conditions for separating components without degradation.

4. Column Operation

This section will illustrate approaches to selecting column conditions, packing material, and mobile phase. A practical guide to packing and developing a

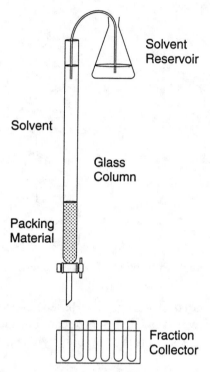

Fig. 9. Fundamentals of column chromatography.

column will then follow. **Figure 9** illustrates a basic column chromatography system. A column contains a stationary phase of a given packing material. The sample is applied to the top of the packing material. A solvent reservoir is located above and fractions are collected below.

The purification of a compound from a crude extract is greatly facilitated if the identity of the compound is known. Its chemical properties can then be used to guide in the selection of appropriate isolation procedures, including the selection of packing materials. In natural products isolation, the identity of the biologically active compound is rarely known, and methods of purification must be determined based on the chemical or chromatographic behavior of the biological activity of interest.

4.1. Selection of Column Conditions

The choice of packing material is based mainly on an arbitrary rating of the sample's polarity. Highly polar compounds are best handled using ion-exchange methods (*see* Chapter 5) or gel-permeation chromatography. If the compound of interest is suspected to be related to certain known compounds, separation methods used for their purification can be used as a starting point.

Table 3
Developing a Solvent System Using TLC

Step	Procedure
1	Make a solution in a volatile solvent of the crude to be separated, that is at least 10 mg/mL.
2	Apply 2–5 µL of this solution to each of several TLC plates 2.5 × 10 cm).
3	Develop each plate using different solvent compositions, and visualize the plates with a UV lamp and/or various spray reagents. (For more detail, *see* Chapter 7.)
4	Choose a solvent system that puts the compound of interest at $R_f = 0.2$–0.3. In the case of a crude sample, choose an initial solvent composition that puts the highest spot at about $R_f = 0.5$, and a final solvent composition that puts the most retained spot at about $R_f = 0.2$.

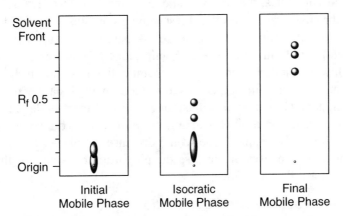

Fig. 10. Thin-layer chromatography plates sprayed with a general purpose detection reagent.

For natural products, probe experiments are an efficient way of determining a starting point for selecting column conditions. Thin-layer chromatography (TLC) plates are available coated with most adsorbents useful in column chromatography. One approach to selecting column conditions would be to run several TLC plates (as shown in **Table 3**) and visually evaluate how well each system fractionates the crude sample. This ensures that the ensuing column chromatography step will lead to some degree of purification. For example, as shown in **Fig. 10**, if TLC conditions are such that all visible components move to a R_f of greater than 0.6, the column chromatography will most likely achieve little separation, and everything will elute in the first few fractions. Similarly, TLC conditions where "nothing moves," i.e., all

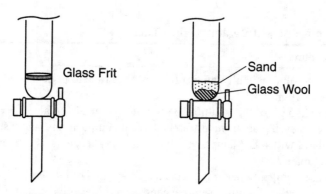

Fig. 11. Supports for column packing material.

material stays on or near the origin, would likely result in unrecoverable material from the chromatography column. Prescreening conditions using TLC do not guarantee that the compound of interest—usually the biologically active compound(s)—will elute in a useful fraction range from the chromatography column. However, it does increase the probability that the column chromatography step can achieve some degree of success. Following bioassay results of the fractions, in general, one would adjust the polarity of the mobile phase to optimize the separation on a given packing material. If the compound of interest were not sufficiently retained, one would decrease the proportion of the polar solvent for normal phases or increase the proportion of water for the reverse phases and repeat the experiment.

4.2. Column Packing and Equilibration

In practice, columns are usually packed by the chemist immediately prior to use. Alternatively, it is now also possible to purchase prepacked columns. The least expensive packing materials are usually discarded after a separation to prevent the risk of contaminating future samples with strongly retained compounds from a previous separation. More expensive materials can be washed and recycled. However, whether a column is freshly packed, recycled, or purchased prepacked should make little difference for its use.

The packing material is introduced into the column either dry or as a slurry in a solvent. Columns used for low-pressure chromatography are usually made out of glass. Glass is resistant to solvents, and thick-wall glass can tolerate the low-to-medium pressures used during column development. As shown in **Fig. 11**, a glass frit can be used to support the packing material. Alternatively, a plug of glass wool, covered with a layer of sand, can also be used.

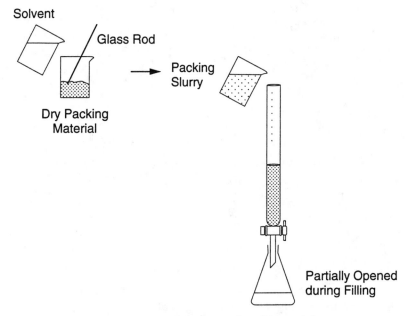

Fig. 12. Slurry preparation and packing a column.

The amount of adsorbent to use depends on sample loading. This varies depending on the difficulty of the separation and the adsorbent being used. In general, 100–500 g of packing material is used per gram of crude sample.

4.2.1. Slurry Packing

Slurry packing is the oldest and most reliable way for the novice to pack a column. It is the only packing mode available for materials that swell in the mobile phase, such as the carbohydrate packings. The desired amount of adsorbent is placed in a beaker and a solvent added (*see* **Fig. 12**). The mixture is stirred and additional solvent added if needed, to obtain a pourable slurry. The slurry must not be so thick that air bubbles are trapped in the column or so thin that the column cannot be packed in "one pour." For adsorbents that swell, sufficient time has to be allowed for the adsorbent to be fully solvated. Typically, one might add enough solvent to wet the adsorbent and produce a thick slurry and then wait overnight before adding additional solvent to produce the pourable slurry.

4.2.2. Dry Packing

Dry packing is another very efficient way to pack a column. It is most often used in conjunction with regular or bonded silica gel. If done well, a dry packed column will give excellent resolution. As the name implies, dry packing

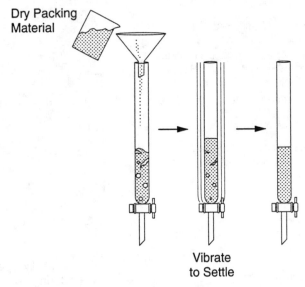

Fig. 13. Dry packing a column.

involves pouring the dry adsorbent directly into the column (*see* **Fig. 13**). This is then followed by a "wetting" step, where a suitable solvent is passed through the adsorbent, and finally by an equilibration step as the initial mobile phase is passed through the column. The key to dry packing is to get most of the air out of the dry pack. When the dry adsorbent is poured into the column, the column should be vibrated to ensure good packing. As an alternative to vibration, the column can be tapped with a cork ring during the fill operation. Note that the better the packing of the dry material, the better the performance of the column. Both slurry packing and dry packing can give excellent chromatographic results if care is taken in preparing the column.

4.3. Sample Application

Sample loading can be effected in several ways depending on the type of column used and development mode used. Preferentially, the sample is dissolved in a small amount of the initial mobile phase and applied with a long pipet to the top of the column bed (*see* **Fig. 14**). The exit valve is opened to allow the sample solution to be adsorbed on the stationary phase and then closed. The top of the column can then be carefully filled with mobile phase. To prevent disturbing the top of the bed, which now has the sample adsorbed, one can apply to the top of the bed a layer of sand about 5–10 mm thick, or a piece of filter paper the same diameter as the column bed. In a closed, pumped system, an injection valve can be used to introduce the sample solution in the mobile phase path just ahead of the packing material bed.

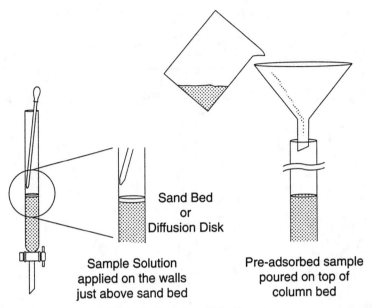

Sand Bed
or
Diffusion Disk

Sample Solution
applied on the walls
just above sand bed

Pre-adsorbed sample
poured on top of
column bed

Fig. 14. Sample application.

If the sample is not soluble in the initial mobile phase, and the top of the column bed is accessible, one can "dry load" the column. This is most often used for silica gel columns where the starting mobile phase might be fairly nonpolar. In this procedure, the sample is dissolved in a solvent (for example, EtOAc or MeOH), and approx 10 times the weight of silica gel, or another inert carrier such as Celite, is added to this solution. Using a large flask (e.g., 20 times the volume of the silica gel that was added), the solvent is removed under reduced pressure using a rotary evaporator. This leaves behind silica gel on which the sample is now adsorbed. The dry powder can now be transferred to the top of the column bed and slurried with a little of the initial mobile phase to remove air bubbles.

4.4. Column Development

Elution can be carried out by gravity, by applying nitrogen pressure at the inlet, by applying vacuum pressure at the outlet, or by pumping the mobile phase through the column at varying pressures. For all of these, it might be desirable to apply a solvent gradient, although isocratic methods are often used.

4.4.1. Gradient Formation

In open column chromatography, step gradients are most often used. Not only are they the simplest to generate, but if compositions are chosen adequately, excellent results are obtained. This is in contrast to ion-exchange separa-

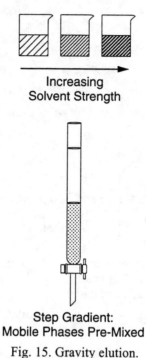

Increasing
Solvent Strength

Step Gradient:
Mobile Phases Pre-Mixed

Fig. 15. Gravity elution.

tions, where step gradients are not desirable, and HPLC, where the instrumentation allows for the easy creation of gradients of any shape. Step gradients are generated simply by preparing a range of mobile phases with varying ratios of polar/nonpolar solvents (*see* **Fig. 15**). One to three column volumes of each step are generally adequate. As the column is developed, the column inlet reservoir is simply refilled with the new solvent. Should a finer gradient be necessary, a gradient maker (*see* **Fig. 16**) can be used.

4.4.2. Gravity

Gravity elution is generally restricted to relatively coarse particle sizes of greater than 60 μm. For finer particles, the resulting back pressure is such that force is necessary to pass solvent through the column at the desired flow rate. Gravity elution is the simplest to set up. Solvent is poured on top of the open column and gravity pushes it through the packing material. A solvent reservoir can be used for added capacity (*see* **Fig. 9**). The flow can be controlled by adjusting the opening of the outlet valve.

4.4.3. Air/Nitrogen Pressure

In flash chromatography, nitrogen pressure is applied to the top of the column (*see* **Fig. 17**). Using a needle release valve, fairly accurate flows can be

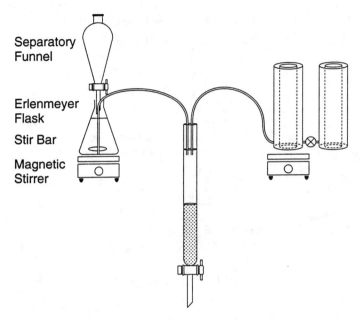

Separatory
Funnel

Erlenmeyer
Flask

Stir Bar

Magnetic
Stirrer

Fig. 16. Examples of gradient generation.

obtained. Particle sizes in the 40–60 μm range can then be used. If applying pressure while using a glass column, it is wise to use a column that has an appropriate wall thickness. Such columns can be purchased for the purpose of flash chromatography. An additional precaution would be to use plastic mesh netting as a column jacket or simply tape the outside of the column. If too high a pressure is applied, the column could literally explode. An outer jacket of netting or tape might help in reducing damages to the surroundings, including the column operator. To reduce chances of such an event, it is essential to use the right equipment and to inspect the glass column for cracks prior to use. If unsure about the setup, ask someone who has been properly trained.

4.4.4. Vacuum

An alternative to air or nitrogen pressure for flash chromatography is to use a vacuum at the column outlet (**Fig. 18**). The resulting flow is similar but the operation is a bit more difficult to set up. However, this is a relatively safe method of running a column. A common use of vacuum is in the rapid purification of a known entity. For example, if it is known that a certain component of a crude matrix can be eluted selectively from an adsorbent using certain conditions, it is possible to carry out chromatography using a scinterred glass funnel filled with the adsorbent. The crude mixture is applied to the adsorbent and the mixture

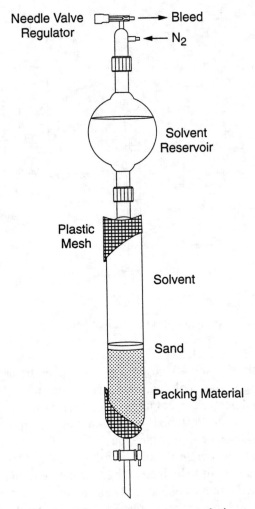

Fig. 17. Air or nitrogen pressure elution.

eluted with a mobile phase directly into a round-bottom flask, ready for concentration. This technique is often known as vacuum liquid chromatography or VLC.

4.4.5. Pumped (Low and Medium Pressure)

A pump is the preferred solvent delivery system (*see* **Fig. 19**). It ensures a smooth and constant flow of solvent. For silica gel chromatography, where organic solvents are used, care must be taken to select a pump that is both inert and designed for use with flammable solvents. Piston or plunger pumps are preferable as they can be purchased with materials inert to hydrocarbons or chlorinated solvents.

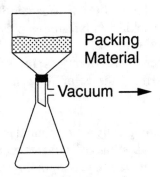

Fig. 18. Vacuum elution.

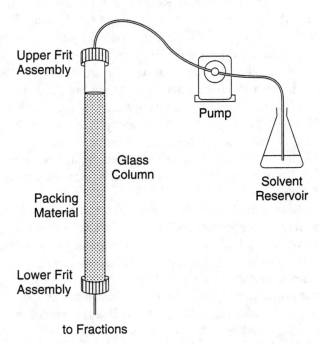

Fig. 19. Low- and medium-pressure pumped elution.

Differences between low-, medium-, and high-pressure chromatography can be summed up essentially on the basis of the particle size of the stationary phase and resulting operating pressure of the packed column. Low-pressure (LPLC) columns are usually run with 40- to 200-μm particles at flow rates that do not generate pressures significantly above atmospheric pressure. Medium-pressure chromatography (MPLC) is usually defined as employing 25- to 40-μm stationary phases and thus runs at pressures between 75 and 600 psi

(5–40 bar). *(7)* By comparison, HPLC (*see* Chapter 6) is run in stainless steel columns with 3- to 10-μm packing with resulting pressures of 500–3000 psi.

The main advantage of MPLC over LPLC is in improved resolution (smaller particle size) and shorter run times. These advantages are even more apparent in HPLC. With the increased access to HPLC, the use of MPLC has diminished considerably.

4.5. Detection

During the isolation of biologically active natural products, the best detector is a robust rapid high-throughput assay. Given the luxury of such bioassay capabilities, every fraction can be assayed for biological activity and appropriate pools prepared for the next step. It is not necessary to have a UV trace to isolate natural products. However, if assay capabilities are limited, it is often necessary to limit the number of samples submitted for bioassay. For example, for a set of 80 fractions, one could arbitrarily pool aliquots of every ten fractions and submit eight fractions for bioassay. In a second round, the ten fractions from the active composite would be assayed separately to determine the active fractions. In this procedure, only 18 bioassays are needed.

Before submitting fractions for bioassay, one can analyze individual fractions by TLC or HPLC (using an autosampler). The analysis of fractions by TLC is the simplest and most efficient method to determine the performance of the chromatography. Small aliquots (approx 5 μL) of each fraction can be spotted on a single TLC plate. After development and staining, a good picture of the performance of the separation is obtained.

If necessary, a classical detector can be attached to the column outlet, preceeding the fraction collector. UV detectors are the easiest to install and use. A variable-wavelength detector allows selection of the monitoring wavelength. Such detectors should be equipped with the appropriate cell. Analytical cells, used on HPLC systems, have path lengths of 6–10 mm and are not suitable for use with preparative open columns, as the detector output will quickly become saturated. A more generally useful cell for open column detectors would be a cell with a path length of less than 0.5 mm.

Refractive index detectors can also be used. Their main advantage is that they can used for compounds with small to no UV absorption coefficients. They are, however, much less sensitive than UV detectors for the majority of compounds encountered as natural products. These detectors are generally more difficult to set up to obtain a stable baseline. They are best used with isocratic mobile phases such as those used in size-exclusion chromatography.

In addition to bioassays, HPLC and TLC analyses, and UV and RI detectors, one can use chemical tests to locate compounds of interest. For example, when desalting a sample with a BioGel P-2 column, the NaCl-containing fractions can be located by adding a small aliquot of each fraction to parallel tubes containing a

1% aqueous silver nitrate solution (+trace of nitric acid). The relative amounts of silver chloride precipitate give a profile of the elution of NaCl from the column.

4.6. Generic Experimental Protocols

4.6.1. SiO₂ Chromatography

4.6.1.1. PREPARE THE COLUMN

1. Select a heavy wall glass column, specifically designed for flash chromatography or rated for pressure, that is about three times the volume of silica gel needed.
2. Use 100 g of silica/g of crude mixture for easy separations, or up to 500 g/g for more difficult ones. A bed height of approx 20–30 cm is desirable, with 40–60 cm head space remaining to hold the solvent.
3. If the bottom of the column is not equipped with a glass frit, plug the column outlet with glass wool and pour in a small bed of sea sand (about 1 cm thick). While tapping the column, carefully pour in the dry silica gel (40–63 µm), being careful not to inhale the material (use fume hood). Apply a thin layer (0.5 cm) of sea sand to the top of the column.

4.6.1.2. EQUILIBRATE THE COLUMN

1. Fill the column with the initial solvent composition, being careful not to disturb the silica bed/sand layer.
2. With the column outlet opened, allow the solvent to percolate down the column by gravity.
3. When the solvent appears at the outlet, apply nitrogen pressure to the column to give a linear flow rate of approx 1–2 cm/min. (It is recommended to use plastic mesh around the column and a nitrogen regulator equipped with a safety valve.)
4. Continue equilibrating the column until the bed has a uniform appearance, i.e., no "dry" areas are visible, reloading the column with solvent if needed. Let the solvent level drop to less than 0.5 cm above the sand level.
5. Remove the nitrogen pressure and close the column outlet.

4.6.1.3. APPLY THE SAMPLE

1. Dissolve the sample in a minimum of mobile phase. Preferably, the volume used (in milliliters) should not exceed $0.4 \times D^2$ (where D is the column diameter in centimeters).
2. Using a long pipet, apply the sample solution to the sand bed, being careful not to disturb the silica below.
3. To prevent diluting the sample in the mobile phase, the sample must be adsorbed on the silica. Using either gravity or a little nitrogen pressure, push the sample solution down into the sand bed without allowing the silica bed to dry out.
4. Rinse the sides of the column with a small amount of the initial mobile phase. Push the solvent level down to the sand bed level.
5. Repeat the previous step two or three times.
6. Fill the column with the initial mobile phase.

4.6.1.4. ELUTE AND COLLECT FRACTIONS

1. As before, apply nitrogen pressure to the column such that the linear flow rate is approx 1–2 cm/min.
2. Collect 10–20 fractions per column bed volumes. For example, for a 100-mL column, one would collect fractions of 5–10 mL. Fewer fractions can be collected if the separation will take place over several column volumes.
3. With each "reloading" of the column with solvent, increase the polarity of the mobile phase. A typical step gradient sequence might be as follows: initial composition of 50% EtOAc/hexane, followed by 1 column volume each of 75% EtOAc/hexane, EtOAc, and 1-5-20% MeOH/EtOAc.

4.6.2. Generic Size-Exclusion Chromatography (LH-20)

4.6.2.1. PREPARE THE COLUMN

Typically, one would choose a glass column with a diameter of 15–25 mm and a length of 40–100 cm. The size of the column can be adjusted according to the desired bed volume. For practical purposes, one should count on using about 1 mL swollen gel per milligram of compounds to be chromatographed. For example, for a sample weight of 200 mg, one would select a column with a 200-mL bed volume.

1. Swell the gel overnight by suspending Sephadex LH-20 in MeOH. Use sufficient methanol to get a free-flowing slurry, and then let it sit overnight to ensure complete swelling. If needed, additional methanol should be added to get a thick but pourable slurry. (Prepare a little more than will be needed to fill the column; for example, swell 60 g for a 200-mL column.) Care should be taken to ensure that enough dry gel is used, since the gel has to swell in the desired solvent prior to column filling, and the packing process should be carried out in one "pour."
2. Use a glass column equipped with a glass frit at the outlet, and fill the column in one slow continuous pour with the outlet valve left in the partially open position. It is important to have solvent flow while filling the column to ensure good sedimentation, but it is even more important not to stop the filling process until complete. Packing in stages does not yield a good bed. Mechanical vibration of the column during the packing process gives a better packing.
3. Continue slow pouring as the bed settles.

4.6.2.2. EQUILIBRATE THE COLUMN

1. Apply a flow rate (approx 1–5 mL/min) to complete the settling of the bed. Let the column equilibrate for several hours with the flow on.
2. Let the MeOH level drop to just above the gel level.

4.6.2.3. APPLY THE SAMPLE

1. Dissolve the sample in MeOH using no more than about 5% of the column volume, i.e., 10 mL for the 200-mL column. For chromatography purposes, the sample should be dissolved in 1–5% of the total bed volume, while the sample

solution viscosity should be kept close to that of the eluant. In "desalting" mode, the sample could be dissolved in as much as 30% of the bed volume.

2. Apply the sample solution to the top of the column; open the outlet valve and allow the solvent level to drop to the same level as the gel bed. If a column fitted with adjustable end pieces is being used, the sample solution must be applied in the same manner as the eluting solvent. For gravity flow columns, the sample solution is fed through the inlet tube. After the sample is introduced on the column, the solvent reservoir is connected to the same inlet tube. For pumping systems, the sample can be injected on the column using an injector design as with HPLC systems or simply pumped on the column.

3. Add enough MeOH (another 10 mL) so that the sample solution flows down into the gel bed and is no longer in contact with the mobile phase in the column head.

4.6.2.4. Elute and Collect Fractions

1. Fill the column head with MeOH and attach either a solvent reservoir (for gravity feed) or a pump outlet tube.

2. Open the column outlet valve and adjust the flow rate to 2–4 mL/min (for the 200-mL column). The desired flow rate for this type of gel should be such as to give a contact time of approx 50–100 min. This is equivalent to a linear flow rate of approx 10–15 cm/h. Such slow flow rates can usually run perfectly well with gravity flow, as these columns generate little back pressure. However, it is generally preferable to use a low-pressure pump. Pumping the solvent through the column allows for better flow-rate control throughout the separation.

3. Collect about 40 fractions per column vol (5-mL fractions in this example). Collect fractions for 2 column volumes or 80 fractions.

5. Practical Examples

5.1. Adsorption from Fermentation Broths

Isolation of kilogram quantities of the potent immunosuppressant macrolactam immunomycin (**Fig. 20**) was required in order to support a medicinal chemistry project and biological evaluation. Although the compound can be readily extracted from fermentation broth with common water-immiscible organic solvents, such as dichloromethane and ethyl acetate, the use of large volumes of these solvents presents certain safety and environmental concerns.

It was found that the immunomycin could be recovered from the fermentation broth using a fluidized adsorption process. A large fermentation batch consisting of 14,000 L of whole broth containing 1.2 kg of product was diluted with an equal volume of methanol. The slurry was fed at 20 L/min to a column of 600 L of SP-207 resin (a brominated polystyrene resin). The immunomycin was eluted with 100% methanol and could be recovered using only 3000 L of solvent. The recovery of product was above 95% and was of sufficient purity to allow the material to be processed to 98% purity with no further use of chromatographic methods.

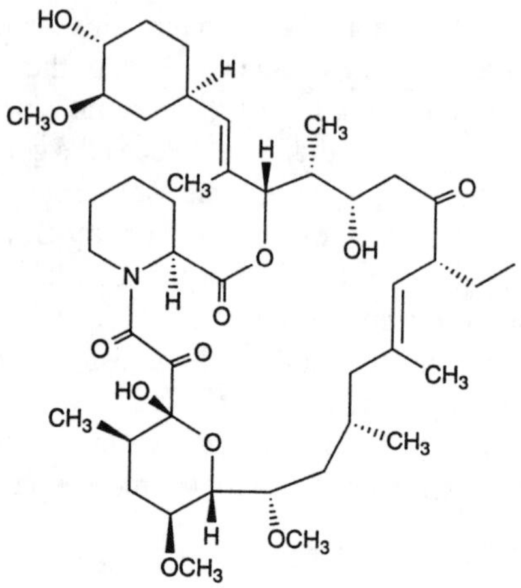

Fig. 20. Structure of immunomycin.

5.2. Reverse Phase Chromatography on Polystyrene Resins

The aqueous-soluble portion of the partitioned MeOH extract of stems of *Terminalia chebula* Retz. was found to be active in a whole-cell bioassay. Initial fractionation studies using 1 g of crude extract indicated that useful purification techniques were limited to liquid–liquid partitioning, LH-20 chromatography used in an adsorption mode, and adsorption chromatography used on polymeric stationary phases such as HP-20. All attempts to purify the active component by HPLC resulted in significant loss of material. A small amount, less than 500 µg, of the major active component was obtained by this method, but this quantity was sufficient only for ^{1}H NMR characterization.

In order to obtain a larger amount of this active compound, 20 g of crude MeOH extract was fractionated by partitioning the aqueous solution with CH_2Cl_2 followed by 2-butanone. The bulk of the activity was distributed into the 2-butanone extract with some remaining in the aqueous spent. The 7 g of active extract was applied to a 1.5 L column of SP-207 and eluted with a step gradient of MeOH in H_2O. This was carried out as a simple adsorption/elution operation. The activity was spread between the 66% MeOH and 100% MeOH eluates. The brown residue (2.6 g) from only the 66% MeOH eluate, which appeared to be less complex than the 100% MeOH eluate, was further fractionated by adsorption chromatography on LH-20. The sample was applied to a 1.5-L column packed in MeOH, and the column was developed with a step gradient of acetone in MeOH. Activity was found in the 20–40% acetone fractions. The fractions were analyzed by RP-HPLC (Primesphere C-8; 0.1% TFA:ACN,90:10), and those fractions enriched in the compound of interest were pooled. This material, 465 mg, was ultimately purified by chromatography on a 450-mL column of CHP20p developed with a gradient of 5–30% MeOH in H_2O. The fractions were analyzed by HPLC and those fractions containing pure compound (2-*O*-galloylpunicallin; *see* **Fig. 21**) were pooled and lyophilized. Approximately 40 mg of purified material was obtained as a light tan powder.

5.3. Sample Desalting

During the purification of an unknown antibacterial agent, the eluate from an anion-exchange experiment had to be desalted. The desalting of a 1% NaCl eluate could be accomplished on a BioGel P-2 column by size exclusion. The small inorganic ions are most retained on such a packing material.

1. A 10-mL aliquot of a previous ion-exchange eluate was freeze-dried.
2. The residue was dissolved in 1 mL water and applied to an 80-mL BioGel P-2 column (1.5-cm ID × 45 cm; water as the mobile phase).
3. The column was eluted with a flow rate of 0.8 mL/min, collecting 2.5-min fractions (2.0 mL).
4. For detection of chloride ions, a 20-µL aliquot was taken from each fraction and added to test tubes containing 100 µL of an acidic silver nitrate solution (1% aqueous). NaCl was detected in fractions 32 and 33.
5. Fractions were bioassayed and antibacterial activity was detected in fractions 27–28.

5.4. Partitioning on SiO_2

The preparative separation of pneumocandins A_0 and B_0 (**Fig. 22**) proved to be fairly difficult. They were fairly well-separated on C18 reverse phase chromatography on an analytical scale, but this separation could not be scaled up at all. For example, 25 mg of the mixture was not separable on a 21.2-mm ID × 250-mm column. These compounds chromatographed poorly on silica gel until water was added to the mobile phase. As seen in **Fig. 23**, the lower phase of the biphasic system CH_2Cl_2/MeOH/H_2O (65:35:10) gave radically improved resolution of the pneumocandins compared to its nonaqueous counterpart.

Eventually, single-phase solvent systems were developed. Either CH_2Cl_2/MeOH/5% aqueous AcOH (80:20:2) or EtOAc/MeOH/5% aqueous AcOH (85:10:5) yielded a baseline separation of pneumocandins A_0 and B_0 *(8)*.

5.5. Adsorption on LH-20

When the biological activity or the compound of interest is not recovered from an LH-20 column within the usual 1.5–2 column volumes, elution should be continued for up to 7 or 8 column volumes. Compounds eluting this "late" from an LH-20 column are usually fairly pure.

This was exemplified by the isolation of the antibiotic rachelmycin from the EtOAc crude extract of a fermentation broth.

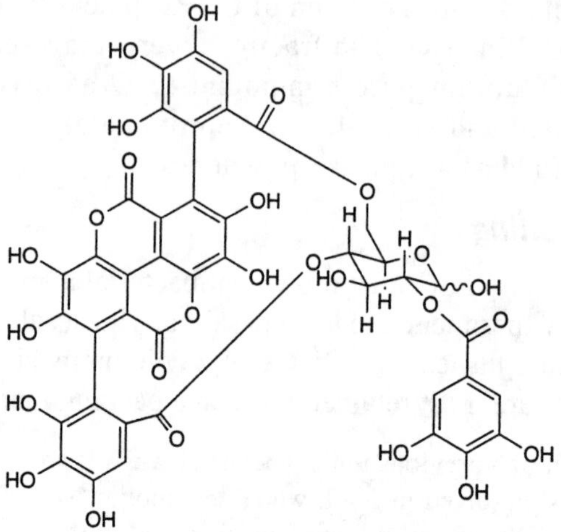

Fig. 21. Structure of 2-*O*-Galloylpunicallin.

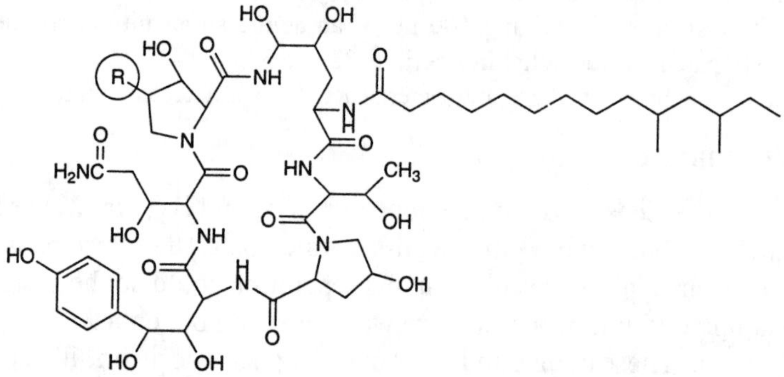

Fig. 22. Structure of pneumocandins A_0: R = CH_3 and B_0: R = H.

1. The EtOAc extract was dried over anhydrous sodium sulfate and evaporated to dryness to yield an oily residue (380 mg).
2. The residue was dissolved in MeOH (10 mL) and applied to a column of Sephadex LH-20 (400 mL bed volume) equilibrated with MeOH.
3. Elution was carried out using MeOH with a flow rate of 20 mL/min, collecting 20-mL fractions (160 fractions).
4. The fractions were bioassayed.
5. Fractions 93–135 were combined and evaporated to dryness to yield 3.2 mg. *Note:* Bioassay of a titration of the composite (fractions 93–135) and of the feed indicated an 80% recovery of activity. HPLC analysis of the composite showed a single major component. Mass spectral and NMR analysis identified the sample as the known antibiotic rachelmycin shown in **Fig. 24**.

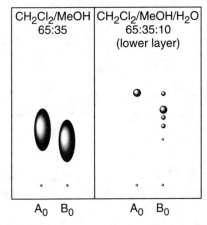

Fig. 23. Silica gel TLC behavior of pneumocandins.

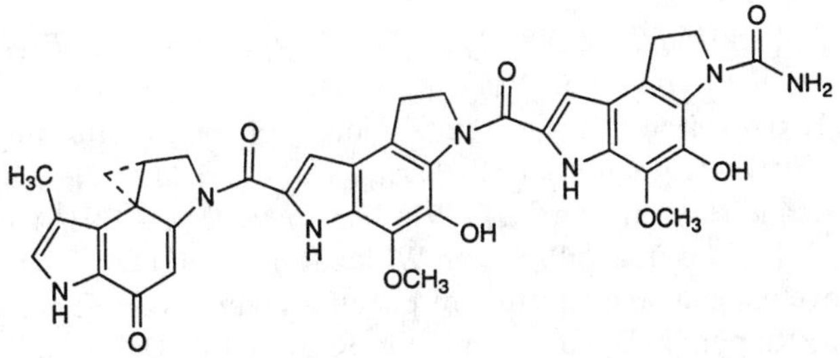

Fig. 24. Structure of rachelmycin.

5.6. Alumina

A good use of alumina is in the purification of alkaloids. The isolation of quinolizidine alkaloids (**Fig. 25**) from *Lupinus argenteus*, a plant of the western United States, exemplifies this process *(9)*.

1. The crude alkaloid mixture (3.3 g) was dissolved in diethyl ether (approx 25 mL).
2. This was applied to a column of basic alumina (Merck, Type T); 250-mL bed volume.
3. The column was eluted sequentially with diethyl ether (1000 mL), 10% MeOH/ether (500 mL), 50% MeOH/ether (300 mL), and MeOH (200 mL).
4. Fractions (approx 50 mL each) were collected and pooled based on TLC analysis. Fractions 6–8 contained (+)-aphyllidine (0.6 g), fractions 25–27 contained a mixture of stereoisomers of hydroxyaphyllidine and dihydroxyaphyllidine, while fractions 28–43 contained a mixture of dihydroxyaphyllidine stereoisomers.

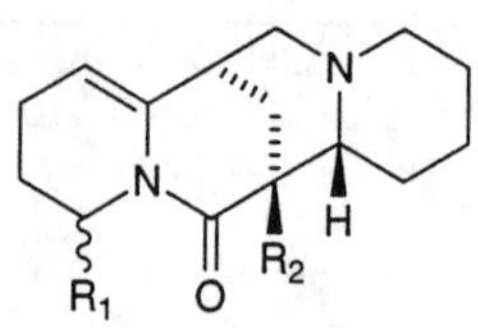

Fig. 25. Structure of some quinolizidine alkaloids. (+) Aphyllidine, $R_1 = R_2 = H$; 2-Hydroxyaphyllidine, $R_1 = OH$, $R_2 = H$; 2,9-Dihydroxyaphyllidine, $R_1 = R_2 = OH$.

References

1. Liteanu, C. and Gocan, S. (1974) *Gradient Liquid Chromatography.* Wiley, New York.
2. Poole, C. F. and Poole, S. K. (1991) *Chromatography Today,* Elsevier, Amsterdam.
3. Deyl, Z., Macek, K., and Janak, J. (eds.) (1975) Liquid column chromatography, in *J. Chromatography Library,* vol. 3, Elsevier, Amsterdam.
4. Wolf, F. J. (1969) *Separation Methods in Organic Chemistry and Biochemistry,* Academic, New York.
5. Yau, W. W., Kirkland, J. J., and Bly, D. D. (1979) *Modern Size-Exclusion Liquid Chromatography.* Wiley, New York.
6. Unger, K. K. (ed.) (1990) Packings and stationary phases in chromatographic techniques, in *Chromatographic Science Series,* vol. 47, Dekker, New York.
7. Marston, A. and Hostettmann, K. (1991) *Nat. Prod. Rep.* **8,** 391–414.
8. Schwartz, R. E., Masurekar, P. S., and White, R. F. (1993) Discovery, production process development, and isolation of pneumocandin B_0, in *Cutaneous Antifungal Agents* (Rippon, J. W. and Fromtling, R. A., eds.), Dekker, New York, pp. 375–393.
9. Arslanian, R. L., Harris, G. H., and Stermitz, F. R. (1990) New quinolizidine alkaloids from *Lupinus argenteus* and its hosted root parasite *Castilleja sulphurea.* Stereochemistry and conformation of some naturally occuring cyclic carbinolamides. *J. Org. Chem.* **55,** 1204–1210.

5

Isolation by Ion-Exchange Methods

Claude Dufresne

1. Introduction

Historically, ion-exchange chromatography has been a popular technique for the isolation of natural products. This technique is used for the separation of ionized or charged substances, a characteristic of a majority of natural products. Ion-exchange chromatography was first reported in the late 1930s, and its application to natural products was first described in the late 1940s as a technique to isolate and separate amino acids from protein hydrolysates. It is still widely used today for the analysis and separation of proteins. As the name implies, the main factor contributing to retention and separation of components is the electrostatic attraction between ionized substances from the sample and ionized centers of opposite charge on the stationary phase. Ion-exchange chromatography is thus widely applicable to the purification and analysis of a large number of molecules.

The practice of ion-exchange chromatography is well-summarized in the literature *(1–8)*. Manufacturers' booklets can also be a very useful source of up-to-date information. The explanations and examples used in this chapter will be geared to the application of ion-exchange separation techniques useful in natural products isolation. For that reason, more emphasis will be placed on selective adsorption/elution conditions as opposed to more conventional chromatography applications.

In the isolation of compounds from natural sources, the desired compound (or solute) is often present in a low titer and in a complex mixture of diverse structures. A charged functional group is most often present and represents a convenient "handle" by which to semiselectively extract the desired compound. An ion-exchange purification step can thus achieve high levels of purification directly from fermentation broths or crude extracts. The technique is easily

From: *Methods in Biotechnology, Vol. 4: Natural Products Isolation*
Edited by: R. J. P. Cannell © Humana Press Inc., Totowa, NJ

scaleable up to manufacturing scales and at low cost. This is exemplified by the wide spread use of ion-exchange processes in the industrial production of antibiotics.

An advantage of the technique is that it opens the door to the pursuit of nonsolvent extractable natural products, long neglected because of difficulties encountered in isolation. On the other hand, the use of the technique often introduces large amounts of inorganic salts and the ensuing need for desalting steps. For this reason, it is presently reserved for difficult problems that cannot otherwise be readily resolved by the use of modern reverse phase/hydrophobic adsorbents, such as, for example, the purification of naturally occurring amino sugars.

2. Theory of Ion Exchange

The basis for ion-exchange separations is the reversible binding of charged molecules. Charged functional groups (G), attached to some support matrix (R), can interact with oppositely charged solute molecules (S), resulting in retention on the column, and displacement of the counter-ion (C). The functional groups on the support matrix can be either positively or negatively charged with an associated counter-ion, resulting in either anion- or cation-exchange columns, respectively. In the following reaction, the positively charged solute is attracted to the negatively charged functional group attached to the support matrix and displaces the counter-ion. The process is generally reversible, allowing for adsorption/elution cycles, along with adsorbent regeneration.

$$\underline{RG^-}\ C^+ + S^+ \rightleftharpoons \underline{RG^-S^+} + C^+$$

or

$$\underline{RG^+}\ C^- + S^- \rightleftharpoons \underline{RG^+S^-} + C^-$$

The charge on solute molecules can often be manipulated by adjusting the pH. Organic acids are negatively charged when the pH of the solution is above the acid's pKa, and amines are positively charged at pH values below the base's pKa value. For example, at pH values above 6.0, the majority of carboxylic acids are deprotonated and exhibit a negative charge. They can be retained on resins bearing functional groups that are positively charged, such as quaternary ammonium groups. Similarly, amines are generally protonated at pH values below 8.0 and would therefore be retained on resins bearing functional groups that are negatively charged at the same pH, such as sulfonic acids or carboxylic acids (above pH 6.0).

In order for the charged solute to be retained, it must displace the counter-ion that is present near the charged functional group. The equilibrium presented above can be summarized in term of a partition constant (K_p). The partition constant is the ratio of the two dissociation constants (K_{dC} and K_{dS}) for binding of the resin-functional group to the counter-ion and solute, respectively:

$$K_p = \frac{[\underline{RGS}][C]}{[\underline{RGC}][S]} = K_{dC}/K_{dS}$$

where

$$K_{dC} = \frac{[\underline{RG}][C]}{[\underline{RGC}]}$$

and

$$K_{dS} = \frac{[\underline{RG}][S]}{[\underline{RGS}]}$$

The success or failure of an ion-exchange experiment then clearly depends on the relative affinity of a functional group toward various ions and their relative concentrations. Polyvalent ions have, in general, greater affinity for a charged stationary phase than do monovalent ions, as they can interact with more than one charged site of the stationary phase. Ions that are more polarizable or have a higher oxidation state will have a higher affinity for the ion exchanger. The affinity of some common anions toward anion exchangers is generally as follows, although it can change with various resins:

hydroxide < acetate < bicarbonate, formate < chloride < phosphate, citrate

The affinity of some common cations towards cation exchangers is generally as follows:

lithium < hydrogen < sodium < ammonium < calcium

These relative affinities explain in part why chloride ions (high affinity) are effective in eluting carboxylates (lower affinity) from an anion-exchange column. Similarly, sodium ions are not very effective at eluting positively charged amines (ammonium ions having a higher affinity than sodium ions). These relative selectivities constitute one of the major factors involved in designing an ion-exchange experiment.

The simple picture presented above, based on Coulombic interactions, is unfortunately a poor representation of the actual adsorption/retention process. There are also important interactions between sample molecules (large and small) and nonionic regions of the support matrix. Although these nonionic interactions can be minimized by the use of organic modifiers, or nonaqueous systems, they remain a problem that has to be evaluated experimentally, as will be discussed later.

The stationary phase contains a fixed number of charged functional groups per unit volume. This fact is illustrated by the measure of capacity of an ion exchanger. For example, a resin with a capacity of 3 milliequivalents per gram of ion exchanger (meq/g) has the theoretical capacity to adsorb 3 meq, i.e., 3 mmol of a monovalent charged molecule, or 1 mmol of a trivalent one, per gram of ion exchanger used.

The kinetics of the ion-exchange process are very much dependent on the surface area of the stationary phase. In the exchange process shown below, as equilibrium is approached, counter-ion S^+ diffuses into the bead as counter-ion C^+ diffuses out of the bead. To maintain electroneutrality, both steps must occur at the same time. This diffusion step is the rate-limiting step with the actual chemical exchange being a fast step.

$$\underline{RG^-}\ C^+ + S^+ = \underline{RG^-}S^+ + C^+$$

Decreasing the bead size increases the surface area and therefore increases the efficiency of the diffusion step by lowering the time needed for the ion-exchange process to take place.

3. Materials for Ion Exchangers

Ion-exchange packing materials consist of water-insoluble particles bearing covalently bound positively and negatively charged functional groups. Free counter-ions are associated with these functional groups. The support matrices making up the insoluble particles can be based on a variety of polymeric materials, including polysaccharides and synthetic resins. This section will discuss the various materials used for support matrices and ion-exchange functional groups.

3.1. Support Matrices

The physical properties of the ion-exchange column are determined by the nature of the packing material's support matrix. There are three major groups of materials useful as matrices for natural products isolation: polystyrene resins, carbohydrate polymers, and silica gel. Important properties arising from the nature of the support matrix include the column's flow characteristics, its resistance to mechanical shock, and the porosity of the particle. Both porous and nonporous support matrices are available. Highly porous particles are also termed macroreticular; these have rigid pores that are fixed into the resin structure, as shown in **Fig. 1**. Porous gels must be swollen to expose the majority of the functional groups. Nonporous materials, such as silica gel, offer the benefit of speed, with separation times as much as five times faster than on porous material.

When a bead of the ion-exchange resin is placed in water, water molecules diffuse into the resin and hydrate the charged functional groups and their associated counter-ions. This hydration results in swelling. The amount of swelling varies with the type of polymer used. In general, the higher the percentage of crosslinking, the less hydration water per unit charge will be achieved, and thus the less swelling will be observed. Support matrices are usually classified as either hydrophobic or hydrophilic.

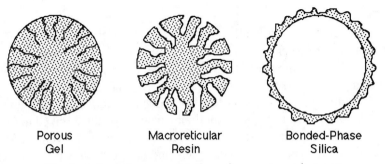

| Porous
Gel | Macroreticular
Resin | Bonded-Phase
Silica |

Fig. 1. Schematic representation of support matrix types.

Bead diameters for polymeric materials are usually given in mesh sizes, whereas silica-based supports are reported in microns. A useful size for polymeric materials is the 100- to 200-mesh range. Larger beads (50–100 mesh) could be used for large preparative columns while smaller ones (200–400 mesh), or silica-based supports (5- to 10-μm range) would be better suited for analytical or rapid separations.

3.1.1. Polystyrene Resins

The most widely used ion-exchange support materials are hydrophobic polymers, such as polystyrene or methacrylate, which are highly substituted with charged functional groups. These matrices are rigid and offer very good mechanical strength. They are both thermally and chemically stable. Polystyrene backbones can tolerate a pH range of 1–14 while methacrylate backbones can be used over a range of pH 2.0–10.

One of the most widely used hydrophobic resins is Dowex (Dow Chemicals). The resin is made by reacting styrene with divinylbenzene (DVB). The resulting polymer is then said to be crosslinked and is formed into beads. The amount of DVB used in the reaction is variable and leads to different degrees of crosslinking. This is indicated by the designations X-2, X-4, or X-8, that reflect the percentage of DVB used as 2, 4, or 8%, respectively, leading to the equivalent percentage of crosslinking, with 8% being a popular choice. The capacity and selectivity of the resin increase with the amount of crosslinkage. This is due to the presence of a higher density of ionic sites, which in turn is the result of reduced swelling. However, highly crosslinked resins have a slower equilibration time as access to the interior regions of the matrix becomes more and more restricted.

A major problem with hydrophobic supports, especially polystyrene, is the possible interaction of the solutes to be separated, with the support matrix itself. Termed "backbone interactions," these forces can be significant enough to impede solute recovery from the ion-exchange column.

3.1.2. Carbohydrate Polymers

These supports were originally designed as polysaccharides for the separation of biomolecules such as proteins. Being hydrophilic, these matrices do not lead to protein denaturation. One of the most widely available supports is Sephadex, a crosslinked dextran from Pharmacia (Uppsala, Sweden). Because of its hydrophilicity, it shows very few backbone interactions or very few nonspecific adsorption of substrates. Functional groups are ether-linked to the glucose units of the support. The dextran is bead-formed and swells readily in water, resulting in a gel that is easy to pack and has good flow properties. Bed volumes also change with ionic strength. Two types of Sephadex resins are available, −25 and −50, referring to their degree of porosity. The −25 types are more tightly crosslinked than the −50 types and are better suited to natural products isolation work. They swell less and are more resistant to mechanical pressures. The −50 types, being more porous, are better suited for separations of large biomolecules. Other supports include crosslinked agarose (such as Sepharose) and cellulose.

3.1.3. Silica Gel

More recently, silica-based matrices have been introduced. As opposed to the organic polymers mentioned earlier, silica does not shrink or swell with changes in solvent composition. The main disadvantage of silica-based support matrices is their pH stability requirements. Silica is stable in the pH range of 2.0 to 7.5, which precludes prolonged operation at higher pH values. They can be exposed to a broader pH range for only brief periods of time. Since they are available in small particle sizes (5–50 µm), equilibration times are shorter, and consequently, short exposure to high pH values is not necessarily a big problem. The small particle sizes also give rise to back pressure. These materials are thus best suited for high-performance separations.

3.2. Functional Groups

The charge and nature of the functional group present on the stationary phase determine the type of ion-exchange resin. The number of these groups per unit volume of resin determines the column's capacity. The pKa of the functional group determines the strength of the exchanger and its usefulness to effect a given separation. Apparent pKa values for various functional groups used in ion exchange are shown in **Table 1**.

3.2.1. Anion Exchangers

Since a large number of natural products bear a negative charge, such as a carboxylate anion, anion exchangers are used for their purification. Both strong and weak anion exchangers are available. A representative sampling of strong

Table 1
Approximate pKa's for Various Functional Groups

Functional group	Approximate pKa
$-SO_3H$	<1
$-PO_3H$	2.5, 7.5
$-CO_2H$	5
$-NR_2$	8
$-NR_3^+$	>13

anion exchangers is listed in **Table 2**. Examples include quaternary amino groups as in QAE-resins (quaternary amino ethyl). These are positively charged over the full pH range. Primary, secondary, and tertiary amines are protonated over only some of the pH range and are thus considered weak exchangers. A sampling of weak exchangers is shown in **Table 3**.

3.2.2. Cation Exchangers

Strong cation exchangers are exemplified by sulphonic acids, which are negatively charged over the full pH range. Examples include SP-resins (sulphopropyl). Phosphoric acids are also considered strong exchangers, even though they lose their charge below pH 2.0. **Table 4** shows a representative sampling of commercial materials. Carboxylic acids are negatively charged above pH 6.0 and are thus considered weak exchangers. Examples include CM-resins (carboxymethyl), as shown in **Table 5**.

4. Column Operation

This section will attempt to present practical considerations in setting up and carrying out an ion-exchange separation. In general, as with most chromatography methods, the process starts by selecting a packing material and loading the sample, followed by appropriate washes and elution steps. Since control of pH is an essential part of the ion-exchange process, adequate buffering should be maintained while loading and eluting columns. **Table 6** shows a few buffers useful in ion-exchange separations.

4.1. Packing-Material Selection

The selection of a packing material is largely empirical and often based on what is available in your lab or from your favorite local suppliers. If the charge of the solute to be separated is known, the choice of ion-exchanger type is obvious. For example, if you are designing an isolation process for a compound that bears a carboxylic acid, you would first investigate strong anion-

Table 2
Selection of Commercially Available Strong Anion Exchangers

Resin	Manufacturer	Functional group	Counter-ion	Support	Capacity, meq/100 mL	pH Range	Bead mesh range and size, μm
Dowex–1X2-100	Dow Chemicals	Trimethyl benzyl ammonium	Cl⁻	Polystyrene gel 2% crosslink	70	0–14.0	50–100 150–250
Dowex–1X8-400	Dow Chemicals	Trimethyl benzyl ammonium	Cl⁻	Polystyrene gel 8% crosslink	120	0–14.0	200–400 35–75
Amberlite IRA-400	Rohm and Haas	Quaternary ammonium	Cl⁻	Polystyrene gel 8% crosslink	140	0–14.0	16–50 500–1000
Diaion SA10A	Mitsubishi	Trimethyl benzyl ammonium	Cl⁻	Polystyrene gel	130	0–14.0	40–60 350–550
Diaion SA20A	Mitsubishi	Dimethyl benzyl hydroxyethyl ammonium	Cl⁻	Polystyrene gel	130	0–14.0	40–60 350–550
Amberlite IRA-900	Rohm and Haas	Trimethyl benzyl ammonium	Cl⁻	Polystyrene porous	100	0–14.0	16–50 500–1000
Diaion PA 312	Mitsubishi	Trimethyl benzyl ammonium	Cl⁻	Polystyrene porous 6% crosslink	120	0–14.0	16–50 500–1000
QAE-Sephadex A-25	Pharmacia	Quaternary amino ethyl	Cl⁻	Dextran	50	2.0–12.0	100–400 40–120
TSKgel SAX	TosoHaas	Quaternary ammonium	Cl⁻	Polystyrene divinylbenzene	>370	1.0–14.0	>400 5

Table 3
Selection of Commercially Available Weak Anion Exchangers

Resin	Manufacturer	Functional group	Counter-ion	Support	Capacity, meq/100 mL	pH Range	Bead mesh range and size, μm
DEAE-Sephadex A-25	Pharmacia	Diethyl amino ethyl	Cl⁻	Dextran	50	2.0–12.0	100–400 40–120
Amberlite IRA-35	Rohm and Haas	Diethyl amino ethyl	Free base	Acrylic DVB macroreticular	110	0–9.0	16–50 500–1000
Amberlite IRA-68	Rohm and Haas	Diethyl amino ethyl	Free base	Acrylic DVB	160	0–7.0	16–50 500–1000
Amberlyst A-21	Rohm and Haas	Diethyl amino benzyl	Cl⁻	Sytrene DVB macroreticular	260	0–9.0	500
Diaion WA10	Mitsubishi	Dimethyl amino ethyl	Free base	Polyacrylate gel	120	0–9.0	40–60 350–550
Diaion WA20	Mitsubishi	Polyamine	Free base	Polystyrene porous	250	0–9.0	40–60 350–550
TSKgel DEAE-5PW	TosoHaas	Diethyl amino ethyl	Cl⁻	Methacrylate porous	>10	2.0–12.0	>400 10
TSKgel DEAE-2SW	TosoHaas	Diethyl amino ethyl	Cl⁻	Silica	>30	2.0–7.5	>400 5

Table 4
Selection of Commercially Available Strong Cation Exchangers

Resin	Manufacturer	Functional group	Counter-ion	Support	Capacity, meq/100 mL	pH Range	Bead mesh range and size, µm
SP-Sephadex A-25	Pharmacia	Sulfopropyl	Na^+	Dextran	30	2.0–12.0	100–400 40–120
Dowex– 50X2-100	Dow chemicals	Sulfonic acid	H^+	Polystyrene 2% crosslink	60	0–14.0	50–100
Dowex– 50X8-100	Dow chemicals	Sulfonic acid	H^+	Polystyrene 8% crosslink	170	0–14.0	50–100
Diaion SK1B	Mitsubishi	Sulfonic acid	Na^+	Polystyrene gel	190	0–14.0	40–60 400–600
Amberlite IR-122	Rohm and Haas	Sulfonic acid	Na^+	Polystyrene 10% crosslink	210	0–14.0	16–50 500–1000
Diaion SK112	Mitsubishi	Sulfonic acid	Na^+	Polystyrene 12% crosslink	210	0–9.0	16–50 500–1000
TSKgel SP-5PW	TosoHaas	Sulfonic acid	Na^+	Methacrylate	>10	2.0–12.0	> 400 10
TSKgel SCX	TosoHaas	Sulfonic acid	Na^+	Polystyrene/ divinylbenzene	>420	1.0–14.0	> 400 5

Table 5
Selection of Commercially Available Weak Cation Exchangers

Resin	Manufacturer	Functional group	Counter-ion	Support	Capacity, meq/100 mL	pH Range	Bead mesh range and size, μm
CM-Sephadex A-25	Pharmacia	Carboxymethyl	Na$^+$	Dextran	56	2.0–12.0	100–400 40–120
Amberlite IRC-50	Rohm and Haas	Carboxyl acid	H$^+$	Polystyrene macroreticular 4% crosslink	350	5.0–14.0	16–50 500–1000
Diaion WK10	Mitsubishi	Carboxyl acid	H$^+$	Polymethacrylate porous	250	5.0–14.0	40–60 350–550
Duolite C-433	Rohm and Haas	Carboxyl acid	H$^+$	Polystyrene gel	420	5.0–14.0	16–50 500–1000
Diaion CR10	Mitsubishi	Carboxyl acid (chelating)	Na$^+$	Polystyrene	50	1.0–5.0	40–60 350–550
Cellex CM	Bio-Rad	Carboxymethyl (chelating)	H$^+$	Cellulose	70	5.0–12.0	200–400
TSKgel CM-3SW	TosoHaas	Carboxymethyl	Na$^+$	Silica	>30	2.0–7.5	>400 10

Table 6
Useful Buffers in Ion-Exchange Separations

Buffer	pH Range
Citrate	2.0–6.0
Phosphate	2.0–3.0
	7.1–8.0
Formate	3.0–4.5
Acetate	4.2–5.4
Triethanolamine	6.7–8.7
Borate	8.0–9.8
Ammonia	8.2–10.2

Table 7
Example of a Resin-Selection Experiment

Step	Procedure
1	pH stability study
2	Equilibrate the column (2 mL bed) by washing with 5 mL water
3	Adjust the pH of the centifuged broth (*see* **Table 8**) and load onto column
4	Wash the column with 5 mL water
5	Elute with 5 mL of eluate 1 (*see* **Table 8**)
6	Elute with 5 mL of eluate 2 (*see* **Table 8**)
7	Submit sample to a bioassay
	(Adjust the eluate pH to 7.0 if necessary.)

exchange packing materials (SAX). SAX columns are readily available in a wide array of formats from several suppliers.

Given that in natural products research the structure of the compound of interest is often unknown, the best approach to resin selection is through the use of probe columns. This is especially the case for fermentation broths and crude extracts as these may contain a number of competing ions, such as salts, present in various concentrations. For this reason, it is often advisable first to desalt the broth before probing ion-exchange methods.

As several biologically active molecules may be unstable to extreme pH values, it is also important to carry out a pH-stability study. In such a study, the fermentation sample is adjusted to several pH values (for example: 2, 4, 9, 11) for various lengths of time (for example: 30 min, 3 h, 24 h). At the end of the time interval, the solution is adjusted back to pH 7.0 and the sample bioassayed. The pH-stability profile will often dictate the type of separation to be performed and hence the resin to be used.

A small amount of centrifuged fermentation broth (or similarly clarified aqueous extract) is thus adjusted to the proper pH and loaded onto a small bed

Table 8
Examples of Cartridge Columns and Elution Conditions

Conditions	Anion exchange		Cation exchange	
	Silica-based	Polymer-based	Silica-based	Polymer-based
Minicolumn Examples:	Waters Accell Plus QMA or Aminopropyl NH_2 Sep-Pak Cartridges EM Sciences Adsorbex SAX	Self-packed Dowex 1 (Cl^- cycle)	Waters Accell Plus CM Sep-Pak Cartridge EM Science Adsorbex SCX	Self-packed Dowex 50 (Na^+ cycle)
Loading pH	$6.5 < pH < 8.0$	$6.5 < pH < 8.0$	$4.0 < pH < 6.0$	$4.0 < pH < 6.0$
Loading Time	1–2 min	5–10 min	1–2 min	5–10 min
Eluate 1	1% $NaCl/H_2O$	0.1 N aq $NaHCO_3$	5% NaCl	0.1 N aq NH_4OH
Eluate 2	3% NH_4Cl in 90% $MeOH/H_2O$	0.5 N aq HCl	2% aq pyridine (may dissolve some packing material)	1 N aq NH4OH

volume of resin. After a wash of the column, several elution conditions are examined. The biological activity is monitored in both the column spent and eluates. Such a process is illustrated in **Tables 7** and **8**. The use of commercial disposable prepacked columns (available in a wide variety of matrix/functional group combinations) is advantageous. A number of these are based on a silica support and are thus somewhat limited to uses at pH values below approx 8.0. However, since they offer much faster kinetics than other resin forms, a greater number of probe experiments can be carried out in a shorter time.

For example, a 10-mL aliquot can be loaded onto a 1-mL column bed, with collection of two 5-mL spent fractions. The column is then washed with water (2 mL) and bound material eluted (*see* **Subheading 4.5.**). The purpose of collecting two or more spent fractions is to monitor for sample breakthrough. An important factor in resin selection is loading capacity. One may wish to load as much broth as possible per unit volume of resin in order to render the isolation process practical. This becomes especially important when scaling up to larger fermentation processes. A well-chosen resin can allow for very selective adsorption/elution of the desired compound and for an efficient process.

An additional factor in selecting a resin is recovery of biological activity. The choice of elution conditions is critical to effect a good recovery. A proper pH-stability study must have been carried out and the biologically active compound must have been found to be stable over the range of pH values utilized.

If the identity of the molecule to be isolated is known, then resin selection should take advantage of any unusual structural feature(s) that may make the adsorption/elution process more selective. If a sample is retained on an exchanger but poor, or no, recovery is observed, a weaker exchanger, perhaps also with a lower charge density (lower capacity), should be tried.

4.2. Resin Preparation

The preparation of the ion-exchange resin has a large impact on the success of an ion-exchange separation. The commercial resin is rarely ready to use straight from the bottle.

4.2.1. Washing

At the very least, the resin should be washed. There are two important reasons for doing so: removing impurities and fines from the manufacturing process, and swelling the resin. Even a high-purity resin can often undergo some degree of degradation during storage. Column manufacturers often recommend specific washing conditions for their resins. Washing polymeric resins with MeOH, or under conditions that resemble the elution conditions, is a good way to minimize the introduction of contaminants. Remember that the process of natural products isolation is complex enough without the added complications brought about by introducing contaminants from the resin into the active eluates.

4.2.2. Swelling

Swelling the resin exposes a larger percentage of the functional groups to the mobile phase. In the case of carbohydrate supports, suspending the resin in water may not in itself give rise to complete swelling. A number of charged functional groups will remain tightly bound internally through hydrogen bonding and will therefore not be available for the ion-exchange process. A precycling step can help ensure that the resin achieves its full potential for capacity. Precycling involves treating the resin alternately with dilute HCl and NaOH solutions (for example, 0.5 N). In the case of a diethylaminoethyl (DEAE) resin, for example, washing with dilute acid protonates all of the functional groups, breaks up internal hydrogen bonding, and hence gives rise to maximum swelling. The resin can then be neutralized with base and subsequently equilibrated with the proper buffer system.

4.2.3. Resin Cycle

The cycle of the resin, i.e., the nature of the associated counter-ion, is very important. For example, whereas most anion-exchange resins are available in the chloride cycle, this may not always be optimal (or desirable). Conversion of the resin from one cycle to another can be accomplished simply by passing a large volume of a concentrated solution of the desired counter-ion over the resin. Following conversion, the resin is washed with large volumes of water. The most common cycle conversions involve hydrogen-to-sodium cycle for cation exchangers and chloride-to-acetate cycle for anion exchangers.

For example, to convert 100 mL of Dowex-50 (H) resin to its sodium cycle, one would wash the resin with several hundred milliliters of 1 N NaOH at a flow rate of approx 5–10 mL/min. The conversion is complete when the pH of the eluate goes above 9.0. The resin is then washed with water until the pH drops below 9.0. To convert a Dowex-1 (Cl) resin to an acetate or formate cycle, one must first convert the resin to the hydroxide cycle. This can be accomplished by washing the resin with a large volume of 1 N NaOH, typically 10 to 20 times the column volume. One can monitor for completeness of conversion by monitoring the eluate for Cl ions (acidify with nitric acid and add a few drops of 1% silver nitrate solution; a white precipitate indicates the presence of chloride ions). After washing with water to below pH 9.0, the resin is washed with 1 N formic or acetic acid (approx 2 column volumes) with a flow rate of about 5–10 mL/min for a 100-mL column. The conversion is complete when the pH of the washes drops to below 2.0. The resin is finally washed with water until the pH rises above 5.0.

4.3. Column-Size Selection

Two factors are important in choosing a column: its volume and its shape. A resin-bed volume is chosen such that several times the required exchange capacity is obtained. If the amount of the solute to be adsorbed is known, the capacity figure supplied by the resin manufacturer (*see* **Tables 2–5**) can be used to estimate the resin-bed volume needed. For samples such as fermentation broths, the required exchange capacity is generally not known. A good rule of thumb is to use a resin-bed volume that is 1/10 to 1/20 of the broth volume. As the process is scaled up, larger ratios may be achievable. The size of the column used to contain the resin is not critical.

A short column that accomodates the desired volume should be selected. The ion-exchange chromatography process is different from classical chromatography. The process can be considered as an on/off event. For example, during gradient elution, when the right conditions are reached, the solute becomes unbound. Once unbound, solute molecules remain free for the remainder of their journey down the column. For this reason, long columns are not desirable for ion-exchange separations. In fact, long bed heights can create back-pressure problems, as well as band-broadening due to effects of Eddy diffusion and longitudinal diffusion, during elution. A short, wide diameter column bed is much better suited, giving the same chromatographic result but with a much lower back pressure. On a laboratory bench scale, bed heights of 10–20 cm are generally used.

4.4. Sample Loading

A fermentation broth should be clarified prior to loading on an ion-exchange resin. Cellular mass can coat the resin particles and significantly hinder access to the exchange sites. Experimentation will determine the extent of this problem for a given sample. Centrifugation is the preferred and safest method of clarification. Filtration is often necessary when the size of the sample to be clarified is too large for laboratory-scale centrifuges and too small for pilot-plant-size continuous-flow centrifuges. The problem with filtration is nonspecific adsorption of the solutes on the filter paper (cellulose) or Celite (deactivated silica).

There are two methods of adsorbing compounds on the ion-exchange resin: "batch" mode or "column" mode. In batch mode, an appropriate amount of resin is added to a vessel containing the clarified broth. The mixture is then stirred for an appropriate amount of time, typically 15–30 min, and the resin is filtered. Such a batch or slurry mode of operation is advantageous in cases in which the broth cannot be easily filtered, a state that will rapidly block column frits. The resin can be recovered by filtration through a very coarse medium such as a fine wire screen or sometimes simply by decanting the supernatant "spent" broth.

In "column" mode, the resin is poured as a slurry into an appropriate-size column. After the resin has settled into a bed, the clarified broth (the "feed") is applied. A good rule of thumb is to allow for 10–20 min contact time between the feed and the resin (less for silica-based small particles). For example, a flow rate of approx 5–10 mL/min would be appropriate for a 100-mL column. This relatively slow flow rate is necessary to allow sufficient time for unbound molecules to diffuse past already adsorbed molecules and into resin pores, so that the ion-exchange reaction can take place, as explained earlier.

4.5. Elution

There are two strategies for eluting bound solutes from an ion-exchange column: changes in ionic strength or changes in pH. In each case, the use of organic cosolvents may be desirable. The use of a high-salt solution is effective and displaces solutes from the charged resin sites by a mass balance effect. For example, sodium chloride is often used to elute charged solutes from both cation- or anion-exchange columns. A change in pH can provide more selectivity in desorption of bound solutes. The pH can be adjusted such that solutes are no longer charged and are thus no longer retained. For example, carboxylic acids can be adsorbed at pH 6.0 and eluted at pH 4.0, a level at which carboxylate anions are protonated to form neutral molecules.

The use of organic cosolvents in the elution step can help to minimize backbone interactions. Backbone interactions result from the adsorption of the hydrophobic portions of molecules onto the hydrophobic portions of the resin support. This phenomenon is most noticeable with aromatic compounds on polystyrene-based supports. The use of a solvent–salt combination may be the only way to disrupt these interactions and thus recover some of these compounds from the resin. Additionally, use of solvent–salt eluents can lead to a much sharper elution profile. As charged molecules are rendered neutral by a change in pH, their hydrophilicity will likely decrease substantially and may cause the molecules not only to bind to the resin backbone but also to precipitate. Methanol or acetonitrile are often used as water-miscible cosolvents to help counter these problems. For example, one of the best eluent compositions for elution of various organic anions adsorbed on an anion-exchange resin such as Dowex-1, is a solution of 3% ammonium chloride (approx 0.5 M) in 90% methanol/water. Similarly, organic salts such as mixtures of pyridine and acetic acid, which can be adjusted to give a wide range of pH values (*see* **Table 9**) give rise to good recoveries. These offer the additional advantage of being volatile and thus removable by evaporation.

If resolution of sample components is important, several factors can be optimized: ionic strength, pH, temperature, flow rate, organic modifier concentration, and buffer concentration. Since the ionic strength of the eluting mobile phase has the greatest impact on the performance of the separation, it is wise to optimize this factor first. Similarly, choices between opting for a pH gradient or a salt gradient should be made early in the experiment design process.

Table 9
Compositions for Pyridine/Acetic-Acid Buffers

Composition	pH 3.0	pH 5.0	pH 8.0
Water	970	970	980
Acetic acid	28	14	0.2
Pyridine	2	16	20

The size and shape of the gradient used has a large impact on the success of the chromatography. A smooth gradient is usually more effective than a step gradient and can be generated with the use of a gradient maker. However, for probe experiments, adequate results can easily be obtained using stepped gradients. Gradients are generated by increasing addition of a second component to a mixing flask containing the starting solution. Gradients with variable slopes, linear, convex, or concave, can be generated by varying the equipment used in its generation. A simple gradient maker is shown in **Fig. 2**. It allows for the simple preparation of a gradient from 100% A to 100% B. Variations in the volume and variations in the slope of the gradient are in effect variations in its slope. Large-gradient volumes give rise to better resolution at the expense of somewhat increased band broadening and the necessity of collecting larger fractions. Small-gradient volumes tend to give poor separations. In general, a total elution volume of 5–10 column volumes should be used to ensure full recoveries.

Elution can be carried out at a flow rate greater than that used for adsorption. Typically, one might use a contact time of 2–5 min between the eluting mobile phase and the stationary phase. Fractions should be of a small enough volume so as to take advantage of the resolution achieved on the column, such as 5–10 fractions per column volume. For example, for the elution of a 100-mL bed column volume, one might use a gradient total volume of 600 mL, collecting 10- to 20-mL fractions.

5. Applications

There are several types of compounds that one might attempt typically to isolate from a crude extract using an ion-exchange method: strong and weak acids and bases, as well as amphoteric compounds. As both adsorption and elution processes will generally involve pH adjustments, it is wise first to determine the stability of the compound of interest at various pH values, as mentioned earlier. With information on the stability of the compound of interest at hand, one can then choose an appropriate ion-exchange process.

5.1. Anionic Compounds

For best selectivity, anionic compounds should be adsorbed at a low pH on either strong or weak anion exchangers. At pH 4.0 or less, carboxylic acids

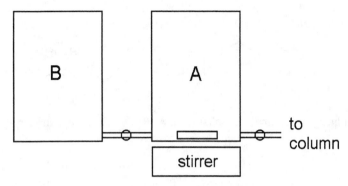

Fig. 2. Typical gradient maker

will not be retained, resulting in a fairly selective adsorption of stronger acids. If the compound is not stable at acidic pH values, a separation based on its pKa is not possible, but it can still be adsorbed on a strong anion-exchange resin at neutral pH, along with monocarboxylic acids. If a strong anion exchanger is used, elution can be carried out with a salt concentration gradient. If a weak anion exchanger is used, elution can be carried out with an alkaline mobile phase, unless of course, the compound is unstable to basic conditions.

5.1.1. Cephamycins A and B

These cephalosporin antibiotics (**Fig. 3**) were discovered in the early 1970s. The isolation procedure shown below *(9)* makes use of ion exchange after desalting the fermentation broth on XAD-2. This is often necessary for broths that contain very high salt concentrations. The compounds are then adsorbed on a weak anion exchanger and eluted with nitrate ions. After a desalting step, they are chromatographed on a different weak anion exchanger but at a lower pH than the first ion-exchange step.

1. Acidify the fermentation broth and filter.
2. Pass the filtrate through a column of XAD-2 and elute with 60% aqueous MeOH.
3. Concentrate the eluate and adjust the pH to 3.5 with aqueous NH$_4$OH.
4. Dilute with an equal volume of H$_2$O and pass through a column of Amberlite IRA-68 (Cl).
5. Elute with 1 M NaNO$_3$ in 0.1 M NaOAc (pH 7.5), collecting fractions.
6. Bioassay and combine active fractions; adjust to pH 3.0 and desalt on XAD-2.
7. Adjust concentrated eluate to pH 4.0 and lyophilize.
8. Dissolve the powder in a small volume of 0.5 M NH$_4$Br–0.05 M AcOH buffer.
9. Chromatograph on a column of DEAE Sephadex A-25, eluting with the same buffer.
10. Bioassay fractions and pool active fractions (cephamycins A and B).
11. Each pool is desalted by adsorbing on XAD-2 and eluting with 90% aqueous MeOH.

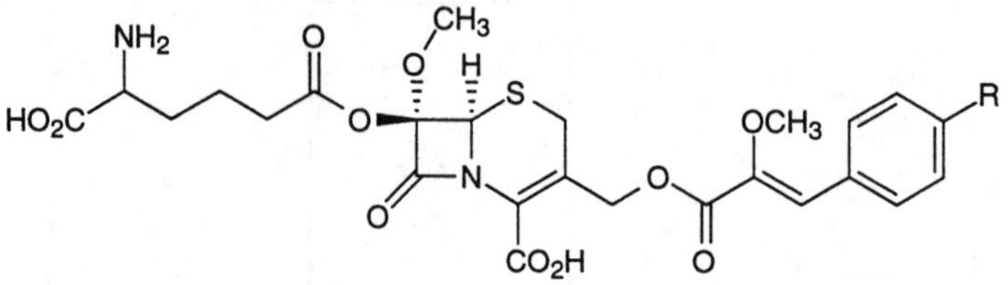

Fig. 3. Cephamycins A and B. Cephamycin A: R = OSO₃H; cephamycin B: R = OH.

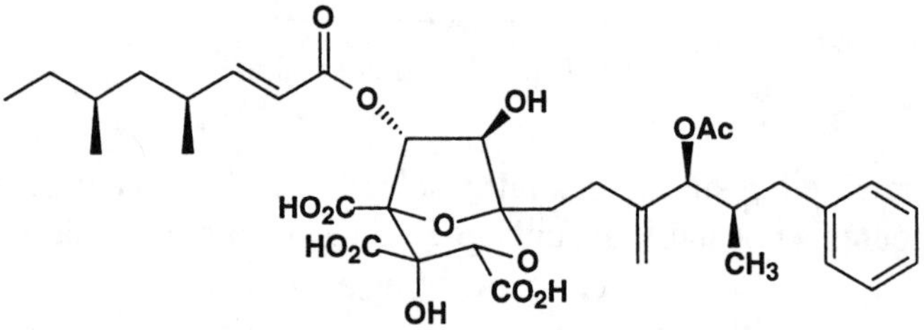

Fig. 4. Structure of Zaragozic Acid A.

5.1.2. Zaragozic Acids

Zaragozic acids (**Fig. 4**; also known as squalestatins) were discovered while screening for squalene synthase inhibitors *(10)*. They contain an unusual tricarboxylic acid core flanked by two lipophilic side chains. This amphipathic nature caused some difficulties in early isolations by ion-exchange processes. Significant tailing was observed during elution from Dowex-1 giving rise to, at best, modest recoveries. This was presumably caused by backbone interactions with the polystyrene matrix. In designing an ion-exchange purification step for these compounds, we tried to adapt the process to the special features of the compounds and of the isolation process itself. For example, we had found that the zaragozic acids were present in both the filtered broth and in the mycelial cake. However, they could be efficiently extracted from whole fermentation broth, without the need for filtration of the mycelia, by extracting with EtOAc at pH 2.0. The ion-exchange step would have to selectively adsorb these compounds from the crude nonaqueous extract. We used an Amberlyst resin, a macroreticular resin that is solvent-resistant. A weakly basic functional group was selected (Amberlyst A-21) and used in the acetate cycle. The acetate counter-ions are sufficiently basic (pK_a = 5) to deprotonate the zaragozic acids (pK_a1 = 3.5). The resulting monocarboxylate ions are then selectively adsorbed on the resin. The elution condition giving rise to the sharpest elution (smallest volume) was found to be a mobile phase of high salt concentration, specifically

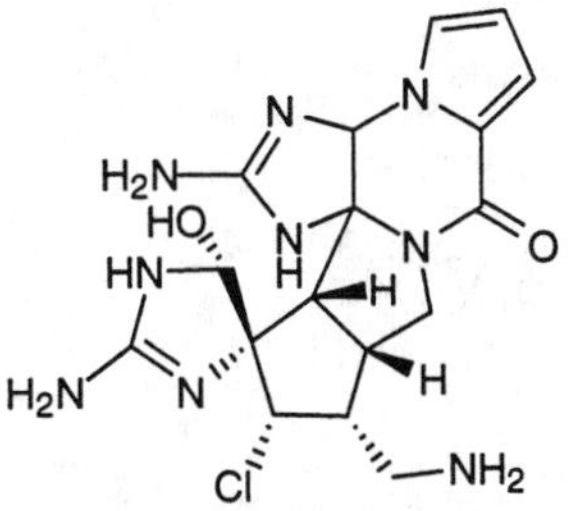

Fig. 5. Structure of Palau'amine.

3% ammonium chloride in 90% methanol/water. The eluate could then be desalted using Diaion HP-20 to give a product of better than 80% purity.

5.2. Cationic Compounds

As with strong acids, strong bases are separated with best selectivity if the adsorption is carried out at high pH values on either strong or weak acid ion exchangers. Under these conditions, weak bases are not protonated and will not be retained. If a strong acid exchanger is used, elution can be carried out with a salt solution. If a weak acid exchanger is used, the compound can also be eluted using a solution of sufficiently low pH to repress ionization of the resin. If the compound is unstable to alkaline pH values, it may not be possible to effect separation from other bases present. In this case, the compound could be adsorbed on a weak cation exchanger at neutral pH, followed by elution with salt or with a strong acid solution if stability permits.

Weak bases should be adsorbed on a strong cation exchanger. Separation from strong bases is achieved by elution with a weak base, buffered one or two pH units above the compound's pKa. Aqueous pyridine is often used for this purpose. If the compound is unstable to alkaline conditions, it may not be possible to separate it from strong bases by an ion-exchange process.

5.2.1. Palau'amine

Marine natural products often incorporate guanidine, a basic functionality. These can be efficiently extracted from aqueous extracts by the use of weak cation exchangers. Near neutral pH, the carboxylate ion exchanger is negatively charged, while guanidine is protonated. The antibiotic palau'amine (**Fig. 5**) was isolated from a marine sponge collected in the South Pacific *(11)*, using such an ion-exchange process.

1. Lyophilize the sponge and extract the residue with MeOH.
2. Evaporate the extract and triturate with water.
3. Pass this aqueous solution through a column of Cellex CM (Na cycle).

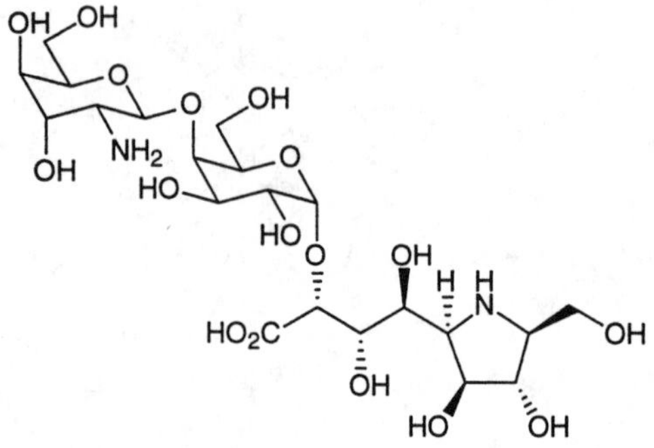

Fig. 6. Structure of Gualamycin.

4. Elute with a step gradient of NaCl.
5. Bioassay the eluate fractions (activity is in the 0.5 M NaCl fraction).
6. Lyophilize and triturate with ethanol as a desalting step.
7. Chromatograph the ethanol-soluble portion on Sephadex LH-20 (MeOH) to afford essentially pure palau'amine.

5.2.2. Gualamycin

Small basic water-soluble compounds are difficult to isolate. They are not solvent-extractable and are not easily amenable to chromatography by traditional techniques such as silica gel or RP-HPLC. Furthermore, the lack of any chromophore often renders detection difficult. Fortunately, in many cases, amino functionalities provide a "handle" for the isolation of such compounds. Gualamycin (**Fig. 6**) was found with a screen for new acaricides from the culture broth of a *Streptomyces* sp. *(12)*.

1. Pass the filtered broth through a charcoal column.
2. Wash with water and elute with a step gradient of aqueous MeOH.
3. Bioassay the eluate fractions; combine the active fractions.
4. Pass the pooled eluate through a column of Dowex-50W (H⁺ cycle).
5. Wash the column with water and elute with 2.8% aqueous ammonia.
6. Bioassay the eluate fractions, lyophilize, and redissolve in water.
7. Pass through a column of CM-Sephadex C-25 (Na⁺).
8. Elute with a step gradient of aqueous NaCl.
9. Bioassay the eluate fractions and desalt to afford pure gualamycin.

5.2.3. Paromomycins

Paromomycin (**Fig. 7**) *(13)* is an example of the large class of basic water-soluble aminoglycoside antibiotics isolated during the 1960s and 1970s. As an antibiotic, it is chiefly effective against Gram-negative organisms. As with most of the compounds of this class, they are purified by ion-exchange methods.

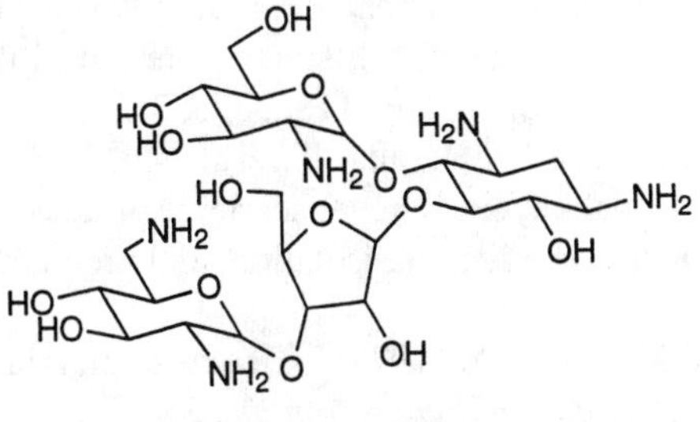

Fig. 7. Structure of paromomycin.

1. Adjust the whole fermentation broth to pH 3.0 and filter.
2. Collect the filtrate and adjust to pH 7.0 with NaOH.
3. Pass through a column of Amberlite IRC-50 (NH_4^+ cycle).
4. Wash the column with water; elute with 0.5 N aqueous NH_4OH, collecting fractions.
5. Bioassay eluate fractions; concentrate active fractions *in vacuo*; adjust to pH 7.0.
6. Pass through a column of Amberlite CG-50 (NH_3 cycle).
7. Wash with water (3 column volumes).
8. Elute with a step gradient of aqueous NH_4OH (0.05–0.3 N).
9. Bioassay eluate fractions; evaporate active fractions to dryness.

References

1. Cooper, T. G. (1977) *The Tools of Biochemistry*, Wiley, New York, pp. 136–168.
2. Walton, H. F. (1976) I*on-Exchange Chromatography*, Dowden, Hutchinson & Ross, Stoudsburg, PA.
3. Pietrzyk, D. J. (1990) Ion exchangers, in *Packings and Stationary Phases in Chromatographic Techniques* (Unger, K. K., ed.), Chromatographic Science Series, vol. 47, Marcel Dekker, New York, pp. 585–720.
4. Mikes, O. (1975) Fundamentals of ion-exchange chromatography, in *Liquid Column Chromatography* (Deyl, Z., Macek, K., and Janak, J., eds.), Elsevier, New York, pp. 69–87.
5. Poole, C. F. and Poole, S. K. (1991) *Chromatography Today*, Elsevier, Amsterdam, pp. 422–439.
6. Liteanu, S. and Gocan, S. (1974) *Gradient Liquid Chromatography*,Wiley, New York, p. 337.
7. Wolf, F. J., (1969) *Separation Methods in Organic Chemistry and Biochemistry*, Academic, New York, pp. 137–182.
8. Harland, C. E. (1994) *Ion Exchange: Theory and Practice*, 2nd ed., Royal Society of Chemistry, London.
9. Hamill, R. L. and Crandall, L. W. (1978) Cephalosporin antibiotics; in *Antibiotics; Isolation, Separation and Purification*, vol. 15 (Weinstein, M. J., and Wagman, G. H., eds.), Journal of Chromatography Library, pp. 87–91.
10. Bergstrom, J., Dufresne, C., Bills, G., Nallin-Omstead, M., and Byrne, K. (1995) Discovery, biosynthesis, and mechanism of action of the zaragozic acids: potent inhibitors of squalene synthase. *Ann. Rev. Microbiol.* **49,** 607–639.

11. Kinnel, R. B., Gehrken, H.-P., and Scheuer, P. J. (1993) Palau'amine: a cytotoxic and immunosuppresive hexacyclic bisguanidine antibiotic from the sponge *Stylotella agminata. J. Am.Chem.Soc.* **115**, 3376, 3377.

12. Tsuchiya, K., Kobayashi, S., Harada, T., Takashi, N.T., Nakagawa, T., and Shimada, N. (1995) Gualamycin, a novel acaricide produced by *Streptomyces* sp. NK11687. I. Taxonomy, production, isolation, and preliminary characterization. *J.Antibiotics* **48**, 626–629.

13. Marquez, J. A. and Kershner, A. (1978) 2-Deoxystreptamine-Containing Antibiotics; in, *Antibiotics; Isolation, Separation and Purification*, vol. 15 (Weinstein, M. J., and Wagman, G. H., eds.), Journal of Chromatography Library, 202–207.

6

Isolation by Preparative HPLC

Paul Stead

1. Introduction

Preparative high-performance (or high-pressure) liquid chromatography (HPLC), is a versatile, robust, and widely used technique for the isolation of natural products. The main difference between HPLC and other modes of column chromatography is that the diameter of stationary phase particles is comparatively low (3–10 μm), and these particles are tightly packed to give a very uniform column bed structure. The low particle diameter means that a high pressure is needed to drive the chromatographic solvent (or "eluent") through the bed. However, because of the very high total surface area available for interaction with solutes (approx 100–300 m²/g for a typical 5-μm-diameter stationary phase) and the uniformity of the column bed structure, the resolving power of HPLC is very high. Preparative HPLC is increasingly widely applied to both laboratory and pilot-plant scale isolation work, and recent developments in instrumentation and column-packing materials mean that scale up is now relatively straightforward.

Natural products are frequently isolated following the evaluation of a relatively crude extract in a biological assay in order to fully characterize the active entity. In this setting, the requirement for speed will dictate that rapid, scaleable, high-resolution techniques such as preparative HPLC are most usefully applied very early in an extraction process so that the first milligrams of an active compound are provided in a timely manner. The biologically active entity is often present only as a minor component in the extract, and the resolving power of HPLC is ideally suited to the rapid processing of such multicomponent samples on both an analytical and preparative scale. Larger scale isolations are often required in order to provide more of a metabolite of interest for further biological or chemical studies. The concentration of the metabolite

From: *Methods in Biotechnology, Vol. 4: Natural Products Isolation*
Edited by: R. J. P. Cannell © Humana Press Inc., Totowa, NJ

in the crude source material (e.g., fermentation broth or plant material) will ideally have been substantially increased through appropriate development processes; in such cases, the desired metabolite might be isolated using a high-capacity, low-resolution technique such as ion-exchange or adsorption-elution from a polymer resin, with preparative HPLC applied as the final purification step, if required. Preparative HPLC on such a scale is not often carried out, though the frequency of this is increasing *(1,2)*. When operating at scales greater than the original isolation, many additional metabolites related to the principal component of interest (termed minor metabolites) may be revealed, and preparative HPLC is often an ideal technique to apply to their isolation *(3–5)*. HPLC has been applied to the isolation of virtually all classes of natural products of both plant and microbial origin; separations that were considered extremely challenging a few decades ago are now relatively routine, and in that time, preparative HPLC has become an indispensable tool for most natural products chemistry laboratories.

This chapter addresses the practical application of laboratory-scale preparative HPLC to the isolation of natural products. It comprises a discussion of the principal separation modes used in HPLC, column-packing materials and solvents, preparative HPLC instrumentation and detection methods, chromatographic method development, and the practicalities of carrying out a preparative HPLC-based natural product isolation. Discussion of basic chromatographic theory underlying HPLC is kept to a minimum since this is discussed in Chapter 1 and is the subject of many excellent reviews (*see Suggested Readings*). Included within the discussion are examples drawn both from the author's own experience and from the literature, which emphasize the great versatility and utility of preparative HPLC in natural products isolation work.

1.1. HPLC Separation Modes, Column-Packing Materials, and Solvents

The modes of separation most commonly applied to natural product isolations are normal phase, reverse phase, and, to a lesser extent, gel permeation and ion-exchange chromatography. They vary in their applicability to different sample types and are discussed in turn in the following section. The choice of packing material is governed by the physicochemical properties of the target metabolite and of the other metabolites present in the sample, as well as by factors such as cost, general applicability, and scale of operation. Numerous manufacturers (e.g., Eka Nobel, Merck, Waters, Rockland, Shandon, YMC, Machery Nagel) offer a wide range of column packing materials for both analytical and preparative applications. Some of the properties of commonly used packing materials are summarized in **Table 1**. Chromatographic eluents used in HPLC typically comprise mixtures of organic solvents, or organic solvents

Table 1
Stationary Phases Commonly Used in HLPC

description	structure*	nature of interaction with solute	uses/comments
C18 octadecyl	$-Si-C_{18}H_{37}$	strong non-polar	the most retentive phase for non-polar solutes. Good general applicability
C8 octyl	$-Si-C_8H_1$	strong non-polar	Similar retentiveness to C18
C6 hexyl	$-Si-C_6H_1$	moderate non-polar	less retentive than C8 or C18
C2 ethyl	$-Si-C_2H_5$	weak non-polar	
C1 methyl	$-Si-CH$	weak non-polar	least retentive of the alkyl-bonded phases
Ph phenyl	$-Si-\langle\rangle$	moderate non-polar	reverse phase. Different selectivity to alkyl-bonded phases. Useful for aromatic compounds
CH cyclohexyl	$-Si-\langle\rangle$	moderate non-polar	
CN cyanopropyl	$-Si-(CH_2)_3CN$	moderate non-polar/polar	Unique selectivity for polar compounds. Can be used in normal and reverse phase modes
2OH diol	$-Si-(CH_2)_3OCH_2CH(OH)CH(OH)$	polar	similar selectivity to silica when used in normal phase mode, though not deactivated by small amounts of water
aminopropyl	$-Si-(CH_2)_3NH$	weak anion exchange/ polar	useful for separating carbohydrates when used in reverse phase mode. Alternative selectivity to silica when used in normal phase mode
silica	$-Si-OH$	polar	
benzenesulphonic acid	$-Si-CH_2CH_2\langle\rangle-SO_3H$	strong cation exchange	
quaternary ammonium	$-Si-(CH_2)_3N+(CH_3)_3Cl-$	strong anion exchange	

(*the length of the alkyl spacer group for some supports varies between manufacturers)

and water, and often contain additives such as buffers, acids, bases, and ion-pair reagents. Choice is governed by the properties of the sample being chromatographed and compatibility with the stationary phase used. Some properties of commonly used HPLC solvents are shown in **Table 2**.

1.1.1. Normal Phase Chromatography

Normal phase chromatography employs a polar stationary phase, usually silica, and less polar (usually nonaqueous) chromatographic eluents. Solutes separate during passage through the column by adsorbing to the surface of the stationary phase particles, from which they may be displaced by solvent molecules. The strength of interaction depends on the nature of the functional groups present in the solute molecules. Thus as a general rule, nonpolar analytes elute more quickly than polar analytes since they interact less strongly with the highly polar surface of the adsorbent particles. Elution is controlled by the polarity of the chromatographic solvent; retention times decrease with increasing solvent polarity.

Solvents commonly used in normal phase chromatography are aliphatic hydrocarbons, such as hexane and heptane, halogenated hydrocarbons (e.g., chloroform and dichloromethane), and oxygenated solvents such as diethyl ether, ethyl acetate, and butyl acetate. More polar mobile phase additives such as isopropanol, acetone, and methanol are frequently used (*see* **Table 2**). The technique is particularly suited to analytes that are very hydrophobic, e.g., fat-soluble vitamins such as tocopherols *(6)* and other hydrocarbon-rich metabolites that exhibit poor solubility in the water-miscible solvents employed in other separation modes. In addition, since the geometry of the polar adsorbent surface is fixed, the technique is useful for the separation of positional isomers; the proximity of functional groups to the adsorbent surface, and hence the strength of interaction, may well differ between isomers.

In adsorption chromatography, care should be taken to ensure that the water level within the eluting solvent is strictly controlled, as water rapidly deactivates silica by adsorbing to it strongly, causing analytes to elute more quickly. In addition, column equilibration times are comparatively long, and this makes reproducible preparative-scale gradient separations challenging (*see* **Subheading 2.1.2.**).

1.1.2. Reverse Phase Chromatography

Reverse phase, as its name implies is the reverse of normal phase operation; the stationary phase is nonpolar and the eluent is polar. The eluent normally comprises mixtures of water and organic cosolvents (or modifiers). Other additives, such as buffers, acids, bases, and ion-pair reagents may be incorporated into the eluting solvent: These are discussed in **Subheading 2.1.3.** The stationary phases most commonly used in reverse phase HPLC are known as

Table 2
Some Properties of Solvents Used in Normal and Reverse Phase HPLC

Solvent	Molecular weight	b.p. (°C)	Refractive index at 20°C	Density relative to water (4°C)	Elutropic value (silica)	UV cutoff, nm[a]
Acetone	58.1	56	1.359	0.79	0.43	330
Acetonitrile	41.1	81	1.344	0.79	0.50	190
Butan-1-ol	74.1	117.8	1.399	0.81	—	215
Butan-2-one	72.1	80	1.379	0.81	0.39	330
Butyl acetate	116.2	124–126	1.394	0.88	—	254
t-Butylmethyl ether	88.2	53–56	1.369	0.74	0.29	—
Carbon tetrachloride	153.8	77	1.460	1.59	0.14	263
Chloroform	119.4	60.5–81	1.426	0.78	0.03	200
1,2-Dichloroethane	99.0	83	1.444	1.26	—	225
N,N-dimethylformamide	73.1	153	1.431	0.94	—	268
1,4-Dioxane	88.1	100–102	1.422	1.02	—	215
Ether	74.1	34.6	1.353	0.71	0.29	215
Ethyl acetate	88.1	76.5–77.5	1.372	0.90	0.45	260
Ethanol	46.1	78	1.360	0.79	—	210
Heptane	100.2	98	1.387	0.68	0	200
Hexane	86.2	69	1.375	0.66	0	200
Methanol	32.0	64.6	1.329	0.79	0.73	205
Methyl sulfoxide	78.1	189	1.479	1.10	—	268
Propan-1-ol	60.1	97	1.384	0.80	—	210
Propan-2-ol	60.1	82.4	1.377	0.79	0.63	210
Tetrahydeofuran	72.1	67	1.407	0.89	0.35	215
Toluene	92.1	111	1.496	0.87	0.22	285
Water	18.0	100	—	1.00	>0.73	—

[a]Wavelength at which A = 1.00 for a good LC-grade solvent.
Reproduced with permission from ref. 7.

"bonded-phase" materials and comprise fused colloidal silica particles chemically derivatized with an alkylsilyl reagent, e.g., octadecyl trichlorosilane, which renders the surface of the "reverse phase" silica hydrophobic. The degree of hydrophobicity and hence retentiveness varies broadly in parallel with the length of the alkyl chain bonded to the silica surface. Packing materials are commonly available with alzkyl chain lengths of 1, 2, 4, 6, 8, and 18 carbon atoms (*see* **Table 1**). The organic solvents most commonly used in reverse phase HPLC are acetonitrile, methanol, and tetrahydrofuran (THF) (**Table 2**). Solutes tend to elute in order of increasing hydrophobicity, and elution is speeded up by increasing the proportion of organic modifier in the eluent.

Reverse phase supports will bind from aqueous solution most analytes that contain a hydrophobic moiety or domain. Since the majority of secondary metabolites do possess some degree of hydrophobicity, such supports are of good general applicability to natural products work. In addition, most crude natural product extracts are, by their nature, highly heterogeneous and tend to exhibit better solubility in the water/water-miscible organic-solvent mixtures used in reverse phase HPLC than in the less polar solvents employed for normal phase chromatography.

1.1.3. Gel Permeation Chromatography

Gel permeation chromatography (GPC, also known as size-exclusion chromatography or gel filtration) separates molecules according to their size, although when applied to the separation of low-molecular-weight (MW) species, solute-solvent-support interactions can also play a significant role. The stationary phase comprises a porous gel (e.g., styrene-divinylbenzene, porous glass, or porous silica) in which the pore size is strictly controlled. Examples of commonly used solvents are chloroform, methanol, THF, toluene, and water. As solutes migrate through a bed of stationary phase, their speed of passage is governed by the extent of diffusion into and out of the porous gel matrix. Large molecules have limited access to the pores and are eluted near to the void volume of the column. Small molecules diffuse more freely into and out of the gel matrix and are therefore retarded. The extent of retardation is a function of molecular size; large molecules elute more quickly than small ones. Historically, GPC has served as a method of choice for the determination of molecular-weight averages and molecular-weight distribution in polymers. However, it has been less frequently applied to the separation and isolation by HPLC of low-molecular-weight compounds from complex natural product samples, which often contain many solutes of similar molecular weight. GPC is a simple and predictive technique to use, however, and recent developments in small-molecule GPC columns make the technique much more widely applicable than has previously been the case. Because of the unique selectivity of GPC, the technique is a very useful adjunct to other modes of separation in HPLC.

1.1.4. Other Types of Support

In addition to the chromatographic supports already described, many other supports are available (both silica-based and organic polymer-based) that exhibit very different properties. The silica-based supports comprise those in which the surface silanol groups are bonded with a short-chain alkyl spacer group that terminates with one or more functional groups or a cyclohexyl or phenyl ring (*see* **Table 2**). Such supports can be very useful for preparative work, e.g., the use of γ-aminopropyl bonded silica columns for the isolation of polar materials such as carbohydrates.

Ion-exchange supports are used for the isolation of ionizable species, e.g., carboxylic acids or amines. Metabolites bearing a net charge bind reversibly to ionized groups on the stationary phase surface through competitive displacement of a counter-ion. The strength of interaction depends on the degree of ionization of the component of interest and its affinity for the stationary phase binding sites. Retention is modified by varying the nature and/or concentration of counter-ion in the eluent and by the choice of counter-ion.

Styrene-divinylbenzene (hydrophobic) supports are also used in preparative HPLC; such supports offer the potential advantage of not being silica-based, and therefore silanol interactions are eliminated.

However, the selectivity of these supports is such that they would not normally be employed in the first instance for the isolation of a molecule of unknown character; a reverse phase silica column offers the best bet in terms of general applicability to the isolation of natural products by preparative HPLC. Since this is, indeed, by far the most commonly employed mode of operation in natural products chemistry, further discussion focuses mainly on the application of this technique.

1.2. HPLC Hardware

1.2.1. Preparative HPLC Instrumentation

Many benchtop preparative HPLC instruments are modular in design and comprise a solvent delivery device (pump), a sample introduction device such as an autosampler or manual injection valve, a column, detector, and detector output device (e.g., a chart recorder or printer). The pump delivers solvent at an accurately controlled flow rate. For gradient elution, a second pump is added and both are controlled using a gradient flow rate controller. In addition, gradient instruments require a mixer to ensure that solvents are completely mixed prior to reaching the column. A pressure monitor is normally employed. In some modern instruments, a single unit acts as a binary pump, mixer, and flow-rate gradient controller. Alternatively, separate modules may be controlled by a computer offering full system control including sample injection, fraction (or peak) collection, and integration (e.g., the Gilson "Autoprep" system).

The injection valve (e.g., Rheodyne valve) allows the sample to be injected onto the top of the column from a filled loop that is temporarily switched away from the flow of eluent while filling is taking place. The loop size varies from approx 10 to 200 μL in the case of a typical analytical scale instrument and from approx 1to 10 mL for a benchtop preparative instrument. For sample introduction, the loop is switched back in series with the flow of eluent and the chromatographic run begins.

1.2.2. HPLC Detectors

UV detectors are popular because they offer high sensitivity, and because the majority of naturally occurring compounds encountered have some UV absorbtivity at low wavelengths (195–210 nm). Some fully saturated (aliphatic) structures are UV-transparent as a result of the absence of chromophores, such as aromatic rings, double bonds, and other conjugated electron systems, but these are an exception rather than the rule. Since most analytes absorb some UV light in the range 195–210 nm (i.e., possess end absorbance), it is at these wavelengths that the investigator will generally be operating when trying to identify and isolate a material of unknown character within a mixture; at that stage the chromogenic properties of the target molecule will not be known.

The organic cosolvents most commonly used in reverse phase preparative HPLC (acetonitrile and methanol) are UV-transparent at wavelengths down to ~215 nm and acetonitrile can be readily obtained as a high-quality "far UV" grade, which is transparent to 190 nm. Some of the solvents used in normal phase chromatography are themselves strong absorbers of UV light, which means that low detector wavelength settings are not possible (*see* **Table 2**). This can prove to be a limiting factor in the general applicability of normal phase HPLC to natural product isolation work.

The high sensitivity of UV detection can be a bonus if a component of interest is only present in small amounts within a sample. However, at the other extreme, large amounts of strongly UV-absorbing compounds injected onto a column might well cause saturation of the UV detection system. Preparative scale detectors are inherently less sensitive than their analytical scale counterparts; even so, detector overload can be a problem when operating with large sample loadings or when working with highly chromogenic solutes. In this case, the investigator has several options. One is to alter the detector wavelength setting to one at which the compound in question absorbs less strongly. This might involve an upward shift of, say, 5–10 nm from a UV_{max}. A second option is to use an alternative means of detection (e.g., refractive index [RI]; *see* **Subheading 1.2.2.3.**). Another option is to split the flow of eluent as it leaves the chromatographic column and direct only a proportion into the detector.

1.2.2.1. UV Diode Array

UV-photodiode array detectors allow the collection of UV absorbance data across many wavelengths simultaneously and are thus very useful as a method-development tool, for peak purity checking and for distinguishing and identifying components. As long as a target metabolite possesses some UV absorptivity, it will be detected by choosing a sufficiently broad range of collection wavelengths. Each chromatographic peak will have associated with it a UV absorption spectrum (e.g., over the range 195–450 nm), which can be very useful when "chasing" a peak during LC method development, for choosing a suitable monitoring wavelength for detection during scale-up, and for revealing possible related components in a crude extract through similarities in their UV absorption profiles.

Figure 1 shows the UV absorption spectrum of cephalochromin, a *bis*-napthopyrone metabolite of *Nectria episphaeria* (*see* **Fig. 6** for structure). This illustrates how distinctive (and thus diagnostic) a UV-absorbance profile can be for certain compound classes, particularly those containing a substantial number of conjugated carbon–carbon double bonds or aromatic rings.

Having isolated a component of interest, an estimate of purity can often be gained by analyzing the compound by HPLC with diode array detection, then interrogating the product peak by comparing UV scans taken across it. "Impure" peaks are often revealed by such comparisons. Some detectors can additionally work in summed absorbance mode, where the sum of total UV absorbance over a set wavelength range is recorded with time to produce a summed UV absorbance chromatogram. This mode of operation is useful for detecting all UV absorbers within an extract of unknown composition, though sensitivity is reduced as the UV absorbance is averaged over the chosen wavelength range. Diode array detectors have traditionally been used as an analytical tool only, but in recent years preparative scale detectors have become readily available.

1.2.2.2. UV Spectral Libraries

When attempting to isolate a material of unknown character, the detection wavelength chosen in the first instance will normally be in the range 195–210 nm. However, as already stated, a significant proportion of natural products do possess distinctive UV absorption spectra. The assimilation of such spectra into a searchable "library" can thus be of considerable use for the identification of known compounds in a crude natural product extract, or for identifying components related to a known structure, through similarities in their UV absorption spectra. The operating software supplied with most modern diode array detectors has the capability for spectral library generation and searching, and

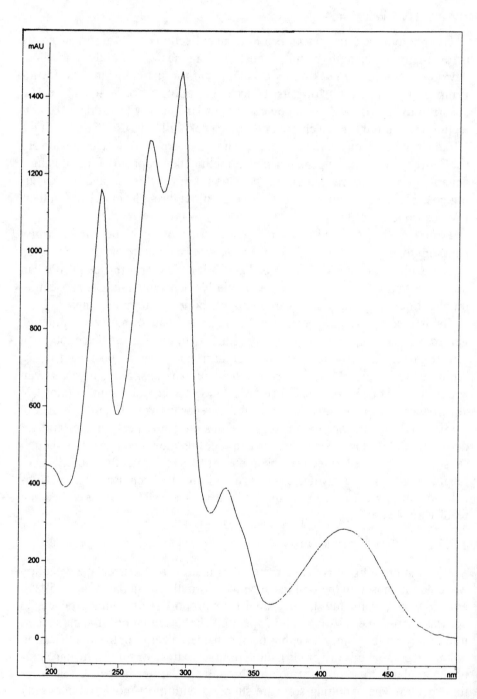

Fig. 1. UV spectrum of cephalochromin.

this offers yet another powerful tool for the process of LC method development and product isolation.

1.2.2.3. REFRACTIVE INDEX

A second and widely used method of detection in preparative HPLC is refractive index (RI). All compounds have a refractive index value, and thus the RI detector is universal in its scope. Only those analytes whose RI is identical to that of the eluting solvent will not be detected. There are two main points to be considered when considering RI over UV as a method of detection. First, RI is in most cases a less sensitive detection method than UV. That is only a problem when the desired compound is present at low levels, possesses a low RI, or possesses an RI similar to the eluting solvent. Conversely, low sensitivity is an advantage when very large (i.e., UV-saturating) quantities of sample are being chromatographed. Thus RI is a popular detection method for process/production-scale operation. Second, RI is limited to isocratic elution (*see* **Subheading 2.1.2.**), and this is perhaps the major disadvantage of the technique. Gradient elution involves the mixing of solvents of differing refractive index, thus giving rise to large baseline drifts and fluctuations in measurements.

2. Carrying Out a Preparative HPLC Separation

Frequently, the objective of preparative HPLC as applied to natural products chemistry is to isolate a metabolite of unknown structure in sufficient quantity and purity to enable structure elucidation and biological assay. Alternatively, the objective might be to scale up the isolation of a known compound to provide material for further biological evaluation or for chemical studies. The purpose for which the compound is required will dictate the compound purity required, and this in turn may dictate the strategy adopted. Many factors may affect the success of a preparative HPLC-based natural product isolation. Some principal considerations—chromatographic method development, sample preparation, scale-up, and fractionation/fraction work-up—are now discussed. Examples are included wherever possible to illustrate the points in question and to emphasize the enormous versatility and resolving power of preparative HPLC.

2.1. Method Development

2.1.1. Initial Studies: Column Selection

The choice of column packing material is dictated by the solubility/polarity of the compound of interest and the other components within the sample, as well as on other factors such as cost and general applicability. In terms of general applicability, reverse phase packing materials are preferred for the majority of preparative HPLC-based natural product isolations. Reverse phase columns are very robust and are suited to the broad spectrum of polarities commonly encountered with natural product samples. Column equilibration times are short, and method development/scale-up is relatively straightforward and predictive in comparison to many other modes of operation.

The choice of reverse phase packing material will depend on the amount of information available on the component of interest and on other sample components. Initial tests such as solvent partitioning behavior, solubility in various solvents, and others (*see* Chapter 1) can be used to estimate polarity and hence be of use in initial column/mobile phase selection. The most retentive of the silica-based reverse phase supports, C18 and C8, are a sensible first choice, as the retention of polar compounds is maximized, while the retention of nonpolar materials can be easily modulated by choice of eluent. If the compound of interest is very nonpolar (or the sample contains components that bind very strongly to retentive phases such as C8/C18), a shorter chain alkyl-bonded phase such as C6 or C4 may be more suitable.

Chromatographic method development (the rapid optimization of column and mobile phase conditions for separation of the component of interest) may begin with a C18 or C8 packed column, and acetonitrile/water or methanol/water as the eluent. As method development progresses, the initial choice of column might need to be reviewed if separation cannot be achieved by manipulation of the mobile phase conditions (*see* **Subheading 2.1.6.**) and as more information is gained about the properties of the compound of interest.

2.1.2. Initial Studies: Isocratic and Gradient Elution

If a chromatographic experiment is performed using a single unchanging eluent, then the elution is termed isocratic. If, however, the composition of the eluent (e.g., the proportion of organic cosolvent to water) is altered with time during a run, then the elution is termed gradient. A typical reverse phase gradient elution experiment with a natural product extract of unknown composition might begin with water or aqueous buffer as the chromatographic eluent, and over time the proportion of organic cosolvent (e.g., acetonitrile) is progressively increased to about 80% (v/v). Polar materials will be eluted first, whereas more strongly retained (nonpolar) materials will require a higher proportion of organic modifier to elute them. An analytical-scale, gradient-elution experiment is often a useful initial means of evaluating a sample that contains many components of wide-ranging polarity. Once a component of interest has been located by such an experiment, the investigator must choose whether to run preparative HPLC separations under isocratic or gradient-elution conditions.

Gradient elution may be desirable if more than one sample component is being sought and these differ from each other significantly in retention under the conditions employed. Isocratic elution may be more appropriate, now that an initial measurement of compound hydrophobicity and sample complexity has been gained. The choice may be governed by availability of instrumentation. One advantage of isocratic elution is that column re-equilibration is not required after each run, and so throughput might be increased.

2.1.2.1. From Gradient to Isocratic Elution

It is often neccessary to "best guess" a suitable isocratic system following an initial analysis run under gradient conditions, as part of the method development process. The percentage of organic modifier required to elute the compound in question isocratically can be estimated by calculating the percentage that the solute in question "sees" as it elutes during a gradient run and lowering it a little to ensure adequate retention.

For example, if a compound elutes after 10 min using a linear gradient of 0–90% acetonitrile in water over 20 min, it follows that the concentration of acetonitrile entering the column top after 10 min is 45% (the gradient is ramping up at 4.5% per min). However, the concentration of acetonitrile in which the compound elutes is somewhat less than 45%. This concentration is calculated by reference to the column "dead volume" (the column volume minus the volume of stationary phase), and this in turn is calculated from the retention time of an "unretained" solute (a solute that passes through the column with the solvent front). Under typical analytical HPLC conditions (flow rate, 1 mL/min, 15 × 0.46 cm column), the solvent front appears after ~1.5 min, so the column dead volume is about 1.5 mL in this example. It follows that the concentration of acetonitrile contained in the product fraction in this example is ~38% (45% less 1.5 min at 4.5%/min). A sensible first guess at a suitable "isocratic" eluent would be a 30–35% acetonitrile/water mixture. As the HPLC method develops, the percentage might be lowered or raised accordingly, but as a first step, this type of calculation should serve reasonably well.

2.1.3. Buffering and Ionization Suppression in Reverse Phase HPLC

2.1.3.1. Ionization and Its Effect on Retention in RP-HPLC

The hydrophobicity and therefore retention of ionizable compounds is strongly influenced by pH; ionizable species are most strongly retained under reverse phase conditions when unionized. In addition, many crude natural product extracts are highly heterogenous and contain a diversity of charged and neutral species whose retention can be affected by the pH of the sample, by the chromatographic eluent, and by other factors such as the presence of free silanol groups on the stationary phase surface. The presence of salts and biological buffers in a sample can also influence the chromatographic behavior of certain classes of compounds. The introduction of heterogeneous samples onto a chromatographic column can lead to poor reproducibility and solute peak shape if the mobile phase is not buffered sufficiently to neutralize such effects. This is particularly true when operating on a preparative scale, where the aim is to increase the sample load to a maximum. For these reasons, it is often a good idea to include a buffer (possibly in combination with an acid) in the eluting solvent.

2.1.3.2. BUFFERS

The presence of a buffer will maintain a constant ionic environment through the chromatographic system and thus contribute to reproducible chromatographic results. Many factors dictate the choice of buffer; if possible, it should be UV-transparent and free from organic contaminants that may end up in the product. Care should be taken to ensure that the buffer is soluble at the appropriate level when the aqueous and organic components are mixed and that the buffer is suited to the pH range employed. Buffers are normally used at a concentration of 10–100 mM for preparative work. Within this concentration range, there is a risk that certain buffers (e.g., phosphates) will either precipitate in the presence of high organic cosolvent concentrations or cause the eluent to partition into two discrete phases. At normal buffer concentrations, this is only an issue where the concentration of organic modifier exceeds approx 60–70% v/v, and in these cases the compatibility of the chosen buffer with other mobile phase constituents should be checked.

Many different buffers are suitable for use in RP-HPLC, and some of the properties of commonly used buffers are summarized in **Table 3**. They are added to the eluent prior to pH adjustment (if required) and degassing. The removal of such buffers from product-containing fractions is straightforward and is described in **Subheading 2.4.3.**

2.1.3.3. IONIZATION SUPPRESSION

Carboxylic acids generally have pKa values between 2 and 4. The use of an acidic eluent (~pH 1.5–2.0) will therefore increase the retention of such acids within a sample by suppressing ionization (and thereby increasing hydrophobicity). Only very strong organic acids (e.g., α-keto acids, sulfonic acids) are ionized at this pH.

Most mineral acids (e.g., sulfuric, hydrochloric), are suitable for use in RP-HPLC. Alternatively, organic acids such as acetic, formic, heptafluorobutyric, and trifluoroacetic acid may be used. Acetic acid is the weakest of these and trifluoroacetic acid (TFA) is the strongest. Some of the characteristics of commonly used acids are summarized in **Table 4**. The organic acids listed here (apart from heptafluorobutyric acid) have the advantage that they are relatively

Table 3
Some Properties of Buffers Commonly Used on RP-HPLC

Name	Formula	Molecular weight	Usual concentration range, mM
Ammonium acetate	CH₃COONH₄	77.1	5–20
Ammonium dihydrogen phosphate	NH₄H₂PO₄	115	10–100
Ammonium formate	HCOONH₄	63.1	5–20
Sodium phosphate	Na₂H₂PO₄	120	10–100
Sodium phosphate (dibasic)	Na₂HPO₄	142	10–100
Potassium phosphate (monobasic)	KH₂PO₄	136.1	10–100
Potassium phosphate (dibasic)	K₂HPO₄	174.2	10–100

volatile and may be removed from a product fraction by freeze-drying (TFA) or by rotary evaporation at ambient temperature (acetic, formic acid).

Figure 2 shows gradient HPLC chromatograms of an extract of *Pseudomonas aeruginosa* ATCC 10145, a producer of phenazine metabolites including phenazine-1-carboxylic acid (*see* **Fig. 3**). Fermentation broth supernatant was analyzed by gradient HPLC using a reverse phase column (Kromasil 5 μm C8) and an eluting gradient of 100% aqueous phosphate buffer to 75% acetonitrile/phosphate buffer. The pH of the mobile phase had a profound effect on the retentiveness of this compound (**Fig. 2A–C**; peak i) due to the ionizability of the C-1 carboxylic acid group. The compound was poorly retained at pH 6.0, and in this case, retention was increased as the pH was lowered. The compound was most strongly retained and separated from other fermentation metabolites at pH 2.0 (**Fig. 2C**).

Another phenazine metabolite of *P. aeruginosa* ATCC 10145, pyocyanine, is weakly basic and tautomerizes between the free base and protonated hydroxyphenazinium salt at different pH values. In this example, the retention of pyocyanine (**Fig. 2A–C**; peak ii) was greater under reverse phase conditions at pH 4.0–6.0 than at pH 2.0. Pyocyanine was not well-resolved from other fermentation metabolites at any of these pH values because of the predomination of the polar hydroxyphenazinium tautomer, and raising the pH further was not an option by reason of suspected chemical instability of the free base. However, an alternative approach to the analysis of pyocyanine involved increasing the retention of the hydroxyphenazinium salt by the use of an ion-pair reagent.

2.1.4. Ion-Pair HPLC

It is not possible in all cases to increase retention in RP-HPLC by suppressing ionization. Strong acids and strong bases might be ionized at all pH values

Table 4
Some Properties of Acids Commonly Used in RP-HPLC

Name	Formula	Molecular weight	Usual conc. range used (% v/v)	pKa	Azeotropic mixture with water ? (% w/w of component in azeotrope)	b.p. of azeotrope (if formed)	Method of removal from HPLC fraction[a]
Acetic acid	CH_3COOH	60.05	0.01–0.1	4.74	Yes (zeotropic)		1
Formic acid	HCOOH	46	0.01–0.1	3.74	Yes (77.4)	107.2	1
Heptafluorobutyric acid	$CF_3(CF_2)_2COOH$	214	0.01	0.1	Yes (29)	97	2, 3
Hydrochloric acid	HCl	36.5	0.01–0.2		Yes (20.2)	108.6	2, 3
Phosphoric acid (Orthophosphoric acid)	H_3PO_4	98	0.01–0.3	2.1, 7.1, 12.3	No		3
Sulfuric acid	H_2SO_4	98	0.01–0.2		No		3
Trifluoroacetic acid	CF_3COOH	114	0.01–0.2	0.3			2, 3

[a]1, azeotropic removal (e.g., rotary evaporation); 2, freeze-drying; 3, desalting procedure (*see* **Subheading 2.4.3.**).

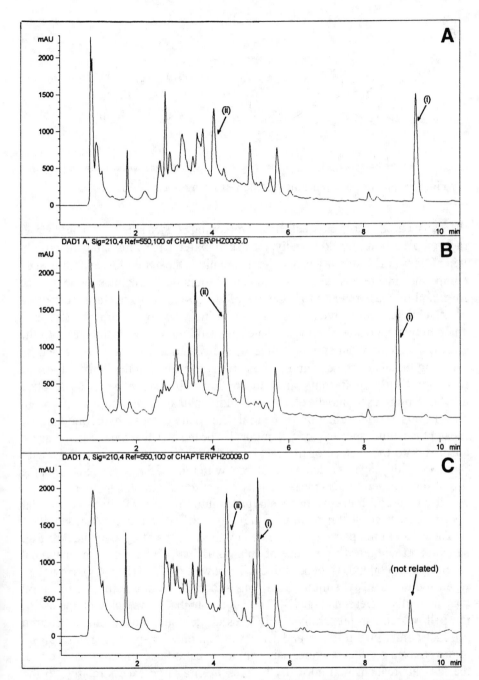

Fig. 2. HPLC analysis of *P. aeruginosa* ATCC 10145 fermentation broth extract. HPLC conditions: Column: Kromasil 5 μm C8 19 × 0.46 cm. Mobile phase A: 50 m*M* NH₄H₂PO₄ in water. Mobile phase B: 60% v/v acetonitrile/50 m*M* NH₄H₂PO₄ in water. The pH of A and B was adjusted to 2.0 **(A)**, 4.0 **(B)**, or 6.0 **(C)** with H₃PO₄ (A–B). Linear gradient 100%A–100%B in 10 min at 2 mL/min with a 5-min hold at 100%B. Detection wavelength: 210 nm. Peaks corresponding to pyocyanine (peak i) and phenazine-1-carboxylic acid (peak ii) are labeled.

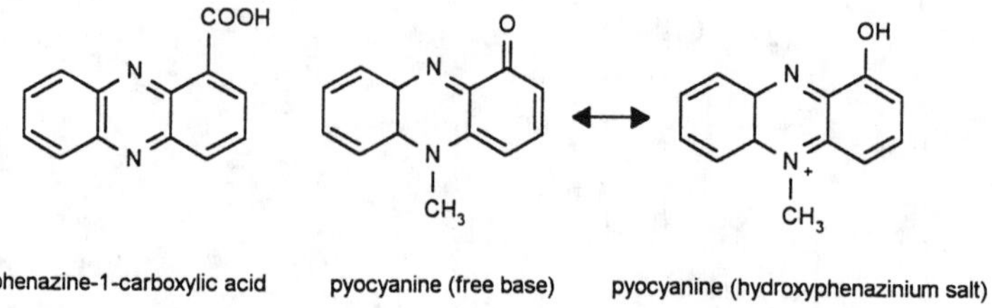

phenazine-1-carboxylic acid   pyocyanine (free base)   pyocyanine (hydroxyphenazinium salt)

Fig. 3. Structures of phenazine metabolites from *P. aeruginosa* ATCC 10145.

that can be used in conventional HPLC employing bonded silica stationary phases (approx pH 2.0–8.0). Additionally, the use of extreme pH values may be prohibited by chemical instability of a target metabolite. One option for separating such compounds in a reverse phase system is to chromatograph solutes in the ionized form and increase retention by the use of an ion-pair reagent. In the case of a positively charged analyte, retention can be increased by incorporating a long chain alkylsulphonate or alkylsulphate (e.g., sodium dodecylsulphate) into the eluent. Conversely, an anionic solute whose retention cannot be increased by lowering the pH of the eluent may be chromatographed in the ionized form by incorporating a quaternary ammonium ion-pair reagent such as a tetraalkylammonium salt into the eluent. The addition of such ion-pair reagents probably results in the formation of neutral "ion pairs" whose hydrophobicity is greater than either species alone. It might also be the case that the ion-pair reagent adsorbs onto the surface of the packing material, acting as an ion exchanger. Since ion-pair reagents selectively interact with ions of the opposite charge, the use of such reagents alters the selectivity of a chromatographic method, and this can also be useful for separating a charged solute from neutral species of similar hydrophobicity present in a crude or partially purified natural product sample.

The effect of ion pairing is illustrated by the analysis of pyocyanine (*see* **Fig. 3**) with and without the presence of an anionic ion-pair reagent. Under typical reverse phase conditions, pyocyanine was not well retained (**Fig. 4A**). However, when sodium dodecyl sulfate (SDS) was added to the mobile phase, retention was markedly increased (**Fig. 4B**). The main potential drawback with the use of ion-pair reagents in preparative HPLC lies in their subsequent removal from a product-containing fraction and from the column. Ion-pair reagents can be removed from product fractions using anion- or cation-exchange resins: even so, the ion-pair reagent will normally be present in a large excess relative to the product, and its complete removal is generally not straightforward.

2.1.5. Silanol Interactions

Most silica-based reverse phase chromatographic supports contain a small percentage of free (underivatized) silanol groups, and this can adversely affect

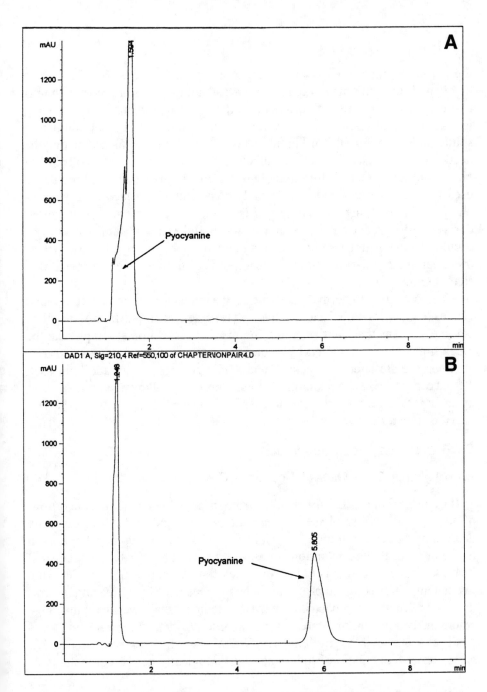

Fig. 4. Ion-pair HPLC analysis of *P. aeruginosa* ATCC 10145 fermentation broth extract. HPLC conditions: Column: Kromasil 5 μm C8 19 × 0.46 cm. Mobile phase: 40% v/v aceto-nitrile/10 mM NH$_4$H$_2$PO$_4$, 0.3% v/v H$_3$PO$_4$. After degassing, 14 g SDS was added to each liter of mobile phase and dissolved by slow mixing. Flow rate: 2 mL/min. Detection wave-length: 210 nm. Broth extract was mixed 1:1 with mobile phase prior to injection.

the chromatographic behavior of certain compound classes. Strongly basic compounds may chromatograph as very broad tailing peaks or may not elute at all during a run. The use of buffers may alleviate this problem, by minimizing localized pH variations caused by free silanol groups and by out-competing solute molecules for silanol-binding sites, although further measures may be needed in some cases. Several manufacturers offer "base-deactivated" reverse phase supports, in which free silanol groups are eliminated either through the use of silicas characterized by extremely homogeneous surfaces, or by a second process involving end-capping of free silanols remaining after the initial derivatization reaction, by a shorter alkylsilyl reagent such as methyltrichlorosilane. Alternatively, a small amount of a tertiary organic base such as triethylamine (0.05–0.1%) may be incorporated into the eluent to mask free silanol groups.

When operating in normal phase mode, the interaction of certain compound classes (e.g., bases with the acidic hydroxyls present on the surface of the silica particles) means that their retention in normal phase chromatography can be much greater than predicted by hydrophobicity considerations alone. Bases commonly elute later than neutral and acidic compounds; in addition, such effects can give rise to peak tailing, though this can be alleviated in most cases by incorporating a tertiary organic base (e.g., triethylamine, 0.01–0.1% v/v) into the eluent.

2.1.6. Improving Peak Separation

2.1.6.1. ALTERING THE ORGANIC COSOLVENT CONCENTRATION

If a component is not fully resolved from its neighbors under the conditions of an isocratic reverse phase analysis, the peaks might be fully resolved by decreasing the concentration of cosolvent in a stepwise manner. Separation may improve, though retention times, and hence the overall run time, will increase. If the objective is to improve peak separation during a gradient run, two incompletely resolved peaks might be fully resolved by increasing the gradient time. Another approach is to make the gradient "shallower" over the range where the component of interest elutes, in order to spread the peaks out.

Figure 5 shows a gradient HPLC analysis of an extract of *Nectria episphaeria* fermentation broth. The two biologically active compounds of

---

Fig. 5. *(opposite)* Gradient HPLC analysis of *Nectria episphaeria* fermentation broth extract. HPLC conditions: Column: Kromasil 5 μm C8 15 × 0.46 cm. Mobile phase A: water. Mobile phase B: 60% v/v acetonitrile/water. Linear gradient A to B in 15 min at 1.5 mL/min, with a 10-min hold at 100%B. Detection wavelength: 210 nm.

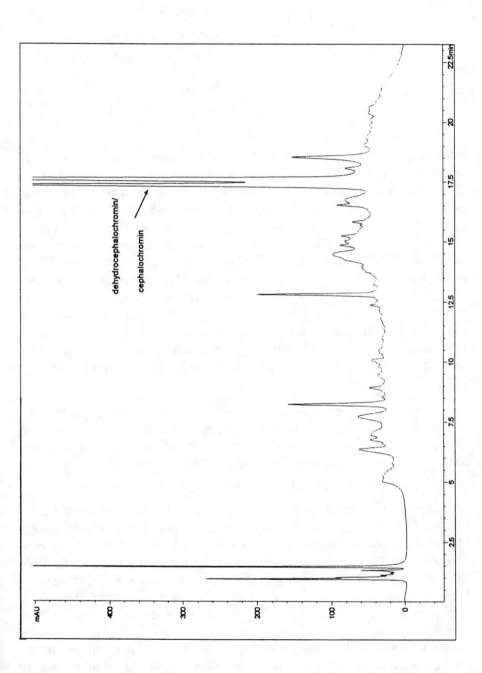

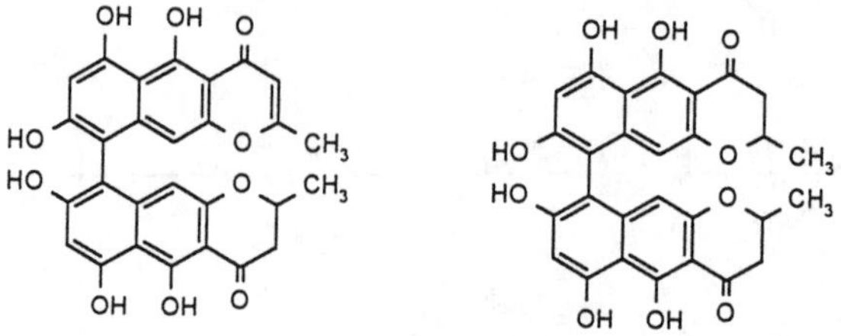

Fig. 6. Structures of 2,3-dehydrocephalochromin and cephalochromin.

interest, cephalochromin and 2,3-dehydrocephalochromin (CC, DCC; **Fig. 6**) are incompletely resolved under these conditions.

Figure 7 illustrates how an isocratic method was developed for the resolution of the two compounds. The compounds coeluted after 2.4 min using an eluent of 65% v/v acetonitrile/water (**Fig. 7A**). As the acetonitrile concentration was progressively decreased, resolution was improved and retention was increased. It can be seen that this also results in much broader peaks. Partial resolution was observed when the organic modifier concentration was 55% v/v (**Fig. 7B**), near-baseline resolution was seen at 50% v/v (**Fig. 7C**), and complete resolution was achieved when the organic modifier concentration was 45% v/v (**Fig. 7D**). It can be seen from the structures that these metabolites bear an abundance of ionizable phenolic hydroxyls, and this feature necessitated the use of a buffered eluent for preparative work (*see* **Subheading 2.3.2.**).

2.1.6.2. ALTERING SELECTIVITY

The approach outlined above is not always successful, and an alternative approach is to alter the selectivity of the chromatographic method. Selectivity is a function of the interaction of sample components with both the mobile phase and stationary phase, and altering the nature of one or both of these might achieve a better separation.

2.1.6.3. MOBILE PHASE CONSIDERATIONS

A change in solvent from acetonitrile to methanol, for example, might alter selectivity sufficiently to allow incompletely resolved components to be fully resolved. Methanol is a weaker eluting solvent than acetonitrile in RP-HPLC (except at concentrations approaching 100%), and a change from, say, 50% v/v acetonitrile/water to 60% v/v methanol/water should give broadly similar retention times, though, one hopes, with improved separation of a target metabolite from interfering peaks. A third common choice of solvent is THF. THF is a strong eluent (70% THF/water is approximately equivalent to 100% methanol or acetonitrile), though it is more unpleasant to work with and can form explosive peroxides, and it is normally considered for preparative work when separation is not achieved by other means. Optionally, a combination of organic cosolvents and water is employed.

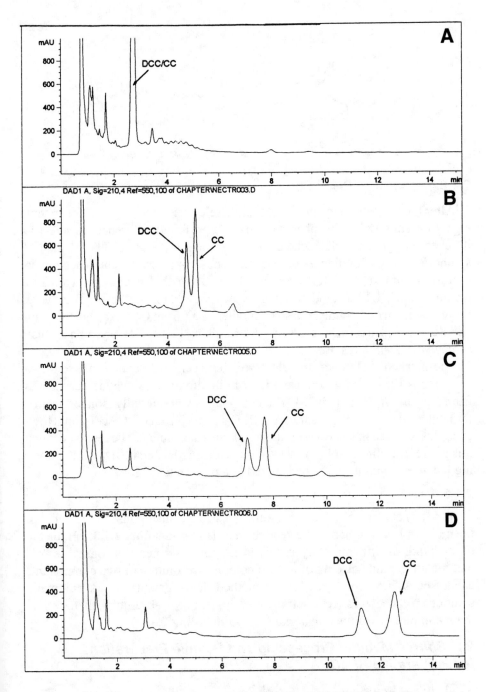

Fig. 7. Resolution of cephalochromins by isocratic HPLC. HPLC conditions: Column: Kromasil 5 µm C8 15 × 0.46 cm. Mobile phases: **(A)** 65% v/v acetonitrile/water. **(B)** 55% v/v acetonitrile/water. **(C)** 50% v/v acetonitrile/water. **(D)** 45% v/v acetonitrile/water. Flow rate: 1.5 mL/min. Detection wavelength: 210 nm.

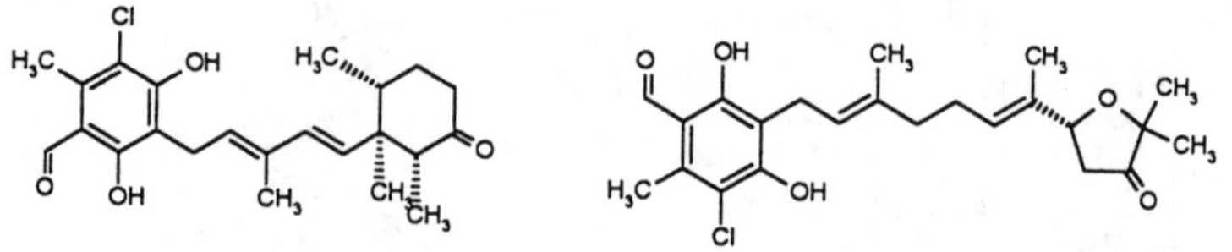

Fig. 8. Structures of dihydroxybenzaldehydes from *Sesquicillium* sp.

2.1.6.4. STATIONARY PHASE CONSIDERATIONS

Altering the stationary phase can alter selectivity to a significant extent; e.g., different C18 bonded phases can exhibit profound differences in selectivity even though the surface chemistry is nominally the same. The method of synthesis and postbonding treatment (e.g., end-capping) varies between manufacturers, and such differences can be enough that a change from one manufacturer's C18 to another will give the required resolution. Alternatively, switching from one bonded phase to another (e.g., from C18 to a shorter chain alkyl bonded phase such as C8 or C6 or a phenyl or cyclohexyl phase) may achieve the desired result.

The marked difference in selectivity between two reverse phase silica packings is illustrated by the isolation of dihydroxybenzaldehyde derivatives from *Sesquicillium* sp. (**Fig. 8**). The compounds were initially isolated from a fermentation extract by preparative HPLC using a Kromasil C8 column. However, this resulted in a two-component mixture that could not be resolved using this phase. Baseline resolution was achieved using Hypersil BDS C18, allowing the three components to be isolated in a pure state (**Fig. 9**).

2.1.6.5. pH

If the target metabolite contains ionizable groups, manipulation of the pH of the mobile phase might prove effective (*see* also **Subheading 2.1.3.**). If, on the other hand, an incompletely resolved neighboring peak is ionizable, pH manipulation might also work well. If complete resolution of two components cannot be achieved in a reasonable method development time, a pragmatic solution might be to collect fractions at each side of a peak doublet, then recycle the incompletely resolved material (*see* **Subheading 2.3.4.**).

2.2. Source Material Processing and Sample Preparation for Preparative HPLC

2.2.1. Initial Extraction

The processing of a crude source material to provide a sample suitable for preparative HPLC, as well as other considerations, such as the choice of solvent for sample reconstitution/dissolution, can have a significant bearing on

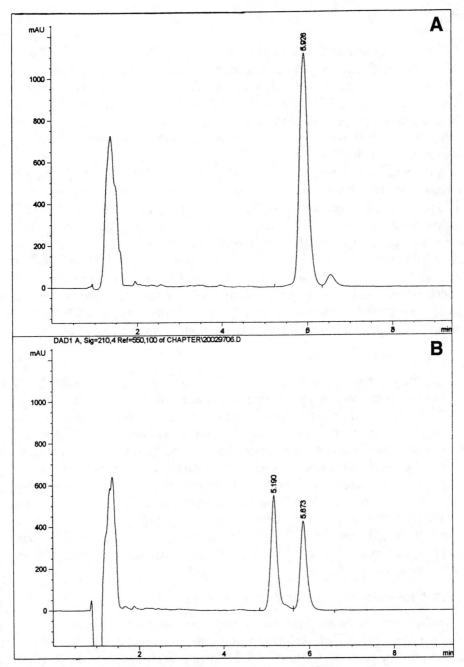

Fig. 9. Analysis of dihydroxybenzaldehydes from *Sesquicillium* sp. HPLC conditions: **(A)** Column: Kromasil 5 μm C8 15 × 0.46 cm. Mobile phase: 60% v/v acetonitrile/50 mM NH$_4$H$_2$PO$_4$, 0.3% v/v H$_3$PO$_4$. **(B)** Column: Hypersil C18 BDS 5 μm 15 × 0.46 cm. Mobile phase: 60% v/v acetonitrile/10 mM NH$_4$OAc, 0.1% v/v TFA. Flow rate: 1.5. mL/min.

the overall success of a natural product isolation. The source material, e.g., dried powdered plant or whole fermentation broth, will initially need to be treated in such a way as to ensure that the compound of interest is efficiently liberated into solution. In the case of dried plant material, an organic solvent (e.g., acetone, methanol, chloroform) may be used as the initial extractant, and following a period of maceration, solid material is then removed by decanting off the extract or by filtration.

Microbial fermentation broths will contain cells and cell debris, and the compound of interest may be located in solution in the broth supernatant or associated with the cell (either bound to the cell surface or contained intracellularly). If the metabolite is cell surface-associated, measures must be taken to release/solvate the target compound, after which cells and cell debris may be removed by filtration or centrifugation. Addition of a water-miscible organic solvent such as methanol or acetonitrile to whole broth is a good technique for liberating cell-bound metabolites into solution. Alternatively, whole fermentation broth may be lyophilized, then the solid residue extracted with a suitable organic solvent. Cell disruption might be required for the release of intracellular metabolites.

2.2.1.1. SOLVENT EXTRACTION

In those cases where the target metabolite exists in solution within a broth supernatant, extraction of the supernatant with an organic solvent (e.g., butan-1-ol, ethyl acetate, or dichloromethane) is often a useful means of obtaining an initial crude extract. If a water-miscible solvent has been used as the initial extractant, volatile organic solvent can be removed by rotary evaporation, to leave an aqueous solution/suspension that can be solvent-extracted in the same way. In certain cases, considerable sample enrichment can be achieved by choosing a solvent into which the desired component partitions efficiently, but into which other sample components do not. Shelley *(8)* showed that toluene (rather than methanol) extraction of the fermentation broth of a Streptomycete yielded an extract rich in the desired metabolite, rapamycin, but devoid of an undesired impurity, elaiophylin.

2.2.1.2. ION-PAIR–ASSISTED SOLVENT EXTRACTION

Highly polar charged solutes can sometimes be partitioned effectively into water-immiscible organic solvents using ion-pair reagents (also known as phase-transfer catalysts). **Figure 10A** shows a chromatogram of *Serratia marcescens* ATCC39006 filtered broth supernatant. This organism produces polar β-lactam metabolites (**Fig. 11**), which retain poorly under RP-HPLC conditions *(9)*; in addition, the instability of the strained β-lactam ring system negates the use of ionization suppression by acidification of the chromatographic eluent in order to increase retention.

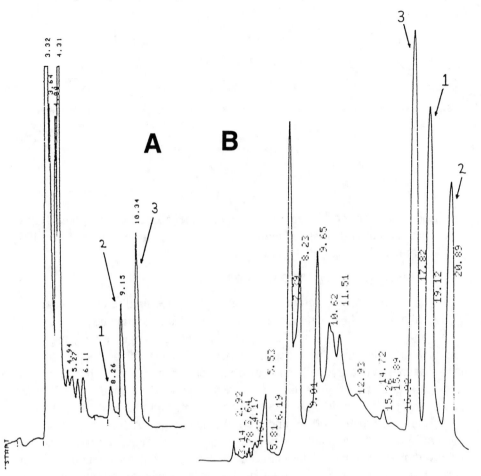

Fig. 10. Analytical and semipreparative HPLC of β-lactams from *Serratia marcescens* ATCC39006. **(A)** Analytical HPLC chromatogram of the β-lactam free acids. **(B)** Semipreparative HPLC chromatogram of the *p*-nitrobenzyl esters. HPLC conditions: Column: Spherisorb 5 μm ODS2 (C18) 25 × 1 cm. Mobile Phases: (A) 0.1 M KH_2PO_4 in water pH 7.0. (B) 40% v/v acetonitrile/water. Flow rate: 2 mL/min. Detection wavelength: (A) 210 nm. (B) 254 nm. The peaks corresponding to (*3S, 5S*)-1-carbapenam-3-carboxylic acid, (*5S*)-1-carbapen-2-em-3-carboxylic acid, and (*3S, 5R*)-1-carbapenam-3-carboxylic acid are labeled as peaks 1–3, respectively (*see* **Fig. 11** for structures). Sample loading for the semipreparative experiment: 5 mg containing 2 mg total products, dissolved in 0.5 mL mobile phase.

The compounds were partitioned efficiently into dichloromethane containing 4% w/v trioctylmethyl ammonium chloride (Aliquat 336: Aldrich, Milwaukee, WI), and after drying of the organic layer with magnesium sulfate, the compounds were derivatized to the more stable *p*-nitrobenzyl esters using

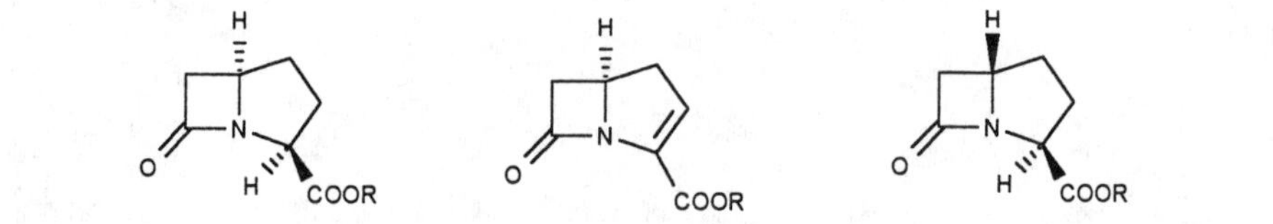

(3S,5S)-1-carbapenam-3-carboxylic acid   (5S)-1-carbapen-2-em-3-carboxylic acid   (3S,5R)-1-carbapenam-3-carboxylic acid

Natural products: R=Na,
Derivatised compounds: R=p-nitrobenzyl

Fig. 11. β-Lactams produced by *S. marcescens* ATCC39006.

p-nitrobenzyl bromide. The esters were more amenable to reverse phase HPLC and were subsequently isolated under reverse phase conditions employing 40% v/v acetonitrile/water as eluent (**Fig. 10B**).

2.2.2. Desalting and Sample Concentration

Further processing of a crude extract is normally required prior to preparative HPLC, although if the initial extract is relatively "clean" it might be possible to go to preparative HPLC directly. The objective in this second processing stage is to enrich the sample with respect to the compound of interest and to remove inorganic salts that are present. Lyophilization of whole fermentation broth followed by solvent extraction of the dry residue is a convenient way of obtaining a crude extract substantially free from inorganic salts. Where whole broth has been mixed with a water-miscible organic solvent and then filtered/centrifuged, removal of organic solvent by rotary evaporation is necessary prior to desalting. Desalting is then achieved by passing the aqueous concentrate through a column containing an adsorbent to which the target compound binds but to which inorganic salts and highly polar materials do not. Many such adsorbents are available, and the choice depends on the characteristics of the target compound. Most secondary metabolites bind to some extent to hydrophobic supports from aqueous solution. Commonly used adsorbents are reverse phase silicas, e.g., Whatman "Partisil 40" (a 40-μm-diameter reverse phase C18-bonded silica), or styrene-divinylbenzene copolymer resins, e.g., Amberlite XAD-16 (Rohm and Haas) or Diaion HP20 (Mitsubishi). After a water wash, the compound of interest is eluted from the adsorbent usually with aqueous or pure organic solvents such as methanol, acetonitrile, or acetone. By carefully choosing the eluting solvent strength and by fractionating the eluate, considerable sample clean-up may be achieved, as well as desalting.

2.2.3. Sample Preparation for Preparative HPLC

The solvent composition of the sample to be injected onto the preparative HPLC column is extremely important and should be as close as possible to that of the eluent. The aim is to achieve an optimal balance between sample concentration and volume; the volume of the sample should be manageable, i.e., able to be processed by HPLC in a reasonable number of runs. Ideally, the sample should be dissolved in the eluent itself and, in the case of a gradient system, in the initial solvent in which the column has been equilibrated. This is frequently not possible, owing to the heterogeneous nature of many natural product extracts or because the volume of solvent required to dissolve the sample might be too large for subsequent processing by HPLC. The sample may not be sufficiently soluble in the chromatographic solvent to permit the concentrated loads required in preparative HPLC. In this case, further sample enrichment procedures might be required prior to HPLC. Alternatively, the sample might be dissolved by adding a higher proportion of organic modifier than is present in the eluent. A small amount of a second organic modifier might be required to effect dissolution.

The final solvent composition of the sample will vary from case to case, but as a rule, the level of organic modifier should be kept as close as possible to that of the eluent. A higher proportion of organic modifier in the sample than in the eluent will generally result in peak broadening, and, hence loss of resolution in reverse phase HPLC, particularly in the case of poorly retained (polar) metabolites. Even if the chromatographic eluent is buffered, it is a good idea to check the pH of the sample and adjust it to that of the mobile phase. This is particularly relevant in those cases where the target metabolite is ionizable and pH is critical to the separation process.

2.2.3.1. Guard Columns

Many natural product source materials contain significant levels of strongly binding components, such as chlorophylls and other extraneous material, that may in the long term compromise column performance if left unchecked. This rarely causes problems if sample preparation methods are tailored to take account of this and columns are regularly cleaned/maintained. Optionally a small precolumn (or "guard column") is installed prior to the chromatographic column. This is packed with the same stationary phase as that employed for the main column; after repeated use the precolumn may be emptied, used packing material discarded, and the column repacked with fresh material, thus acting as a reservoir to remove strongly binding material from the sample prior to it reaching the main column.

2.3. Scale-Up

2.3.1. Scale of Operation

The size of column required will depend on the quantity of material to be isolated and its abundance within the sample mixture being chromatographed.

In general, 1–2 mg of a compound is sufficient for full structural characterization by NMR and mass spectrometry. If this is the total requirement, it may be possible to isolate such amounts by repeated injections using an analytical scale column (e.g., 15 cm × 0.46 cm internal diameter [i.d.]). 1–5 mg total weight of sample (in a volume of up to approx 200 μL) can often be injected without serious loss of resolution, and for the occasional purification using HPLC, an analytical scale column might suffice. A larger column would be advisable if: (1) the abundance of the required material in the sample is low, necessitating many injections of sample; (2) the loss of resolution is marked as the sample load increases; or (3) more than approx 5–10 mg of material is required in total.

2.3.2. Scaling Up

2.3.2.1. COLUMN DIMENSIONS

It is convenient (and will save method development time) to use identical column-packing material in both analytical and preparative scale chromatography. For a typical 5-μm-diameter packing, this means that conventional preparative HPLC columns up to ~2 cm in diameter (and ~25 cm in length) can be used at flow rates of 20–30 mL/min without unduly high column back pressure. When using longer columns or viscous solvents, high column back pressure can compromise method development by limiting the flow rate. As a very rough guide, a 5 -μm bonded phase is suited to preparative HPLC applications with columns up to ~25 × 2 cm i.d., a 7- to 10-μm-diameter phase with columns up to ~25 × 5 cm i.d., and a 10- to 20-μm-diameter phase for columns larger than these.

As a general rule, the increase in sample loading for preparative HPLC is proportional to the increase in column volumes (i.e., column cross-sectional area and length) from analytical to preparative scale operation. It is simplest to consider scaling up initially by alteration of the column diameter. Comparison of the cross-sectional areas of an analytical HPLC column of 0.46 cm i.d. and a lab scale preparative HPLC column of 2 cm i.d. shows that the cross-sectional area (proportional to d^2) varies by a factor of 19. Thus, if the same packing material is used for both columns and they are both of the same lengths, it should be the case that sample load may be increased by a factor of 19 without impairment of chromatographic performance. Loading then varies according to the relative lengths of the analytical and preparative columns. In practice, other considerations, such as the solvent distribution characteristics at the column top and column-packing density/homogeneity, come into play during scale-up, but the guidelines outlined above should serve reasonably well. Chromatographic variability is also minimized by performing initial scale-up experiments using an analytical column packed with the same packing material (preferably the same batch of packing material) that is to be used throughout the scale-up process. We can also say directly from the above example that the retention time of a solute (under identical mobile phase conditions) will vary by a factor of 19. Alternatively, if the flow rate through the preparative column is increased by a factor of 19, the retention time of a given solute will be equal (1 mL/min through the analytical column is equivalent to 19 mL/min through the preparative column).

2.3.2.2. SAMPLE PREPARATION

The importance of sample preparation and choice of eluent is illustrated by the scale-up isolation of cephalochromin and 2,3-dehydrocephalochromin from cultures of *Nectria epishaeria* (*see* **Subheading 2.1.3.**). Baseline resolution of these closely related metabolites was achieved under analytical conditions using a column packed with Kromasil 5 μm C8 and an eluent of 45% v/v acetonitrile/water. However, an increase in sample loading rapidly resulted in loss of resolution and peak shape (**Fig. 12A**), even when the sample was acidified prior to injection. When the sample was chromatographed using an eluent buffered with ammonium dihydrogen phosphate/phosphoric acid (pH 2.0), near-baseline resolution was again established at high analytical-scale sample loadings (**Fig. 12B**). This was maintained as the scale of operation was increased to the preparative scale (25 × 5-cm column; **Fig. 13**).

2.3.3. Peak Broadening, Overload, and Displacement Effects

In conventional elution chromatography, solute peaks might begin to broaden as the sample load is increased and solutes begin to compete for adsorption sites on the column stationary phase. Provided that components are well-resolved at low sample loadings (e.g., α >1.3), a slight increase in peak broadness might not affect the purity of the product fraction. Purity will be compromised as the column capacity is exceeded and solute peak shape is lost. The choice of sample loading for preparative HPLC will depend on many factors; for example, the nature of the components present in the sample and their chromatographic proximity to the component of interest, the purity of product required, the column capacity, and the total amount of sample to be processed.

Mass overload refers to overload of a column due to total mass of sample injected and can sometimes be used to increase the throughput of a preparative HPLC separation as long as the degree of overloading is controlled. Peaks neighboring a solute of interest may begin to merge with it under such conditions, but if the central region or "heart" of the product peak is pure, it may be collected and the incompletely resolved side fractions reprocessed. Volume overload results when the volume of sample injected exceeds 10–20% of the column dead volume (at normal sample concentrations, this is usually 5–20% w/w). For poorly retained solutes (i.e., those with low k' values), this results in excessive broadening of peaks and hence loss of resolution.

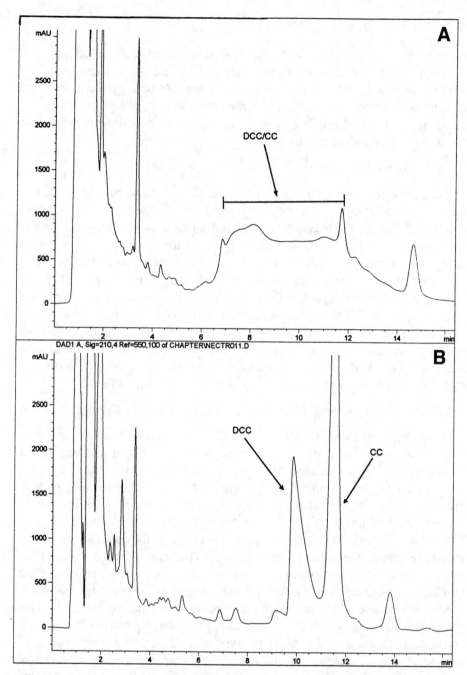

Fig. 12. Analytical HPLC of cephalochromins from *Nectria episphaeria*. HPLC conditions: Column: Kromasil 5 μm C8 15 × 0.46 cm. Mobile phases: **(A)** 50% v/v acetonitrile/water. **(B)** 50% v/v acetonitrile/50 m*M* NH$_4$H$_2$PO$_4$, 0.3% v/v H$_3$PO$_4$. Sample load: 3 mg (containing 0.8 mg dehydrocephalochromin/cephalochromin) in 80 μL mobile phase. Flow rate: 1.5 mL/min. Detection wavelength: 210 nm.

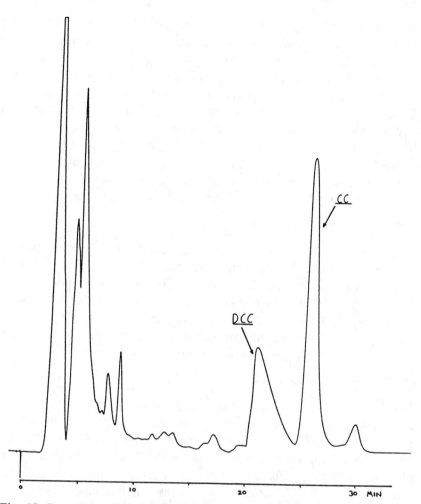

Fig. 13. Preparative HPLC of cephalochromin from *Nectria episphaeria*. HPLC conditions: Column: Kromasil 7 μm C8 25 × 5 cm. Mobile phase: 50% v/v acetonitrile/50 mM NH$_4$H$_2$PO$_4$, 0.3.% v/v H$_3$PO$_4$. Flow rate: 80 mL/min. Detection wavelength: 210 nm. Sample load: 190 mg (containing approx 50 mg dehydrocephalochromin/cephalochromin) in 20 mL mobile phase.

2.3.3.1. DISPLACEMENT EFFECTS

A strongly retained solute may displace a more weakly retained solute by simple competition for binding sites on an adsorbent surface. In displacement chromatography, very high sample loadings are introduced onto a column using a weakly eluting solvent (the carrier), and thus all sample components bind initially, forming an adsorbed band at the column top. A displacer (a very strongly retained solute) is then pumped onto the column. Thus, the band of adsorbed sample components is displaced, with sample components displacing each other according to their relative adsorption strength. The effect is to create a train of displaced sample components that becomes focused into sharp bands during migration through the column by competition with neighboring component bands. An example of the application of this technique in natural products isolation is the separation of 1- and 2-naphthol using a β-cyclodextrin silica column with tetradecyltrimethylammonium bromide (cetrimide) as displacer *(10)*. The disadvantage of this technique is that method development times are long. However, the increases in efficiency and throughput under optimized conditions can make this time well-spent for very large scale isolation processes.

2.3.4. Preparative Recycling HPLC

It is not always possible to obtain complete resolution of components following a single preparative HPLC run. An alternative to further method development, or to the use of a longer HPLC column, is to recycle that portion of the eluent that contains the incompletely resolved components through the column a second time. Preparative LC instruments equipped with a recycling valve can provide a speedy solution to difficult separations, at the same time offering additional substantial savings in solvent consumption in certain cases.

2.3.4.1. RECYCLING THE PRODUCT

Provided band-broadening is kept to a minimum during the recycling event, an incompletely resolved product can be recycled many times in order to achieve the desired degree of resolution. Kubo and Nakatsu *(11)* separated two phytoecdysteroids, ajugasterone and vitexirone (**Fig. 14**), which differ by only a single side-chain double bond, using recycling HPLC with a polyvinyl alcohol resin column. Complete resolution was achieved after three cycles.

2.3.4.2. RECYCLING THE ELUTING SOLVENT

When operating isocratically, it is efficient to recycle that portion of the eluting solvent that is clean, that is, does not contain sample components. However, it is often not possible to recycle the eluting solvent during preparative HPLC processing of natural product extracts because of the presence of a multitude of other components, which elute over a wide timespan. But, for certain isocratic separations where the sample contains predominantly the desired material(s), recycling a proportion of the eluent is a potentially useful option.

2.3.4.3. SHAVE AND RECYCLE CHROMATOGRAPHY

Partial resolution of two peaks following a first pass through the chromatographic column enables pure products to be obtained by collecting the leading

ajugasterone   vitexirone

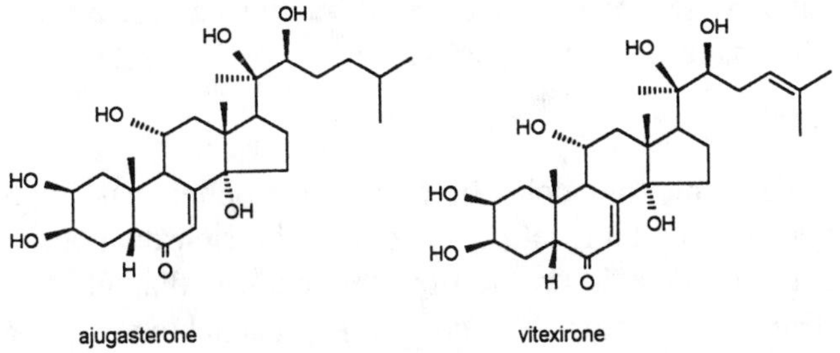

Fig. 14. Structures of phytoecdysteroids.

and tailing edges of the peak doublet. The incompletely resolved material is then recycled, and the process of "shaving and recycling" is repeated as many times as necessary.

2.4. Fraction Collection and Work-Up

2.4.1. Fractionation

The two main methods of fraction collection are collection of material relating to individual chromatographic peaks and time slicing. If the objective is to collect all components with a view to characterizing the biological activity in a complex multicomponent sample, one might choose to time slice, i.e., collect fractions on a time-per-fraction basis rather than collect individual peaks. Time-slicing a chromatogram into 0.5- or 1-min fractions is a pragmatic way of fractionating a complex sample; the investigator might end up with 30–40 fractions from a typical analytical or lab-scale preparative HPLC experiment.

In this way a complex mixture might be split into fractions, each containing perhaps five or less components. If the operation is performed on a reasonably large scale (e.g., using a lab scale "preparative" column [15 × 2 cm i.d.], a flow rate of 10–25 mL/min, and a sample loading equivalent to 10–100 mg dry weight of extract in a sample volume of 2–5 mL), the investigator might process enough material in a single run for both biological evaluation of each fraction and subsequent resolution of the active fraction(s) into single components. Occasionally, the desired material might be in sufficient abundance to provide enough material from a single run for full structural characterization, but more often than not, the resolved (active) component will serve as an analytical standard for subsequent LC method development.

If the compound of interest is already characterized and the object is to isolate such a component from a source material using a fully developed preparative LC method, then the investigator may choose to collect a single fraction, pooling the target "peak" from each chromatographic run in a single collection vessel. It might be wise also to collect small fractions across a peak of interest to maximize the chances of obtaining pure material.

2.4.2. Time Delays

There is an inevitable time delay between a component passing through the flow cell of a detector and it reaching the outlet of the chromatographic instrument. The delay will depend on the flow rate and the diameter/length of the outlet tubing from the detector. With conventional benchtop preparative HPLC equipment operating at flow rates above approx 10 mL/min, the delay is normally insignificant; but when collecting components using an analytical-scale instrument and low flow rates (1–2 mL/min), the delay can amount to several seconds, and this should be borne in mind when operating at this scale, particularly when peak resolution is incomplete.

2.4.3. Fraction Work-Up

If the chromatographic eluent is a mixture of organic modifier and water and contains no additives such as involatile buffers/acids, then product recovery can be effected simply by removing solvent, e.g., by rotary evaporation. Alternatively, if the solvent volumes are large, the organic modifier can be removed by rotary evaporation and the product recovered by adsorption/elution from a suitable adsorbent such as a reverse phase silica or an organic copolymer resin. This is also a method of choice where additives such as involatile buffers (phosphates, acetates) and acids (orthophosphoric) are present in the fraction and need to be removed.

2.4.3.1. DESALTING USING THE HPLC COLUMN

It is possible in nearly all cases to use the same HPLC column for subsequent desalting that was used in the purification. The preparative HPLC column is often a good choice, as the purified compound in question will certainly bind. Care should be taken to wash the column through with water, then with a strongly eluting solvent, e.g., 90% v/v acetonitrile/water, in order to remove strongly bound components. The column should then be equilibrated in water again prior to pumping the product-containing fraction back on the column, and the bulk of the organic modifier should be removed from the fraction prior to this step. This is normally achieved by rotary evaporation at ambient temperature. Should the solution become cloudy (as with very hydrophobic compounds), organic modifier may be added drop-wise until dissolution is just effected. Having pumped the fraction back on to the column, the column resin is washed thoroughly with water until all buffer has been removed. Monitoring the pH of the effluent is a good way to judge when buffer removal is complete. Otherwise, about 3–4 column volumes of water should be enough. The adsorbed component can then be eluted using, e.g., 90% methanol/water or acetonitrile/water.

2.4.3.2. REVERSE PHASE SILICA CARTRIDGES

Reverse phase silica cartridges (e.g., Bond-Elut [Varian], Sep-Pak [Waters]) are convenient to use since they contain preweighed adsorbent in a disposable syringe-like column. The resin bed is first wetted with organic solvent (methanol, acetonitrile) or an organic solvent/water mixture, then equilibrated in water prior to use. It follows that a component that has been purified by RP-HPLC should bind to (and subsequently elute from) such a resin, providing that the bulk of the organic modifier present in the HPLC fraction has been removed prior to the adsorption step. Inorganic buffers/acids are not retained and pass through the column to waste. After the adsorption is complete, the resin is washed through with water to remove the last traces of buffer/acid, and the adsorbed components may then be eluted with methanol or a methanol/water mixture. Other resin types are available in a cartridge format (e.g., silica, ion-exchange resins, and so on), and the reader is referred to the manufacturer's product literature for data on sample/solvent suitability.

2.4.3.3. ORGANIC COPOLYMERS

An alternative to reverse phase silica for desalting is the use of organic copolymers [e.g., the Amberlite XAD range of styrene-divinylbenzene copolymer resins (Rohm and Haas)]. Such resins have broadly similar retention characteristics to reverse phase silica supports though selectivity is frequently altered. The resins may be packed into columns, then wetted with organic solvent and equilibrated in water in the same manner as reverse phase silica cartridges. The sample loading, washing, and elution flow rates are comparatively low (~5 bed vol/h compared to ~50–100 bed vol/h for reverse phase silica cartridges), but the resins are robust, cheap, have a high loading capacity, and may be reused many times.

2.4.3.4. OBTAINING THE FINAL PRODUCT

The component of interest must finally be isolated from a small volume of organic solvent or solvent/water mix to yield the requisite pure product. This can be achieved by rotary evaporation, freeze-drying, or vacuum centrifugation. The choice of method depends on the equipment available, the amount of product isolated, and the purpose for which it is intended. These techniques are discussed further in Chapter 9.

2.5. Some Special Considerations for Preparative-Scale HPLC in Natural Products Chemistry

2.5.1. Tannins

Tannins are a commonly occurring class of phenolic metabolites found mainly in plants. They comprise two main groups. Hydrolysable tannins are

hydrolysable tannin (pentagalloyl glucose)   condensed tannin (polymeric flavan-3-ol)

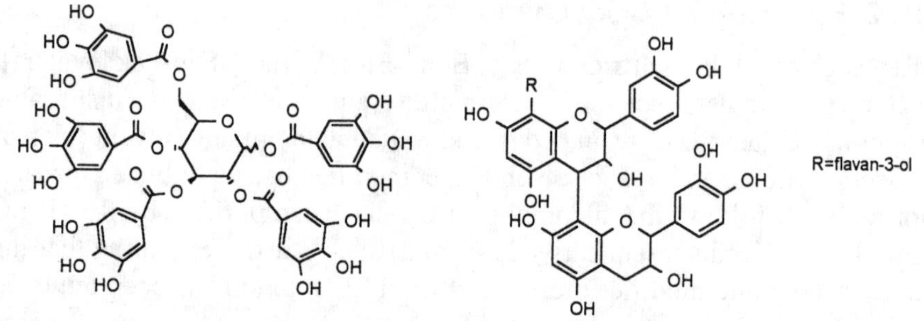

Fig. 15. Examples of hydroyzable and condensed tannins.

esters of phenolic acids, e.g., 3,4,5-trihydroxybenzoic acid (gallic acid), and glucose (**Fig. 15**). There may be several phenolic acids esterified to a central carbohydrate core. Condensed tannins are more resistant to hydrolytic degradation than hydrolysable tannins and appear to derive from flavan-3,4-diols (**Fig. 15**), having a polymeric flavan-3-ol structure *(12)*. These polyhydroxylated aromatic metabolites represent a very large family of natural products. As a class, they have the general property of binding nonspecifically to protein, causing precipitation, and can thus give rise to nonspecific "activity" during the screening of crude plant extracts for biological activity.

The presence of tannins in a natural product sample frequently correlates chromatographically with a broad "hump" eluting over the polar/moderately polar region of the HPLC chromatogram (e.g., between approx 15–30% organic modifier concentration during a typical gradient RP-HPLC analysis). In complex plant extracts, it is often not possible to discern discrete tannin peaks by manipulation of the mobile phase conditions, perhaps because the broad hump seen on the chromatogram actually comprises numerous (chromatographically) similar metabolites eluting over a broad timespan, thus giving rise to the "hump"-like effect.

The tannins, by virtue of their polyphenolic nature are, however, both strongly hydrogen bonding and ionizable and thus can be removed (even from methanolic solution) by batchwise treatment with either a hydrogen-bonding polymer resin such as polyvinyl pyrrolidone, or polyamide, or a weakly basic anion exchanger such as diethylaminoethyl cellulose. It is by no means certain that all polyphenolic metabolites bind to these resins or that tannins are the only species capable of binding, and this should be borne in mind when considering tannin removal as a preliminary step in the fractionation of plant-derived material.

2.5.2. Very Strongly Retained Materials

Many partially characterized natural product samples contain hydrophobic components that are very strongly retained under reverse phase conditions. If the desired metabolite falls into this category, a switch from reverse phase to normal phase operation may be indicated *(see below)*. In many cases, very strongly retained components are not of interest as products but nevertheless need to be accounted for during chromatographic method development.

Many natural product extracts are highly colored, and this may be associated with discoloration of the top of column packing material following repeated analytical or preparative chromatography of relatively crude extracts. This is especially true when dealing with plant material that might contain mixtures of chlorophylls/chlorophyll degradation products, which, by virtue of their basic porphyrin structure, are very strongly retained. This is not normally associated with an accelerated decline in column performance, providing that the column is washed through periodically with a strong eluent (e.g., 75% v/v acetonitrile, 0.025 M ammonium dihydrogen phosphate, 0.3% v/v orthophosphoric acid in water or 90% v/v acetonitrile, 10 mM ammonium acetate, 0.2% v/v TFA in water).

Very strongly retained materials such as porphyrins and long-chain fatty acids can cause more serious problems if they are not eluted during an initial chromatographic run, only to appear having eluted much later in a subsequent experiment. Such components can cause confusion and product contamination, so due care should be taken to ensure that such materials are eluted between runs with an appropriate washing cycle.

As already discussed, RP-HPLC is suitable for the majority of natural product isolations, though the hydrophobicity of the desired matabolite/s might dictate the use of normal phase operation. An example of the application of this mode of operation to natural products work is the isolation of tocopherols from soya bean oil and wheat germ *(6)*. This example also emphasizes the power of normal phase (adsorption) chromatography for the separation of positional isomers. Baseline resolution of α, β, γ, and δ-tocopherol (**Fig. 16**) was achieved under semipreparative HPLC conditions utilizing a 10-μm silica stationary phase (Alltech Econosil). It is notable that β- and γ-tocopherols were completely resolved even though they differ only in the position of one methyl substituent on the benzopyran nucleus.

2.5.3. Preparative Separations of Enantiomers

The application of chiral preparative chromatography (including HPLC) to natural products isolation is rare, since most chiral natural products (of which there are a great many examples) are produced in a single chiral form. However, racemates do occur, and their separation on a preparative scale poses a particular challenge, though recent developments in chiral chromatographic methodology mean that such resolutions can often be performed quite readily.

Enantiomers may be separated directly or indirectly; a direct separation involves chromatographing a racemate utilizing either a chiral stationary phase

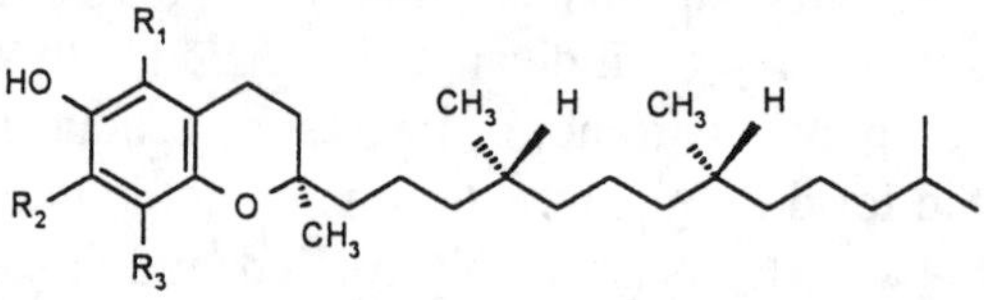

R1	R2	R3	
CH₃	CH₃	CH₃	α-tocopherol
CH₃	H	CH₃	β-tocopherol
H	CH₃	CH₃	γ-tocopherol
H	H	CH₃	δ-tocopherol

Fig. 16. Structures of tocopherols.

or chiral mobile phase. Both naturally derived modified polysaccharides (e.g., potato starch, cellulose esters, carbamates) and synthetic stationary phases, particularly derivatives of commercial silica, have been widely employed for the direct preparative separation of racemates, including natural products. An indirect separation requires derivatization of an enantiomeric mixture with a chiral reagent (e.g., MTPA) to yield diastereoisomers that may be separated by conventional means. Indirect methods require removal of the derivatizing group to yield enantiomerically pure product.

2.5.3.1. EXAMPLES OF DIRECT CHIRAL SEPARATIONS

The enantiomers of *trans,trans-* and *cis,trans-*2,8-dimethyl-1,7-dioxaspiro-[5.5]undecane (**Fig. 17**), the main pheromone components of *Adrena* bees, were directly resolved on a preparative scale utilizing triacetyl cellulose by Isaksson et al. *(13)*. In a single run, 140 mg of the *trans,trans-*racemate was chromatographed through a column containing 180 g adsorbent to yield 50 mg of each enantiomer.

[R]-N-(3,5-dinitrobenzoyl)-phenylglycine bound ionically to γ-amino-propyl-bonded silica was used *(14)* to resolve naturally occurring dihydro- and tetrahydrodiols of benzo[a]pyrene and benz[a]anthracene (**Fig. 18**) into the respective pure enantiomers.

2.5.3.2. INDIRECT SEPARATIONS

Kubo and Nakatsu *(11)* separated the racemic pheromone ipsdienol into pure enantiomers using an indirect approach. (±)-Ipsdienol was derivatized with (+)-α-methoxy-α-(trifluoromethyl)-phenylacetic acid (MTPA) to yield a mixture of diastereoisomers (**Fig. 19**), which were separated by conventional normal phase preparative HPLC using a nucleosil silica column with product recycling (*see* **Subheading 2.3.4.**). After seven cycles the diastereomers were

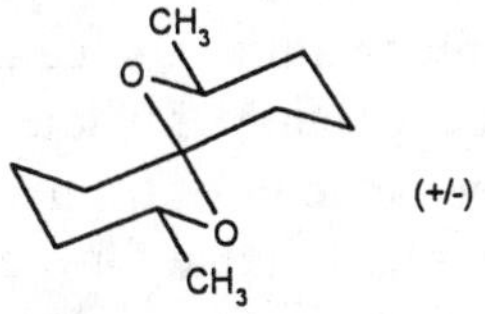

Fig. 17. *Trans,trans*-2,8-dimethyl-1,7-dioxaspiro[5.5]undecane.

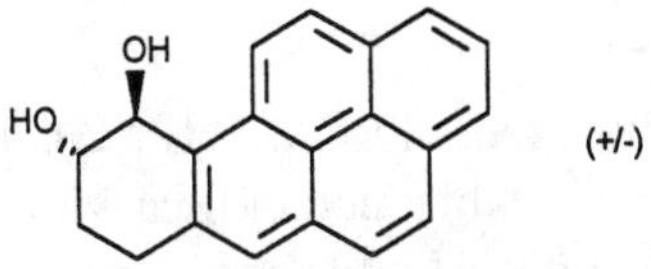

Fig. 18. Example of racemic benzo[a]pyrene.

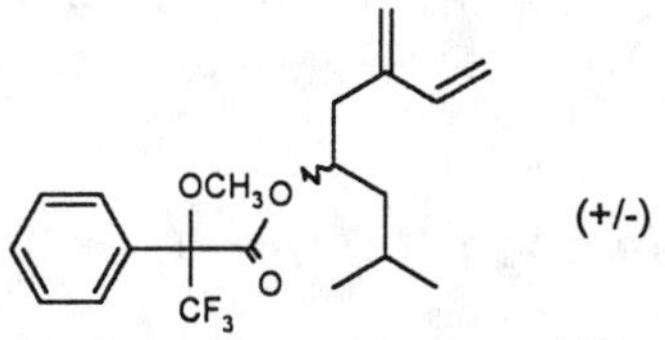

Fig. 19. Diastereomeric MTPA-esters of ipsdienol.

completely resolved, collected separately, then converted back to optically pure (+)- and (−)-ipsdienol using sodium borohydride in methanol.

3. Summary and Conclusions

It is clear that preparative HPLC has been widely applied to the isolation of diverse natural products that are often minor components of highly complex biological mixtures. The power of the technique to separate and isolate metabolites that differ only slightly in chemistry and/or stereochemistry is formidable. The examples shown constitute just a few cases in which HPLC has been employed to achieve quick separations and isolations that until relatively recently were extremely laborious.

3.1. The Increasing Use of HPLC

Traditionally, HPLC has been used as a final step in often complex isolation procedures that involve many different lower resolution techniques prior to preparative HPLC. The increasingly widespread use of HPLC, and associated developments in stationary phase and hardware design and performance, mean that HPLC can frequently be applied much earlier in the isolation process, particularly where the objective is to characterize rapidly the biological activity in a sample. In many cases, a crude natural source material can be processed in one or two steps, e.g., solvent extraction of whole fermentation broth followed by adsorption/elution of target metabolites from a column containing a hydrophobic resin, to provide an extract suitable for preparative HPLC. Once sufficient material has been isolated for structural identification, the investigator can capitalize on this knowledge in the design of more refined HPLC methodologies for further isolation.

3.2. Sample Preparation

The importance of sample preparation for HPLC cannot be overemphasized. This is particularly true for ionizable metabolites whose retention under reverse phase conditions will vary with pH and for polar metabolites whose retention is relatively poor. The nearer the solvent composition of the sample is to that of the mobile phase, the greater the chance of success in a preparative HPLC experiment. If possible, the proportion of organic solvent in the sample should be kept to less than, or equal to, its proportion in the mobile phase for reverse phase chromatography.

3.3. Mobile Phase Buffering/pH Control

When isolating a metabolite from a highly heterogeneous natural source material, this author recommends the general use of mobile phase additives such as acids and inorganic buffers; the heterogeneous (and often uncharacterized) nature of many natural product samples means that such additives frequently enhance chromatographic performance and reproducibility. When scaling up and increasing sample load to a maximum, this can be particularly relevant. Such mobile phase additives are easy to remove from product-containing fractions, and concerns about buffer removal should not be a deterrent to their use.

In conclusion, therefore, the increasing availability of high-quality chromatographic supports, solvents, and robust reliable instrumentation means that HPLC is now a mainstream technique in the natural products chemistry laboratory and should be considered along with other chromatographic techniques as early as is practicable during a natural product isolation. In this author's opinion, a reverse phase column provides the most sensible first choice when seeking to isolate a metabolite of unknown character from a natural extract, since most metabolites bind to some extent to such supports and will be soluble in either water, a water-miscible organic solvent (e.g., methanol, acetonitrile, THF), or a mixture of these. The choice of stationary and mobile phase will obviously be influenced by the information available concerning the target metabolite(s) and on the other components of the sample.

References

1. Edwards, C., Lawton, L. A., Coyle, S. M., and Ross, P. (1996) Automated purification of microcystins. *J. Chromatogr. A* **734,** 175–182.
2. Sakuma, S. and Motomura, H. (1987) Purification of saikosaponins a, c and d. Application of large scale reversed-phase high-performance liquid chromatography. *J. Chromatogr.* **400,** 293–295.
3. Blows, W. M., Foster, G., Lane, S. L., Noble, D., Piercey, J. E., Sidebottom, P. J., and Webb, G. (1994) The squalestatins, novel inhibitors of squalene synthase produced by a species of *Phomac.* V. Minor metobolites. *J. Antibiotics* **47,** 740–754.
4. Takesako, K., Ikai, K., Haruna, F., Endo, M., Shimanaka, K., Sono, E., Nakamura, T., and Kato, I. (1991) Aureobasidins, new antifungal antibiotics. Taxonomy, fermentation, isolation and properties. *J. Antibiotics* **44,** 919–924.
5. Ritzau, M., Phillips, S., and Zeeck, A. (1993) Metabolic products of microorganisms 268. Obscurolides, a novel class of phosphodiesterase inhibitors from *Streptomyces.* II. Minor components belonging to the obscurolide B to D series. *J. Antibiot.* **46,** 1625–1628.
6. Shin, T.-S. and Godber, S. (1994) Isolation of four tocopherols and four tocotrienols from a variety of natural sources by semi-preparative HPLC. *J. Chromatogr. A* **678,** 49–58.
7. Grant, R. (1992) Properties of chromatographic solvents. *LC/GC Int.* **5,** 25 (selected data reproduced with permission).
8. Shelley, P. R. (1996) High performance liquid chromatography, in *Downstream Processing of Natural Products* (Verrall, M. S., ed.), Wiley, Chichester, UK.
9. Bycroft, B. W., Maslen, C., Box, S. J., Brown, A. G., and Tyler, J. W. (1987) The isolation of (3R,5R) and (3S,5R)-carbapenam-3-carboxylic acid from *Serratia* and *Erwinia* sp. and their putative biosynthetic role. *J. Chem. Soc. Chem. Comm.* 1623–1625.
10. Vigh, G., Quintero, G., and Farkas, G. (1989) Displacement chromatography on cyclodextrin-silicas. 1. Separation of positional and geometrical isomers in the reversed-phase mode. *J. Chromatogr.* **484,** 237–250.
11. Kubo, I. and Nakatsu, T. (1991) Recent examples of preparative-scale recycling high performance liquid chromatography in natural products chemistry. *LC/GC Int.* **4,** 37–42.
12. Trease, G. E. and Evans, W. C. (1983) Phenols and phenol glycosides, in *Pharmacognosy,* Balliere Tindall, Eastbourne, UK, pp. 368–415.
13. Isaksson, R., Liljefors, T., and Reinholdsson, P. (1984) Preparative separation of the enantiomers of trans,trans- and cis,trans-dimethyl 1,7-dioxaspiro-[5.5]undecane, main pheromone component of *Adrena* bees, by liquid chromatography on triacetylcellulose. *J. Chem. Soc. Chem. Commun.* 137–138.
14. Weems, H. B. and Yang, S. K. (1982) Resolution of optical isomers by chiral high performance liquid chromatography: separation of dihydrodiols and tetrahydrodiols of benzo[a]pyrene and benz[a]anthracene. *Anal. Biochem.* **125,** 156–161.

Suggested Readings

1. Bidlingmeyer, B. A., ed. (1987) *Preparative Liquid Chromatography, J. Chromatography Library 38,* Elsevier, Amsterdam.

2. Bidlingmeyer, B. A. (1992) *Practical HPLC Methodology and Applications*, Wiley, New York.
3. Lim, C. K., ed. (1986) *HPLC of Small Molecules; A Practical Approach*, IRL, Oxford, UK.
4. Hostettmann, K., Hostettmann, M., and Marston, A. (1986) *Preparative Chromatography Techniques; Applications in Natural Product Isolation*, Springer-Verlag, Berlin, Germany.
5. Shelley, P. R. (1996) High performance liquid chromatography, in *Downstream Processing of Natural Products* (Verrall, M. S., ed.), Wiley, Chichester, UK.
6. Dolan, J. W., ed. LC troubleshooting; monthly articles published in *LC/GC Int.* Aster, Eugene, OR.

7

Isolation by Planar Chromatography

Simon Gibbons and Alexander I. Gray

1. Introduction

Planar liquid chromatography (PLC) involves the separation of mixtures on thin layers of adsorbents that are usually coated on glass, plastic, or aluminium sheets. The most common form of planar liquid chromatography is thin-layer chromatography (TLC); and this particular technique is the easiest, cheapest, and most widely used method for the isolation of natural products. TLC is one of the oldest forms of chromatography, the simplest example being the school experiment of spotting a plant extract near the bottom of thin strips of blotting paper and "developing" in a jar with water or alcohol. As the water moves up the blotting paper, the dark extract is separated into its component colors of light and dark greens and yellows.

The aim of this chapter is to describe the basic principles behind this technique and to give procedures for analyzing extracts and isolating natural products so that the worker unfamiliar with TLC and related techniques may use this simple method to follow and to isolate novel natural products. Examples of TLC isolations, chiefly from plants, will be given and the methodology behind the isolation of unknown products will be discussed. Success in TLC (like all forms of chromatography!) relies on a flexible approach and—by having a variety of methods at your disposal—versatility almost always guarantees success.

Natural product extracts are generally complex and comprise mixtures of neutral, acidic, basic, lipophilic, hydrophilic, and amphiphilic (e.g., amino acids) compounds and, as a consequence, there is rarely one method that will serve for all eventualities. It is sometimes worthwhile to carry out ^{1}H or ^{13}C NMR spectroscopy of the extract or fraction to determine the class of compound(s) to be separated (1)—deuterated NMR solvents are cheap ($1.00 for CDCl$_3$) and 1 D NMR experiments are quicker to run than the extensive

From: *Methods in Biotechnology, Vol. 4: Natural Products Isolation*
Edited by: R. J. P. Cannell © Humana Press Inc., Totowa, NJ

development of mobile and stationary phases that may be needed. The starting point should always be the simplest method; examples for the isolation of a variety of natural products are given in **Subheading 5.**

1.1. Basic Principles of TLC

Separation by TLC is effected by the application of the mixture or extract as a spot or thin line onto a sorbent that has been applied to a backing plate (**Fig. 1**). Analytical TLC plates (thickness 0.1–0.2 mm) are commercially available; e.g., the commonest analytical silica gel plate is the 20 × 20-cm, plastic or aluminium backed Kieselgel 60 F_{254} plate, which has a 0.2 -mm thickness of silica sorbent (Merck no. 5554, Darmstadt, Germany).

The plate is then placed into a tank with sufficient suitable solvent to just wet the lower edge of the plate/sorbent but not enough to wet the part of the plate where the spots were applied (origin). The solvent front then migrates up the plate through the sorbent by capillary action, a process known as development (**Fig. 2**).

An important factor in quantifying migration of a compound on a particular sorbent and solvent system is the R_f value. This is defined as:

$$R_f = \frac{\text{Compound distance from origin (midpoint)}}{\text{Solvent front distance from origin}}$$

In the example shown in **Fig. 2**:

$$R_f = \frac{\text{Compound distance from origin}}{\text{Solvent front distance from origin}} = \frac{2.3 \text{ cm}}{2.8 \text{ cm}}$$

$$R_f = 0.82$$

R_f values are always ratios, are never greater than 1, and vary depending on sorbent and/or solvent system. These values are sometimes quoted as hR_f, i.e., relative to solvent front = 100, $hR_f = R_f \times 100$ (in our case $hR_f = 82$). In the case of adsorption chromatography (*see* **Subheading 1.2.1.**), where the sorbent is silica (i.e., a normal phase), polar compounds (e.g., 2) have a higher affinity for the sorbent (stationary phase), "stick" to the sorbent, and move slowly up the plate as the solvent (mobile phase) migrates. These compounds will have relatively small R_f values in this example. Nonpolar compounds (e.g., Compound 1) have less affinity for the stationary phase, will move comparatively quickly up the plate, and therefore have relatively larger R_f values. As a consequence of development, compounds of a mixture will separate according to their relative polarities. Polarity is related to the type and number of functional groups present on a molecule capable of hydrogen-bonding (cf. 1.2):

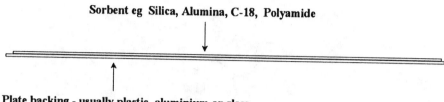

Fig. 1. Basic TLC plate layout.

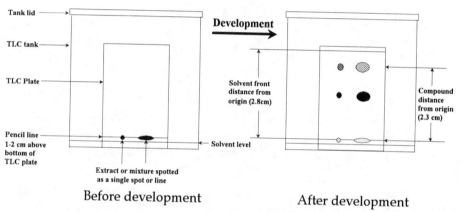

Before development   After development

Fig. 2. Simple TLC equipment and procedure.

1. Nonpolar groups: CH_3-, CH_3O-, $Ph-$, CH_3CH_2, and
2. Polar groups: $-CO_2H$, $-OH$, $-NH_2$, SO_3H, PO_3H_2.

Compound 1 would be considered to be a relatively nonpolar compound compared with **Compound 2**, but it should be noted that this relative polarity will vary according to the type of stationary phase and mobile phase used.

Solvent strengths are also measured in terms of polarity, and dielectric constants are generally used to quantify relative strengths (**Table 1**). A high dielectric constant indicates a polar solvent with a strong power of elution, and a low dielectric constant indicates a nonpolar solvent with a lower ability to elute a component from a sorbent. This elution strength applies to normal phase adsorption chromatography.

1.2. Mechanisms of Separation

There are four basic mechanisms of chromatography by which separation can occur, and more than one mechanism may be responsible during a given separation:

1. Adsorption chromatography—The most commonly used sorbents utilized in this form of chromatography are silica and alumina. As the components move through

Compound 1. Artemisinin (from the antimalarial herb *Artemisia annua*).

Compound 2. Psilocybin (from the fungus *Psilocybe mexicana*).

Table 1
Dielectric Constants of Solvents

Solvent	Dielectric constant (20°C)
Pentane	1.8
Hexane	1.9
Cyclohexane	2.0
Benzene[a]	2.3
Toluene	2.4
Diethyl ether	4.3
Dimethyl sulfoxide	4.7
Chloroform	4.8
Ethyl acetate[a]	6.0
Acetic acid	6.2
Dichloromethane	9.1
Pyridine	12.3
Acetone[a]	20.7
Methanol	32.6
Acetonitrile	37.5
Water	78.5

[a]Compounds recorded at 25°C *(2)*.

the sorbent, their relative rates of migration are affected by their individual affinities for the sorbent. Separation occurs when one compound is more strongly adsorbed by the sorbent than the other components. When the sorbent is silica or alumina, polar natural products move slowly compared to nonpolar natural products. Adsorption takes place because of the interaction between the compound and groups associated with the sorbent; in the case of silica, which has silanol groups (**Fig. 3**), binding occurs between the compound and free hydroxyls on the sorbent. In this particular case, adsorption involves hydrogen bonding between compound functional groups and adsorbent surface hydroxyl groups.

2. Partition chromatography—This mechanism involves the relative solubility of the compound between the sorbent (stationary phase) and the solvent (mobile phase). Compounds that are more soluble in the mobile phase will migrate up the plate to a greater extent than components that are more soluble in the stationary phase. Reverse phase TLC utilizes sorbents that partition natural products between a hydrophobic, fatty (lipid) stationary phase, and an aqueous mobile phase. The most commonly used reverse phase sorbent is silica that has been reacted with a straight-chain 18 carbon alkyl unit to form an octadecasilyl phase (ODS), and there are a variety of slightly more polar phases commercially available (**Fig. 4**). Nonpolar "fatty" compounds such as the sesquiterpene artemisinin (**Compound 1**) are readily "soluble" in stationary phases such as ODS; and during solvent development a partition is set up between the two phases. Separation is effected by compounds partitioning to different extents between the stationary phase and mobile phase.

3. Size-inclusion/-exclusion chromatography—Compounds may be separated by their relative sizes and by their inclusion (or exclusion) into the sorbent. The most commonly used size-inclusion sorbents are the dextran gels, particularly the lipophilic versions such as Sephadex LH-20, which are of most use for the separation of small hydrophobic natural products from their larger "contaminants," usually chlorophylls, and so on. In organic solvents such as chloroform and methanol these gels swell to form a matrix. As compounds migrate with the solvent through the gel, small molecules become included into the gel matrix and larger molecules are excluded and migrate at a greater rate. It should be noted that separations on gels such as Sephadex LH-20 also involve the mechanisms of adsorption, partition, and possibly ion exchange, and occasionally the trend of larger molecules eluting first and smaller molecules eluting last may be reversed. This form of chromatography has found considerable use in the removal of "interfering" plant pigments such as the chlorophylls, which tend to be larger and more lipophilic than many plant products. This class of chromatography is more usually carried out in open-column form and is less commonly used as a mechanism of separation for TLC, which generally relies on the mechanisms of adsorption and partition.

4. Ion-exchange chromatography—This technique is limited to mixtures containing components that can carry a charge. In this form of chromatography, the sorbent is usually a polymeric resin that contains charged groups and mobile counter-ions, which may exchange with ions of a component as the mobile phase

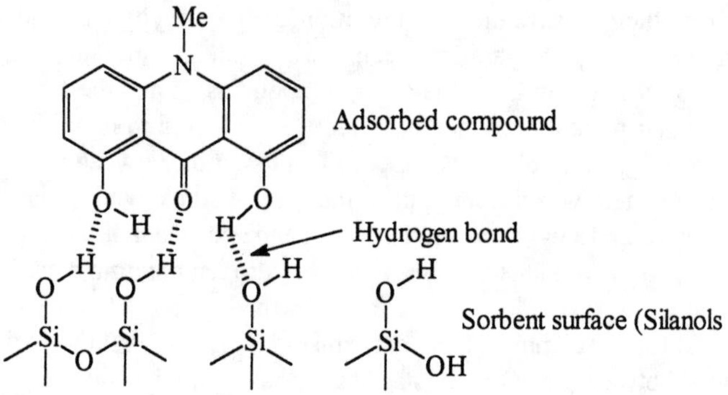

Fig. 3. Adsorption and hydrogen bonding between compound and sorbent face.

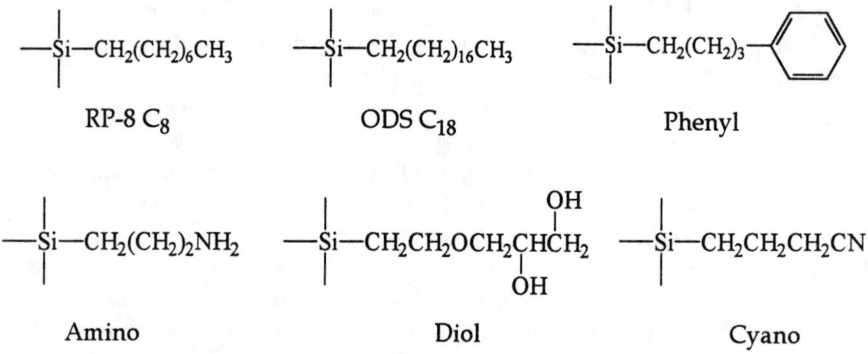

Fig. 4. Common phases for partition chromatography.

migrates through the sorbent. Separation is achieved by differences in affinity between ionic components and the stationary phase.

In cation exchange, acidic groups such as $-CO_2H$ and $-SO_3H$ are incorporated into the resin and are able to exchange their protons with other cations of components to form $-CO_2^-$, H_3O^+, and $-SO_3^-$, H_3O^+, respectively, at particular pH ranges. In anion exchange, basic groups such as quaternary ammonium moieties ($-N^+R_3$), are incorporated into the resin and are able to exchange their anions with anions of components. As with size-exclusion chromatography, this form of separation is generally used in columns, but can be utilized for separations on thin layers.

1.3. Applications of TLC

Traditionally, analytical TLC has found application in the detection and monitoring of compounds through a separation process. In the case of known natural products or other compounds (e.g., pharmaceuticals), qualitative and quantitative information can be gathered concerning the presence or absence

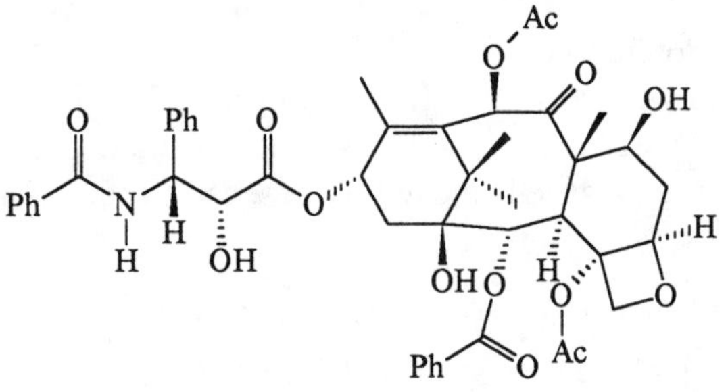

Solvent System
(1) CHCl$_3$-MeCN, (7:3)
(2) CHCl$_3$-MeOH, (7:1)
(3) CH$_2$Cl$_2$-THF, (6:2)
(4) EtOAc-iPrOH (95:5)

(3)

Fig. 5. TLC solvent systems for the resolution of taxol (Compound 3).

of a metabolite or breakdown product. An excellent example of this is the production of the antitumor diterpene taxol (**Compound 3**), from the endophytic fungus *Taxomyces andreanae*. Stierle et al. *(3)* isolated fungal taxol that had R_f values identical to that of taxol from the Pacific Yew, *Taxus brevifolia*, on four different solvent systems (**Fig. 5**). Use of the four solvent systems gave a higher degree of confidence that the fungal compound was identical to taxol, although the authors did confirm this by mass spectrometry and immunochemistry. Analytical TLC has been used to chemically classify organisms by their chemical constituents, in particular the filamentous bacteria, the Actinomycetes. The important genus *Streptomyces* generally contains a LL stereoisomer of a cell-wall metabolite known as diaminopimelic acid, whereas the rarer genera possess the *meso* form of this metabolite. By hydrolyzing the organism cell wall and running a TLC of the hydrolysate against the two standards, it is possible to classify loosely the actinomycete *(4)*.

Natural products may be "tracked" by running analytical TLC of fractions from other separation processes, such as column chromatography or HPLC. More than one solvent system should always be used for a TLC separation, as even apparently "pure" spots may consist of several compounds with identical R_f values. The similarity of different extracts from the same species can also be assessed in this way, and the decision to combine nonpolar and polar extracts can be made on the basis of identical or similar TLC chromatograms. Qualitative initial screening of extracts should be routinely performed, and the presence of ubiquitous compounds such as plant sterols and certain phenolics can be ascertained at an early stage by running the appropriate standard alongside an extract. In certain cases; classes of compounds may be determined by spraying developed plates with stains that give a color reaction with a particular compound class (*see* **Subheading 3.**).

Many natural products are still isolated by conventional preparative TLC (PTLC) and examples can be found in the journals *Phytochemistry* and *Journal of Natural Products*. Although preparative HPLC is in "vogue" and is often the method of choice, PTLC is still a very useful isolation method in many cases because of its simplicity, cost, speed, and ability to separate compounds in the 1 mg to 1 g range.

2. System Selection

As much information as possible regarding the extract-producing organism should be gathered—this will aid in the selection of a separation system. After a full literature search, the following points will need to be addressed: Has the species been studied before? If so, what metabolites were isolated? Are there standard TLC methods available? If the chemistry of a species has not been studied, is there any information at the generic level? Chemotaxonomy, or the classification of an organism according to its natural products, may assist in assigning chemically undefined genera *(5)*—related species *may* produce related secondary metabolites—forewarned is forearmed!

Databases such as NAPRALERT, Berdy, The Dictionary of Natural Products, Chemical Abstracts, and, in the case of plants, certain excellent classical texts such as Hegnauers' "Chemotaxonomie der Pflanzen" *(6)* can give a great deal of information regarding the classes of natural products present in certain taxa.

Information about semipurified samples (e.g., column fractions) can also be invaluable. Several workers *(1,7)* routinely record ^{1}H NMR spectra of column fractions prior to TLC purification. This may seem a rather expensive detection system, but much information can be gathered about the classes of compounds present, and a separation method can be tailored accordingly.

TLC on silica gel is still the most common method of TLC though it suffers from some drawbacks. These however, may usually be overcome easily:

1. Acidic compounds "tail" on silica because of interactions between acidic groups (e.g., –CO_2H, –OH) and silanols—This may be reduced by the addition of a small amount of acid (e.g., 1% trifluroacetic acid or acetic acid) to the mobile phase, which will maintain acidic groups in a nonionized form.
2. Basic compounds also may behave poorly (i.e., tail, streak) on silica; the addition of weak bases (e.g., 1% diethylamine or triethylamine) should eradicate poor chromatography.
3. Highly nonpolar compounds such as fatty acids, glycerides, alkanes, and some lower terpenoids require simple nonpolar solvent systems (e.g., cyclohexane, hexane, pentane, diethyl ether:hexane mixtures) and may be difficult to detect by UV (i.e., no chromophore) or by spray detection (use charring reagents, e.g., vanillin-sulfuric acid).
4. Highly polar metabolites such as sugars, glycosides, tannins, polyphenolics, and certain alkaloids require the development of polar mobile phases, and in some

cases such compounds may be irreversibly adsorbed onto silica. Choice of mobile phase should evolve through use of a mono or binary system, i.e., 100% $CHCl_3$ or Hexane:EtOAc (1:1) as a starting point and then on to the addition of acids or bases to improve chromatography, i.e., a ternary system such as toluene:ethyl acetate:acetic acid (60:38:2) and as a last resort to use of quaternary system, e.g., hexane:ethyl acetate:formic acid:water (4:4:1:1).

Normal phase plates (silica, alumina) should be stored in a dessicator, as they are prone to pick up water from the atmosphere and become deactivated (lose their ability to resolve compounds). In some cases, plates may be activated by drying in an oven before use.

2.1. Forms of Development

In isocratic development, a solvent of constant composition is used to effect separation; for example, 40% ethyl acetate in hexane. This may be extended to continuous development, in which the TLC plate is left in an isocratic system after the solvent front has reached the top of the TLC plate. This has the advantage that closely eluting bands may be resolved through the use of a nonpolar solvent over several hours. A major disadvantage of this technique is that unstable compounds may degenerate on the adsorbent during this lengthy time period.

In multiple development, the plate is developed, removed from the tank, dried, and then subjected to further development(s). Multiple development may be run isocratically or by use of a step gradient.

In step-gradient TLC, the plate is developed in a nonpolar system (e.g., 10% ethyl acetate in hexane), dried, and then developed in a system of increased polarity (e.g., 20% ethyl acetate in hexane). This method allows great control over a separation in that the polarity may be very gradually increased to achieve separation of closely eluting bands.

2.1.1. Choice of Development

The decision as to whether the system is to be run isocratically or by using a step gradient can be made by running a series of analytical plates with the sample and varying the mobile phase composition. **Table 2** lists some of the more commonly used systems.

3. Detection of Natural Products in TLC

Both at the analytical and preparative stages of TLC, effective visualization or detection is crucial to obtain pure compounds, and poor detection may result in low recovery of product from the sorbent. Detection is either nondestructive, following which the compounds may be recovered from the sorbent (e.g., ultraviolet [UV] detection), or destructive, by which the compounds are contaminated by the detection reagent and are unrecoverable from the sorbent

Table 2
Simple Systems for TLC

Solvent system	Sorbent	Notes
Hexane:Ethyl acetate (EtOAc)	Silica gel	Universal system—can substitute hexane for petroleum spirit or pentane.
Petrol:Diethyl ether (Et$_2$O)	Silica gel	A universal system for relatively nonpolar metabolites. Excellent for terpenes and fatty acids. Care should be taken with Et$_2$O as explosive mixtures are formed with air.
Petrol:Chloroform (CHCl$_3$)	Silica gel	Considerably useful for the separation of cinnamic acid derivatives, particularly coumarins.
Toluene:Ethyl acetate:Acetic acid (TEA)	Silica gel	Vary the composition, e.g., 80:18:2 or 60:38:2—excellent for acidic metabolites.
CHCl$_3$:Acetone	Silica gel	A general system for medium-polarity products.
Benzene:Acetone	Silica gel	Useful for the separation of aromatic products. Care should be taken as benzene is a highly carcinogenic solvent. Substitute toluene for benzene.
Butanol:Acetic acid:Water	Silica gel	A polar system for flavonoid and glycosides.
Butanol:Water:Pyridine: Toluene	Silica gel	Sugar analysis system. Try 10:6:6:1. Development may take 4 h on a standard 20 × 20-cm plate.
Methanol:Water	C$_{18}$	Start with 100% MeOH to determine if metabolite will move from the origin. Increase water concentration to slow migration of metabolites. The addition of small amounts of acid or base may improve chromatography.
Acetonitrile:Water	C$_{18}$/C$_2$	A universal simple reverse phase system.
Methanol:Water	Polyamide	Universal.
Methanol:Water	Cellulose	Used for the separation of highly polar compounds such as sugars and glycosides.

(spray detection). There are some excellent texts available on this subject, such as Wagner, Bladt, and Zgainski's *Plant Drug Analysis (8)* or *The Merck Handbook of Dyeing Reagents for Thin Layer and Paper Chromatography (9)*; these will cover most eventualities.

3.1. Ultraviolet Detection

UV detection involves the use of UV active compounds (indicators) that are incorporated into the sorbent of TLC plates by the manufacturer. Typical examples of plates with these sorbents include the range of analytical plates produced by Merck: Alumina, 0.2 mm thick, 20 × 20 cm, with a 254-nm UV indicator (Merck no. 5550). Under short-wavelength UV light (254 nm), the indicator, which is usually a manganese-activated zinc silicate, will emit a pale green light. Under long-wave UV light (366 nm), a further indicator will emit a pale purple light. Compounds that absorb light at either 254 or 366 nm will appear as dark spots against a light background when UV light is shone onto the plate. Many compounds, such as the furocoumarins, will also emit a distinctive blue or yellow fluorescence under UV light. Long wavelength (366 nm) light is normally used for compounds that fluoresce, e.g., yellow, orange, blue, or red, as is the case for some chlorophylls. The major disadvantage with UV detection is that compounds that do not absorb UV light at 254 or 366 nm will be invisible and will require spray detection. The primary advantage of UV detection is that it is generally nondestructive and detection of compounds can be observed very readily through a separation process. It should be noted, however, that UV light can promote free radical reactions with certain natural products. UV lamps are widely commercially available from suppliers such as CAMAG (Camag Ref. 022.9230). Care should be taken not to shine light from these lamps into eyes or onto skin, as UV light is mutagenic.

3.2. Spray Detection

This relies on a color reaction between the compound on the TLC plate and a spray reagent (stain) introduced onto the plate as a fine mist from a spray canister. Ten of the most common spray reagents are listed in **Table 3**. Most are universal reagents and will react with many classes of natural products; the most widely used sprays are (1)–(3). Dragendorffs reagent (spray [6]) is especially useful for the detection of many classes of alkaloids and is well worth the effort required to make it. In some cases, heat is required to assist the color reaction and this can be supplied in the form of a hand-held heater (hair dryer!) or a drying oven. All of the compounds required to make the spray reagents are readily available as are the ready-made spray solutions themselves, from suppliers such as Sigma or Aldrich. Each of the spray reagents should be made up and used in a fume cupboard. The subject of partial identification of natural products by spray detection is also discussed in Chapter 10.

When using spray detection in preparative TLC, most of the plate should be covered and only a small proportion of the edge (2 cm) sprayed with reagent. Ideally, a scalpel should be used to score a line 2 cm in from the plate edge so that after spraying, corrosive spray reagent does not migrate into the sorbent and react with compounds to be recovered.

Table 3
Some Simple Spray Reagents for Natural Products TLC Visualization

Detection spray	Recipe	Treatment	Notes
(1) Vanillin/Sulfuric acid	Dissolve vanillin (4 g) in concentrated H_2SO_4 (100 mL).	Heat at 100°C until coloration appears.	A universal spray. Many terpenes give red and blue colors. Natural products with little functionality may give poor coloration—try spray (2). Spray and heat in a fume cupboard.
(2) Phosphomolybdic acid (PMA)	Dissolve PMA in ethanol to make a 5% (w/v) solution.	Heat at 100°C until coloration appears.	Useful to detect many terpenes as blue spots on a yellow background. Spray and heat in a fume cupboard.
(3) Ammonium molybdate (VI)	Dissolve ammonium molybdate (VI) (10 g) in concentrated H_2SO_4 (100 mL).	Spray onto plate and heat at 100°C until coloration appears.	A universal spray. Many diterpenes give a blue color. Spray and heat in a fume cupboard.
(4) Antimony (III) chloride	Dissolve antimony (III) chloride in a mixture of glacial acetic acid (20 mL) and chloroform (60 mL).	Spray onto plate and heat at 100°C for 2–5 min or until coloration appears.	Di- and triterpenes give a red-to-blue coloration. Care should be taken when handling this spray as antimony compounds are highly poisonous. Spray and heat in a fume cupboard.
(5) Tin (IV) chloride	Add tin (IV) chloride (10 mL) to a mixture of chloroform (80 mL) and glacial acetic acid (80 mL).	Spray onto plate and heat for 5 min at 100°C or until coloration appears.	Useful for the detection of flavanoids and terpenes. Tin (IV) chloride is poisonous and a lachrymator. Spray and heat in a fume cupboard.

Reagent	Preparation	Procedure	Notes
(6) Dragendorff's Reagent	Add 10 mL of 40% aqueous solution of KI to 10 mL of solution of 0.85 g of basic bismuth subnitrate in acetic acid (10 mL) and distilled water (50 mL). Dilute the resulting solution with acetic acid and water in the ratio 1:2:10.	Generally no heat is required, but if reaction is not spontaneous, heat until coloration appears. The procedure may be enhanced by decolorizing the plate with concentrated ammonia vapor.	This is the traditional method for alkaloid detection although care should be taken as some non-alkaloids such as iridoids and some flavonoids give a positive reaction. Alkaloids give a dark orange-to-red coloration.
(7) 2,4 Dinitro-phenyl hydrazine	Dissolve 2,4-dinitro-phenylhydrazine (0.2 g) in 2 N HCl (50 mL).	Generally no heat is required, but if reaction is not spontaneous heat until coloration appears.	Detects aldehydes and ketones with a yellow-to-red coloration.
(8) Perchloric acid	A 20% (w/v) aqueous perchloric acid solution.	Heat at 100°C until coloration appears.	A universal spray but is especially useful for steroids and triterpenes.
(9) Borntrager Reagent	A 10% (w/v) ethanolic solution of KOH.	Heat until coloration appears.	For the detection of coumarins and anthraquinones.
(10) Ninhydrin	Add ninhydrin (0.3 g) to a mixture of butanol (100 mL) and acetic acid (3 mL).	Heat at 100°C until coloration appears.	Especially useful for amino acids, amines, and as a general alkaloid spray. Alkaloids appear as a red coloration.

(continued)

Detection spray	Recipe	Treatment	Notes
(11) Ehrlich Reagent	Spray first with solution of 1 g 4-dimethylamino benzaldehyde in 100 mL 36% HCl/MeOH (3:1), then dimethylamino benzaldehyde in 100 mL ethanol.	Place for 5 min in tank saturated with HCl vapour (or spray with 25% HCl). Gently warm.	Detection of amines, indoles, ergot alkaloids.
(12) Anisaldehyde/sulfuric	Add 1 mL conc. H_2SO_4 to 50 mL acetic acid containing 0.5 mL anisaldehyde.	Heat at 100°C until coloration appears.	Detection of many compounds, especially terpenes, sugars, phenols, and steroids.
(13) Bial's Reagent (Orcinol-ferric chloride)	Add 10 mL 10% H_2SO_4 containing 1 g ferric chloride to 1 mL 6% orcinol/ethanol.	Heat at 100°C for 10–15 min or until coloration appears.	Particularly useful for detection of sugars.
(14) Triphenyl-tetrazolium chloride	Add 10 mL 4% triphenyl-tetrazolium chloride/MeOH to 10 mL 1 N NaOH.	Heat at 100°C until coloration appears.	Detection of reducing sugars, corticosteroids.
(15) Fluorescein	0.01% fluorescein/ethanol.	Heat gently, then spray lightly with water or treat with steam.	Detection of lipids.
(16) Ferric chloride	5% ferric chloride in 0.5 N HCl.	Generally no heat required, or heat gently.	For detection of phenolics.

4. Preparative TLC (PTLC)

Preparative TLC (PTLC) has long been a popular method of isolation, primarily because of its simplicity and universal accessibility to students and researchers working in natural products chemistry. This popularity has been diminished in recent years because of the success of high-performance liquid chromatography and countercurrent chromatography. Unlike these two techniques, however, PTLC does not require expensive equipment; separations can be effected rapidly and the amount of material isolated generally falls into the 1 mg to 1 g range, which is certainly sufficient for structure elucidation purposes. This section gives a breakdown of the basic steps of PTLC, with emphasis on preparing and running plates, and some of the advantages and disadvantages of PTLC.

4.1. When to Use PTLC

Although separations depend on the level of complexity of an extract, PTLC is nearly always used as a final purification step in an isolation procedure. A broad procedure is given below.

Biomass (Plant,   Nonpolar extract   Column Chromatography
Microbe, Insect, $\xrightarrow{\text{Extraction}}$ Partition $\nearrow$ $\searrow$ VLC, CC, Flash, HPLC → PTLC
or Marine) $\searrow$Polar extract $\nearrow$ More than one step?

The number of compounds that can be separated on a preparative plate will ultimately depend on how those compounds behave on a particular system, but as a general rule, the separation of no more than a mixture of four major components should be attempted. The separation of complex mixtures can be carried out on preparative TLC as a first stage but larger amounts of material are needed, and as the process of running many plates can be time-consuming, it is more usual to separate partially purified mixtures. Complex extracts can, in the first instance, be separated by vacuum liquid chromatography, flash chromatography, or column chromatography prior to PTLC. These first purification steps are covered in Chapter 4.

The friedelane triterpene (**Compund 4**) was isolated from the bark of the Camerounian rainforest tree *Phyllobotryon spathulatum (10)* using the separation process in **Table 4**.

This triterpene needed only one purification step prior to preparative TLC, and because of its lack of distinctive chromophore, required visualization by spray detection using vanillin reagent (**Table 3**).

4.2. Scale-Up from Analytical to PTLC

The scale-up procedure from analytical (0.1- to 0.2-mm sorbent thickness) to preparative TLC (0.5- to 4-mm sorbent thickness) is of paramount impor-

Species	Extract	Step (1)	Step (2)	Structure
Phyllobotryon *spathulatum*	Petrol and CHCl$_3$ (Bark)	VLC on Silica gel. Fraction eluted with 25% EtOAc in Hexane.	Prep TLC Toluene 80 EtOAc 18 AcOH 2	4

tance, as changing the size of a separation can drastically affect the chromatography of natural products. The chromatography of a compound separated on analytical plates where 1 mg of material is involved can alter significantly when milligrams or tens of milligrams are employed. This is possibly attributable to sorbent particle size. On normal phase silica, when moving from analytical to preparative scale, it may be necessary to reduce the polarity of the solvent markedly in order to achieve the same R_f values. Very often this is a trial and error procedure, but as an example, the separation of a mixture of two components achieved using hexane:EtOAc (60:40) as a mobile phase on an analytical plate would possibly require the less polar system hexane:EtOAc (90:10) on a preparative plate to give comparable R_f values. This is a general rule and will vary according to compound class and the types of stationary phases used—the best method being the sacrifice of a small portion of mixture, and experimentation.

4.3. Commercially Available PTLC plates

These plates are usually limited to the sorbents, silica, alumina, C$_{18}$, and cellulose and are usually of thicknesses 0.5, 1.0, and 2.0 mm. The glass-backed silica-gel 60 plates from Merck have a particle-size distribution of 5–40 µm, compared to the corresponding analytical plate of 5–20 µm. These silica plates have a high specific surface area, are very homogeneous, and usually give excellent results.

The use of commercially available preparative plates with a concentration zone will enhance separation. This zone is a layer of inert large-pore silica at the bottom of the plate onto which the sample is applied. As the solvent migrates through this zone, the mixture is unretained and focuses at the interface between the zone and "normal" sorbent. Uneven applications of mixtures are focused as discrete lines, and this will greatly improve separation/resolution.

Normal phase plates such as the 2-mm Merck Kieselgel 60F$_{254}$ 20 × 20-cm plate (Merck no. 5717) require pre-elution with a nonpolar solvent such as dichloromethane to "clean" and remove contaminants. These impurities will be carried with the solvent to the top of the plate, and then the plates should be dried prior to use. When a new box is opened, unused plates should be stored in a desiccator as moisture from the air will affect the activity of the sorbent (especially in the case of silica), resulting in poor resolution and poor separation.

4.4. Homemade Preparative Plates

Making your own plates allows greater flexibility of choice of sorbent and, whereas commercial plates are restricted to three or four sorbents, with the correct recipe, homemade plates offer much wider scope for experimentation. These plates also allow the variation of thickness to accommodate the separation of large amounts of material. Binders such as calcium sulphate (gypsum) are require to bind the sorbent to the plate, but some silica sorbents (e.g., Merck 7749) contain sufficient binder for the purpose. Preparing your own plates will also give you the choice of selecting a sorbent with or without a UV indicator and will also enable the incorporation of additives that enhance separation into the sorbent. An example of this (recipe shown below) is the addition of a small quantity of silver nitrate to a silica sorbent that aids the resolution of olefinic compounds.

If cost is an issue, making plates is cheaper than the commercial alternative, and the removal of sorbent from the plate backing during the desorption process is easier than on commercial plates—a point to consider if compounds are poorly resolved. The following example is a method for making silica preparative plates of 0.5 mm thickness with optional silver nitrate additive. For plates of 1 or 2 mm thickness, two or four times the amount of water and sorbent are required, and all of the equipment is readily available from suppliers such as CAMAG or Merck.

Equipment: 5 glass backing plates (20 × 20 cm), adjustable gate applicator, 2 glass spacer plates (5 × 20 cm), Kieselgel 60 (45 g) Merck 7749, plate holder, silver nitrate (1 g) (optional), TLC plate coater, distilled water (90 mL), 200-mL conical flask, and stopper.

4.4.1. Procedure

1. Clean the glass backing plates with 1 N aqueous KOH and then acetone and dry prior to spreading.
2. Place the plates into the TLC plate coater with spacer plates at either end. Adjust the applicator to the correct plate thickness required (0.5 mm in this case) and place at one end on the spacer plate.
3. Put silica (45 g) or alternative sorbent and the silver nitrate (if required) into the conical flask and add deionized water (90 mL). Shake the stoppered conical flask vigorously for 30 s and ensure that a homogeneous slurry is produced.
4. Immediately pour the slurry into the applicator, and in one steady movement pull the applicator across the plate faces to rest on the far plate spacer.
5. Air-dry the plates for 1 h and then put into a plate holder and activate in an oven at 115°C for 4 h prior to use.

This general method may be applied to other sorbents though additional binder may be necessary. When incorporating silver nitrate into the sorbent, the plates should be stored and developed in the dark to avoid discoloration and degeneration of the sorbent.

4.5. Sample Application

Preparative plates such as those mentioned above should be removed from the oven and allowed to cool to room temperature before use. The sample to be separated should be dissolved in the minimum volume of solvent possible (usually in the concentration range 10–20 mg/mL). This sample is then applied near to the bottom of the plate (~1.5 cm from the bottom) as a thin line (2–4 mm wide) using either a microsyringe, a capillary, or a pasteur pipet that has been drawn out over a Bunsen burner. Thinner capillaries (5–10 µL) give greater control over sample application and result in a finer, more concentrated zone. In order to apply the sample in a straight fashion, it is preferable to lightly draw a pencil line (without scoring the sorbent!) approx 1.5 cm above the plate edge, or alternatively use a piece of A4 paper placed on the plate as a guide, or use a template. Application of the sample as a straight line is necessary as this forms the origin, and assuming that the plate is homogeneous, the sample will separate during development into even bands of individual compounds. If the sample is applied in an irregular fashion (i.e., a wavy line), then during development the sample will separate into compounds as irregular bands that are difficult to remove in a pure form from the plate during the desorption process.

The sample should not be applied right up to the edges of the plate as "edge effects" (the rapid movement of solvent up the plate sides or poor sorbent homogeneity) will lead to uneven movement of solvent up the plate during development, and as a consequence, irregular band shape will result (**Fig. 6**).

4.6. Development and Detection

A suitable solvent system and sorbent phase will have been chosen and some of the simpler cases are given in **Subheading 2.** and in the examples (**Subheading 7.**). Mobile phases for preparative systems should be freshly made up, and usually 100-mL volumes are suitable to run one or two plates in the same tank. A solvent-saturated atmosphere in the tank is favored to improve chromatography, and this can be facilitated by adding some filter paper (e.g., 15 × 15 cm) to the inside walls of the tank.

Silica gel is quite a "reactive" sorbent, and some natural products are unstable on this phase. It should be noted that during development, plates should be kept out of direct sunlight, as degradation of the natural products may occur.

Development is achieved by allowing the solvent front to reach the plate top or within a few millimeters of it and then removing the plate from the tank and

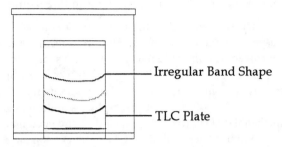

Fig. 6. Irregular band shape resulting from "edge effects."

air-drying in a fume cupboard. Handheld dryers should be avoided to remove excess solvent from plates due to the risk of degradation.

Most semipurified samples have some residual color, or the natural products of interest may be colored; in such cases, it is possible to gage how far the compounds have migrated up the plate. In the case of plant extracts, nonpolar pigments such as the chlorophylls or carotenes can give a visual aid to separation and an idea of how far the compounds of interest have migrated relative to the pigments. If the natural products of interest absorb long- or short-wavelength UV light, then the success of the separation can be readily observed—this is especially useful in multiple development—and it is rewarding to see compounds resolved through the isolation process! With poorly UV-absorbing products, use of a spray reagent is required (**Subheading 3.**), and spraying only the plate edge will give an idea of how far the natural products of interest have migrated. If, after spray detection, the compounds have not migrated far enough up the plate to effect separation, then the contaminated sprayed silica (or other sorbent) must be removed to avoid contamination of the solvent system before further redevelopment.

4.7. Desorption and Recovery of Natural Products

Once the decision has been made that the separation of compounds has been satisfactorily achieved, the natural products need to be effectively recovered from the sorbent, dried, and stored for structure elucidation. On the silica example given above, where a UV fluorescent indicator is incorporated into the sorbent, UV-absorbing bands (compounds) may be marked out by a pencil or scalpel and scraped off the backing plate onto tin foil or paper.* With spray detection, bands may be cut from the spray-colored edge (but not incorporating it!) along the plate using a ruler. These bands may be scraped from the plate onto foil.

*The procedure of sorbent removal (especially silica and alumina) from plate backings should always be performed in a fume cupboard, and a dust mask should be worn to avoid breathing dangerous fine particulate material coated in substances of (presumably) unknown composition.

Compounds may be desorbed from the sorbent in three simple ways:

1. The compound-rich sorbent can be transferred to a conical flask and solvent added. The suspension should be left for 30 min to facilitate leaching of compound into the solvent and then filtered. This process should be repeated two or three times to ensure good recovery. The type of solvent used should be slightly more polar than is normally required to dissolve the sample; e.g., if the sample dissolves readily in chloroform, then desorption should be carried out using chloroform:methanol (9:1) or (8:2). This should ensure maximum recovery from the sorbent and minimize the possibility of the product remaining strongly bound to the solid phase.

2. The compound-rich sorbent should be placed in a sintered glass funnel (3 porosity frit) attached to a glass Buchner flask to which a vacuum is applied. The sorbent is then washed with solvent, and the resulting solution can be recovered in the flask and evaporated to yield the product. Repeated washings with solvent will lead to effective recovery of compounds. This is the method of choice for recovery of components from preparative TLC plates.

3. A Pasteur pipet fitted with a cotton wool (defatted) plug or a micro column with a 3-porosity frit can be packed with compound-rich sorbent. This "mini" column can then be eluted with solvent to recover the pure compound. Care should be taken not to overpack these columns as compound elution time may be considerable. However, one benefit of these desorption methods, assuming that the natural products of interest are sufficiently stable, is that they may be set up with sufficient solvent and left to desorb for a long period of time.

In all three cases, where silica is the sorbent, methanol can be used as a final wash stage to ensure full compound recovery—many natural products such as the glycosides of flavonoids and triterpenes are highly polar and may require the addition of 1 or 2% acetic acid in this final methanol elution.

Products should be dried quickly after elution, preferably using a high-purity N_2 blow-down apparatus, and stored in a freezer. Rotary evaporators using heat and turbovaps using air should be avoided because of the risk of heat decomposition and oxidation or loss by evaporation.

4.8. Assessing Purity by TLC

After desorption, analytical TLC should be performed on recovered products to ascertain their purity. The smaller particle size of analytical plates compared to PTLC enables better resolution and a greater ability to measure purity. At least two different solvent systems should be used in order to distinguish between compounds that have similar (or identical!) R_f values on a particular system. It should be noted that if a recovered compound appears to be impure, even after what promised to be a successful purification by PTLC, then it is possible that the natural product was unstable on the sorbent or in solution, and an alternative stationary phase or separation process should be sought.

4.9. Advantages and Disadvantages of PTLC

In the last 10 yr, there has been quite a considerable movement away from "wet" techniques (such as PTLC and conventional column chromatography) and toward instrumental techniques such as HPLC and countercurrent chromatography. Many natural products chemists prefer these instrumental methods because of the greater control they afford over a separation process and reproducibility, although the high cost and need for routine servicing of these machines will maintain a significant role for PTLC in isolation procedures. The following lists detail some pros and cons of PTLC.

4.9.1. Advantages

1. PTLC is cost-effective compared to the instrumentation required for HPLC and droplet countercurrent chromatography.
2. PTLC is a simple technique that requires little training or knowledge of chromatography.
3. An analytical method may be easily scaled up to a preparative method.
4. Natural products can be quickly isolated in the milligram to gram range.
5. Solvent and stationary phase choice are flexible; i.e., the solvent system can be changed quickly during a run.
6. The separation can be optimized readily for one component: It is relatively easy to "zero in" on a particular product.
7. Methods are quickly developed.
8. Almost any separation can be achieved with the correct stationary phase and mobile phase.
9. A large number of samples can be analyzed or separated simultaneously.

4.9.2. Disadvantages

1. There is poor detection when compared to diode array HPLC.
2. There is poor control of elution compared to HPLC.
3. Loading of the sample and speed of operation are poor compared to vacuum liquid chromatography.
4. Multiple development methods to isolate grams of material may be time-consuming.
5. PTLC is restricted to simple sorbents such as silica, alumina, cellulose, and RP-2.

5. Centrifugal PTLC (CPTLC)

This excellent and underexploited technique can be utilized as a primary "clean-up" process of natural products extracts or as a final purification step. CPTLC makes use of a rotor that is coated with a sorbent to form a circular plate that is then attached to a spindle and rotated using a motor. Solvent is then introduced into the middle of the circular plate by a pump to equilibrate the sorbent. Plates should be saturated with solvent and allowed to equilibrate at a given flow rate for 10 min. The sample mixture can then be introduced to the plate in the same fashion. As the plate rotates and solvent migrates through the sorbent, the sample is separated into circular compound bands that may be readily collected as they elute from the plate (**Fig. 7**) (cf. TLC in which bands are not generally allowed to reach the edge of the plate).

The plate and motor are housed in an apparatus where a nitrogen atmosphere can be applied. A good example of CPTLC apparatus is the Chromatotron (Harrison Research Model 7924), which has a duct to collect eluting bands and a quartz window that fits over the plate allowing visualization of the plate with UV light.

CPTLC has a number of advantages over PTLC. First, because development is accelerated centrifugally by plate rotation, separation can be rapid. Sample component zones expand continuously and consequently are drawn into increasingly narrow concentric rings. The mobile phase expands outward so that it is faster at the trailing edge than at the front, and this will compress the component bands. Both of these factors lead to narrow bands and better chromatography than linear development. Solvent changes can be made quickly and one may operate in a gradient or isocratic mode. Larger amounts of material (1–2 g) may be loaded onto the plate at once, than is the case with PTLC. As with homemade preparative plates, CPTLC plates allow the choice of sorbent, additives, and binders.

Recipes for making a variety of plates with different sorbents accompany CPTLC apparatus manuals. However, 2- or 4-mm thickness silica-gel plates may be made in the following way:

Add silica (Kieselgel 60 PF254 Merck Art 7749) (65 or 100 g; for 2 or 4 mm thick) and binder ($CaSO_4$; 4 or 6 g) to distilled water (100 or 190 mL), and shake thoroughly. The resulting slurry should be poured onto the rotor at the edge and the plate tapped gently to remove air bubbles and to ensure a homogeneous layer. Air-dry the plate for 30 min and oven-dry at 50°C for 12 h. The resulting plate should then be scraped to the required thickness and stored in an oven at 50°C prior to use.

The correct choice of solvent system should be ascertained by using a series of analytical plates with increasingly polar solvent to determine R_f values. When using an isocratic system, a solvent system can be used where the R_f of the highest eluting compound is about 0.3. This will result in a steady separation in which fractions (and compound bands) can be collected and analyzed by TLC. A more polar system (e.g., R_f of the least polar component is 0.8) can be used in which concentrated compounds will appear as discrete bands that move quickly through the plate—smaller volume fractions should be collected and analyzed. As with PTLC, use of a sorbent incorporating a UV indicator will aid in the monitoring of UV active compounds.

Khan et al. *(11)* used a Chromatotron CPTLC apparatus in the separation of some unusual clerodane diterpenes (e.g., **Compound 5**) in a chemotaxonomic study of the flacourtiaceous species *Zuelania guidonia*. Silica gel sorbent and a

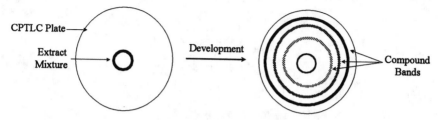

Fig. 7. Circular band separation through CPTLC development.

Compound 5.

mobile phase of petrol/ethyl acetate (49:1) were used and the compound was visualized under UV light.

Waterman and Ampofo *(12)* used CPTLC to isolate the cytotoxic quassinoids, ailanthinone (**Compound 6**), 2'-acetylglaucarubinone (**Compound 7**) and the alkaloid 8-hydroxycanthin-6-one (**Compound 8**) from the rainforest tree *Odyendyea gabonensis* (Simaroubaceae).

6. Over-Pressure TLC (OPTLC)

Over-pressure TLC (OPTLC) was introduced by Tyihak et al. in 1979 *(13)* in an attempt to combine the advantages of conventional TLC and HPLC. This technique employs the use of a pressurized circular ultra microchamber (PUM chamber), which houses a TLC plate and inlets for the introduction of sample and solvent onto the sorbent. The thin sorbent layer is covered by a membrane kept under external pressure so that the vapor phase above the sorbent is nearly eliminated. A substantially shorter time is required for separation than in conventional TLC and classical column chromatography (CC) and greater resolution and separation efficiency is achieved. The rate at which solvent migrates is as stable as HPLC and consequently the technique can be used to model CC

Compound 6 and 7. (6) R = COCH(Me)CH$_2$CH$_3$. (7) R = COC(OAc)(Me)CH$_2$CH$_3$ (silica gel; CH$_2$Cl$_2$:isopropanol [49:1]).

Compound 8. (silica gel; toluene:EtOAc:AcOH [5:4:1]).

methods. Separations can be carried out 5–20 times faster than conventional TLC, and so this method may be applicable to high throughput/repetitions.

Tyihak et al. validated this technique using the separation of the synthetic dyes indophenol, Sudan G, and Butter Yellow. Natural products such as capsaicin from *Capsicum anuum* and furocoumarins from *Heracleum sphondylium* have been separated by Nyirdey et al. *(14)*.

6.1. Automated Multiple Development (AMD)

This method utilizes a fully automated developing chamber that consists of a sensor to optically detect the solvent front position, a mechanism to lift the plate out of the developing chamber, multiple solvent reservoirs, a solvent pump, and an integrated fan to dry the plate and remove solvent vapor. Modern systems contain microprocessor-controlled programming to vary solvent composition after each run. Multiple development dramatically increases separation power, improves reproducibility and precision, and can be set up to run without continuous supervision. This apparatus can also be used in conjunction with a TLC plate scanner that will detect UV-active bands. This can be interfaced with a PC and linked to a printer for hard copy. An excellent example of an AMD device is the CAMAG AMD system (Merck).

6.2. Two-Dimensional TLC

Two-dimensional TLC is frequently used for the screening of complex mixtures. If the object is to find known compounds, and standards are available,

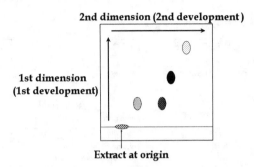

Fig. 8. Two-dimensional TLC plate after two developments.

then this is a very powerful form of TLC. The extract is spotted onto the plate in the normal fashion and the plate is developed, dried, and then turned through 90° and developed a second time (**Fig. 8**). This has the advantage of resolving compounds into the second dimension, which gives further resolution. Also, different solvent systems may be used for the second elution, which further enhances the resolving power of this technique. The resulting chromatogram may then be observed under UV light or stained for detection purposes.

7. Examples of Preparative TLC

The examples in **Table 5** are taken from the natural products literature, from our own experience, and in particular from the excellent PhD dissertations (University of Strathclyde) of Monira Ahsan *(15)* and Satyajit D. Sarker *(22)*. They cover a range of different classes of plant and microbial natural products. Only the final preparative TLC stage is given in the isolation; further details may be obtained from the reference.

8. TLC Bioassays

TLC bioassays against fungi and bacteria have proved exceptionally popular because of their ease of use, low cost, speed, and their ability to be scaled up to assess the antimicrobial activity of a large number of samples. Generally, TLC plates are run and then the microorganism is introduced to the plate as a spray (in the case of direct bioautography), or the plate is covered with a growth medium containing the microorganism in a dish or tray (overlay assay). With the occurrence of multiple drug-resistant bacteria (such as methicillin-resistant *Staphylococcus aureus*) and the need for new antimycotic drugs, these simple bioassays will continue to prove useful in the assessment of antimicrobial activity of natural product extracts. A critical review of key antifungal and antibacterial assays has been made by Cole *(46)*, and the reader is referred to a number of authors; namely, Spooner and Sykes *(47)*, Holt *(48)*, Rios et al. *(49)*, Homans and Fuchs *(50)*, Betina *(51)*, Leven et al. *(52)*, and Begue and Kline *(53)*.

Table 5
Examples of Preparative TLC

Species and Compound class	Reference	PTLC Method	Structure
Boronia inornata Sesquiterpene **Spathulenol**	(15) Ahsan (1993)	Silica gel Toluene: EtOAc (97:3) $R_f = 0.39$ Toluene: EtOAc:AcOH, (89:10:1) Three developments	
Boronia inornata Sesquiterpene	(15) Ahsan, (1993)	Silica gel Toluene:EtOAc (96:4) $R_f = 0.5$ Toluene:EtOAc, (92:8)	
Calea divaricata Sesquiterpene **Hydroxyeupatolide-8-O-angellate**	(16) Ober *et al.*, (1984)	Silica gel Me$_2$CO:Hexane (4:1)	
Leonitis ocymifolia Diterpene ester	(17) Habtemariam *et al.*, (1994)	Silica gel Hexane:CHCl$_3$:EtOAc (2:3:2)	
Cupressus goveniana Diterpene **Cupresol**	(18) Jolad *et al.*, (1984)	Silica gel 60 PF$_{254}$ CH$_2$Cl$_2$:EtOAc (94:6)	
Casearia tremula Diterpene ester	(19) Gibbons *et al.*, (1996)	Silica gel Toluene:EtOAc:AcOH (88:10:2) $R_f = 0.71$ Petrol: EtOAc, (1:1) Two developments	
Boronia inornata Triterpene	(15) Ahsan (1993)	1. Toluene:EtOAc, AcOH (80:18:12) 2. Petrol:EtOAc, 6:4 $R_f = 0.20$ Toluene:EtOAc, AcOH (80:18:12)	
Boronia inornata Triterpene	(15) Ahsan (1993)	Silica gel Toluene:EtOAc, (96:4) $R_f = 0.49$ Toluene:EtOAc, (96:4)	
Castilleja rhexifolia Iridoid **Catalpol**	(20) Roby and Stermitz (1984)	Alumina *n*-BuOH:H$_2$O:MeOH (7:3:1)	

Species and Compound class	Reference	PTLC Method	Structure
Asterolasia trymalioides Coumarin	(21) Sarker *et al.,* (1995)	Silica gel CHCl₃ Two developments	OMe
Asterolasia drummondii Coumarin **Dipetalolactone**	(22) Sarker (1995)	Silica gel (CHCl₃:EtOAc, 9:1) Two developments	
Eriostemon myoporoides Coumarin	(23) Sarker (1995)	Silica gel Hexane:EtOAc, (8:2) $R_f = 0.31$	OOH
Drummondita hassellii Coumarin	(24) Rashid *et al.,* (1992)	Silica gel Toluene:EtOAc, (8:1)	OMe
Cotoneaster acutifolius Dibenzofuran δ-**cotonefuran**	(25) Kokubun *et al.,* (1995)	Silica gel (1) CHCl₃-Me₂CO (19:1) $R_f = 0.57$ (2) Toluene:EtOAc, (2:1) $R_f = 0.70$	OH MeO OMe OMe
Imperata cylindrica Lignan **Graminone B**	(26) Matsunaga *et al.,* (1994)	Silica gel C₆H₆:EtOAc (1:1)	OH OMe OMe MeO OH
Steganotaenia araliacea Bisbenzocyclo-octadiene lignan **Neoisostegane**	(27) Taafrout *et al.,* (1984)	Silica gel 60 EtOAc:Hexane (1:1) Three developments.	CH₃O CH₃O OCH₃ CH₃O OCH₃
Drummondita hassellii Flavonoid	(24) Rashid *et al.,* (1992)	Silica gel Toluene:EtOAc (8:3)	OMe MeO MeO OMe OH O
Boronia coerulescens ssp *spicata* Flavonoid	(28) Ahsan *et al.,* (1993)	Silica gel Toluene:EtOAc (8:2)	HO MeO OH O OMe
Boronia inconspicua Flavonoid	(15) Ahsan (1993)	Silica gel CHCl₃:EtOAc, (95:5) Three developments	OH HO OH geranyl OH O

Species and Compound class	Reference	PTLC Method	Structure
Seiridium sp. Butenolide **7'-Hydroxyseiridin**	(29) Evidente and Sparapano (1994)	Silica gel (1) Petrol:Acetone, (6:4) (2) CHCl$_3$:*iso*-Propanol (9:1)	
Homalium longifolium Glycoside	(30) Shaari *et al.,* (1995)	Silica gel EtOAc:MeOH (1:1)	
Eriostemon myoporoides Geranylated phenol	(22) Sarker (1995) and (23) Sarker *et al.,* (1994)	Silica gel CHCl$_3$:EtOAc, (8:2) R_f = 0.30	
Asterolasia drummondii Quinoline alkaloid **Maculosidine**	(22) Sarker (1995)	Silica gel CHCl$_3$:EtOAc, (8:2)	
Eriostemon gardneri Quinoline alkaloid	(31) Sarker (1995)	Silica gel 1. Hexane:EtOAc, (8:2) 2. CHCl$_3$:EtOAc, (8:2)	
Papaver somniferum Alkaloid **N-allylnorreticuline**	(32) Brochmann, Hannssen and Cheng (1984)	Silica gel CHCl$_3$:MeOH, 8:2	
Berberis sp. Benzylisoquinoline alkaloid **Dihydrorugosinone**	(33) Valencia *et al.,* (1984)	Silica gel 1. CHCl$_3$:MeOH:NH$_4$OH (90:10:1) 2. C$_6$H$_6$:Me$_2$CO:MeOH: NH$_4$OH (45:45:10:1)	
Brunsvigia josephinae Alkaloid	(34) Viladomat *et al.,* (1994)	Silica gel Pure MeOH	
Citrus decumana Acridone alkaloid	(35) Basa and Tripathy (1984)	Silica gel C$_6$H$_6$:EtOAc (19:1)	
Aconitum forrestii Diterpene alkaloid **Forestine**	(36) Pelletier *et al.,* (1984)	Alumina, PF$_{254}$ Thick Layer Chromatography (20cm x 20cm x 3mm) Me$_2$CO:Hexane (45:55)	

Species and Compound class	Reference	PTLC Method	Structure
Thalictrum faberi Alkaloid **Thalifaberidine**	(37) Lin, *et al.*, (1994)	Silica gel Cyclohexane:EtOAc: Diethylamine (6:4:1 to 4:8:1)	
Sternbergia lutea Alkaloid **Hippamine**	(38) Evidente, *et al.*, (1984)	Silica gel CHCl$_3$:MeOH (9:1)	
Uvaria angolense Indole alkaloid **Uvarindole B**	(39) Muhammad and Waterman (1985)	Silica gel G CHCl$_3$:MeOH (49:1)	
Senna multiglandulosa Anthraquinone dimer	(40) Abegaz *et al.*, (1994)	Silica gel CHCl$_3$:MeOH (100:2)	
Penicillium sclerotiorum Azaphilone	(41) Pairet *et al.*, (1995)	Silica gel CH$_2$Cl$_2$:MeOH (19:1)	
Streptomyces griseoviridis Lactone **Cineromycin B**	(42) Burkhardt *et al.*, (1996)	Analytical silica gel TLC CHCl$_3$:MeOH (9:1)	
Picea abies Flavonol glucoside	(43) Slimestad *et al.*, (1994)	Silica gel *n*-BuOH:AcOH:H$_2$O (4:1:5) Upper layer	
Morus alba *nor*-tropane alkaloid **Calystegine C$_1$**	(44) Asano *et al.*, (1994)	HPTLC Silica gel PrOH:AcOH:H$_2$O (4:1:1)	
Castanospermum australe Indolizidine alkaloid **Castanospermine**	(45) Molyneux *et al.*, (1988)	CPTLC Silica gel 2mm plate 1. CHCl$_3$:MeOH:NH$_4$OH:H$_2$O (70:26:2:2) 2. EtOH:NH$_4$OH (98:2)	

8.1. TLC Direct Bioautography

This technique may be utilized with either spore-forming fungi or bacteria and can be used to track activity through a separation process. It is a very sensitive assay and gives accurate localization of active compounds (Rahalison et al. *[54]*). For the assessment of antifungal activity, the plant pathogen *Cladosporium cucumerinum* (IMI-299104) can be used, as it is nonpathogenic to humans, readily forms spores, and can be easily grown on TLC plates with the correct medium. A simple method is outlined as follows:

1. Spot extracts or pure compounds onto analytical TLC plates in duplicate (plastic-backed, Kieselgel 60 PF254, Merck Art 5735), develop with the appropriate mobile phase, and dry.
2. Prepare a slope of *Cladosporium cucumerinum* (IMI-299104) from a culture and allow to sporulate for 2 d.
3. Prepare a TLC growth medium as follows: NaCl (1 g), KH_2PO_4 (7 g), $Na_2HPO_4·2H_2O$ (3 g), KNO_3 (4 g), $MgSO_4$ (1 g), and Tween-80 (20 drops added to water [100 mL]). To 60 mL of this solution should be added 10 mL of aqueous glucose (30% w/v).
4. Prepare a fungal spore suspension by adding the above solution to the fungal slope and shaking.
5. Spray the suspension onto one of the TLC plates and incubate at 25°C for 2 d in an assay tray with moist cotton wool to ensure a moist atmosphere. This spraying should be performed in a laminar flow cabinet.
6. Observe the inoculated TLC plate at regular intervals—the presence of antifungal compounds are indicated by inhibition or reduced lack of mycelial growth. This is frequently observed as light spots against a dark-green background.
7. Visualize the remaining TLC plate using a spray reagent and/or UV detection and compare with the incubated plate.

Aspergillus niger, another readily sporulating fungus, may be used in the place of *Cladosporium* sp., but care must be taken with this organism because of risk of aspergillosis—all microbes should be handled aseptically in a laminar flow cabinet. Controls of antifungal compounds such as amphotericin B should be used each time this assay is performed. This assay does not distinguish between fungicidal and fungistatic metabolites, and further assays, such as a liquid broth assay, will be needed to measure Minimum Inhibitory Concentration (MIC) *(47)*.

Dellar et al. *(55)* isolated the antifungal sesquiterpenes aristolen-2-one (**Compound 9**) and prostantherol (**Compound 10**) from two species of *Prostanthera* (Labiatae). Activity was assessed and tracked through the separation procedure by the use of direct bioautography with *Cladosporium cucumerinum* as the target fungus.

Compound 9 inhibited the growth of *C. cucumerinum* for 70 h at a dose of 1 µg and **Compound 10** caused inhibition at 10 µg for the same duration.

Compound 9.

Compound 10.

Compound 11. (Dose = 0.25 µg).

Compound 12. (Dose = 3 µg).

Compound 13. (Dose = 3 µg).

Compound 14.

The antifungal activity of many natural products, including plant phenolic compounds, can be readily assessed using this simple procedure. Hostettmann and Marston *(56)* have investigated a series of xanthones (**Compounds 11–13**) from *Hypericum brasiliense* (Guttiferae) for activity against *C. cucumerinum*. One of these compounds, **Compound 11**, exhibited a very low inhibitory dose (0.25 μg), which may warrant further investigation of the antimycotic function of these interesting compounds.

8.2. TLC Bioautographic Overlay Assay

In this form of assay, the extract or pure compound is run on a TLC plate, which is then covered by a medium seeded with the appropriate microorganism. As with direct bioautographic assays, both fungi and bacteria may be investigated. Rahalison et al. *(54)* have applied this technique for the evaluation of antimicrobial extracts against the yeast *Candida albicans* and the bacterium *Bacillus subtilis*.

A simple overlay assay against *Staphylococcus aureus* (Manohar *[57]*) may be carried out as follows:

1. A base of nutrient agar is poured into an assay dish and allowed to set.
2. The extract, fraction, or pure compound, is run on a TLC plate (in duplicate) with the appropriate developing solvent. One of these plates should be visualized under UV light and then stained to observe developed compounds. R_f values are then accurately measured.
3. An innoculum of *S. aureus* at a titer of 10^9 colony-forming units (CFU)/mL in Mueller Hinton Broth is prepared, and nutrient agar is added at 7.5 g/L to thicken the medium. This is then diluted to give a final titer of 10^5 CFU/mL.
4. The remaining TLC plate is placed on the nutrient agar base and then the medium containing the test organism is poured over the plate and incubated at 37°C for 24 h.
5. Antibacterial zones appear as clear spots against a background of bacterial colonies. Zones may be visualized more clearly by the use of tetrazolium salts (such as *p*-iodonitrotetrazolium chloride [INT] or methylthiazoyltetrazolium chloride [MMT]), which indicate bacterial dehydrogenase activity. These solutions may be sprayed onto the face of the medium. Zones of inhibition (and therefore antimicrobial compounds) appear as clear zones against a purple background.

6. Zones of inhibition can be compared with the previously developed TLC plate, so that active metabolites may be readily isolated.
7. An appropriate control substance such as ampicillin or chloramphenicol should be used.

Drug-resistant bacteria, such as methicillin-resistant *Staphylococcus aureus,* will need to be cultured in the presence of methicillin (1 mg/L) to minimize the risk of loss of resistance.

Batista et al. *(58)* used an overlay method in the bioassay-guided fractionation of an acetone extract of the roots of *Plectranthus hereroensis* (Labiatae) to isolate the antibacterial diterpene **(Compound 14)**. *Staphylococcus aureus* was used as the test organism.

This compound was then assessed in a broth-dilution assay and found to have an MIC of 31.2 µg/mL.

Hamburger and Cordell *(59)* have used a variant of this assay to investigate the activity of some simple plant sterols and phenolic compounds. An overlay of nutrient broth containing the test organism was spread over the TLC plate and then incubated. Interestingly, this assay was insensitive to some cytotoxic compounds, including camptothecin, glaucarubolone, and β-peltatin, when tested at 5 µg. This might be because of poor migration of these compounds through the nutrient medium, and it should be noted that this phenomenon could be a problem with this method.

Acknowledgment

Dr. Dave Kau is thanked for useful discussions.

References

1. Gray, A. I. (1993) Quinoline alkaloids related to anthranilic acid. *Meth. Plant Biochem.* vol. 8, p. 288, Academic, London.
2. *CRC Handbook of Chemistry and Physics* (1991–1992), 72nd ed. CRC, Boston, MA.
3. Stierle, A., Strobel, G., Stierle, D., Grothaus, P., and Bignami (1995) The search for a taxol producing micro-organism among the endophytic fungi of the Pacific yew *Taxus brevifolia. J. Nat. Prod.* **58,** 1315–1324.
4. Staneck, J. L. and Roberts, G. D. (1974) Simplified approach to identification of aerobic actinomycetes by thin layer chromatography. *App. Microbiol.* **28,** 226–231.
5. Waterman, P. G. and Grundon, M. F. (eds.) (1983) *Chemistry and Chemical taxonomy of the Rutales.* Academic, London.
6. Hegnauer, R. (1989) *Chemotaxonomie der Pflanzen,* vol. 1–10 Birkhäuser-Verlag, Berlin.
7. Gibbons, S. (1994) Ph.D. dissertation, University of Strathclyde, UK.
8. Wagner, H., Bladt, S., and Zgainski, E. M. (1984) *Plant Drug Analysis—A Thin Layer Chromatography Atlas.* Springer-Verlag, Berlin.

9. *Merck Handbook—Dyeing Reagents for Thin Layer and Paper Chromatography* (1980) E. Merck, Darmstadt, Germany.

10. Gibbons, S., Gray, A. I., Hockless, D. C. R., Lavaud, C., Nuzillard, J., Massiot, G., Waterman, P. G., and White, A. H. (1993) Novel D:A *friedo*-oleanane triterpenes from the stem bark of *Phyllobotryon spathulatum. Phytochemistry* **34**, 273–277.

11. Khan, M. R., Gray, A. I., and Waterman, P. G. (1990) Clerodane diterpenes from *Zuelania guidonia* stem bark. *Phytochemistry* **29**, 2939–2942.

12. Ampofo, S. and Waterman, P. G. (1984) Cytotoxic quassinoids from *Odyendyea gabonensis* stem bark: isolation and high field NMR. *Planta Medica* 261–263.

13. Tyihak, E., Mincsovics, E., and Kalasz, H. (1979) New planar liquid chromatographic technique: overpressured thin layer chromatography. *J. Chromatogr.* **174**, 75–81.

14. Nyiredy, S., Dallenbach-Tölke, K., Erdelmeier, C. A. J., Meier, B., and Sticher, O. (1985) *Abstracts, 33rd Ann. Congr. Society for Medicinal Plant Research*, Regensburg.

15. Ahsan, M. (1993) Ph.D. dissertation, University of Strathclyde, UK.

16. Ober, A. G., Fronczek, F. R., and Fischer, N. H. (1985) Sesquiterpene lactones of *Calea divaricata* and the molecular structure of leptocarpin acetate. *J. Nat. Prod.* **48**, 302–305.

17. Habtemariam, S., Gray, A. I., and Waterman, P. G. (1994) Diterpenes from the leaves of *Leonotis ocymifolia* var. *raineriana. J. Nat. Prod.* **57**, 1570–1574.

18. Jolad, S. D., Hoffmann, J. J., Schram, K. H., Cole, J. R., Bates, R. B., and Tempesta, M. S. (1984) A new diterpene from *Cupressus govenia* var. *abramasiana*: 5β-hydroxy-6-oxasugiol (cupresol). *J. Nat. Prod.* **47**, 983–987.

19. Gibbons, S., Gray, A. I., and Waterman, P. G. (1996) Clerodane diterpenes from the bark of *Casearia tremula. Phytochemistry* **41**, 565–570.

20. Roby, M. R. and Stermitz, F. R. (1984) Penstemonoside and other iridoids from *Castilleja rhexifolia*. Conversion of penstemonoside to the pyridine monoterpene alkaloid rhexifoline. *J. Nat. Prod.* **47**, 854–857.

21. Sarker, S. D., Gray, A. I., and Waterman, P. G. (1995) Coumarins from *Asterolasia trymalioides. J. Nat. Prod.* **57**, 1549–1551.

22. Sarker, S. (1994) Ph.D. dissertation, University of Strathclyde, UK.

23. Sarker, S. D., Armstrong, J. A., and Waterman, P. G. (1994) Sesquiterpenyl coumarins and geranyl benzaldehyde derivatives from the aerial parts of *Eriostemon myoporoides. Phytochemistry* **37**, 1287–1294.

24. Rashid, M. A., Armstrong, J. A., Gray, A. I., and Waterman, P. G. (1992) Alkaloids, flavonols and coumarins from *Drummondita hassellii* and *D. calida. Phytochemistry* **31**, 1265–1269.

25. Kokubun, T., Harborne, J. B., Eagles, J., and Waterman, P. G. (1995) Dibenzofuran phytoalexins from the sapwood of *Cotoneaster acutifolius* and five related species. *Phytochemistry* **38**, 57–60.

26. Matsunaga, K., Shibuya, M., and Ohizumi, Y. (1994) Graminone β, a novel lignan with vasodilative activity from *Imperata cylindrica. J. Nat. Prod.* **57**, 1734,1735.

27. Taafrout, M., Rouessac, F., Robin, J-P., Hicks, R. P., Shillady, D. D., and Sneden, A. T. (1984) Neoisostegane, a new bisbenzocyclooctadiene lignan lactone from *Steganotaenia araliacea. J. Nat. Prod.* **47**, 600–605.

28. Ahsan, M., Armstrong, J. A., Gibbons, S., Gray, A. I., and Waterman, P. G. (1994) Novel *o*-prenylated flavonoids from two varieties of *Boronia coerulescens*. *Phytochemistry* **37**, 259–266.

29. Evidente, A. and Sparapano, L. (1994) 7-hydroxyseiridin and the 7'-hydroxyisoseiridin, two new phytotoxic $\Delta^{\alpha,\beta}$-butenolides from three species of *Seiridium* pathogenic to cypresses. *J. Nat. Prod.* **57**, 1720–1725.

30. Shaari, K. and Waterman, P. G. (1995) Further glucosides and simple isocoumarins from *Homalium longifolium*. *Nat. Prod. Lett.* **7**, 243–250.

31. Sarker, S. D., Waterman, P. G., and Armstrong, J. A. (1995) 3,4,8-trimethoxy-2-quinolone—a new alkaloid from *Eriostemon gardneri*. *J. Nat. Prod.* **58**, 574–576.

32. Brochmann-Hanssen, E. and Cheng, C. Y. (1984) Biosynthesis of a narcotic antagonist: conversion of N-allylnorreticuline to n-allylnormorphine in *Papaver somniferum*. *J. Nat. Prod.* **47**, 175,176.

33. Valencia, E., Weiss, I., Shamma, M., Urzua, A., and Fajardo, V. (1984) Dihydrorugosine, a pseudobenzylisoquinoline alkaloid from *Berberis darwinii* and *Berberis actinacantha*. *J. Nat. Prod.* **47**, 1050,1051.

34. Viladomat, F., Bastida, J., Codina, C., Campbell, W. E., and Mathee, S. (1994) Alkaloids from *Brunsvigia josepinœ*. *Phytochemistry* **35**, 809–812.

35. Basa, S. C. and Tripathy, R. N. (1984) A new acridone alkaloid from *Citrus decumana*. *J. Nat. Prod.* **47**, 325–330.

36. Pelletier, S. W., Ying, C. S., Joshi, B. S., and Desai, H. K. (1984) The structures of forestine and foresticine, two new C_{19}-diterpenoid alkaloids from *Aconitum forrestii* stapf. *J. Nat. Prod.* **47**, 474–477.

37. Lin, L.-Z., Hu, S.-H., Zaw, K., Angerhofer, C. K., Chai, H., Pezzuto, J. M., Cordell, G. A., Lin, J., and Zheng, D.-M. (1994) Thalfaberidine, a cytotoxic aporphine-benzylisoquinoline alkaloid from *Thalictrum faberi*. *J. Nat. Prod.* **57**, 1430–1435.

38. Evidente, A., Iasiello, I., and Randazzo, G. (1984) Isolation of Sternbergine, a new alkaloid from the bulbs of *Sternbergia lutea*. *J. Nat. Prod.* **47**, 1003–1007.

39. Muhammad, I. and Waterman, P. G. (1985) Chemistry of the Annonaceae, part 18. Benzylated indoles and dihydrochalcones in *Uvaria angolensis* from Tanzania. *J. Nat. Prod.* **48**, 571–580.

40. Abegaz, B. M., Bezabeh, M., Alemayehu, G., and Duddeck, H. (1994) Anthraquinones from *Senna multigladulosa*. *Phytochemistry* **35**, 465–468.

41. Pairet, L., Wrigley, S. K., Chetland, I., Reynolds, E. E., Hayes, M. A., Holloway, J., Ainsworth, A. M., Katzer, W., Cheng, X.-M., Hupe, D. J., Charlton, P., and Doherty, A. M. (1995) Azaphilones with endothelin receptor binding activity produced by *Penicillium sclerotiorum*: taxonomy, fermentation, isolation, structure elucidation and biological activity. *J. Antibiot.* **48**, 913–918.

42. Burkhardt, K., Fiedler, H.-P., Grabley, S., Thiericke, R., and Zeeck, A. (1996) New cineromycins and musacins obtained by metabolite pattern analysis of *Streptomyces griseoviridis* (FH-S 1832). *J. Antibiot.* **49**, 432–437.

43. Slimestad, R., Andersen, O. M., and Francis, G. W. (1994) Ampelopsin 7-glucoside and other dihydroflavonol 7-glucosides from needles of *Picea abies*. *Phytochemistry* **35**, 550–552.

44. Asano, N., Oseki, K., Tomioka, E., Kizu, H., and Matsui, K. (1994) N-containing sugars from *Morus alba* and their glucosidase inhibitory activities. *Carbohydrate Res.* **259**, 243–255.
45. Molyneux, R. J., Benson, M., Wong, R. Y., Tropea, J. E., and Elbein, A. D. (1988) Australine, a novel pyrrolizidine alkaloid glucosidase inhibitor from *Castanospermum australe. J. Nat. Prod.* **51**, 1198–1206.
46. Cole, M. D. (1994) Key antifungal and antibacterial assays—a critical review. *Biochem. Systematics Ecol.* **22**, 837–857.
47. Spooner, D. F. and Sykes, G. Laboratory assessment of antibacterial activity. *Meth. Microbiol.* **7B**, 211–276.
48. Holt, R. J. (1975) Laboratory tests of antifungal drugs. *J. Clin. Pathol.* **28**, 767–774.
49. Rios, J. L., Recio, M. C., and Villar, A. (1988) Screening methods for natural products with antimicrobial activity: a review of the literature. *J. Ethnopharmacol.* **23**, 127–149.
50. Homans, A. L. and Fuchs, A. (1970) Direct bioautography on thin-layer chromatograms as a method for detecting fungitoxic substances. *J. Chromatogr.* **51**, 327–329.
51. Betina, V. (1973) Bioautography in paper and thin layer chromatography and its scope in the antibiotic field. *J. Chromatogr.* **78**, 41–51.
52. Leven, M., Vanden Berghe, D. A., Mertens, F., Vlietinck, A., and Lammens, E. (1979) Screening of higher plants for biological activity I. Antimicrobial activity. *Planta Medica* **36**, 311–321.
53. Begue, W. J. and Kline, R. M. (1972) The use of tetrazolium salts in bioautographic procedures. *J. Chromatogr.* **64**, 182–184.
54. Rahalison, L., Hamburger, M., Hostettmann, K., Monod, M., and Frenk, E. (1991) A bioautographic agar overlay method for the detection of antifungal compounds from higher plants. *Phytochem. Anal.* **2**, 199–203.
55. Dellar, J. E., Cole, M. D., Gray, A. I., Gibbons, S., and Waterman, P. G. (1994) Antimicrobial sesquiterpenes from *Prostanthera* aff. *melissifolia* and *P. rotundifolia. Phytochemistry* **36**, 957–960.
56. Hostettmann, K. and Marston, A. (1994) Search for new antifungal compounds from higher plants. *Pure Appl. Chem.* **66**, 2231–2234.
57. Manohar, R. (1996) Personal communication.
58. Batista, O., Simoes, M. F., Duarte, A., Valdeira, M. L., De la Torre, M. C., and Rodriguez, B. (1995) An antimicrobial abietane from the roots of *Plectranthus hereroensis. Phytochemistry* **38**, 167–169.
59. Hamburger, M. O. and Cordell, G. A. (1987) A direct bioautographic TLC assay for compounds possessing antibacterial activity. *J. Nat. Prod.* **50**, 19–22.

Bibliography

General TLC Texts

Wagner, H., Bladt, S., and Zgainski, E. M. (1984) *Plant Drug Analysis—A Thin Layer Chromatography Atlas, Springer-Verlag, Berlin.* (The "bible" of plant analysis by TLC—many excellent examples of systems and detection sprays.)

Bauer, K., Gros, L., and Sauer, W. (1991) *Thin Layer Chromatography*, Huthig Buch Verlag GmbH, Heidelberg. (A superb introduction to TLC, an essential text for any interested in this subject.)

E. Merck Handbook—Dyeing Reagents for Thin Layer and Paper Chromatography, E. Merck, Darmstadt, Germany. (A comprehensive set of spray reagents.)

Hostettmann, K., Hostettmann, M., and Marston, A. (1985) *Preparative Chromatography Techniques*, Springer-Verlag Berlin. (Chapter 3 has many examples of preparative TLC from plants.)

Touchstone, J. C. (1992) *Practice of Thin Layer Chromatography*, Wiley, Chichester, UK.

Grinberg, N., ed. (1990) *Modern Thin Layer Chromatography*, Chromatographic Science Series, vol. 52, Marcel Dekker.

Bioautographic TLC Assays

Aszalos, A. and Issaq, H. J. (1980) Thin Layer Chromatographic systems for the classification and identification of antibiotics. *J. Liquid Chromatogr.* **3,** 867–883.

8

Separation by High-Speed Countercurrent Chromatography

James McAlpine

1. Introduction

Modern high-speed countercurrent chromatography (HSCC) has arisen only over the last 15 or so years and offers the natural product chemist a new separation tool with many unique advantages. It is inherently the mildest form of chromatography with no solid support and hence no chance of loss of substrate by binding to the column. The only media encountered by the sample are solvent and Teflon tubing. The former is common to all forms of chromatography and the latter to most. It is true that the solvent systems have more components than many other forms of chromatography, but these can be chosen from the most nonreactive and innocuous solvents. Hence the chromatographer is virtually assured of near 100% recovery of sample from a chromatography. The number of two-phase systems that can be employed is limited only by the imagination of the chromatographer, and the systems can be explored by any of several simple tests, prior to a preparative separation, to ensure success. Two similar compounds of almost identical polarity can have surprisingly different partition coefficients in a specific two-phase system resulting in baseline separation by countercurrent chromatography.

Countercurrent methodology had its beginning in the 1950s with the Craig machine *(1)*, a mechanical system of sequential separating cells in which one phase of a two-phase solvent system could be equilibrated with the other phase in successive cells, thereby carrying a solute along according to its partition coefficient between the two phases. Solutes would be washed from the train in the order their partition coefficients favored the mobile phase. These instruments were cumbersome, delicate, and required a major air-handling system as they invariably leaked organic solvents to some extent. A typical system would

From: *Methods in Biotechnology, Vol. 4: Natural Products Isolation*
Edited by: R. J. P. Cannell © Humana Press Inc., Totowa, NJ

involve 200–400 cells, and a separation using such an instrument would take in the order of a week to accomplish. They were used because they could achieve separations that could not be otherwise effected. They were both displaced and replaced. Displaced by the high-pressure liquid chromatography (HPLC) and the large number of possible solid supports available for this methodology, and replaced by droplet countercurrent instruments that could be used to effect that same separation method in a fraction of the laboratory space. Replaced, where a countercurrent chromatography was needed by commercial droplet counter-current instruments. Droplet countercurrent instruments are still available. They are composed of vertical tubes of a diameter that will allow droplets of one phase of a two-phase solvent system to rise (or fall) through the other phase. These mixing tubes are then connected top to bottom, with fine tubing such that the droplets would completely fill the tubing and exclude the station-ary phase from these interconnecting tubes. Thus the mobile phase is added slowly and allowed to percolate through the mixing chambers under the force of gravity, to achieve a distribution of solute according to partition coefficient. Droplet countercurrent systems, while sharing the high separatory power of the Craig machine and the high overall recovery of load sample, still suffer from the problem of being slow, and this is further complicated by the need to maintain constant temperature during the course of a chromatography.

High-speed countercurrent instruments became commercially available around 1980 and have overcome all of the drawbacks of these earlier instru-ments. They make countercurrent chromatography a useful means of achiev-ing delicate separations on the milligram-to-gram scale in a few hours. This chapter offers the reader a primer in the use of this technique for separations in natural product isolations.

2. Current Instruments

Although several minor variants are available, instruments are basically of two types: the Centrifugal Partition Chromatography instrument, sold by Sanki Instruments; and the Coil Planet Centrifuge, designed by Yochiro Ito and sold by PC Inc. The former effectively replaces gravity as the driving force of a drop-let countercurrent procedure with centrifugal force and thus achieves a remark-able increase in the speed of the process. It does necessitate the use of a rotating seal. The Teflon tubing is replaced by small solid blocks of Tefzel, honey-combed with a channel system replicating the tubing of a droplet system. The blocks (cartridges) are connected by Teflon tubing and can be individually replaced should one become clogged or spring a leak. A typical instrument would contain 12 such cartridges. A distinct advantage of this instrument is the ability to use solvent systems containing relatively viscous solvents, such as *n*-butanol at room temperature. Although *n*-butanol containing solvent systems can be used in the Coil Planet Centrifuge, they usually result in poor retention of stationary phase and hence suboptimal performance. An obvious weak point in the design of the Centrifugal Partition Chromatograph is the rotating seal, which must remain solvent resistant and leak-proof to a wide variety of solvents under speeds as high as 1000 rpm. The commercial instrument has a ceramic-graphite spring-loaded seal with a specified 1500-h life expectancy. The author's limited experience with one of these instruments would suggest that this seal is surprisingly robust. One distinct advantage of this system over the Coil Planet centrifuge is that as cartridges are arranged symmetrically the system is in balance at the time the mobile phase starts to exit the column and there is no need for a counter balance.

The Coil Planet Centrifuge is just one of a large number of instruments that have been the life work of Yochiri Ito. His study of the movement of one phase of a two-phase solvent system with respect to the other under a variety of imposed vectors and the use of this behavior as a separatory tool is without equal. The Coil Planet Centrifuge is available both in horizontal and vertical configurations, and although the forces imposed on the solvents are slightly different, the practical effects are essentially equivalent and the two systems can be used interchangeably to effect a separation. The Coil Planet Centrifuge consists of Teflon tubing wound in a spiral around a central cylinder. When the coil is filled with liquid and spun around its axis, an Archimedean screw force is exerted on the liquid, tending to drive it toward the center (head) of the spiral or toward the outside (tail), depending on the direction of spin. This Archimedean screw force provides the counter to the flow and the means by which one phase is held stationary while the other is pumped through it. Moreover, if the coil is spun in a synchronous planetary motion such that the period of orbital rotation is the same as that for spin around the axis of the coil, it is possible to thread the feed and exit lines through the center spindle of the coil and out the center spindle of the orbit. These two lines do not entwine as the instrument spins and so the need for a rotating seal is removed. In practice, the orbital axis is the drive axis and the coil spin is driven from that by two identical cogs. Given that the usual operating speed is around 800 rpm and that a typical chromatography takes 2–3 h and therefore involves more than 100,000 rotations, it is not surprising that the inlet and outlet do become twisted with constant use and it is necessary to inspect and occasionally untwist them. For an instrument in steady use this need only be done about once a month or even less frequently and should never be done while the instrument is in motion.

The two-phase system undergoes some interesting dynamics during operation as explained theoretically by Ito *(2)* and demonstrated by strobe light photography by Conway and Ito *(3)*. Within each orbital rotation the two phases undergo a mixing and a separation step; and this is reasonably postulated to increase the partition efficiency and hence the separatory resolution of the method. Typical instruments of both types hold approx 300 mL in a column, although analytical coils are available for the Coil Planet Centrifuge with a capacity of 90 mL are common as are larger coils with up to a 1-L capacity. The system must be counter balanced and the counter balance has to be tailored to the solvent system. Newer instruments have as many as four identical coils connected in series and symmetrically placed around the center axis. This provides an internal counterbalance; however the system is only in balance to the extent that each coil is maintaining the same amount of stationary and mobile phases. The difficulty with increasing the scale lies in the large centrifugal forces generated and the need to keep such a system in balance as the solvent system changes in composition while filling the columns or if any significant bleeding of stationary phase should occur during a chromatography.

2.1. Vendors

HSCC has not caught the attention of the large instrument makers and their manufacture tends to be a "cottage industry." The Sanki Instrument is an exception. Horizontal coil planet centrifuges are available from:

P.C. Inc., 11805 Kim Place, Potomac, MD 20854. Tel: 301-299-9386.
Conway Centri Chrom Inc., 52 MacArthur Drive, Williamsville, NY 14221. Tel: 716-634-3825.
AECS, PO Box 80 Bridgend, South Wales, UK CF31 4LH. Tel: 1656-649-073.
S.E.A.B. (Socit d Etudes et d Application Industrielle de Brevets) 64 Rue Pasteur 94807 Villejuif Cedex, France. Tel: 33-1-4678-9111.
Vertical coil planet centrifuges are available from Pharma-Tech Research Corporation, 6807 York Road, Baltimore, MD 21218. Tel: 301-377-7018.
The centrifugal droplet countercurrent instrument is available from Sanki Engineering, Ltd., Imazato 2-16-17, Nagaoka-cho, Kyoto, Japan 617.

3. Operation

The use of HSCC as a separation tool in natural product chemistry can have various aspects. Scientists at PanLabs in Bothell, WA, have chosen to use it as a dereplication tool (4) by choosing a single solvent system and building a database of the elution times of known bioactive microbial metabolites. All bioactive extracts, while still at the crude extract stage, are subjected to HSCC on an Ito coil. The retention time of the bioactivity eluted from the column can then be correlated with those of similar activities in the database, and the presumptive identity of the bioactive component can be checked spectoscopically. A much more common usage will be as a preparative chromatographic method, either for the purification of crude or semipurified mixtures, or alternatively to separate two closely related congeners, which have already been the subject of several other separation steps. The initial approach may be tailored to the particular problem.

3.1. Separation of Crude Mixtures

One can liken the course of an HSCC chromatography to a TLC. Analytes that strongly favor the stationary phase tend to behave as would those in a TLC that have an R_f of zero, whereas those that strongly favor the mobile phase behave like those with an R_f of 1.0. When running a TLC, the highest resolving power is usually obtained for those analytes with R_f in the vicinity of 0.4. Similarly, there are optimal partition coefficients to effect the highest chance of separation. Thus, if the researcher knows some analytical aspect of the metabolite or chemical entity he or she wishes to isolate, a solvent system can be selected to maximize the chances of a successful purification. In many cases this will be a certain bioactivity. Here a crude partition coefficient can be determined by distributing the mixture in the two-phase system and bioassaying both phases. Optimal partition coefficients for the Ito coil planet centrifuge are between 1.0 and 2.0 favoring the stationary phase, whereas for the Sanki centrifugal partition chromatograph they are between 2.0 and 5.0, again favoring the stationary phase. Partition coefficients based on bioactivity of crude mixtures have the inherent problem that several congeners of a natural product extract may be bioactive and the determined value is a weighted mean based on potencies, quantities, and partition coefficients of individual components. Although this is theoretically disturbing, in practice it seldom seems to present a problem as one of two situations will prevail. Either the congeners will have similar partition coefficients and one will have chosen a system in which they fall in the area of maximum resolution leading to separation from other components in the mixture and at worst case no separation from one another; or the bioactive components will have different partition coefficients and the system will be useful in separating them from one another, even if less effective in separating them from other components. Other analytical determinants can be used to estimate the partition coefficients. If the desired compounds are known to be colored, this feature can be used to rapidly assess solvent systems either by the eye or with a spectrometer. If the desired isolate can be detected on TLC plates, comparison of the spot intensity from TLC chromatography of equal aliquots of the two phases can give an adequate assessment of the system.

3.2. Separation of Two Closely Related Congeners

In the course of a natural product isolation, the chemist is often presented with mixtures containing very closely related biosynthetic relatives that may differ only by one or two methylenes, the placement of an olefin, or the stereochemistry of a nonpolar substituent. If the molecules have strongly polar groups common to their structure, the difference in polarity associated with these structural difference can be insignificant and render an adsorption type chromatographic method useless. In this situation, HSCC is often the separation method of choice, especially if the mixture has already been the subject of multiple chromatographic steps. Although the methods given above for choice of a solvent system may well work, this may be the time to employ more sophisticated analytical techniques to ensure success. TLC or analytical HPLC of each phase in the two-phase system will work if the congeners are sufficiently separated in such a system to assay them; if not, it is worth examining the two phases by ^{1}H-NMR or some other technique in which the relative partition coefficients of the congeners can be assessed.

3.3. Choosing and Tailoring the Solvent System

A cursory glance at the solvent systems used in the table of examples will reveal that most of the two-phase systems are multicomponent, and many different systems can arise from the same three or four components by differing the ratio of those components. In the early literature, carbon tetrachloride was a common component in solvent systems. It had several desirable properties, including low viscosity and high density. But, as use of it is effectively proscribed for health reasons, examples containing it have been omitted from the table. Examples including chloroform have been included as this solvent is still available. Tetrachloroethylene is also still available and this often will substitute surprisingly well for carbon tetrachloride. Methylene chloride and diethyl ether can both be used, but the researcher should be aware that a vapor lock will force the stationary phase from the system and abort the chromatography. Hence these solvents need to be used only if the ambient temperature permits. A common approach to a four component system such as the hexane-ethyl acetate-methanol-water system is to assume that: (1) for organics of medium polarity, hexane and water will be poor solvents and ethyl acetate and methanol good solvents; (2) the lower phase will consist mainly of methanol and water; and (3) the upper phase will consist mainly of hexane and ethyl acetate. Hence, if in the 1:1:1:1 system the desired compound favors the upper phase, it can be displaced toward the lower by increasing the proportion of hexane or methanol. Increasing the proportion of methanol has its limits since, at some level, the system will become monophasic. In choosing the solvent system it is necessary to avoid those that form an emulsion. A useful practical test is to shake well together a milliliter of each of the two phases and allow the mixture to separate under gravity. The separation should be complete in 5 s.

When working with ionizable compounds it is advisable to be sure that these are maintained in the same ionization state throughout the chromatography and that this has been taken into account when the solvent system is being chosen. This can be effected by including small amounts of an acid or a base in the solvent system or by including low concentration buffers as the aqueous component. In any of these approaches it is important to take into account the effect on the solubility of the load sample. The amount of material that can be successfully chromatographed is determined by this solubility (and of course by the differences in partition coefficients of the components). Typical loads for a 300-mL coil are in the order of 200 mg, but this can vary by almost an order of magnitude in either direction depending on solubility.

3.4. Physical Aspects of Operation

All HSCC instruments are effectively closed systems, and it is not necessary to locate the actual instrument in an exhaust hood. However. the solvent will be pumped from reservoirs and the eluent is usually collected in a fraction collector; and, since almost all systems involve volatile organic solvents, it is advisable to locate these peripherals in a hood. The pump must be capable of delivering between 2 and 5 mL/min and should not produce large pulses. A typical three-way injection valve is required and the sample can be loaded in any volume from 1 to 10 mL. It is of paramount importance that the sample be completely dissolved. To avoid any possibility of salting out, it is common to load the sample in a mixture of the two phases. The machine should be fully loaded, and at least the initial parts of the instrument should be equilibrated and rotating before the sample is loaded.

3.5. Use of the Ito Coil Planet Centrifuge

When using the Ito coil, the researcher is presented with making a choice of three twofold variables:

1. The question of which phase to select as the stationary phase, i.e., which phase to fill the column with.
2. The choice of the inlet tube, either the "head" or the "tail" of the column.
3. The question of which direction to spin the column, i.e., to have the Archimedean force directed to the inside or outside of the spiral.

Two of the eight possibilities will usually work well, two poorly, and the other four will result in no retention of stationary phase.

The tubing to the columns are labeled "head" and "tail" and spin directions as "forward" and "reverse." It is advisable to fill the column with the stationary phase while it is spinning with an Archimedean force against the fill. This ensures that the column is filled without any vapor blocks. The column does not have to be spun at normal running speed as this will create balancing problems. When the column is filled with stationary phase it should be spun at 800–1000 rpm while pumping the mobile phase. It is possible to introduce the sample load with the solvent front of the mobile phase, but in a new system this is usually unwise. The system can be tested to ascertain the displacement of stationary phase before introducing the sample. In the better systems only about 10% of the stationary phase is displaced before breakthrough of the mobile phase. After that, only the mobile phase is eluted from the column.

It is useful to keep in mind the theoretical shape of the elution curves. Components with partition coefficients strongly favoring the mobile phase will be eluted very early in chromatography and will be in a sharp peak. As the chromatography continues, the peaks eluted with the mobile phase broaden. After two to three column volumes of mobile phase have been eluted it is possible to reverse the direction of spin and displace the stationary phase either by continuing to pump mobile phase, or preferably, by a stream of nitrogen. The stationary phase should also be collected in fractions, as separations may have been effected but the compounds not yet eluted. Components eluted with the stationary phase will also come as sharp peaks. If the stationary phase is displaced with nitrogen, the researcher should be wary of the increasing flow rate as the column empties.

4. Examples of the Use of HSCC
for the Separation of Natural Products

The following few examples from the literature have been chosen to represent the power of the method. In each case, baseline or near baseline separation of two close structurally related congeners has been obtained. Each represents by any method a considerable challenge.

4.1. Separation of Pristinamycins (Fig. 1)

The pristinamycins, produced by *Streptomyces pristinaespiralis,* are an unusual complex of antibiotics in that they consist of two pairs of peptolide antibiotics very closely related within the two pairs but with virtually no structural relationship from one pair to the other. Pristinamycins IA and IB differ only in the degree of *N*-methylation of a 4'-aminophenylalanine moiety, whereas pristinamycins IIA and IIB differ only in that IIA has a 2,3-dehydroproline moiety where IIB has a proline. Thibaut and his group *(5)* were able to achieve baseline separations between IIA and IIB with a system comprising chloroform-ethyl acetate-methanol-water (12:8:15:10) on a triple planetary coil instrument at 1400 rpm with the upper phase mobile. Pristinamycins IA and IB were best separated with a system in which the same components were in the ratio 6:4:8:1 where the last component was formic acid "to control the pH" but of otherwise unspecified strength.

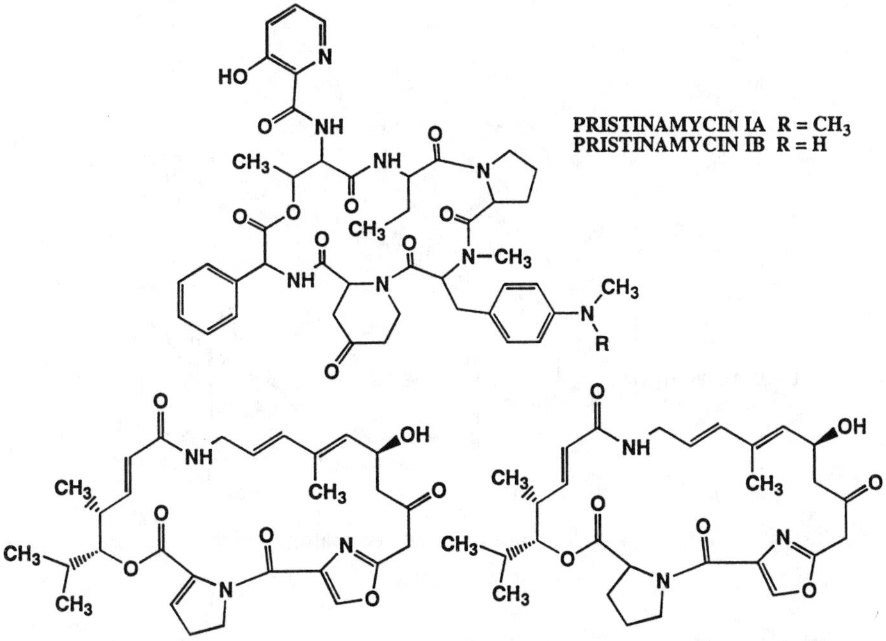

PRISTINAMYCIN IA R = CH₃
PRISTINAMYCIN IB R = H

PRISTINAMYCIN IIA   PRISTINAMYCIN IIB

Fig. 1. Separation of pristinamycins.

4.2. Separation of Taxol and Cephalomannine (Fig. 2)

The anticancer agent, taxol, is now obtained from a number of *Taxus* species but invariably occurs with with sizeable amounts of the congener, cephalomannine. These complex diterpenes differ only in the nature of the amide carboxylic acid attached to the amine of the phenylisoserine side chain. In the case of taxol this is a benzoic acid moiety, whereas in cephalomannine it is a tiglic acid group. These two impart very little selective polarity to the two natural products, and separation of them is notoriously difficult. Almost baseline separation of a small sample (6.1 mg) was achieved, however, by Chu and his coworkers *(6)*, using a system of hexane-ethyl acetate-methanol-ethanol-water (10:14:10:2:13) with the aqueous phase mobile. In this system, taxol had a partition coefficient of 1.8 and cephalomannine of 1.42.

4.3. Separation of Niddamycins (Fig. 3)

The 16-membered antibacterial macrolide niddamycin is produced by *Streptomyces djakartensis* as a mixture of aliphatic esters of the 3"-hydroxyl, the secondary alcohol on the neutral sugar mycarose. Niddamycin A1 has a butyryl ester, whereas niddamycin has the isovaleryl ester at this position. In addition,

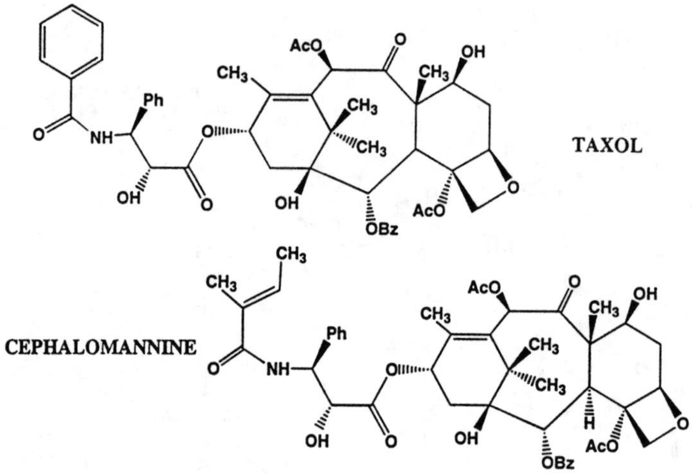

TAXOL

CEPHALOMANNINE

Fig. 2. Separation of taxol and cephalomannine.

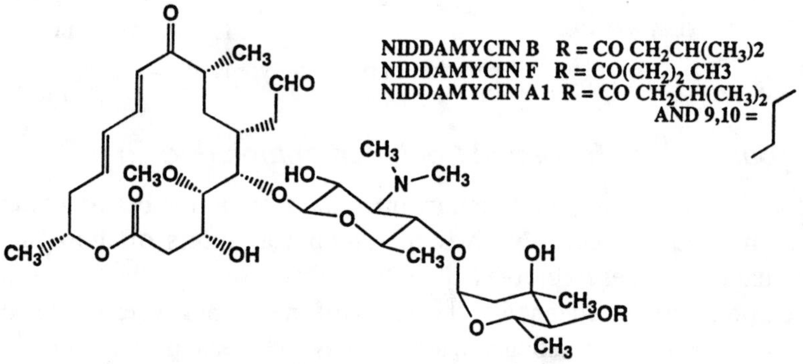

NIDDAMYCIN B   R = CO CH$_2$CH(CH$_3$)2
NIDDAMYCIN F   R = CO(CH$_2$)$_2$ CH3
NIDDAMYCIN A1 R = CO CH$_2$CH(CH$_3$)$_2$
                              AND 9,10 =

Fig. 3. Separation of niddamycins.

another congener, niddamycin F is similar to niddamycin A1 except that the 9,10 olefinic bond in the macrolide ring of A1 is fully reduced in niddamycin F. Chen and coworkers (7) achieved baseline separation of a 200-mg sample of all three niddamycins on an Ito coil in a system of carbon tetrachloride-methanol-0.01 M aqueous phosphate buffer at pH 7.0 with a ratio of 2:3:2. With the aqueous phase, mobile niddamycin F was eluted first followed by niddamycin B while niddamycin A1 was retained and recovered from fractions of the stationary phase when it was pumped from the column.

Table 1
**Table of HSCC Systems Used in the Isolation
and Separation of Natural Products**

Solvent system	Compounds	Ref.
n-Hexane-EtOAc-MeOH-H$_2$O 70:30:15:6	Tirandamycins A and B	*8*
n-Hexane-EtOAc-MeOH-H$_2$O 1:1:1:1	Arizonins B2 and C3	*9*
	Concamycins	*10*
n-Hexane-EtOAc-MeOH-H$_2$O (0.01 *N* H$_2$SO$_4$) 5:6:5:6	Squalestatins	*11*
n-Hexane-EtOAc-MeOH-H$_2$O 2:3:3:2	Arizonins A1, A2, B1, and C2	*9*
n-Hexane-EtOAc-MeOH-H$_2$O 3:7:5:5	Auxins	*12*
n-Hexane-EtOAc-MeOH-H$_2$O (25 m*M* PO$_4$$^{3-}$ buffer p*H* 6.9) 7:3:5:5	Australifungins	*13*
n-Hexane-EtOAc-MeOH-H$_2$O 2:2:2:1	Phomopsolides	*14*
n-Hexane-EtOAc-MeOH-H$_2$O 10:14:10:2:13	Taxol and Cephalomannine	*6*
n-Hexane-CHCl$_3$-MeOH-H$_2$O 1:1:1:1	Trichoverroids	*15*
n-Hexane-CH$_2$Cl$_2$-MeOH-H$_2$O 5:1:1:1	Bu 2313 B (A tetramic acid)	*8*
	5-*N*-Acetylardeemin	*16*
n-Hexane-CH$_2$Cl$_2$-MeOH-H$_2$O 10:40:17:8	Steroids	*17*
Heptane-EtOAc-MeOH-H$_2$O 1:1:1:1	Oxysporidinone	*18*
CHCl$_3$-EtOAc-MeOH-H$_2$O 12:8:15:10	Pristinamycins	*5*
CHCl$_3$-MeOH-H$_2$O 1:1:1	Coloradocin	*7*
	2-Norerythromycins	*19*
	Pentelenolactone	*8*
	Ascelacins	*20*
CHCl$_3$-MeOH-H$_2$O 7:13:8	Siderochelin	*8*
CHCl$_3$-MeOH-H$_2$O 4:3:3	1,3-Dimethylisoguanine	*21*
CHCl$_3$-MeOH-H$_2$O (0.5% HBr) 5:5:2	Michellamines	*22*
n-Hexane-EtOAc-CH$_3$CN-MeOH 5:4:5:2	Triterpene acetates	*23*
n-Heptant-C$_6$H$_6$-IPA-acetone-H$_2$O 5:10:3:2:5	2-Norerythromycins	*19*
	6-*O*-Methylerythromycin A metabolites	*24*
n-Hexane-EtOAc-H$_2$O 3:7:5	2-Norerythromycins	*19*
EtOAc-EtOH-H$_2$O 3:1:2	Dorrigocins	*25*
EtOAc-MeOH-H$_2$O i-AmOH-*n*-BuOH-*n*-PrOH-H$_2$O-HOAc-tBu$_2$S 8:12:10:30:25:1	Tunichromes	*27*
Et$_2$O-MeOH-H$_2$O (PO$_4$$^{3-}$) 3:1:2	Giberellins	*12*
n-BuOH-H$_2$O (0.01 *N* HCl)	Tetracyclines	*28*

References

1. Craig, L. C. and Craig, D. (1956) in *Techniques in Organic Chemistry, volume III, Separation and Purification* (Weissberger, A., ed.), Interscience Publishers, New York, pp. 247–254.

2. Ito, Y. (1986) High-speed countercurrent chromatography. CRC Critical Reviews in *Anal. Chem.* **17,** 65–143.

3. Conway, W. and Ito, Y. (1984) *Analytical Chemistry-Applied Spectroscopy Section,* Pittsburgh Conference and Exposition. Atlantic City, Abstract 472.

4. Baker, D. (1997) Optimizing Microbial Fermentation Diversity for Natural Product Discovery. *IBC Conference on Natural Products Drug Discovery-New Technologies to Increase Effciency and Speed.* March 17, 18, Coronado, California.

5. Drogue, S., Rolet, M.-C., Thiebaut, D. and Rosset5 R. (1992) Separation of prisitinamycins by high-speed countercurrent chromatography I. Selection of solvent system and preliminary preparative studies. *J. Chromatogr.* **395,** 363–371.

6. Chiou, F.-Y., Kan, P., Chu, I.-M., and Lee, C.-J. (1997) Sepatation of taxol and cephalomannine by countercurrent chromatography. *J. Liquid Chromatogr. Rel. Tech.* **20,** 57–61.

7. Chen, R. H., Hochlowski, J. E., McAlpine, J. B., and Rasmussen. R. R. (1988) Separation and purification of macrolides using the Ito multi-layer horizontal coil planet centrifuge. *J. Liquid Chromatogr.* **11,** 191–201.

8. Brill, G. M., McAlpine, J. B., and Hochlowski, J. E. (1985) Use of coil planet centrifuge in the isolation of antibiotics. *J. Liquid Chromatogr.* **8,** 2259–2280.

9. Hochlowski, J. E., Brill, G. M., Andres, W. W., Spanton, S. G., and McAlpine, J. B. (1987) Arizonins, a new complex of antibiotcs related to Kalafungin II. Isolation and characterization. *J. Antibiotics* **40,** 401–407.

10. Martin, D. G., Biles, C., and Peltonen, R. E. (1986) Countercurrent chromatography in the fractionation of natural products. *Amer. Lab.* **18(10),** 21–26.

11. Dawson, M. J., Farthing, J. E., Marshall, P. S., Middleton, R. F., O'Neill, M. J., Shuttleworth, A., Stylli, C., Tait, R. M., Taylor, P. M., Wildman, H. G., Buss, A. D., Langely, D., and Hayes, M. V. (1992) The Squalestatins, novel inhibitors of squalene synthase produced by a species of *Phoma.* I. Taxonomy, fermentation, isolation, physico-chemical properties and biological activity. *J. Antibiotics* **45,** 639–647.

12. Mandava, N. B. and Ito, Y. (1982) Separation of plant hormones by countercurrent chromatography. *J. Chromatogr.* **247,** 315–325.

13. Mandala, S. M., Thorton, R. A., Frommer, B. R. Curotto, J. E., Rozdilsky, W., Kurtz, M. B., Giacobbe, R. A., Bills, G. R., Cabello, M. A., Martin, I., Pelaez, F., and Harris, G. H. (1995) The discovery of Australifungin, a novel inhibitor of sphinganine N-acyltransferase from *Sporormiella australis.* producing organism, fermentation, isolation, and biological activity. *J. Antibiotics* **48,** 349–356.

14. Stierle, D. B., Stierle, A. A., and Ganser B. (1997) New phomopsolides from a *Penicillium sp. J. Nat Prod.* **60,** 1207–1209.

15. Jarvis, B. B., DeSilva, T., McAlpine, J. B., Swanson, S. J., and Whittern, D. N. (1992) New trichoverroids from *Myrothecium verrucaria* Isolated by high speed countercurrent chromatography. *J. Nat. Prod.* **55,** 1441–1446.

16. Hochlowski, J. E., Mullally, M. M., Spanton, S. G., Whittern, D. N., Hill, P., and McAlpine, J. B. (1993) 5-N-Acetylardeemin, a novel heterocyclic compound which reverses multiple drug resistance in tumor cells II. Isolation and elucidation of the structure of 5-N-acetylardeemin and two congeners. *J. Antibiotics* **46,** 380–386.

17. Williams R. G. (1985) *Analytical Chemistry-Applied Spectroscopy Section,* Pittsburgh Conference and Exposition. New Orleans, LA, Abstract 300.

18. Breinholt, J., Ludvigsen, S., Rassing, B. R,. Rosendahl, C. N., Nielsen, S. E., and Olsen, C. E (1997) Oxysporidinone: a novel, antifungal N-methyl-4-hydroxy-2-pyridinone form *Fusarium oxysporum. J. Nat. Prod.* **60**, 33–35.

19. McAlpine, J. B., Tuan, J. S., Brown, D. P., Grebner, K. D., Whittern, D. N., Buko, A., and Katz, L. (1987) New antibiotics from geneticallly engineered actinomycetes I. 2-norerythromycins, isolation and structural determinations. *J. Antibiotics* **40**, 1115–1122.

20. Hochlowski, J. E., Hill, P., Whittern, D. N., Scherr, M. FI., Rasmussen, R. R., Dorwin, S. A., and McAlpine, J. B. (1994) Ascelacins, novel compounds that inhibit binding of endothelin to its receptor II. Isolation and elucidation of structures. *J. Antibiotics* **47**, 528– 535.

21. Mitchell, S. S., Whitehall, A. B., Trapido-Rosenthal, H. O., and Ireland, C. M. (1997) Isolation and characterization of 1,3-dimethylisoguanine from the Bermudian sponge *Amphimedon viridis. J. Nat. Prod.* **60**, 727, 728.

22. Hallock, Y. F., Manfredi, K. P., Dai, J.-R., Cardellina, J. H. II., Gulakowski, R. J., McMahon, J. B., Schaffer, M., Stahl, M., Gluden, K.-P., Bringmann,G., François, G., and Boyd, M. R. (1997) Michellamines D-F, new HIV-inhibitory dimeric naphthylisoquinoline alkaloids, and korupensamine E, a new antimalarial monomer, from *Ancistrocladus korupensis. J. Nat Prod.* **60**, 677–683.

23. Abbott, T., Peterson, R., McAlpine, J., Tjarks, L., and Bagby, M. (1989) Comparing centrifugal countercurrent chromatography, nonaqueous reversed phase HPLC and Ag ion exchange HPLC for the separation and characterization of triterpene acetates. *J. Liquid Chromatogr.* **12**, 2281–2301.

24. McAlpine, J. B., Theriault, R. J., Grebner, K. D., Hardy, D. J., and Fernandes, P. B. (1987) Minor products from the microbial transformation of 6-O-methylerythromicin A by *Mucor circinelloides. 27th Interscience Conference on Antimicrobial Agents and Chemotherapy,* New York, Abstract.

25. Hochlowski, J. E., Whittern, D. N., Hill, P., and McAlpine, J. B. (1994) Dorrigocins: novel antifungal antibiotics that change the morphology of rag-transformed NW3T3 cells to that of normal cells II. Isolation and elucidation of structures. *J. Antibiotics* **47**, 870–874.

26. Kobayashi, J., Tsuda, M., Fuse, H., Sasaki, T., and Mikami, Y. (1997) Halishigamides A-D, new cytotoxic oxazole-containing metabolites from Okinawan sponge *Halichondria sp. J. Nat. Prod* **60**, 150–154.

27. Bruening, R. C., Oltz, E. M., Furukawa, J., Nakanishi, K., and Kustin, K. (1985) Isolation and structure of tunichrome B-1, a reducing blood pigment from the tunicate *Ascidia nigra* L. *J. Amer. Chem. Soc.* **107**, 5298–5300.

28. Zhang, T. (1984) Horizontal flow-through coil planet centrifuge: some practical applications of countercurrent chromatography. *J. Chromatogr.* **31S**, 287–297.

9

Crystallization and Final Stages of Purification

Norman Shankland, Alastair J. Florence,
and Richard J. P. Cannell

1. Introduction

The hard work has been done and the purification is "complete"—the target compound has been separated from the other organic compounds in the mixture but is still in solution, and may possibly be "contaminated" by buffer salts or other inorganic compounds. The final, relatively easy, but necessary, step is to prepare the target compound in a usable form. This generally means producing a concentrated solution of pure compound or the pure dry solid, which may or may not be crystalline. The process of crystallization from solution can be used as a purification step in its own right or used to produce crystals for molecular structure determination by single-crystal X-ray diffraction—these two aspects are discussed in **Subheading 5.**

2. What is "Purity"?

The prelude to this final stage is to establish that the purification is complete. Analysis will have been ongoing during the isolation process, and so a suitable analytical system should be in place. However, because no further purification work is anticipated, additional analysis may be useful at this stage in order to ascertain with greater certainty the level at which contaminants are present.

A single peak on one (or preferably more than one) high-performance liquid chromatography (HPLC) system suggests only one component in the sample being analyzed. Similarly, a single spot on a number of different thin-layer chromatography (TLC) systems is suggestive of a single component. However, to be confident in this conclusion, we need to know that the systems being used actually do separate and detect all components. With HPLC, it is a

From: *Methods in Biotechnology, Vol. 4: Natural Products Isolation*
Edited by: R. J. P. Cannell © Humana Press Inc., Totowa, NJ

good idea to use a gradient system to elute compounds of a wide polarity range and to detect at a low wavelength, where compounds without a characteristic chromophore are likely to at least have some end absorbance. The use of two different systems reduces the possibility of impurities going undetected because of coelution. Whereas TLC does not have the resolving power of HPLC, it has the advantage that compounds do not require a chromophore to be detected— almost all compounds can be visualized by staining, and specific sensitive stains can be used to look for particular suspected contaminants. Although nuclear magnetic resonance (NMR) and mass spectrometry are also powerful tools for the detection and quantification of contaminants, it is preferable to know in advance that impurities are not going to interfere with the structure-elucidation process to a significant degree.

The definition of the word "pure" is fairly arbitrary *(1)*. To say that a purification process is "complete" and that the target natural product compound is now "pure" does not necessarily imply that it is absolutely free of other chemicals. It simply means that the amount of any impurity present does not exceed some arbitrarily defined "acceptable" level.

3. Desalting and Concentration

3.1. Gel Filtration

The target natural product molecules typically have a mass of several hundred atomic mass units (amu) and can be separated from smaller inorganic ions (and from larger macromolecules) by running on a small gel-filtration column. The larger components elute from the column first, leaving the smaller components to take a slower, more tortuous route down the column. The target natural product compounds therefore elute first and the inorganic ions elute last. Such a column can be set up quickly using some gel-filtration medium (e.g., Sephadex G15) retained in a Pasteur pipet with some glass wool.

3.2. Liquid–Liquid Extraction

Organic natural product compounds can often be separated from more polar components such as buffer ions and acids by partitioning between water and an immiscible organic phase. The relative affinity of a component for the liquid phases is indicated by the magnitude of its partition coefficient, which is approximately equal to the ratio of the solubility of the component in the organic phase to its solubility in water. Therefore, for the separation to be successful, the target natural product compound should have a high partition coefficient, and the more polar "impurities" should have low partition coefficients. The efficiency of the process can be increased by using repeated extractions with small volumes of liquid in preference to a single extraction with the equivalent combined volume. Thus, a greater percentage of polar water-soluble impurities will be removed from an organic phase extracted with 4×25 mL vol of water, compared with a single extraction with 100 mL water.

3.3. Solid Phase Extraction

This is a commonly used method for both removing common impurities and concentrating samples and can be achieved with commercially available solid phase extraction cartridges packed as columns in syringes through which the solutions can be forced. The process can also be carried out by pumping onto reverse phase HPLC columns. In any case, the sample solution containing the target compounds should be concentrated, perhaps by rotary evaporation, or diluted with an appropriate solvent to increase polarity so that the target compounds adsorb onto the reverse phase stationary phase when pumped onto a water-equilibrated column. Most natural product compounds that have a degree of lipophilicity will be adsorbed onto the stationary phase, and the more-polar contaminants will pass straight through. The remaining polar material can be washed away with several bed volumes of water and the pH of the wash can be monitored to ensure removal of any traces of acid or alkali. The target compounds can then be eluted from the column in a small volume of organic solvent. This technique is described more fully in Chapters 1 and 6.

4. Drying

The final stage is to evaporate solvent from liquid samples and then dry the solid product obtained. This may sound fairly straightforward but it is worth considering briefly why and how the purified natural products might be dried.

4.1. Reasons for Drying

1. Chemical and physical stability—The compound is more likely to remain stable in a dry form than in solution.
2. Yield—In order to determine the yield of compound isolated, it usually needs to be weighed as a dry solid.
3. NMR—In many cases, the aim of the purification will be to carry out NMR spectroscopy in order to elucidate molecular structure. Any water present in the sample shows up as a large signal in the middle of a 1H-NMR spectrum and may make it difficult, or impossible, to interpret the spectrum. This is not a problem with a properly dried sample dissolved in a deuterated or nonprotonated solvent.

4.2. Methods of Drying

Whereas drying on an industrial scale can be a costly and complex part of an industrial process *(2)*, on a laboratory scale it should be a relatively minor part of an isolation. However, the method of drying may well be determined by the nature of the sample and by what we wish to do subsequently with the solid.

4.2.1. Drying Under Inert Gas

As a sample is dried, a dynamic equilibrium is established between the sample surface and the vapor phase. By removing solvent vapor from the immediate vicinity of the surface, the equilibrium is shifted in favor of evaporation and drying. This can be done by passing an inert gas such as nitrogen over a sample either with or without additional heating. This method may leave the solid as a film on the bottom of the vessel, dry, but not always easy to manipulate.

4.2.2. Rotary Evaporation

Rotary evaporators are familiar to most chemical laboratories, and the process is simply one of boiling the sample under a reduced pressure to lower the boiling point while rotating the sample to maximize the surface area over which evaporation takes place. The vapor is trapped by a condenser and collects in a separate vessel. Again the material may end up as a thin film across the inside of a glass round-bottomed flask. An additional disadvantage is that solutions may be prone to "bump," or boil unevenly, spilling over into the waste vessel. Solutions containing surface-active material are also prone to frothing, forming a foam that can spill out of the containing vessel. This can sometimes be reduced by the addition of a small amount of a surface-active organic solvent such as *n*-octanol.

4.2.3. Vacuum Drying

This process essentially follows the principle just described, with an applied vacuum facilitating drying by lowering the boiling point of the solvent. If the solvent is water, a hygroscopic material such as phosphorus pentoxide is normally put in the dryer to absorb water as it comes off the sample. The sample can be heated as necessary.

4.2.4. Vacuum Centrifugation

Vacuum centrifugation combines the advantages of low vapor pressure and heating with centrifugation, so that as samples dry, they are concentrated in the bottom of a tube rather than spread as a thin film over a relatively large area. This method is particularly useful for handling relatively large numbers of liquid samples such as drying and concentrating fractions prior to assay.

4.2.5. Freeze-Drying/Lyophilization

Freeze-drying takes place under high vacuum and involves sublimation of water from a frozen solid. The sample to be dried is first frozen, using solid carbon dioxide or Freon, and then placed under vacuum and the water removed by sublimation. This process has the advantage that it tends to leave the sample as a manageable solid with a fine porous structure that allows it to be readily redissolved or resuspended in liquid. It tends not to denature proteins and can be used as a means of storing viable microbial cells.

In order to determine whether a solid is dry, the principle of constant weight is often used. When a solid undergoing a drying step ceases to lose weight, it has no more solvent left to lose and is therefore dry.

5. Crystallization

5.1. Introduction

This section provides guidance on laboratory-scale crystallization of "small" organic compounds. It does not deal with the more specialized area of crystallization of proteins. Crystal structure reports in journals rarely, if ever, detail crystallization information beyond the solvent used. Textbooks also tend to be limited in value because they vary so much in scope and focus. What we present here combines information gathered from textbooks with our own experience of growing single crystals for X-ray and neutron diffraction experiments, and keeps the natural products chemist very much in mind.

5.1.1. What is a Crystal?

Crystallinity is synonymous with order, and it is this order that enables us to recognize crystalline material through properties such as a definite melting point, the diffraction of X-rays, and the presence of ordered flat surfaces (faces) with straight edges. The sparkling of crystalline sugar, for example, is caused by light reflecting off the flat faces that bound individual crystals. The term *poly*crystalline describes aggregates of crystals that are too small for any crystallinity to be instantly obvious to the naked eye. In marked contrast to crystalline solids, amorphous materials such as liquids, glasses, and rubbers have no long-range atomic order.

There is an obvious connection between crystal chemistry and natural products. Crystals appear in plant material *(3,4)*—calcium oxalate is extremely common; potassium acid tartrate in outer perisperm cells of nutmeg; hesperidin and diosmin in cells of many of the Rutaceae; calcium carbonate in cells of Cannabinaceae; silica in the cells of the sclerenchymatous layer of cardamom seeds. The crystallizing temperature of the solid complex between 1,8-cineole and *o*-cresol forms the basis for official assay of oil of eucalyptus *(4)*. Also worth noting is the fact that alkaloids, particularly brucine, are widely used to resolve optically active acids by diastereoisomer fractional crystallization *(5)*.

5.1.2. Why Crystallize?

Single-crystal X-ray diffraction allows us to "see" atom positions in 3D space, and as such is more direct than NMR, which uses radio frequency to "hear" nuclei resonating in a magnetic field. Single-crystal X-ray diffraction

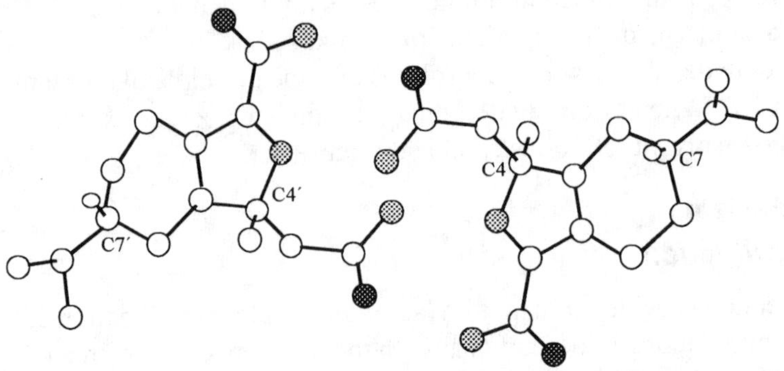

Fig. 1. Manicoline B (after **ref. 6**).

can be used to determine, confirm, or complete molecular structures routinely and unambiguously and thereby establish conformation and relative stereochemistry. For example, the crystal structure of the alkaloid manicoline B (**Fig. 1**) shows that the molecule occurs as diastereoisomers with the same configuration at C-7 and different configurations at C-4. Single-crystal X-ray diffraction can also be used to determine absolute configuration. Heavy atom (e.g., bromo-) derivatives are preferred if the parent compound contains only C, N, and O, because bromine has appreciable anomalous scattering and renders the determination of absolute configuration easier (for an example, *see* **ref. 7**).

On a point of interest, the Cambridge Structural Database *(8)* archives crystal structure data (currently approx 153,000 "small" molecules) and enables searches to be performed using a graphical interface. Entries for terpenes, alkaloids, and miscellaneous natural products are identified as such, which is useful for searching these classes of compounds. The number of compounds in these three categories, with coordinates to enable 3D representation of structure, currently stands at approx 3700.

Subheadings 5.2.–5.4. are written from the point of view of the natural products chemist who has compound(s) of acceptable chemical purity and who wants to grow crystals, usually for the purposes of molecular structure determination by single-crystal X-ray diffraction. **Subheading 5.5.**, on the other hand, illustrates how crystallization can be used to achieve separation. Bear in mind that, on a scale smaller than 100 mg, chromatographic techniques are usually more appropriate for separations but, as the examples in **Subheading 5.5.** show, crystallization often occurs as part of a concentration step in an extraction.

5.2. Obtaining Crystals

The most practical method of crystallizing natural products is from solution, and the process can be described as one in which:

1. A saturated solution containing one or more compounds of interest becomes supersaturated.
2. Nucleation occurs and crystal growth ensues.

Crystallization is essentially a collision process: Molecules collide to form a cluster called the nucleus, which then develops into a crystal with a characteristic internal structure and external shape. It therefore follows that factors such as stirring and degree of supersaturation, which influence the number of molecular collisions in solution, will affect the crystallization process.

5.2.1. Solvent Selection

Solvent is chosen such that the compound of interest is neither excessively soluble nor insoluble. The common solvents include water, the short-chain alcohols (methanol to hexanol), halogenated solvents (chloroform and carbon tetrachloride), ketones such as acetone and methyl-isobutylketone, pyridine, 1,4-dioxane, ethyl acetate, diethyl ether, petroleum ether, hexane, and toluene. Solubility varies tremendously with solvent. The solubility of naphthalene, for example, is approximately doubled going from methanol to ethanol, while the addition of water to either drastically reduces solubility *(9)*. Thus, solvent selection is important, and solvent mixtures provide a convenient way of tailoring solubility to a required level. Any miscible pair of solvents is worth investigating, especially if compound solubility differs significantly between the two.

5.2.2. Preparation of Solution and Crystallization

In instances in which there is no shortage of sample compound, a saturated solution can be prepared by dissolving some of the sample in the crystallizing solvent, then incrementally adding more solid up to the point where no more will dissolve, i.e., the point of saturation. Note that the maximum concentration of compound that can be dissolved at a particular temperature, i.e., the saturation solubility, generally increases with increasing temperature.

When only small quantities of sample compound are available, an alternative approach is to dissolve the compound in Solvent 1 and then add a second, miscible solvent dropwise to produce a mixed solvent system in which the compound is less soluble than in Solvent 1 alone. When the solution turns turbid, it is saturated.

Once the solution has been filtered to remove gross particulate contamination—glass wool in a Pasteur pipet is convenient for small volumes—proceed to the supersaturation stage. The most common methods of supersaturating a solution (i.e., raising the concentration of a dissolved compound above its saturation solubility) are evaporation and cooling.

5.2.2.1. EVAPORATION

Leave the solution open to the atmosphere at constant temperature, or alternatively:

1. Reduce the rate of evaporation by covering with perforated aluminium foil.
2. Enhance evaporation by directing a gentle stream of nitrogen gas over the solution surface.

One obvious question is, "Does temperature matter?" Strictly speaking, the answer is yes. The exact way in which organic molecules pack together to form the crystal lattice is often dependent on temperature. A racemic aqueous solution of sodium ammonium tartrate, for example, spontaneously resolves into dextrorotatory and levorotatory crystals when crystallized below 28°C, but yields racemic compound crystals at temperatures above 28°C *(10)*. Furthermore, the single enantiomer crystals are tetrahydrate (i.e., four molecules of water cocrystallize with each molecule of sodium ammonium tartrate), whereas the racemic compound crystals are monohydrate. This is an example of solid-state polymorphism (**Subheading 5.4.2.**) and a historically important one: Louis Pasteur effected the chiral separation of sodium ammonium tartrate by crystallization in 1848 *(11)*. However, it is by no means unique; in fact, quite the opposite. Polymorphism is widespread among organic compounds *(12)*, and temperature often has an important effect on the polymorphic form of an organic compound obtained by crystallization from solution.

In many instances, if all that is required from a single-crystal X-ray diffraction experiment is a proof of molecular structure, then the occurrence of polymorphism is not necessarily a problem, other than to note that single crystals of one physical form of a compound may be more suitable for a diffraction experiment than single crystals of a different form.

5.2.2.2. COOLING

The solubility of "small" organic molecules generally decreases with decreasing temperature. By controlling the rate and extent of cooling, thereby controlling the degree of supersaturation, it is possible to control the degree of nucleation and the rate of crystal growth. Cooling rate can be conveniently controlled using a water bath and simply making adjustments based on observations of whether nucleation and growth are proceeding too rapidly or too slowly. Microcrystals are indicative of too rapid cooling—this tends to result in the formation of excessive numbers of nuclei and hence a large number of small crystals.

5.2.2.3. CRYSTALLIZATION BY VAPOR DIFFUSION

If growth by slow evaporation or controlled cooling is not proving to be successful, crystallization by vapor diffusion can be useful *(13–15)*:

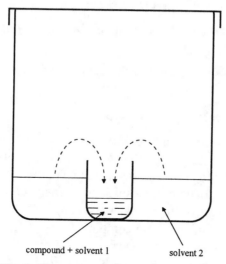

compound + solvent 1   solvent 2

Fig. 2. Supersaturation by vapor diffusion.

1. Place the sample in a small test tube and add just enough of Solvent 1 to produce a solution.
2. Place the test tube in a larger sealed beaker containing Solvent 2 (**Fig. 2**). Solvent 2 should be sufficiently volatile to diffuse into Solvent 1, producing a mixed system in which the compound is less soluble than in Solvent 1 alone.
3. Evaporation of Solvent 1 will help supersaturate the solution, although it can be advantageous when the process actually increases the volume of recrystallizing solution, since this helps avoid "crusting" (**Subheading 5.3.1.**). Ideally, Solvent 2 should be more volatile, more dense and a poorer solvent for the compound than Solvent 1.

5.2.3. Growth of High-Quality Single Crystals for Diffraction

Growth of diffraction-quality crystals necessitates *(13)*:

1. A limited number of nuclei.
2. A slow rate of growth—days rather than hours.

As a general rule, good single crystals are produced by slow growth from unstirred solutions. These conditions limit nucleation, whereas high degrees of supersaturation result in the rapid formation of a large number of nuclei and tend to yield less suitable crystals. Major multiple nucleation can sometimes be prevented by scratching the inside of the beaker, or seeding the solution with a small crystal of the compound. Remember that a seed crystal will still grow in a solution where the degree of supersaturation is so low that the rate of nucleation is zero or close to zero. Thus, the solution will "fatten up" the seed in preference to depositing "new" crystals.

5.3. Common Problems and Solutions

5.3.1. Polycrystalline Crust Forms as Solvent Recedes During Evaporation

Reduce the rate of solvent evaporation, and introduce one or two seed crystals into the solution, if available.

5.3.2. Product is Not a Crystalline Solid

"Oiling" is common and can be overcome by varying the crystallizing temperature and/or the crystallizing solvent. It may be that nucleation is a problem, in which case stirring or seeding may help. Failing that, derivatization is a possibility. Many cyanogenic glycosides are difficult to crystallize, whereas their peracetates readily form crystals *(16)*. The hydrochloride and hydrobromide salts of organic base compounds are often easier to crystallize than the parent compound itself. Derivatives are also useful in fractional crystallisations *(17)*; for example, picrates of alkaloids and osazones of sugars.

5.3.3. Crystallization is Reluctant to Proceed

Supersaturated solutions can often sit for very long periods of time without producing crystals *(9)*. This seems counterintuitive, but it stems from the fact that nuclei below a certain critical size find it energetically unfavorable to expand against the surrounding solvent. Chemical impurities also tend to impede crystallization. However, if purity is not the problem, then try the following:

1. Stirring can enhance nucleation by promoting the frequency of collisions in solution, although excessive agitation can actually have the opposite effect *(18)*.
2. Crystals are quite happy to grow on foreign surfaces *(19)* and leaving the flask open to atmospheric dust might be all that is needed to get the crystallization going. However, if seed crystals of the sample compound are available, it is even better.
3. Filtering a hot solution into a cold flask to achieve very rapid cooling is often sufficient to induce rapid crystallization. Roughening the inside of the glass flask with a spatula is also often helpful.
4. Temperature cycling can be advantageous—Cool a supersaturated solution to refrigerator or freezer temperatures to reduce solubility and hopefully induce nucleation (**Subheading 5.2.2.**) and then warm to room temperature to encourage the nuclei to develop into crystals. This circumvents the possibility that excessive cooling might actually impede progress by increasing viscosity.

5.3.4. Crystals Grow but Are Unsuitable for Single-Crystal X-Ray Diffraction

It is often the case that single crystals are too small in one or more dimensions to give good-quality diffraction data (**Subheading 5.4.1.**). If so, change the crystallizing solvent or try the following:

1. Reduce the number of nuclei formed by reducing the degree of supersaturation and by filtering off any gross particulate contamination.
2. If the crystals are large enough to handle, use one or two to seed a separate crystallization.
3. Disperse a small quantity of the crystals in a drop of saturated mother liquor on a glass microscope slide and observe the crystals with a microscope, paying particular attention to those dispersed around the periphery of the droplet. Providing that the rate of evaporation is not too high, significant increases in crystal size can be observed fairly readily as the droplet evaporates. Water droplets evaporate at a reasonable rate at room temperature, whereas a highly volatile organic solvent such as diethyl ether tends to evaporate far too rapidly for this approach to be useful.

5.3.5. Only a Small Quantity of Compound Is Available for Crystallization

A hanging-drop variation of the vapor-diffusion technique described in **Subheading 5.2.2.** has proved to be a popular and effective method of crystallizing milligram quantities of proteins *(13–15)*. In principle, the method is not restricted to macromolecules, and a simple modification of the vapor-diffusion scheme described in **Subheading 5.2.2.** is worth trying with very small quantities of natural product extract. The compound should be dissolved in a drop of Solvent 1, but in place of the test tube shown in **Fig. 2**, the drop should be suspended from a glass cover slip over a reservoir of Solvent 2, and the system sealed with grease to prevent solvent from escaping. Vapor diffusion results in supersaturation and hopefully crystal growth. Crystals growing in the hanging drop can be observed and retrieved easily, and the method has been used to grow protein crystals in drop volumes as low as 5–15 μL, over a reservoir of 500 μL *(13)*.

5.4. Selecting a Crystal

5.4.1. Crystal Quality

Once the compound of interest has been crystallized, the question then arises, "What makes a single crystal 'good'?" Size, shape, and quality are essential for obtaining good single-crystal X-ray diffraction data *(14)*. The crystal should ideally be equidimensional, with edges in the range approx 0.1–0.3 mm. Thus, the volume of the crystal should be large enough to ensure adequate diffraction of the X-ray beam, but not too large, otherwise absorption of X-rays becomes problematic. The crystal must be single in the sense that it is neither twinned nor is it an aggregate of microcrystals. It should not be physically distorted or fractured, but beyond that, it does not have to have well-developed faces, and hygroscopicity is not necessarily a problem. Crystal quality is conveniently checked using a polarizing microscope *(14)*:

1. Place a crystal on a glass microscope slide—A fine paintbrush is good for gently manipulating small crystals.

2. Rotate the crystal about an axis normal to the polarizer, or alternatively rotate the polarizer itself.

A single crystal should ideally appear either uniformly dark, irrespective of position, or else undergo a sharp change in appearance from uniformly dark to uniformly bright every 90°. Undulatory extinction is indicative of strain in the crystal lattice. A composite crystal, i.e., an intergrowth of two or more crystals, will often show light and dark simultaneously. A twin is a composite of two crystals joined symmetrically about a twin axis, or a twin plane, and often appears as a "V," "L," or "+" shape *(20)*.

5.4.2. Solid-State Polymorphism

It is not uncommon for microscopic examination to reveal two or more populations of crystals with characteristically different shapes. Assuming the sample is sufficiently pure to rule out the possibility that the populations are in fact different compounds, there is the possibility that the compound is polymorphic. Polymorphs of the same chemical compound have different crystal lattice structures, i.e., they have different internal molecular packing arrangements, which necessarily gives rise to different external crystal shapes. An example is shown in **Fig. 3**. L-glutamic acid can be crystallized from hot aqueous solution to yield the α-polymorph, the β-polymorph or mixtures of the two, depending on factors that include temperature and rate of stirring *(21)*. As pointed out in **Subheading 5.2.2.**, if all that is required is a proof of molecular structure, then polymorphic form is not necessarily a problem, or even important on this scale, other than to note once again that single crystals of one physical form of the compound may be more suitable for a diffraction experiment than single crystals of a different form. However, the existence of polymorphism should always be documented and may well assume significance should the compound reach the stage of industrial production. (For a comprehensive review of polymorphism, *see* **ref. 12**.)

Having selected one or more high-quality single crystals for a diffraction experiment, it is essential to store the samples to prevent chemical or physical degradation. Common mechanisms of physical degradation include:

1. Moisture gain. Hygroscopic crystals are best stored under nitrogen or in a dry atmosphere.
2. Solvent loss. It is fairly common for compounds to crystallize as solvates, i.e., with molecules of solvent incorporated into the crystal structure (*see*, for example, **Subheadings 5.2.2. and 5.5.2.**). Single-crystal solvates may become polycrystalline as a result of desolvation and are best stored in a sealed glass vial.

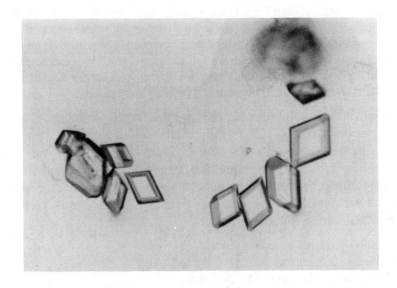

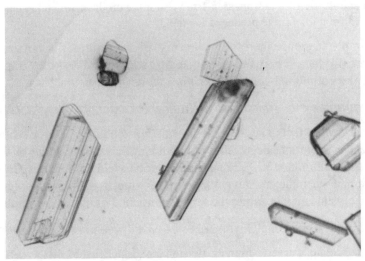

Fig. 3. L-glutamic acid α-crystals (top) and β-crystals (bottom).

5.5. Crystallization as a Separation Method

5.5.1. General

The principle of crystallization as a separation method is fairly simple and draws on what has already been outlined in **Subheading 5.2.** For example, assuming we have a product comprising component A mixed in with components B and C:

1. Dissolve a sample of the mixture in hot solvent. Choose the solvent such that B and C are soluble at any temperature reached in the crystallization, while compound A is not.
2. Cooling yields a crop of A, with a reduced content of components B and C.
3. Repeat **steps 1** and **2** using fresh solvent each time, until the required degree of separation is achieved (note that one crystallization step from a mixture of compounds does not guarantee a chemically pure crystal product).

The disadvantage of this approach is that losses can be prohibitive, and on a scale smaller than 100 mg, chromatographic techniques are more appropriate for separating the components of a sample. There are variations on the above scheme, designed to recycle the liquid filtrates produced by successive crystallization steps and to conserve the target compound. A good general account of these fractional crystallisation schemes is given in *(1)*, and one other scheme is mentioned here for completeness:

1. Crystallize product and retain filtrate.
2. Dissolve product in fresh solvent.
3. Recrystallize product and retain filtrate.
4. Concentrate the filtrate from **step 1** to yield more product, which is then recrystallized from the filtrate produced in **step 3**.

This simple sequence therefore makes use of both filtrates to obtain twice-crystallized product. It may be, of course, that component A is the "impurity," not the target compound—examples of both cases follow.

5.5.2. Examples of Purification of Natural Products by Crystallization

Concentrated extracts may deposit crystals on standing by virtue of the fact that solvent evaporation, decreasing temperature, or a combination of the two results in supersaturation *(22)*. For example, good yields of crystals are sometimes obtained when the hot solvent used in a Soxhlet extraction is cooled overnight. The crystals may be either the target compound of interest or impurities.

5.5.2.1. TARGET COMPOUND CRYSTALLIZES LEAVING "IMPURITIES" IN SOLUTION

1. Crude solanine, extracted from the potato plant, is purified by dissolving in boiling methanol, filtering, and concentrating until the alkaloid crystallizes out *(23)*.
2. Naringin is isolated from grapefruit peel by extracting into hot water, filtering through celite, and concentrating the filtrate to the extent that naringin crystallizes at refreigerator temperatures as the octahydrate (melting point 83°C) *(24)*. Recrystallization from isopropanol (100 mL to 8.6 g naringin) yields the dihydrate (melting point 171°C). The di- and octahydrate compounds are examples of crystalline solvates (**Subheading 5.4.**).
3. Piperine, extracted from powdered black pepper with 95% ethanol. The extract is filtered, concentrated, 10% alcoholic KOH added, and the residue formed is discarded. The solution is then left overnight to yield yellow needles of piperine *(25)*.

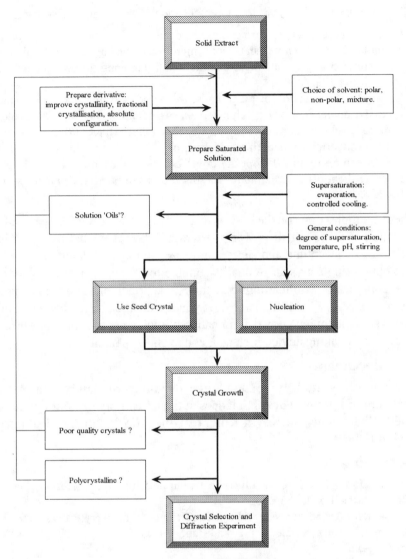

Fig. 4. Summary flowchart.

4. Capsanthin, isolated from red pepper or paprika. A 20-mL volume of concentrated ether extract diluted with 60 mL petroleum and left to stand for 24 h in a refrigerator produces crystals of almost pure capsanthin *(26)*.

5. Salicin, extracted from willow bark into hot water. The solution is filtered and concentrated, and the tannin removed by treatment with lead acetate. Further concentration and cooling yields salicin crystals *(27)*.

Subheading 5.3.2. makes reference to the use of derivatives such as sugar osazones in fractional crystallisation.

276 *Shankland et al.*

5.5.2.2. "Impurities" Crystallize Leaving Target Compound in Solution

1. Concentrated extracts of carotenoids are occasionally contaminated with large amounts of sterols. These can be conveniently removed by leaving a light petroleum solution to stand at $-10°C$ overnight and removing the precipitated sterol by centrifugation *(26)*.
2. During the purification of plant acids, oxalic acid, which may be present in excessive amounts, can be precipitated out as calcium oxalate by adding calcium hydroxide solution to a concentrated alcoholic plant extract *(28)*.
3. In the production of medicinal cod-liver oils, saturated acylglycerols such as stearin can be removed from the crude cod-liver oil simply by cooling and filtering them off as precipitate, leaving the unsaturated acylglycerols in the liquid *(29,30)*.

These examples draw on the basic principles of **Subheading 5.2.**, particularly evaporation and cooling. It is worth reiterating, however, that using a rotary evaporator to concentrate and supersaturate a solution is certainly not the best way to obtain single crystals of quality suitable for X-ray diffraction. The more genteel approach of **Subheadings 5.2.** and **5.3.** is preferable, and the key points are summarized in **Fig. 4.** Remember, if you are unsure about whether a single crystal is suitable for an X-ray determination of molecular structure, never redissolve it without taking advice first, and, above all, be patient!

Acknowledgments

The authors gratefully acknowledge the input of Sandy Gray of the Department of Pharmaceutical Sciences at the University of Strathclyde, and Kenneth Shankland and Kevin Knight of the *ISIS* Facility at Rutherford Appleton Laboratory.

References

1. Mullin, J. W. (1972) Crystallisation techniques, in *Crystallisation*, 2nd ed., Butterworths, London, pp. 233–257.
2. Hossain, M. A. and Kennedy, J. F. (1993) Drying, in *Recovery Processes for Biological Materials* (Kennedy, J. F. and Cabral, J. M. S., eds.), Wiley, New York, pp. 543–558.
3. Trease, G. E. and Evans, W. C. (1996) Cell differentiation and ergastic cell contents, in *Pharmacognosy*, 14th ed., W. B. Saunders, London, pp. 554–567.
4. *ibid.* Volatile oils and resins, pp. 255–292.
5. Jacques, J., Collet, A., and Wilen, S. H. (1981) Formation and separation of diastereomers, in *Enantiomers, Racemates and Resolutions*, Wiley, New York, pp. 251–368.
6. Polonsky, J., Prangé, T., Pascard, C., Jacquemin, H., and Fournet, A. (1984) Structure (x-ray analysis) of Manicoline B, a mixture of two diastereoisomers of a new alkaloid from *Dulacia guianensis* (Olacaceae). *Tetrahedon Letts.* **25,** 2359–2362.

7. Ghisalberti, E. L., Jefferies, P. R., Skelton, B. W., White, A. H., and Williams, R. S. F. (1989) A new stereochemical class of bicyclic sesquiterpenes from *Eremophila virgata* W. V. Fitzg. (Myoporaceae). *Tetrahedron* **45**, 6297–6308.

8. Allen, F. H., Kennard, O., and Watson, D. G. (1994) Crystallographic databases: search and retrieval of information from the Cambridge Structural Database, in *Structure Correlation*, vol. 1 (Bürgi, H.-B. and Dunitz, J. D., eds.), VCH, Weinheim, pp. 71–110.

9. VanHook, A. (1961) Crystallization in the laboratory and in the plant, in *Crystallization Theory and Practice*, Reinhold, New York, pp. 192–237.

10. Jacques, J., Collet, A., and Wilen, S. H. (1981) Solution properties of enantiomers and their mixtures, in *Enantiomers, Racemates and Resolutions*, Wiley, New York, pp. 167–213.

11 *ibid.* Resolution by direct crystallization, pp. 217–250.

12. Threlfall, T. L. (1995) Analysis of organic polymorphs. *Analyst* **120**, 2435–2460.

13. Glusker, J. P., Lewis, M., and Rossi, M. (1994) Crystals, in *Crystal Structure Analysis for Chemists and Biologists*, VCH, New York, pp. 33–72.

14. Stout, G. H. and Jensen, L. H. (1989) Crystals and their properties, in *X-ray Structure Determination. A Practical Guide*, Wiley, New York, pp. 74–92.

15. Glusker, J. P. and Trueblood, K. N. (1985) Crystals, in *Crystal Structure Analysis. A Primer*, Oxford University Press, New York, pp. 8–19.

16. Seigler, D. S. and Brinker, A. M. (1993) Characterisation of cyanogenic glycosides, cyanolipids, nitroglycosides, organic nitro compounds and nitrile glucosides from plants, in *Methods in Plant Biochemistry*, vol. 8 (Waterman, P. G., ed.), Academic, London, pp. 51–131.

17. Trease, G. E. and Evans, W. C. (1996) Introduction and general methods, in *Pharmacognosy*, 14th ed., W. B. Saunders, London, pp. 119–130.

18. Mullin, J. W. (1972) Crystallisation kinetics, in *Crystallisation*, 2nd ed., Butterworths, London, pp. 174–232.

19. VanHook, A. (1961) Historical review, in *Crystallization Theory and Practice*, Reinhold, New York, pp.1–44.

20. Mullin, J. W. (1972) The crystalline state, in *Crystallisation*, 2nd ed., Butterworths, London, pp. 1–27.

21. Kitamura, M. (1989) Polymorphism in the crystallization of L-glutamic acid. *J. Crystal Growth* **96**, 541–546.

22. Harborne, J. B. (1984) Methods of plant analysis, in *Phytochemical Methods*, 2nd ed., Chapman and Hall, London, pp.1–36.

23. *ibid.* Nitrogen compounds, pp. 176–221.

24. *ibid.* Sugars and their derivatives, pp. 222–242.

25. Harborne, J. B. (1973) Nitrogen compounds, in *Phytochemical Methods*, 1st ed., Chapman and Hall, London, pp. 166–211.

26. Harborne, J. B. (1984) The terpenoids, in *Phytochemical Methods*, 2nd ed., Chapman and Hall, London, pp. 100–141.

27. Trease, G. E. and Evans, W. C. (1996) Phenols and phenolic glycosides, in *Pharmacognosy*, 14th ed., W. B. Saunders, London, pp. 218–254.

28. Harborne, J. B. (1984) Organic acids, lipids and related compounds, in *Phytochemical Methods*, 2nd ed., Chapman and Hall, London, pp. 142–175.
29. Trease, G. E. and Evans, W. C. (1996) Vitamins and hormones, in *Pharmacognosy*, 14th ed., W. B. Saunders, London, pp. 441–450.
30. *ibid.* Hydrocarbons and derivatives, pp. 172–190.

Suggested Reading

Laboratory Manual on Crystal Growth (1972) (Tarján, I. and Mátrai, M., eds., translated by Morlin, Z.), Akadémiai Kiadó, Budapest.

10

Dereplication and Partial Identification of Natural Products

Frank VanMiddlesworth and Richard J. P. Cannell

1. Introduction

Since the "Golden Age of Antibiotics" in the 1950s, natural products chemists have faced the steadily increasing problem of how to maximize the discovery of new compounds and minimize the re-evaluation of natural products already described in the literature. If a compound has been isolated, identified, and reported, it should be possible to use the published information to identify the compound when it appears again, without having to repeat the entire isolation and structure-determination process. In addition, in many instances, the questions being asked in a study can be answered simply by partial identification of the unknown structure. These complementary processes of rapid identification of known compounds from a partially purified mixture and identification of enough of an unknown structure to prioritize or conclude an isolation, have come to be termed "dereplication" by the natural products community.

The origin of the term dereplication as currently used in natural products chemistry is obscure, but it seems to have predated 1978, since that year's edition of the CRC Handbook of Antibiotic Compounds *(1)* contains the following historical analysis:

> . . .early recognition of duplication in a new active agent was essential. . . In the earliest procedures extensive use of biological activity and resistance patterns served to detect similarities. . . Now however, the great convenience of chemical and physical instrumental methods lays the groundwork for more specific identification and *dereplication*.

The aims of dereplication and partial identification procedures are to identify a chemical entity to a level that will successfully conclude the extraction as

From: *Methods in Biotechnology, Vol. 4: Natural Products Isolation*
Edited by: R. J. P. Cannell © Humana Press Inc., Totowa, NJ

efficiently as possible. This can mean either a full identification of a natural product after only partial purification, or a partial identification to the level of a family of known compounds. Full identification in such cases normally relies on comparison of the compound with a characterized standard.

Reasons for carrying out a partial identification include:

1. To identify the compound as a member of a set that is not "desired." These classes might include common "interfering" groups of compounds such as tannins and polyphenols, fatty acids, or proteins, that may show nonspecific biological activity. The natural product might be one or a mixture of such compounds and may even include novel compounds.

2. To group a number of samples into related chemical classes and therefore prioritize samples for the extraction procedure. Often when natural extracts are assayed in high-throughput screens against biological targets, a relatively large primary "hit" rate is observed, which tends to suggest that one or more commonly recurring compounds are active in that assay. This filtering mechanism should identify rapidly the most diverse extracts on which to concentrate further efforts.

3. To obtain information that will progress the extraction; e.g., determination of the compound as an alkaloid means that it is basic and might be isolated by ion-exchange techniques.

This process of dereplication is becoming increasingly important and occupies a significant proportion of the time of many natural products chemists. Certain groups of organisms, such as marine invertebrates, were once very productive sources of novel compounds, but as they have been progressively investigated, the isolation of structurally novel components is becoming less routine, and more time is spent on dereplication. Faulkner's observations about marine natural products can be extended to many areas of natural products discovery:

> The good old days of 'grind and find'—when nearly every organism contained new and interesting molecules—are fast disappearing. Most bioactive extracts now contain only known compounds and developing rapid methods to avoid duplication of earlier research has become a priority *(2)*.

This is not to say that the large proportion of natural products are not waiting to be discovered, but that we need methods for bypassing those already discovered that effectively stand in the way.

In order to carry out dereplication procedures, a number of general characterization techniques are routinely employed to build information about the natural product that can be compared with other characterized compounds or sets of compounds. These techniques include chromatographic and other separation methods, chemical, spectroscopic, and biological approaches. Essentially, the process involves a series of questions at each stage of the extraction based on characteristics of the compound that allow it to be assigned to either a known compound, a general class of compounds, or an unknown structure. No single piece of data is conclusive on its own, but the partial structure identification is, instead, a process of building increasing levels of confidence in a putative structure.

The last two decades have seen tremendous breakthroughs in each of these technologies as well as in information transfer. This chapter attempts to outline the scope of the dereplication problems and show how these technological advances, along with long-established methods, can be applied to these processes of natural product dereplication and partial identification.

2. Separation Sciences

2.1. Solvent Partitions

The first physical characteristics of an unknown natural product are determined during the initial extraction and concentration steps of natural product isolation. If partitioning experiments are performed using solvents exhibiting a range of polarities and at various pH values, then some indication of the hydrophobicity of the natural product can be determined at this stage, as well as some indication of whether the compound contains an ionizable functional group.

2.2. TLC and HPLC

If the natural product is suspected to be a known compound that is available as a standard, then various chromatographic techniques such as TLC and HPLC may be used to establish with a fairly high degree of confidence, the coidentity of the natural product with another compound. If two compounds have different t_R (HPLC), or R_f (TLC) values on identical chromatographic systems, they cannot be the same compound and, conversely, two samples of the same compound will always have the same retention time on a given system. The usefulness of this depends on the accuracy with which the t_R of a natural product can be measured. By HPLC, retention times can usually be measured to an accuracy of about 0.5%.

Experimental variability in retention times between chromatographic runs means that, in order to maximize the degree of certainty of identification, the sample and the reference standard should be injected together (coinjection/spiking/overspiking). If more than a single peak is observed—e.g., two peaks, or a peak shoulder—the two compounds are certainly different (assuming no artifactual effects from the chromatographic system). If a single peak is seen, the two compounds may be the same. However, different compounds may have the same retention time, and an additional identification technique should be used in order to establish coidentity with more certainty.

Chromatographic behavior also provides useful information about the nature of the compound; e.g., one is often led to suspect the presence of fatty acids from their long retention times observed in acidic media using a reverse phase column. Theoretical treatments have appeared that attempt to link a compound's physical characteristics, such as hydrophobicity, logP, surface area, and dipole moment, to its behavior in a series of HPLC experiments *(3)*. If this theory is born out by empirical evidence, HPLC retention time could impart more structural information than presently.

2.2.1. TLC and Bioassay Overlay

When TLC is combined directly with bioassay, more information about an unknown bioactive component may be gathered simultaneously. This is most readily seen with antimicrobial compounds. Following development, the TLC plate is dried and then overlaid with a thin layer of agar containing a test organism against which the natural product is active. Following incubation, zones of growth inhibition in the agar can be seen in regions of the plate containing the active compound *(4,5)*. This allows characterization of an unknown bioactive compound within a mixture, or comparison of the unknown compound against a standard, without the requirement for preparative isolation.

2.3. Solid Phase Extraction

One expeditious but low-resolution method of obtaining physical characterization of an unknown extract is the use of solid phase extraction (SPE) cartridges. SPE has been widely used in other analytical fields such as drug metabolism as an initial concentration and fractionation step, followed by further high-resolution analysis, in order to quantify a small number of compounds of interest. However, there are also reports of the use of SPE for dereplication of a wide range of unidentified natural products. In one instance reported from the NCI *(6)*, a panel of several different SPE packings was employed to augment the low resolution obtained from a single SPE cartridge. A panel of different SPE packings including Sephadex G-25, C4, and C18 was employed, and the activity elution pattern was used to categorize samples. With each sample, four fractions were eluted from each column and then assayed for anti-HIV activity. The fractions were all aqueous for G-25 and comprised a step gradient ranging from 100% aqueous to 100% methanol for the RP columns. The elution profiles obtained from this experiment for dextran sulfate—cyclosporin and an extract of *Topsentia sp.*, which gave rise to the novel compound ibesterol sulfate—are shown in **Fig. 1**. The comparison of large numbers of composite data represented by such patterns, can be enhanced by pattern-recognition computer algorithms.

2.4. Countercurrent Chromatography

Another separation technique that has shown utility as a prefractionation method for dereplication is countercurrent chromatography (CCC) or centrifugal partition chromatography (CPC). This separation method is based on the

SPE Packing Material

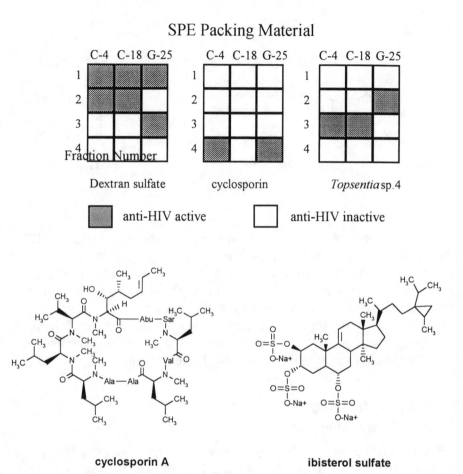

Fig. 1. Anti-HIV activity patterns from SPE separations (adapted from **ref. 8**).

distribution constant (K_D) of a compound between two immiscible liquid phases. Researchers at Panlabs and Wyeth-Ayerst reported a rapid method involving CPC in which they identified the known bioactive compounds geldanamycin and elaiophylin (**Scheme 1**) in an extract of *Streptomyces violaceusniger (7)*. The resolving power of CPC generally is not as high as that of HPLC; but, when combined with other techniques, such as UV analysis and LC-MS, the retention time of a compound on CPC is complementary evidence for the presence or absence of a known compound.

2.5. Capillary Electrochromatography

A technology that is likely to be of great use for natural product dereplication, once it becomes more established, is capillary electrochromatography (CEC)

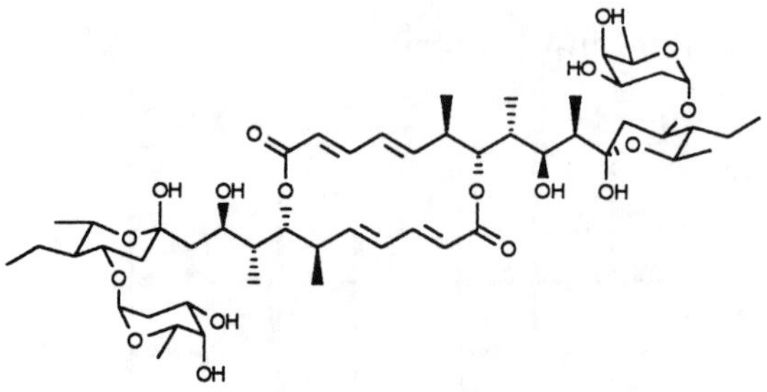

Elaiophylin

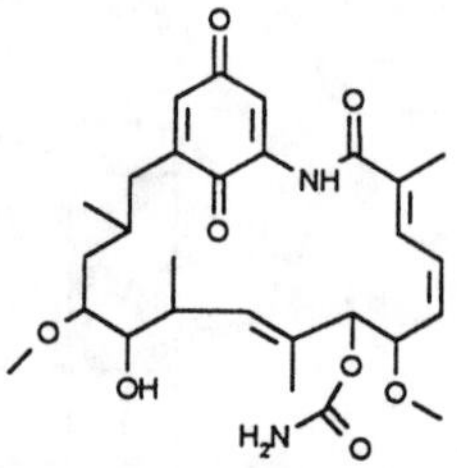

Geldanamycin

Scheme 1.

(8). CEC is a hybrid separation technique that combines capillary HPLC (50-μm capillary diameter) with capillary zone electrophoresis, and its main advantage is the enormous number of theoretical plates that can be achieved. This is a result of the uniform, plug-like flow that electro-endoosmosis generates and the fact that this allows the use of very small particles (3 μm diameter). The technology is at an early stage of development (as there are problems inherent in packing columns of such small particle size *[9]*), but has already resulted in efficiency values of up to 387,000 theoretical plates per meter *(10)*.

3. Chemical Identification

3.1. TLC Spray Reagents

For a natural product mixture that has been separated on a TLC plate, the most common chemical tests are the TLC colorimetric stain reagents that give a visual indication of the presence of various functional groups. These spray reagents are usually applied as an aerosol to form a thin uniform layer on the TLC plate and, most commonly, heated to hasten the reactions which result in color formation. There are numerous stains listed in several standard texts on the subject *(11,12)*. Table 3 of Chapter 7 lists some of the most useful and widely used of these. Whereas these tests are very useful and easy to perform, it is important to remember that very few are very specific, i.e., they rarely detect compounds solely of the given class, and they often will not detect every single compound of that class.

This approach has been used to give a secondary metabolic "fingerprint" of a range of organisms, which can allow for the classification of those organisms that appear to be producing the same range of metabolites and highlighting those that appear to exhibit a particularly different or interesting profile *(13)*.

3.2. Common Nonselective Bioactive Natural Products (see Fig. 2)

In the case of bioassay-directed isolation studies, the goal is to identify compounds that interact with a particular biological target, often a specific receptor or enzyme. Since these interactions are rarely observable directly, indirect reporter systems are often employed, involving the production of some measurable quantity, such as color or light, or radioactivity, which can be used as a monitor of the biochemical process and which allows the assay to be carried out at a high throughput. Unfortunately, these assays are prone to various artifactual compounds that appear to give hits in the assay but actually interact with some component of the assay system other than the target; e.g., they quench the light produced in a light emission-based assay and hence block its detection, or they react with a colorimetric assay product such that the product appears not to have been formed. These compounds therefore interfere with the assay and register as false positives. Similarly, some compounds give rise to hits by interaction with the target but on such a nonselective basis as to be meaningless in the context of the specific target. This class of compounds may include those that nonspecifically form complexes with proteins and hence inhibit many enzyme assays, or those that are toxic to a variety of cells. Such distinctions of selectivity are of course subjective but, in practice, these compounds tend to recur often and their early elimination is desirable.

Some assays are more robust than others, but some commonly occurring natural products that frequently cause interference in typical assays are listed in **Table 1**. In general, the activities of these artifacts can be loosely classified into major categories: detergent-like, toxic, polyphenol, antioxidant, and UV quenchers.

3.2.1. Detergent-Like Compounds

These have a tendency to disrupt membranes and therefore interfere with assays that are carried out in whole cells or membrane preparations, in which only one part of the cell's activity is being monitored; e.g., uptake by the cell of a particular compound or receptor binding using a radiolabeled ligand. If the cell is damaged by a substance that has no direct action on these systems, the assay may break down and give a misleading result.

3.2.2. Toxic Compounds

Compounds that show general eukaryotic cell toxicity may give rise to false positives, or show nonspecific activity, in cell-based assays. (Some of these also act by damaging membranes and may overlap with the detergent-like class of compounds.)

3.2.3. Polyphenols (Vegetable Tannins)

These are ubiquitous in plant extracts (*see* Chapter 12) and show activity in a large number of assays. In general, their nonspecific activity has been ascribed

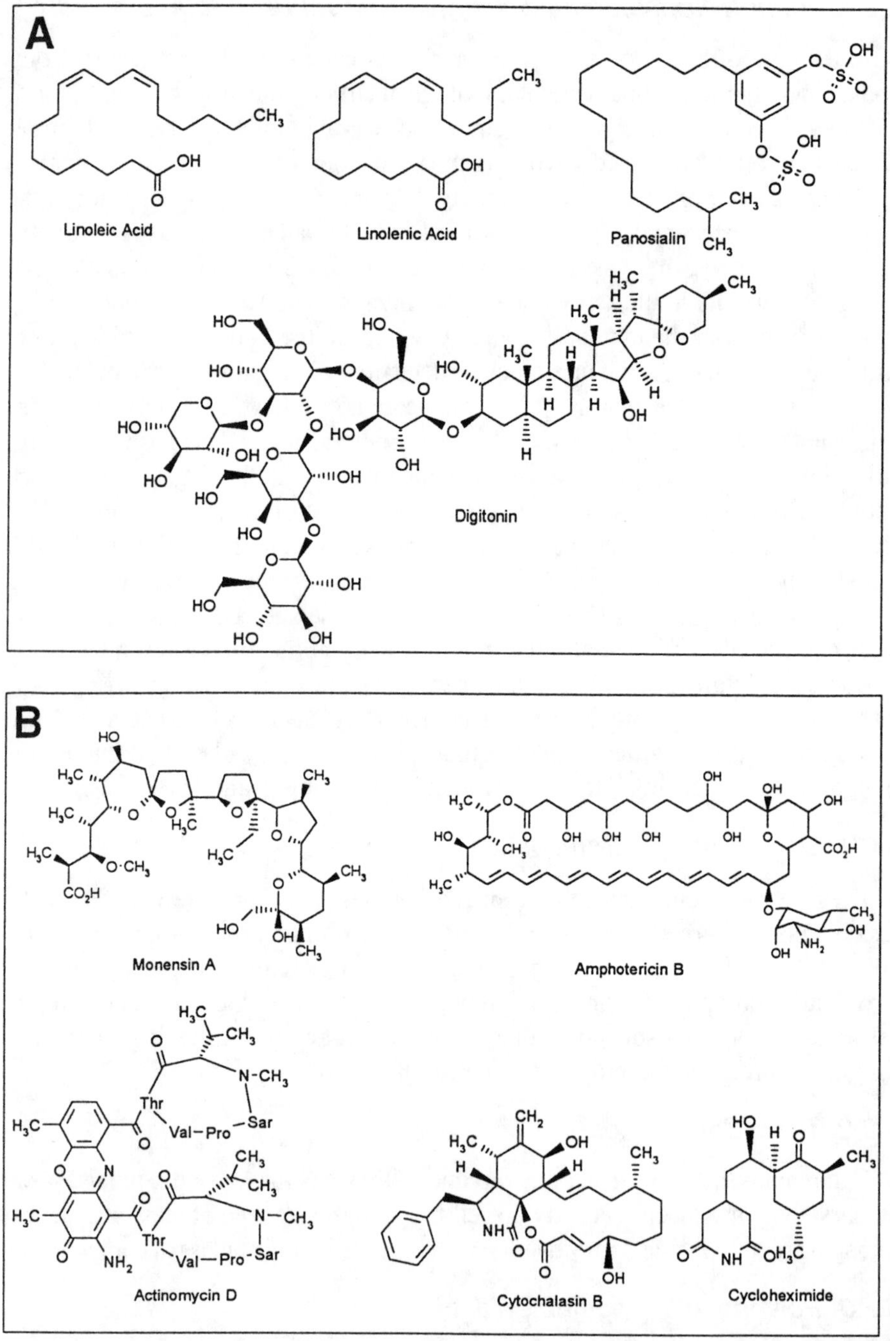

Fig. 2. Structures of some common bioactive natural products. **(A)** Detergent-like. **(B)** Toxic.

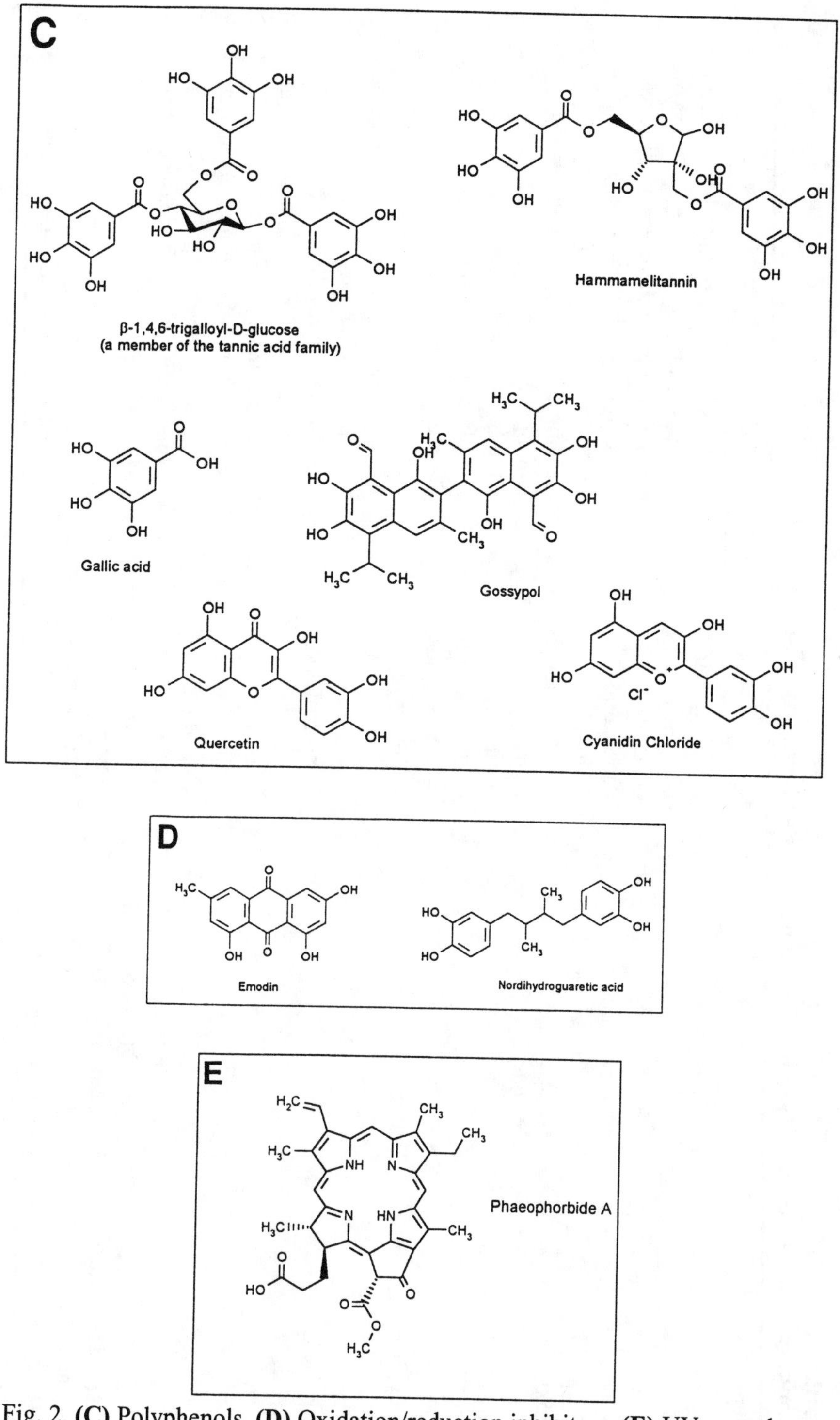

Fig. 2. **(C)** Polyphenols. **(D)** Oxidation/reduction inhibitors. **(E)** UV quencher.

Table 1
Common Classes of Bioassay-Interfering Natural Products (*see also* Fig. 2)

Type	Chemical class	Example	Note
Detergent-like	Fatty acid	Linolenic acid	These are three of the most common
		Linoleic acid	fatty acids, but there are a plethora of
		Oleic acid	less common members of this class
	Amphoteric sulfates	Panosialin	Common in Streptomycetes
	Saponin (triterpene glycoside)	Digitonin	Common component of plants
Toxic	Polyene	Amphotericin B	Membrane-damaging agent
	Polyether	Monensin	Ionophore
		Actinomycin D	Inhibits DNA transcription
		Cytochalasin B	Inhibits cell division
		Cycloheximide	Protein synthesis inhibitor
Polyphenols	Tannin	Tannic acid	Commercially available mixture of
			hydrolyzable tannins usually ranging
			from tri- to nona-galloyl glucose
		Hammamelitannin	Commercially available extract of
			Hammamelis, a plant containing high
			concentrations of tannins
	Phenol	Gallic acid	Basic subunit of hydrolysable tannins
		Gossypol	
	Flavonoid (Flavonol)	Quercetin	
	Flavonoid (Anthocyanin)	Cyanidin	
Oxidation/reduction inhibitors	Quinone (oxidant)	Emodin	Nonselective tyrosine kinase inhibitor
	Resorcinol (antioxidant)	Nordihydroguaretic acid	Basic subunit of many plant pigments
UV Quenchers	Phaeophorbide A		Chlorophyll breakdown product

to their ability to complex metal ions, scavenge radicals and reduce active oxygen species, and form tight complexes with a wide array of proteins and polysaccharides *(14)*. They will therefore often give a false-positive result in most assays involving a purified protein by forming a precipitate with the protein.

3.2.4. Antioxidants

These will interfere with assays that are based on oxidative/reductive processes.

3.2.5. UV Quenchers

Many assays are based on a measurement of light either in the ultraviolet or visible range (e.g., those utilizing a colorimetric product, scintillation proximity assays, assays utilizing green fluorescent protein, or recombinant cell-based assays containing reporter systems involving transcription of light-generating proteins). Compounds that strongly absorb or quench this radiation will appear to be interacting with the target. These may include pigments or simply, in some cases, various colored compounds.

The capricious nature of the distinction between "interfering" compounds and genuine "hits" in an assay can be demonstrated by the fact that digitonin could be chemically classified as a saponin—a class normally considered to be one of nonselective membrane-damaging agents. However, digitonin is sufficiently selective to serve as a highly successful human cardiotonic therapy. Similarly, polyphenols generally exhibit nonspecific biological activity, yet many have warranted investigation on the basis of their specific bioactivity, e.g., inhibition of HIV reverse transcriptase *(15)*. Many so-called toxic compounds that are often regarded as nuisances in natural products chemistry have proved to be very useful and important tools for biochemical studies (e.g., actinomycin D, cycloheximide and brefeldin A). In addition, many "cytotoxic" compounds have exhibited enough selectivity to be clinically beneficial as anticancer therapeutics (e.g., camptothecin, taxol, etoposide, actinomycin D, and vincristine).

Table 1 lists examples of commonly occurring natural products that often give rise to apparent activity in bioassays or representatives of chemical classes that give rise to such nonspecific, "interfering" activity. Such a list is useful as a checklist when attempting to isolate compounds exhibiting biological activity, or as a set of compounds that can be tested in a biological assay in order to give some idea of the types of "interfering" compounds that might give a false-positive result in a biological assay. Some of the compounds listed are representatives of general chemical classes that tend to "interfere" or that are commonly occurring (e.g., tannins, fatty acids, saponins); others fall less readily into such broad chemical classes (e.g., actinomycin D). Many of these are plant metabolites, discussed further in Chapter 12.

If the search for novel and "interesting" natural products is to be carried out over a large number of assays and using a large number of organism extracts, it may be worthwhile putting into the assay as a first step, not just commonly interfering natural products, but all of the characterized natural products available at the time. This will help to give a better overall picture of the sorts of compounds that might be expected to be detected in the extracts and may even be the same as those active in the extracts.

3.3. Biochemical/Chemical Tests For Some Common Nonselective Bioactive Natural Products

Chemical and biochemical tests are often used in natural products chemistry to identify the class of compound or to ascertain the presence or absence of certain functional groups. For the common bioactive natural products listed in **Subheading 3.2.**, several tests have been developed to identify their presence. Some of these are listed below (*see* **Subheadings 3.3.1.–3.3.4.**).

3.3.1. Fatty Acids

The strongly hydrophobic nature of fatty acids will result in a long retention time on RP-HPLC at low pH. If the active component elutes after most of the rest of the extract, this can be an indication that fatty acids are responsible. The most commonly occurring fatty acids are oleic, linoleic, and linolenic acids, and these can be tested for by the use of standards.

3.3.2. Panosialins

β-Lactamase Inhibition—Panosialins are commonly found as constituents of bacterial extracts. They are characterized by their β-lactamase inhibitory activity *(16)*. This can be assayed by overlaying a TLC plate on which the sample has been chromatographed, or just spotted, with a thin layer of agar containing β-lactamase. When this is set, it is overlaid with agar containing nitrocefin (**Scheme 2**)—a colorimetric substrate for β-lactamase that is converted to a colored product by the enzyme. Following incubation for 30 min at 37°C, the agar will be red except for a clear zone in the region of panosialins.

3.3.3. Saponins

1. Hemolysis—Saponins (steroid glycosides) are present in many organisms, particularly plants, and their presence (as well as that of other membrane-damaging agents) can be detected by their ability to lyse red blood cells. In one assay format *(17)*, 1 mL of a 10-μM methanol solution of saponin was added to 9 mL of a sheep erythrocyte suspension (8.1×10^3 cells/mL) in 0.9% NaCl. At various time points, 1 mL of the mixture was withdrawn and centrifuged at 2000g for 1 min. The absorbance of the supernatant at 540 nm was then measured. The percent hemolysis value can be determined as a ratio of this absorbance to that caused by hypotonicity.

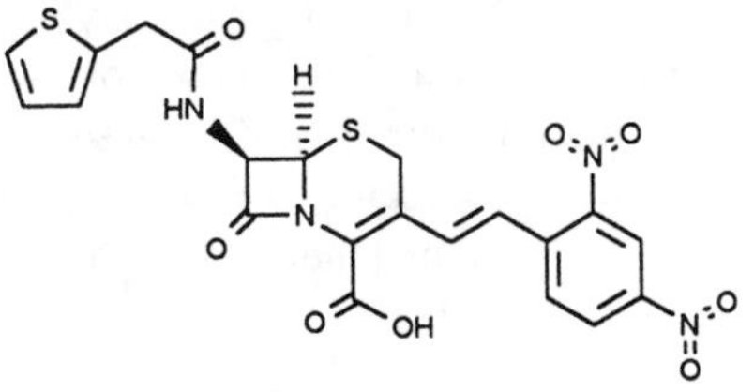

nitrocefin

Scheme 2.

2. Foaming—Saponins, and other amphoteric compounds that reduce surface tension, exhibit a fairly characteristic tendency to form stable, persistent foams from aqueous alcohol solutions.

3.3.4. Tannins

One reason that precise and quantitative assays for tannin determinations have been difficult to develop is that tannins encompass a heterogeneous group of compounds and polymers. However, several assays have been developed to estimate tannin levels in extracts, and an excellent review is available *(18)*. Many of these assays are based on either the reduction capabilities of polyphenols or the propensity of tannins to form precipitates with various proteins. The following two assays are best used as a qualitative analysis for the presence or absence of particular tannins, but can be used with standards for approximate tannin determinations.

1. Ferric-to-Ferrous Reduction—Polyphenols are able to reduce Fe^{3+} to Fe^{2+} with varying efficiencies. The production of Fe^{2+} ions can be monitored by the formation of Prussian blue, $Fe_4[Fe(CN)_6]_3$. In one assay format *(19)*, 0.2 mL of 8 mM $K_3Fe(CN)_6$ was added to 3 mL of a 50-µM tannin solution, followed by the addition of 0.2 mL of 0.1 M $FeCl_3$ in 0.1 M HCl. The optical density was read after 5 min at 700 nm. In a cruder format, the presence of tannins can be determined by the addition of 5% $FeCl_3$/methanol (w/v) solution to an equal volume of sample; a brown coloration indicates the presence of polyphenolics.
2. Protein Binding—Tannins, as the name implies, characteristically form complexes with proteins based on multipoint hydrogen bonding, and this feature can be used to detect and remove tannins from crude extracts. A visible protein-tannin precipitate should be formed on addition of the tannin-containing extract to a relatively concentrated (approx 5%) solution of bovine serum albumin (BSA). The amount of BSA either remaining in solution or in the precipitate can be analyzed by various protein determination assays.
3. Adsorbent Binding—In the same way that tannins bind to proteins through multipoint hydrogen bonding, so do they also bind to a number of other polymeric materials. These include the adsorbents commonly used to remove tannins

from crude extracts prior to testing in biological assays, such as polyvinylpyrroli-done (PVP), polyamide, and (in the authors' laboratory at least), the ion-exchange resin Whatman DE52. Therefore, the loss of bioactivity following treatment of an extract with one of these adsorbents, either in a column or a batch mode, suggests that the activity is caused by tannins/polyphenolics. (*See* Chapter 13 for details of methods.)

3.4. Artifacts

A common feature of natural product extractions is the occurrence of natural product derivatives formed during the extraction process and the concentration of contaminants from materials used during the process. To minimize these artifacts, a prudent approach is to use the mildest possible conditions in order to avoid side reactions. Also, biological material that is as fresh as possible should be used. Some extractions may even have to be carried out under an inert atmosphere in order to prevent oxidation of the metabolites.

At every step of the extraction there exists the possibility of artifact forma-tion. During concentration steps, the presence of inorganic salts and traces of acid can catalyze reactions. Some solvents such as acetone, methanol, ethylene glycol, and dimethylformamide may give rise to adducts. Materials used for separations may also lead to artefacts. A range of reactions can occur on acti-vated alumina including aldol condensations, rearrangements, hydration, and dehydration. Silica, too, can catalyse a number of reactions that include oxida-tion, rearrangements, and N- and O-demethylation. Other materials with which the extract comes into contact are a potential source of artifacts and, hence, of confusion. This was exemplified by the isolation of tricontanol (**Scheme 3**) during an extraction of a fungus with plant-growth-promoting activity. This compound possesses plant-growth-promoting activity but is also known to be a contaminant of some filter papers *(20)*. Some natural products may be stable while contained within the crude extract but, once isolated, may be unstable—to air, solvents, or light.

Plasticizers, often phthalic acid and dialkylphthalates, are common contami-nants, especially in small-scale work, and are very diffficult to avoid as they are common additives in polymerization processes used in the manufacture of plastic vessels and tubing that may be used during an extraction. An example of this was the identification of a compound widely used as a light stabilizer in plastics, Tinuvin 770 (**Scheme 3**), as a potent L-type calcium channel blocker *(21)*. Natural products extraction artifacts have been briefly reviewed by Ghisalberti *(20)* and general artifacts arising from the various forms of chro-matography and analysis often used in natural products work have been reviewed by Middleditch *(22)*.

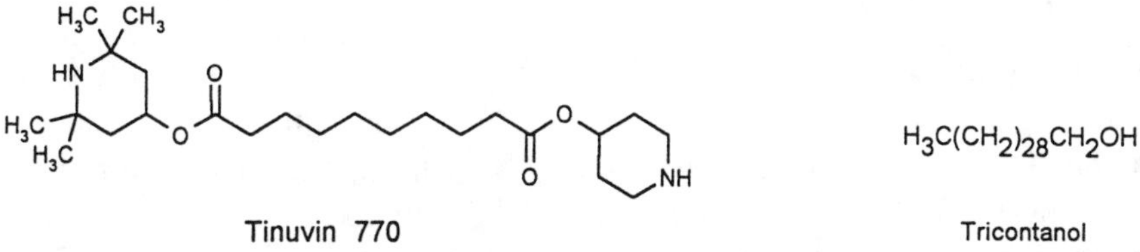

Tinuvin 770   Tricontanol

Scheme 3.

4. Spectroscopic and Hyphenated Techniques

Various forms of spectroscopy are used to carry out full identification of a natural product that has been purified, but many spectroscopic methods can also be used at an earlier stage on compounds in mixtures. The aim may be to "eliminate" an artifactual compound, to assign it to a particular class, or to detect the presence/absence of a particular chemical group within a mixture. The distinction between these latter functions and full structure determination is becoming increasingly blurred as technological advances translate to more complete characterization of natural products in mixtures. Hence, whereas this chapter does not deal with full structure determination, the techniques outlined here can often be used to characterize fully natural products in mixtures. These generally involve "hyphenated," or "tandem" techniques in which separation (usually HPLC or GC) is carried out with the components analyzed "on-line" by a physical method such as ultraviolet (UV) absorbance, mass spectrometry (MS), or nuclear magnetic resonance (NMR). Thus, in reality, the spectroscopy often is not carried out on a mixture but rather on mixture components as they are separated, effectively combining separation and structure determination.

4.1. UV Absorbance

Historically, Woodward and Fieser's early empirical correlation of various organic substructures with their associated UV spectra *(23,24)* could be considered one of the first attempts to partially identify organic compounds on the basis of nondestructive physical characterization. Woodward was able to predict the λ_{max} for a number of conjugated systems, such as variously substituted enones and dienes, based on literature precedent. Contemporary structure determination of purified compounds now relies most heavily on NMR and MS techniques, the UV spectrum normally contributing only a minor component to this process. However, the advent of HPLC and UV diode array detectors has enabled the acquisition of a UV spectrum for every component represented in an HPLC chromatogram. Consequently, the UV spectrum has become one of the most readily accessible pieces of information pertaining to structure, and interest has revived in exploiting its usefulness.

4.1.1. LC-UV Libraries

In the last 20 yr, HPLC and UV diode array detection have both grown from infancy to become essential components of the natural product chemist's dereplication arsenal. Today, most natural products experts have analyzed hundreds of purified natural products by HPLC-UV, and many libraries of UV spectra with associated chromatographic behavior have been generated. In 1993, one of the most extensive LC/UV libraries described in the literature consisted of data from 380 purified compounds and was used extensively in the laboratories of Fiedler with various actinomycete fermentations for dereplication purposes, in order to determine the presence of previously reported secondary metabolites *(25)*. By comparing the UV spectra and chromatographic retention times of unidentified components obtained from HPLC-UV analysis of crude fermentation extracts, Fiedler et al. were able to obtain a rapid indication of the presence of known compounds. In addition, previously undescribed compound family members that share the same UV chromophore but exhibit different retention times were also identified. Some of the novel compounds identified by this technique as being similar to but different from previously reported compounds include naphthgeranine F (similar to naphthgeranine E) *(26)*, juglomycin Z (similar to juglomycin C) *(27)*, echinoserine (similar to echinomycin) *(25)*, and several nikkomycins, including K_z and O_z (similar to nikkomycin Z) (*see* **Scheme 4**).

4.1.2. LC-UV Measures of Peak Purity

UV diode array and fast scanning detectors not only enable the generation and use of libraries of known natural product standards, but can also enhance chromatographic resolution. This enhancement is due to "peak purity" assessment, which allows the researcher automatically to compare UV spectra at different time points across a peak of interest and thus detect the presence or absence of multiple poorly resolved components. This feature is generally included in the standard software of most commercially available diode array detectors.

4.2. Mass Spectrometry and LC-MS

In most cases, mass spectrometry (MS) is the most sensitive method for obtaining dereplication information about an unknown compound. Microgram amounts are usually enough for several MS experiments, even though <1% of any sample undergoes ion formation by any single ionization technique.

Mass spectrometry depends on the determination of a mass-to-charge ratio (m/z); so, by definition, mass spectrometry is only useful for characterizing molecules that can be ionized to a positive or negative charged state under controlled conditions. Fortunately, a number of mass spectrometer ionization conditions have been developed (**Table 2**), and most natural products can be ionized using a variety of these techniques.

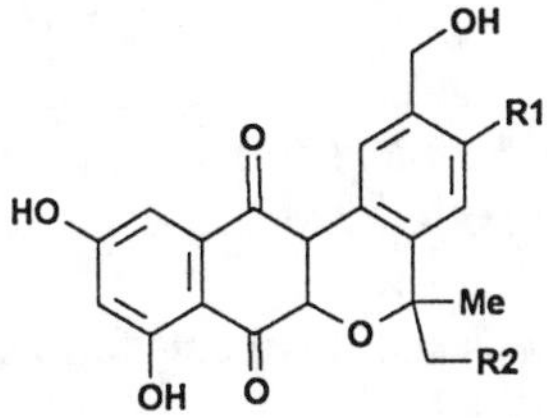

naphthgeranine E R1 = OH, R2 = H
naphthgeranine F R1 = H, R2 = OH

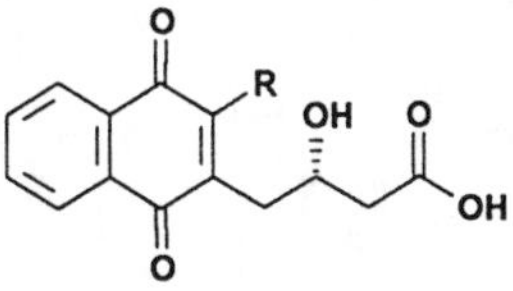

juglomycin C R = H
juglomycin Z R = Me

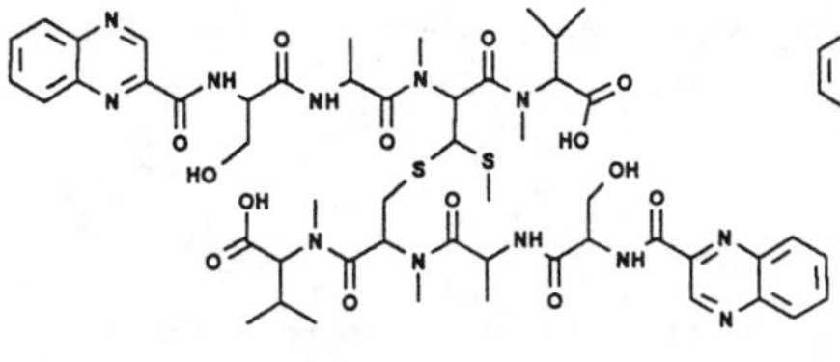

echinoserine

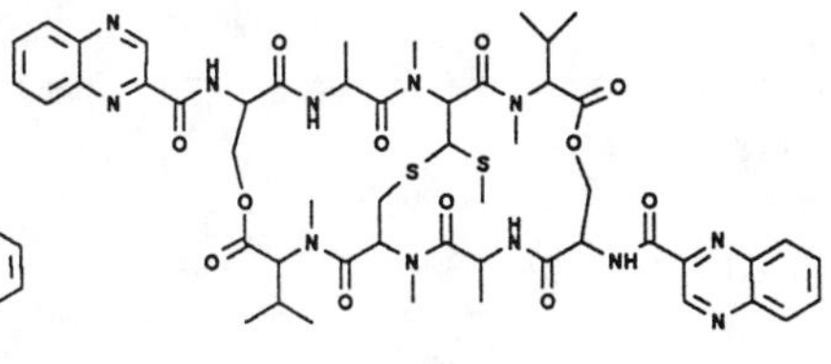

echinomycin

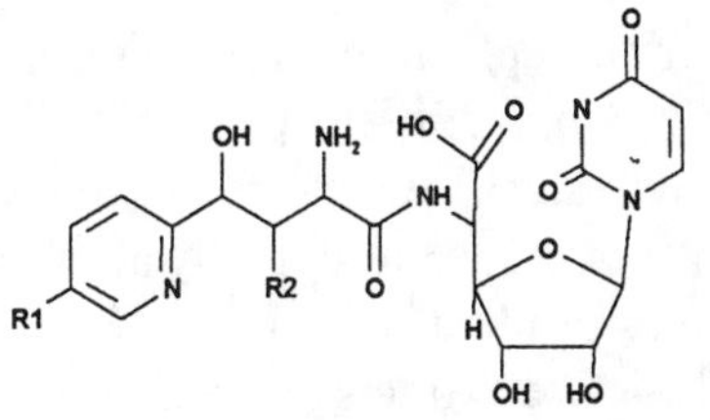

nikkomycin Kz R1 = H, R2 = H
nikkomycin Oz R1 = OH, R2 = H
nikkomycin Z   R1 = OH, R2 = Me

Scheme 4.

One difficulty in employing mass spectrometry in natural product dereplication is the lack of a "universal" ionization condition under which any unknown compound could be expected to be ionized. Optimization of ionization conditions involves many factors. In addition to the mode of ionization, the pH modifiers used in the HPLC solvent can be critical to the ionization process, and the choice of ion source and strength of electric field are all critical parameters.

An attempt to develop generic ionization conditions was made via an analysis of 46 "representative" natural products under several HPLC and ionization conditions *(30)*. Two of the conclusions from this study were:

1. For unknown samples, electrospray is the recommended choice of ionization for polar extracts (e.g., MeOH, EtOH, acetone).
2. Atmospheric pressure chemical ionization gave the most sensitive response for moderately polar extracts (e.g., CHCl₃, EtOAc).

Table 2
Common Modes of MS Ionization

Electron impact (EI)	Harsh, many fragment ions formed, +ve or −ve
Chemical ionization	Soft, quasimolecular ions (MH+, MNH$_4$+, and so on), +ve or −ve
Fast atom bombardment (FAB)	Quasimolecular ions and fragments formed, +ve and −ve
Thermospray ionization	First to interface with HPLC, quasimoleular ions, +ve or −ve
Electrospray ionization (ES)	Interfaces to HPLC, current method of choice for quasimolecular ions in both +ve and −ve modes
Atmospheric pressure chemical ionization (APCI)	Interfaces to HPLC
Matrix-assisted laser desorption (MALDI)	

A compromise solution for dereplication procedures is to use a combination of ionization modes. In one report *(31)*, electrospray MS in both positive and negative modes was coupled to an HPLC interface and used to obtain information on unknown components of crude biologically active extracts. The authors of this report claimed successful identification of a known natural product in two out of eight biologically active extracts examined, another two compounds were identified as novel, and they assumed that the active components in the remaining four did not ionize or were present at a concentration below the limits of MS detection.

The main limitation to nebulizer HPLC-MS interfaces is that many common HPLC solvent modifiers such as H_3PO_4 are not tolerated, as they are not volatile and will saturate the mass detector, causing unacceptable losses in sensitivity. This problem can be circumvented using a belt-drive-interface system, but this interface presents other more mechanical problems.

Another MS parameter that can affect sensitivity is the choice of available mass analyzers. Some of the instrument designs commonly used for analysis of natural products are listed in **Table 3**.

For dereplication and structure determination purposes, one of the most useful results from an LC-MS study is the identification of a compound's molecular ion. From the molecular ion, it is usually possible to determine the compound's molecular weight to the nearest atomic mass unit. This can be carried out by experimentally changing the mobile phase buffer and observing the resulting adduct ions in order to determine the adduct composition of the molecular ion; e.g., M$^+$+H, M$^+$+Li, M$^+$+Na, M$^-$−H. The unit-molecular-weight

Table 3
Common Mass Analyzers for Natural Products

Magnetic deflection mass analyzer	
Double focusing sector spectrometer	Capable of accurate mass measurements
Quadrapole mass analyzer	
Triple quadrapole analyzer	Capable of identifying tandem MS/MS (or daughter) ions
Ion trap	Capable of identifying multiple tandem MS/MS (or daughter) ions (up to MS^{10})
Time-of-flight spectrometer	
Ion cyclotron resonance spectrometer	Potential for accurate mass measurements of multiple components in mixtures

information for an unknown compound can be used to reduce dramatically the number of possible structures under consideration for structure elucidation.

To illustrate how useful the unit-molecular-weight information is in natural product dereplication, **Fig. 3A** shows the unit-molecular-weight distribution of the approx 78,000 known natural products contained in the Chapman and Hall database *(32)*. It can be seen that, for the reported natural products, determination of the molecular weight will narrow the reported structural possibilities to <800, and the largest number of known natural products that share a common unit molecular weight is only 759 (mol wt = 318). For that molecular weight, there are known natural products that exhibit 45 different empirical (or molecular) formulas, each of which adds up to approx 318 Dalton.

One method of obtaining an empirical formula is from a precise mass determination of the molecular ion. No atom has a mass equal to a whole number (except by definition, carbon, which has a mass of exactly 12 Dalton), e.g., $^{1}H = 1.0078$, $^{16}O = 15.9949$, $^{14}N = 14.0031$. Therefore, the accurate mass of a compound (to four decimal places) can represent only one possible molecular formula. **Figure 3B** shows the distribution of the number of known natural products that share a given accurate molecular weight. Of the reported natural products, the most common molecular formula is $C_{15}H_{20}O_4$, which occurs 517 times and gives rise to a molecular weight of 264.1356. Most empirical formulas occur far less than this, and it can be seen from **Fig. 3B** that accurate mass information significantly narrows the structural possibilities even further.

Also striking as seen from the graph is the difference in the occurrence of natural products with odd and even unit molecular weights. Those with a molecular weight of x, where x is even, are far more common than those with a molecular weight of $x \pm 1$. To a large extent, this can be related to the presence

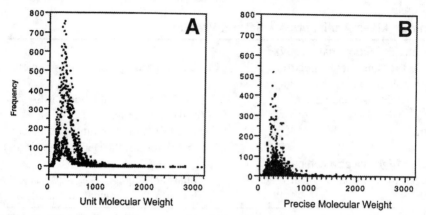

Fig. 3. Distribution of compounds within *Dictionary of Natural Products (68)* according to **(A)** unit molecular weight and **(B)** accurate molecular weight (i.e., same empirical formula).

in the molecule of no, or an even number, of nitrogen atoms—any molecule with one or an odd number of nitrogens must have an odd molecular weight.

4.2.1. LC-MS-MS

In addition to the structural information obtained from the molecular ion, a great deal of information can be obtained using various mass spectral fragmentation and derivatization techniques. In the mass spectrometer, the molecular ion exists in a metastable high energy state and fragmentation, or bond breakage, can usually be induced. This is most commonly carried out by EI-MS or laser desorption MS or by further subjecting each ion to another round of ionization in a process of MS-MS. The pattern of fragmentation is reproducible, and if sufficient ions are detected, the profile can give nearly unique characteristic information.

Such fingerprints of mass spectral fragmentation have been useful in dereplication and in identification of family similarities. For instance, a family of 18 different naturally occurring taxol analogs were each identified from crude extracts of *Taxus brevifolia* and *Taxus baccata* by a procedure primarily based on analysis of their behavior under LC-MS-MS conditions *(33)*. Fourteen different molecular ions were obtained for the eighteen compounds, but after the four or five fragmentations depicted in **Fig. 4**, each compound exhibited an identical "template" ion of 327 m/z, representing the ionized taxol core.

4.2.2. Common MS Derivatizations

One of the strengths of mass spectral analysis is that only minute quantities of material are required for a full set of experiments. This enables microscale

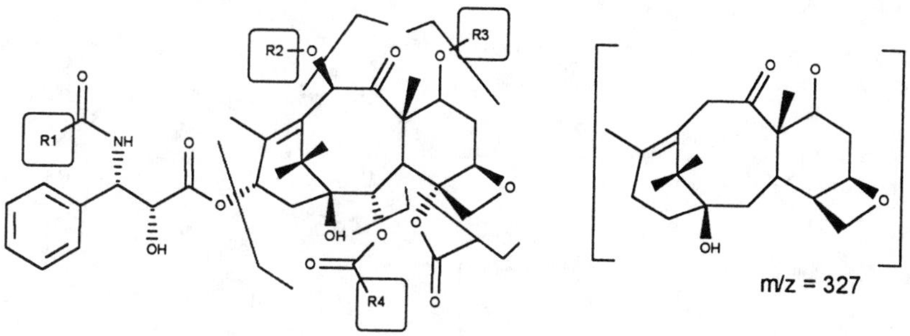

Fig. 4. MS fragmentations observed for 18 taxol analogs.

derivatizations of natural products to be carried out and monitored using mass spectrometry. Several high-yielding derivatizations are commonly carried out in order to improve the ionization or volatility of the original natural product, and the results can be useful in dereplication *(34)*. The most common functional groups that are derivatized are OH, CO_2H, and NH, but a myriad of other functionalities can also be specifically derivatized such as aldehydes and ketones, glycols, α amino acids, α hydroxy acids, α keto acids, esters, amides, and amino alcohols.

Three of the most common derivatives are trimethyl silyl, acetyl, and methyl. Some of the common reagents that give rise to these deriatives and some of the functional groups with which they react are shown in **Fig. 5**.

A dereplication example that illustrates the use of microscale derivatization and analysis by GC-MS is an identification of a series of bioactive diterpenes by NCI researchers *(35)*. The extract from *Croton cuneatus* showed activity in a phorbol dibutyrate receptor, binding assay, and, on analysis, could be separated by HPLC into a group of seven very minor, related components. Following hydrolysis and acetylation, all seven components appeared to give rise to only two peaks, which by GC-CIMS analysis were judged to be phorbol tetraacetates. It was concluded that the seven compounds were probably various esters of 4α-, or 16-hydroxylated phorbol analogs (**Fig. 6**).

4.3. LC-NMR

The advantages of directly interfacing HPLC separation with NMR analyses have so far been limited by the time and amount of material required to obtain various NMR spectra. However, two different types of HPLC interface have been developed for LC-NMR analysis. In "stopped-flow" techniques, the material of interest is directed into an NMR sample cell within the magnetic field after HPLC separation has occurred, and the pumps are then stopped to allow the necessary NMR experiments to be performed. The second type of

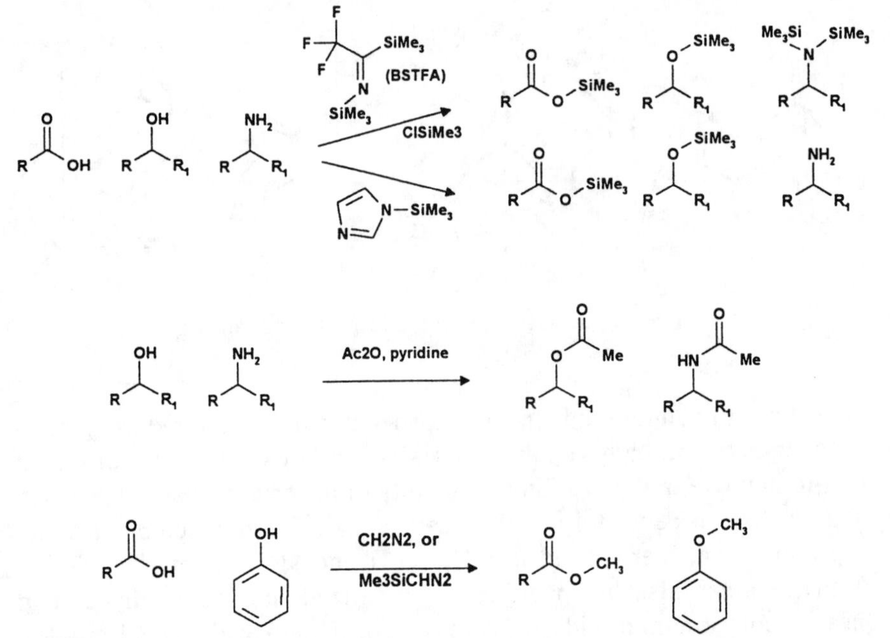

Fig. 5. Some common derivatization methods to enhance mass spectral properties.

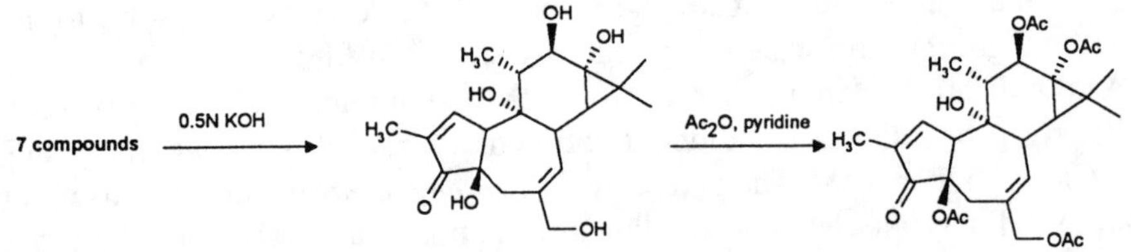

Fig. 6. Derivatization of diterpenes from *Croton cuneatus*.

interface is an off-line method in which the material corresponding to each peak is retained in a separate loop that can be automatically scanned. In this way, it is possible to obtain NMR spectra for all the peaks in a chromatogram without the need for preparative isolation, provided that baseline resolution be achieved *(36–38)*.

There are also reports of HPLC-NMR-MS in which the separation system is coupled to both NMR and MS *(39)*. The power and potential of LC-NMR and related hyphenated techniques are likely to be enormous, extending the scope of analytical separations and obviating the need for much time-consuming preparative scale work and reducing the risk of chemical degradation of the compounds. This will allow extraction work to concentrate on natural products that are known to be of interest and that are required as pure materials in larger amounts for further study. Natural product examples of the use of this technology include the use of on line LC-NMR to help determine the structures of three sesquiterpene lactones from the plant *Zaluzania grayana (40)* (**Fig. 7**).

4.3.1. NMR of Mixtures

A procedure has also been reported in which NMR experiments can be carried out on some mixtures without any prior separation. Spectra of different compounds within a mixture were separated by the use of 2D diffusional methods. Pulsed-field gradient spin-echo NMR measurements gave 2D spectra in which signals from different molecules were separated in a second dimension according to their diffusion constant. All signals from a given molecule showed the same diffusion constant, thus allowing differentiation of signals from different molecules *(41)*. Improvements in pulsed-field-gradient hardware and data-processing methods have given rise to these high-resolution diffusion-ordered spectroscopy (HR-DOSY) techniques that can analyze NMR spectra of mixtures of small molecules with a resolution comparable to that of HPLC-NMR. Even if the NMR spectra obtained in this way are insufficient to assign a structure fully, they are often sufficient to dereplicate a compound or to characterize it partially.

4.4. LC-IR

Fourier Transform infrared spectroscopy (FTIR) can be coupled to an LC system by directing a portion of the eluate onto a heated rotating germanium disk from which the mobile phase evaporates, leaving a deposition of sample. IR spectra can be obtained directly from the disk without the problem of swamping of IR absorbance by the mobile phase components. This technique has not been widely used for the analysis of natural products, but it does represent another form of physical measurement that can be carried out on samples as they are separated *(42)*.

4.5. Computer-Enhanced Structure Determination

If dereplication methods show that a natural product has not been previously reported in the scientific literature, then full structure elucidation can be undertaken if the interest warrants the effort. The complete theory and practice of the science of structure determination are beyond the scope of this chapter, but the efficiency of determining structures is increasing dramatically, with most determinations being accomplished now in hours or days rather than weeks or months.

Although there is no inviolate structure determination procedure, the two general processes that constitute the process are: first, the "virtual" generation of all possible structures; second, the elimination of candidates based on inter-

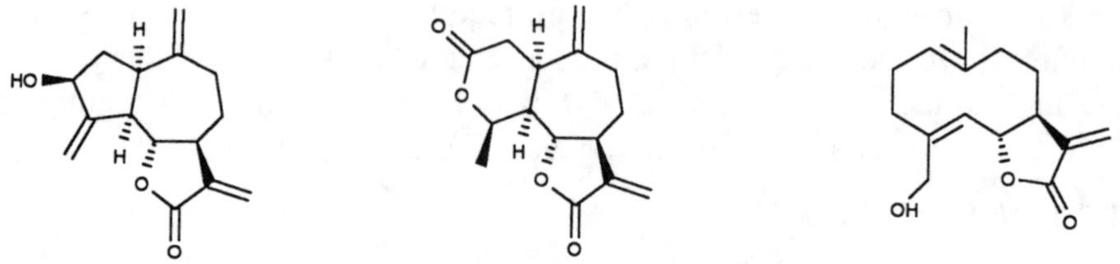

Fig. 7. Sequiterpene lactones from *Zaluzania grayana.*

pretation of physical data The obvious difference in complete and partial structure determination is simply a matter of the number of possible structures
remaining when the elimination process is halted.

Since the virtual generation of all possible structures is a logical process and
completeness is required, attempts have been made to develop artificial intelligence programs to automate this part of the procedure, as well as to assist in
the translation of spectral data into substructure information. Djerassi's pio-
neering contributions to the field resulted in several computer programs
addressing both needs. His GENOA and CONGEN *(43,44)* programs addressed
most of the theoretical issues involved in generating all possible structures
based on substructures obtained from analysis of a limited set of spectral data.
Based on their analysis of several incomplete literature structure determinations, an interesting suggestion was made that these programs be used as aids
for referees to determine whether all possible structures had been considered
when a new structure determination manuscript is under review. These academic forerunners have given rise to structure generation packages that are
now commercially available such as MOLGEN *(45).*

Djerassi was also a pioneer in the more challenging field of automated interpretation of spectral data. His DENDRAL program *(46)* was one of the first
attempts to analyze the interpretation of mass spectral data and add some degree
of artificial intelligence to the process. Another advance in the automated
interpretation of mass spectral data is the FRANZ (fragmentation and rearrangement analyzer) program *(47),* in which the most common fragmentation
reactions have been taken into consideration and, if given a structure and a
mass spectrum, the "explainable" fragments that are consistent with the structure can be readily obtained.

With the advent of powerful 2D NMR experiments, a heavier reliance in
structure determination has been put on this technique, and some efforts have
been directed at automating NMR interpretation as well. Munk has developed
several interrelated programs for this purpose *(48).* All of these programs are
combined under the general name of SESAMI (systematic elucidation of structure applying machine intelligence). Maier has also developed some pattern-

recognition algorithms for application to splitting patterns for interpretation of ^{1}H-NMR and ^{13}C-NMR spectra *(49)*.

4.5.1. Simulating NMR and MS Spectra

During the structure determination process, partial structures can be proposed from interpretation of various pieces of data, and, if the proposed partial structure can be corroborated by other spectral data, then confidence is raised in the proposed partial structure. To make this process more efficient, a number of commercial sources now provide simulation software that can approximate various spectra for a given structure. Three of the most common commercially available software packages for NMR simulation are: WIN-SPECEDIT *(50)*, CSEARCH *(51)*, and ACD *(52)*.

Software is also being developed to simulate mass spectral data of given structure. One such program, MASSIMO (mass spectra simulator), has been developed in parallel with the FRANZ algorithms and gives predictions for both peaks and intensities of fragment ions.

5. Bioassay Profiling

In the drug discovery process, the therapeutic utility of a given compound is reflected by its pattern and potency of activity in a variety of bioassays. Antibiotics, for instance, are tested initially for their effectiveness against a panel of microorganisms, and anticancer agents are routinely tested against a panel of tumor-cell lines to determine their selectivity and range of activity. The specificity, or "therapeutic window," of a compound is also predicted by its activity in a panel of "side effect" assays. Other bioassays required for compounds in the drug discovery process are aimed at pharmacokinetic and toxicity parameters. This process of biological profiling of compounds can be a lengthy and compound-consuming endeavor, but many of the assays have been miniaturized and automated and can now be used as aids in dereplication of crude natural product extracts.

5.1. Antibiotic Activity

One method of compound classification and dereplication that has been used in the field of antibiotics research since the 1950s, is based on a compound's spectrum of activity. In fact, in formulating his classification database for antibiotics *(53)*, Berdy considered basing the classification system on a compound's "summarized activity." Among the test organisms considered were: Gram-positive and Gram-negative bacteria, mycobacteria, fungi, yeasts, and protozoa. Most antibiotics exhibit various degrees of activity against such a panel of organisms. Compounds at the extremes in this classification system would be the broad-spectrum antibiotics, which show potent activity against most organisms tested, and the narrow-spectrum antibiotics, which are active only against one or two distinct organisms. Berdy eventually chose a structure-based approach over this activity profile method because of the lack of consistency in the protocols used to generate antibiotic spectra in reports obtained from the literature.

5.2. Anticancer Activity

As part of their efforts to identify clinically useful antitumor compounds, the U. S. National Cancer Institute (NCI) in 1989 established a panel of 60 human tumor cell lines representing seven major categories of human cancer. They have found that the activity profile for various compounds is sufficiently characteristic to be employed as a means of identification, using specialized pattern-recognition algorithms.

For instance, cardenolide glycosides, such as 2'-acetylneriifolin, exhibited a specific pattern of cytotoxic activity in the NCI panel of cell lines *(54)*. Certain cell lines, particularly those among the non–small-cell lung, brain tumor, and renal-cell lines are exceptionally sensitive to 2'-acetylneriifolin, whereas most of the leukemia and colon cell lines were less sensitive to it. From the similar pattern of activity produced by crude extracts of plants of the classes Apocyanaceae and Asclepiadaceae, NCI scientists concluded in this study that similar cardenolide glycosides are present in these extracts.

A second example of this same NCI procedure resulted in the rapid identification of cucurbitacin D from a novel source *(55)*. The pattern of cytotoxic activity observed from a crude extract of *Gonystylus keithii* against renal, brain, and melanoma subpanels correlated strongly with the pattern observed earlier for purified cucurbitacins B, E, and I (**Scheme 5**). This bioprofile indication led to the expeditious fractionation and identification of cucurbitacin D as the anticancer active component in the extract.

The NCI's real purpose in establishing this sort of bioprofiling was to identify a compound that exhibits properties unique among all those in the database. A successful example of the NCI's screening procedure for identifying unique compounds is the identification of betulinic acid (**Scheme 6**) as a highly selective potential antimelanoma agent isolated from stem bark of *Ziziphus mauritiana (56)*.

5.3. Affinity Fingerprints

An analogous but more speculative and potentially much more powerful "biofingerprint" approach is championed by Terrapin Technologies (San Francisco, CA). The basic premise is that the active site of any enzyme or receptor can be simulated by combinations of a limited number of steric and electronic "shapes." If the complementary "stereo-electronic shape" is present in a com-

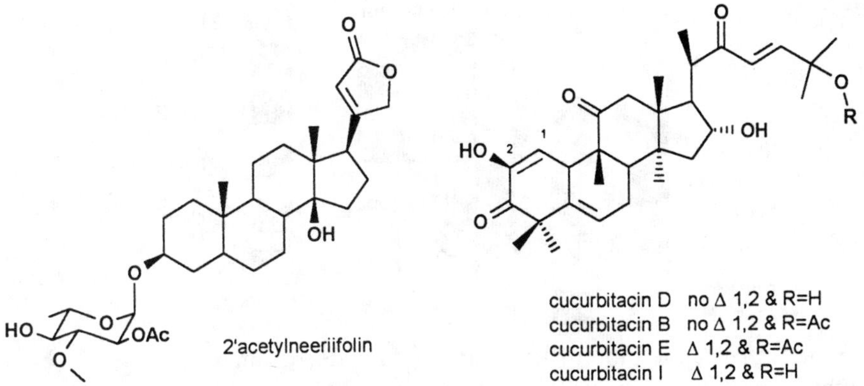

cucurbitacin D   no Δ 1,2 & R=H
cucurbitacin B   no Δ 1,2 & R=Ac
cucurbitacin E   Δ 1,2 & R=Ac
cucurbitacin I   Δ 1,2 & R=H

2'acetylneeriifolin

Scheme 5.

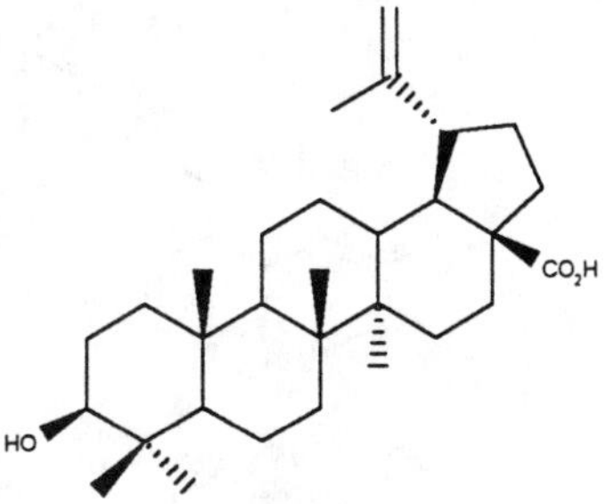

betulinic acid
Scheme 6.

pound, then some binding will occur, and higher affinity is indicative of a composite of complementary "shapes." Furthermore, they have identified a panel of proteins, each of which exhibits a representative "shape" at their active site, and have developed assays to quantitate the complementary "shapes" of compounds including natural products. In this way, it is intended that compounds will be identified that bind strongly to specific biotargets and will lead to candidates for new drugs.

It was found that, when 5000 randomly chosen synthetic and natural compounds were tested against a panel of only 18 proteins, unique patterns could be generated for 95% of the compounds. Since the most important character of a compound for drug discovery is its biological activity, this biofingerprint approach is very appealing for pharmaceutical research, though for dereplication studies it is largely speculative at this stage. The binding-reactivity fingerprints of nine natural products tested by this method are shown in **Fig. 8** *(57) (see also* **Scheme 7**).

A1
R8
S1
HF2
DAO
BCh
Pap
PDE
harmaline
quinine
citrinin
lasalocid
scopoletin
NDG
naringenin
colchicine
taxol
approximate IC_{50}
<4 μM
4-40 μM
40-400 μM
400-1000 μM
>1000 μM

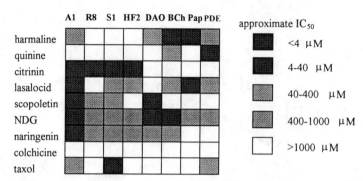

Fig. 8. Terrapin bioprofiling pattern (adapted from **ref.** ***47***). A1, human gluthathione-*S*-transferase; R8, rat glutathione-*S*-tranferase; S1, schistosome glutathione-*S*-transferase; HF2, housefly glutathione-*S*-transferase; DAO, porcine D-amino acid oxidase; BCh, equine butyryl cholinesterase; Pap, papain; PDE, snake venom phosphodiesterase I.

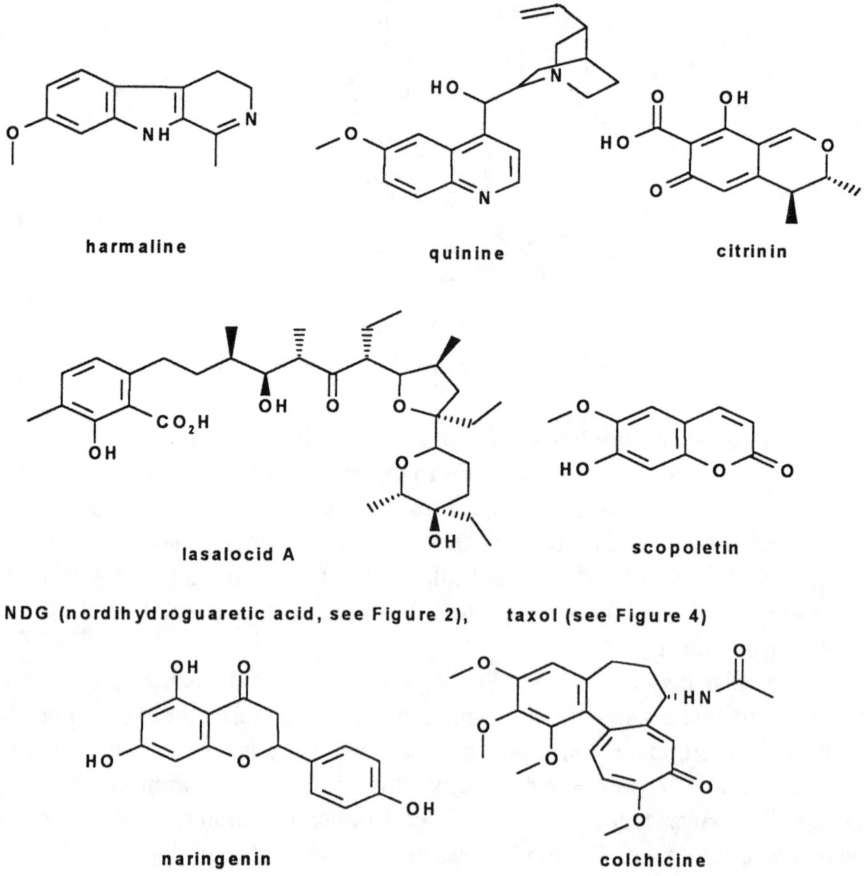

harmaline
quinine
citrinin
lasalocid A
scopoletin
NDG (nordihydroguaretic acid, see Figure 2),
taxol (see Figure 4)
naringenin
colchicine

Scheme 7.

5.4. Immunochemical Techniques

The exquisite "dereplication" ability of the mammalian immune systems to identify and remove unwanted xenobiotics has been utilized by some natural products chemists. Application of antibody-based detection methods for natural products have thus far been limited to those natural products that are of significant economic interest, either as agricultural contaminants or as potential pharmaceutical constituents. However, the development of more readily available microbially derived antibody fragments *(58)* and the advent of various methods for increasing their affinity *(59)* augur well for more widespread use of these technologies for dereplication in the future. Of the numerous reports of the use of this technique of antibody-based detection to identify natural products and related family members, two representative examples follow.

In one study *(60)* aimed at identifying and quantifying, from various plant extracts, new compounds related to the anticancer drug taxol, polyclonal antibodies were raised using 2-succinyl taxol-bovine serum albumin (**Fig. 9**) as the immunogen. These antibodies were then used to develop an enzyme-linked immunosorbent assay (ELISA) that was specific for the taxol family. This taxol ELISA assay was used to monitor solvent partitions and chromatographic fractions of extracts of *Taxus brevifolia* from different sources. Five different ELISA-positive taxoids were isolated, one of which was previously unreported.

A specific type of dereplication is required by the agricultural industry to identify harmful secondary metabolite contaminants present in various feedstocks. The antibody-based technologies have proven to be the method of choice for this application because of their robustness, reliability, and minimal requirements for specialized equipment. In addition, the antibody-based approaches are amenable to quantitation of secondary metabolites. An example is the development of an assay to detect paxilline and related neurotoxic contaminants of ryegrass *(61)* (**Fig. 10**). Monoclonal antibodies were raised against conjugates of paxilline *O*-(carboxymethyl)oxime, and these were used to develop a TLC-ELISAgram for paxilline-related compounds. The TLC-ELISAgram technique *(62)* is similar to the gel overlay method and is analogous to Western blotting. In this case, the antibody was bound to a nitrocellulose sheet and allowed to capture crossreacting compounds through contact with a TLC plate on which a sample of ryegrass had been chromatographed. The nitrocellulose sheet was then incubated with a paxilline-enzyme conjugate that bound to the rest of the plate. Substrate for the enzyme was then added, which gave rise to a colored product and hence clear zones in a uniform colored background identified the paxilline-related compounds. Using this technique to analyze an extract of *Penicillium paxilli*, paxilline was identified as was the previously unreported, but crossreacting, paxinorol.

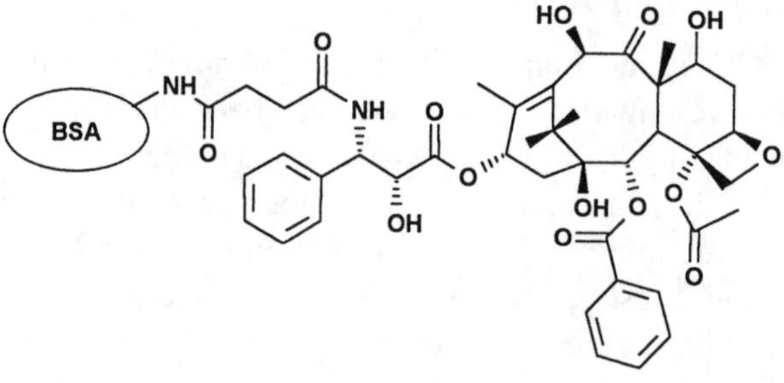

Fig. 9. Taxol BSA conjugate.

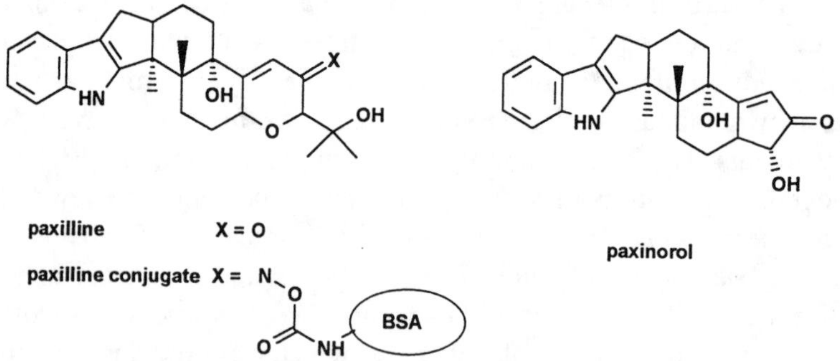

paxilline   **X = O**

paxilline conjugate X = N

paxinorol

Fig. 10. Paxilline-related compounds.

5.4.1. Polyene Mode of Action

In some cases, it is desirable to identify compounds that exhibit similar bio-logical activities but whose structures represent diverse chemical classes; dereplication methodologies can be used for this purpose. For instance, amphotericin's antifungal activity is known to be related to its ability to bind ergosterol and thus disrupt fungal membrane integrity, but amphotericin is also toxic to many mammalian cells, which severely restricts its therapeutic useful-ness. In one study *(63)*, Molinski et al. attempted to discover novel natural products with the same mode of antifungal activity to that of amphotericin, in the hope that they might possess the benefits of amphotericin without some of the unwanted side effects. A large number of extracts were found that exhib-ited antifungal activity and in order to prioritize them, a secondary assay was devised that measures whether an antifungal agent's activity is reduced in the presence of exogenous ergosterol. The use of this assay for bioactivity-guided fractionations, and comparison with standard samples of amphotericin, led to the discovery of jaspamide, a novel depsipeptide (**Fig. 11**). Jaspamide appeared to fulfill the requirements and could be identified without recourse to isolation of all the antifungal compounds initially under consideration.

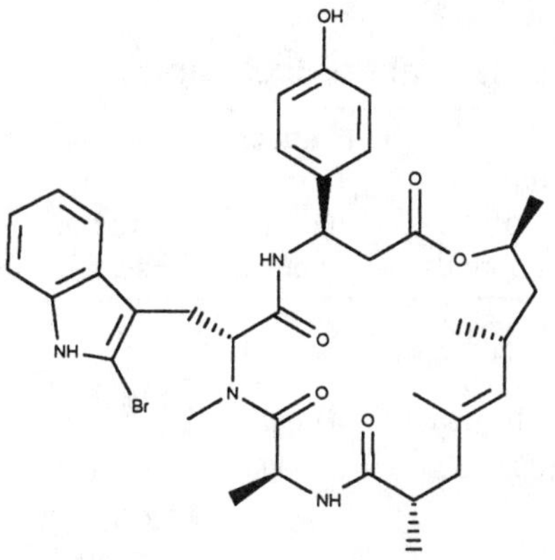

Fig. 11. Jaspamide.

6. Literature Databases

Since natural product dereplication is an attempt to minimize effort by using that which is already known, efficient use of literature databases is critical to most dereplication procedures. The use of commercially available databases for natural products dereplication has been reviewed, and it has been estimated that a $300 investment in literature searches could avoid a $50,000 investment in reisolation and identification of a complex compound already described in the literature *(64)*.

In general, three categories of query are asked of literature database searches in order to obtain an early indication of whether the natural product of interest is a known compound:

1. Compounds exhibiting similar biological activity to the compound of interest.
2. Information on compounds known to be produced by the taxonomic source/organism under study.
3. Quantifiable physical and chemical characteristics of known compounds.

Some of the most useful databases for natural product dereplication with their particular attributes are summarized in **Table 4**. The search mechanics vary between databases and those details should be obtained directly from the database vendors. However, a successful typical overall process is described below.

To dereplicate an unknown natural product as rapidly as possible, any new information on the unknown compound should be compared as early as possible with literature data obtained from a database search. For instance, if the aim is to isolate the bioactive component from a natural extract that has given a positive result in a bioassay, then a literature search for natural products exhibiting the same, similar, or associated biological activities could be carried out even before any extracts are tested. The disadvantage of this approach is

Table 4
Databases Containing Natural Product Information

Database	Number of compounds	Number of natural products	Structure search	Mol wt	UV
CAS *(65)*	>12,000,000		Yes	Yes	
Beilstein *(66)*	>5,000,000	91,000	Yes	Yes	Yes
NAPRALERT *(67)*	100,000	100,000	Yes (search by registry file)	Yes (search by registry file)	
Dictionary Natural Products *(68)*	115,000	70,000	Yes	Yes	
Berdy *(69)*	26,000	26,000		Yes	Yes
KMC-plus *(70)*	16,000	16,000		Yes	Yes
Antibase *(71)*	14,000	14,000	Yes	Yes	Yes
DEREP *(72)*	7000	7000		Yes	Yes
Marinlit *(73)*	6000	6000	Yes	Yes	Yes
MNP *(74)*	4000	4000	Yes	Yes	Yes

Database	NMR, ^{1}H, ^{13}C	Mass spec.	Bio-activity	Source organism	Access	Contents
CAS *(65)*			Yes	Yes	STN	All sources
Beilstein *(66)*	Ref. only	Ref. only	Yes	Yes	STN	All sources
NAPRALERT *(67)*			Yes	Yes	STN	Mainly plants
Dictionary Natural Products *(68)*				Yes	CD-ROM	All sources
Berdy *(69)*			Yes	Yes	MS-DOS	All sources
KMC-plus *(70)*			Yes	Yes	MS-DOS	All sources
Antibase *(71)*	Yes	Yes	Yes	Yes	ISIS/Base	Microorganisms
DEREP *(72)*			Yes	Yes	MS-DOS	All sources
Marinlit *(73)*			Yes	Yes	Mac	Marine organisms
MNP *(74)*			Yes	Yes	Mac	Marine organisms

that assay protocols are likely to vary between different literature reports leading to apparent differences between observed and reported results. Even if the exact assay has not been described in the literature, the compounds may have been reported as active in cruder multiple target assays, or as giving rise to more general, associated in vivo pharmacological effects of undetermined mode of action.

A second database search can be carried out if taxonomic information is available on the organism source of the extract. Not only is it useful to obtain literature information on compounds reportedly produced by the species under investigation, but any other chemotaxonomic information can be used to crossreference with the earlier bioactivity search to highlight natural products expected to be identified from the extract.

For example, numerous crude organism extracts are producers of antimicrobial activity as detected by whole-cell assays against various microorganisms; hence, when faced with a large number of "hits," it is often difficult to prioritize those worth extracting over those that produce compounds that have been previously reported. One approach in such cases might be to search activity in the Berdy database that consists of antibiotic secondary metabolites (mainly from microorganisms). A search on the basis of the source organism (e.g., *Aspergillus nidulans*) and the test organism against which it shows activity (e.g., *Candida* sp.) would quickly lead to the suggestion that the active components were likely to be echinocandins. If an echinocandin standard is available, using this simply to show (perhaps by HPLC or TLC) that the extract contains echinocandins, and in approximately sufficient quantities to account for the observed level of activity, may well be sufficient to halt the extraction. If a standard is not available, the hypothesis could be tested by employing a physical test such as mass spectrometry, looking for ions of the appropriate molecular weight.

Once fractionation has led to some physical characteristics of the active component, such as UV spectra or putative molecular weight, another literature search can be executed. During the isolation and structure identification of the zaragozic acids (also known as squalestatins) *(75)*, a literature search of the Chemical Abstracts database was carried out within hours of isolating sufficient material to obtain a COSY spectrum, since the two substructures (A and B) were readily identified from these data (*see* **Fig. 12**). When the Chemical Abstracts search revealed that no known compounds contained either of these substructures, it was obvious that the compound was novel and therefore patentable. It was several more days before enough NMR and MS experiments had been carried out and an exhaustive structure determination completed, at which point the truly novel 2,8-dioxabicyclo[3.2.1]octane-3,4,5-tricarboxylate core of the zaragozic acids could be searched for in Chemical Abstracts and shown to be unprecedented in the natural product literature.

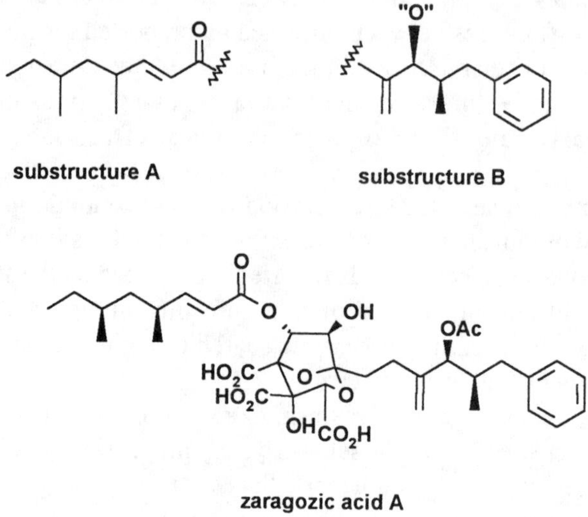

substructure A   substructure B

zaragozic acid A

Fig. 12. Zaragozic acid substructures.

Some of the databases (**Table 4**) are beginning to incorporate searchable fields containing other physical characteristics, such as ^{13}C-NMR chemical shifts and mass spectral fragment ions. Some of these are simulated data that are less accurate for the more unusual compounds. The most readily obtained physical data is normally a UV spectrum, and several of the commercial databases are searchable by this characteristic. Each new characteristic that agrees with the literature value adds a level of confidence to the identification of an unknown compound as a literature compound. The level of confidence required depends on the questions being asked.

7. Scope for Natural Products Dereplication

7.1. History of Natural Product Identification

The pace of natural product discovery has been increasing throughout this century. The number of structurally assigned natural products that have been reported in the literature now stands at >100,000 *(66)*, of which >26,000 *(69)* have reported biological activity (*see* **Fig. 13**).

The majority of the reported natural products have been isolated from plants, fungi, or bacteria. Since a large percentage of natural products have shown some sort of biological activity, it can be assumed that much natural product isolation has been bioassay-directed. Except in a few cases, little effort has been expended in determining the complete range of secondary metabolites that are biosynthesized by any one organism.

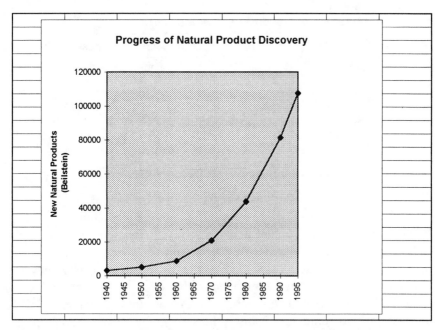

Fig. 13. Numbers of new natural products discovered over past 60 yr (data from **ref. 66**).

7.2. Earth's Natural Product Repertoire

Based on the approx 320,000 described species of higher plants, bacteria, and fungi, the estimated total number of reported natural products (most of which derive from these sources), of 100,000 (<1 per 3 organisms) can reasonably be judged to be well below the total produced by these organisms—probably by several orders of magnitude (*see* **Table 5**). (Most organisms have not been examined chemically and, of those that have, very few have been exhaustively studied with regard to their secondary metabolites.) If insects, other animals, protozoa, and algae are included—species not traditionally associated with natural products but also likely to be rich sources of chemistry—the proportion of the total already discovered is even lower. However, most organisms have not yet been described, and if the estimates of the total numbers of species (which range from approx 3 to 30 million) are used in this consideration, it can be seen that we have yet identified only a tiny proportion of the earth's natural product repertoire. If this vast unknown is to be explored seriously, it is inevitable that dereplication and rapid identification methods play an ever-increasing role.

7.3. Confidence Factors

The underlying theme throughout this chapter is the process of proposing and building confidence in chemical structure information for a natural prod-

Table 5
Numbers of Described Species *(76)*

Organism	Number of described species
Insects	751,000
Other animals	281,000
Higher plants	248,400
Algae	26,900
Protozoa	30,800
Fungi	69,000
Bacteria	4800

uct under investigation. As has been stated, no single technique gives 100% confidence in a structure (except perhaps X-ray diffraction analysis, which requires milligram amounts of pure material and considerable time), but the confidence inherent in each technique is different. When comparing physical data obtained for an unknown compound to that of a standard, the resolving power of the technique is the critical issue in determining confidence levels. For instance, if two compounds exhibit the same t_R by HPLC, then there is a higher level of confidence that the compounds are identical than if they exhibit the same R_f by TLC in a single solvent system. This is due to the higher resolving power of HPLC. **Table 6** illustrates the resolving power or "unique identifier" factor for various physical measurements that leads to different confidence levels. We have defined the "unique identifiers" as the maximum number of different compounds that could be separated by various techniques, and it has been calculated by dividing the range of possible values for a physical measurement (maximum − minimum) by the techniques' resolution. Some "typical" conditions have been considered for the techniques shown, and the number of unique identifiers varies with different experimental conditions.

Another important conclusion of this chapter is that combinations of data greatly increase confidence over a single set of data. To illustrate this point, a theoretical treatment has again been formulated (**Table 7**) showing the calculated number of unique identifiers for various combinations of characteristics. Because no chromatographic or spectroscopic measurement of all known natural products will give an even distribution (*see* **Fig. 3**), these "unique identifier" calculations have little meaning. However, they can give an indication of which combinations of techniques might be most powerful as dereplication tools.

7.4. Prioritization of Natural Product Extracts

Often the natural products chemist is faced with a large number of extracts with some common feature that require prioritization. This might be a set of

Table 6
Theoretical Limits of Unique Identifiers

Technique	Minimum	Maximum	Resolution	Unique identifiers
TLC	0.0 cm	10 cm	0.5 cm	20
HPLC	1.5 min	30 min	0.2 min	142
UV max	200 nm	350 nm	2 nm	75
MS	150 m/z	900 m/z	1 m/z	750
IR (fingerprint region)	700/cm	1800/cm	5/cm	220

Table 7
Theoretical Limits of Identifier Combinations

LC/UV	$142 \times 75 = 10{,}650$
LC-MS	$142 \times 1{,}350 = 191{,}700$
MS/MS	$750 \times 750 = 562{,}500$
4 IR peaks	$220^4 = 2{,}342{,}560{,}000$

bioactive hits from a screen of organism extracts out of which the aim is to isolate the most "interesting" (usually synonymous with novel and potent) biologically active components. There is no set protocol for dealing with such a set—or indeed, any dereplication problem—but there are a number of steps that can be taken at this stage that might help to limit the amount of work involved in rediscovering known compounds and allowing efforts to concentrate on the novel natural products.

7.4.1. Information About the Organism

The first step might be to find out from the literature as much as possible about the active organisms in terms of their taxonomy and chemistry.

1. What metabolites are these sources known to produce?
2. Do any of these metabolites have reported biological activity that is the same or suggestive of the screen activity?
3. Do any have physicochemical properties that might suggest they are responsible for the activity?
4. Are standards of the metabolites available for comparison?

This is more applicable for metabolites of plants or larger animals, as these are better described taxonomically compared to bacteria, which are much more difficult to classify with any degree of consistency (and which tend to be much more variable with regard to their secondary metabolite production).

7.4.2. Information About the Biological Target

Additionally, the same question can be asked the other way around: What is known about the biological target—either a specific molecular assay or the more general biological area from which it derives? What compounds and, specifically, what natural products are known to act in these systems. And is it possible that any of these account for, or even give a clue as to, the positive results from the assays?

One might even ask, "Which of these compounds are likely to act specifically and which are likely to be general nonspecific 'interfering' compounds?"

In this way, it may be possible to eliminate a large proportion of the extracts by dereplicating for a relatively small number of natural products known to show activity against the biological target.

7.4.3. Clustering Organism Extracts

If there are still a large number of extracts worthy of investigation, the next step might be an attempt at dereplication within the set of extracts to prevent duplication of isolation work. This can be approached by grouping those that have an active component that appears to be alike, perhaps with respect to some of the physicochemical properties outlined above.

More tentatively, one might group samples using less direct parameters. For example, crude extracts from different sources that have the same chromatographic profile may be grouped together on the basis that they are likely to produce the same secondary metabolites. Extracts from organisms that are taxonomically similar or indistinguishable may be grouped together on the basis that they are more likely to produce similar chemistry and may be the same species.

A decision might then be taken to work on only one of each of these groups on the basis that this is more likely to yield the widest range of compounds and to lower the probability of isolating the same compound numerous times. The active compound from each group, once isolated, can then be used as a standard to compare against the active extracts of the other members of the group. This approach is by no means a sure method of dereplicating or prioritizing—the production of secondary metabolites often does not tie in so conveniently with these other characteristics—but it is a way of increasing the odds in favor of discovering the most diverse range of natural products from the screen.

7.4.4. Targeting Novelty

The complementary approach might be to ask of the collection of active extracts, "Which seem particularly unusual or interesting?" Attention might then be focused on these—perhaps because they derive from an unusual source, e.g., a marine animal among a collection of streptomycetes, or an organism from a group of organisms that have been little studied with regard to their natural products; or possibly because they have an unusual UV spectrum. The aim of this approach is to increase the chances of finding novel compounds.

7.4.5. Selectivity of Bioactivity

An additional approach for prioritizing high-throughput screen "hits" would be to make judgments informed by the results of secondary assays and other biological assays. For instance, if the ultimate aim of an isolation program is drug discovery, an extract might be considered progressible only if it showed activity against phosphodiesterase V (PDE V) together with >100× less activity against a related isoform PDE I. If a number of extracts showed activity in a PDE I assay, they could be prioritized using the results of the same extract in the other assay on the basis that a selectively acting compound is preferable. The decision might be taken not to pursue the isolation of the active components from an extract that is active in both assays, even though there is a risk that the activity is due to different compounds each of which is selective.

All such judgments of prioritization are, of course, to some extent subjective and depend on the overall aim of the extraction program, the time and resources available, and to a certain extent, luck—the only sure way of not missing the most exciting compounds is to isolate them all. The strategies outlined above are not guaranteed ways of getting to the best compounds; they are only meant to shift the balance in favor of doing so. The order in which they are applied will depend on particular circumstances. One of the most valuable tools in this process is experience. The necessity for this may have been replaced somewhat by technology, but experience is still invaluable in picking out and isolating novel and interesting natural products.

7.5. Future

7.5.1. Technology Development

A few decades ago, the purification and structural elucidation of almost any natural product was an enormous undertaking. As a result of advances in technology, this process has become almost routine. The speed and ease with which natural products can be isolated and characterized will continue to increase with increasing miniturization and automation of every step from biological assay to structure determination. Developments in structural elucidation techniques, such as high-field NMR and highly sensitive MS, mean that it is often possible to determine structures using orders-of-magnitude-less material than would have been required a decade or so ago. For instance, high-resolution microcoil NMR has been used to obtain spectra on a 300-MHz machine using 19 ng of sample in a 1-min acquisition time *(77)*. This is leading to a blurring of the division between analytical and preparative purifications. Techniques that are, or were, considered solely analytical, may soon be suitable in some circumstances for the natural product chemist to generate sufficient material to determine a structure. The speed and resolving power of techniques such as microbore LC, capillary electrophoresis, and capillary electrochromatography, can then be harnessed to be used alongside the methods outlined in this book. The increased use of "hyphenated" techniques as are described in this chapter is also blurring the division between the once very separate steps of natural product extraction and structure determination, which can, in some cases, now be carried out as effectively one step.

7.5.2. High-Throughput Screening

The extraction of many natural products is undertaken as a result of activity in a biological assay. High-throughput screening technology has developed greatly in recent years through robotic automation, high-density format screens, and the enormous increase in identification of specific molecular targets—largely as a result of molecular biological techniques—that form the basis of high-throughput screens. The application of this technology to the search for novel natural products will result in a large number of "hits" from screens of crude organism extracts. In order to focus on the extracts of most interest as quickly as possible and to avoid isolating repeatedly the same common natural products, effficient dereplication processes are of the utmost importance.

7.5.3. Combinatorial Biosynthesis (*Fig. 14*)

An exciting development that is unfolding in the natural products field is the finding that, in some cases, genes coding for enzymes involved in different biosynthetic pathways can be recombined in such a way that hybrid end products are produced. The first example of this technology yielded a number of novel compounds including dihydrogranatirhodin, a slight variant of actinorhodin and granaticin. Dihydrogranatirhodin was produced as a minor component of a random insertion of actinorhodin biosynthetic genes into the granaticin producer.

In order to efficiently and systematically exchange and recombine biosynthetic genes, the biosynthetic genes responsible for various polyketide natural products must be sequenced, and a host-vector system must be available. Several complete biosynthetic gene clusters have now succumbed to cloning and sequencing *(78–84)*, and a host-vector system has been developed in *Streptomyces (85)*. In initial recombination and truncation efforts, compounds exhibiting dramatically different carbon skeletons have been produced. A sample of some of the hybrid structures produced with enzymes taken from the biosynthetic pathways that normally lead to actinorhodin and tetracenomycin (**Fig. 15**) are shown in **Fig. 16**.

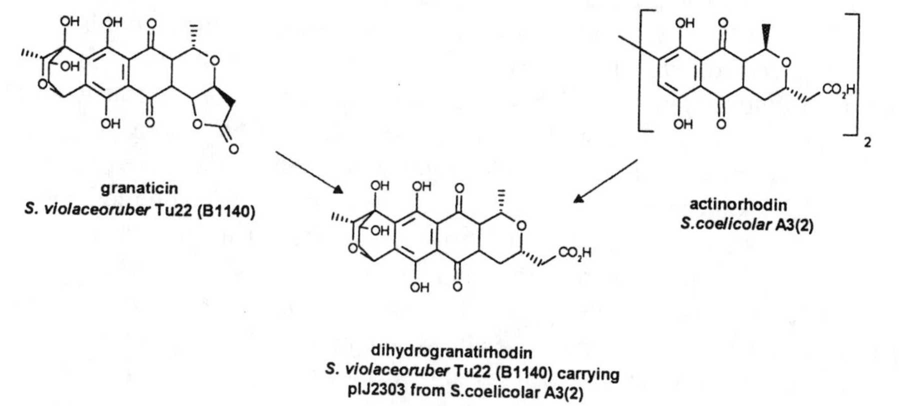

Fig. 14. Combinatorial biosynthesis leading to "unnatural" natural products.

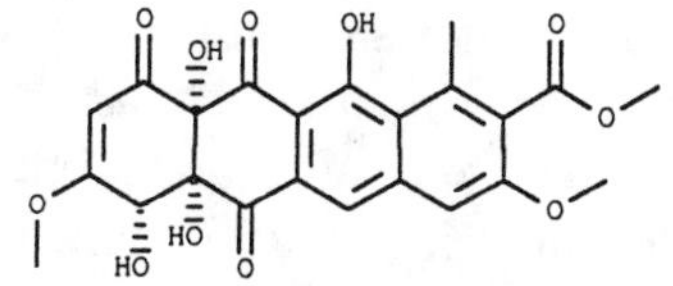

Fig. 15. Tetracenomycin C, a natural product isolated from *S. glaucescens*.

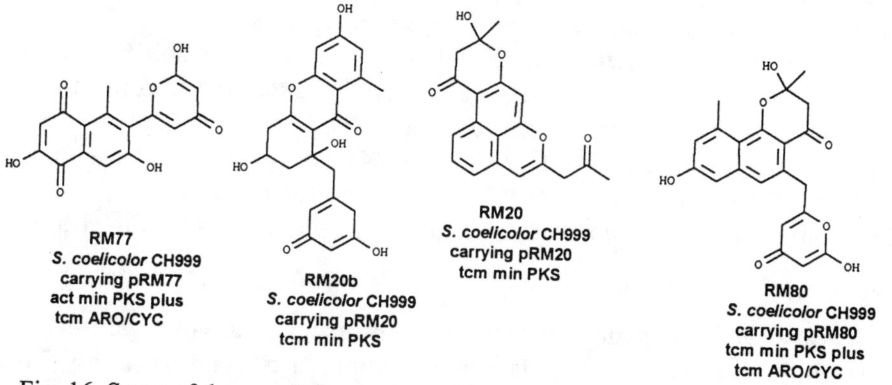

Fig. 16. Some of the novel structures produced from truncations and combinations of actinorhodin and tetracenomycin pathways.

The potential for producing novel macrocyclic polyketides is even more promising, since, in this case, the physical and temporal functioning of biosynthetic enzymes has been implicated as being a sequential process *(86)*. If substrate specificities can be overcome, then an enormous number of compounds could be produced representing all of the possible combinations of oxidation state, stereochemistry, and methyl substituents for macrocycles, as well as several complete libraries of variously sized macrocycles. Progress in this direction using erythromycin genes has resulted in erythromycin analogs exhibiting altered oxidation states as well as compounds with altered ring-size lactones of 6 and 12 carbons rather than the normal 14-membered lactone (**Fig. 17**).

If this technology fulfills its exciting potential, then the dereplication problem could to some extent be addressed genetically. In principle, one could identify the biosynthetic genes present in the producing organism and from this analysis predict the structure of the natural product that should be formed from that sequence of biosynthetic machinery. However, the "rules" regulating these pathways are only beginning to be elucidated, and physical analyses of these "unnatural natural products" will certainly be essential for some time.

7.5.4. Combinatorial Chemistry

As a source of novel chemical structures, natural products are now rivaled by the revolution that is combinatorial chemistry by which a vast number of compounds may be made from a relatively small number of starting compounds, or monomers *(87)*. An alliance of natural products chemistry with combinatorial chemistry has resulted in the development of several libraries of natural product derivatives, using natural products as templates *(88)* and as targets for total synthesis on solid phase *(89)*. Whereas natural products have often been the target or the starting point for synthetic chemists, the use of natural products as combinatorial chemistry monomers is likely to increase enormously the numbers of natural product-derived structures available for testing.

Lessons learned from natural products dereplication and prioritization in high-throughput assays can also be applied to the "deconvolution" problems, faced by combinatorial chemists when assaying pools of compounds. With limited resynthesis capabilities, not every active pool can be followed up, and the use of prioritization methods will be required, similar to those outlined above.

7.5.5. Novel Organisms

It is also worth remembering that there exist many groups of organisms that have not been explored with regard to natural products. As discussed in **Subheading 7.2.**, most species have not been described, let alone examined chemically, and it may be that natural products chemistry leads taxonomy rather than the other way around; i.e., undescribed organisms that appear to produce interesting or useful natural products will be those that receive the most attention in taxonomic terms. Some major groups of organisms not traditionally regarded as rich sources of natural products may yet prove fruitful (e.g., insects have hardly been explored yet represent the largest group of reported species). Some organisms may be rich sources yet difficult to study. For example, DNA stud-

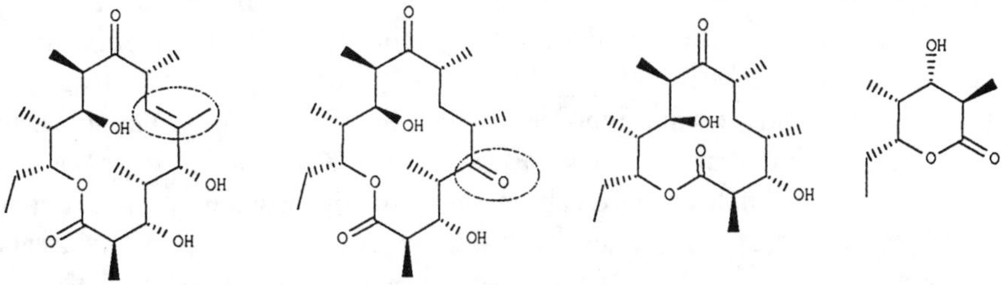

Fig. 17. Some of the alternative structures produced from truncations and combinations of erthromycin biosynthetic genes.

ies suggest that there are orders-of-magnitude-more bacterial species than was once suspected, but many of these are "nonculturable" (at least for the present) *(90,91)*. We are only beginning to recognize the wide diversity of groups such as marine bacteria. Some habitats such as sea floor, hydrothermal vents, and forest canopies have hardly been explored; in some cases, their long isolation from other habitats may have resulted in the evolution of a radically different range of secondary metabolites. However, the increasing rediscovery of marine natural products mentioned above illustrates the fact that different approaches and more efficient processes are required both for new discoveries and dereplication of natural products *(92)*.

7.5.6. Chemical Ecology

The study of natural products will be enhanced if we learn more about the biological role of secondary metabolites. Although it is generally agreed, for instance, that many microbial secondary metabolites must play some defensive role, there is almost no evidence that they do indeed act as such in vivo. Many marine invertebrates produce a large number of structurally diverse secondary metabolites, many of which have some form of potent biological activity; this is probably associated with the fact that these organisms are often soft, sessile, and highly colored. As we learn more about chemical ecology and the evolutionary origins of secondary metabolites, and hence the original reason for their prevalence, we may also learn how best to look for secondary metabolites of interest.

7.5.7. Information Sharing

With funding for research under increasing scrutiny, the natural products community should encourage the most efficient use of any research allocations that are available. One step in this direction could be an attempt to capitalize on the low-cost, high-capacity, instant availability of the Internet for creation of an internationally accessible dereplication database. If a core of interested

maintainers could be identified and sufficient funding obtained, then a reposi-
tory of spectral and biological data might be created that would make
dereplication much less problematic. Successful precedent for creation and use
of such a shared database is the highly acclaimed Cambridge Crystallographic Data
Centre (CCDC). One reason for the success of the CCDC is that deposition of
X-ray structure coordinates in the database is required by most journals as a prereq-
uisite for publication of X-ray data. These authors propose that such a database be
established, in order to facilitate the discovery of new and useful natural products
internationally, and for the benefit of all natural products research.

However, if the reliability of spectral simulation algorithms continues to
improve, then it is conceivable that, at some point in the future, reporting of
UV, NMR, MS, and IR data may no longer be required and it will only be
necessary to report anomalous findings that do not agree with the predicted
spectra. Such an advance would be analogous to the present redundant nature
of reporting elemental analysis data or precise mass data in support of empirical formulas. Of course, collection of this data would still be essential for structure elucidation, but reporting correlation between spectral data and structures
may at some point no longer advance the science and thus become redundant.
If the calculated spectra become so advanced, then a dereplication database
might essentially consist of a list of all of the reported natural product structures with supporting software to generate the associated spectra.

Acknowledgments

The helpful input and advice of John Bradshaw, John Hardwick, and Chris
Coulson are gratefully acknowledged.

References

1. Langlykke, A. (1980) Foreword to *CRC Handbook of Antibiotic Compounds*
   (Berdy, J., ed), CRC, Boca Raton, FL.
2. Faulkner, D. J. (1995) Chemical riches from the oceans. *Chemistry in Britain* **31,**
   680–684.
3. Valko, K. (1995) Retention prediction of pharmaceutical compounds. *J.
   Chromatogr. Libr.* **57,** 4792.
4. Noble, M., Noble, D., and Fletton, R. A. (1978) G2201-C, a new
   cyclopentenedione antibiotic isolated from the fermentation broth of *Streptomyces cattleya. J. Antibiot.* **31,** 15–18.
5. Hamburger, M. O. and Cordell, G. A. (1987) A direct bioautographic TLC assay
   for compounds possessing antibacterial activity. *J. Nat. Prod.* **50,** 19–22.
6. Cardellina, J. H., Munro, M. H. G., Fuller, R. W., Manfredi, K. P., McKee, T. C.,
   Tischler, M., Bokesch, H., Gustatson, K., Beutler, J., and Boyd, M. (1993) A
   chemical screening strategy for the dereplication and prioritisation of
   HIV-inhibitory aqueous natural product extracts. *J. Nat. Prod.* **56,** 1123–1129.

7. Alvi, K. A., Peterson, J., and Hofman, B. (1995) Rapid identification of elaiophylin and geldanamycin in *Streptomyces* fermentation broths using CPC coupled with a photodiode array detector and LC-MS methodologies. *J. Ind. Microb.* **15**, 80–84.

8. Dittmann, M. M., Wienand, K., Bek, F., and Rozing, G. P. (1995) Theory and practice of capillary electrochromatography. *LC-GC* **13**, 800–814.

9. Boughtflower, R. J., Underwood, T., and Paterson, C. J. (1996) Capillary electrochromatography—some important considerations in the preparation of packed capillaries and the choice of mobile phase buffers. *Chromatographia* **40**, 329–335.

10. Smith, N. W. and Evans, M. B. (1994) The analysis of pharmaceutical compounds using capillary electrochromatography. *Chromatographia* **38**, 649–657.

11. Stahl, E. (ed.) (1969) *Thin-Layer Chromatography*, Springer-Verlag, Berlin.

12. *TLC Visualization Reagents and Chromatographic Solvents.* (1973) Publication JJ-5, Eastman Kodak Company, Rochester, NY.

13. Burkhardt, K., Fiedler, H., Grabley, S., Thiericke, R., and Zeeck, A. (1996) New cineromycins and musacins obtained by a metabolite pattern analysis of *Streptomyces griseoviridis* (FH-S 1832) I. Taxonomy, fermentation, isolation and biological activity. *J. Antibiot.* **49**, 432–437.

14. Haslam, E. (1996) Natural polyphenols (vegetable tannins) as drugs: possible modes of action. *J. Nat. Prod.* **59**, 205–215.

15. Nonaka, G.-I., Nishioka, I., Yamagishsi, T., Kashiwadw, Y., Dutschman, G. E., Bodner, A. J., Kilkuskie, R. E., Cheng, Y.-C., and Lee, K.-H. (1990) Anti-AIDS agents, 2: Inhibitory effects of tannins on HIV reverse transcriptase and HIV replication in H9 Iymphocyte cells. *J. Nat. Prod.* **53**, 587–595.

16. Bush, K., Freudenberger, J., and Sykes, R. (1980) Inhibition of *Escherichia coli* tem-2 beta-lactamase by the sulfated compounds izumenolide, panosialin and sodium dodecyl sulfate. *J. Antibiot.* **32**, 1560–1562.

17. Takechi, M., Shimada, S., and Tanaka, Y. (1992) Time course and inhibition of saponin-induced hemolysis. *Planta Med.* **58**, 128–130.

18. Scalbert, A. (1992) Quantitative methods for the estimation of tannins in plant tissues. *Basic Life Sci.: Plant Polyphenols* **59**, 259–280.

19. Budini, R., Tonelli, D., and Girotti, S. (1980) Analysis of total phenols using the Prussian blue method. *J. Agric. Food Chem.* **28**, 1236–1238.

20. Ghisalberti, E. (1993) Detection and isolation of bioactive natural products, in *Bioactive Natural Products* (Colegate, S. and Molyneux, R., eds.), CRC, Boca Raton, FL, pp. 9–57.

21. Glossmann, H., Hering, S., Savchenko, A., Berger, W., Friedrich, K., Garcia, M. L., Goetz, M. A., Liesch, J. M., Zink, D. L., and Kaczorowski ,G. J. (1993) A light stabilizer (Tinuvin 770) that elutes from polypropylene plastic tubes is a potent L-type Ca^{2+}-channel blocker. *Proc. Natl. Acad. Sci. USA* **90**, 9523–9527.

22. Middleditch, B.S. (1989) Analytical artifacts: gc, ms, hplc, tlc and pc. *J. Chromatogr. Library*, vol. **44**, Elsevier, Amsterdam.

23. Woodward, R. B. (1941) Structure and the absorption spectra of a,b-unsaturated ketones. *J. Am. Chem. Soc.* **63**, 1123–1126.

24. Gordan, A. J. and Ford, R. A. (eds.) (1972) *The Chemist's Companion*, Wiley, Chichester, UK, p. 217 (and references therein).
25. Fiedler, H. P. (1993) Biosynthetic capacities of Actinomycetes. 1. Screening for secondary metabolites by HPLC and UV-visible absorbance spectral libraries. *Nat. Prod. Lett.* **2**, 119–128.
26. Volkmann, C., Hartjen, U., Zeeck, A., and Fiedler, H. P. (1995) Biosynthetic capacities of *Actinomycetes*. 3. Naphthgeranine F, a minor congener of the naphthgeranine group produced by *Streptomyces violaceus. J. Antibiot.* **48**, 522–524.
27. Fiedler, H. P., Kulik, A., and Schuz, T. C. (1994) Biosynthetic capacities of *Actinomycetes*. 2. Juglomycin Z, a new naphthoquinone antibiotic from *Streptomyces tendae. J. Antibiot.* **47**, 1116–1122.
28. Blum, S., Fiedler, H. P., Groth, I., Kempter, C., Stephan, H., Nicholson, G., Metzger, J., and Jung, G. (1995) Biosynthetic capacities of *Actinomycetes*. 4. Echinoserine, a new member of the quinoxaline group, produced by *Streptomyces tendae. J. Antibiot.* **48**, 619–625.
29. Fiedler, H. P. (1984) Screening for new microbial products by HPLC using a photodiode array detector. *J. Chromatogr.* **316**, 487–494.
30. Zhou, S. and Hamburger, M. (1996) Application of liquid chromatography-atmospheric pressure ionisation mass spectrometry in natural product analysis: evaluation and optimization of electrospray and heated nebulizer interfaces. *J. Chromatogr. A* **755**, 189–204.
31. Constant, H. and Beecher, C. (1995) A method for the dereplication of natural product extracts using electrospray HPLC-MS. *Nat. Prod. Lett.* **6**, 193–196.
32. Bradshaw, J. (1996) personal communication. Data adapted from *Dictionary of Organic Compounds*, Electronic Publishing Div., Chapman & Hall, London.
33. Kerns, E. H., Yolk, K. J., Hill, S. E., and Lee, M. S. (1994) Profiling taxanes in *Taxus* extracts using LC-MS and LC-MS/MS techniques. *J. Nat. Prod.* **57**, 1391–1403.
34. Blau, K. and Halket, J. (eds.) (1993) *Handbook of Derivatives for Chromatography*, Wiley, Chichester, UK.
35. Beutler, J., Alvarado, A., Schaufelberger, D., Andrews, P., and McCloud, T. (1990) Dereplication of phorbol bioactives: *Lyngbya majuscula* and *Croton cuneatus. J. Nat. Prod.* **53**, 867–874.
36. Spraul, M., Hofmann, M., Dvortsark, P., Nicholson, J. K., and Wilson, I. D. (1993) High-performace liquid chromatography coupled to high-field proton nuclear magnetic resonance spectroscopy: application to the urinary metabolites of ibuprofen. *Anal. Chem.* **65**, 327.
37. Sidelmann, U. G., Gavaghan, C., Carless, H. A. J., Spraul, M., Hoffmann, M., Lindon, J. C., Wilson I. D., and Nicholson, J. K. (1995) 750MHz directly coupled HPLC-NMR: application to the sequential characterisation of the positional isomers and anomers of the 2-, 3- and 4-fluorobenzoic acid glucuronides in equilibrium mixtures. *Anal. Chem.* **67**, 4441–4445.
38. Sidelmann, U. G., Lenz, E. M., Spraul, M., Hoffmann, M., Troke, J., Sanderson, P. N., Wilson, I. D., and Nicholson, J. K. (1996) 750 MHz HPLC-NMR spectroscopic stud-

ies on the separation and characterisation of the positional isomers of the glucuronides of 6, 11-dihydro-11-oxodibenz[*b,e*]oxepin-2-acetic acid. *Anal. Chem.* **68**, 106–110.

39. Pullen, F. S., Swanson, A. G., Newman, M. J., and Richards, D. S. (1995) On-line liquid chromatography/nuclear magnetic resonance/mass spectrometry—a powerful spectrometric tool for the analysis of mixtures of pharmaceutical interest. *Rapid Commun. Mass Spectrometry* **9**, 1003–1006.

40. Spring, O., Buschmann, H., Vogler, B., Schilling, E. E., Spraul, M., and Hoffmann, M. (1995) Sesquiterpene lactone chemistry of Zaluzania grayana from online LC-NMR measurements. *Phytochemistry* **39**, 609–612.

41. Barjat, H., Morris, G. A., Smart, S., Swanson, A. G., and Williams, S. C. R. (1995) High-resolution diffusion-ordered 2D spectroscopy (HR-DOSY)—a new tool for the analysis of complex mixtures. *J. Mag. Reson. Ser. B* **108**, 170–172.

42. Dwyer, J. L., Chapman, A. E., and Liu, X. (1995) Analysis of steroids by combined chromatography-infrared spectroscopy. *LC-GC* **13**, 240–253.

43. Djerassi, C., Smith, D. H., and Varkony, T. H. (1979) A novel role of computers in the natural products field. *Naturwiss.* **66**, 9–21.

44. Nourse, J., Smith, R., Carhart, R., and Djerassi, C. (1979) Exhaustive generation of stereoisomers for structure elucidation. *J. Am. Chem. Soc.* **101**, 1216–1223.

45. Benecke, C., Grund, R., Hohberger, R., Kerber, A., Laue, R., and Wieland, T. (1995) MOLGEN+, a generator of connectivity isomers and stereoisomers for molecular structure eludication. *Anal. Chim. Acta* **314**, 141–147.

46. Djerassi, C., Smith, D., Crandell, C., Gray, N., Nourse, J., and Lindley, M. (1982) Applications of artificial intelligence for chemical inference. XLII. The DENDRAL project: computational aids to natural products structure elucidation. *Pure Appl. Chem.* **54**, 2425–2442.

47. Gasteiger, H., Hanebeck, W., Schulz, K., Bauerschmidt, S., and Hollering, R. (1993) Automatic analysis and simulation of mass spectra, in *Computer-Enhanced Analytical Spectroscopy*, vol. 4 (Wilkins, C., ed.), Plenum, NY, pp. 97–133.

48. Christie, B. and Munk, M. (1991) The role of two-dimensional nuclear magnetic resonance spectroscopy in computer-enhanced structure elucidation. *J. Am. Chem. Soc.* **113**, 3750–3757.

49. Maier, W. (1993) New approaches to computer-aided NMR interpretation and structure prediction, in *Computer-Enhanced Analytical Spectroscopy*, vol **4**, (Wilkins, C., ed.), Plenum, NY. pp. 37–54.

50. Thiele, H., Paape, R., Maier, W., and Grzonka, M. (1995) WIN-SPECEDIT. *Bruker Report* **141**, 7–9 (http://www.braker.de/).

51. CSEARCH system of software and databases, Version 5.1, Sadtler Division, Bio-Rad Laboratories, Hercules, CA.

52. Advanced Chemistry Development Inc., 141 Adelaide St. West, Suite 1501, Toronto, Ontario M5H 3L5 Canada (http://www.acdlabs.com).

53. Berdy, J. (1974) Recent developments of antibiotic research and classification of antibiotics according to chemical structure. *Adv. Appl. Microb.* **18**, 309–406.

54. Decosterd, L., Gustafson, K. R., Cardellina, J. H., Cragg, G. M., and Boyd, M. R. (1994) The differential cytotoxicity of cardenolides from Thevetia ahouia. *Phytother. Res.* **8**, 74–77.

55. Fuller, R. W., Cardellina, J. H., Cragg, G. M., and Boyd, M. R. (1994) Cucurb–itacins: differential cytotoxicity, dereplication and first isolation from *Gonystylus keithii. J. Nat. Prod.* **57,** 1442–1445.
56. Pisha, E., Chai, H., Lee, K, Chagwedera, T., Farnsworth, N, Cordell, G., Beecher, C., Fong, H., Kinghorn, D., Brown, D., Wani, M., Wall, M., Hieken, T., Gupta, T., and Pezzuto, J. (1995) Discovery of betulinic acid as a selective inhibitor of human melanoma that functions by induction of apoptosis. *Nat. Med.* **1,** 1046–1051.
57. Kauver, L. M., Higgins, D. L., Villar, H. O., Sportsman, J. R., Engqvist-Goldstein, A., Bukar, R., et al. (1995) Predicting ligand binding to proteins by affinity fingerprinting. *Chem. and Biol.* **2,** 107–118.
58. O'Neil, K. and Hoess, R. (1995) Phage display: protein engineering by directed evolution. *Cur. Opin. Struct. Biol.* **5,** 443–449.
59. Stemmer, W. P. (1994) Rapid evolution of a protein in vitro by DNA shuffling. *Nature* **370,** 389–391.
60. Guo, Y., Vanhaelen-Fastre, R., Diallo, B., Vanhaelen, M., Jarziri, M., Homes, J., and Ottinger, R. (1995) Immunoenzymatic methods applied to the search for bioactive taxoids from *Taxus baccata. J. Nat. Prod.* **58,** 1015–1023.
61. Miles, C., Wilkens, A., Garthwaite, I., Ede, R., and Munday-Finch, S. (1995) Immunochemical techniques in natural products chemistry: isolation and structure determination of a novel indolediterpenoid aided by TLC- ELISAgram. *J. Org. Chem.* **60,** 6067–6069.
62. Pestka, J. J. (1991) High performarnce thin layer chromatography ELISAgram. Application of a multi-hapten immunoassay to analysis of the zearalenone and aflatoxinmycotoxin families. *J. Immunol. Meth.* **136,** 177–183.
63. Antonio, J. and Molinski, T. F. (1993) Screening, of marine invertebrates for the presence of ergosterol-sensitive antifungal compounds. *J. Nat. Prod.* **56,** 54–61.
64. Corley, D. G. and Durley, R. C. (1994) Strategies for database dereplication of natural products. *J. Nat. Prod.* **57,** 1484–1490.
65. Chemical Abstracts Service, 2540 Olentangy River Road, PO Box 3012, Columbus, OH 43210-0012.
66. Beilstein Informationssysteme, Carl-Bosch-Haus, Varrentrappstr. 40-42, D-60486 Frankfurt am Main, Germany.
67. NAPRALERT, Programm for Collaborative Research in the Pharmaceutical Sciences, College of Pharmacy, University of Illinois at Chicago, Chicago, IL 60680.
68. *Dictionary of Natural Products,* Electronic Publishing Division, Chapman & Hall, 2-6 Boundary Row, London SE 1 8HN, UK.
69. Institute of Drug Research, Microbiological and Documentation Department, H-1325 Budapest, Hungary.
70. KMC, USACO Corporation Sales Dept., Tsutsumi Bldg 1-13-12, Simbashi, Minato-Ku, Tokyo 105, Japan.
71. Chemical Concepts GmbH, Bochstr. 12, D-69469 Weinheim, Germany.
72. 3150 Rumsey Drive, Ann Arbor, MI 48105-1466.
73. Department of Chemistry, University of Canterbury, Private Bag 4800, Christchurch, New Zealand.

74. Prof. D. J. Faulkner, University of California, San Diego, La Jolla, CA 92093-0212.
75. Hensens, O., Dufresne, C., Liesch, J., Zink, D., Reamer, R., and VanMiddlesworth, F. (1993) The zaragozic acids: structure elucidation of a new class of squalene synthase inhibitors. *Tet. Lett.* **34,** 399–402.
76. Wilson, E. O. (1994) *The Diversity of Life.* Penguin, London, UK.
77. Olson, D. L., Peck, T. L., Webb, A. G., Magin, R. L., and Sweedler, J. V. (1995) High-resolution microcoil ^{1}H-NMR for mass-limited, nanoliter volume samples. *Science* **270,** 1967–1970.
78. Hopwood, D. A. and Sherman, D. (1990) Molecular genetics of polyketide synthesis and its comparison to fatty acid biosynthesis. *Annu. Rev. Genet.* **24,** 37–66.
79. Hopwood, D. A. (1993) Genetic engineering of Streptomyces to create hybrid antibiotics. *Curr. Opin. Biotechnol.* **4,** 531–537 (and references therein).
80. Hutchinson, C. R. (1994) Drug synthesis by genetically engineered microorganisms. *Bio/Technology* **12,** 375–380 (and references therein).
81. Hutchinson, C. R. and Fujii, I. (1995) Polyketide synthase gene manipulation: a structure:function approach in engineering novel antibiotics. *Annu. Rev. Microbiol.* **49,** 201–238.
82. Tsoi, C. J. and Khosla, C. (1995) Combinatorial biosynthesis of "unnatural" natural products: The polyketide example. *Chem. Biol.* **2,** 355–362.
83. Khosla, C. and Zawada, R. (1996) Generation of polyketide libraries via combinatorial biosynthesis. *Trends Biotechnol.* **14,** 335–341.
84. Aparicio, J., Molnar, I., Schwecke, T., Konig, A., Haydock, S., Khaw, L., Staunton, J., and Leadlay, P. F. (1996) Organization of the biosynthetic gene cluster for rapamycin in *Streptomyces hygroscopicus:* analysis of the enzymatic domains in the modular polyketide synthase. *Gene* **169,** 916.
85. McDaniel, R., Ebert-Khosla, S., Hopwood, D., and Khosla, C. (1993) Engineered biosynthesis of novel polyketides. *Science* **262,** 1546–1550.
86. Cortes, J., Haydock, S., Bevitt, D., and Leadley, P. F. (1990) An unusually large multifunctional polypeptide in the erythromycin-producing polyketide synthase of *Saccharopolyspora erythrea. Nature* **348,** 176–178.
87. Thompson, L. and Ellman, J. (1996) Synthesis and applications of small molecule libraries. *Chem. Rev.* **96,** 555–600.
88. Atuegbu, A., Maclean, D., Nguyen, C., Gordan, E., and Jacobs, J. (1996) Combinatorial modification of natural products: preparation of unencoded and encoded libraries of Rauwolfia alkaloids. *Biorg. Med. Chem.* **4,** 1097–1106.
89. Green, J. (1995) Solid phase synthesis of lavendustin A and analogs. *J. Org. Chem.* **60,** 4287–4290.
90. Hugenholtz, P. and Pace, N. R. (1996) Identifying microbial diversity in the natural environment: a molecular phylogenetic approach. *Trends Biotechnol.* **14,** 190–197.
91. McVeigh, H. P., Munro, J., and Embley, T. M. (1996) Molecular evidence for the presence of novel actinomycete lineages in a temperate forest soil. *J. Ind. Micro. Biotechnol.* **17,** 197–204.
92. de Vries, D. J. and Hall, M. R. (1994) Marine biodiversity as a source of chemical diversity. *Drug Dev. Res.* **33,** 161–173.

11

Purification of Water-Soluble Natural Products

Yuzuru Shimizu

1. Introduction

Recent advancement in separation and structure elucidation methods has been remarkable. It is not unusual for submicrograms of substances to be purified from vast amounts of biological material and their structures elucidated. The major contributing factors are progress in high-performance chromatography technique and computer-aided high-resolution nuclear magnetic resonance (NMR). With the help of these two techniques, a number of minute biologically important substances have been brought to light, which would have been inconceivable a few decades ago. Despite all this, the purification of small water-soluble molecules is still shunned by most researchers. For example, a glance at the natural products section of *Chemical Abstracts* shows that about 95% of new substances reported are in the lipid-soluble category. There may be more lipid-soluble compounds than water-soluble compounds in nature, but this ratio seems to be greatly disproportionate. Clearly, this reflects the difficulty in purifying small-molecular-weight water-soluble compounds. About 10 yr ago, this author wrote a guide for the purification of marine natural products with an emphasis on the water-soluble compounds *(1)*. This chapter is intended to present an updated general procedure with new specific examples.

1.1. General Extraction Procedure

In line with the principle, "like dissolves like," one might think that the most suitable solvent for the extraction of water-soluble compounds is water. More often than not, however, simple maceration of fresh biological material with water or aqueous buffers fails to extract water-soluble compounds because they are mostly stored in protected states. The mechanism of such protection is varied: binding to the membranes, compartmentalization, protection by lipophilic

From: *Methods in Biotechnology, Vol. 4: Natural Products Isolation*
Edited by: R. J. P. Cannell © Humana Press Inc., Totowa, NJ

material, and so on. This problem is usually not encountered in the extraction of lipophilic compounds, because organic solvents break up the compartmental structures. For that reason, polar organic solvents such as methanol or ethanol are often used in the extraction of water-soluble compounds even if they may not be the best solvents to dissolve the target molecules. Also, these organic solvents are much easier to evaporate than water.

Other methods to break up the compartmentalization are sonication, freezing-thawing, freeze-drying, heating, and enzyme digestion. These methods can be used singularly or in combination.

Use of organic solvents also prevents microbial growth, one of the most serious problems associated with the isolation of water-soluble compounds. It is imperative that all isolation work be done in a cold room. Use of antimicrobial agents, such as sodium azide, has sometimes been recommended, but this author discourages the use of azide in isolation, because there is evidence that azide can react with certain molecules to form triaza derivatives. If azide is used for the preservation of gel columns or other supports, care should be taken to wash it out thoroughly before use. Another problem associated with aqueous systems is the activation of enzymes such as peptidases, glycosidases, sulfatases, and oxidases by solubilization. If the desirable compounds are susceptible to enzymes, the native natural products will not be isolated. A well-known example is *Digitalis* cardiac glycosides. The genuine glycosides are purpurea glycoside A and purpurea glycoside B. In the normal extraction process, it is difficult to isolate the native glycosides because the terminal glucose unit is lost by the action of indigenous β-glucosidase and only digitoxin and gitoxin can be isolated. Deactivation or denaturation of the enzymes can be carried out by quick heating or treatment with alcohols, but alcohol treatment does not necessarily deactivate the enzymes. Therefore, it is strongly recommended that the large-molecular-weight fraction containing liberated enzymes be removed as quickly as possible by methods such as ultrafiltration or gel filtration.

1.2. Desalting and Choice of Buffer Solutions

Desalting is probably the most important step in the handling of water-soluble compounds. It is not necessarily difficult to fractionate water-soluble compounds to a single chromatographic peak. In fact, strongly hydrophilic compounds are routinely analyzed on high-performance liquid chromatography (HPLC) without any trouble. However, what makes the preparative separation of water-soluble compounds so difficult is the separation of inorganic salts, often from minute amounts of the target molecule. This is the step in which organic chemists may simply give up their efforts, since most of them are used to removing inorganic salts by simple partition between water-immiscible organic solvents and aqueous solutions.

If the compounds have some lipophilicity, the standard method for desalting is the use of reverse phase columns such as C18 silica gel or various other organic polymers such as XAD-2, -4, and -7. Usually, the aqueous solution is passed through the column and salts are washed out with water; subsequently, the organic compounds are eluted with a solvent system containing organic solvents. This method cannot be applied to strongly polar or ionized compounds such as polar amino acids or sugars. Another commonly used method for desalting is the use of size-exclusion columns such as Sephadex G-10 and Bio-Gel P-2. Inorganic ions are presumed to be the smallest in the mixture, and hence their elution should be expected to be retarded the most. This, however, is not always the case because there are unpredictable interactions between the compounds and column support, such that the predicted elution order can often be reversed. These interactions can hold advantages for the extractor and can be used to isolate specific types of compounds. The purification of paralytic shellfish toxins such as saxitoxin and gonyautoxins was done by taking advantage of their specific adsorption on Bio-Gel P-2 of Sephadex G-10.

In most cases, the extraction and fractionation of water-soluble compounds necessitates the use of buffer solutions. After all is said, the key to the isolation of water-soluble compounds is finding a suitable pH and ionic concentration to keep the molecules as individual molecular entities separable on a given matrix. However, the separation of the buffer salts from the compound is not an easy task. Several volatile buffers are suggested to avoid this problem (**Table 1**). They are mostly combinations of weak bases and weak acids, which are bound only by weak ionic interactions and are volatile under reduced pressure or lyophilization. However, in reality, these buffers are not so easy to handle. For example, the organic buffers containing pyridine and other aromatic bases have intolerable, noxious odors and are difficult to use in a closed, cold room. They also may not be acceptable in the modern laboratory for safety reasons. They also retain lipohilic nature and interact with the solutes just like alcohols. Ammonium acetate and ammonium carbonate buffers are removable by evaporation or lyophilization, but, in practice, these are not so easy to evaporate. The first lyophilization often results in a sticky mixture of ammonium acetate or carbonate and solutes. Sometimes this process has to be repeated several times. It is usually necessary to redissolve the residue in a large amount of water, freeze, and lyophilize again. In either case, one has to expect drastic pH changes during evaporation, which may affect the desired compounds.

1.3. Selection of Chromatographic Supports

Without the help of some kind of chromatographic method, the purification of water-soluble compounds would be difficult to accomplish. There are a variety of column-packing materials with many choices of interacting func-

Table 1
Examples of Volatile Buffers

Buffer	pH
Ammonim biocarbonate	5.0–7.0
Ammonium acetate	7.0–8.0
Pyridine-acetic acid	3.1
16.1:278.5	
Pyridine-acetic acid	5.0
161.2:143.2	
Pyridine-acetic acid-α-picoline	8.0
11.8:0.1:28.2	
Pyridine-acetic acid-2,4,5-collidine	8.3
10:0.4:10	
Pyridine-acetic acid-N-ethylmorpholine	9.3
7.5:0.1–0.5:12.5	

tional groups. Their interaction mechanisms include weak, moderate and strong, anion and cation exchange, ligand exchange, reverse phase, and ion- and size-exclusion, among others. Here, special attention must be paid to the possible irreversible adsorption of certain substances onto the support material.

We all know from experience that the recovery of substances from chromatography is rarely 100%. Same compounds tend to "disappear" on the column. In the case of water-soluble compounds, the tendency is greatly enhanced, especially with silica gel-based supports. Some compounds, including amino acids, are virtually impossible to separate preparatively on silica gel-based supports. The mechanism for such irreversible retention is not fully understood, but trapping by hydrogen bonding in suitably shaped pores or matrices may be the greatest contributing factor. For some compounds, covalent bonding by Michael addition or hemiketal formation is also suspected. With respect to irreversible adsorption, there seems to be a strong relationship between the shape of the molecule and pore size. For example, linear polycyclic ether brevetoxins are easily trapped in silica gel-60, and never eluted even after washing with very polar solvents. The use of used silica gel or large pore silica gel can lessen this irreversible adsorption, but it also results in poor separation. Similar observations were made with some cyclic peptides. Use of material with larger pore sizes is sometimes helpful. Materials based on a range of silica gels each having a different pore-size are available. For example, EM Corporation sells silica gel-based columns of pore size up to 1000 Å. Needless to say, however, the larger the pore size, the smaller the surface area and, consequently, the lower the number of theoretical plates. Capping of free hydroxyl groups on the silica helps to prevent undesirable adsorption, and many such "end-capped" silica-based HPLC columns are commercially available. Fast chromatography or elevated temperature can also help to improve recovery, but often the problem still remains.

In any case, for such compounds, silica gel-based column material should be avoided as much as possible. Fortunately, various type of non-silica gel-based C-18 and other reverse-phase columns are now widely available. They include matrices such as polystyrenedivinylbenzene and hydroxyethyl methacrylate/dimethylacrylate copolymers with various functional groups. Recovery rates are generally much better on these polymeric materials, and are accompanied by a much longer column life. These alternative supports are also more tolerant to extreme pH and high concentrations of buffers such as ammonium acetate.

1.4. General Fractionation Scheme

Prior to the 1950s, water-soluble natural products isolated were mostly limited to molecules stable to strongly acidic and basic conditions. In the case of amphoteric compounds such as amino acids, for example, a combination of strongly acidic and basic ion-exchange resins can easily separate them from other components. The procedure, however, is not applicable for esters and other acid- or alkali-labile compounds that do not survive in the extreme pH conditions of the resins or buffers. Epimerization of chiral centers can also be a problem. Thus, for an unknown compound, a fractionation scheme involving any drastic conditions should be avoided. On the other hand, weakly acidic or weakly basic ion-exchange resins can be used under less drastic conditions. In particular, the combination of ionic interaction and reversed phase and/or gel filtration (size exclusion) properties exerts tremendous separation capability. Recently, a large number of this type of column materials have become available. **Table 2** shows the chromatographic supports often used in the author's laboratory and their applications.

Scheme 1 illustrates the general isolation procedure for the first trial. Once the chemical nature of the target molecule becomes known, the procedure can be altered or shortened.

1.5. Heavy Metal Contamination

In modern natural product research, most purified samples are examined by high-resolution NMR. In this respect, this author wants to draw your special attention to a problem that is unique to water-soluble compounds and rarely encountered with lipophilic compounds: contamination of the sample with paramagnetic heavy metals, which can be derived from the original extract, equipment, labware, or reagents used in the isolation.

As mentioned, most purification procedures involve chromatographic separation and thus use solvent delivery systems. Most delivery systems use stain-

Table 2
Chromatographic Supports Often Used in the Author's
Laboratory for Separation of Water-Soluble Components

Type of compounds	Column packing
Mono- and oligosaccharides	Sephadex G-10, G-15, polymer-based gels, e.g., Bio-Gel P-2, Ca-loaded gels (e.g., Supelcogel Ca), strong cation exchange ($-SO_3H$) resins, weakly basic anion exchange resins
Polysaccharides	Sephadex G-50, G-100, G-200, Bio-Gel P-6 ~P-100, styrene divinyl-benzene-based size-exclusion resins (e.g., Bio-Gel SEC), and their DEAE-bonded material
Oligopeptides	Sephadex G-10, G-15, Bio-Gel P-2 ~P-6 and other polymer-based size-exclusion gels and reverse phase gels
Proteins and glycoproteins	Sephadex G-15 ~G-200, Bio-Gel P-6 ~P-100, other polymer-based size-exclusion material and their DEAE-bonded forms, C18 on large-pore (300Å) support and C18 on polymer-based material (e.g., HEMA and Hamilton PRP)
Amine, guanidine, and amino acid derivatives	Strongly acidic cation exchange resins ($-SO_3^-$), weakly acidic ($-COOH$) cation-exchange resins, especially, polymer supports (e.g., HEMA CM and Bio-Rex 70), RP (C18, C8, and Hamilton PRP), Bio-Gel P-2
Polar carboxylic acids	Anion-exchange resins, RP (C18 and Hamilton PRP)
Glycosides	RP (C18, C8, and polymer-based), Sephadex G-10, LH-20
Desalting	Bio-Gel P-2, Sephadex G-10, RP (C18, PRP)

Sephadex, Pharmacia Fine Chemicals; Bio-Gel, Bio-Rad; HEMA, Altech; and Supelcogel, Supelco.

less steel (SUS 13~32) in pumps, lines, and injectors, which releases Ni and Fe ions when buffer solutions are used. The amount of the leached metal ions may be small but can be enough to cause problems in NMR measurements. The contamination can also come from the surface of glassware. The problem is especially troublesome if the final purification step is the concentration of a large amount of an aqueous acidic solution to obtain just a microgram quantity of a substance. In an ^{15}N NMR experi-

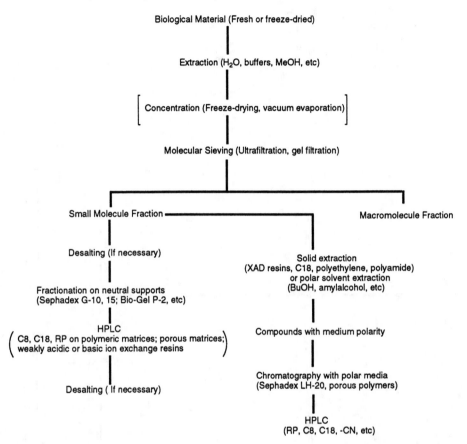

Scheme 1. General isolation scheme for unknown small water-soluble molecules.

ment of biosynthetically enriched small amounts of PSP toxins, we found it absolutely necessary to pass the sample solution through Chelex 100, a metal chelating resin. Otherwise no signals would be observed in ^{15}N NMR *(2)*. **Figure 1** shows an alarming example from our laboratory. The apparently clean carbon NMR spectrum of "chromatographically pure" domoic acid *(see* **Fig. 1**), obtained by elution with 0.1% acetic acid, has several carbon signals missing or collapsed owing to metal chelation. Treatment of the sample with Chelex 100 restored the missing signals. Without treatment, there could have been a serious misinterpretation of the structure, or the identity, of the compound. Therefore, this author strongly recommends the use of Chelex 100 for the preparation of all NMR samples of water-soluble compounds. Generally, a remarkable improvement is seen in the spectrum quality.

The following are two typical examples of isolation of water-soluble compounds carried out in the author's laboratory.

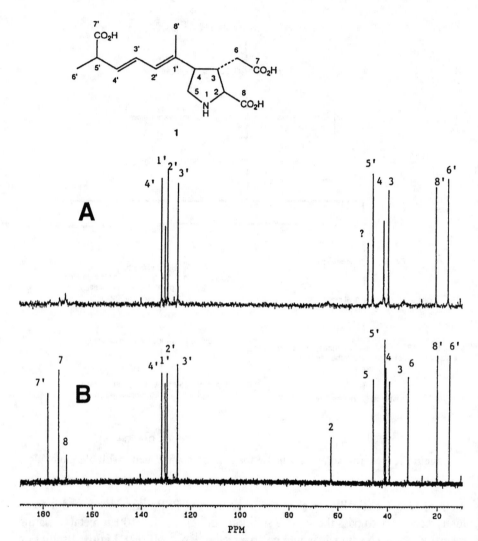

Fig. 1. 13C NMR spectra of domoic acid (**1**), isolated from culture of the diatom, *Pseudonitzschia*. The spectrum (**A**) is of a sample without treatment with Chelex 100 (Bio-Rad, Hercules, CA) and (**B**) after treatment with Chelex 100. In A, several signals are missing and chemical shift changes are seen (spectra of an identical isolate in D_2O).

2. Isolation of 1-Hydroxy-5,11-dideoxytetrodotoxin (*see* Fig. 2) and Other Tetrodotoxin Derivatives from the Newt, *Taricha granulosa (3)*

2.1. Materials

1. The newts, *Taricha granulosa* (collected in Oregon), were obtained through Carolina Biological Supply. Ultrafiltration apparatus: Amicon High Performance

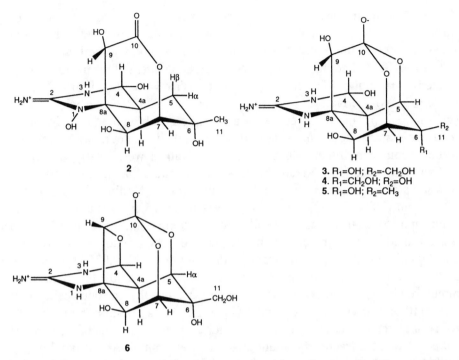

Fig. 2. Structures of tetrodotoxin derivatives isolated from the newt, *Taricha granulosa*.

Ultrafiltration Cell Model 2000B with membrane filters (15-cm diameter), XM100A (100,000 Dalton cutoff), and PM10 (10,000 Dalton cutoff) were used.

2. Chromatography columns: Bio-Gel P-2, 5.0 × 70 cm, Bio-Rad; Bio-Rex 70 H$^+$ form, –400 mesh, 2.8 × 55 cm and 1.8 × 56 cm, Bio-Rad; Hitachi gel 3013-C H$^+$ form, 0.4 × 15 cm, Hitachi; and HEMA-IEC BIO CM column, 0.75 × 25 cm, Alltech; Chelex 100, H$^+$ acetate form, –400 mesh, Bio-Rad.

3. Solvents: HPLC-grade methanol and analytical-grade acetic acid were distilled before use. Water used for HPLC was glass-distilled deionized water passed through a high-purity organic remover.

2.2. Methods

The live newts (1400 g, 112 bodies) were frozen in liquid nitrogen and stored before extraction. The animal bodies were minced, extracted in a homogenizer with a threefold volume of 0.1% acetic acid in methanol for 4 min, and centrifuged; and the residue was re-extracted twice with a twofold volume of the same solvent. The combined extract was centrifuged and the supernatant was evaporated to about 500 mL, at which no methanol was left in the solution. After removal of precipitates by centrifugation, the supernatant was diluted with 1 *N* acetic acid to 1000 mL and subjected to ultrafiltration.

The ultrafiltration was done in two steps, first through XM100A and then through PM 10 membranes at approx 50 psi in a cold room (5°C). The dialysate (<10,000 Dalton mol wt) was evaporated *in vacuo* to 300 mL and loaded onto a Bio-Gel P-2 column (5.0 × 70 cm) after adjustment of the pH to 5.5 with dilute NaOH solution. The column was first washed with 700 mL of water, and the tetrodotoxin derivatives were eluted with a 0.03–0.06 N acetic acid gradient (total 1000 mL). The combined toxin fractions were rechromatographed again in the same system. Upon completion of the second chromatography run, water-soluble components other than tetrodotoxin derivatives were mostly removed.

The toxin fractions were combined and concentrated *in vacuo*, and the pH was adjusted to 6.5 with dilute NaOH solution prior to loading onto a Bio-Rex 70 column (2.8 × 55 cm). The column was washed with a small amount of water, and 15-mL fractions were collected. The toxin fractions eluted with 0.05 N acetic acid were combined and further purified by chromatography on a Bio-Rex 70 column (1.8 × 56 cm, linear gradient elution with 0.03–0.06 N acetic acid, 2 × 250 mL, followed by 0.06 N and 0.5 N acetic acid). Fractions were monitored by TLC (Whatman HP-KF with pyridine/ethyl acetate/acetic acid/water (10:5:2:3); visualization under UV at 305 nm after spraying with 10% KOH in methanol and heating at 130°C for 10 min). Fractions of 5 mL were collected, and the fractions containing toxins were combined and lyophilized. In this chromatography, tetrodotoxin (**3** in **Fig. 2**), and three known tetrodotoxin derivatives—6-*epi*-tetrodotoxin (**4** in **Fig. 2**), 11-deoxytetrodotoxin (**5** in **Fig. 2**), and 4,9-anhydrotetrodotoxin (**6** in **Fig. 2**), were obtained in pure form. The desired compound (**2** in **Fig. 2**), which showed the highest R_f value on thin-layer chromatography (TLC), was further purified by HPLC.

The new compound fraction was chromatographed on a Hitachi gel 3013-C column with 0.05 N acetic acid as eluting solvent. Fractions of 2 mL were collected and monitored by a UV detector at 225 nm. The toxin was further purified on a HEMA-IEC BIO CM column with 0.05 N ammonium acetate (pH 5.75) (**Fig. 3**).

The new tetrodotoxin derivative fractions were collected and lyophilized three times by adding water to eliminate ammonium acetate completely. The combined fractions were then rechromatographed on the same column using 0.1 N acetic acid as eluent. After passing through small Chelex 100 and Bio-Gel P-2 columns (0.5 × 1.5 cm, elution with 0.1 N acetic acid), the new compound was obtained in spectroscopically (MS and NMR) pure state. (Yield: 1.2 mg.)

2.3. Comments

The direct application of a crude extract on a small-pore size membrane (e.g., <10,000) usually causes clogging and results in a very slow filtration rate. It is always better to do the filtration in two or more steps, even if it is not necessary to subfractionate the macromolecules. In this experiment, the target

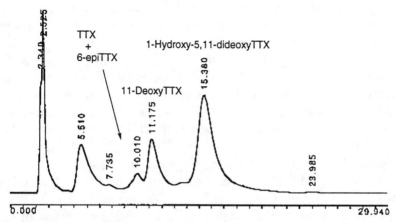

Fig. 3. Chromatographic elution pattern of tetrodotoxin (TTX) derivatives (3-mg total) from a HEMA-IEC Bio 1000 CM column (7.5 × 250 mm); 3 mL/min, 0.05 M ammonium acetate, pH 5.75; detection at 225 nm.

molecule has an *N*-hydroxyl guanidine group, which is known to be reduced easily by endogenous enzymes or bacterial action. Low temperature operation and quick removal of macromolecular fractions raise the yield.

Tetrodotoxin derivatives have been found in many different types of organisms. The structural variation among them gives very important clues about the biosynthetic origin of the important toxin. However, separation of the closely related toxins is not so trivial. Silica-based columns used by most researchers give poor yields. We found that the carboxylic acid form of HEMA gives an excellent separation and a relatively high yield (*see* **Fig. 3**).

3. Isolation of Domoic Acid, a Glutamate Agonist from the Diatom, *Pseudonitzschia pungens* f. *multiseries* Culture Medium *(4)*

3.1. Materials

1. *Pseudonitzschia pungens* f. *multiseries* strain B99I-K from Narragansett Bay, RI *(5)*, was cultured in 8 L of Guillard f/2 medium for 50 d.
2. C18 silica gel: Bondesil preparative grade, 40 μm (Analytichem).
3. Sephadex LH-20 (Pharmacia Fine Chemicals).
4. Solvents: HPLC grade methanol and acetic acid were distilled before use. Water used for HPLC was glass-distilled deionized water passed through a high-purity organic remover.

3.2. Methods

The 50-d-old *Pseudonitzschia* culture was centrifuged and the algal cells were separated. After adjustment of the pH to 3.0 with dilute HCl, the supernatant was passed under weak suction through C18 silica gel (300 g) packed in a Büchner funnel. The silica gel was washed with 100 mL of distilled water and the adsorbed material eluted with 300 mL of methanol. The methanol eluate was evaporated to dryness *in vacuo* and loaded on an LH-20 column (1.5 × 40 cm). The column was developed with methanol (~200 mL) and monitored by a UV detector (254 nm) and TLC. Domoic acid fractions were combined, evaporated, and chromatographed on a C18 column (1.5 × 12 cm, medium pressure). The column was developed consecutively with 0.1% acetic acid in 10% MeOH (50 mL), 0.1% acetic acid in 30% methanol (100 mL), and 0.1% acetic acid in 50% methanol (50 mL). Domoic acid was mostly eluted with the 30% methanol. The domoic acid fractions were rechromatographed on a C18 silica gel column (1 × 7 cm) using 0.1% acetic acid in 28% methanol. The domoic acid fractions were combined and evaporated to a crystalline mass with faintly brown color. (Yield: 4.76 mg.) For NMR measurements, this sample was passed through 2 g of Chelex 100 (prewashed with HCl and distilled water) in a Pasteur pipet using 0.1 *N* HCl as eluent.

3.3. Comments

Domoic acid is known as the culprit of amnesic shellfish poisoning (ASP) *(5,6)*. It is a strong glutamate agonist and known to bind to kinate receptors in brain. It is produced by a few species of diatom. We found that the strain used in these studies exudes most of the domoic acid into the medium. The isolation of the water-soluble amino acid from a large amount of the seawater-based medium was done by ionization-suppression of three carboxylic acid functions by acidification and adsorption on C18. As mentioned in **Subheading 1.**, the compound easily forms a chelate with heavy metal ions. We found that even recrystallized samples contained enough metals to create a disturbance in NMR.

References

1. Shimizu, Y. (1985) Bioactive marine natural products, with emphasis on handling of water-soluble compounds. *J. Natl. Prod.* **48,** 223–235.
2. Hori, A. and Shimizu, Y. (1983) Biosynthetic N-enrichment and N-nmr spectra of neosaxitoxin and gonyautoxin-II: application to the structure determination. *J. Chem. Soc. Chem. Commun.* 790–792.
3. Kotaki, Y. and Shimizu, Y. (1993) 1-Hydroxy-5,11-dideoxytetrodotoxin, the first N-hydroxy and ring-deoxy derivative of tetrodotoxin found in the newt *Taricha granulosa. J. Am. Chem. Soc.* **115,** 827–830.
4. Unpublished experiment.
5. Maranda, L., Wang, R., Masuda, K., and Shimizu, Y. (1990) Investigation of the source of domoic acid in mussels; in *Toxic Marine Phytoplankton* (Granèli, E., Sundström, B., Edler, L., and Anderson, D. M., eds.), Elsevier, Amsterdam, 300–304.

6. Wright, J. L. C., Boyd, R. K., de Freitas, A. S. W., Falk, M., Foxall, R. A., Jamieson, W. D., Laycock, M. V., McCulloch, A. W., McInnes, A. G., Odense, P., Pathak, V. P., Quilliam, M. A., Ragan, M. A., Sim, P. G., Thibault, P., Walter, J. A., Gilgan, M., Richard, D. J. A., and Dewar, D. (1989) Identification of domoic acid, a neuroexcitatory amino acid in toxic mussels from eastern Prince Edward Island. *Can. J. Chem.* **67,** 481–490.

12

Special Problems with the Extraction of Plants

Gloria L. Silva, Ik-Soo Lee, and A. Douglas Kinghorn

1. Introduction

There is increasing scientific interest in the extraction and isolation of secondary metabolites from plants; for example, as part of biosynthetic, biochemical, chemotaxonomic, ecological, phytochemical, pharmacological, and plant tissue culture studies. This chapter is intended to provide guidance for those interested in phytochemistry and intending to work on the isolation of secondary metabolites from plants of new and known structure. The secondary metabolites of plants are compounds with no apparent function in the primary metabolism of the organism, and these substances tend to be of restricted taxonomic distribution (1). Such metabolites have an extensive history of use as therapeutic agents (2,3). The most common plant secondary metabolites occur in the following groups: alkaloids, anthraquinones, coumarins, essential oils (lower terpenoids and phenylpropanoids), flavonoids, steroids, and terpenoids (cardenolides, diterpenoids, iridoids, monoterpenoids, sesquiterpenoids [including sesquiterpene lactones], and triterpenoids) (4).

The selection, collection, and identification of the plant material to be studied are the first steps in carrying out a phytochemical investigation, and several basic factors involved with these activities will be discussed. The drying and grinding of plant material are also of importance, particularly in the case of labile bioactive constituents, and this aspect will also be mentioned. The effective extraction of a plant compound or compounds of interest from a natural source depends largely on solubility, stability, and functional-group considerations. Extraction methods to be employed to obtain a crude plant extract, as well as precautions that must be taken to avoid compound decomposition, side reactions, or rearrangements during the extraction process, will be discussed.

From: Methods in Biotechnology, Vol. 4: Natural Products Isolation
Edited by: R. J. P. Cannell © Humana Press Inc., Totowa, NJ

Several plant constituents are generally regarded as interfering substances either during purification steps or when biological assays are conducted, including chlorophylls and polyphenols (vegetable tannins). Moreover, other extraneous impurities such as plasticizers and silicone grease may be introduced during the plant extraction process. Methods to recognize and eliminate these impurities from plant extracts will also be discussed. In a final section, several useful general reagents are given for the preliminary recognition of different types of plant secondary metabolites, which, it is hoped, will have particular value in chemotaxonomic investigations. Notes with more specific information on certain topics are also provided where deemed necessary, in order to be of further assistance to the interested reader.

2. Method

The overall procedures for the extraction of plant material during a phytochemical investigation consist of a series of apparently simple steps. However, the ultimate success of this type of research project depends on the care devoted to each individual aspect of the work.

2.1. Selection, Collection, and Identification of the Plant Material

1. The many considerations involved in the proper selection of a plant for the study of its bioactive or other secondary metabolite constituents have been discussed previously *(5,6)*. Selection of plant material for study in drug-discovery programs may be performed by different approaches, such as totally random selection, or by selective selection using ethnopharmacological reports, or by restricting the plants of interest to groups based on chemotaxonomic, geographical, or compound structural-type preferences *(6–8)*. However, plant selection should normally involve a literature survey of the floristic diversity of the area of interest and should include the plant medicinal uses in the region where collection will take place *(7)*. In this manner, biologically active metabolites may be investigated in plant material selected because of local use in traditional medicine *(4,5)* (*see* **Note 1**), while chemotaxonomic studies may be performed on genera or species that have not been previously studied or when there is relatively little information already available (*see* **Note 2**). Scrutiny of existing chemical reports on medicinal plants is also important, and it is to be noted that even if an isolate is of known structure, a newly observed bioactivity may be of great interest if studied in depth *(9,10)*. A novel approach to plant selection is a computer-based selection method or Literature Information Selection Technique (L.I.S.T.) that correlates biological activity, botanical facts, and chemotaxonomic information using the NAPRALERT® database *(11–13)*. For example, in a recent study, the NAPRALERT database was used to indicate that species in the genus *Selaginella* have been used to treat a variety of diseases in traditional medicine in several countries, and that, although in-depth studies on the chemical constituents of the genus have already been performed, very little information on their pharmaco-

logical activity has appeared in the scientific literature. Bioactivity-guided fraction-ation of an active ethyl acetate extract from *Selaginella willdenowii* afforded three known biflavonoids with significant cytotoxicity against a panel of human cancer cell lines. This plant was preselected for study using the NAPRALERT database *(14)*. Totally random plant collection, without giving any consideration to the dupli-cation of work conducted previously by others, is considered expensive and is not regarded as being very practical in drug-discovery programs *(5,7)*. In recent years, considerable discourse has been accorded to the proper compensation of indigenous peoples and their governments in plant drug discovery efforts *(7)*; this has become an important consideration in the selection of plant samples for phytochemical study.

2. During the collection of a plant, it should be kept in mind that the specimens to be studied should be healthy, since microbial and other infections may change the metabolites produced by the specimen, e.g., by phytoalexin formation *(15)*. Varia-tions in collection-site altitude, plant age, climate, and soil type can all influence the concentration levels of secondary metabolites and even the kinds of compounds biosynthesized in certain cases *(15–18)*. Different organs in the plant are known to produce and/or accumulate different profiles of secondary metabolites; e.g., fla-vonoids may be present in the flowers and leaves of a particular species, whereas tropane alkaloids occur in the roots *(16)*, and sesquiterpene lactones and essential oils may be restricted to glandular hairs or other glands *(19)* (*see* **Note 3**). The fact that plant-secondary-metabolite profiles may vary both qualitatively and quantitatively among different batches of the same plant part collected at different times has impor-tant consequences in making plant recollections for scale-up work (*see* **Note 4**).

3. Once a plant part(s) is collected, at least three herbarium samples should be pre-pared, and each organism concerned should be identified or authenticated by a taxonomist. One of these samples should be deposited in a local national her-barium, and the others should be deposited in a specialist museum or herbarium. All voucher specimens should be kept in an appropriate protected place for future reference. A card with details of the place, altitude, environment, and character-istics of each collection should be attached to the herbarium sample, which is of vital importance in case a recollection of the plant material is necessary (*see* **Note 5**). Although depositing herbarium samples is a basic step in performing phy-tochemical investigation, many researchers in the past neglected this step and thus were unable to reproduce their work. Unfortunately, if an erroneous identifi-cation of a plant sample occurs, this might mislead future workers on the same species and may produce confusion in the scientific literature. Also, it may be noted that the taxonomic identification of a plant at an early stage of a phy-tochemical investigation may assist in later compound identification and "dereplication" efforts, since perusal of the published literature on the species, genus, or family concerned is then possible (*see* **Note 6**).

2.2. Drying and Grinding

In most cases, plant material is dried in the atmosphere prior to workup. It may be dried at room temperature or in the oven at no more than 30°C; it must be kept away from direct sunlight because ultraviolet radiation may produce chemical reactions giving rise to compound artifacts. Compacted samples of fresh plant material with little air circulation may experience fungal infestation and elevated temperatures by fermentation if left to stand for several days, hence well-ventilated places and homogeneous distribution of the material should be ensured. Fresh plant material is sometimes specifically required for study, and in these cases it should be immediately extracted with solvent to prevent enzymatic processes or reactions that start after the plant is collected, or during grinding. For instance, decomposition or rearrangements by pH changes may occur, leading to hydrolysis of constituents such as iridoid and flavonoid glycosides. These reactions may be prevented by denaturing the plant enzymes responsible by soaking the samples in methanol or ethanol soon after collection and/or by controlling the pH by adding a buffer. When studying essential oils, fresh plant material is processed preferentially to avoid loss of metabolites by volatilization. The constituents of plant material stored for some time may decompose; e.g., *Antireha putminosa* loses 50% of its alkaloids after 2 mo of storage *(4)*, whereas some flavonoid glycosides may hydrolyze *(20)*. It is therefore advisable to fully extract a small portion of the fresh material and keep a TLC chromatogram of the extract for future comparison purposes and for the later detection of changes (*see* **Note 7**).

For the grinding (comminution) of plant material, several types of equipment can be used, from sophisticated mills and blenders, to simple axes, scissors, or knives. When the secondary metabolites to be extracted are thermolabile or volatile, the milling stage may be omitted to avoid losses by heat generated during comminution *(4,8)*. The plant material may also be frozen with liquid nitrogen and pounded in a chilled mortar or thick polyethylene bag, even with fresh material. This process may be helped by adding purified sand (Merck Art. 7712) to the mortar, with the semidry mixture then transferred to a flask and extracted with appropriate solvent, and the final solid residue then filtered off *(21)*. The grinding process assists the penetration of the solvent to the cellular structure of the plant tissues, thereby helping to dissolve the secondary metabolites and increase the yields of extraction. Generally, it has been found that the smaller the particle size of the plant material the more efficient the extraction.

2.3. Extraction

Some general points should be considered in terms of the extraction process, such as the overall characteristics of the secondary metabolites to be extracted (e.g., some glycosides are thermolabile or pH-sensitive). In general, the solvents to be employed and the extraction processes will follow the information provided in Chapter 2 of this volume. Although the normal practice is to apply a standard technique to obtain a crude extract from a plant material, e.g., an acid-base shakeout to prepare an alkaloidal extract (*see* **Subheading 2.3.1.**), the reader should bear in mind that, because of the structural diversity within a given natural product group and their possible special requirements, it is advisable to consult specific reviews, papers, and books in order to prevent the avoidable loss of desired bioactive metabolites caused by the use of an inappropriate extraction technique.

2.3.1. Choice of Solvents

Usually, lipophilic plant secondary metabolites of different degrees of polarity are studied; however, more rarely, water-soluble plant constituents may be of interest. The solvent(s) chosen for the extraction should be considered carefully. They should dissolve the secondary metabolites under study, be easy to remove, and be inert, nontoxic, and not easily flammable (*see* **Note 8**). Solvents should be distilled or even double distilled before use if they are of low or unknown quality. Several plasticizers are commonly found as impurities in solvents, e.g., dialkyl phthalate, tri-*n*-butyl acetyl citrate and tri-butyl phosphate; these may be incorporated during solvent manufacture or on storage in plastic-lined or plastic-stoppered containers. Methanol and chloroform usually contain dioctylphthalate [di-(2-ethylhexyl)phthalate or *bis*-2 ethylhexyl-phthalate] *(22)*, which in our experience is frequently erroneously isolated in phytochemical investigations. This substance has even proven to be active in certain bioassays and may contaminate plant extracts and the isolates purified from them when solvent is used in bulk and the extract reduced in volume *(15)*. The characterization and elimination of dioctylphthalate are discussed in **Subheading 2.3.3.** Chloroform, methylene chloride, and methanol are usually the solvents of choice in a preliminary extraction of a plant part. It has been shown that chloroform and its impurities, CH_2Cl_2 and CH_2ClBr, may react with some compounds as in the case of certain alkaloids (e.g., brucine, strychnine, and ephedrine), producing quaternary salts and other artifacts *(23)*. Similarly, the presence of traces of HCl may either produce decomposition, dehydration, or isomerization in other compounds *(24)*. Owing to its nephro- and hepatotoxic effects *(22)*, chloroform should be manipulated in ventilated areas using a respiratory mask, or used under a fumehood. Methylene chloride is less toxic and more volatile than chloroform, and it may produce artifacts, as previously indicated. Methanol and 80% ethanol are solvents that are more polar than the chlorinated hydrocarbons. It is thought that alcoholic solvents efficiently penetrate cell membranes, permitting the extraction of high amounts of endocellular components. In contrast, chloroform, being of lower polarity, may wash out mostly extracellular material *(25)*. In this manner, alcohols dissolve chiefly polar metabolites together with medium- and low-polarity compounds extracted by cosolubilization. In general, aqueous-alcoholic solvents seem to possess the optimum solubility characteristics for initial extraction *(8)*, bearing in mind the possible problems already discussed.

However, it has also been demonstrated that some artifacts may be produced when using methanol during the extraction procedure. For example, trechonolide A obtained from *Trechonaetes laciniata* was converted into trechonolide B by methylation when heated with methanol containing traces of acid *(26)*, and methyl 12-cystisineacetic acid isolated from *Euchresta japonica* was suggested as arising from an esterification of the corresponding acid during extraction *(27)*. Also, decomposition of 1-hydroxytropacocaine was observed when *Erythroxylum novogranatense* was extracted in warm methanol *(28)*.

Water is seldom used alone to obtain a crude plant extract; instead, an aqueous-methanolic extract is generated as shown in **Fig. 1** and partitioned between different solvents *(29)*. Using this procedure, ethyl acetate and diethyl ether are prone to form emulsions with water, so the addition of sodium chloride to saturation may break the emulsion, although on certain occasions it is necessary to "break" the emulsion by centrifugation. Extraction by steam distillation is widely used to obtain volatile terpenes *(30)*, although it has been observed that a fall of up to 2 pH units may occur because of the rupture of vacuoles, which may produce undesired reactions on sensitive compounds *(31)*.

Diethyl ether is rarely used for plant extractions because of its volatility, flammability, and toxicity, as well as its tendency to form explosive peroxides. Peroxides of diethyl ether are reactive and may produce oxidations of polyunsaturated compounds such as carotenoids. Peroxides can be removed from diethyl ether by shaking with $FeSO_4$, and can be avoided altogether by purchasing diethyl ether in metal cans containing only small volumes of solvent. In turn, acetone may produce acetonides if 1,2-*cis*-diols are present in an acidic medium. Extraction under acid or basic conditions is often conducted for specific separations; e.g., anthocyanins are extracted by crushing fresh plant material with methanol containing 1% w/v hydrochloric acid *(20)*, and alkaloids may be extracted in either acid or basic media. It has been reported that the acid-base treatment of extracts may produce artifacts because of rearrangements, e.g., dihydroquercetin from *Pseudotsuga menziesii*, under basic/acid catalysis and high temperature (>100°C) undergoes epimerization at C-2 and C-3 and ring contraction, producing alphitonin *(32)*; scopine from *Hyoscyamus albus* produces oscine by rearrangement of the epoxide *(16)*; and the decomposition and hydrolysis of glycosides has been reported *(20)*. As pointed out in this section, it is important to know the characteristics of the plant secondary metabolites to be extracted (solubility, reactivity, stability) in order to select the appropriate solvent for the extraction to avoid solute decomposition and the formation of artifacts. A solvent conveniently purified by distillation may be satisfactory for use (*see* **Note 9**).

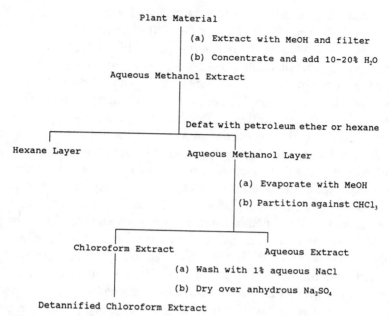

Fig. 1. General procedure for preparing detannified chloroform and aqueous extracts from methanolic crude plant extracts.

After extraction, the solvent is eliminated by rotary evaporation at no more than 30–40°C since some thermolabile compounds may be degraded by higher temperatures. The remaining gummy or resinous residue from the plant extract (dry extract) is then weighed and processed by different methods according to the target metabolites (*see* **Note 10**).

In the following section we will refer to several common extraction processes (and their advantages and disadvantages) that are usually employed in phytochemical research. The actual selection of one or more of these methods depends on the specific needs of the researcher.

2.3.2. Processes for Plant Extraction

The most simple extraction processes employed may be classified as follows: extraction with organic solvents: percolation, maceration, and extraction using a Soxhlet apparatus; and extraction with water: infusion, decoction, and steam distillation.

Percolation is usually one of the most widespread methods employed for plant extraction since it does not require much manipulation or time. The equipment used is a conical glass container with a tap at the base of the apparatus used to set the rate of the solvent elution. Hot or cold solvent may be used. In the former case, a metallic percolator is required, and a complete description of the equipment and procedures for use can be found in the *United States Pharmacopoeia* (USP), *The National Formulary* (NF), the *British Pharmaceutical Codex* (BPC), *Pharmacopoeia Internationalis* (PhI), and elsewhere *(8,33)*. Very fine powders, resins, and powders that swell or give a viscous eluent cannot be extracted by this method since percolation would be disrupted. The sample should be coarsely fragmented, and particles that pass through a 3-mm sieve would be adequate. Particles of too large a size may produce a high elution rate precluding the necessary equilibrium for the dissolution of the metabolites, and the menstruum (solvent) would percolate unsaturated. Percolation is more efficient than maceration (discussed *below*), since it is a continuous process in which the saturated solvent is constantly being displaced by fresh menstruum. Normally, percolation is not used as a continuous method because the sample is steeped in solvent in the percolator for 24 h (for up to three times), and then the extracted materials are collected and pooled. It has been observed that, after a triple-solvent extraction, the remaining marc does not contain valuable material *(8)*. For example, the third extractive of the whole plant of an *Ambrosia* species with chloroform has been shown to afford a residue devoid of sesquiterpene lactones (a major group of plant secondary metabolites originally present in the plant) (Silva, 1988, unpublished observations). The completion of percolation may be determined in several ways, and a few examples will illustrate this. Thus, when extracting alkaloids, a few drops of the eluent may be tested for the presence of these compounds, via the formation of precipitates, with specific reagents such as Dragendorff reagent, Mayer reagent, or ammonium reineckate salt. Also, flavonoids are usually colored compounds, and thus a colorless eluent would be indicative of the exhaustion of the drug on extraction. When extracting lipid materials, the concentration *in vacuo* of a portion of the eluant and the subsequent absence of residue will indicate the end of the extraction. In the case of sesquiterpene lactones and cardiac glycosides, the Kedde reaction could be used to indicate their presence, and either the Molisch reagent or the aniline acetate reaction might indicate the presence of carbohydrates (*see* phytochemical detection reagents listed in **Subheading 3.**).

Maceration has no real advantages over percolation and consists simply in placing the powdered plant sample in any shaped glass or stainless steel container that is stoppered and in contact with the solvent, in order to allow penetration into the cellular structure to dissolve the soluble compounds. The efficiency of this method may be increased by occasionally shaking the container or by using a mechanical or magnetic stirrer to allow homogenization of the final solution and saturation of the solvent. It is a discontinuous method, and the solvent should be renewed until the plant material is exhausted. This requires occasional filtration steps that may produce loss of solvent, metabolites, and/or plant material. Such problems may be avoided in part by suspending the ground material in a tied bag in the upper part of the solvent.

The use of a commercially available Soxhlet extractor is a convenient way to prepare crude plant extracts. This procedure is used mainly with pure solvents, although some authors have reported the use of binary or ternary solvent mixtures. Mixed solvents suffer the inconvenience that individual components may distill at different temperatures, so that the resulting mixture in the chamber containing the drug is enriched in the solvent of lower boiling point. Thus actual solvent proportions in the extracting chamber differ from that originally used in the collector, and this fact may introduce errors when trying to reproduce the experiment using other extraction methods. The main advantage of extraction using a Soxhlet apparatus is that it is an automatic, continuous method that does not require further manipulation other than concentration of the extractive and saves solvent by recycling it over the sample. Moreover, this method is not time-consuming, since for a standard-sized sample (500 g), the extraction time is less than 24 h. An obvious disadvantage is that the extractives are heated during the period of extraction at the boiling point of the solvent employed and thermally labile compounds such as carotenoids may hydrolyze, decompose, or produce artifacts *(26)*.

Infusion and decoction are simple methods for extraction with water. In the former case, boiling or cold water is added to the milled drug; in the latter, the sample is boiled for about 15 min in water. Extraction with water as the sole solvent is seldom used for plant material, although some plant constituents are water-soluble, such as carbohydrates, flavonoid polyglycosides, quaternary alkaloids, saponins, and tannins. As an example, taxifolin, or dihydroquercetin is believed to undergo certain enzymatic reductions, forming water-soluble oligomeric flavonoids that give adhesive properties to Douglas fir *(Pseudotsuga menziesii)* bark extracts. Douglas fir extract is prepared by boiling the dry bark with water for 40 min and extracting the aqueous filtrate with diethyl ether (yield: 11% of dry weight) *(32)*. Water-soluble compounds are usually extracted using mixtures of methanol-water or ethanol-water by one of the methods mentioned previously for organic solvents. A very interesting comparison between different solvent and extraction methods (Soxhlet, reflux, infusion) has been described for the isolation of coumarins, revealing that solubility is not always the prevailing factor for an efficient extraction and that the concentration of the compound of interest in the plant material also plays an important role *(34)*. As mentioned, steam distillation is used particularly for the extraction of plant volatile oils *(30,31)*.

Figures 1–3 show general protocols that may be used for plant extraction. **Figure 1** shows a general procedure to obtain a detannified chloroform extract from a plant crude methanolic extract. Direct extraction of the plant material

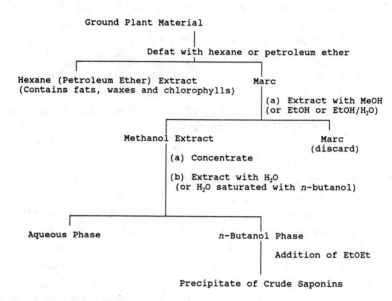

Fig. 2. General fractionation method to obtain a precipitate of crude saponin from plants, adapted from the literature *(35)*.

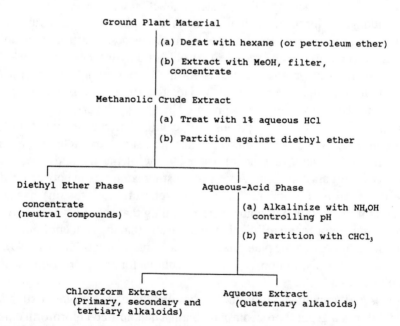

Fig. 3. General procedure to obtain alkaloidal extracts from a methanolic crude extract.

with chloroform may also be employed, with the concentration of the extract to dryness *in vacuo* affording a gummy residue that is then treated with 80% aqueous methanol; partition between hexane (to defat and hence remove the lipids such as alkanes, fatty acids, and waxes) and evaporation of the methanol from the aqueous layer give an aqueous extract that may be partitioned against different solvents according to the polarity of the desired metabolites. Different structural groups of flavonoids may be partially purified with some modification of **Fig. 1**, in which successive partitioning into diethyl ether, chloroform, and ethyl acetate will often afford, in turn, flavones and flavonols, methoxylated flavonoids, and flavonoid monoglycosides. Di- and polyglycosylated flavonoids will remain in the residual aqueous phase. Saponins are water-soluble compounds, and the crude saponin fractions may be obtained as depicted in **Fig. 2** *(35)*. For alkaloids, use may be made of the fact that they are basic compounds and may be extracted either into aqueous acid solution after removal of neutral impurities with an organic solvent, or by treating the ground wet plant material with an alkaline substance such as $CaCO_3$ powder and extracting with diethyl ether after standing overnight. **Figure 3** outlines the first of these two procedures. It is worth reiterating, however, that as far as possible, specific literature should be consulted for specific plant-extraction problems.

2.3.3. Interfering Compounds

It has been found that many naturally occurring compounds may interfere with the isolation and purification of a desired bioactive plant constituent. A few general procedures are mentioned below that may help the investigator to realize that contamination may have taken place during extraction.

2.3.3.1. LIPIDS

Whereas lipids are usually extracted with solvents of low polarity, they may coextract when polar solvents are used. These compounds may be visualized by running a TLC plate and using iodine vapor in a closed chamber to reveal brown spots or by performing a ^{1}H-NMR spectral measurement in which a high broad peak at approx δ 1.2–1.4 is observed. To remove the fats and waxes from an extract, the ground plant material may be percolated with petroleum ether or hexanes and allowed to dry prior to the full extraction process (**Fig. 2**); the material also may be directly extracted with the solvent of choice and defatted later (**Fig. 1**). Column chromatography or vacuum-liquid chromatography (VLC) *(36,37)* using petroleum ether or hexane as eluents may also be used to wash out the nonpolar lipid compounds, allowing the subsequent fractionation of the extract. Fats and waxes can be eliminated from a contaminated sample by filtering the sample through a reverse phase chromatographic column, a result of which being that the lipids are retained. An alternative approach is to add methanol or methanol-water in sufficient volume to dissolve the desired compound, assisting the dissolution by sonication if necessary and then filtering off the precipitate.

2.3.3.2. Pigments

Unwanted pigments such as chlorophylls and flavonoids may be present at high concentration levels depending on the plant part processed. They are not easily eliminated, but some of the following methods may be applied. Activated charcoal or activated carbon is known to decolorize solutions by a selective adsorption phenomenon. The solution may be either percolated through a relatively short charcoal column, or the powder can be mixed with the liquid to be decolorized, left to stand for a period of time, and filtered *(29)*. The efficiency of the adsorption is increased by heating. Charcoal has the disadvantage that many active medicinal compounds can also be adsorbed, as in the case of morphine, strychnine, and quinine (it is because of this that charcoal has been used as an antidote for alkaloid poisoning). Chlorophylls are commonly eliminated in substantial amounts from the extracts by solvent partitioning (**Fig. 1**) and can also be retained at the head of a neutral alumina column. A trial with a small sample and a subsequent TLC analysis may be suggested in order to evaluate the effects of decolorizing by these methods. Extracts and fractions may also be clarified by filtering them through Celite® (*see* **Note 11**). An aqueous solution of 2–5% lead-(II) acetate (general precipitation reagent) has been also used for the removal of fatty acids, chlorophylls, and other colored materials. The gummy extract from the plant is dissolved in 95% aqueous ethanol, with warming if necessary, and the lead-(II) acetate solution is then added producing an insoluble precipitate, which is filtered off by suction through Celite or diatomaceous earth *(38)*. This method has been used extensively to obtain prepurified fractions containing sesquiterpene lactones, but many other compounds may be coprecipitated, thereby reducing their overall compound yields.

2.3.3.3. Tannins

Vegetable tannins are polyphenols commonly found in plant extracts, often in high concentrations *(1)*, and give false-positive results in many biological assays usually because of their tendency to precipitate proteins through multipoint hydrogen bonding. The vegetable tannins (plant polyphenols) may be divided structurally into two broad groups, namely, polyesters based on gallic acid and/or hexahydroxydiphenic acid and their derivatives (the so-called hydrolyzable tannins), and the proanthocyanidins (the so-called condensed tannins) *(39)*. These compounds are extracted when using polar solvents, and it has been observed that aqueous and organic extracts containing tannins inhibit enzymes, such as topoisomerases 1 and 2 (T-1 and T-2), viral reverse transcriptase (RT), and other enzymes, leading to false-positive results. For example, T-2 enzyme may be inhibited at tannin concentrations as low as 0.05 µg/mL *(40–43)*. The bioactivity of a plant extract when due to tannins can be detected by assaying the extract before and after treatment with polyvinylpyrrolidone *(40,41)*. The presence of tannins can be inferred by the formation of a precipitate with ferric chloride (*see* **Subheading 3.**), and they can also be removed from aqueous and nonpolar extracts by passage over polyamide, collagen, Sephadex LH-20, or silica gel *(42)*. To eliminate tannins from a chloroform extract, the extract may be washed with 1% aqueous sodium chloride, with the upper phase discarded and the chloroform phase then dried with anhydrous Na_2SO_4 for a few hours. Tannins may also be precipitated by gelatin-sodium chloride solution (5% w/v NaCl and 0.5% w/v gelatin), caffeine *(43)*, nylon, or protein. They are retained by soluble polyvinyl pyrrolidone (PVP) *(44)* or polyamide resins *(40–43)*, by the formation of hydrogen bonds between the tannin phenolic hydroxy groups and the amide units of the retaining agent. PVP/Polyamide may be used batch-wise, or in the form of a small column over which the extract is passed, with monitoring of the supernatant or eluate by the ferric-chloride reaction, to ascertain that tannins have been removed (*see* **Note 12**). Using methanolic extracts, DE52 (diethylaminoethyl cellulose-based ion exchanger) may also be used as an effective removal agent for tannins and does not retain so many nonpolyphenolic compounds as does PVP (Cannell and Noble, 1995, unpublished observations). Phenolic compounds can also be removed by washing with 1% NaOH solution *(45)*.

2.3.3.4. PLASTICIZERS

Plasticizers (*see* **Subheading 2.3.1.**) may contaminate solvents, filter papers, plastic apparatus, and chromatographic solid phases stored in plastic containers. Dioctylphthalate ester has been commonly found to contaminate isolates from plants, and in pure form it is a yellow oil that exhibits significant cytotoxic activity for P-388 murine lymphocytic leukemia cells. By TLC on silica gel, it shows a pink-violet spot when sprayed with concentrated sulfuric acid or concentrated sulfuric acid-acetic acid (4:1), and heated at 110° for 5 min with $R_f = 0.4$ (petroleum ether-ethyl acetate, 19:1) (*see* **Note 13**). Plasticizers can be eliminated by distilling the solvents, filtering the sample through a reverse phase chromatographic column (Gerado Burton, unpublished observations), or by filtering the extract or sample through porous alumina *(15)*.

2.3.3.5. GREASE

Silicone grease is used as a lubricant in ground-glass joints in extraction apparatus and in stopcocks in columns and vacuum lines. It may contaminate plant samples and can be recognized by the following mass spectral fragmentation ions: m/z 429, 355, 281, 207, and 133. When hydrocarbon grease is used, the ion pattern shows losses at every 14 mass unit intervals because of the degradation of the aliphatic chains *(15)*.

3. General Reagents for the Detection of Various Phytochemical Groups

In this section, some characteristic general reagents are described for a few of the most common types of natural products found as plant secondary metabolites (some of these are also listed in Chapter 10). It should be taken into consideration that none of these reactions is specific, and a positive reaction allows only the presumption of the presence of a certain type of secondary metabolite, since certain structural similarities with compounds of completely different types may result in false-positive reactions. A negative reaction does not exclude the presence of any compound by reason of the fact that such a compound may occur in too low a concentration for unambiguous detection.

3.1. Alkaloids

The following reagents may produce false-positive reactions with coumarins, polyphenols, purines, amino acids, proteins, and other nitrogenous compounds that might also occur in plant extracts. In contrast, not all the alkaloids that might be present in a plant extract give a positive reaction because of structural idiosyncrasies. Other alkaloid-detecting reagents are also described in the literature *(46)*.

1. Mayer reagent: Dissolve 1.36 g $HgCl_2$ in 60 mL water and 5 g KI in 10 mL water. Combine both solutions and make up with water to 100 mL. Add a few drops to an acidified solution (HCl or diluted H_2SO_4) containing the alkaloids, and if alkaloids are present, a white to yellowish precipitate will appear. Special care should be taken since the precipitate may be redissolved by AcOH or EtOH in the solution or excess of reagent.

2. Dragendorff reagent: Dissolve 8.0 g $Bi(NO_3)_3.H_2O$ in 30% w/v HNO_3 and 27.2 g KI in 50 mL water. Combine the solutions and stand for 24 h, filter, and make up with water to 100 mL. Use only in acid solutions where an orange-brownish precipitate will appear. The alkaloids may be recovered by treatment with sodium carbonate and subsequent extraction with ethyl ether. This reaction may also be performed on a filter paper or on a TLC plate by adding a drop of the reagent onto a spot of the sample.

3. Wagner reagent: Dissolve 1.27 g I_2 (sublimed) and 2 g KI in 20 mL water, and make up with water to 100 mL. A brown precipitate in acidic solutions would suggest the presence of alkaloids.

4. Ammonium reineckate: Add 0.2 g hydroxylamine to a saturated solution of 4% ammonium reineckate, and acidify with dilute HCl. A pink precipitate will appear

if alkaloids are present. The precipitate is soluble in 50% acetone that may also be used to recrystallize it.

3.2. Sesquiterpene Lactones and Cardiac Glycosides

Many compounds containing α,β-unsaturated lactones may also give a positive reaction with the following tests. Other reactions for sesquiterpene lactones and cardiac glycosides may be found in the literature *(47)*.

1. Kedde reagent: Solution I: 2% of 3,5-dinitrobenzoic acid in MeOH; solution II: 5.7% KOH in water. Add one drop of each solution to 0.2–0.4 mL of the sample solution, and a bluish to purple color will appear within 5 min. The solution should not contain acetone, which gives a deep bluish color.
2. Baljet reagent: Solution I—1 g picric acid in 100 mL EtOH; solution II—10 g NaOH in 100 mL water. Combine solution I and II (1:1) before use and add two to three drops to 2–3 mg of sample; a positive reaction is indicated by orange to deep red color.
3. Legal reagent: Solution I—0.5% of a recently prepared sodium nitroprussiate in water; solution II—0.2 *N* NaOH. Dissolve 2 mg of sample into pyridine (two to three drops), add one drop solution I, and four drops solution II (one at a time). A deep red color will be observed for cardiac glycosides and pink for α,β-unsaturated lactones and some β–,γ-lactones. (These should be kept under controlled pH since they may isomerize in alkaline solution.)

3.3. Flavonoids

Many reagents have been described for the recognition of flavonoids although they may give a false-positive reaction with other polyphenols. The reagents are generally described in published monographs *(4,20,48)*.

1. Shinoda test: To an alcoholic solution of the sample, add magnesium powder and a few drops of concentrated HCl; orange, pink, red to purple colors will appear when flavones, flavonols, the corresponding 2, 3-dihydro derivatives, and/or xanthones are present. It is advisable to add *t*-butyl alcohol before adding the acid to avoid accidents from a violent reaction; the colored compounds will dissolve into the upper phase. By using zinc instead of magnesium, only flavanonols give a deep-red to magenta color; flavanones and flavonols will give weak pink to magenta colors or no color at all.
2. Sulfuric acid: Flavones and flavonols dissolve into concentrated sulfuric acid giving a deep yellow solution. Chalcones and aurones produce red or red-bluish solutions. Flavanones give orange to red colors.

3.4. Other Polyphenols

Ferric chloride (5%) dissolved in water or ethanol produces a brown precipitate *(4,48)* in the presence of polyphenols.

3.5. Sterols

As in the case of all the reagents listed so far, the following are not specific reactions that can indicate the presence of sterols without a reasonable doubt. Additional sterol-detecting reactions have been described in the literature *(46,47)*.

1. Liebermann-Buchard test: Combine 1 mL anhydrous acetic acid and 1 mL chloroform and cool to 0°C, and add one drop concentrated sulfuric acid. When the sample is added, either in the solid form or in solution in chloroform, blue, green, red, or orange colors that change with time will indicate a positive reaction; a blue-greenish color in particular is observed for Δ^5-sterols, with maximum intensity at 30 min.
2. Salkowski reaction: Dissolve 1–2 mg of the sample in 1 mL chloroform and add 1 mL concentrated sulfuric acid, forming two phases, with a red or yellow color indicating the presence of sterols and methylated sterols.

3.6. Saponins

Because of their surface-active properties, they may be recognized by shaking an aqueous solution of the sample and observing the production of foam, which is stable for approx 15 min. They are additionally recognized by the ability to haemolyze red blood cells *(4,35)*.

3.7. Carbohydrates

The following general reactions may be useful for the identification of carbohydrates.

1. Molisch reagent: Solution I—1% α-naphthol in 80% EtOH; solution II—concentrated H_2SO_4. Add two to three drops of solution I to a sample solution and acid, without mixing, to form an upper phase. A purple ring will appear in the interface as a result of the reaction between α-naphthol and furfural and 5-hydroxymethyl furfural aldehydes produced by dehydration of saccharides. A red color will appear if α-naphthol is replaced by 5% thymol. This reagent may be used with crude aqueous extracts as well as pure compounds.
2. Aniline acetate reaction: The solid sample is heated over a flame, and the vapors are allowed to react with aniline acetate impregnated on a filter paper placed on the vapors. A red color will appear in presence of heterocyclic aldehydes produced from carbohydrate dehydration.

4. Notes

1. Sources of published ethnomedical information to facilitate the plant selection process may be difficult to find because such data are usually compiled in botanical texts of limited distribution. Another reliable source of such information are notes made by taxonomists on herbaria samples. Also, useful literature sources are *Medicinal and Aromatic Plant Abstracts*, published by the Publications & Information Directorate, CSIR, Hillside Road, New Delhi 110 012, India *(5)*; and journals such as *Economic Botany* and the *Journal of Ethnopharmacology*.

2. Sources of chemotaxonomic information may be found in different databases, e.g., *Chemical Abstracts* and NAPRALERT, the latter also providing cross-information of ethnomedical, pharmacological, and chemical data *(5,11,12)*.
3. Usually, the whole plant material is processed unless previous information on a particular plant part that specifically accumulates a metabolite of interest is available. Preliminary chromatographic tests may be performed for separate part plants (leaf, stem, root, bark), and qualitative/quantitative comparison may lead to the preferred choice *(4)*.
4. It is preferable if herbarium samples include either flowers or fruits, to assist in subsequent taxonomic identification. Obtaining these plant parts from tree species in rainforests, however, may cause logistical problems.
5. For maximum assurance that a recollected sample will contain the same constituents as the original collected plant material, recollections should as far as possible be carried out in the same location, on the same plant part, at the same time of the year. However, care should be taken not to destroy all of the specimens growing at a particular collection location.
6. In the context of plant drug discovery, the term "dereplication" may be defined as the attempt to remove duplicate leads. In addition to relying on previous literature information, bioactive components of already known structure in crude plant extracts may be identified by monitoring by HPLC/UV/MS (e.g., **ref.** *49*; *see* Chapter 10).
7. Old stored material is commonly used for phytochemical studies, and whereas the results obtained are usually satisfactory *(50)*, critical analysis of evidence for compound lability is suggested as a routine practice.
8. Highly flammable, explosive, and/or toxic solvents should normally be avoided, e.g., benzene, diethyl ether, and carbon tetrachloride *(8)*.
9. Reagent-grade solvents after redistillation and when stored in glass containers are of sufficient purity for solvent extraction.
10. Plant extracts should not be stored for long periods in organic solvent at room temperature or in the sunlight. It is advisable to eliminate any solvent residue from a stored extract to avoid side reactions *(51)*.
11. Celite is a commercial brand of diatomaceous earth used as a filter aid. Different-purity grades of Celite can be purchased from many manufacturers; Celite consists of approx 90% SiO_2, and also contains small percentages of CaO, Al_2O_3, and Fe_2O_3.
12. Although PVP is a standard treatment for tannin removal, it is also capable of retaining compounds other than polyphenols (at least under certain conditions) (Cannell, 1995, unpublished observations).
13. There are some specific spray reagents for the detection of phthalate esters; namely, spray solution I (add some zinc powder to a 20% ethanolic resorcinol solution), spray solution II (2 M sulfuric acid), and spray solution III (40% aqueous potassium hydroxide solution). Procedure: Spray with I, heat for 10 min at 150°C, spray with II, heat 10 min at 120°C, and spray with III. Phthalate esters will appear as orange spots on a yellow background *(48)*. Spectroscopic data: UV

λ_{max} 275 nm (log ϵ 3.17), shoulder at 282 nm; ^{1}H nmr (δ, CDCl$_3$) 7.70 (2H, dd, H-3 and H-6 aromatic protons), 7.52 (2H, dd, H-4 and H-5 aromatic protons), 4.20 (4H, dd, H-1' and H-1" 2-ethylhexyl residue), 1.2–1.8 (14H, m, CH and CH$_2$s of 2-ethylhexyl residue), 0.90 (12H, CH$_3$ groups); eims (*m/z*) 279, 167, and 149 (100%). These ions are common to dialkyl-phthalates, while tri-*n*-butyl acetyl citrate shows ions at *m/z* 329, 259, 185, and 129, and tri-butyl phosphate exhibits significant fragment peaks at *m/z* 211, 155, and 99 *(15)*.

References

1. Robinson, T. (1991) T*he Organic Constituents of Higher Plants*, 6th edn., Cordus Press, North Amherst, MA.
2. Tyler, V. E., Brady, L. R., and Robbers, J. E. (1988) *Pharmacognosy*, 9th edn., Lea and Febiger, Philadelphia.
3. Farnsworth, N. R. and Soejarto, D. D. (1991) Global importance of medicinal plants, in *Conservation of Medicinal Plants* (Akerele, O., Heywood, V., and Synge, H., eds.), Cambridge University Press, New York, pp. 25–51.
4. Farnsworth, N. R. (1966) Biological and phytochemical screening of plants. *J. Pharm. Sci.* **55,** 225–276.
5. Farnsworth, N. R. (1990) The role of ethnopharmacology in drug development, in *Bioactive Compounds from Plants* (Chadwick, D. J. and Marsh, J., eds.), Wiley, New York, pp. 2–21.
6. Cordell, G. A., Farnsworth, N. R., Beecher, C. W. W., Soejarto, D. D., Kinghorn, A. D., Pezzuto, J. M., Wall, M. E., Wani, M. C., Brown, D. M., O'Neill, M. J., Lewis, J. A., Tait, R. M., and Harris, T. J. R. (1993) Novel strategies for the discovery of plant-derived anticancer agents, in *Human Medicinal Agents from Plants* (Kinghorn, A. D. and Balandrin, M. F., eds.), American Chemical Society, Washington DC, Symp. Ser. 534, pp. 191–204.
7. Soejarto, D. D. (1993) Logistics and politics in plant drug discovery: the other end of the spectrum, in *Human Medicinal Agents from Plants* (Kinghorn, A. D. and Balandrin, M. F., eds.), American Chemical Society, Washington DC, Symp. Ser. 534, pp. 96–111.
8. Kinghorn, A. D. (1985) A phytochemical approach to bioscreening of natural products, in *Drug Bioscreening: Fundamentals of Drug Evaluation Techniques in Pharmacology* (Thompson, E. B., ed.), Graceway Publishing, New York, pp. 113–132.
9. You, M., Ma, X., Mukherjee, R., Farnsworth, N. R., Cordell, G. A., Kinghorn, A. D., and Pezzuto, J. M. (1994) Indole alkaloids from *Peschiera laeta* that enhance vinblastine-mediated cytotoxicity with multidrug-resistant cells. *J. Nat. Prod.* **57,** 1517–1522.
10. You, M., Wickramaratne, D. B. M., Silva, G. L., Chai, H., Chagwedera, T. E., Farnsworth, N. R., Cordell, G. A., Kinghorn, A. D., and Pezzuto, J. M. (1995) (-)-Roemerine, an aporphine alkaloid from *Annona senegalensis* that reverses the multidrug-resistance phenotype with cultured cells. *J. Nat. Prod.* **58,** 598–604.
11. Farnsworth, N. R., Loub, W. D., Soejarto, D. D., Cordell, G. A., Quinn, M. L., Mulholland, K. (1981) Computer services for research on plants for fertility regulation. *Kor. J. Pharmacogn.* **12,** 98–109.

12. Loub, W. D., Farnsworth, N. R., Soejarto, D. D., and Quinn, M. L. (1985) NAPRALERT: computer handling of natural product research data. *J. Chem. Inf. Comput. Sci.* **25,** 99–103.

13. Cordell, G. A., Beecher, C. W. W., and Pezzuto, J. M. (1991) Can ethnopharmacology contribute to the development of new anticancer agents? *J. Ethnopharmacol.* **32,** 117–133.

14. Silva, G. L., Chai, H., Gupta, M. P., Farnsworth, N. R., Cordell, G. A., Pezzuto, J. M., Beecher, C. W. W., and Kinghorn, A. D. (1995) Cytotoxic biflavonoids from *Selaginella willdenowii. Phytochemistry* **40,** 129–134.

15. Banthorpe, D. V. (1991) Classification of terpenoids and general procedures for their characterization, in *Methods in Plant Biochemistry,* vol. 7 (Dey, P. M. and Harborne, J. B. eds.), Academic, New York, pp. 2–41.

16. Doerk-Schmitz, K., Witte, L., and Alfermann, A. W. (1994) Tropane alkaloid patterns in plants and hairy roots of *Hyoscyamus albus. Phytochemistry* **35,** 107–110.

17. Kinghorn, A D. (1994) The discovery of drugs from higher plants, in *The Discovery of Drugs with Therapeutic Potential* (Gullo, V., ed.), Butterworth-Heineman, Boston, pp. 81–108.

18. Oberti, J. C., Silva, G. L., Sosa, V. E., Kulanthaivel, P., and Herz, W. (1986) Ambrosanolides and secoambrosanolides from *Ambrosia tenuifolia. Phytochemistry* **25,** 1355–1358.

19. Kleinig, H. (1989) The role of plastids in isoprenoid biosynthesis. *Ann. Rev. Plant Physiol.* **40,** 39–59.

20. Markham, K. R. (1982) *Techniques of Flavonoid Identification,* Academic, New York, pp. 1–113.

21. van Beek, T. A., van Dam, N., de Groot, A., Geelen, T. A. M., and van der Plas, L. H. W. (1994) Determination of the sesquiterpene dialdehyde polygodial by high-pressure liquid chromatography. *Phytochem. Anal.* **5,** 19–23.

22. Fawell, J. K. and Hunt, S. (eds.) (1988) Chloroform, in *Environmental Toxicology: Organic Pollutants.* Wiley, New York, pp. 15–24.

23. Phillipson, J. D. and Bisset, N. G. (1972) Quaternisation and oxidation of strychnine and brucine during plant extraction. *Phytochemistry* **11,** 2547–2553.

24. Britton, G. (1991) Carotenoids, in *Methods in Plant Biochemistry,* vol. 7 (Dey, P. M. and Harborne, J. B., eds.), Academic, New York, pp. 474–517.

25. Ghisalberti, E. L. (1993) Detection and isolation of bioactive natural products, in *Bioactive Natural Products: Detection, Isolation and Structural Determination* (Colegate, S. M. and Molyneux, R. J., eds.), CRC, Boca Raton, FL, pp. 9–57.

26. Lavie, D., Bessalle, R., Pestchanker, M. J., Gottlieb, H. E., Frolow F., and Giordano, O. S. (1987) Trechonolide A, a new withanolide type from *Trechonaetes laciniata. Phytochemistry* **26,** 1791–1795.

27. Ohmiya, S., Otomasu, H., Haginiwa, J., and Murakoshi, I. (1979) (-)-12-Cystisineacetic acid, a new lupin alkaloid in *Euchresta japonica. Phytochemistry* **18,** 649,650.

28. Moore, J. M., Hays, P. A., Cooper, D. A., Casale, J. F., and Lydon, J. (1994) 1-Hydroxytropacocaine: an abundant alkaloid of *Erythroxylum novogranatense* var. *novogranatense* and var. *truxillense. Phytochemistry* **36,** 357–360.

29. Lee, I.-K., Ma, X., Chai, H.-B., Madulid, D. A., Lamont, R. B., O'Neill, M. J., Besterman, J. M., Farnsworth, N. R., Soejarto, D. D., Cordell, G. A., Pezzuto, J. M., and Kinghorn, A. D. (1995) Novel cytotoxic labdane diterpenoids from *Neouvaria acuminatissima. Tetrahedron* **51,** 21–28.

30. Weurman, C. (1969) Isolation and concentration of volatiles in food odor research. *J. Agric. Food Chem.* **17,** 370–384.

31. Charlwood, B. V. and Charlwood, K. A. (1991) Monoterpenoids, in *Methods in Plant Biochemistry,* vol. 7 (Dey, P. M. and Harborne, J. B., eds.), Academic, New York, pp. 43–98.

32. Kiehlmann, E. and Li, E. P. M. (1995) Isomerization of dihydroquercetin. *J. Nat. Prod.* **58,** 450–455.

33. Matoasca, G. and Walker, G. C. (1970) Extraction and Extractives, in *Remington's Pharmaceutical Sciences* 14th ed. (Osol, A., ed.), Mack, Easton, PA, pp. 1578–1593.

34. Bourgaud, F., Poutaraud, A., and Guckert, A. (1994) Extraction of coumarins from plant material (Leguminosae). *Phytochem. Anal.* **5,** 127–132.

35. Hostettmann, K., Hostettmann, M., and Marston, A. (1991) Saponins, in *Methods in Plant Biochemistry,* vol. 7 (Dey, P. M. and Harborne, J. B., eds.), Academic, New York, pp. 435–471.

36. Coll, J. C. and Bowden, B. F. (1986) The application of vacuum liquid chromatography to the separation of terpene mixtures. *J. Nat. Prod.* **49,** 934–936.

37. Pelletier, S. W., Chokshi, H. P., and Desai, H. K. (1986) Separation of diterpenoid alkaloid mixtures using vacuum liquid chromatography. *J. Nat. Prod.* **49,** 892–900.

38. Herz, W. and Högenauer, G. C. (1961) Isolation and structure of coronopilin, a new sesquiterpene lactone. *J. Org. Chem.* **26,** 5011–5013.

39. Haslam, E. (1989) *Plant Polyphenols: Vegetable Tannins Revisited* in *Chemistry and Pharmacology of Natural Products* (Phillipson, J. D., Ayres, D. C., and Baxter, H., eds.), Cambridge University Press, Cambridge, UK, pp. 1–230.

40. Tan, G. T., Pezzuto, J. M., Kinghorn, A. D., and Hughes, S. H. (1991) Evaluation of natural products as inhibitors of human immunodeficiency virus type 1 (HIV-1) reverse transcriptase. *J. Nat. Prod.* **54,** 143–154.

41. Tan, G. T., Pezzuto, J. M., and Kinghorn, A. D. (1992) Screening of natural products as HIV-1 and HIV-2 reverse transcriptase (RT) inhibitors, in *Natural Products as Antiviral Agents* (Chu, C. K. and Cutler, H. G., eds.), Plenum, New York, pp. 195–222.

42. Wall, M. E., Wani, M. C., Brown, D. M., Fullas, F., Oswald, J. B., Josephson, F. F., Thornton, N. M., Pezzuto, J. M., Farnsworth, N. R., Cordell, G. A., and Kinghorn, A. D. (1993) Effect of tannins on screening of plant extracts for bioactivity based on inhibition of enzyme activity. 34th Annual Meeting of the American Society of Pharmacognosy, San Diego, CA, July 18–22, Abstract 0–2.

43. Wall, M. E., Taylor, H., Ambrosio, L., and Davis, K. (1969) Plant antitumor agents. III. Convenient separation of tannins from other constituents. *J. Pharm. Sci.* **58,** 839–841.

44. Loomis, W. D. and Battaile, J. (1966) Plant phenolic compounds and the isolation of plant enzymes. *Phytochemistry* **5,** 423–438.

45. Gosmann, G., Guillaume, D., Takeda, A. T. C., and Schenkel, E. P. (1995) Triterpenoid saponins from *Ilex paraguariensis. J. Nat. Prod.* **58,** 438–441.

46. Dominguez, X. A. (1973) *Métodos de Investigación Fitoquimica* (Editorial Limusa, ed.), Mexico D.F., Mexico, pp. 1–281.
47. Klyne, W. (1970) *Química de los Esteroides* (Compañiá Editorial Continental S. A., ed.), Barcelona, Spain, pp. 126–149.
48. Copius-Peereboom, J. W. (1960) The analysis of plasticizers by micro-adsorption chromatography. *J. Chromatogr.* **4**, 323–328.
49. Constant, H. L. and Beecher, C. W. W. (1995) A method for the dereplication of natural product extracts using electrospray HPLC/MS. *Nat. Prod. Lett.* **6**, 193–196.
50. Luyengi, L., Lee, I.-K., Mar, W., Fong, H. H. S., Pezzuto, J. M., and Kinghorn, A. D. (1994) Rotenoids and chalcones from *Mundulea sericea* that inhibit phorbol ester-induced ornithine decarboxylase activity. *Phytochemistry* **36**, 1523–1526.
51. Rodrigues, A. A., Garcia, M., and Rabi, J. A. (1978) Facile biomimetic synthesis of costunolide-1,10-epoxide, santamarin and reynosin. *Phytochemistry* **17**, 953,954.

13

Isolation of Marine Natural Products

Amy E. Wright

1. Introduction

The world's oceans cover more than 70% of the earth's surface and contain over 200,000 invertebrate and algal species *(1)*. These organisms live in complex communities and in close association with other organisms both macro- (e.g., algae, sponges, ascidians) and micro- (e.g., nonfilamentous bacteria, fungi, actinomycetes). Some organisms derive their chemistry from dietary sources, while others synthesize the compounds *de novo*. Some compounds may be produced by associated microorganisms, while others may require an association between the host and microorganism to produce the compounds. The chemistry of any particular specimen can be affected by the habitat as well as by geographic and seasonal factors *(2)*. In fact, the true biogenetic origin of most marine natural products remains a topic for debate within the marine natural products community.

Because of the diversity of marine organisms and habitats, marine natural products encompass a wide variety of chemical classes, including terpenes, shikimates, polyketides, acetogenins, peptides, alkaloids of varying structures, and a multitude of compounds of mixed biosynthesis. In the past decade alone, the structures of over 5000 marine natural products have been published *(3–10)*.

In many instances, the class of compound present in the organism can be predicted based on the taxonomic classification of the source organism. Unfortunately, even knowing the class of compound does not always allow one to define a simple purification method. Series of marine natural products can often contain a variety of chemical functionalities (e.g., OH, OCH_3, OAc, OSO_3^- Na^+). Each change in functionality has the potential to radically change the polarity of the compounds and therefore the method required for purification. For example, specimens of the deep-water sponge genus *Spongosorites* typically contain bis(indole) alkaloids. Topsentin (**Scheme 1**), the simplest com-

From: *Methods in Biotechnology, Vol. 4: Natural Products Isolation*
Edited by: R. J. P. Cannell © Humana Press Inc., Totowa, NJ

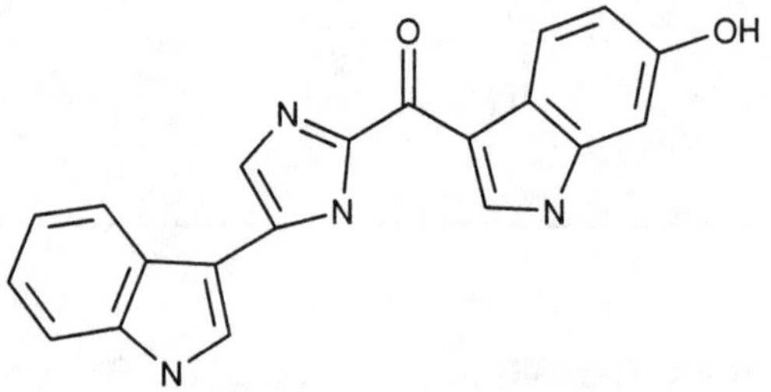

Scheme 1. Topsentin.

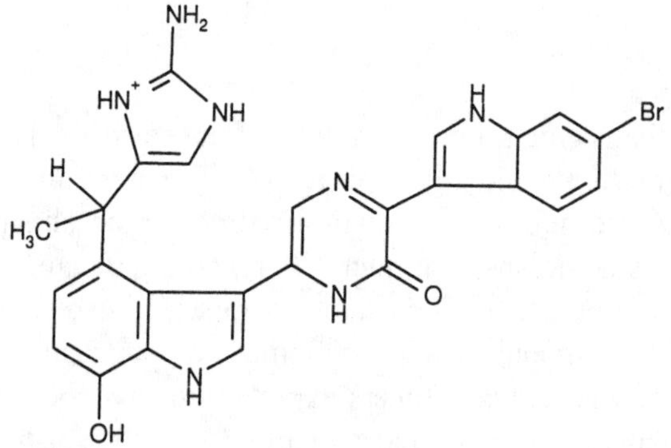

Scheme 2. Dragmacidin d.

pound of the series, can be purified by chromatography on silica gel using CHCl₃-MeOH mixtures as the eluent *(11,12)*. Dragmacidin d (**Scheme 2**), which possesses a 2-aminoimidazole side chain, is much more polar and requires chromatography on reverse phase stationary phases and elution with acetonitrile-water-trifluoroacetic acid (TFA) mixtures *(13)*. In this instance, knowing the taxonomy of the organism assisted in assigning the structure of the pure compounds, but did not assist in defining the purification method for the more polar metabolite which possesses an unexpected functionalization.

In order to gain insight into the methods that are used most in the purification of marine natural products, 115 reports of marine natural products published in 1995 in *The Journal of the American Chemical Society, The Journal of Organic Chemistry, Tetrahedron,* and the *Journal of Natural Products* were reviewed. Each publication was categorized as follows:

1. The phylum of the source organism.
2. The class of chemical compound(s) reported.
3. The preservation method of the organism (fresh/frozen vs lyophilized).
4. The extraction method. "Nonpolar": solvents such as CH_2Cl_2, hexanes, acetone,

EtOAc, Et$_2$O, toluene, petroleum ether; "nonpolar plus alcohol": any of the above mixed with an alcohol; "alcohol": usually ethanol, methanol, or isopropanol; "complex scheme": includes either sequential extraction or very complex unusual mixtures of solvents; "aqueous": either 100% water or mixtures of water and another solvent where water is > 50% of the mixture.

5. The method used, if any, of solvent partitioning. These were separated into:
   a. "Simple," such as a one-step partition (e.g., butanol-water) or a two-step partition (e.g., EtOAc-water) followed by subsequent partitioning of the aqueous phase with butanol.
   b. "Kupchan" includes any true or modified Kupchan scheme in which the percentage of aqueous phase is adjusted sequentially.
   c. "Complex" comprises any scheme in which either an unusual sequence of solvents and/or very unusual complex mixtures of solvents were used (e.g., EtOAc:MeOH:CHCl$_3$:AcOH:heptane mixtures, used in the isolation of the batzellidines).

6. The type, if any, of open-column, flash, or vacuum-column chromatography used. These were divided into silica gel; bonded phases (e.g., ODS, C-8, Diol, CN); or gel permeation on nonfunctionalized resins, including both size and partition chromatography systems (e.g., Sephadex LH-20, Sephadex LH-60, NS Gels, BioBeads SX-2, SX-4, SX-8, AMBERLITE XAD-2, XAD-4, and XAD-7, TSK-G3000S gel).

7. The type, if any, of HPLC method used. These were separated into normal phase, reverse phase (C-18, C-8, C-4), other bonded phases (e.g., DIOL, CN, NH$_2$), and instances in which some combination of the above were used.

8. Whether medium-pressure liquid chromatography (MPLC), counter-current chromatography (CCC), or preparative thin-layer chromatography (PTLC) was used.

9. Whether any other methods were used (e.g., trituration, crystallization, anion/cation exchange, ultrafiltration).

The results of this review are tabulated in **Tables 1–3**. **Table 1** shows the distribution of compounds within phyla. **Table 2** shows the most commonly used purification methods for different phyla. **Table 3** shows the most commonly used purification methods for different classes of compounds. Some general conclusions are:

1. Preservation of samples: In 77% of the reports, fresh or frozen materials were extracted. In 23% of the reports, the organism was lyophilized or air-dried (two instances) prior to extraction.

2. Extraction: The most commonly used extraction solvents were alcohols (46%) or mixtures of alcohol and less polar solvents (25%).

3. Partitioning: No solvent partitioning was used in 28% of the cases. Simple partitions were carried out 41% of the time. Kupchan schemes were used 25% of the time, and complex schemes were used 5% of the time.

4. Column chromatography (VCC, flash, or open-gravity):
   a. 10% of the isolation procedures did not use any form of open-column chromatography.

Table 1
Types of Compounds vs Phyla

	Bryozoan	Chlorophyta	Chordata	Cnidaria	Echinodermata	Micro-alga	Micro-Organisms	Mollusca	Phaeophyta	Porifera	Rhodophyta
ACETOGENIN				2	1	1				7	
ALKALOID	1	1	3	1	1	1	1			12	
AMINE										1	
AMINE POLYMER										1	
GLYCOSIDE										1	
MIXED BIOSYNTHESIS			1					1		6	
NUCLEOSIDE										1	
PEPTIDE			5	2		1		1		6	
PHENOL/HYDROQUINONE										4	
POLYETHER	1						1		1	1	
POLYKETIDE						2				3	
SAPONINS					3						
STEROL				4	1					1	
SULFATE ESTERS						1			1	1	
TERPENE	1			17				2	1	9	1
TOTALS	3	1	9	26	6	6	2	4	3	54	1

b. 56% of the isolations used silica-gel stationary phases.

c. 12% of the isolations used bonded phase (e.g., ODS, DIOL, CN) stationary phases.

d. 10% of the isolations used both silica-gel and bonded phase stationary phases (i.e., there were multiple column-chromatography steps).

e. 46% of the isolations used gel-permeation chromatography on non-functionalized resins. LH-20 was used in 42% of the isolations.

f. 44% of the isolations used only silica or reverse phase stationary phases (no "gel" chromatography).

g. 13% of the isolations used only nonfunctionalized resins such as Sephadex LH-20.

h. 33% of the isolations used a combination of silica or bonded phase chromatography and chromatography on nonfunctionalized resins.

5. MPLC was used in 9% of the studies.

6. CCC was used in 7% of the studies.

7. PTLC was used in 10% of the studies.

8. HPLC:

a. 27 % of the isolations did not use HPLC.

b. 6% used solely normal phase stationary phases (e.g., silica).

c. 49% used reverse phase stationary phases (RP-18, RP-8, RP-4).

d. 3% used other bonded phases (e.g., CN, DIOL, NH_2).

Table 2
Phyla of Source Organisms vs Purification Methods

Phylum	Total #	1		2					3				4								5	6	7	8					9
		Fresh/Frozen	Lyophilized or air dried	Nonpolar	Alcohol + Nonpolar	Alcohol	Complex Scheme	Aqueous	No partitioning	Simple Partitions	Kupchan-type Partitions	Complex Partitions	No Column Chromatography	Silica/Bonded Phase Based Only	Gel Based only	Gel and Si/Bonded Phase	Silica gel Stationary phase	Bonded Stationary Phase	Multiple Stationary Phases	LH-20 or Other Gel	MPLC Used	CCC Used	PTLC Used	No HPLC Used	Regular Phase HPLC	Reverse Phase HPLC	Other Bonded Phase HPLC	Multiple HPLC Types	Other Methods
BRYOZOA	3	3					3			1	2			1		2	2			3						3			
CHLOROPHYTA	1	1				1			1					1			1								1				1
CHORDATE	9	8	1	1		7	1			2	1	5	1	4	5			4	4	1	5	2			1		4	2	1	2
CNIDARIA	26	19	7	4	6	12	4		7	11	6	2		16	1	9	22	1	2	10			3	10	3	8	2	3	3
ECHINODERM	6	4	2	1		2		3	2	4				2		4					1	4							
MICRO-ALGA	6	4	2			4	1	1	2	3	1			4			2	1	2	1	1		1			4			2
MICRO-ORGANISM	2	2			1	1			1	1				1		1	1	1		2			1				1	1	
MOLLUSC	4	4		1		2	1		1	2	1			3		1	2	1	1	1			1		2	2			
PHAEOPHYTA	3	3		1		2			2	1				1		2	2			2				3					3
PORIFERA	54	39	15	5	16	24	8		16	22	14	2	9	21	6	18	26	8	5	24	5	4	3	13	7	29	1	4	6
RHODOPHYTA	1	1				1			1					1			1						1					1	
TOTALS	115	87	28	13	28	53	16	4	33	47	29	6	11	51	15	38	63	14	11	49	10	8	11	31	13	56	4	11	14
Percentages		76	24	11	24	46	14	3	29	41	25	5	10	44	13	33	55	12	10	43	9	7	10	27	11	49	3	10	12

1, form of organism when extraced (choices: fresh/frozen or lyophilized/air-dried); 2, extraction method; 3, liquid–liquid partitioning schemes; 4, column chromatography; 5, medium pressure liquid chromatography (MPLC) used? (Y/N); 6, countercurrent chromatography (CCC) used? (Y/N); 7, preparative thin-layer chromatography used? (Y/N); 8, types of HPLC used; 9, other methods used? (Y/N).

    e. 10% used multiple HPLC separations on both normal and reverse-phase stationary phases.

9. 14% of the studies used other separation methods such as trituration, crystallization, ultrafiltration, and/or cation/anion exchange chromatography.

1.1. General Approach Used at HBOI

This chapter provides an outline of the general approach used in the author's laboratory to purify marine natural products. An outline is given in **Fig. 1**. In our approach, all separations are carried out on a small scale until pure compounds are reproducibly isolated. A variety of purification methods are used to ensure isolation of all compounds of interest, and all fractions are characterized by either bioassay, NMR, HPLC, and/or TLC. Our overall procedure includes the following steps:

1. Collection and field identification of the marine organism.
2. Initial extraction of the organism.
3. Biological assay of the extract.
4. Partitioning to confirm and enrich bioactivity.
5. Determination of the polarity of the natural products present in the extract/ dereplication of known compounds.

Table 3
Types of Compounds vs Purification Methods

Compound Type	Total #	[1] Fresh/Frozen	Freeze or air dried	[2] Nonpolar	Alcohol + Nonpolar	Alcohol	Complex Scheme	Aqueous	[3] No partitioning	Simple Partitions	Kupchan-type Partitions	Complex Partitions	[4] No Column Chromatography	Silica/Bonded Phase Based Only	Gel Based only	Both Gel and Silica Based	Silica gel Stationary Phase	Bonded Stationary Phase	Multiple Stationary Phases	LH-20 or Other Gel	[5] MPLC Used	[6] CCC Used	[7] PTLC Used	[8] No HPLC Used	Regular Phase HPLC	Reverse Phase HPLC	Other Bonded Phase HPLC	Multiple HPLC Types	[9] Other Methods
ACETOGENIN	11	7	4	2	4	3	2		4	4	3			2		9	7	1	1		1		2	3	2	3	1	2	2
ALKALOID	21	16	5	2	6	11	2		4	7	7	3	3	4	2	12	11	2	3	14	1	3	4	6	4	9	1	1	5
AMINE	1	1				1				1				1			1									1			1
AMINE POLYMER	1	1			1					1			1								1								1
GLYCOSIDE	1	1				1				1						1	1			1						1			
MIXED BIOSYNTHESIS	8	6	2		1	6				2	3	3		5		3	2	3	3	3	2			7					1
NUCLEOSIDE	1	1				1					1				1					1						1			
PEPTIDE	15	14	1	1	4	7	3		6	4	4	1	1	6	4	4	6		1	8	1		1	8	1	3		2	
PHENOL/HYDROQUINONE	4	3	1		3	1			3		1			3		1	4			1			1	3	1	1			
POLYETHER	3	3				1	1	1	1	1	1			1		2	1	1			3		1		1	2			3
POLYKETIDE	6	5	1		1	3	2			1	2	3		3	1	2	1	3	1	3	1			5		1			
SAPONINS	3	1	2					3	1	2				1		2				2		3		3					
STEROL	6	3	3			1	5			5	1			2	1	3	4		1	4					2	3		1	1
SULFATE ESTERS	3	3				3			3					1		2				2					1	2			
TERPENE	31	23	8	7	5	12	7		9	15	5	2	2	17	2	10	26			12	4		3	11		10		3	3
TOTALS	115	87	28	13	28	53	16	4	33	47	29	6	11	51	15	38	64	14	11	53	10	8	11	31	7	56	3	11	16
Percentages		76	24	11	24	46	14	3	29	41	25	5	10	44	13	33	56	12	10	46	9	7	10	27	6	49	3	10	14

1, form of organism when extracted (choices: fresh/frozen or lyophilized/air-dried); 2, extraction method; 3, liquid–liquid partitioning schemes; 4, column chromatography; 5, medium pressure liquid chromatography (MPLC) used? (Y/N); 6, countercurrent chromatography (CCC) used? (Y/N); 7, preparative thin-layer chromatography used? (Y/N); 8, types of HPLC used; 9, other methods used? (Y/N).

6. Selection of a first chromatographic step based on the polarity.
7. Further chromatography.
8. Development of an HPLC separation, if possible.
9. Scale-up of the isolation for additional biological testing and/or structure elucidation.

2. Collection and Storage of Marine Organisms
2.1. Handling of Marine Organisms

Marine organisms have been the source of thousands of different natural products. Many of these compounds have been shown to be extremely toxic in mammalian systems. Palytoxin, for example, originally found in the zooanthid *Palythoa toxica,* remains one of the most toxic nonproteinaceous compounds discovered to date. The tide pool in which the zooanthid grew was known in local legends to be toxic and scientists working with the organism fell ill with flu-like symptoms both during collection and later work *(14)*. Other compounds, such as mycalamide *(15)* and aplysiatoxin, *(16)* are strong irritants. Aplysiatoxin also has strong tumor-promoting properties. In general, when working with any new organism, it is safest to assume that the exact nature of

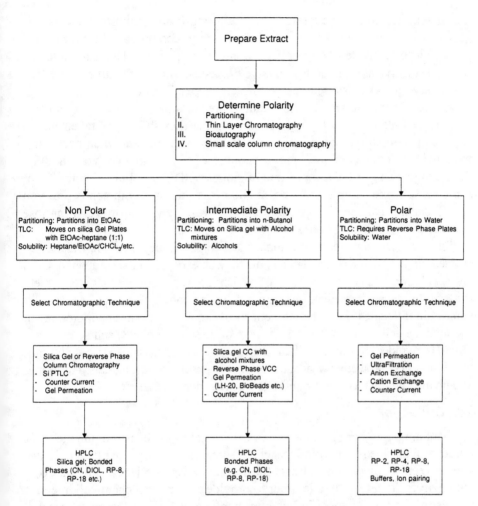

Fig. 1. General isolation approach used at HBOI.

the compounds present in the organism and the biological properties of the compounds are not known. Caution should always be used in handling marine organisms. Proper protective equipment such as gloves and eye protection should always be worn. Many researchers (including the author) have experienced instances of extreme eye irritation caused during collection of organisms where "sea water" from the organism has squirted from the animal and into the eye. In addition, many organisms such as hydroids and sponges such as *Neofibularia nolitangere* and *Tedania ignis* ("fire sponge"), have highly irritating components that cause immediate itching and rash formation in some individuals. Typically, a single encounter with the sponge *Neofibularia* is all that is required to motivate researchers working in the author's lab to put on gloves when processing specimens. It is strongly recommended that one wear proper clothing while diving or snorkeling for organisms. This can include a wet suit (or dive skin) and gloves. Dive masks can protect the diver/snorkeler, and safety glasses or sunglasses can protect the wading collector.

Workup in the lab should use standard precautions for working with compounds of unknown biological properties. Caution should be taken not to expose oneself to the compounds in any way. Wear gloves when necessary, work in chemical fume hoods, prevent contact of any compounds with the skin, do not ingest any of the sample, and do not "smell" the sample directly. If for some reason, the sample must be smelled (the author recommends that you don't), use normal chemical precautions, and waft the vapor towards your nose in order to minimize exposure.

If extracts, fractions, or pure compounds are spilled, they must immediately be cleaned up. If not, others may be unknowingly be exposed to the compound. Even one small drop of a compound such as myclamide A, a substance that is extremely irritating and causes immediate blistering of the skin upon exposure, can be extremely unpleasant if touched. The long-term effects of exposure, such as tumor promotion, and teratogenicity, are not known for most of these compounds, and so exposure should be avoided. In summary, handle all marine specimens and extracts with caution. Use proper protective wear and minimize exposure to the materials. This is true of both the raw organism and extracts or fractions derived thereof.

2.2. Collection

There are a number of philosophies as to which organisms provide the most interesting marine natural products chemistry. Many groups involved in large-scale screening of marine extracts for drug discovery collect as great a taxonomic diversity as possible in order to provide the greatest chemical diversity for testing in highly specific enzyme or receptor-binding-based bioassays. Other groups specialize in the natural products chemistry of specific taxonomic groups known to be rich in natural products. Still other groups focus on organisms in which there appear to be an ecological reason for production of compounds. Sponges or ascidians with surfaces free of fouling organisms may produce compounds that inhibit fouling *(17–19)*. Thin encrusting and boring organisms are often rich in secondary metabolites, and it has been proposed that these compounds are produced to inhibit the growth of neighboring organisms, allowing the encrusting or boring organism to colonize additional space *(20,21)*. Organisms that occur in areas of high herbivory or predation often produce toxic or unpalatable compounds that act to deter predation *(2)*. Ultimately, the choice of organisms to collect depends on the preference and experience level of the collectors as well as the ultimate goal of the research program.

The collection of organisms should be carefully documented. Notes on latitude, longitude, depth, current, surge, water temperature, salinity, and dates of collection should be recorded. Notes on the habitat of collection (e.g., reef face, in crevice, under rock, on bottom side of rock, on front face of rock, on surface of another organism) and any observed interactions with other organisms (being fed upon by nudibranch, overgrown with cyanophyte, dead at edges due to neighboring organism) should be recorded. Careful descriptions of the organisms including color, morphology, consistency, presence of mucus, odor, and reproductive state, if obvious, should be recorded. *In situ* and deckside photography are important for later taxonomic evaluation. The presence of associated organisms both exterior and interior should be noted. It is often common to find worms, molluscs, copepods, brittle stars, anemones, and even small fish living within larger marine invertebrates. Epiphytes and zooanthids are commonly observed in association with marine invertebrates and may affect the chemistry encountered. In many instances, less-experienced collectors may not be able to identify all of the associated organisms, but detailed field notes and carefully prepared vouchers may allow a more experienced taxonomist or field biologist to identify the associated organisms at a later date.

Voucher specimens should be prepared to allow for complete identification. Vouchers are also necessary to document an invention should a patent be filed. Voucher specimens should be representative of the entire specimen. If different color or morphologies of the same species are collected, vouchers of each should be preserved. If specimens are small, a complete specimen should be retained if possible. In our lab, voucher specimens typically fit into 100- to 40-mL jars, dependent on the specimen shape.

Typically, sponges are vouchered by cutting off a representative piece that illustrates both the exterior surface, interior architecture, and overall morphology of the organism. Spicules that are important in the identification of most families of sponges may be localized, and it is necessary to voucher all parts of the sponge. In addition, a single "specimen" can often be an association in which one sponge encrusts or bores into the surface of a second sponge. An example is the Caribbean sponge *Myriastra kalitetilla,* which occurs as a grooved spherical sponge with a red-orange exterior and a cream interior. The red surface is due to a very thin encrusting association by a *Desmacella* sp. Extraction of the red surface layer yields a different suite of compounds than extraction of the cream interior of the "sponge." Sponge voucher specimens are typically stored in 70% aqueous ethanol (30 mL water per 70 mL 100% ethanol). Octocorals and hard corals can be vouchered in the same manner as sponges.

Ascidians and other soft-bodied organisms (e.g., alcyonaceans, anemones, annelids, some brittle stars) are more difficult to preserve. These organisms are relaxed prior to long-term preservation to allow them to remain open after preservation. This is done by placing the voucher specimen into sea water containing a few crystals of menthol. The specimen is then stored overnight in a refrigerator (if possible), and then the sea water is decanted. Ascidians are stored permanently in 10% formalin solution made by diluting "full strength" formaldehyde solution (37%) by 1:10 (1 mL formaldehyde solution per 9 mL water) while other soft-bodied invertebrates (alcyonaceans, anemones, brittle stars) can be stored permanently in 70% ethanol. Colonial ascidians can be very difficult to identify as they are difficult to preserve. It can be of value to obtain exact preservation steps directly from the taxonomist who will identify the specimens. Jellyfish and very soft-bodied echinoderms can be stored indefinitely in 10% formalin solution after relaxation with menthol. These often lose shape rapidly and therefore photo-documentation can be important. Algae are typically stored as dry-pressed specimens but they can also be stored in 5% formalin solution.

If one plans to return the samples to the laboratory aboard a commercial air plane, the transport of large quantities of ethanol is often not allowed. In these instances, the vouchers can be stored in 10% formalin (everything except algae) or 5% formalin (algae) until returned to the laboratory. In our laboratory, when air travel is required, the voucher specimens are placed into WhirlPak® (Nasco) sample bags with 10% formalin solution. These are then stored in sealed dry-pak shipping canisters for transport. Upon return to the lab, they can be transferred to the appropriate preservative for long-term storage.

As with all specimens collected for natural products research, all collections of marine organisms should be made with the informed consent of the host country or state. Permits are required for most collections of marine organisms and come under local and/or federal laws. Some marine species are protected by CITES and cannot be collected or exported without special permits. A review by Baker et al. *(22)* outlines general philosophies and policies with respect to the collection of both terrestrial and marine organisms.

2.3. Storage of Marine Organisms

Marine organisms are often collected at remote places where laboratory facilities are limited. Many die immediately on exposure to air and rapidly begin to decompose. Compounds present in the organisms can be rapidly degraded by oxidative, enzymatic, or polymerization processes, and therefore the organisms need to be either dried, extracted, or frozen immediately to reduce spoilage and chemical degradation. The compounds present in some organisms, such as the Verongid sponges, can begin to degrade and polymerize immediately upon being touched. This is indicated by a rapid color change from white, yellow, or orange to dark blue-black, even when maintained in sea water.

Many groups freeze the organisms at –20°C immediately after collection and store them frozen until further work up can be carried out. In some cases, the organisms are placed into an alcohol such as methanol, ethanol, or isopropanol, and then the preserved organism is stored either at room temperature or in a freezer (*see* **Note 1**). Algae and some gorgonians are often air-dried and then stored either at room temperature or in a freezer until further workup. If facilities are available, the samples can be lyophilized immediately after collection and then stored either at room temperature or in a freezer until further workup (*see* **Note 2**). One group, which works in very limited field-laboratory facilities, immerses the organism in EtOH-H$_2$O (50:50) for approx 24 h. This solution is then decanted and discarded. The organisms are placed in Nalgene bottles and shipped back to the home laboratory at ambient temperature *(23)*.

In our group, organisms are photo-documented, a taxonomic voucher taken, a subsample taken for extraction, field collection and taxonomic notes are recorded, and the remainder of the specimen is frozen at –20°C until further workup (*see* **Note 3**). Every attempt is made to have the specimen in the freezer within 1 h of collection to minimize degradation of the compounds. Where this is not possible, the samples are stored on ice until processing is complete.

3. Extraction
3.1. Invertebrates

A typical extraction scheme for marine invertebrates (frozen, dried, or lyophilized): Invertebrates are cut into small pieces and macerated in a high-speed blender with solvent (*see* **Note 4**). The resulting extracts are filtered either through Whatman no. 1 filter paper (gravity or vacuum), or a bed of Celite 521 packed in a Büchner funnel (*see* **Note 5**). After filtration, the tissue residue (marc) is returned to the blender and extracted with a second portion of solvent. This process is continued until no further color is extracted. In cases where the extracts are colorless, the successive extracts can be concentrated separately and the mass of residue after concentration determined. Extraction can be considered complete when little or no additional residue is obtained after concentration. When following bioassay-guided purification, successive extracts can be concentrated and assayed separately. Extraction is considered complete when no further activity is detected in the extracts. In our lab, samples are extracted three to six times to ensure complete extraction.

Some laboratories prepare successive extracts of each organism using solvents of increasing polarity. This affords some measure of preliminary separation of components. Organisms are first extracted exhaustively with a nonpolar solvent such as diethyl ether, hexanes, ethyl acetate, or a halogenated solvent (dichloromethane, chloroform), then exhaustively with an alcohol (methanol or ethanol), and then exhaustively with water or water-alcohol mixtures. Some groups use acetone for extraction, but care must be taken that adducts are not formed.

Scientists at the National Cancer Institute, US National Institutes of Health have an extensive screening program of natural products to detect compounds with antitumor or anti-HIV properties. They have developed an extraction method in which the frozen organism is ground with dry ice (CO_2) and extracted with H_2O at 4°C. The aqueous extract is removed by centrifugation and lyophilized. The organism residue is also lyophilized. The dry marc is then extracted sequentially with MeOH-CH_2Cl_2 followed by methanol. The organic extracts are combined and dried *in vacuo*. The aqueous and combined organic extracts are then available for assay and subsequent chemical isolation (*see*, for example, Hallock et al. *[24]*).

3.2. Macro Algae

Most researchers air-dry or lyophilize specimens of brown algae (Phaeophyta) and red algae (Rhodophyta) prior to extraction. Specimens of calcareous green algae (Chlorophyta) are sometimes dried prior to extraction but often are not. The dried algae is often ground with a mortar and pestle or ground with a Wiley Mill to pass through a 2-mm sieve. The ground material is then extracted successively with solvents of increasing polarity (hexanes, dichloromethane, methanol) using a Soxhlet extractor. Alternatively, the dried, fresh, or frozen material can be extracted by maceration in a high-speed blender (*see* **Note 4**). The extracts are filtered either by gravity using fluted filter paper (Whatman no. 1) or by vacuum using a Buchner funnel with fritted glass disk. The algal tissue is returned to the blender and extracted again. In both the Soxhlet and blender methods, extraction with each solvent is continued until no further color is extracted. Extracts are concentrated *in vacuo* by distillation under reduced pressure on a rotatory evaporator.

3.3. Outline of Procedure Used in the Author's Laboratory at HBOI

A quick procedure used at HBOI to prepare extracts for biological testing is given below. In this procedure, ethanol is used as the extraction solvent, as it is compatible with the bioassays run in our lab (which include a battery of receptor binding and enzyme assays as well as whole-cell assays). To confirm that ethanol was a suitable extraction solvent, a series of organisms were extracted with methanol, ethanol, or methanol-toluene (3:1). Comparable hit rates were observed for all three sets of extracts when assayed against the P388 tumor cell line, the HSV-1 virus, and the fungal pathogen *Candida albicans*. As ethanol is tolerated better than the other solvents in the assays, it is currently the extraction solvent of choice at HBOI.

Procedure outline:

1. Grind approx 8 g of frozen organism in 20 mL nondenatured 100% ethanol for 2 min, using a Virtis™ grinder.

2. Transfer the extract and organism residue into a 20-mL scintillation vial and steep overnight at –20°C.

3. Filter the extract by gravity through fluted (pleated) filter paper (*see* **Note 5**).

The average concentration of extracts prepared in this manner is 9 mg/mL with a range of 1–20 mg/mL depending on the nature of the organism extracted. Stony organisms, such as Scleractinian corals and Lithistid sponges, tend to give low yields. Extracts are stored at –20°C indefinitely. A TLC comparison of freshly prepared extracts with those that had been prepared by the same procedure 3–5 yr earlier indicated that there was no significant difference in the major components of the extracts after long-term storage.

4. Planning the Isolation Method

The separation system to be used depends to a large extent on the polarity of the compounds of interest. A number of methods can be used to determine the polarity of the natural products present in the extracts. Those used at HBOI include partitioning between aqueous and organic solvents, thin-layer chromatographic analysis with eluents of varying polarity, and small-scale characterization of chromatographic properties. The behavior of biologically active compounds in each method can be followed by bioassay of resultant fractions, or by direct bioautography in the case of TLC.

4.1. Partitioning Schemes

In our lab, extracts are partitioned routinely between *n*-butanol and water. In some instances extracts are partitioned first between ethyl acetate and water and the water phase is subsequently partitioned against *n*-butanol. Nonpolar compounds will partition into the ethyl acetate whereas compounds of intermediate polarity will partition into the *n*-butanol. Water-soluble metabolites usually remain in the aqueous phase. In some cases, partitioning between hexanes or heptane and methanol can be useful to remove lipids from more polar materials prior to chromatography (lipids typically partition into the hexane or heptane phase). A number of groups use a modified Kupchan scheme to assess polarity of the compounds. This involves successive partitioning of the extracts between nonpolar solvents and increasingly aqueous alcohol solutions.

With marine extracts in particular, care must be taken in the interpretation of results of such partitioning experiments. An example that illustrates this is the purification of the dragmacidin d series of compounds. Partitioning of a crude extract between ethyl acetate and water will result in the enrichment by a small amount of dragmacidin d as the major component of the ethyl acetate partition. Bioassay against the fungal pathogen *Cryptococcus neoformans* results in a fairly high activity for this fraction (Minimum inhibitory concentration [MIC] = 6.25 μg/mL). Bioassay of the water partition results in an MIC = 50 μg/mL for this fraction. Based on bioactivity alone, one might assume that the antifungal compound has partitioned fairly cleanly into the ethyl acetate phase. TLC and NMR analyses of the two fractions, however, show that the major component of the ethyl acetate phase is also present in the aqueous phase, but due to the high salt content of the extract and hence of the aqueous phase, the compound is simply present as a lower percentage of the overall fraction. In effect, the activity of the compound has been diluted out due to the enrichment of the salt in the aqueous phase. In fact, the best route of purification of this class of metabolites is either to partition the crude extract between *n*-butanol and water or go directly to vacuum column chromatography (VCC) on a reverse phase stationary phase using a step gradient of acetonitrile-water-trifluroacetic acid. This example illustrates two rules:

1. It is important to compare all fractions by TLC, HPLC, and/or NMR to look for similarities.
2. During bioassay-guided purifications, never discard a fraction until an analytical method is available that distinguishes the active compound(s) from the other components of the mixture. The compounds may be present but their effects masked by other components of the mixture. This is especially important in instances where the supply of organism is limited and recollection is difficult if not impossible. It is important not to waste any of the specimen.

4.2. Solid Phase Extraction

Solid phase extraction provides the opportunity to carry out very small-scale chromatographic separations using a variety of stationary phases (also discussed in Chapter 1). Two separation systems commonly used by this author, which are suitable for most natural products including most marine natural products are as follows:

1. Chromatography of the extract on silica gel using a step gradient of ethyl acetate or a halogenated solvent (CH_2Cl_2, $CHCl_3$, Cl_2CHCH_3) in heptane or hexanes. For example, a typical elution series would be: heptane; ethyl acetate-heptane (1:3 v/v); ethyl acetate-heptane (1:1v/v); ethyl acetate-heptane (3:1 v/v); ethyl acetate; ethyl acetate-methanol (1:1 v/v).
2. A reverse phase separation using a C-18 bonded silica gel. In this case, the column is developed with a step gradient of water-methanol or water-acetonitrile. A typical elution series would be: 100% water; methanol-water (1:3 v/v); methanol-water (1:1 v/v); methanol-water (3:1 v/v); 100% methanol; 100% dichloromethane. For very polar organic soluble compounds (e.g., those that have an R_f of 0.5–0.6 in the *n*-propanol-ethyl acetate-water [7:2:1] TLC system, described below), it can be useful to add 0.1% TFA as an ion-pairing reagent. This eliminates tailing and is useful in the separation of nitrogen-containing heterocycles such as stevensine *(25)*, dragmacidin d *(13)*, and the ecteinascidins *(26)*.

4.3. Bioautography

An excellent method for identifying the bioactive component(s), including their polarity, is bioautography (*see also* Chapters 1 and 7). Although the most common form of bioautography detects antimicrobial compounds *(27)*, the method has also been extended to detect antitumor compounds *(28)*. In bioautography, thin-layer plates of the extracts of interest are placed in contact with agar plates seeded with the microorganism of interest. For bioautography against tumor cell lines, agar overlays are often used. The TLC plate may be removed after a short incubation time or may remain in contact while the assay plate is incubated to allow for growth of the microorganism. After an appropriate incubation time, a zone of growth inhibition will be observed at the R_f values of the active compounds. In the author's laboratory, three thin-layer systems are used to characterize polarity:

1. For nonpolar compounds:ethyl acetate-heptane (1:1) on silica plates.
2. For intermediate polarity compounds: ethyl acetate-methanol (19:1) on silica-gel plates.
3. For polar organic soluble compounds: *n*-propanol-ethyl acetate-water (7:2:1) on silica gel plates.

5. Column Chromatography

Column chromatography is typically the next step after determination of the polarity of the extract components. Nonpolar compounds are usually chromatographed on silica-gel stationary phases. Vacuum column chromatography (VCC) or vacuum flash chromatography can provide a fast and simple first separation of an extract. This can be followed by additional VCC or by HPLC. Both silica-gel and reverse phase packings can be used *(29,30)*.

5.1. Vacuum Column Chromatography

In this method, the column is a Buchner funnel with a medium-porosity fritted glass disk. A piece of filter paper is cut to fit flat into the bottom of the funnel. The stationary phase is then poured in. TLC-grade silica gel can be used for normal phase separations (EM Science Kieselgel 60H is used in the author's laboratory), whereas reverse phase separations require column-chromatography grade reverse phase packings (40–63 μm). A number of reverse packings are commercially available, but the author's group prepares their own reverse phase packings using a modification of the method published by Evans et al. *(31)* (*see* **Note 6**).

After addition of the stationary phase, the funnel is tapped lightly on the countertop to allow the stationary phase to settle uniformly. Normal phase silica gel will settle substantially (to approximately half its original depth); reverse phase packings will not. If additional height of the column is desired, more packing material can be added at this stage and then tapped again to settle the column. The funnel is then placed onto the top of a vacuum flask fitted with a rubber vacuum seal and a vacuum applied. The stationary phase will again settle. The top surface is tamped down using a small vial or beaker with a flat bottom. It is important to tamp down the edges to make sure the packing is uniformly thick. If the edges are not well-tamped down, the extract will simply run down the edges of the glass and will not adsorb to the column packing. With reverse phase packings, it is difficult to get the top surface completely flat, as the packing is very flocculant. This will not affect the separation as long as the column has been firmly tamped down.

The column is then pre-equilibrated with the first solvent in the elution series. Enough solvent is put through the column to completely wet the column (e.g., for a 60-mL column, put through approx 75–100 mL). Release the vacuum before the column goes dry and pour off the wash solvent. It is very important that the column not be allowed to go dry at this point. Allowing reverse phase columns to go dry at this point can lead to "icing up" of the column and extremely slow flow rates.

For separations on silica gel, the extract is applied as a solution in the first eluent. If it will not go into solution in this solvent, a small amount of a more polar solvent can be added to bring it into solution. It is important not to add too much of the more polar solvent or the compounds may elute in the first fraction rather than adsorb to the column. It is acceptable to have some materials that are not completely in solution, as long as they can be suspended and transferred to the column. If a significant quantity of material is not soluble, it may be necessary either to:

1. Carry out a rough polarity separation by partitioning the extract between heptane/methanol, CH_2Cl_2/water, or n-BuOH/water prior to VCC, or;
2. Begin the separation with a more polar eluent (e.g., 25% ethyl actetate-75% heptane).

For reverse phase VCC, the extract is often applied as a slurry preadsorbed onto the stationary phase. This can be done by dissolving the extract in methanol and then adding 2–20 g of stationary phase. The solution is swirled to make sure that the packing is well-coated. The methanol is removed *in vacuo*, and the first eluent (typically water) is added to form a slurry. The slurry is poured onto the top of the column after applying a vacuum to the column.

The column is then eluted with portions of solvent of increasing or decreasing polarity (a step gradient). Typical step gradients used in our lab include:

1. Silica-gel stationary phases: 100% heptane, 20% ethyl acetate-80% heptane; 40% ethyl acetate-60% heptane; 60% ethyl acetate-40% heptane; 80% ethyl acetate-20% heptane; 100% ethyl acetate; 25% methanol-75% ethyl acetate; 50% methanol-50% ethyl acetate; 100% methanol. For less polar compounds such as many compounds from the red alga *Laurencia*, a step gradient using 20% steps of dichloromethane in heptane can be used.

2. Reverse phase (RP-18) stationary phases: 100% H_2O, 80% H_2O-20% Acetonitrile (ACN); 60% H_2O-40% ACN; 40% H_2O-60% ACN, 20% H_2O- 80% ACN; 100% ACN, 100% MeOH. For compounds with basic functionality, addition of 0.1% by volume of TFA can greatly improve the separation.

It is important that a vacuum be applied to the column prior to pouring any solvent onto the column. If no vacuum is applied, the top surface of the column may be deeply grooved on addition of the solvent. This will greatly affect the separation. A piece of filter paper can be placed on the top of the column after the sample has been applied, to help minimize channeling in the column.

6. Other Factors that Can Complicate Marine Natural Products Isolations

6.1. Taxonomic Uncertainty

Although knowledge of the taxonomy of the organism does not always assist in defining the best purification scheme for new metabolites, incorrect or incomplete taxonomic assignments can lead to difficulties if assumptions are made about the chemistry that an organism may contain. Taxonomic identification of many species, especially sponges and colonial ascidians, can be extremely difficult. In some instances, different taxonomists have identified the same sponge with different species (and even genus) names. Application of molecular taxonomic methods is clarifying this field, but in some instances this can lead to a change in both the name and the overall classification of an organism. As can be imagined, this has complicated the chemical literature. One example is the sponge *Verongia aerophoba,* which is now called *Pseudoceratina crassa.* A search of the chemical databases based on the new name may not reveal the majority of the references for this organism, which were published under the original taxonomic classification.

6.2. Purification of Water-Soluble Compounds; Effects of Salt

Water-soluble marine natural products provide an interesting isolation challenge. These compounds are typically purified by chromatography on the basis of ion exchange, molecular weight, and/or adsorption on nonfunctionalized resins *(32).* The presence of large quantities of inorganic salts can present significant difficulties in the isolation of low-molecular-weight compounds as no simple universal method for desalting small molecular-weight compounds exists. Repetitive trituration with methanol or other alcohols can be effective if the compound has alcohol solubility. In some cases Sephadex G-10, Bio-Gel P-2, nonionic resins, such as Amberlite XAD-2 or XAD-7, or active charcoal can be used. The isolation of water-soluble compounds is covered in Chapter 11.

An example of the isolation of a low-molecular-weight water-soluble compound is 3-amino-1-(2-aminoimidazolyl)-prop-1-ene (**Scheme 3**), isolated

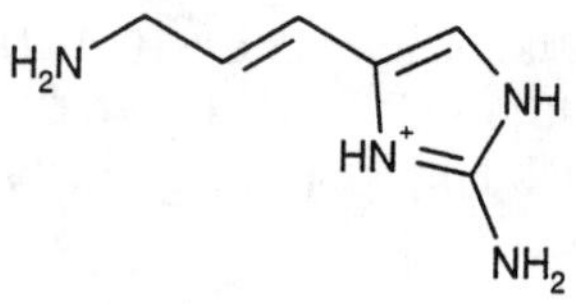

Scheme 3. 3-Amino-1-(2-aminoimidazoyl)-prop-1-ene.

from the sponge *Teichaxinella morchella* *(25)*. The frozen sponge was extracted exhaustively with methanol. After concentration, the methanol extract was partitioned between *n*-butanol and water. The water partition was chromatographed on BioRex-70, a weak cation-exchange resin, using 0.2 *N* AcOH as eluent. Chromatography was monitored by thin-layer chromatography (silica gel:*n*-BuOH-AcOH-H_2O 4:1:1) with detection of compound by reaction with ninhydrin. In all cases, small amounts of inorganic salts remained in the material, making it impossible to determine true bioactivity values. Fortunately, in this instance, the presence of salts in the sample did not hinder the NMR analysis of the compound.

6.3. Polyamines

A number of marine organisms, particularly sponges, contain large-molecular-weight cationic polymeric amines that show activity in a variety of bioassays. The most common of these is halitoxin (**Scheme 4**), which was first reported from *Amphimedon compressa* (formerly called *Haliclona rubens*). Polyamines have also been isolated from *Cinachyra* sp., *Hispidopetra* sp., and *Desmacidon* sp. (Wright, unpublished results). Typically these sponges contain a series of compounds with molecular weights ranging from 1000 to over 25,000 amu. The compounds are difficult to separate and tend to tail significantly when chromatographed on most reverse phase and normal phase stationary phases. Some success has been observed using cation-exchange resins and molecular-weight separations on LH-20 (for methanol-soluble halitoxins) or Sephadex G-200 (water-soluble compounds). CCC using *n*-BuOH/H_2O/AcOH (4:4:1, BuOH mobile phase) or *n*-BuOH/H_2O (1:1, *n*-BuOH mobile phase) has also been used. Ultrafiltration was found to be the most effective method to purify halitoxin *(33)*.

6.4. Polar Sulfate Ester-Containing Compounds

Many marine organisms contain compounds that possess a sulfate ester functionality. These compounds tend to be active in a number of receptor binding and enzyme bioassays and can often be difficult to purify. They tend to occur as a series of closely related compounds that are both very polar and labile to acid or base treatment. Perhaps the most commonly occurring sulfate ester is halistanol sulfate (**Scheme 5**), first reported from *Halichondria* cf. *moorei* *(34)*.

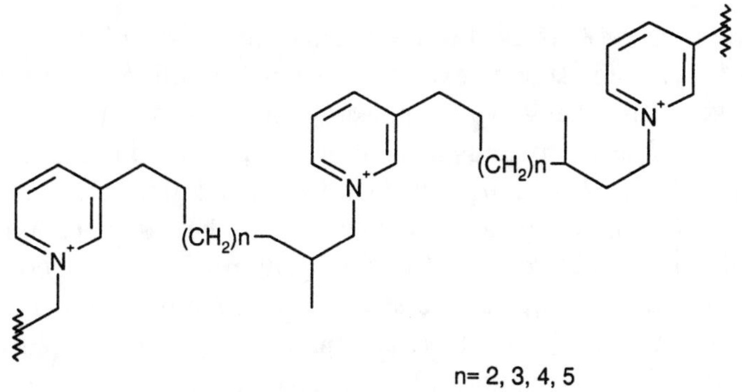

n= 2, 3, 4, 5

Scheme 4. Halitoxin (*n* = 2, 3, 4, 5).

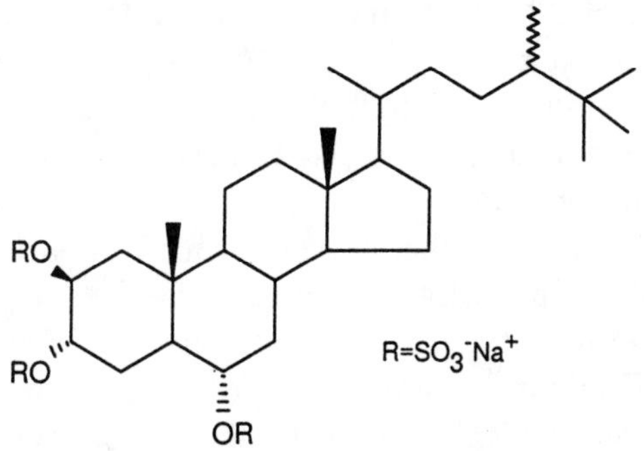

R=SO$_3^-$Na$^+$

Scheme 5. Halistanol sulfate (R = SO$_3^-$Na$^+$).

This compound also occurs in a number of related Haplosclerid sponges, such as *Topsentia* spp., *Monanthus ciocalyptoides*, *Foliolina* sp., and *Xestospongia* spp., as well as from *Aaptos* sp., *Trachyopsis* sp., and two species of *Pseudaxynissa* *(35)*. Halistanol sulfate was purified by successive chromatography of the water-soluble portion of an aqueous ethanol extract using a TSK G3000S gel, silica gel, and a Sephadex LH-20 stationary phase. Antimicrobial fractions from the LH-20 separation were further purified by recrystallization from EtOH-H$_2$O.

These sterol sulfate esters show activity in a number of enzyme and receptor-binding assays and are also active in the anti-HIV screen run at the US National Cancer Institute. A dereplication scheme for this class of compounds has been published by Cardellina et al. *(36)*, in which extracts are chromatographed in three systems: Sephadex G-25 for molecular weight; C4 wide pore (300); and C18 narrow pore (60 Å). Fractions are assayed against HIV and the patterns of activity compared to that observed for halistanol sulfate. Sterol sulfates from six sponge extracts were eluted with methanol:H$_2$O (2:1 v/v) and allowed for the rapid dereplication of this class of compound. In the author's lab, TLC is used to dereplicate for halistanol sulfate and related compounds. A crude sponge extract or butanol partition is chromatographed on silica-gel plates using *n*-propanol-ethyl acetate-water (7:2:1 v/v/v) as the mobile phase. The compounds have an R_f of approx 0.5 and turn dark purple when sprayed with 2% vanillin in sulfuric-acid solution followed by heating. Many of these compounds are associated with a heterocyclic amine counterion, which turns bright yellow after visualization with the reagent.

A number of aromatic sulfate esters have been reported. These include 34-sulfatobastadin-13 sulfate *(37)*, aplysillin a *(38)*, *bis*(sulfato)cyclosiphonodictyol a *(39)*, and siphonodictyol g *(20)*. Most of these compounds were isolated by repeated chromatography on LH-20 using methanol as the eluent. In our experience, many sulfated metabolites tend to be retained on LH-20 stationary phases for 10–15 column volumes. Late elution of an active metabolite from LH-20 packings may be indicative of sulfate functionality in the molecule. A strong absorption at 1250 cm^{-1} in the IR spectrum can also be used initially to confirm the presence of sulfate ester functionality.

Another class of compound that can be difficult to purify is the saponins found in Echinoderms. Almost all echinoderms examined to date contain either polyhydroxylated sterols or terpene glycosides, many of which contain sulfate ester functionality. The purification of compounds (**Schemes 6–9**) *(40)* from the starfish *Nardoa tuberculata* exemplifies the procedure most often used to purify these metabolites (**Fig. 2**).

The animals (1.85 kg) were chopped and soaked in H_2O (twice, 2 L for 8 h each). The combined aqueous extracts were settled and after centrifugation passed through a column of 1 kg Amberlite XAD-2. The column was first washed with 1 L H_2O and then eluted with 2 L methanol to yield 3.24 g of crude extract, after concentration of the methanol eluate. This extract was chromatographed on a Sephadex LH-60 column (4 × 100 cm), using MeOH-H_2O (2:1) as eluent (flow rate approx 10 mL/h); 5-mL fractions were collected and monitored by TLC (Si plates; *n*-BuOH-HOAc-H_2O (12:3:5), detected by ceric sulfate/H_2SO_4). Fractions 125–200 from Sephadex LH-60 were submitted to dccc using $CHCl_3$-MeOH-H_2O (7:13:8) ascending mode, lower phase as stationary. Fractions were once again monitored by TLC as above and combined accordingly. Early fractions (1–61) from the dccc separation were further separated by a second dccc separation using *n*-BuOH-Me_2CO-H_2O (3:1:5) ascending mode, lower phase as stationary phase (flow = 10 mL/min). Fractions were monitored by TLC and then submitted to HPLC on a C18 μ-Bondapak column (30 cm × 7.8 mm) with MeOH-H_2O (55:45) (5 mL/min flow rate) to afford pure compounds (**Schemes 6–9**) (yields: 6, 2, 2, and 3 mg, respectively).

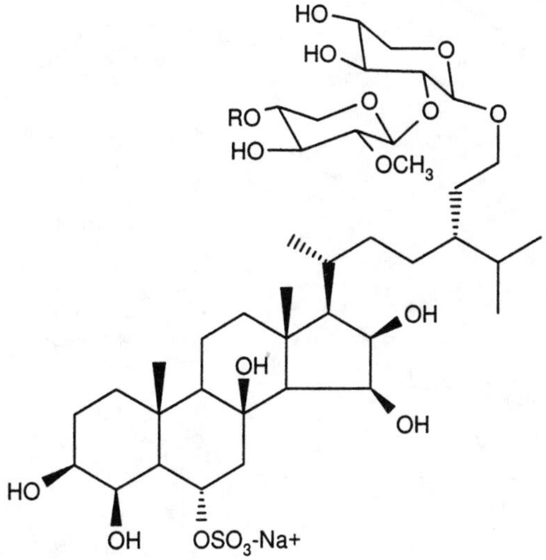

Schemes 6–8. Scheme 6, R = H; Scheme 7, R = CH$_3$; Scheme 8, R = H, Δ^{22E}.

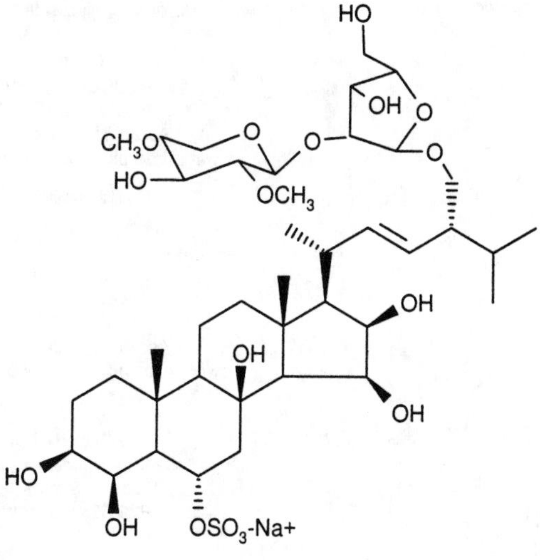

Scheme 9.

6.5. Complex Mixtures of Polar Metabolites: The Ptilomycalins/ Crambescidins/Batzelladines

A series of complex pentacyclic guanidines linked by a linear ω-hydroxy fatty acid to a spermidine or hydroxy spermidine unit have been reported from the sponges *Ptilocaulis spiculifer* *(41)*, *Hemimycale* sp. *(42)*, *Crambe crambe*

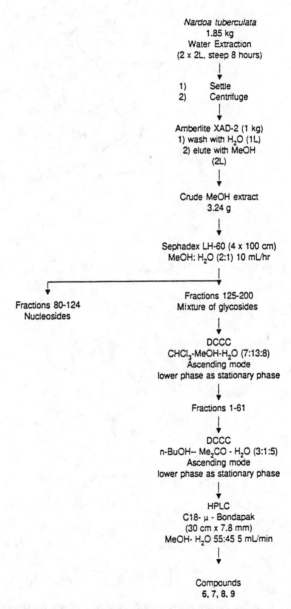

Fig. 2. Purification scheme for Echinoderm saponins (**Schemes 6–9**).

(43,44), *Batzella* sp. *(45)*, and *Monanchora arbuscula (46)*, and also from the starfish *Fromia monilis* and *Celerina heffernani (47)*. These compounds are very polar and can exist as mixtures that are difficult to separate. The majority of the

compounds lack a significant chromophore complicating the HPLC separation requiring that less-sensitive methods such as refractive-index-based detection must be used.

The complexity of the purification is exemplified by the scheme used to purify ptilocaulin (**Scheme 10**), ptilocaulin ester (**Scheme 11**), ptilomycalin (**Scheme 12**), crambescidin 800 (**Scheme 13**), crambescidin 816 (**Scheme 14**), crambescin a (**Scheme 15**), and batzellidines a–e (**Schemes 16–20**), all from a large collection of *Batzella* sp. *(45)* (**Fig. 3**). Crude extracts of this sponge inhibited binding of HIVgp-120 to CD4 and all fractionation was followed using this assay. The freeze-dried sponge was extracted with methanol and the extract triturated successively with ethyl acetate, dichloromethane, and methanol. The bioactive dichloromethane fraction was chromatographed on Sephadex LH-20 using a mixture of methanol/dichloromethane/hexane (1:1:1). The active fractions were then taken on through silica-gel chromatography using a gradient of methanol/CH_2Cl_2/H_2O/AcOH. Fractions were monitored by TLC and similar fractions combined. These were then further purified by either PTLC or repetitive silica-gel chromatography using complex solvent mixtures (e.g., acetone/methanol/dichloromethane/water/acetic acid 30:20:50: 2.5:3.5). Other approaches to the purification of this class of compound included the use of DCCC (*n*-BuOH-Me$_2$CO-H$_2$O [45:15:75], descending mode, monitored by TLC [*n*-BuOH-AcOH-H$_2$O 60:15:25, Dragendorff spray reagent]), followed by Sephadex LH-20 (MeOH) and Biogel P2 (H$_2$O-EtOH 8:2) *(43)*.

This series of compounds also serves to illustrate the level of complexity that can be encountered in the marine natural products literature. Ptylomycalin was first reported from two different sponges, *Ptilocaulis spiculifer* and *Hemimycale* sp. The voucher specimen of *P. spiculifer* was re-evaluated and found to be identical to the *Batzella* sp. studied by Patil et al. *(45)*, and the taxonomy has been revised *(46)*. In addition, the presence of this series of related compounds in the sponge genera *Batzella*, *Crambe*, and *Monanchora* has led Tavares et al. *(46)* to propose a closer taxonomic relationship than previously accepted for these three genera. The recent publication of the compounds in a different phylum (Echinodermata) and the impact of this on the chemotaxonomic questions have yet to be addressed. It is possible that the compounds isolated from the starfish are derived from a sponge diet.

6.6. Compounds with pH-Sensitive Chromatographic Properties— Polyacridine Alkaloids

A series of brightly colored polyacridine alkaloids have been isolated from marine sponges of the family Pachastrellidae *(48)*, an unidentified ascidian *(49)*, and ascidians of the genus *Cystodytes (48)* and *Eudistoma (50)*. These

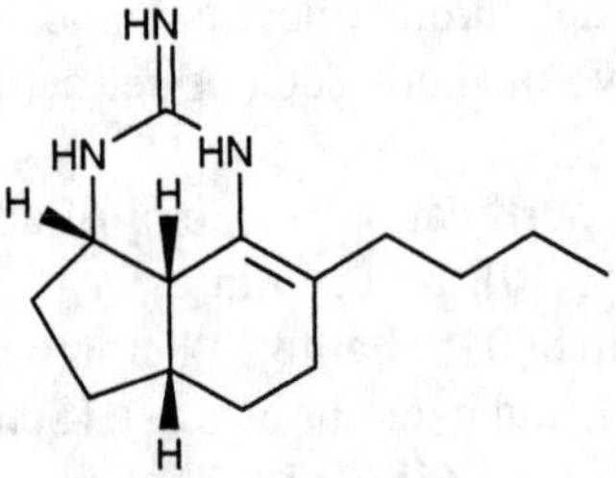

Scheme 10. Ptilocaulin.

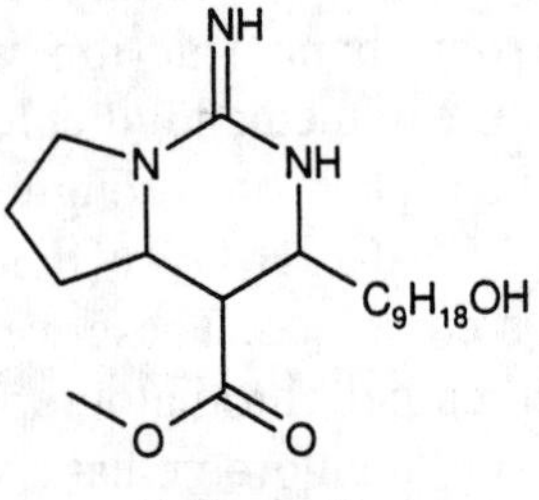

Scheme 11.

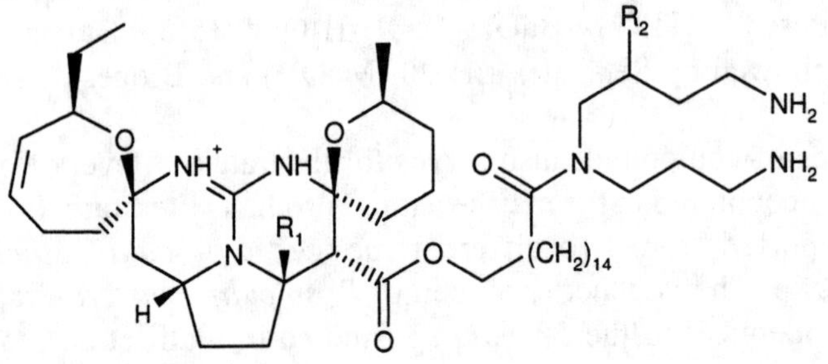

Scheme 12–14. Scheme 12, $R_1 = R_2 = H$; Scheme 13, $R_1 = H$, $R_2 = OH$; Scheme 14, $R_1 = R_2 = OH$.

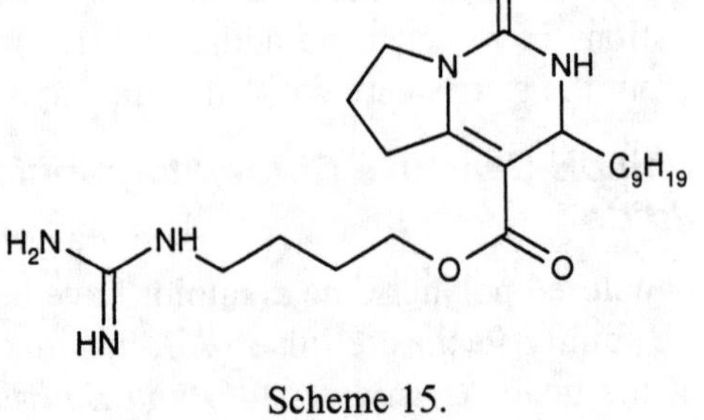

Scheme 15.

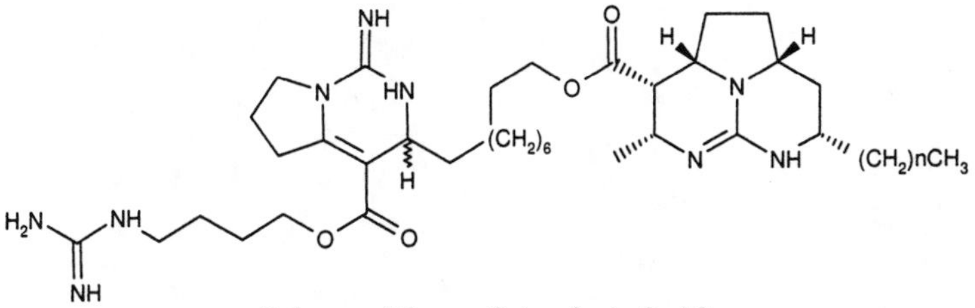

Scheme 16. $n = 8$ (major), 9, 10.

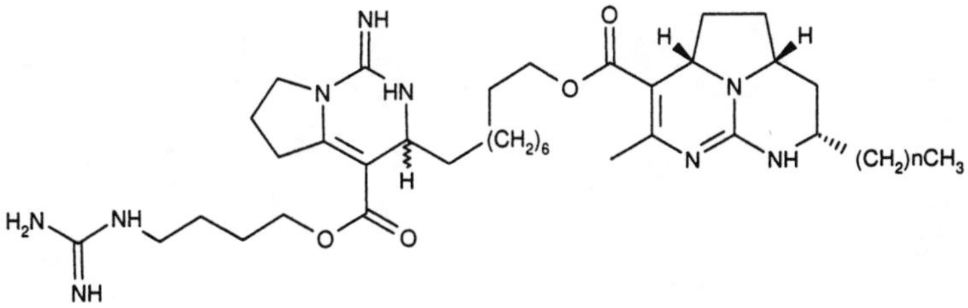

Scheme 17. $n = 6$ (major), 7, 8.

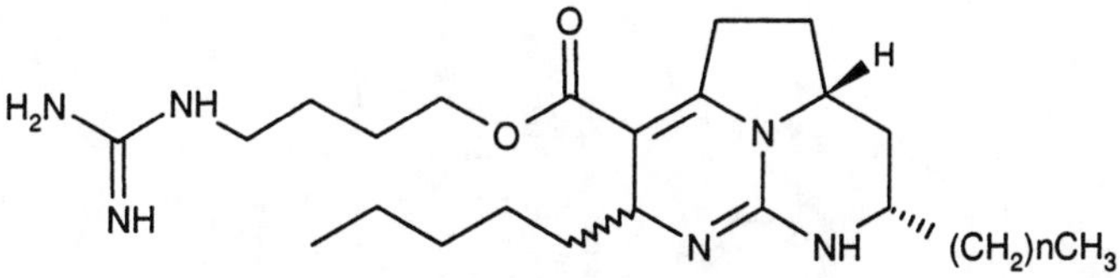

Scheme 18. $n = 6$ (major), 9, 10.

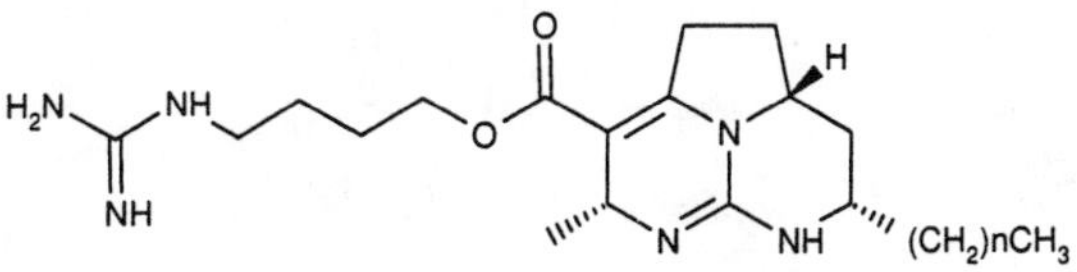

Scheme 19. $n = 8$ (major), 9, 10.

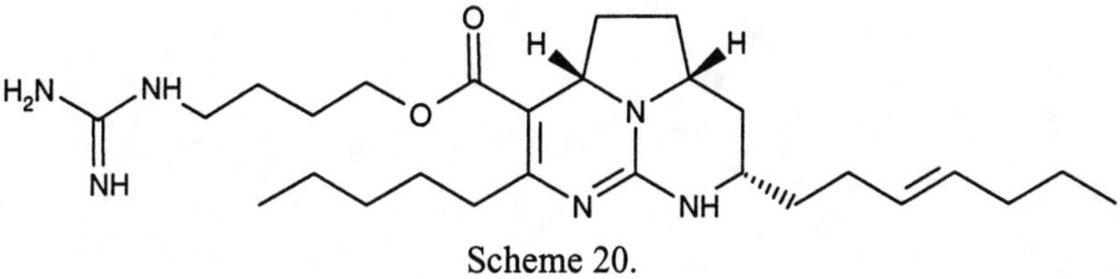

Scheme 20.

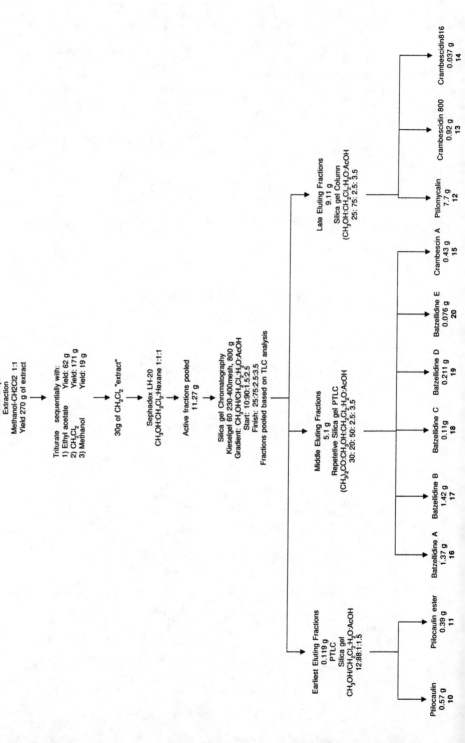

compounds can be difficult to separate on RP-18 or silica-gel stationary phases as they are extremely susceptible to small changes in pH, causing tailing in many chromatographic systems. Purification of the compounds has utilized centrifugal countercurrent chromatography, selective precipitation after simple LH-20 chromatography, and HPLC on ODS and amino stationary phases (**Fig. 4**).

A methanol-toluene extract of a deep-water sponge of the genus *Dercitus* was found to inhibit growth of P388 murine leukemia cells *(51)*. The frozen sponge was extracted with either methanol or dichloromethane containing 5% NH_4OH to yield a dark purple extract. Fractionation of the crude extract by centrifugal CCC using MeOH:CH_2Cl_2:H_2O (5:5:3) gave pure dercitin (**Scheme 21**) as a dark maroon pigment. Further fractionation of CCC fractions that contained minor related components (TLC and NMR analysis) was achieved using HPLC on an amino stationary phase with CH_3CN:MeOH:CH_2Cl_2 (4:4:1) as eluant to yield nordercitin (**Scheme 22**), dercitamine (**Scheme 23**), dercitamide (= kuanoniamine c) (**Scheme 24**), and cyclodercitin (**Scheme 25**).

The ascidian *Cystodytes* sp. was the source of kuanoniamine D (**Scheme 26**) and dercitamide (**Scheme 24**). In this approach to the purification, the ascidian was extracted successively with hexane, followed by CH_2Cl_2-MeOH (1:2) *(48)*. Chromatography of the combined crude extract on Sephadex LH-20 using MeOH as eluant yielded two fractions. The first fraction was concentrated to a gum, washed with $CHCl_3$, and redissolved in MeOH at 45°C. After sitting at room temperature, a purple solid precipitated. The solid was dissolved in water and the solution basified with 1% NaOH to pH 9.0. At this point, a yellow solid precipitated, which could be chromatographed by HPLC on an RP-18 stationary phase with MeOH-H_2O (20:1) as eluant to yield kuanoniamine D (**Scheme 26**) and dercitamide (**Scheme 24**). The second fraction from LH-20 chromatography was dissolved in warm MeOH and, after cooling, debromoshermilamine (**Scheme 27**) was obtained as a purple precipitate.

The acid-base characteristics of the compounds were used to advantage in the purification of the kuanoniamines a (**Scheme 28**), b (**Scheme 29**), and d (**Scheme 26**), by Caroll and Scheuer *(49)* (**Fig. 4**). An unidentified ascidian was extracted first with methanol and then with $CHCl_3$-MeOH (1:1) containing 1% of a 30% NH_4OH solution. The extracts were combined and concentrated to an aqueous residue, which was acidified with 1 M hydrochloric acid and partitioned against $CHCl_3$. The aqueous phase was basified with 10% NH_4OH and partitioned against chloroform. The basic $CHCl_3$ extract was then concentrated and the residue chromatographed on a silica-gel cartridge column with $CHCl_3$-MeOH (8:2) as eluant. HPLC of the active fractions using an

---

Fig. 3. *(opposite)* Purification scheme for the Ptilocaulin/Crambescidin class of guanidine alkaloids.

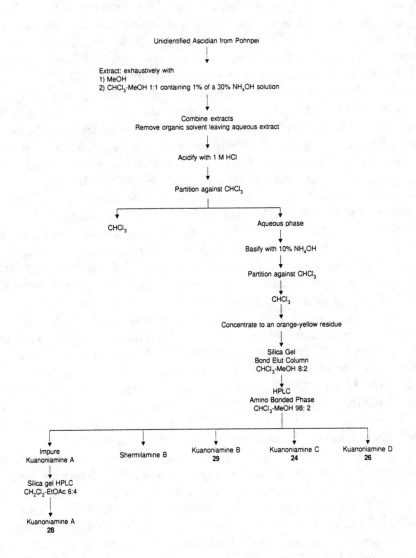

Fig. 4. Isolation of Pyridinoacridine alkaloids; Kouaniamune A–D.

amino-bonded phase and CHCl$_3$-MeOH (98:2) as eluant led to pure shermilamine b and kuanoniamines b–d. A semipure fraction of kuanoniamine A from the amino separation was further purified by HPLC on a silica stationary phase with CH$_2$Cl$_2$-

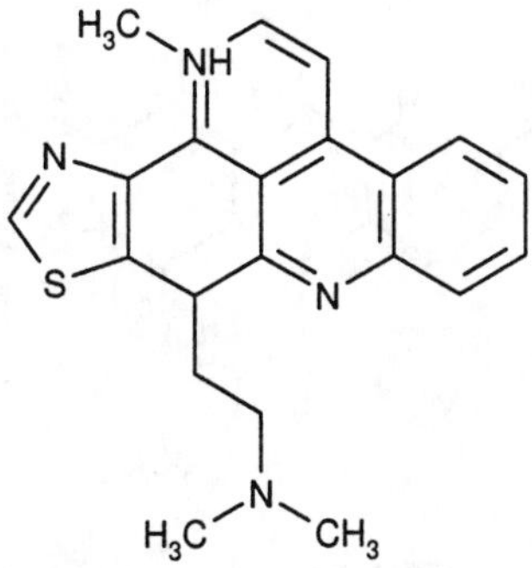

Scheme 21. Dercitin.

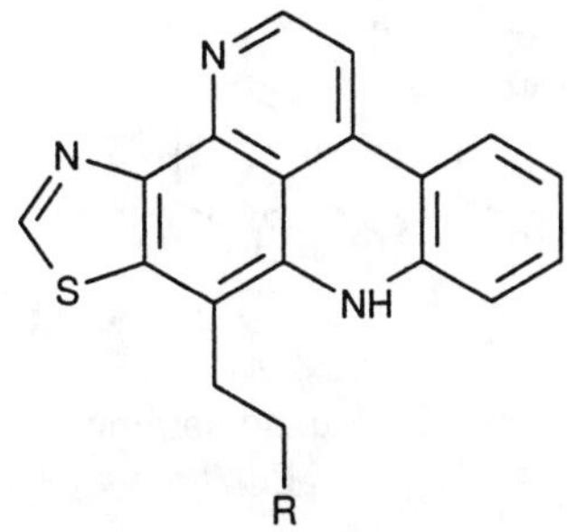

Schemes 22–24, 26, and 29. Scheme 22, R = N(CH$_3$)$_2$; Scheme 23, R = NHCH$_3$; Scheme 24, R = NHCOC$_2$H$_5$; Scheme 26, R = NHCOCH$_3$; Scheme 29, R = NHCOCH$_2$CH(CH$_3$)$_2$.

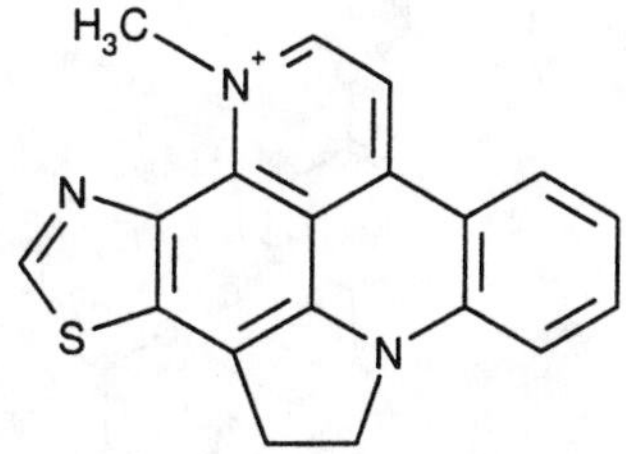

Scheme 25. Cyclodercitin.

EtOAc (6:4) as eluant to yield pure kuanoniamine A. These metabolites were also isolated from a mollusk *Chelynotus semperi*, which was observed to eat the ascidian.

6.7. Exceptionally Trace Metabolites—The Spongistatins

A series of extremely potent antitumor macrolides, known as the spongistatins, have been reported from four different sponges, *Spongia* sp. *(52)*,

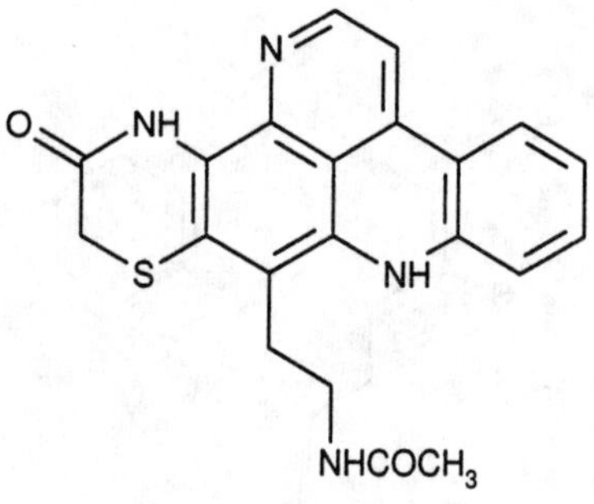

Scheme 27. Debromoshermilamine.

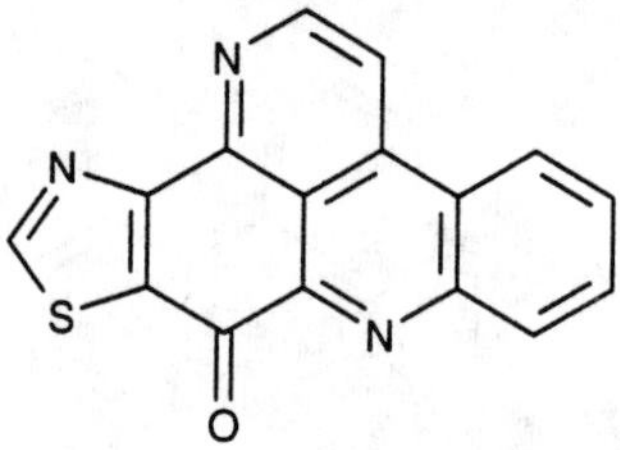

Scheme 28. Kuanoniamine a.

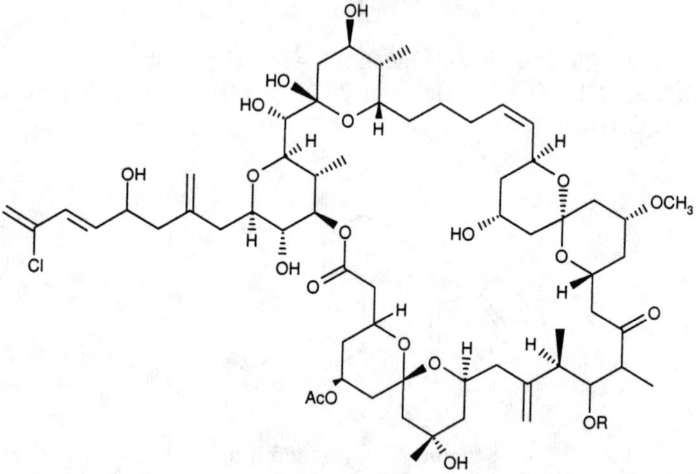

Schemes 30 and 31. Scheme 30, R = OAc; Scheme 31, R = H.

Spirastrella spinispirulifera (53), *Hyrtios altrum (54)*, and *Cinachyra* sp. *(55)*. These compounds are present as very trace metabolites. The first compound in the series, spongistatin 1 (**Scheme 30**), was reported from a *Spongia* sp. collected from the Republic of the Maldives *(52)*. The isolation was bioassay-guided and exceptionally complex. Over 400 kg of wet sponge mass were processed, providing extra challenges to the scientist. Although the reported details are somewhat sketchy, the isolation began with extraction of the fresh or frozen sponge using methanol followed by CH_2Cl_2-MeOH. This extract was then partitioned between methanol-water 9:1 and hexane and then the aqueous phase adjusted to MeOH-H_2O 3:2 and partitioned with dichloromethane. This dichloromethane fraction is the starting point for a series of chromatographic experiments including a series of steric exclusion and partition-chromatography steps on Sephadex LH-20, partition chromatography on silica gel, and (ultimately) HPLC using a Prepex 5–20 μM, C8 column eluted with ACN-MeOH-H_2O (5:5:7) to yield 13.8 mg of spongistatin (3.4 × 10^{-7}% yield). The compound is extremely active against a subset of chemoresistant tumor types with GI_{50} values typically in the range of 2.5–3.5 × 10^{-11} M.

In the isolation of spongistatin 4 (**Scheme 31**), the CH_2Cl_2 fraction from 2409 kg of *Spirastrella spinispirulifera* was initially separated by HPLC employing a pilot scale HPLC system on a silica-gel column, 3 × 0.15 m, operated at 150 psi. This was followed by a series of Sephadex LH-20 separations and multiple HPLC steps using the following columns: Merck RP-2, Prepex- RP-8, and LiChrospher 100 RP-18 to yield 10.7 mg of spongistatin 4 *(53)*.

Kobayashi et al. isolated spongistatin 1 (originally called altohytrin a) from the sponge *Hyrtios altum (54)*. The isolation procedure included acetone extraction of 112 kg of the fresh sponge. This extract was partitioned between water and EtOAc with the activity remaining in the EtOAc phase. Repeated silica-gel column chromatography and HPLC of the active ethyl acetate fraction led to the isolation of 0.5 mg of spongistatin 1 (altohytrin A). Because of the brevity of the communication, exact chromatography conditions were not reported.

Fusetani et al. isolated spongistatin 4 (**Scheme 31**) (cinachyrolide a) from a sponge of the genus *Cinachyra (55)* (**Fig. 5**). In their procedure, 6.6 kg of the fresh sponge were diced and then extracted with ethanol followed by acetone. The combined extracts were concentrated and then partitioned between Et_2O and water. After concentration, the ethereal extract was partitioned between 90% aqueous methanol and hexane. The aqueous methanol phase was then subjected to flash chromatography on an ODS stationary phase using a methanol/water step gradient as eluant. Active fractions from this separation were then successively chromatographed using three different HPLC systems: CapCall Pak C18 AG120-5 with gradient elution (50–80% MeOH/H_2O (v/v); Cosmosil 5C18-AR with isocratic elution using 40% MeCN/H_2O (v/v); Cosmosil 5C18-AR with isocratic elution using 70% MeOH/H_2O (v/v). The final yield of spongistatin 4 was 1.1 mg (1.8 × 10^{-5}% of wet weight).

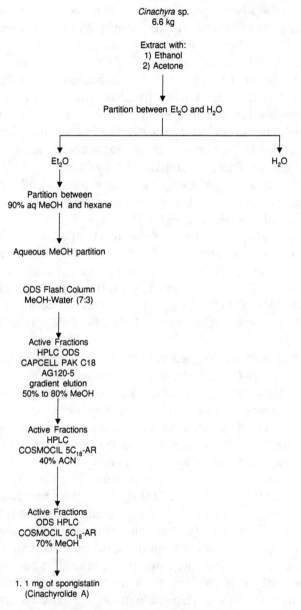

Fig. 5. Isolation flowchart for Spongistatin 1(Cinachyrolide A).

6.8. Microbial Production of Plant- or Invertebrate-Derived Metabolites

The extremely trace nature of compounds such as the spongistatins, as well as their presence in taxonomically unrelated organisms collected from different geographic locations, suggest that these compounds may have a common dietary, or associated microorganism source. Debate continues as to the true source organism of many compounds that have been isolated from marine invertebrates *(56)*. In general, if a marine natural product meets one or more of the following criteria, a microorganism source of the compound can be suspected:

1. The presence of the same or closely related compounds in multiple phyla in instances in which a predator/prey relationship cannot be established for the organisms. The isolation of pyridinoacridine alkaloids, such as dercitamide (**Scheme 24**), from both the sponge *Dercitus* sp. and the ascidian *Cystodytes (47)* is an example of this.
2. Structural similarity of the compounds to known microbial products. An example of this is ecteinascidin 729 (**Scheme 32**), derived from the ascidian *Ecteinascidia turbinata (26)*. This compound is structurally similar to the actinomycete-produced saframycin a (**Scheme 33**) and related compounds *(57)*.
3. Extremely low yield of compound. Both the ecteinascidins and the spongistatins are examples of this.

Likely exceptions to these "rules" are compounds that have relatively simple biosyntheses, as it is possible that phylogenetically different organisms could have given rise to convergent evolution of simple pathways (i.e., simple indole alkaloids and terpenes). Because of the difficulty of isolating and culturing symbiotic marine microorganisms, failure to culture a microorganism that produces the compound cannot be taken as strong evidence for invertebrate production of the metabolite. A primary goal of research within a number of groups is to define culture conditions for microorganisms associated with marine plants and invertebrates *(58,59)*. Until this is accomplished, other methods must be used to define the organism responsible for production of the metabolites.

Localization of compounds within sponge cells have been successfully carried out by a number of groups *(60–63)*. In these studies, the compounds were found within the spherolous or choanocyte cells of sponges. In most of these studies, the presence of endosymbionts was ruled out by light or electron microscopy; it was therefore concluded that the compounds are produced by the sponge itself.

Cell types are separated by first dissociating the sponge in calcium- and magnesium-free sea water (CMF-ASW), followed by differential centrifugation on a discontinuous Ficoll (cesium chloride) or Percoll gradient. For example, Thompson et al. *(60)* separated cells of *Aplysina fistularis* using a 5-mL centrifuge tube to which 0.5-mL solutions of 30, 25, 20, 15, and 10% Ficoll in CMF-ASW were sequentially added bottom to top. After centrifugation at 1000 rpm for a set of period of time, cells are pelleted out at the interface between successive densities. They are then aspirated with a pipet and after rinsing, the cells are extracted and analyzed for the presence of metabolites. In this way, the differing sponge cell types can be separated from bacterial components.

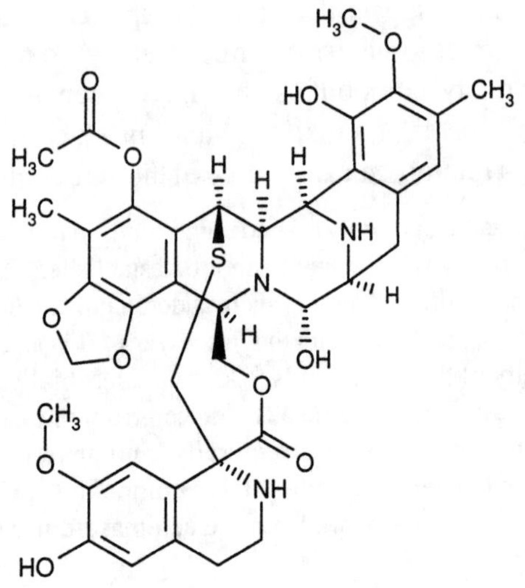

Scheme 32. Esteinascidin 729.

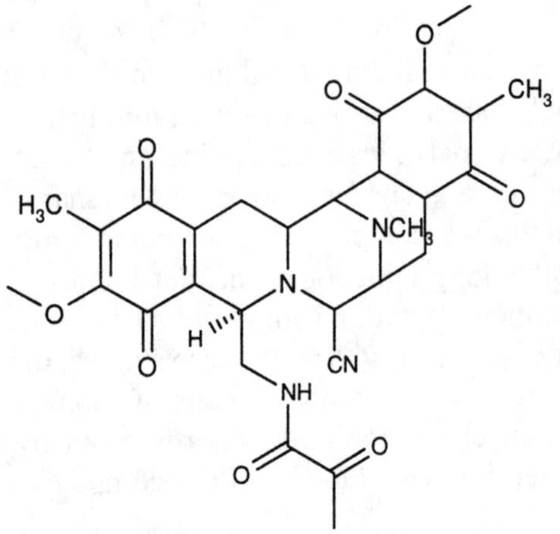

Scheme 33. Saframycin a.

A different approach was used by Bewley et al. *(64)* to localize metabolites of the Lithistid sponge *Theonella swinhoei*. *T. swinhoei* has four distinct cell populations: sponge cells, unicellular heterotrophic bacteria, unicellular cyanobacteria, and filamentous heterotrophic bacteria. This sponge contains two major compounds: swinholide a **(Scheme 34)**, which is related structurally to scytophycin c; a cyanobacterial metabolite; and peptide-P951 **(Scheme 35)**, which contains AHMP (3-amino-4-hydroxy-6-methyl-8-phenylocta-5,7-

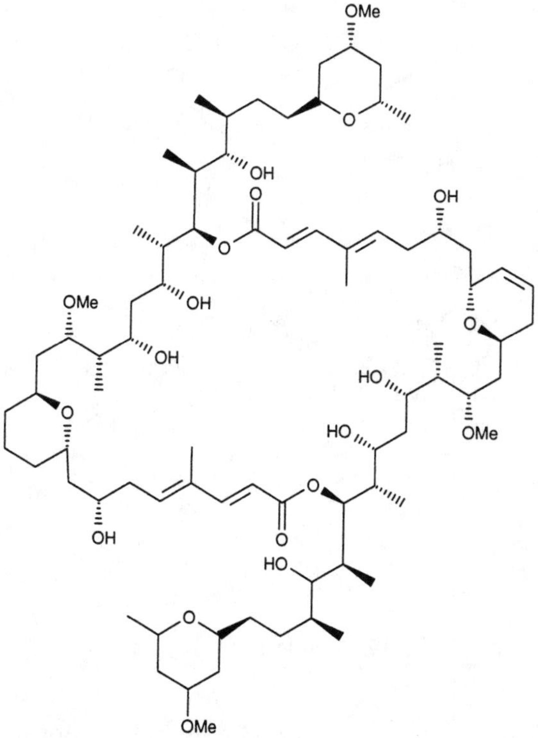

Scheme 34. Swinholide a.

dienoic acid), an amino acid that is similar to ADDA, found in cyanobacterial metabolites such as the microcystins.

In *T. swinhoei*, the cyanobacteria are localized in the ectosome of the sponge, and the filamentous heterotrophic bacteria are localized in the endosome of the sponge. Gross dissection of the endosome from the ectosome followed by differential centrifugation of the dissociated sponge led to separation of the four cell types. Filamentous bacteria could be pelleted by centrifugation at 200*g* for 5 min. The sponge cells could be pelleted by centrifugation at 600*g* for 5 min. The supernatant after these centrifugations contained >95% unicellular bacteria. The cyanobacteria could be pelleted by centrifugation at 1000*g* for 7 min. TLC, HPLC, and NMR analyses of the separated cell types indicated that swinholide a was localized in a mixed population of heterotrophic unicellular bacteria, whereas the peptide P951 was localized in the filamentous heterotrophic bacteria. Neither compound was associated with sponge cells.

In a third approach at localization of metabolites, flow cytometry was used to separate cell types of the sponge *Dysidea herbacea (65)*. *D. herbacea* has

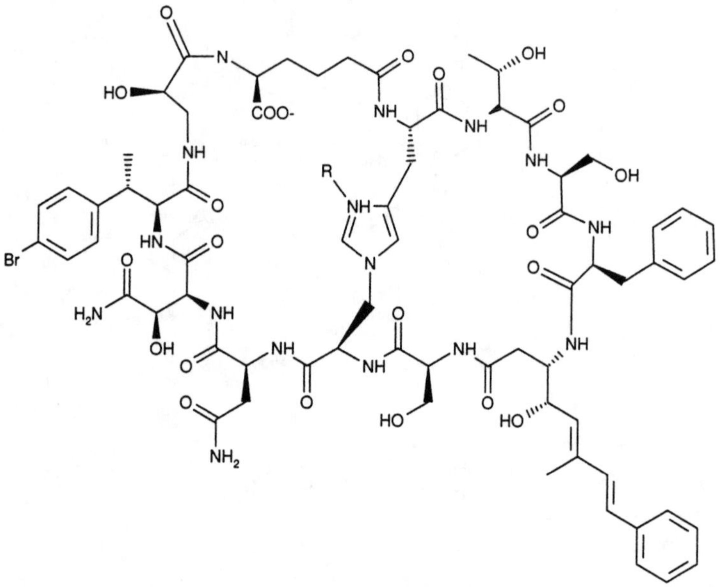

Scheme 35. Peptide-P951. R = hexose.

been shown to support large populations of the symbiotic filamentous cyanobacterium *Oscillatoria spongeliae*. Two chemotypes of the sponge exist. The first contains sesquiterpenes and polychlorinated amino acid-derived metabolites and the second contains only polybrominated diphenyl ethers. A Becton-Dickinson FACStar Plus cell-sorter was used to separate cyanobacterial cells from sponge cells in the two chemotypes based on fluorescence. NMR and GC/MS analysis suggested that the sesquiterpenes, herbadysidolide (**Scheme 36**), and spirodysin (**Scheme 37**) are localized in the nonfluorescent sponge-cell fraction, and 13-demethylisodysidenin (**Scheme 38**) is localized in the cyanobacterial cells. In the second chemotype, 2-(2',4'-dibromophenyl)-4,6-dibromophenol (**Scheme 39**) was localized in the cyanobacterial fraction.

A number of extremely toxic compounds originally observed in marine invertebrates have since been demonstrated to be produced by marine bacteria or dinoflagellates associated with these organisms. A number of excellent review articles have been published on this topic *(56,65)*. An example is okadaic acid (**Scheme 40**), a potent toxin originally reported from the sponge *Halichondria okadai*. It has since been shown to be produced by the dinoflagellates *Prorocentrum lima* and *Dinophysis* sp. and is one of the causative agents of diarrhetic shellfish poisoning *(65)*.

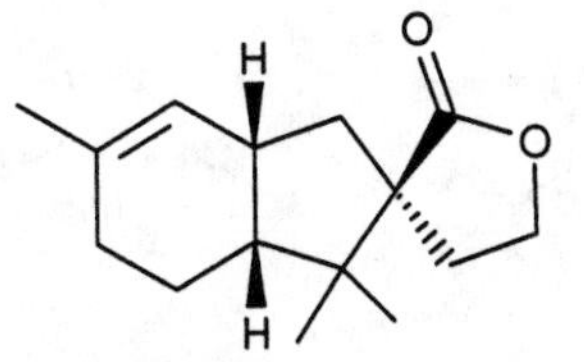

Scheme 36. Herbadysidolide.

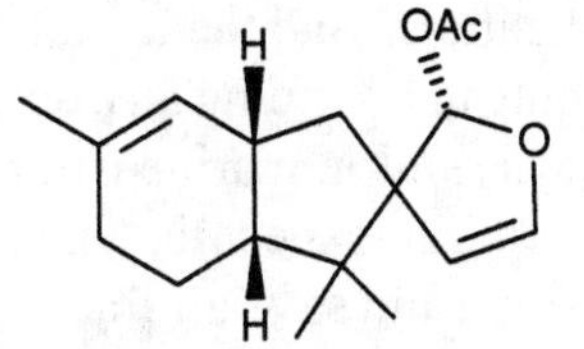

Scheme 37. Spirodysin.

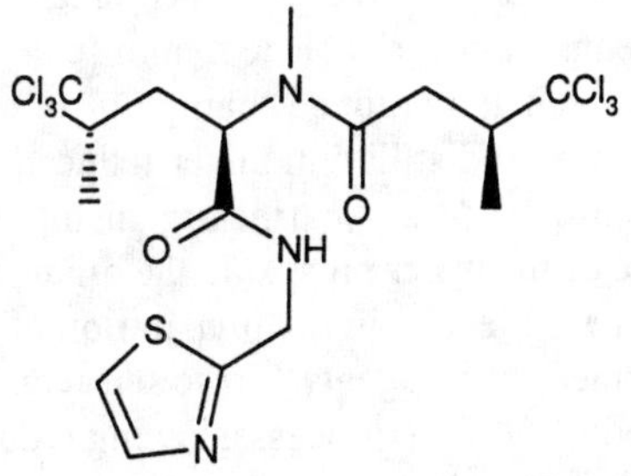

Scheme 38. 13-Demethylisodysidenin.

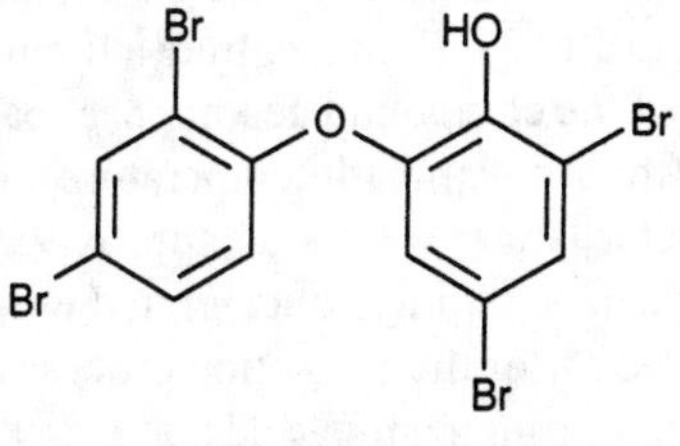

Scheme 39. 2-(2',4'-dibromophenyl)4,6-dibromophenol.

7. Summary

Factors such as uncertainty in the identification of the source organism, crosscontamination by other organisms, the trace nature of some extremely

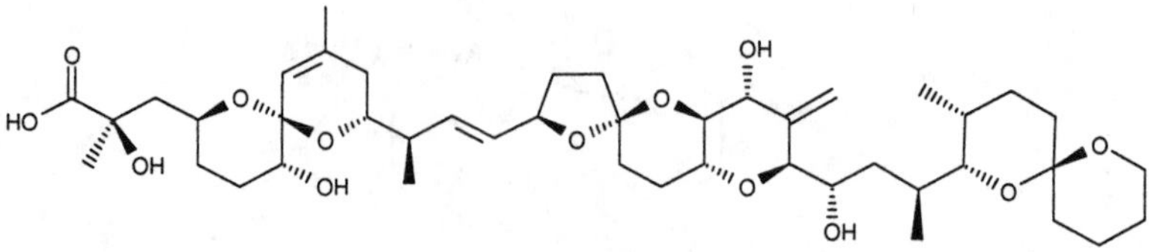

Scheme 40. Okadaic acid.

bioactive compounds, dietary and microbial synthesis of metabolites, unexpected chemical functionalizations, and the overall diversity of marine organisms and habitats all contribute to providing an exciting challenge to the natural products chemist. To be successful in marine natural products chemistry, one should always keep an open mind, expect the unexpected, use as many methods for purification as possible, and save all fractions.

8. Notes

1. Storing extracts in solvent at room temperature can lead to degradation of the compounds and lower overall yields. It is strongly recommended that organisms be maintained at the coldest temperature possible to minimize degradation of compounds.
2. Lyophilization can often help to reduce "bumping" of extracts during concentration of the extract *in vacuo* (distillation under reduced pressure using a rotatory evaporator ["rotovapping"]). Many marine organisms contain significant quantities of water. Because of the water present in the organisms, even extraction with 100% ethanol or methanol results in the preparation of aqueous alcohol extracts that often contain surface active agents. These surfactants can cause foaming and bumping during the concentration process, slowing it down significantly. Freeze-drying the organism prior to extraction allows for the preparation of nonaqueous alcohol extracts that minimizes extraction of surfactants. An example that illustrates this: Methanol extraction of the ascidian *Ecteinascidia turbinata* without lyophilization leads to an extract that foams excessively during concentration. It can take anywhere from 1 to 2 d to concentrate a liter of extract. During this time, a significant quantity of the compound decomposes caused by extended exposure to methanol at 30°C (the rotovap bath temperature). If the organism is first lyophilized to remove water (water makes up approx 95% of the wet weight of the organism), the extract can be rapidly concentrated within approx 3–5 h. The yield of compound and efficiency of the extraction process are significantly increased. In instances in which significant foaming and bumping are encountered, it can sometimes be useful to use a large pear-shaped flask as the distillation flask (at least 1000-mL vol). Small amounts of extract (25–50 mL) are added to the flask, and the rate of spinning of the flask is adjusted to minimize foaming. In some cases, a very fast rate will accomplish this, whereas, in others, a slow rate is effective. It can also be useful to add a small amount of isopropanol (10–20 mL), which can ease the removal of water through formation of an azeotrope, thus reducing foaming.

3. In some instances, freezing the organism can lead to degradation of the compounds. We have observed that extracts prepared from freshly collected material can, in rare instances, vary from those of frozen material. Example: Ethanol extracts prepared from freshly collected specimens of the deep-water sponge of the family Pachastrellidae were observed to inhibit binding of [^{125}I]-endothelin to porcine thoracic aorta. Re-extraction of the frozen sponge yielded extracts devoid of activity. The sponge was recollected and extracted immediately with ethanol. These extracts retained activity. The compound, although not wholly characterized structurally, was shown to be a polymeric material of large molecular weight (>30,000 amu), which apparently is degraded during the freezing process.

4. In the author's lab a Virtis™ grinder is used for 1- to 20-g samples (20–50 mL solvent), whereas a 1-L Waring™ blender is used for 20- to 500-g samples (100–500 mL solvent) and a large (4 L) commercial Waring Blender is used for larger samples (up to 1 kg, 1–2 L solvent). When specimens larger than 1 kg are being extracted, it is usually done in multiple steps on smaller portions. Some compounds are unstable to extensive storage in solution at room temperature, and unless a high-capacity concentration apparatus is available, we have found that it is more effective to extract the organism in batches.

5. Many Haplosclerid and Choristid sponges tend to form a gelatinous mass when extracted with ethanol. Other sponges, such as *Myrmekioderma*, which has a high polysaccharide mucus content, form gelatins when extracted with nonpolar solvents such as EtOAc. In our laboratory, Celite 521 is used in the filtration of these extracts. A Büchner funnel is fitted with a piece of filter paper and then a 2- to 3-cm high layer of Celite is added to the funnel. A vacuum is applied and the Celite layer tamped down. A portion of the extract is poured onto the Celite bed and allowed to filter. As the filtration rate slows, the top surface of the Celite is scraped gently with a spatula to expose new Celite. This process is continued until filtration is complete. If the extract still does not filter, solvents of different polarity can be added to the extract. In most cases, this changes the consistency of the gelatin and allows for filtration. Alternatively, lyophilization of these specimens prior to extraction can reduce filtration problems.

6. Preparation of reverse phase packing (modification of Evans *[31]*).
   a. Using a clean, dry syringe, transfer 20 g (20.2 mL) of octadecyltrichlorosilane into 500 mL anhydrous CCl$_4$ in a 1000-mL round-bottom flask. (To ensure a good packing, all glassware should be dried in a drying oven to remove residual water from the surface.) To this add 200 g dry silica gel (0.040–0.063 mm, 230–400 mesh ASTM). Shake to produce a suspension, and allow the reaction to proceed with stirring for 2 h at room temperature.
   b. Filter off the resulting RP-18 bonded silica gel using a Buchner funnel, and wash with 250 mL anhydrous CCl$_4$ to remove unreacted silane. Place the silica in a beaker and add 500 mL methanol to convert residual chlorines to methoxy groups.
   c. Filter off the silica-gel product using a Buchner funnel, immediately wash with 500 mL CH$_2$Cl$_2$, and allow to suck dry.
   d. Place the RP-18 packing in a 40°C oven overnight prior to endcapping.

Endcapping:

1. Using a clean, dry syringe transfer 20 g of trimethylchlorosilane into 500 mL anhydrous CCl_4 in a dry 1000-mL round-bottom flask. To this add the dried RP-18 product prepared above. Shake the mixture to produce a suspension, and allow the reaction to proceed with stirring for 2 h at room temperature.
2. Filter off the resulting endcapped-RP-18 silica gel using a Buchner funnel, and wash with 250 mL anhydrous CCl_4 to remove unreacted silane. Wash the funnel with 500 mL methanol followed by 500 mL CH_2Cl_2 and allow to suck dry.
3. Place the endcapped-RP-18 packing in a 40°C oven overnight prior to use.

A number of the reagents used in this procedure are very water-sensitive, reactive, and/or constitute health hazards. It is extremely important to use proper protective equipment as outlined in the MSDS information. The silanes will rapidly eat through plastic caps and cannot be stored for long periods of time. It is recommended that only the minimum reagent necessary to prepare the desired quantity of packing material be bought, as long-term storage is nearly impossible.

References

1. McConnell, O. J., Longley, R. E., and Koehn, F. E. (1990) The discovery of marine natural products with therapeutic potential, in *The Discovery of Natural Products with Therapeutic Potential* (Gullo, V. P. ed.), Butterworth-Heineman, Boston, MA, pp. 109–174.
2. Paul, V. J. (1992) *Ecological Roles of Marine Natural Products.* Comstock Pub. Assoc., Ithaca, NY.
3. Faulkner, D. J. (1984) Marine natural products: metabolites of marine algae and herbivorous marine molluscs, *Nat. Prod. Rep.* **1,** 251–280.
4. Faulkner, D. J. (1984) Marine natural products: metabolites of marine marine invertebrates. *Nat. Prod. Rep.* **1,** 551–598.
5. Faulkner, D. J. (1986) Marine natural products, *Nat. Prod. Rep.* **3,** 1–33.
6. Faulkner, D. J. (1987) Marine natural products, *Nat. Prod. Rep.* **4,** 539–576.
7. Faulkner, D. J. (1990) Marine natural products, *Nat. Prod. Rep.* **7,** 269–309.
8. Faulkner, D. J. (1991) Marine natural products, *Nat. Prod. Rep.* **8,** 97–147.
9. Faulkner, D. J. (1992) Marine natural products, *Nat. Prod. Rep.* **9,** 323–364.
10. Faulkner, D. J. (1993) Marine natural products chemistry. *Chem. Rev.* **93,** 1671–1944.
11. Bartik, K., Braekman, J.-C., Daloze, D., Stoller, C., Huysecom, J., Vandevyver, G., and Ottinger, R. (1987) Topsentins, new toxic bis-indole alkaloids from the marine sponge *Topsentia genitrix. Can. J. Chem.* **65,** 2118–2121.
12. Tsujii, S., Rinehart, K. L., Gunasekera, S., Kashman, Y., Cross, S., Lui, M., Pomponi, S., and Diaz, M. C. (1988) Topsentin, bromotopsentin, dihydrodeoxybromotopsentin: antiviral and antitumor bis(indolyl)imidazoles from Caribbean deep-sea sponges of the family Halichondriidae. Structural and synthetic studies. *J. Org. Chem.* **53,** 5446–5453.
13. Wright, A. E., Pomponi, S. A., Cross, S. S., and McCarthy, P. M. (1992) A new bis(indole) alkaloid from a deep water marine sponge of the genus *Spongosorites. J. Org. Chem.* **57,** 4772–4775.

14. Moore R. E., Helfrich, P., and Patterson, G. M. L. (1982) The deadly seaweed of Hana. *Oceanus* **25,** 54–63.
15. Perry, N. B., Blunt, J. W., Munro, M. H. G., and Pannell, L. K. (1988) Mycalamide a, an antiviral compound from a New Zealand sponge of the genus *Mycale. J. Am. Chem. Soc.* **110,** 4850–4851.
16. Moore, R. E., Blackman, A. J., Cheuk, C. E., Mynderse, J. S., Matsumoto, G. K., Clardy, J., Woodward, R. W., and Craig J. C. (1984) Absolute stereochemistries of the aplysiatoxins and oscillatoxin a. *J. Org. Chem.* **49,** 2484–2489.
17. Davis, A. R. and Wright, A. E. (1990) Inhibition of larval settlement by natural products from the ascidian *Eudistoma olivaceum* (van Name). *J. Chem. Ecol.* **16,** 1349–1357.
18. Davis, A. R., Targett, N. M., Mcconnell, O. J., and Young, C. M. (1989) Epibiosis of marine algae and benthic invertebrates: natural products chemistry and other mechanisms inhibiting settlement and overgrowth. *Bio-org. Marine Chem.* **3,** 85–114.
19. Pawlik, J. R. (1993) Marine invertebrate chemical defenses. *Chem. Rev.* **93,** 1911–1922.
20. Sullivan, B. W., Faulkner, D. J., Matsumoto, G. K., Cun-hens H., and Clardy, J. (1986) Metabolites of the burrowing sponge *Siphonodictyon coralliphagum. J. Org. Chem.* **51,** 4568–4573.
21. Sullivan, B. J., Faulkner, D. J., and Webb, L. (1983) Siphonodictidine, a metabolite of the burrowing sponge *Siphonodictyon* sp. that inhibits coral growth. *Science* **221,** 1175,1176.
22. Baker, J. T., Borris, R. P., Carté, B., Cordell, G. A., Soejarto, D. D., Cragg, G. M., Gupta, M. P., Iwu, M. M., Mdulid, D. R., and Tyler, V. E. (1995) Natural product drug discovery and development: new perspectives on international collaboration. *J. Nat. Prod.* **58,** 1325–1357.
23. Rodriguez, J., Nieto, R. M., and Crews, P. (1993) New structures and bioactivity patterns of bengazole alkaloids from a Choristid sponge. *J. Nat. Prod.* **56,** 2034–2040.
24. Hallock, Y. F., Cardellina, J. H. , Balaschak, M. S., Alexander, M. R., Prather, T. R., Shoemaker, R. H., and Boyd, M. R. (1995) Antitumor activity and stereochemistry of acetylenic alcohols from the sponge *Cribrochalina vasculum. J. Nat. Prod.* **58,** 1801–1807.
25. Wright, A. E., Chiles, S. A., and Cross, S. S. (1991) 3-amino-1-(2-aminoimidazolyl)-prop-1-ene from the marine sponges *Teichaxinella morchella* and *Ptilocaulis walpersi. J. Nat. Prod.* **54,** 1684–1686.
26. Wright, A., Forleo, D., Gunawardana, G., Gunasekera, S., Koehn F., and McConnell, O. J. (1990) Antitumor tetrahydroisoquinoline alkaloids from the colonial ascidian *Ecteinascidia turbinata. J. Org. Chem.* **55,** 4508–4512.
27. Hamburger M. O. and Cordell, G. A. (1987) A direct bioautographic TLC assay for compounds possessing antibacterial activity. *J. Nat. Prod.* **50,** 19–22.
28. Burres, N. S., Hunter, J. E., and Wright, A. E. (1989) A mammalian cell agar-diffusion assay for the detection of toxic compounds. *J. Nat. Prod.* **52,** 522–527.
29. Brennan, M. R. and Erickson, K. L. (1982) Austradiol acetate and austradiol diacetate, 4,6-dihydroxy-(+)-selinane derivatives from an Australian *Laurencia* sp. *J. Org. Chem.* **47,** 3917–3921.
30. Blunt, J. W., Calder, V. L., Fenwick, G. D., Lake, R. J., McCombs, J. D., Munro M. H. G., and Perry, N. (1987) Reverse phase flash chromatography: a method for the rapid partitioning of natural product extracts. *J. Nat. Prod.* **50,** 290–292.

31. Evans, M. B., Dale, A. D., and Little, C. J. (1980) The preparation and evaluation of superior bonded phases reversed-phase, high performance liquid chromatography. *Chromatographia* **13**, 5–10.

32. Shimuzu, Y. (1985) Bioactive marine natural products with emphasis on handling of water-soluble compounds. *J. Nat. Prod.* **48**, 223–235.

33. Schmitz, F. J., Hollenbeak, K. H., and Campbell, D. C. (1978) Marine natural products: halitoxin, toxic complex of several marine sponges of the genus *Haliclona. J. Org. Chem.* **43**, 3916–3922.

34. Fusetani, N., Matsunaga, S., and Konosu, S. (1981) Bioactive marine metabolites ii. halistanol sulfate, an antimicrobial novel steroid from the marine sponge *Halichondria* cf. *moorei* Berquist. *Tetrahed. Lett.* **21**, 1985–1988.

35. McKee, T., Cardellina, J. H., Tischler, M., Snader, K. M., Boyd, M. R. (1993) Ibisterol sulfate, a novel HIV-inhibitory sulfated sterol from the deep water sponge *Topsentia* sp. *J. Nat. Prod.* **34**, 389–392.

36. Cardellina J. H., Munro, M. H. G., Fuller, R. W., Manfredi, K. P., McKee, T. C., Tischler, M., Bokesh, H. R., Gustafson, K. R., Beutler, J. A., and Boyd, M. R. (1993) A chemical screening strategy for the dereplication and prioritization of HIV-inhibitory aqueous natural products extracts. *J. Nat. Prod.* **56**, 1123–1129.

37. Gulavita, N. K., Wright, A. E., McCarthy, P. J., Pomponi, S. A., Kelly-Borges, M., Chin, M., and Sills, M. A. (1993) Isolation and structure elucidation of 34-sulfatobastadin 13, an inhibitor of the endothelin A receptor, from a marine sponge of the genus *Ianthella. J. Nat. Prod.* **56**, 1613–1617.

38. Gulavita, N. K., Pomponi, S. A., Wright, A. E., Garay, M., and Sills, M. A. (1995) Aplysillin A, a thrombin receptor antagonist from the marine sponge *Aplysina fistularis fulva. J. Nat. Prod.* **58**, 954–957.

39. Killday, K. B., Wright, A. E., Jackson, R. H., and Sills, M. A. (1995) Bis-(sulfato)-cyclosiphonodictyol A, a new disulfated sesquiterpene-hydroquinone from a deep water collection of the marine sponge *Siphonodictyon coralliphagum. J. Nat. Prod.* **58**, 958–960.

40. Bruno, I., Minale, L., Riccio, R., Cariello, L., Higa, T., and Tanaka, J. (1993) Starfish saponins, Part 50. Steroidal Glycosides from the Okinawan starfish *Nardoa tuberculata. J. Nat. Prod.* **56**, 1057–1064.

41. Kashman Y., Hirsh, S., McConnell, O., Ohtani, I., Kusumi, T., and Kakisawa, H., (1989) Ptilomycalin A: a novel polycyclic alkaloid of marine origin. *J. Am. Chem. Soc.* **111**, 8925,8926.

42. Jares-Erijman, E. A., Sakai, R., and Rinehart, K. L. (1991) Crambescidins: New antiviral and cytotoxic compounds from the sponge *Crambe crambe. J. Org. Chem.* **56**, 5712–5715.

43. Berlinck R. G. S., Braekman, J. C., Daloze, D., Bruno, I., Riccio, R., Ferri, S., Spampinato, S., and Speroni, E. (1993) Polycyclic guanidine alkaloids from the marine sponge *Crambe crambe* and Ca^{+2} channel blocker activity of crambescidin 816. *J. Nat. Prod.* **56**, 1007–1015.

44. Jares-Erijman, E. A., Ingrum, A. A., Sun, F., and Rinehart, K. L. (1993) On the structures of crambescins B and C1. *J. Nat. Prod.* **56**, 2186–2188.

45. Patil D. A., Vasant Kumar, N. V., Kokke, W. C., Bean, M. F., Freyer, A. J., De Brosse, C., Mai., S., Truneh, A., Faulkner, D. J., Carté, B., Breen, A. L., Hertzberg, R. P., Johnson, R. K., Westley, J. W., and Potts, B. C. M. (1995) Novel alkaloids from the sponge *Batzella* sp.: inhibitors of HIV gp-120 human cd4 binding. *J. Org. Chem.* **60,** 1182–1188.

46. Tavares, R., Daloze, D., Braekman, J. C., Hajdu, E., and van Soest, R. W. M. (1995) 8b-Hydroxyptilocaulin, a new guanidine alkaloid from the marine sponge *Monanchora arbuscula. J. Nat. Prod.* **58,** 1139–1142.

47. Palagiano, E., de Marino, S., Minale, L., Riccio, R., Zollo, F., Iorizzi, M., Carre, J. B., Debitus, C., Lucarain, L., and Provost, J. (1995) Ptilomycalin A, crembescidin 800 and related highly cytotoxic guanidine alkaloids from the starfishes *Fromia monilis* and *Celerina heffernani. Tetradedron* **51,** 3675–3682.

48. Gunawardana, G. P., Koehn. F. E., Lee, A. Y., Clardy, J., He, H., and Faulkner, D. J. (1992) Pyridoacridine alkaloids from deep-water marine sponges of the family Pachastrellidae: structure revision of dercitin and related compounds and correlation with the kuanoniamines. *J. Org. Chem.* **57,** 1523–1526.

49. Caroll, A. R. and Scheuer, P. J. (1990) Kuanoniamines A, B, C, and D: pentacyclic alkaloids from a tunicate and its prosobranch mollusk predator *Chelynotus semperi. J. Org. Chem.* **55,** 4426–4431.

50. Rudi, A. and Kashman, Y. (1989) Six new alkaloids from the purple red sea tunicate *Eudistoma* sp. *J. Org. Chem.* **54,** 5331–5337.

51. Gunawardana, G. P., Kohnmoto, S., and Burres, N. S. (1989) New cytotoxic alkaloids from two deep water marine sponges of the family Pachastrellida. *Tetrahed. Lett.* **30,** 4359–4362.

52. Pettit, G. R., Cichacz, Z., Gao, F., Herald, C. L., Boyd, M. R., Schmidt, J. M., and Hooper, J. N. A. (1993) Isolation and structure of spongistatin 1. *J. Org. Chem.* **58,** 1302–1304.

53. Pettit, G. R., Cichacz, Z., Gao, F., Herald, C. L., Boyd, M. R., Schmidt, J. M., Hamel E., and Bai, R., (1994) Antineoplastic agents 300. Isolation and structure of the rare human cancer inhibitory macrocyclic lactones spongistatins 8 and 9. *J. Chem. Soc. Chem. Commun.* 1605,1606.

54. Kobayashi, M., Aoki, S., Sakai, H., Kawazoe, K., Kihara, N., Sasaki, T., and Kitagawa, I. (1993) Altohytrin A, a potent antitumor macrolide from the Okinawan marine sponge *Hyrtios altum. Tetrahed. Lett.* **34,** 2795–2798.

55. Fusetani, N., Shinoda, K., and Matsunaga, S. (1993) Cinachyrolide A: a potent cytotoxic macrolide possessing two spiro ketals from marine sponge *Cinachyra* sp. *J. Am. Chem. Soc.* **115,** 3977–3981.

56. Kobayashi, J. and Ishibashi, M. (1993) Bioactive metabolites of symbiotic marine micro-organisms. *Chem. Rev.* **93,** 1753–1769.

57. Arai, T., Katsuhiro T., Ishiguro K., and Yazawa, K. (1980) Increased production of saframycin A and isolation of saframycin S. *J. Antibiot.* **33,** 951–959.

58. Fenical, W. and Jensen, P. R. (1993) Marine microorganisms: A new biomedical resource, in *Marine Biotechnology, vol. 1: Pharmaceutical and Bioactive Natural Products* (Attaway, D. H. and Zaborsky, O. R., eds.), Plenum, New York.

59. Fenical W. (1993) Chemical studies of marine bacteria: developing a new resource. *Chem. Rev.* **93,** 1673–1683.

60. Thompson, J. E., Barrow, K. D., and Faulkner, D. J. (1983) Localization of two brominated metabolites, aerothionin and homoaerothionin in spherulous cell of the marine sponge *Aplysina fistularis (=-verongia thiona)*. *Acta Zoologica* **64**, 199–210.

61. Muller, W. E., Diehl-Seifert, B., Sobel, C., Bechtold, A., Kljajicand Z., and Dorn, A. (1986) Sponge secondary metabolites: biochemical and ultrastructural localization of the antimitotic agent avarol in *Dysidea avara*. *J. Histochem. Cytochem.* **34**, 1687–1690.

62. Uriz M. J., Turon, X., Gordi, J., and Tur, J. M. (1996) New light on the cell location of avarol within the sponge *Dysidea avara* (Dendroceratida). *Cell Tissue Res.* **285**, 519–527.

63. Uriz, M. J., Becerro, M. A., Tur, J. N. M., and Turon, X. (1996) Location of toxicity with the Mediterranean sponge *Crambe crambe* (Demospongiae: Poecilosclerida) *Marine Biol.* **124**, 583–590.

64. Bewley, C. A., Holland, N. D., and Faulkner, D. J. (1996) Two classses of metabolites from *Theonella swinhoei* are localized in distinct populations of bacterial symbionts. *Experientia* **52**, 716–722.

65. Faulkner, D. J., Unson, M. D., and Bewley, C. A. (1994) The chemistry of some sponges and their symbionts. *Pure Appl. Chem.* **66**, 1983–1990.

66. Yasumoto, Y. and Murata, M. (1993) Marine toxins. *Chem. Rev.* **93**, 1897–1909.

14

Scale-Up of Natural Products Isolation

Michael S. Verrall and Stephen R. C. Warr

1. Introduction

The term "scale-up" has been interpreted here as increasing the output of the product. This can be achieved by increasing the scale of the operation or increasing the concentration of product in the starting material. In the former case, this chapter considers increasing scale to the maximum that can be conveniently operated in a laboratory environment. It thus excludes operations requiring "process-scale" facilities and chemical-engineering expertise. The chapter will consider mainly secondary microbial metabolites, but many aspects of isolation can also be applied to plant products. Although laboratory-scale facilities are assumed (and indeed all procedures discussed can be performed in an average chemical laboratory), for the larger scales of operation, e.g., the manipulation of 5- to 10-L volumes, a 750-mm-high bench is preferable to the standard 900-mm height. For operations requiring a fume cupboard, a "walk-in" type (i.e., having adjustable or removable benching) is recommended for the same reason. It has been assumed that 10-L fermenters and the apparatus associated with the processing of their contents is the maximum comfortable "laboratory" scale.

The term "natural products" encompasses a wide range of chemically diverse molecules produced by a number of different groups of microorganisms. This diversity renders generic extraction processes difficult to formulate. However, some prior knowledge of at least the chemical class, if not the structure, of the compound of interest enables useful comparisons to be made with existing processes to provide a rational starting method for purification.

In very basic terms, whether for intracellular or extracellular products, downstream processing usually involves a clarification step followed either by adsorption onto a resin, or solvent extraction followed by concentration. In

From: *Methods in Biotechnology, Vol. 4: Natural Products Isolation*
Edited by: R. J. P. Cannell © Humana Press Inc., Totowa, NJ

both cases, further chromatography to remove impurities is usually followed by concentration, and then crystallization or freeze drying to produce the final product.

Typically during early development, each stage in the process may have an 80% yield and therefore after six stages, only 26% of the original product will remain. This highlights the advantage of starting with as high a level of material as possible. Furthermore, in the processing of high titer broths, the proportion of losses due to nonspecific adsorption and rejection of impure chromatographic fractions will be reduced.

Therefore, although process development for natural product isolation generally involves the optimization of downstream operations (i.e., postfermenter harvest), the efficiency of the total process is greatly facilitated by increasing the product titer in the fermenter broth at harvest.

The initial quantities of a novel compound may well have been produced with time as the principal criterion, to obtain data on potency/selectivity of the purified product leading to the earliest possible patent filing. With progression of the work, not only scale-up but also the increase of yield and improvements in economy become increasingly important. Any process developed may be taken to the further stage of pilot-plant scale-up, and it should be designed to be "robust" i.e., not greatly influenced by small changes in feedstock composition and not dependent on precise control of process parameters. As a guide, one should aim for each stage to have a yield of 90%. Each stage should be as effective as possible with respect to removing impurities, since it is apparent that the number of stages still must not exceed six in order to achieve an overall 50% yield. Successful optimization work of this nature relies heavily on a reliable quantitative assay for the compound of interest.

2. Assay Systems

Many natural products are discovered as the result of biological screening, where the detection methods do not need to be particularly quantitative. However, all aspects of scale-up require a reliable quantitative assay for the compound under consideration. The screening assay will be based on a biochemical response and is designed for a particular type of sample (e.g., a fermentation broth). Most secondary metabolites are produced as mixtures of closely related compounds, and such an assay gives only a total value of activity in the test system. The assay response may be due to compounds with varying degrees of activity or different kinetics in the test system. It is also possible that there may be synergy or antagonism between components of the mixture. When developing a method for scale-up, it is essential to be able to assess the increase in concentration of the product in the fermentation and to assess the increase in purity after each purification stage. For these reasons, it is desirable to use a chromatographic method with physical detection. HPLC with UV detection is ideal where components have a suitable chromophore. In the absence of a chromophore, refractive-index detection is useful but normally less sensitive. Now that mass-spectroscopy-based detectors are readily available, these are often more convenient and informative; HPLC eluant can be monitored for total ion current, selected parent ion or selected fragment ion. In some cases, the same fragment ion is obtained from different members of a series of analogs and may be diagnostic for the series.

Regardless of assay system, it is essential to have good quantitation of increases in product yield resulting from optimization experiments.

3. Fermentation Development

3.1. Scale of Operation

Initial growth of the producing organism will be on agar and transfer to liquid culture and then scale-up to provide up to 10-L vol of culture broth will generally be required for the isolation of larger quantities of compound.

3.1.1. Transfer to Liquid Medium

Usually, up to three plugs of agar (10-mm diameter) are transferred aseptically to either 50 or 100 mL medium in a 500-mL shake flask, followed by incubation under defined shaking and temperature conditions (240 rpm orbital shaker, 50-mm throw, at 28°C are typical for streptomycetes). For an extended program of work, a homogeneous stock of spores or vegetative culture is often prepared by resuspending growth from an agar plate in a cryopreservative (e.g., 20% glycerol/10% lactose) and storing as 1-mL aliquots in liquid nitrogen or at –80°C.

3.1.2. Scale-Up

Initial liquid cultures in, e.g., 500-mL shake flasks can provide a sufficient volume of fermentation broth for the generation of growth and production profiles and for preliminary isolation experiments relating to clarification, stability, solvent solubility, and affinity for chromatographic resins.

Scale up to 10-L vol will generally require the use of small-scale fermenters rather than shake flasks. Production of 10 L of broth in shake flasks requires large-scale shaker capacity (34 × 2-L flasks each containing 300-mL medium), which may not be available in many laboratories. In contrast, autoclavable "benchtop" fermenters with up to 10 L working volume are available from a number of manufacturers. Moreover, they have the advantage of providing continuous-process monitoring and control and the opportunity to carry out nutrient feeding experiments and optimization of operating parameters *(1)*. The difficulty of transferring a fermentation from shaken flasks to fermenters should not be underestimated. Although 10 L of broth may be obtained from a single vessel, carrying out a fermentation improvement program will require at least four and preferably eight vessels.

There is no single "rule of thumb" for successful transfer of shake-flask cultures to fermenters. For many groups of organisms producing known compounds, a literature search will provide useful data on aeration, agitation, temperature, pressure, and foaming. When no data are available, sulfite oxidation can be used to estimate the oxygen transfer rates in shake flasks, and incubation conditions in fermenters can then be adjusted to give similar or increased rates in vessels. This is carried out by measuring the kinetics of the oxidation of sulfite to sulfate in an aerated fermenter running under model incubation conditions. In this way, the effect of different agitation/aeration regimes within a fermenter on mass transfer rates can be determined. However, it should be realized that the absolute mass transfer rates determined in a synthetic system may be different from those in an actual fermentation as a result of the effect of factors such as pH, ionic strength, and the presence of catalytic impurities *(2)*. However, in many cases, shake flasks are unlikely to provide optimum conditions; and, once initial fermentation conditions have been established, significant increases in productivity should be achieved by further experimentation.

A number of different parameters may be used to achieve successful scaling between different-sized fermenters. In general, a single factor, such as agitator tip speed, is kept constant when the fermentation is operated in different-sized vessels. The specific parameter used will depend on the nature of the fermentation broth. Thus, agitator tip speed determines the shear rate, which can influence the size of microbial flocs and damage to viable cells; Reynolds Number and the power input per unit volume affect mass-transfer coefficients within the reactor; and power input during aeration will determine the motor size required for the fermenter (particularly important for highly viscous fermentations). In well-mixed fermenters, a characteristic mixing time exists that determines the length of time fluid may spend away from the impeller. In large vessels, this parameter should also be considered to ensure a high degree of homogeneity within the fermentation broth.

In addition to the physical parameters discussed above, a number of other factors related to the culture and to the medium should be considered for both transfer of a process from shake flasks to fermenters and for scale-up to larger vessels. These include the provision of a culture stock giving reproducible growth after regeneration, the method of inoculum build-up that may require a number of shake flask and fermenter seed stages, an assessment of the variability within the process, the cost and availability of the medium components, and the method of sterilization within the fermenter.

"Mini-fermenters" with up to 2 L working volume provide an intermediate step in the scale-up process. At this scale, fermenter geometry is often significantly different from their larger counterparts, and the number of probes and other vessel entries lead to completely different mixing regimens within the vessels compared to larger fermenters. This can make successful scaling between these and other vessels more difficult.

At each stage of culture scale-up, the main criterion for success is production of the desired product, and it is important this be routinely monitored. The importance of reliable assay methods has already been emphasized. Although some loss of activity may occur in early scale-up experiments, this will generally be overcome by optimization of the factors discussed above.

3.2. Fermentation Improvement to Increase Titer

A number of strategies can be used to increase titer or productivity within a fermentation. In the short term, these include medium development, optimization of fermentation conditions, and development of the inoculum; these are discussed below. In the longer term, genetic approaches (e.g., cloning for overexpression, mutation of the producing organism, reisolation of the producer strain), biochemical manipulation of the biosynthetic pathway, metabolic control theory, and optimization of the culture storage and regeneration steps have all been used successfully but are beyond the scope of this book. There are numerous examples in the literature describing the increased production of specific metabolites, usually as a result of a single approach to titer improvement, e.g., medium development. One of the more comprehensive reviews concerns the fermentation development and process improvement for the production of avermectin *(3)*; this provides a valuable insight into the relative improvements resulting from, and the interactions between, specific approaches to titer improvement.

3.2.1. Medium Development

A "typical" medium for natural product accretion must supply the necessary nutrients for cell growth and product biosynthesis. The nutrients include sources of carbon, nitrogen, phosphorus, sulfur, potassium, and traces of elements such as iron and cobalt. In many cases, the use of undefined or complex nitrogen sources such as soya flour will provide sufficient levels of phosphate, sulfate, and other ions. Indeed, some simple media may consist of nothing more than a carbon source and a nitrogen source supplemented with a mixture of trace elements. In some cases, significant quantities of calcium carbonate or phosphate ions may be added to buffer the pH rather than to satisfy a specific elemental requirement *(4)*.

At its simplest, medium development takes the starting medium and asks these questions:

1. What are the effects of different concentrations of each medium component?
2. What is the limiting nutrient?
3. What is the effect of substituting each component with an alternative nutrient source?
4. Are there alternative combinations of major nutrient sources that support the production of higher titers?

In many cases, the formation of secondary metabolites is determined by nutrient limitation and examples of regulation by carbon, nitrogen, and phosphate are well-known. Production of certain natural products can also be influenced by low levels of trace elements, such as cobalt, or other minor components of the medium, such as sulfate. However, in the absence of any prior knowledge of medium development, preliminary experiments to manipulate the type and level of carbon and nitrogen sources are likely to lead to significant increases in titer. A large number and diversity of carbon and nitrogen sources have been used in fermentation processes, and to test the effects of all of these on the production of a specific metabolite would be impossible. A useful approach is to categorize available carbon and nitrogen sources into a small number of chemically distinct classes and then test nominated representatives of each class.

Possible types of carbon source: six carbon sugars, four and five carbon sugars, mono-, di-, polysaccharides, oils and fats, organic acids, and so on.

Possible types of nitrogen source: Yeast products, peptones, meat-based extracts, meals and flours, inorganics, and so on.

If prior knowledge exists of either the type of microorganism or type of product, then a literature search may provide useful data on the effect of different nutrient sources. If the product structure is known, then a theoretical consideration of possible biosynthetic routes might indicate benefits in using specific sources (for example, a nitrogen source with high levels of a specific amino acid). However, an initial random medium screen might involve testing two or three candidates from each class of carbon and nitrogen source. These should be selected on the basis of availability, cost, and possible effects on downstream processing.

3.2.2. Experimental Design

A large amount of medium development can be carried out in shake flasks with the exact experimental strategy dependent on the amount and quality of prior knowledge.

One simplistic approach to medium development is to randomly screen a range of alternative media. This is a valid approach in the absence of any prior information and may be useful for completely novel products or groups of organisms with which a worker has little experience. However, in most cases, at least, some data will be available on the requirements for growth and/or production (either from the literature or from previous experience), and a more rational approach will enable faster progress toward increased titers.

There are a number of different experimental design techniques that can be used for medium optimization. Four simple methods that have been used successfully in titer improvement programs are discussed below. These should provide the basis for initial medium-improvement studies that can be carried out in the average laboratory. Other techniques requiring a deeper knowledge of statistics, including simplex optimization, multivariate analysis, and principle-component analysis, have been reviewed *(5,6)*.

1. One factor at a time—This traditional type of experiment holds everything constant and varies only one component at a time. This approach is valid if the chosen factor is known to be a critical effector of titer but has the disadvantage of not identifying the critical factors and giving no data on interactions with other factors.

2. Full factorial experiments—These experiments provide comprehensive data on the effects and interactions of the chosen factors but have the disadvantage of being time-, money-, and resource-intensive. For example, to investigate four factors each at four levels requires 256 experimental treatments. Although large amounts of data are obtained on the levels and interactions of the chosen factors, unless these factors are known to have major effects on product titer, there is a danger that much of this will relate to factors having little or no effect on final titer. Therefore, such experiments would generally be carried out in the later stages of medium development after several critical factors had been identified.

3. Fractional factorial experiments—This technique, based on work by Plackett and Burman *(7)*, has been successfully used to determine which medium component(s) have the greatest effect on metabolite production. Such experiments sacrifice some data on interactions between factors to permit more factors to be examined in the same number of experimental treatments as a full factorial experiment. Each medium component is treated as a single factor and is tested at two different levels, usually each side of the control value. Thus, if the control medium contains 2% glucose, then glucose is tested at 1 and 4%. Using standard-order designs, a medium containing seven different components (i.e., seven factors) could be analyzed in as few as eight experimental treatments. This type of experiment is not designed to optimize a medium immediately but rather to identify the critical factors and the direction of their effect on the system. Therefore, an initial fractional factorial experiment on medium components might be carried out in the early stages of medium development to provide a rational basis for future experimentation.

4. Array testing—These experiments investigate pairs of factors, each at three different levels (usually control level, ×2 control and ×0.5 control). Typical pairs of factors might be:
   a. Level of carbon source vs level of nitrogen source.
   b. Type of nitrogen source vs level of carbon source.

Thus, for a control medium containing, for example, 2% glucose and 1% soya flour, example a. above would test 1, 2, and 4% glucose each at 0.5, 1, and 2% soya flour, i.e., a total of nine treatments. Determination of titer in each test medium allows response surfaces to be plotted from which the effects of high and low levels of each factor and their interactions can be readily identified. As with the fractional factorial experiments described above, these experiments are not designed for absolute optimization but will rapidly identify trends leading to increased titer.

3.2.3. Optimization of Fermenter Conditions

Although some data on fermentation conditions can be gained from shake flasks, these experiments should ideally be carried out in fermenters where more accurate control and process monitoring are available. However, an initial shake flask experiment might investigate temperature, aeration (volume of medium), agitation (spiked flasks), inoculum levels, and pH. This could be done either as a fractional factorial design or as a series of array tests (*see* **Subheading 3.2.2.**), e.g., testing aeration (medium volume) vs temperature.

If a number of small fermenters are available, a preliminary experiment in four vessels might be an airflow/agitation cross using, e.g., high airflow/high agitation, high airflow/low agitation, low airflow/high agitation, and low airflow/low agitation.

Such an experiment would normally be carried out with an improved medium (identified from work in shake flasks) and at a temperature already known to support adequate product titers.

Further experiments that can be usefully carried out in fermenters include pH control to specific levels, nutrient feeding regimens and control of dissolved oxygen levels. Depending on the level of instrumentation, a number of strategies for controlling dissolved oxygen (dOT) can be investigated, including ramping the airflow rate or agitator speed to maintain dOT levels during cell growth or changing a specific parameter after the initial growth phase.

Increase in fermentation volume to pilot-plant scale and beyond would generally require more detailed optimization of fermentation conditions to include parameters such as sterilization regime, medium viscosity, impeller shear, and foaming *(8)*.

Any change in fermenter operating conditions will lead to an altered fermentation profile, and changes in growth rate or final biomass levels will affect whole-broth clarification. The morphology of some organisms, particularly fungi, may be completely different in fermenters compared to shake flasks due to inoculum levels, dissolved oxygen levels, agitation regimes, and shear. Changes in morphology can affect not only culture productivity but also subsequent clarification *(9)*. Thus, if possible, as many of the preliminary extraction experiments should be carried out on culture broth obtained from fermenters run with as close to the final conditions as possible.

3.2.4. Seed Stage Development

The production of 10-L vol of culture broth usually requires the use of at least one seed stage to provide adequate inoculum levels. In some cases, this can have a significant effect on final stage titers with passaging, duration of seed stage, incubation temperature, inoculum level, and original inoculum source all contributing to the "quality" of the final-stage fermentation *(8)*.

In most cases, any effect on downstream processing of changes to the seed-stage regimen will be because of differences in biomass affecting clarification. However, the use of altered seed media may also result in a different impurity profile during isolation, necessitating the modification of chromatographic steps to obtain the desired purity of the final product.

4. Effect on Downstream Processing

Of the short-term strategies for titer enhancement, the greatest increases are likely to initially come from medium development. However, this is also likely to have the greatest effect on downstream processing. Even small changes in the fermentation medium may have profound consequences later on in the isolation process. These may be as simple as an altered level of biomass necessitating a slightly modified clarification stage; alternatively, a combination of specific medium components and fermentation conditions may change biomass and suspended-solid levels and result in the production of a number of intractable biochemical impurities that require extensive chromatography for their removal with a concomitant reduction in overall process yield. Some specific examples are given in **Table 1**.

Not all of the effects of altered medium or fermentation conditions will be detrimental to downstream processing. For example, some changes in culture morphology may result in easier clarification.

In many cases, the overall effect of modifying the fermentation will not become apparent until some distance into the isolation process, when data are available on the purity of the product stream. A process developed for a specific medium will contain chromatography stages designed to remove impurities peculiar to that medium. Changing a single medium component may result in a modified impurity profile necessitating modified or additional chromatography steps to obtain a product of the desired purity. Conversely, some media will result in fewer impurities, obviating the need for a series of different chromatography procedures.

Impurities within an extraction process as a result of fermentation fall into two broad categories: physical and biochemical.

Table 1
Effects of Medium on Downstream Processing

Factor affected by medium	Reason for change in medium	Possible effect on downstream processing
Morphology	Dependent on organism and fermentation conditions, especially fungi.	Affects clarification, volume of collected solids. May affect solvent partitioning.
Extracellular polysaccharides	Organism type. Growth phase at harvest. Nutrient limitation.	Clarification. Flocculation and hydrophobicity of cells. Some retained as impurities.
Biomass	Absolute levels determined by limiting nutrient.	Clarification. Volume of collected solids. Altered volumes of solvents for extraction.
Insoluble components	Medium components. (Undefined or bulk components, e.g., soya flour.)	Retained with cells during clarification.
Oils	Carbon source in some media or requirement for specific organisms.	May form emulsions affecting clarification, solvent partitioning, or adsorption to specific resins.
Antifoam	Added to medium in fermenters.	May form emulsions or affect performance of silica chromatography.
Metal ions	Present in trace element mixes or in some undefined components.	Effects on flocculation and clarity. Product stability. Some biochemical assays. Binding in some column chromatography.
Organic acids	Produced by cells. Dependent on metabolism, media components, and fermentation conditions.	Requirement for initial pH adjustment. Impurities. Capacity for adsorption to chromatography columns.

Physical impurities consist mainly of the cells, cell debris, and insoluble medium components, most of which will be removed by the initial clarification stages. This process may be facilitated by preliminary broth conditioning; for example, the addition of flocculating agents, pH adjustment, or heat treatment. Such operations may have the added advantage of promoting the release of intracellular products to the liquid phase, thereby removing the need for whole-cell extraction. Cell lysis will, of course, also increase the biochemical impurity load *(11)*.

Biochemical impurities originate from the media components, antifoams, oils, and metal ions, and may include metabolites closely related to the compound of interest; they can all affect empirical isolation procedures. It is therefore essential to maintain close liaison between the fermentation and extraction scientists during all aspects of scale-up to ensure that fermentation developments are not adversely affecting isolation procedures. The inevitably changing nature of the feedstock further highlights the requirement for a quantitative specific assay for the product and an assessment of product purity throughout the isolation process.

5. Downstream Process Development
5.1. Preliminary Data

Since one of the objectives of scale-up is to increase yield, i.e., proportion of available product isolated, knowledge of the compound's stability is a useful asset. Procedures that employ conditions in which the compound is less stable can then be avoided or operated to minimize loss. If the data have not already been determined, it is useful to determine stability under a range of pH and temperature conditions. It is important to appreciate that a compound in an impure mixture may be more or less stable than in its pure state. Enzymes present in crude extracts or fermentation broth may transform the product; the rate is likely to be highly dependent on pH and temperature. Some compounds that are relatively unstable in the pure state may be stabilized by conjugation with other components.

Microbial secondary metabolites are normally synthesized within growing or viable cells and may be wholly or partially excreted into the surrounding medium. It is worth determining the relative proportions of intra- and extracellular product. For the purposes of this discussion, the term intracellular means that the product is collected with the cellular fraction on filtration or centrifugation. The precise location in or on the cell is unimportant.

Isolation is simpler and yields are increased if the product is located entirely within the cells or culture fluid. It may be possible to manipulate the fermentation to transfer the product entirely to one phase, or this may be achievable by simple pH adjustment or other means, such as heat treatment, after harvest. For example, an acidic compound may appear to be intracellular at pH 4.0 because of reduced water solubility or adsorption on to cellular lipids, but at higher pH values the anionic form may be extracellular.

5.2. Intracellular Products

Intracellular protein products are often released by cell disruption. Thus, the resulting mixture contains all of the cellular material, and no purification is achieved. In contrast, secondary microbial metabolites may normally be selectively leached from cells with water-miscible organic solvents. Sometimes more selective (although slower) extraction may be obtained with less polar water-immiscible solvents. There is also scope for selective extraction using solvent systems based on supercritical carbon dioxide. It is worth spending a little time on this stage to reduce the impurity load on subsequent stages, but it is not possible to definitively optimize a single stage one at a time. The entire fermentation and extraction development process is a dynamic system, and optimization is an iterative process. The aim at this stage is to obtain an extract containing the desired product and related products but free of the majority of contaminants in the source material. Further purification can then be carried out by means of the methods for extracellular products discussed in **Subheading 5.3.**

An often overlooked but potentially troublesome contaminant is fermentation antifoam. Its effects can sometimes be reduced, if not entirely eliminated, by prior extraction with a nonpolar solvent such as hexane.

Scale-up of these procedures is readily achieved using conventional laboratory equipment. A number of laboratory centrifuges are available for use up to the 6-L scale, and the Jouan 5.22 machine has a 9.6-L capacity.

5.3. Extracellular Products

The majority of extracellular secondary metabolites are hydrophilic or ionizable substances. The ionizable substances are often extractable into a water-immiscible solvent in their unionized state. Thus acidic substances may be extracted from an acidified aqueous solution.

Some solvent-extraction techniques are relatively difficult to effect using conventional laboratory apparatus. For example, the classical penicillin G extraction in which acidified broth is contacted with a water-immiscible solvent can only be operated effectively using continuous-flow methods because of the poor stability of the product at low pH values. This extraction can be reproduced on the bench scale using the AKUFVE apparatus, which was designed for extraction studies in the nuclear industry *(12,13)*. Selective extraction may involve the use of a solvent in which the product has a poor partition coefficient. Countercurrent extractors are mostly process scale devices but the smallest four-stage extractor produced by Robatel could be considered a bench scale. It has a throughput of 50–100 mL/min.

Should solvent extraction be inapplicable as a primary purification stage, adsorption methods should be evaluated. Sequential use of ion exchangers and nonionic polymeric resins will often effect considerable purification. If the resins are to be used regularly such that >50 L will be used during a project, it will be more economical to obtain them directly from the manufacturers rather than from laboratory suppliers. Guidance in the use of ion exchangers is relatively sparse; a useful introduction is provided by Harland *(14)* (*see* Chapter 5).

The nonionic polymeric resins such as Amberlite XAD-1180 (Rohm and Haas) or Diaion HP20 (Mitsubishi) can often be used as the primary adsorbent. They act primarily by hydrophobic and pi-bond interactions. They can be surprisingly effective on water-soluble solutes, which have only a small hydrophobic domain in the molecule. Adsorption is enhanced with increasing ionic strength of the solution (salting-out effect). Should the broth applied to such resins require flocculation prior to clarification, inorganic flocculants such as calcium chloride should be used. The added inorganic ions promote adsorption, whereas organic flocculants can foul the resin. Elution of product from such resins is readily achieved using aqueous methanol, propanone, or propan-2-ol. Methanol should be used with caution as it may esterify or methanolyze certain reactive products. Resins of this type are readily available in bulk at an economical cost, having been developed for industrial applications such as cephalosporin C isolation. If higher capacity or stronger binding is required, the brominated polystyrene resins such as Sepabeads SP-207 (Mitsubishi) could be used. Informative technical literature is available from the manufacturers of the resins mentioned.

5.4. Product Purification

Much useful purification can be achieved using medium-pressure liquid chromatography (MPLC). A large variety of stationary phases are available for this technique, which uses particle sizes of 30–100 μm. In addition to silica gel and its usual derivatives, hydrophobic resins such as those mentioned above can be obtained in a fine bead form. Compared to silica gel, the polymeric resins have the advantage of being stable to concentrated alkali, which is useful for clean-up purposes. They have the disadvantage of being less rigid than silica gel and change their volume with change in solvent polarity. Examples of this type of resin include Amberchrom CG 161 (TosoHaas), and Diaion HP20SS (Mitsubishi), which are both polystyrene-divinyl benzene copolymers, and Amberchrom CG 71, a crosslinked methacrylic acid-based resin. MPLC is considerably less expensive than HPLC with respect to stationary phases, particularly since the latter usually involves the purchase of packed columns. Column systems for MPLC are available from a variety of manufacturers such as Büchi and Chromwald.

Preparative HPLC uses stationary phases of 20 μm or less and is used where high-resolution purification is required. This is not uncommon in secondary metabolite purification, as they are frequently produced as complex mixtures of very closely related compounds. At the time of scale-up, it is likely that analytical HPLC methods will have been developed. These can be used as a guide to devising preparative procedures, but the peak of interest must be well separated from impurities because the much higher loading used in preparative HPLC will result in band-broadening. Numerous books on HPLC have been published in the past 20 yr. Two that give practical advice are referenced here *(15,16)* (*see* Chapter 6).

Reverse phase silica (e.g., octadecyl silica) is widely used for analytical purposes and is very effective when used preparatively. However, its capacity is relatively low. It is resistant to fouling by the majority of impurities found in fermentation broths but certain long-chain aliphatics such as may be found in fermentation antifoams can cause problems. Once fouled, these stationary phases are less readily cleaned than the polymeric resins.

If the HPLC eluant contains a buffer salt, an additional stage will be required to obtain pure product. Desalting can often be achieved by passing the product/ salt solution through a column of one of the MPLC resins such as Diaion HP20SS, which will adsorb many compounds containing hydrophobic domains in the molecule, even though it may be highly water-soluble. Pure product can sometimes be obtained by simply washing the resin with water. In other cases, elution with dilute methanol or propanone may be necessary.

Equipment for preparative HPLC is relatively expensive. To maximize its utility, it should be specified with autoinjection to run unattended and collect previously identified peaks. A 30-min cycle is typical so that overnight operation can process over 30 portions of feed solution. This appears to be the best option for maximizing output with bench-scale apparatus. There is also the advantage that the separation can be fine-tuned during the course of the operation. A number of manufacturers supply equipment based on columns of 15–50 mm diameter packed with stationary phases of 5–15 μm. Retention times in reverse phase HPLC can be influenced by temperature. It is recommended that a column used for repetitive injection be housed in an oven set at a temperature slightly higher than ambient, e.g., 30°C.

Preparative MPLC and HPLC can use large amounts of solvent. It is suggested that an analytical grade is not necessary for intermediate stages of chromatography. There may be some virtue in using solvent mixtures that are readily separable by distillation, thus facilitating re-use. Automatic solvent recycle is an option provided by some manufacturers but should be used with caution. Eluant from an apparent "baseline" separation may contain impurities not detectable by the monitoring equipment in use and cause contamination of the bulk eluant.

The final stage of isolation is usually either crystallization or lyophilization. Great care should be taken in handling the dried product as many natural products are highly toxic. It is recommended that any solid product of unknown properties be handled in a glove box.

6. Summary

Scale-up involves more than just increasing volume. An increase in fermentation titer not only gives more available product but will normally increase the ratio of product to impurities, facilitating the isolation process. Isolation procedures can be made more efficient by carefully optimizing each stage with the aim of minimizing the number of stages and hence overall yield. There is still much empiricism in process development for both fermentation and extraction. An efficient overall process is the result of many incremental improvements and depends on reliable quantitative assay methods. Scale-up in a laboratory may satisfy the requirements for a compound. However, if there is any likelihood of further increase in scale involving the use of process plant, "robust" procedures using inexpensive materials should be used.

References

1. Irvine, T. S. (1990) Laboratory fermenters, in *Fermentation, A Practical Approach* (McNeil, B. and Harvey, L. M., eds.), IRL, Oxford, pp.17–38.
2. Bailey, J. E. and Ollis, D. F. (1977) *Biochemical Engineering Fundamentals*, McGraw-Hill, Tokyo, pp. 424–426.
3. Nallin-Omstead, M., Kaplan, L., and Buckland, B. C. (1989) Fermentation development and process improvement, in *Ivermectin and Avermectin* (Campbell, W. C., ed.), Springer-Verlag, Berlin, pp. 33–54.
4. DeWitt, J. P., Jackson, J. V., and Paulus, T. J. (1989) Actinomycetes, in *Fermentation Process Development and Industrial Microorganisms* (Neway, J. O., ed.), Marcel Dekker, New York, pp. 1–71.
5. Bull, A. T., Huck, T. A., and Bushell, M. E. (1990) Optimization strategies in microbial process development and operation, in *Microbial Growth Dynamics* (Poole, R. K., Bazin, M. J., and Keevil, C. W., eds.), IRL, Oxford, pp. 145–168.
6. Greasham, R. and Inamine, E. (1986) Nutritional improvement of processes, in *Manual of Industrial Microbiology and Biotechnology* (Demain, A. L. and Solomon, N. A., eds.), Americal Society for Microbiology, Washington, DC, pp. 41–48.
7. Plackett, R. L. and Burman, J. P. (1946) The design of multifactorial experiments. *Biometrika* **33**, 305–325.
8. Reisman, H. B. (1993) Problems in scaleup of biotechnology production processes. *Crit. Rev. Biotechnol.* **13**, 195–253.
9. Braun, S. and Vecht-Lifshitz, S. E. (1991) Mycelial morphology and metabolite production. *Tibtech.* **9**, 63–68.
10. Parton, C. and Willis, P. (1990) Strain preservation, inoculum preparation and development, in *Fermentation, A Practical Approach* (McNeil, B. and Harvey, L. M., eds.), IRL, Oxford, pp. 39–64.
11. Van Brakel, L. and Kleizen, H. H. (1990), Problems in downstream processing, in *Chemical Engineering Problems in Biotechnology* (Winkler, M. A., ed.), Elsevier Applied Science, New York, pp. 95–165.
12. Reinhardt, H. and Rydberg, J. (1970) A rapid continuous system for measuring the distribution ratios in solvent extraction. *Chem. Ind.* **11**, 488–491.
13. Rydberg, J., Persson, H., Aronsson, P. O., Selme, A., and Skarnemark, G. (1980) H-10: a new centrifuge for rapid liquid-liquid separations. *Hydrometallurgy* **5**, 273–281.

14. Harland, C. E. (1994) *Ion Exchange: Theory and Practice* (2nd ed.), Royal Society of Chemistry, Cambridge.
15. Dolan, J. W. and Snyder, L. R. (1989) *Troubleshooting LC Systems.* Humana Press, Clifton, NJ, USA.
16. Meyer, V. R. (1994) *Practical High Performance Liquid Chromatography* (2nd ed.), Wiley, Chichester, UK.

15

Follow-Up of Natural Product Isolation

Richard J. P. Cannell

1. Introduction

What do we mean by "follow-up"? Let us assume that the natural product just isolated is of some interest, that is to say, it may have some biological activity worthy of further examination, it may represent a novel structure, or it may be of interest for ecological or chemotaxonomic reasons. In each case, we may want more of the compound, or analogs, biosynthetic precursors, and other related metabolites. If the compound is biologically active, we may look to these related compounds to provide structure–activity relationship data, for compounds that are more active, more chemically or metabolically stable, or in commercial terms will strengthen the patent position of the original compound by describing the wider family of metabolites.

Apart from classical synthetic chemistry approaches, there are a number of ways that we as natural products scientists can utilize the systems that we have already established so far (e.g., organisms, growth/culture conditions, chromatographic systems and separation methods) in order to build on this initial natural product isolation.

2. Further Extraction

Perhaps the most obvious and most important approach is that of carrying out a repeat fermentation (or collection)—probably on a larger scale—in order to isolate either further quantities of the same compound or, any related metabolites that might exist within the same organism. It might also be productive to examine other strains of the organism, or other related species, as these may yield greater levels of, or analogs of, the compound. Armed with knowledge of the original natural product, it is possible to look again at the extract with a better idea of how to find related structures, as follows.

From: *Methods in Biotechnology, Vol. 4: Natural Products Isolation*
Edited by: R. J. P. Cannell © Humana Press Inc., Totowa, NJ

2.1. Similar UV Spectrum

Comparison of UV profiles of the compound with those of materials corresponding to other peaks on a chromatogram can lead to identification of related metabolites. Related compounds often possess features or moieties that give rise to characteristic maxima—a handle by which some peaks can be picked out from the many of no interest.

With high-performance liquid chromatography (HPLC), this kind of analysis may be performed "on-line" by use of a diode array detector, i.e., a detector that measures absorbance over a range of wavelengths simultaneously so that a UV spectrum can be acquired from every point on the chromatogram. Alternatively, material corresponding to various peaks can be collected and their UV absorbance measured individually in a UV spectrophotometer.

The UV spectrum can therefore give a semi-identification that may at least point the extractor to a few selected peaks in an otherwise complex chromatogram.

2.2. Chemical Identification

This principle of identification of compounds from the same structural or chemical family can also be carried out in other ways once the components of a mixture have been partially or fully separated. For example, a TLC plate or paper chromatogram may be sprayed or stained with reagents that react specifically with certain classes of chemical. An example of this was the detection of a number of different secondary amines in a culture broth of *Streptomyces luteogriseus* by staining TLC plates of extracts of the organism with phenothiazine perbromide *(1)*.

This approach of "chemical screening" can also be used to examine related organisms or different strains of the same organism, in order to detect those that exhibit related, or different chemical profiles, which may therefore be the focus of further isolation work.

This principle of detecting specific classes of related compound with relative ease is discussed at greater length as part of the dereplication procedures described in Chapter 10 and also in Chapter 7.

2.3. Mass Spectrometry and LC-MS

Mass spectrometry (MS) is a powerful tool for identifying compounds that are related. Coupled to an LC system, mass spectrometry can often detect the similarities and relatedness of materials corresponding to chromatographic peaks by their characteristic fragmentation pattern and/or by the fact that they contain particular atoms, e.g., Cl and Br, that have characteristic isotope ratios. More simply, it may just be that two compounds have a similar molecular weight or molecular weights separated by expected or explicable differences;

e.g., differences that are multiples of 16 could likely represent the same molecule with and without various oxygen groups.

2.4. Thorough Isolation

The most complete means of ensuring that all of the related metabolites present in an organism extract are isolated, is simply to isolate everything—or at least as many compounds as possible—from the extract. By this means, other unrelated secondary metabolites are often also isolated. Such metabolites may not be obviously structurally related to the original metabolite of interest but may comprise earlier biosynthetic precursors or provide clues as to the biosynthetic pathways in operation and, in addition, may help to build up a secondary metabolic profile of the organism. This process is facilitated by the fact that it is generally carried out on a larger scale repeat extraction, from which it is possible to examine properly the minor peaks of a chromatogram. In the original small-scale separation, these minor peaks may have been overlooked or ignored in favor of more readily obtainable material or may even have not been detectable. This process is often achieved by obtaining a good separation of the extract on preparative HPLC and monitoring the eluate with a high-sensitivity detection system in order to pick out all the minor peaks, barely detectable humps, and perturbations on the chromatogram baseline that might represent minor components. This process—sometimes known as "looking in the grass"—can lead to interesting and surprising results. There is more than one case in which biological activity has been assumed to be solely the result of a major component of an extract only to find later that in fact, most or all of the activity is due to a potent compound present in the extract at very low levels and hence in danger of being overlooked. (*see* **Note 1**).

A subsequent fermentation might also lead to additional, different compounds because, for a number of possible reasons, the secondary metabolic profile of a repeat fermentation may be different. Such reasons might include the effects of scale-up (e.g., oxygenation, shear forces), changes in the organism strain, subtle undetectable differences in the growth of the seed culture, inoculation into growth culture, and so on, all of which can lead to variations in levels and types of secondary metabolite expression.

2.5. Isolation of Squalestatin "Minors"

An example of this approach is given by a group of metabolites: the squalestatins (also known as zaragozic acids), isolated from the fungus, *Phoma* sp. (*see* **Fig. 1**). Extracts of this organism were found to have squalene synthase inhibitory activity, and extraction resulted in the isolation of the major squalestatins of which there were approximately four *(2,3)*. As these compounds appeared to hold potential as leads for the development of cholesterol-

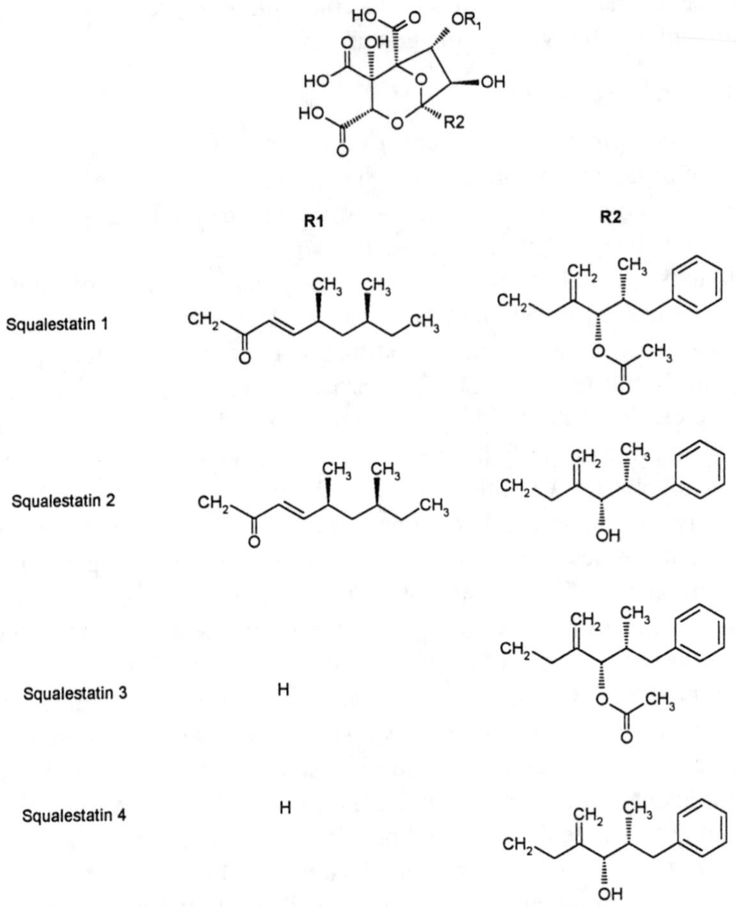

Fig. 1. Some of the squalestatin group of metabolites.

lowering drugs, repeat fermentations were carried out on a larger scale. This enabled more of the previously characterized squalestatins to be isolated, but it also gave the opportunity and will to hunt for related compounds that might be present at much lower levels. By filtration, then adsorption onto a column of a nonionic adsorbent (styrene divinylbenzene; Whatman XAD-16), the concentrated initial extract (from a 500-L fermentation) was clarified and partially purified and then converted to a crude calcium salt, a fairly selective step for this group of tri-carboxylic acids (**Fig. 2**). Large-scale, open-column reverse phase chromatography (Whatman Partisil Prep P40) of acidified extracts of this calcium salt resulted in the isolation of the major squalestatins, some of them as crystalline tripotassium salts. The side fractions and the crystallization

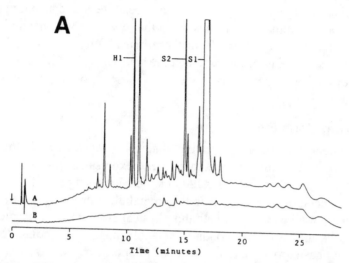

Column: Phase Separations Ltd Spherisorb C6, 5 μm (15 × 0.46 cm). Mobile Phases: A, H₂O-H₂SO₄, 1,000:0.15. B, MeCN-H₂O-H₂SO₄, 500:500:0.15. Linear gradient 0 to 100% B in 15 minutes, hold 10 minutes, 100 to 0% B in 1.5 minutes. Flow: 2 ml/minute. Detection: λ 210 nm. Range: 0.1 AUFS. Chart speed: 1 cm/minute. Trace B is of a blank gradient.

B Broth
    | adjust to pH 10.5
    | pass through rotary drum filter
  Filtrate
    | adjust to pH 6.5
Amberlite XAD-16
    | wash with (NH₄)₂SO₄
    | wash with EDTA (5,000 litre scale)
    | wash with water
    | elute with Me₂CO-H₂O (1:1)
  Eluate
    | Ca(OAc)₂
    | filter (add filter aid on 5,000 litre scale)
Crude Ca salt

C

Squalestatin	Rt (minutes)	Squalestatin	Rt (minutes)
H7	5.8	V1 isomer a	13.6
H9	5.9	V1 isomer b	13.7
H2	6.4	S4	13.7
H6	6.9	W1	14.0
H1	9.4	S8	14.2
H5	9.8	S2	14.3
6-Deoxy H1	10.2	U1	14.5
7-Deoxy H5	11.2	X1	15.4
6-Deoxy H5	11.2	T1	15.6
V2	11.3	S1	15.8
W2	11.4	Y1	16.1
6,7-Dideoxy H5	11.8	S5	16.7
S3	12.6	7-Deoxy S1	16.8
U2	12.9		

HPLC conditions as for Fig. 2 but flow 3 ml/minute.

Fig. 2. Chromatogram of an acidified extract of crude calcium salt of the squalestatins. **(A)** Typical trace after HPLC of an acidified extract of crude calcium salt. **(B)** Isolation of crude calcium salt from fermentation of *Phoma* sp. C2932. **(C)** Squalestatins isolated in the course of this work and their retention times in a gradient HPLC system. (Reproduced with permission from **ref. 4**.)

mother liquors were subjected to further preparative HPLC. By scrutinizing the chromatograms and attempting to isolate almost every component, an additional 24 related metabolites were isolated fom the same organism *(4)*.

Some of these metabolites were extracted in relative abundance, but others were present only in minute quantities, such that it would have been virtually impossible to have isolated them from the initial 200-mL extract. Although this example is something of an extreme case, further related metabolites are frequently found from repeat extractions, even those involving no, or a much more modest, scale-up.

3. Maximizing Gene Expression

A more general method of generating analogs or related metabolites is to attempt to maximize secondary metabolic gene expression in order to maximize the range of products formed. Although there is no single unified concept of secondary metabolism, it is clear that metabolite production does vary according to an organism's chemical and physical environment. In microbial systems at least, the onset of secondary metabolism generally coincides with the end of log phase growth and the onset of idiophase, which itself is generally the result of limitation of a specific nutrient. The nature of this limiting nutrient and the other nutrients in the medium can determine the secondary metabolites produced, through processes such as derepression, or inhibition, of secondary metabolic pathways. For instance, carbon catabolite control is exhibited by glucose, which represses phenoxazinone synthase expression and hence actinomycin production in *Streptomyces antibioticus*; high levels of ammonium suppress the formation of tylosin by *Streptomyces fradiae* and cephalosporin by *Streptomyces clavuligerus*; high inorganic phosphate levels repress enzymes involved in the synthesis of tetracyclins, candicidin, neomycin, and streptomycin; concentrations of trace metals (e.g., iron, zinc, cobalt) often have a profound effect on metabolite production *(5)*. Other compounds may induce or enhance the production of secondary metabolites. These include both commonly occurring molecules, such as various amino acids, which may or may not be components of the metabolites, or less prevalent compounds, such as the autoregulator molecules known to play a role in the related aspects of differentiation and quorum sensing, e.g., A-factor, pamamycin. Overall, the processes that regulate secondary metabolism are poorly understood, a situation that befits a whole form of metabolism whose biological role is still very unclear. Suffice it to say that many physical and chemical parameters can influence secondary metabolite production, and the way in which this can best be used to advantage is generally best determined empirically for any new metabolite or organism.

Hence, varying these factors can lead to a much wider range of metabolites than would be produced by an organism under a single set of conditions. This is most easily carried out for microorganisms, though secondary metabolite production by other organisms is also affected by their local environment. Much has been written about this aspect of microbiology (*see*, for example,

ref. *6*), and will not be discussed in detail here, but some of the most important factors affecting metabolite production are:

1. Medium: carbon source, nitrogen source, phosphorus source, C/N/P ratios, levels of trace nutrients.
2. Autoregulators (e.g., A-factor, pamamycin).
3. Physical conditions: shaken liquid culture, static liquid culture, solid state culture.
4. Oxygen levels.
5. Growth rate.
6. Temperature.
7. pH.

A general rule of thumb is that exposing an organism to various forms of "stress" will lead to an increase in the range of secondary metabolites produced. If the aim is to isolate from a microorganism the greatest possible number of metabolites, then the organism should always be grown in more than one medium and/or in more than one form (e.g., shaken liquid and solid state). Approaches for the more specific aim of maximizing the production of a particular metabolite are discussed in Chapter 14.

4. Blocked Biosynthesis
4.1. Biosynthetic Mutants

The generation from a producing organism of mutant strains that are blocked or altered in the biosynthetic pathway can lead to the isolation of related metabolites that could not otherwise be obtained. These metabolites may be intermediates from the blocked pathway that would normally be transient and detectable only in trace amounts, if at all, or they may represent "shunt" metabolites, whereby the intermediates have gone down a different biosynthetic route, resulting in novel compounds. The products of such mutants may be of interest in their own right, or they may be of interest in biosynthetic studies, biotransformation experiments or as starting points for precursor-directed biosynthesis.

In its simplest form, this might involve mutating isolates of the organism and looking for changes in either the level or type of secondary metabolite produced in the resultant isolates. Mutation can be carried out by the use of UV light or chemical mutagens or by the use of selective media—nutrient-deficient, or toxin-containing—to isolate strains of an organism with a modified genetic make-up, able to survive on such media, and which may result in concomitant modification of the secondary metabolites. The same effect may be obtained by the use of enzyme inhibitors that block a biosynthetic pathway at particular steps.

4.1.1. Pradimicin Biosynthetic Mutants

Spores of *Actinomadura verrucosospora* subsp. *neohibisca*, a producer of the dihydrobenzonaphthacene quinone antibiotic pradimicin, were mutagen-

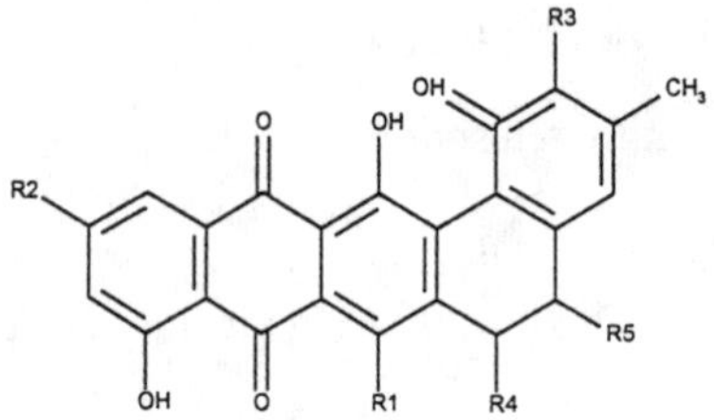

R1	R2	R3	R4	R5
OH	H	COOH	OH	OH
OCH₃	H	COOH	OH	OH
H	H	COOH	OH	OH
H	H	CONHCH(CH₃)COOH	OH	OH
OCH₃	H	CONHCH(CH₃)COOH	OH	OH
OH	CH₃	CONHCH(CH₃)COOH	OH	OH
H	H	COOH	H	OH
H	CH₃	COOH	OH	OH
H	CH₃	CONHCH(CH₃)COOH	OH	OH
OH	H	CONHCH(CH₃)COOH	OH	OH
OH	CH₃	CONHCH(CH₃)COOH	OH	
H	CH₃	CONHCH(CH₃)COOH	OH	

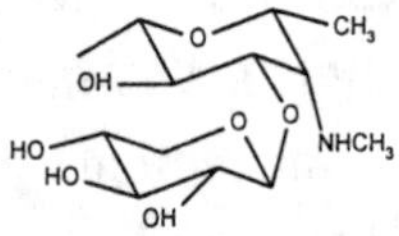

Fig. 3. Structures of pradimicins isolated from biosynthetic mutants.

ized by UV light and/or *N*-methyl-*N*′-nitro-*N*-nitrosoguanidine. As pradimicin is a red pigment, mutants were initially selected from approximately 10,000 colonies on the basis of the production of colorless or non-red pigments, and these were assigned to a number of classes, each of which either accumulated intermediates at a particular stage in the pathway or produced novel shunt metabolites. From these strains were isolated eight novel metabolites and a number of known metabolites *(7,8)* (**Fig. 3**).

4.1.2. Aclacinomycin Biosynthetic Mutants

Similarly, mutants of *Streptomyces galilaeus*, which produces another class of glycosidic anthracyclines, aclacinomycins (**Fig. 4**), yielded a number of novel metabolites. These included novel anthracyclinones devoid of sugars and others with combinations of different sugars. Some were able to produce only one form of the aglycone, others were impaired in their ability to supply rhodosamine as they produced analogs lacking this sugar, others were unable to oxidize the terminal rhodinose to form cinerulose A, and others were unable to supply rhodinose at all *(9–11)*. From the same mutagenesis program were isolated a number of strains capable of producing aclacinomycin A at a 30-fold higher concentration than that of the parent strain.

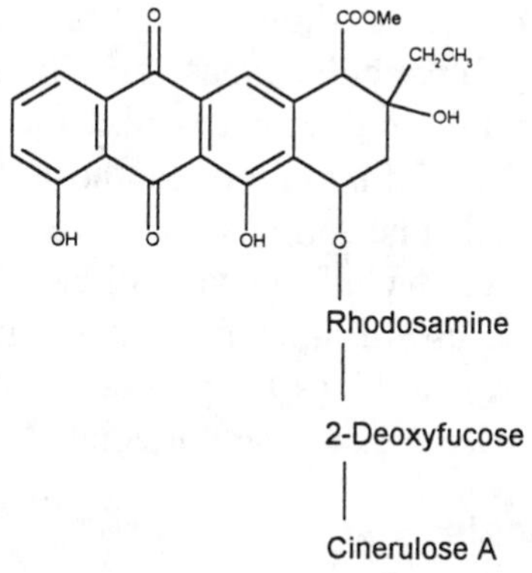

Fig. 4. Aclacinomycin A.

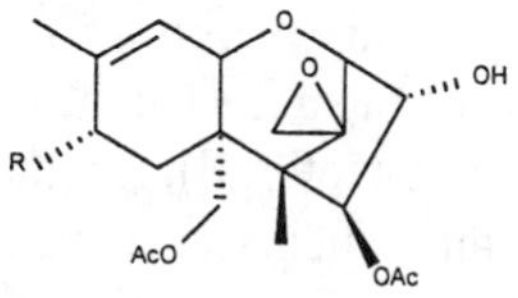

Toxin T-2   R = $OCOCH_2CH(CH_3)_2$

Analogues   R = $OCOCH(CH_3)_2$

R = $OCO(CH_3)_2$

Fig. 5. Trichothecene Toxin T-2 and shunt metabolites isolated from mutant.

4.1.3. Tricothecene Analogs

The tricothecenes are a family of toxic fungal metabolites, and T-2 toxin is the major tricothecene produced by the fungus *Fusarium sporotrichioides* (**Fig. 5**). In studying the biosynthesis of this metabolite, Beremand et al. *(12)* generated a range of amino acid auxotrophs and found that the leucine auxotroph was blocked in the production of T-2 toxin. They found that this mutant, however, produced two analogs that were present only at barely detectable levels in the wild type. The relative concentrations of T-2 and its analogs could be manipulated by controlling the concentration of leucine in the medium, indicating that the metabolites, were shunt metabolites and that all three compounds derive from a common intermediate.

4.2. Enzyme Inhibitors

Enzyme inhibitors can be used to produce the same effect as a genetic mutant, i.e., to block a biosynthetic pathway and lead to the buildup of otherwise transient intermediates or shunt products. Such inhibitors include cerulenin, which inhibits fatty acid synthase and the similar polyketide synthase, and sinefungin and ethionine that inhibit the transfer of methionine groups. Another useful group of inhibitors are those that inhibit cytochromes P450, a group of enzymes that perform oxidative reactions on a wide range of compounds. These inhibitors include ancymidol, metyrapone, and phenytoin. An example of this is the use of ancymidol in fermentations of the fungus *Gibberella pulicaris* in order to block the production of the tricothecenes and allow access to the otherwise transient intermediate trichodiene *(13)*.

5. Directed Biosynthesis

There is a further, more elegant way of attempting to manipulate or "persuade" the organism to produce analogs or derivatives. Most secondary metabolites are largely constructed for the most part from a number of standard building blocks (e.g., terpenoids originate from 5-carbon isoprenyl units; polyketides originate from acetate units [in the case of fungi] or formyl, acetate or malonyl units [in the case of bacteria]). Aromatic groups tend to derive from one of the aromatic amino acids such as tyrosine, phenylalanine, or tryptophan, which themselves derive from shikimic acid or from acetate units. Alkaloids, too, derive in a large part from a number of amino acids such as tyrosine, phenylalanine, tryptophan, lysine, and ornithine, as well as from acetate units, mevalonate, and a number of other simple precursors. Providing organisms with analogs of precursors or intermediates of a secondary metabolite can sometimes lead to these being incorporated by the organism's biosynthetic machinery into a novel secondary metabolite.

This approach assumes some knowledge, or at least some presumption, of the general biosynthetic pathway by which the metabolite is formed. It is usually possible to make a good guess at the biosynthetic origins of a molecule, particularly when biosynthetic information is available on a structurally similar molecule, and these theories can be tested by the use of isotopically labeled precursors. It also relies on the fact that the biosynthetic enzymes are not so specific as to exclude all but the natural precursor. Fortunately, the enzymes of secondary metabolism tend to be less specific than those of primary metabolism.

5.1. Mutasynthesis

As mentioned in **Subheading 4.1.**, the products of a biosynthetic mutant may be of interest in their own right but, in addition, the mutant or its products can be utilized further. The mutant can be used as a reaction system to which can be fed a modified form of the first blocked intermediate, i.e., the product of the blocked enzyme, or subsequent building blocks. Assuming that this is the only blocked step in the pathway and that the remainder of the pathway's enzymes are functioning, the enzymes may well act on the modified intermediate free from competition from the natural substrates to produce a derivatized final product. Mutasynthesis is the term generally used to refer to this process of "blocking and feeding."

The blocked intermediates may also be fed to other organisms in a rational manner—such as to those that usually modify a related precursor—in order to produce "hybrid" metabolites. This process of mutasynthesis usually requires some knowledge of the blocked step and that the biosynthetic enzymes are sufficiently unspecific to accept substrate analogs.

5.2. Methodology

An advantage of this approach is that, once a putative biosynthetic pathway has been elucidated and suitable precursor analogs obtained, there are very few additional experimental procedures, other than those already developed for the isolation of the original "parent" metabolite.

The major processes involved are feeding the precursor to the organism and the development of a separation method to analyze and isolate the products.

5.2.1. Feeding Precursor Analogs

The procedures involved in carrying out directed biosynthesis are largely based on educated guesses, and the best conditions for any given family of metabolites are best determined empirically. There is no right or wrong way, and in many cases it is not worth expending a great effort in adjusting the feeding conditions to obtain the best product titer—it is often enough just to generate the modified metabolite at any level. However, there are a number of general guidelines that it makes sense to follow.

1. Addition of the precursor to a fermentation broth can be carried out at the beginning of the fermentation, i.e., as a medium component, or it can be added at the onset of the biosynthesis of the secondary metabolite, which is very often at the beginning of stationary phase, the period when most secondary metabolites are formed. This latter method is generally preferred as it is more likely to avoid possible toxic effects of the precursor analogs on cell growth and primary metabolism as well as the possibilities of the precursor being catabolized and recycled during the processes of primary metabolism before secondary metabolite formation has begun.

2. The compound may be added as a single aliquot or it may be pulse-fed—perhaps once a day for 4 d from the end of lag phase, or in more sophisticated systems it may be added continuously.

3. The precursor is generally added at levels at which its natural relative might be found in the broth (although in many cases, the natural relative would not be "free" in the broth but would be intracellular and mobilized only in an activated form, e.g., phosphorylated or as a Coenzyme A ester). Obviously, this is a fairly

vague figure but suffice to say that such "physiological" levels are generally assumed to be about 10 mM. An alternative approach is to add the precursor at much higher levels, say 50–100 mM, in order to outcompete the natural precursor for the biosynthetic enzymes' active site (for which the latter probably has greater specificity). The uptake of the unnatural precursor may only be low compared to that of the natural precursor, so by adding excess it may be possible to increase the final amount of a modified product. Disadvantages of this approach are that the high levels of the fed compound may have a toxic or inhibitory effect on the growth or metabolism of the organism and, more specifically, on the general biosynthesis of the secondary metabolite itself. It also requires a greater supply of the precursor analog.

4. The precursor analog is added aseptically, generally as a concentrated, aqueous solution that has been filter-sterilized, autoclaved, or prepared under aseptic conditions. However, if the compound is insoluble in water, it may be added in a small volume of organic solvent or even as a solid. This may cause the compound to precipitate as soon as it enters the aqueous medium but this does not make the experiment a lost cause. The compound may be sparingly soluble and may act in effect as a slow-release feed.

5. The fact that an artificial precursor is not incorporated may reflect problems relating to its uptake across the cell membrane and it may be necessary to modify conditions to create either a cell-free system or a resting cell culture. The former involves growing the culture to stationary phase, separating the cells from the liquid medium by centrifugation, then smashing the cells (e.g., in a sonicating bath) and resuspending in an isotonic buffer to which the precursor analogs are added. This removes the barrier of the cell walls, thus allowing access for exogenous precursor molecules to the biosynthesis enzymes.

In resting cell cultures the cells of the stationary phase culture are separated from the liquid medium by centrifugation, then washed in buffer, centrifuged again, and resuspended in buffer and/or minimal medium to which the precursor is added. Thus, removed of all exogenous substrates, the cells are essentially intact and viable but inert, and with few competing biosynthetic or metabolic pathways in operation, the likelihood of precursor uptake and incorporation is increased. An additional advantage is that the washed-cell system is cleaner than the original cell culture, making purification easier.

There may be problems relating to the conversion of the metabolite to an activated form (e.g., an acetyl coenzyme A ester), which it may require in order to be transported and/or recognized by the relevant enzymes. Other compounds may be rapidly metabolized and "chewed up" by the pathways of primary metabolism before they can be incorporated into the secondary metabolite.

5.2.2. Analysis of Directed-Biosynthesis Products

Presumably, an assay system will already have been established to monitor the natural product during the initial isolation, and this may allow for analysis of the modified product. By comparing the chromatogram of the precursor-fed organism extract with that of an unfed control organism, it should be possible to detect peaks in the former corresponding to the modified product and/or substrate that are not present in the control. If, however, a modified product is undetected by the established analytical system, this can mean either that the precursor has not been incorporated, or simply that the modified product has not been resolved from the natural product. This problem is compounded by the fact that there will be no standard of the compound available. Resolution of potentially coeluting compounds may require gradient HPLC or exploitation of further differences between the modified and natural products by means such as LC-MS—a technique ideal for such analysis. The presence of a particular atom such as a halogen or an additional oxygen can be readily detected by this method. The incorporation of a fluorine-containing precursor can be followed by the use of ^{19}F NMR. Any fluorine-containing metabolites will give a single peak with a characteristic shift on a ^{19}F NMR spectrum, and with no signals from any other molecules, this is a simple and unambiguous technique by which to follow the generation of fluorine-containing metabolites in a complex mixture (**Note 2**).

5.3. Precursor-Directed Biosynthesis of Squalestatins

The squalestatins, described in the previous section, also provide an example of how some knowledge of biosynthetic pathways can lead to interesting directed-biosynthetic products.

The molecule appeared at first sight to be polyketide in nature, and in order to test this assumption and ascertain the biosynthetic origin of the component parts of the molecule, the producing organism—*Phoma* sp.—was fed with isotopically labeled acetate units in the form of [1-^{13}C], [2-^{13}C], and [1,2-^{13}C2] acetate. These demonstrated that the backbone of the molecule was formed from two polyketide chains made up of acetate units. The remaining four carbons of the bicyclic ring structure (carbons *21,3,4,22*) appeared from NMR coupling studies to be incorporated as adjacent intact acetate-derived units at a level lower than the others, suggesting metabolism of the acetate via the TCA cycle to a four-carbon unit; indeed, feeding [2,3-^{13}C succinate] resulted in incorporation of this double-label (albeit scrambled incorporation, suggesting that the succinate had also been metabolized to a large extent by the TCA cycle). Other carbons *(19,20,32,33)* appeared to derive from single carbon units in the form of *S*-adenosyl methionine. The aromatic portion of this molecule was investigated by feeding ^{13}C-labeled forms of phenylalanine and benzoic acid, which resulted in incorporation of both, but the particularly high incorporation of benzoic acid suggested its role as the starter unit of biosynthesis following its formation from phenylalanine *(14)*.

To summarize, it had been established that the backbone of this family of molecules was built from the addition of acetate building blocks to an aromatic starter unit together with the condensation of this to a four-carbon α-keto dicarboxylic acid, followed by esterification/acylation of the tetraketide chain and methylation by methionine-derived carbons and probably hydroxylation at C7. All together this provides a body of information of interest not only for its own sake but as a means of "hitching a ride" on the organism's biosynthetic pathway to make analogs of the compound (**Note 3**).

It was felt, for a number of reasons, that the aromatic moiety represented an area of the molecule suitable for manipulation as a means of generating analogs. It derived from a small simple molecule but with a number of sites for modification that could potentially give rise to a large number of analogs. It had already been shown that feeding labeled benzoic acid resulted in high levels of incorporation into squalestatin—it was the starter unit and presumably relatively little was metabolized by other pathways—maximizing the chances of detecting incorporation. Finally, the methods involved in modifying specific sites on such aromatic groups are generally complex and difficult to carry out by chemical means, so the products were likely to be valuable.

A range of simple analogs of benzoic acid and phenylalanine, easily obtainable from standard chemical suppliers, were chosen as substrates. These included a large number of hydroxy- and dihydroxybenzoic acids, aminobenzoic acids, nitrobenzoic acids, fluoro-, difluoro-, trifluoro-, tetrafluoro- and pentafluorobenzoic acids, chlorobenzoic acids, iodobenzoic acids, and methoxybenzoic acids. A number of structures other than those with a six-membered aromatic ring were also tried, including pyridinecarboxaldehydes, alicyclic carboxylic acids, naphthalenecarboxylic acids, furancarboxylic acids, thiophenecarboxylic acids, nitro-, bromo-, and chlorothiophenecarboxylic acids.

5.3.1. Method

Feeding studies demonstrated that benzoic acid added at the time of inoculation was not incorporated but when added at d 3, 4, or 5 was incorporated at very significant levels. This presumably was because of the fact that the compound added at d 0 was metabolized by the processes of primary metabolism before the culture reached stationary phase where secondary metabolism for the most part takes over.

The samples were added as aqueous solutions (6.25 mg/mL), which were adjusted to neutral pH with sodium hydride and filter sterilized (**Note 4**). 2-mL aliquots of each of these were added to individual cultures (50 mL) to give a final concentration of precursor of 0.25 mg/mL and the cultures reincubated at 25°C with shaking, as they had been for the first part of the fermentation. Four days later (seven days after incubation), the cultures were harvested, analyzed, and the products isolated.

HPLC analysis: Samples of broth were mixed with an equal volume of acetonitrile containing sulfuric acid (5 mL/L), centrifuged, and the supernatant analyzed by reverse phase gradient HPLC (Spherisorb C6 [5-μm particle size,

150 × 4.5 mm] with a gradient of 0–50% acetonitrile/water with sulfuric acid [50 µL/L], flow rate 1 mL/min, detection 210 nm).

HPLC-MS analysis: Samples of broth were prepared for HPLC-MS analysis by mixing with an equal volume of acetonitrile containing trifluoroacetic acid (5 mL/L). The samples were centrifuged and the supernatant analyzed by an isocratic HPLC method (Spherisorb ODS2 [5-µm particle size, 150 × 4.5 mm] acetonitrile/water [55:45] with trifluoroacetic acid [0.1%, v/v], flow rate 0.5 mL/min). This system was connected via a thermospray interface to a (Finnigan Mat TSQ 70B) mass spectrometer. Using the HPLC conditions described, it was not, in fact, possible to differentiate between squalestatin 1 and its fluorinated analogs as they coeluted but they could be detected by MS (*see* **Note 5**).

Purification of the analogs was carried out as before by solvent extraction, adsorption, and elution (solid phase extraction) from a column of Amberlite XAD16, followed by loading of the sample onto a preparative HPLC column (Spherisorb ODS2, 5-µm particle size), which was washed with 25% acetonitrile/water, then squalestatins 1 and analogs were eluted with 60% acetonitrile/water. A set of final preparative HPLC steps were carried out to resolve each of the analogs and the parent compound. The products isolated are shown in **Fig. 6** *(15,16)* (*see* **Note 6**).

So, in the above case, the production of these fluorinated and thiophenylated squalestatins necessitated the following:

1. Some idea of the biosynthesis in order to pick a sensible range of suitable precursor analogs.
2. Some simple optimization of feeding conditions. At its simplest, this might involve determination of whether to:
    a. Add compounds at inoculation, i.e., at the beginning of, or during, growth phase, or after several days growth when log phase growth has stopped (at the onset of, or during, secondary metabolism).
    b. Use whole cells or a washed-cell culture or a cell-free system for optimal incorporation.
3. A method for detection of incorporation, e.g., LC, LC-MS, GC-MS, TLC, NMR.
4. A method for purifying a number of very closely related compounds.

Arguably, the example described above represented a not particularly successful attempt to generate a wide range of metabolites, insofar as a relatively low proportion of the potential precursor analogs were incorporated into the final squalestatin molecule. Presumably, therefore, the active site of one or more of the biosynthetic enzymes exhibits fairly narrow specificity.

Why was it that only the fluorobenzoic acids and the thiophenes were apparently incorporated? In the case of the former, this may reflect the probability that fluorobenzoic acid is structurally the most similar of the analogs to the natural substrate. Fluorine is a fairly inert atom and isosteric with hydrogen. It is not so clear why the thiophenes should have been incorporated.

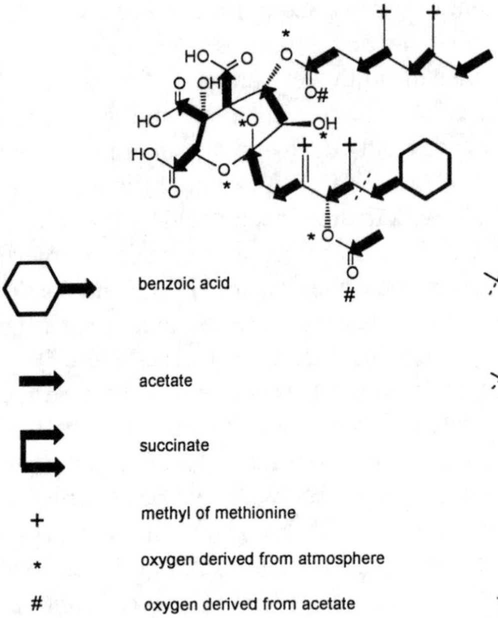

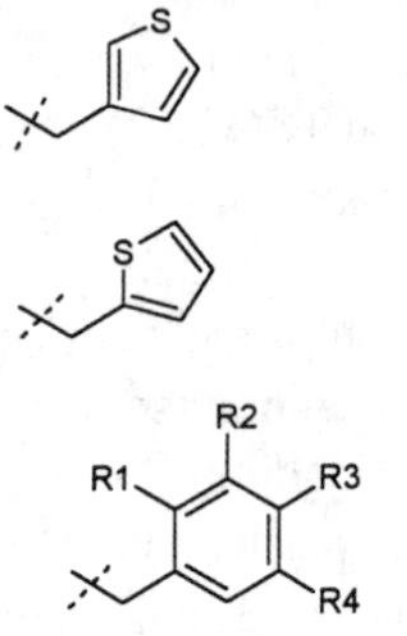

Fig. 6. Biosynthesis of squalestatins and products formed from directed biosynthesis.

	R1	R2	R3	R4
1	H	H	H	H
2	H	H	F	H
3	H	F	H	H
4	F	H	H	H
5	H	F	F	H
6	H	F	H	F
7	F	F	H	H

Legend:
- benzoic acid
- acetate
- succinate
- \+ methyl of methionine
- * oxygen derived from atmosphere
- \# oxygen derived from acetate

Alternative reasons may include:

1. Inability of the other precursors to cross the cell membrane. Had a cell-free system been used, more of the metabolites may have been incorporated (although it is unlikely that any squalestatins would be formed in a cell-free system).
2. Enzyme inhibitory effect of other precursors. (Addition of some of the compounds was associated with a reduction in levels of squalestatins.)
3. Some of the analogs were metabolized by different pathways.

As well as concentrating on the aromatic moiety, attention could also have focused on other parts of the molecule that derive from such as the 4-C unit that comprises part of the bicyclic core, or the various acetate units, by feeding analogs of these precursors. However, there is likely to be more success by using intermediates from later in the pathway.

5.4. Other Examples

There are numerous other examples of precursor-directed biosynthesis involving natural products of various biosynthetic origins *(17)*. Many have utilized

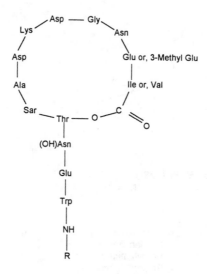

Natural metabolites; R= 8-Methylnonanoyl, 8-Methyldecanoyl or n-Decanoyl

Following feeding of Hexanoic Acid, Caprylic Acid and Nonanoic Acid,
R= Hexanoyl, Capryl and Nonanoyl, respectively

Fig. 7. Directed biosynthesis products of A54145.

intermediates from much later stages in the biosynthetic pathway than the example of the squalestatins.

5.4.1. A54145

This group of lipopeptide antibiotics produced by *Streptomyces fradiae* spawned a wide number of analogs produced by feeding various fatty acids (**Fig. 7**). In addition, the ratios of the various natural metabolites could be controlled by addition of valine or isoleucine *(18)*.

5.4.2. Mitomycins

This group of natural products derived from the shikimate pathway and produced by *Streptomyces caeapitosus* led to a large number of analogues by feeding the organism with a range of primary amines *(19)*. These are summarized in **Fig. 8**.

5.4.3. Cyclosporins

Cyclosporins are a class of cyclic peptides produced by *Beauvaria nivea*, that possess immunosuppressant activity and have spawned a large number of additional modified forms by feeding analogs of the natural amino acid building blocks. A large range of derivatives have been formed via this method with

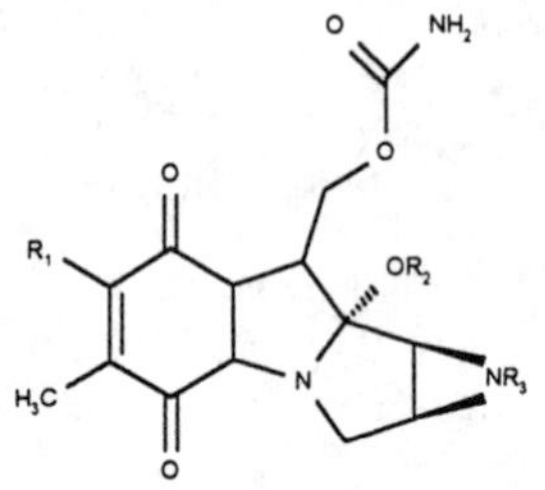

Mitomycin B: R$_1$ = OCH$_3$, R$_2$ = H, R$_3$ = CH$_3$
Mitomycin C: R$_1$= NH$_2$, R$_2$ = CH$_3$, R$_3$ = H

Analogues: R$_1$= Methylamine
               Ethylamine
               Propylamine
               Propargylamine
               Allylamine
               2-Methylallylamine
               2-Chloroethylamine
               3-Chloropropylamine
               Benzylamine
               Aniline

Type I Analogues - Amine incorporated into Mitomycin C nucleus
Type II Analogues - Amine incorporated into Mitomycin B nucleus

Fig. 8. Mitomycin analogs produced by feeding various amine precursors.

modifications at almost all of the amino acid positions *(20,21)*, and more were produced by carrying out the process in a cell-free system. These could not be formed by feeding the precursors to the whole organism, probably because the amino acids involved were normally metabolized *(22)* (**Fig. 9**).

The range of examples that can be drawn from amino acid-derived natural products formed via amide synthases reflect the unspecificity of these enzymes in peptide biosynthesis compared to ribosomal protein synthesis.

5.4.4. Avermectins

One of the most successful attempts at generating a wide range of analogs of a natural product resulted from the isolation of a mutant of the avermectin-producing organism, *Streptomyces avermitilis*. Avermectins types a and b derive their C-25 substituents from isoleucine and valine, via incorporation of these compounds as coenzyme A derivatives of isobutyric and 2-methylbutyric acids, respectively. This mutant lacked the functional branched-chain 2-oxo acid dehydrogenase activity and could not therefore incorporate these likely

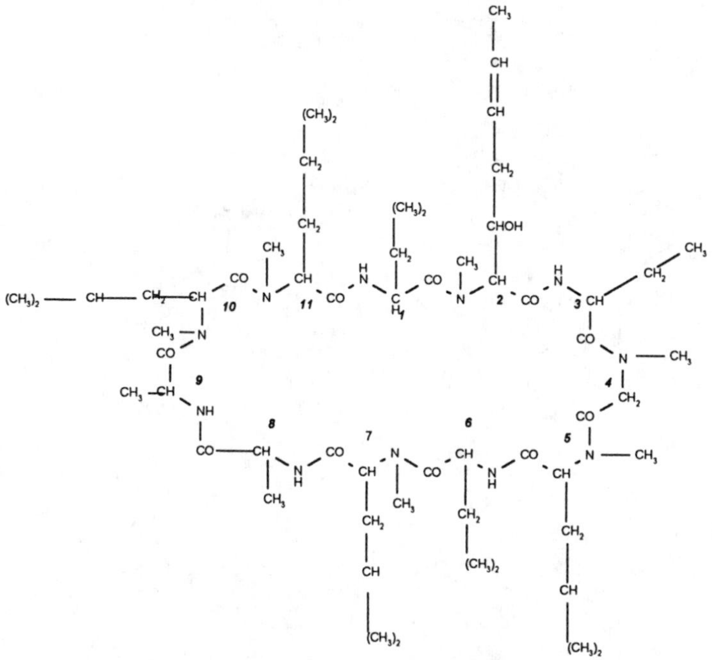

Fig. 9. Some amino acid analogs incorporated into Cyclosporin A by *Beauveria nivea* (numbers in brackets indicate position of incorporation).

L-β-Cyclohexylalanine (1)	**Cell Free Systems:**
DL-α-Allylglycine (2)	N-Methyl-2-amino-3-hydroxy-4,4-dimethyloctanoic acid (1)
D-Serine (8)	N-Methyl-L-Norvaline (11), L-Norvaline (5)
DL-Threonine (2), D-Serine (8)	N-Methyl-L-Norvaline (11), L-Norvaline (2,5)
DL-Valine (2), D-Serine (8)	L-*allo*-Isoleucine (5), N-Methyl-L-*allo*-Isoleucine (11)
DL-Norvaline (2), D-Serine(8)	L-*allo*-Isoleucine (5,11)
3-Fluoro-D-Alanine (8)	D-2-Aminobutyric acid (8), β-Chloro-D-alanine (8)
	2-Deutero-3-Fluoro-D-Alanine (8)

biosynthetic starter units *(23)*. When the fermentation was not supplemented with branched-chain carboxylic acids, no avermectins were produced. However, feeding a range of such acids to the fermentation led to the production of a large number of new avermectins modified at the C-25 position with the corresponding acid substituent as shown in **Fig. 10** *(24)*. The analog containing the cyclohexyl moiety at the C-25 position is now made commercially, by essentially this process, and is marketed as the antiparasitic, doramectin.

5.4.5. Feeding Natural Precursors

This general approach of feeding precursors can also be used just to increase levels of the naturally occurring metabolite by supplementing the culture with the natural precursors. This is illustrated by the simple example of pyrrolnitrin production by *Pseudomonas aureofaciens*, which was increased significantly

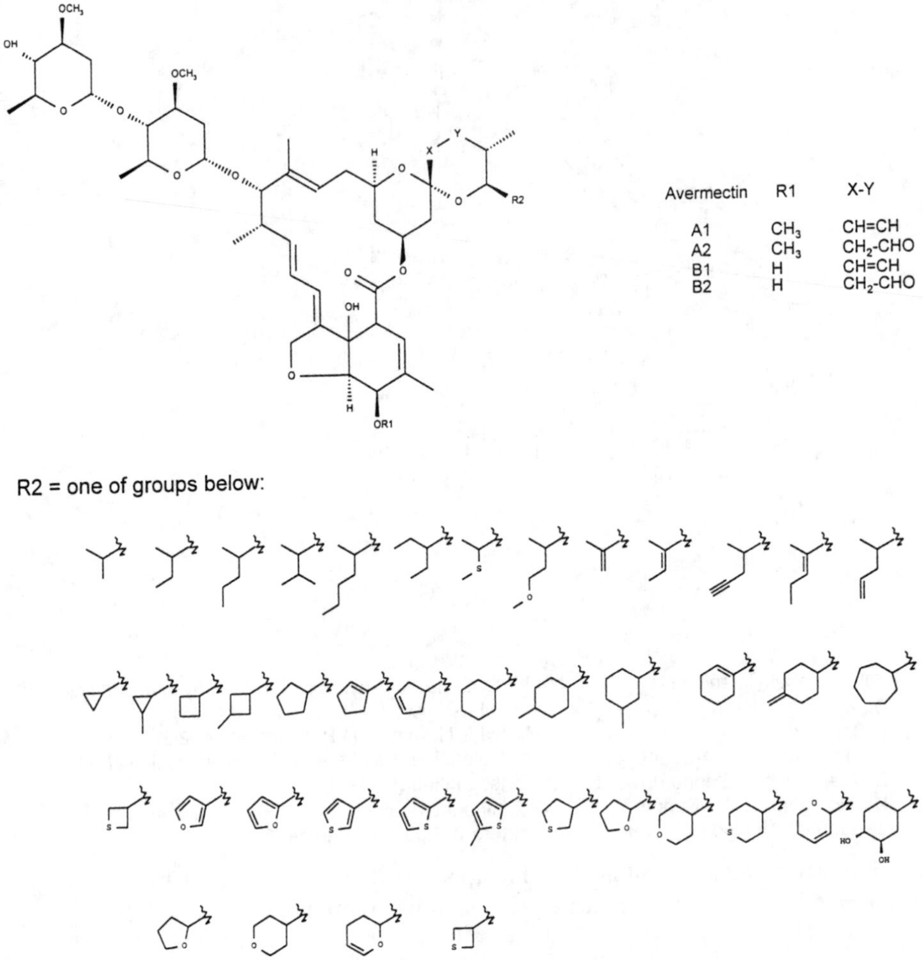

Avermectin	R1	X-Y
A1	CH$_3$	CH=CH
A2	CH$_3$	CH$_2$-CHO
B1	H	CH=CH
B2	H	CH$_2$-CHO

R2 = one of groups below:

Fig.10. Structures of novel avermectins.

by addition of exogenous tryptophan, the direct precursor of pyrrolnitrin (**Fig. 11**). Addition of tryptophan analogs also led to the corresponding analogs of pyrrolnitrin *(25)*.

5.4.6. Halogenation

Other than the method described in **Subheading 5.3.**, other halogens may be introduced or substituted more directly into a natural product by making use of the haloperoxidase activity of various organisms. Organisms producing chlorine-containing metabolites can often be "driven" to produce the same metabolites in a brominated form by addition of an inorganic source of bromine such

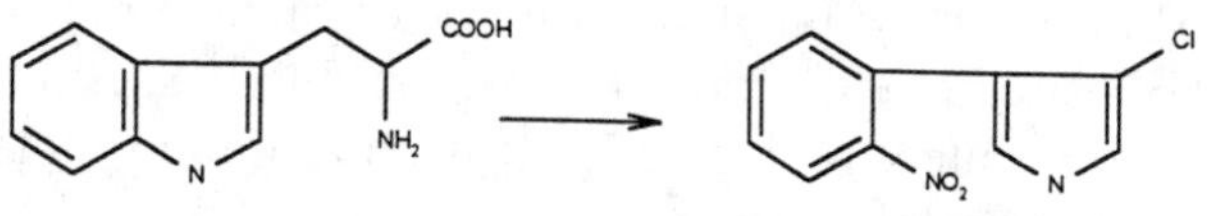

Fig. 11. Tryptophan–precursor of pyrrolnitrin.

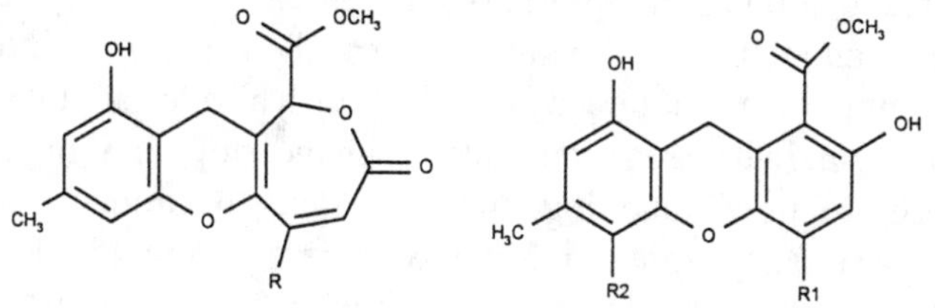

Chloromonilicin R = Cl
Bromomonilicin R = Br

4-Chloropinselin R1 = Cl, R2 = H
4-Bromopinselin R1 = Br, R2 = H
4,5-Dibromopinselin R1,R2 = Br

Fig. 12. Chloromonilicin and 4-Chloropinselin and their brominated forms isolated from *Monilinia fructicola*.

as sodium bromide or potassium bromide. The haloperoxidases that carry out this reaction are fairly unspecific and can often readily utilize bromine in the place of chlorine. Examples include the metabolites of *Monilinia fructicola*, (chloromonilicin and 4-chloropinselin), which were converted to their bromoanalogs following the addition to the medium of NaBr (1 g/L) (**Fig. 12**) *(26)*.

6. Biotransformation

Another method of maximizing diversity from a single natural product is the use of other biological systems, in the form of whole cells or isolated enzymes, to modify the molecule. In its simplest form, this process involves incubation of the isolated natural product with one or several microbial cultures, thus allowing the enzymes of each organism to act on the compound to produce modified forms.

This approach to generating chemical diversity from a single natural product is analogous to a program of chemical modification except that the chemists in this case are microorganisms and the reactions are enzymically mediated. The advantages of biotransformation lie in the fact that many organisms are able to carry out numerous site-specific and stereospecific reactions that are very challenging to a mere human chemist.

For example, chemical hydroxylation of an aromatic group, or at any specific point on a molecule, could involve many protection and deprotection steps and much complex chemistry, but it may well be possible to find an organism that performs the desired modification. This is particularly useful with natural products that, in the context of synthetic chemistry, are big molecules with many functionalities and chiral centers.

The main drawback of biotransformation systems is that the process is not very predictive (except sometimes in the case of purified enzymes). Although it may be possible to build up groups of organisms that tend to carry out certain classes of reaction and to have some knowledge of the general modifications a given type of compound might undergo, such empirical rules are by no means absolute or predictive. In order to maximize the chances of obtaining a particular product, therefore, or of obtaining the widest range of products, it is often necessary to utilize a fairly large number of organisms in the initial screen.

To summarize, it is possible to make use of the various biosynthetic, secondary metabolic, and primary metabolic pathways and enzymes associated with particular organisms by giving them the natural product starting material to work with (*see* **Note 7**).

6.1. Methods

A general outline for carrying out biotransformations on a natural product consists of:

1. An initial screen to identify organisms that biotransform the compound.
2. Incubation of the compound with a range of organisms (or enzymes) alongside a set of controls (organisms with no compound added).
3. Analysis of extracts of both sets of cultures. Metabolites in the fed culture not seen in the control can be presumed to be related to the substrate.
4. Isolation of metabolites either from these or from larger scale cultures.

The issues associated with the practicalities of biotransformations are very much the same as those for precursor-directed biosynthesis. The basic analysis and preparative isolation procedures are likely to have been put in place for the initial isolation of the natural product.

The main aspects for consideration are in **Subheadings 6.1.1.–6.1.4.**

6.1.1. What to Feed

If the aim is to generate a particular derivative of a natural product, then it is necessary to feed either that natural product and/or related metabolites that are structurally closer to the target compound. If the aim is to produce the widest possible range of analogs, then clearly the natural product should be used as starting material. However, it is also worth considering the use of analogs as starting material if they are available (and especially if the natural product is itself in limited supply). The modifications to the main substrate may also occur to the analogs, thus giving a multiplicity of related variants on the original structure. If available, the use of radiolabeled substrate—perhaps with a ^{3}H or ^{14}C atom—can prove advantageous at the analysis stage, as this often allows for easy identification of related metabolites in a complex mixture.

6.1.2. Organisms

The organisms that can be used for biotransformation are limitless. The most circuitous approach is to isolate organisms for a specific biotransformation, perhaps based around the ability of different isolates to utilize particular substrates (e.g., the natural product in question) as a sole carbon source. However, in practice it is easier to use organisms that are already "proven" biotransformers. There exist hundreds of literature reports of specific reactions carried out by specific organisms (or specific enzymes), and many of these organisms are easily obtainable from standard microbial culture collections. Many commonly used microorganisms including, fungi, actinomycetes, and nonfilamentous bacteria, that have shown versatility in carrying out a range of biotransformations and that are available from major culture collections, are listed in **Table 1**. (This covers a wide range of reaction types and organism classes and is a good starting point for anyone establishing a biotransformation program.) Also to be included are organisms previously reported to carry out the types of reactions that are being aimed for. Other organisms that it would make sense to include in such a "panel" of potentially biotransforming organisms are those that are related to the producer of the natural product and those organisms that produce structurally related natural products, on the basis that these might possess biosynthetic/secondary metabolic enzymes that can act on these compounds. (Done in this rational way, this is essentially the same as some of the directed biosynthesis work described in **Subheading 5.**) Plant and animal cell cultures can also be used, though these are usually less convenient than microbial cultures.

Apart from the type of organisms to be used, there is also to be considered the form in which these cultures are used. Types of cultures include:

1. Growing cultures.
2. Stationary cultures.
3. Washed cell cultures/resting cell cultures—prepared by separating cells from a medium by centrifugation and then resuspending in dilute buffer. Washed cell suspensions are often used, as in many cases these behave in essentially the same manner as stationary cultures, but with the advantage that the mixture is much less complex, making analysis and purification more straightforward.
4. Broken cell system/cell-free system—By disrupting the cell wall, the substrate has ready access to the cellular enzymes, and problems of selective permeability are overcome. However, many enzymes will be rendered inactive by this damage to the cell wall.

Table 1
A Selection of "Proven" Biotransformation Organisms

Actinoplanes sp.	ATCC 53771
Amycolatopsis orientalis	NRRL 2452
Aspergillus niger	ATCC 16404
Aspergillus oryzae	ATCC 9102
Bacillus sphaericus	ATCC 13805
Beauveria bassiana	ATCC 7159
Beauveria bassiana	IMI 012939
Cunninghamella bainierii	ATCC9244
Cunninghamella echinulata	IMI 199844
Cunninghamella echinulata var. *elegans*	ATCC 36112
Gibberella fujikuroi	ATCC 12616
Morteriella isabellina	ATCC 38063
Mucor circinelloides	IFO 4563
Mucor rouxii	ATCC 24905
Nocardia corallina	ATCC 31338
Penicillium patulum	IMI 039809
Rhizopus arrhizus	ATCC 11145
Rhizopus stolonifer	ATCC 6227B
Saccharomyces cerevisae	NCYC 1110
Streptomyces griseus	ATCC 13273
Streptomyces lavendulae	CBS 414.59
Stretomyces mashuensis	ISP 5221
Streptomyces punipalus	NRRL 3529
Streptomyces rimosus	NRRL 2234
Verticillium lecanii	IMI 68689

5. Immobilized cultures—Cells can be removed from their medium as for resting cultures and then immobilized on or within a solid support to provide a system that is usually active for longer than with the above systems. Immobilization can be effected by entrapment in a polymer (alginate, polyacrylamide), adsorption onto a solid support (ion-exchange resins, silica), covalent attachment to a support such as cellulose, or chemical crosslinking with glutaraldehyde. The advantages of immobilization are that the system is usually active for relatively long periods and can be re-used for different batches, a system can be created with a high cell density, and the surrounding medium will be fairly clean, making purification of the product straightforward. Also, in some cases, the biotransformation reaction may be affected by immobilization, e.g., in terms of the stereochemistry.

6. Spore suspension—Because spores contain many unique enzymes not expressed in other forms of the organism and because they are relatively stable and active in buffer over a long period of time, spore suspensions are often useful biotransformation systems (*see* **Note 8**).

6.1.3. Feeding Conditions

As with conditions for directed biosynthesis, there are no hard-and-fast predictive rules covering experimental conditions for biotransformations, but there are plenty of literature reports that help to give some idea of the best general practical approaches. Whereas there are limitless permutations of substrate concentrations with time of feeding with different organisms and so on, usually circumstances such as amount of available substrate, numbers of microorganisms, amount of shaker space, and time, all impose practical limitations.

Sample: The substrate itself is added to the culture to give typical concentrations of 0.1–0.5 mg/mL, with 0.25 mg/mL as a standard concentration. The aim is to add sufficient starting material to generate reasonable yields of biotransformed products at the same time remaining below concentrations that are toxic, inhibitory to biotransformation, or that waste valuable substrate. The sample can be added as a filter-sterilized or autoclaved aqueous solution or in a small volume of organic solvent. If the substrate is water-insoluble it may be necessary to dissolve it first in a small volume of organic solvent. As mentioned earlier, even if the compound is only sparingly soluble in water, it may still be transformed. The type and amount of solvent used should be considered as this may damage the cells and may permeabilize the cell walls, which may lead to reduced metabolic activity or to enhanced biotransformation by facilitating substrate uptake by the cells.

Time of feeding and incubation: Again, as with directed biosynthesis, the two points on a growth curve that are deemed most suitable for substrate addition are time of inoculation and at the onset of stationary phase. The latter is perhaps preferable, as by this time there is a high cell concentration, so the substrate cannot significantly inhibit culture growth, and there is the possibility that the substrate might be metabolized by the enzymes of both primary and secondary metabolism, thus maximizing the possible range of biotransformation products.

An alternative, possibly better method, is the pulse feed, or continuous feed. This lessens the potential for toxicity by the compound and can take the form of daily feeds starting from inoculation or from the end of log phase. Continuous feeding can be carried out with the help of advanced and expensive fermentation apparatus or by the use of a wick, with one end in the culture and the other in the solution of substrate. Once fed, the culture is left, typically for several days, to allow reactions to take place.

Typically, then, a bacterial culture might be inoculated from a seed culture and then incubated for approx 24 h, by which time it is likely to have reached the end of growth phase; then the substrate compound is added to the culture, followed by incubation of the mixture for another 3, 4, or even 7 d. Fungal cultures might take longer to reach stationary phase, perhaps 3 d, after which it is again advisable to leave for at least a few days in order to achieve maximum biotransformation.

6.1.4. Other Factors

As the processes and enzymes associated with such biotransformations are often those associated with secondary metabolism, any other experimental conditions that generally affect secondary metabolism should be brought into play whenever possible.

1. Medium: As discussed in **Subheading 2.**, the most important factor in this respect is probably the medium. There are numerous reports of the way in which the nutrient source affects the secondary metabolism. Such factors include carbon, phosphorus and nitrogen source, levels, and ratios; inorganics present in medium; levels of aeration/oxygenation; the physical state of the medium (liquid or solid). The diversity of metabolism elicited by a range of media should be considered insofar as the biotransformation reactions are a product of secondary metabolism.

   Ideally, the medium should be one that promotes dispersed growth such that the organism does not stick to the side of the vessel or, as is often the case with many fungi, grow in the form of a tight mycelial pellet. The physical form in which organisms grow can affect secondary metabolism, and many culture flasks contain internal baffles that promote dispersal of the organism. Whereas pelleting may be difficult to control and may not affect biotransformation, a pellet tends to be hydrophobic and generally less amenable to the diffusion of substrate.

   If only a single medium for each organism is to be used, this should be a liquid medium (to allow for dispersal and diffusion of substrate) that is sufficiently rich to result in a high biomass and contains Arkasoy to promote cytochrome P450 activity.

2. Induction of cytochromes P450: These enzymes are a family of monooxygenases ubiquitous in animals, plants, and many microorganisms, which perform many of the reactions that are carried out by an organism when challenged with a xenobiotic compound, i.e., a compound foreign to the organism, such as a drug. These reactions include many that are commonly associated with biotransformations (in both animals and microbes) such as hydroxylation and demethylation, as well as many reactions that involve conjugation of a metabolite with other groups, such as glucuronic acid, sugars, amino acids, and others.

   In most situations, the activity of cytochromes P450 is seen as a means by which the organism modifies a foreign compound in order to make it more polar and more water-soluble and therefore more readily excreted. As natural products scientists, we can view cytochrome P450 activity as a means of carrying out often subtle and site/stereo-specific reactions on a complex molecule to produce a range of closely related analogs, many of which would be difficult to carry out chemically. Cytochromes P450 have been shown to be expressed, either constitutively or inducibly, in many microorganisms that have been reported as capable of performing such reactions. Arkasoy (soya wheat flour) has been found to induce cytochrome P450 expression in some microbial species; an active component is genistein *(27,28)*, so Arkasoy should be considered as a carbon source or at least as a medium component. (*see* **Note 9**).

3. Scale-up: Scaling up a fermentation for biotransformation purposes may bring with it the possibility of the biotransformation not reproducing. If a different, larger vessel is used, this may result in subtle differences in physicochemical conditions, such as oxygen limitation, mixing, and so on, that result in differences in metabolism. In such cases where it is practically possible, it is sometimes best to carry out the scale-up simply by increasing the number of original vessels.

4. Analysis: An analytical system is also required in much the same way as that described for directed biosynthesis work, i.e., as a means of comparing the biotransformation culture with a control culture to determine those components present only in the former, which are therefore presumably biotransformation-associated. This can take the form of gradient HPLC, HPLC-MS, TLC, and so on. The aim of such an analytical system is to identify that biotransformation products have been produced and that there is something worth isolating from the cultures. The use of MS may give further information about the compounds; e.g., M+16 molecular ion would lead to a suspicion that oxygenation has occurred, but in order to properly identify and test the product, it is always necessary to isolate the compound.

5. Isolation of products: Again, as in the case of directed biosynthesis products, isolation is likely to be guided to a large extent by conditions used for the original isolation of the natural product. Many typical biotransformation reactions are oxidative, and it is therefore likely that a high proportion of the products will be more polar than the substrate. Therefore, a reverse phase system in which the substrate elutes after a reaonable length of time is probably desirable, though it is possible that some products will be less polar and will elute later from a reverse phase chromatography system.

6.2. Biotransformation of Squalestatins

Continuing with squalestatins as models of natural products that can be further exploited following their initial isolation, these molecules were also used as biotransformation substrates *(29)*. The aim of generating biotransformation products from this class of compounds was to generate chemical diversity in the form of natural product analogs and for SAR studies, and to functionalize particular atoms to facilitate further chemistry.

In order to identify organisms that would biotransform the squalestatins, the compound was fed to a range of microbes isolated from soil samples, followed by HPLC analysis of crude extracts of the broths simply to look for a significant decrease in the substrate peak that would imply utilization of the substrate. These isolates were then analyzed more closely and compared with their control cultures (no squalestatin added) and the products identified.

Shake cultures were inoculated from seed cultures (2–3%, v/v) and incubated for 1 d (actinomycetes; 28°C) or 3 d (fungi; 25°C) before addition of the tripotassium salt of squalestatin 1 (0.1 and 0.5 mg/mL), followed by further incubation for up to 7 d.

Analysis and Product Isolation: Gradient HPLC analysis and product isolation could be carried out essentially as described for the squalestatin analogs described in the previous sections. The use of LC-MS allowed the identification of peaks corresponding to related metabolites with more certainty than LC alone. Additionally, MS often gives a strong indication of how the molecule has changed. In cultures in which squalestatin had apparently been metabolized, LC-MS indicated that in most cases the biotransformation had involved addition of oxygen and/or deacetylation. The fragmentation pattern suggested that these had occurred on the ester and the alkyl (C6 and C7) side chains, respectively. The isolation was carried out largely as described in **Subheading 5.3.1.**, except at the final stages when the resolution of compounds with hydroxyl groups on C23 and C24, respectively, required further HPLC.

The products generated by this particular biotransformation experiment are shown in **Fig. 13**. Six analogs were formed, but considering the complexity of the substrate and the number of potential reaction sites, this is perhaps a fairly meager tally compared to many instances of other simple molecules that generate a plethora of different metabolites. This highlights one of the problems of employing biotransformations as a means of modifying natural products—the unpredictability of such systems. For a given molecule, there are a number of reactions that would be predicted as being more likely than others, but this presumably indicates something about the active site specificity of the cytochrome P450 monooxygenases and the other enzymes involved. However, one of the advantages of biotransformations is exemplified in the products that represent extremely difficult targets for chemical modification.

Compound 7, while not a direct biotransformation product, may have been the result of the inhibition of squalene synthase leading to the buildup of farnesyl pyrophosphate, which was converted to 7 by one of the test organisms.

Possible reasons for the relatively poor "rate of return" of novel metabolites, for microbial cultures screened in the case of the squalestatins, may include the poor solubility of the compound resulting in only a small proportion of the substrate in solution at any one time, that the best organisms were not tested/selected, or that other conditions were unfavorable such as media, feeding time, and so on. These compounds are tricarboxylic acids, and this may have rendered them unsuitable substrates; feeding the compounds in their trimethylester forms may have led to more biotransformation. It may also have been that squalestatins, as antifungal agents, may have had some toxic effect on the organisms with which they were incubated.

Fig. 13. *(opposite)* Biotransformation of squalestatins.

	R1	R2	R3
1	CH₂–C(=O)–CH=CH–CH(CH₃)–CH₂–CH(CH₃)–CH₂–CH₃	CH₂–C(=O)–CH₃	H
2	CH₂–C(=O)–CH=CH–CH(CH₃)–CH₂–CH(CH₃)–CH₂–CH₃	H	H
3	H	CH₂–C(=O)–CH₃	H
4	CH₂–C(=O)–CH=CH–CH(CH₃)–CH₂–CH(CH₃)–CH(OH)–CH₃	H	H
5	CH₂–C(=O)–CH=CH–CH(CH₃)–CH₂–C(OH)(CH₃)–CH₂–CH₃	H	H
6	CH₂–C(=O)–CH=CH–CH(CH₃)–CH₂–CH(CH₃)–CH₂–CH₃	CH₂–C(=O)–CH₃	CH₃

7 HO–C(=O)–CH₂–CH(CH₃)–CH₂–CH₂–CH=C(CH₃)–CH₂–CH₂–CH=C(CH₃)–CH₃

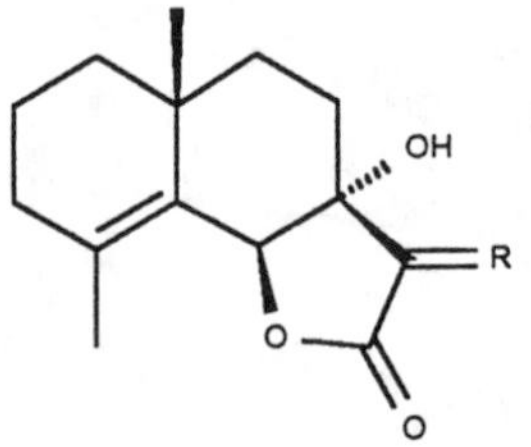

Fig. 14. Biotransformation of frullanolide (R = CH$_2$) to two products where R = CH$_3$ and R = CH$_2$COCH$_3$, respectively.

6.3. Other Examples of Biotransformations

An example of a simple biotransformation of a small natural product is shown in **Fig. 14**, in which the sesquiterpene lactone, 7α-hydroxyfrullanolide from the plant *Sphaeranthus indicus* was acetylated and reduced by two different *Aspergillus* species to give the two products shown *(30)*.

At the other extreme, Borghi et al. reported the biotransformation of the teicoplanin family of antibiotics. They found that these large, complex glycopeptides produced by *Actinoplanes teichomyceticus* could be demannosylated by cultures of *Nocardia orientalis* NRRL 2450, or *Streptomyces candidus* NRRL 3218. Interestingly, they also found that the demannosylated teicoplanin and other de-mannosylated derivatives could be converted back to the mannosylated form by the original producing organism *(31)*.

Chen et al. *(32)* reported that one of the cytochalasin family of natural products, fed to a culture of *Actinoplanes* sp. (4 × 50 mL) at a concentration of 0.05 mg/mL and incubation for a further 30 h, led to the isolation of six biotransformation products, resulting in functionalization at four new points on the molecule (**Fig. 15**).

6.3.1. Anthracycline antibiotics

As with many commercially important groups of natural products, anthracycline antibiotics and their analogs have undergone a whole range of microbial transformations including oxidation, reduction, acylation, and alkylation *(33)*. These main reaction types can be illustrated with one of this family of compounds, daunomycin (**Fig. 16**). The methyl group α to the side-chain ketone of daunomycin is oxygenated by a mutant of *Streptomyces peuceticus* to give adriamycin *(34)*. This was also found to be the final step in the biosynthesis of adriamycin. This ketone group can also be reduced by a variety of organisms, including both filamentous and nonfilamentous bacteria, and fungi, to give 13-dihydrodaunomycin *(35)*. This reaction is also the first step in the mammalian metabolism of daunomycin (*see* **Note 9**). A *Streptomyces*

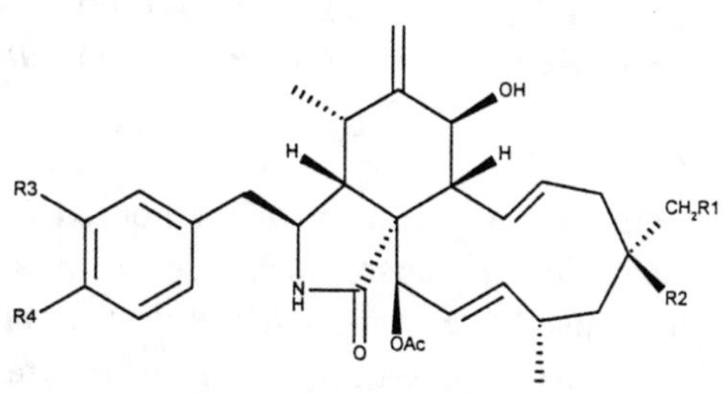

	R1	R2	R3	R4
L-696,474	H	H	H	H
Biotransformation products	OH	H	H	H
	OH	H	H	OH
	OH	H	OH	H
	OH	H	OH	OH
	OH	OH	H	H
	OH	OH	OH	H

Fig. 15. Biotransformation products of cytochalasin L-696,474.

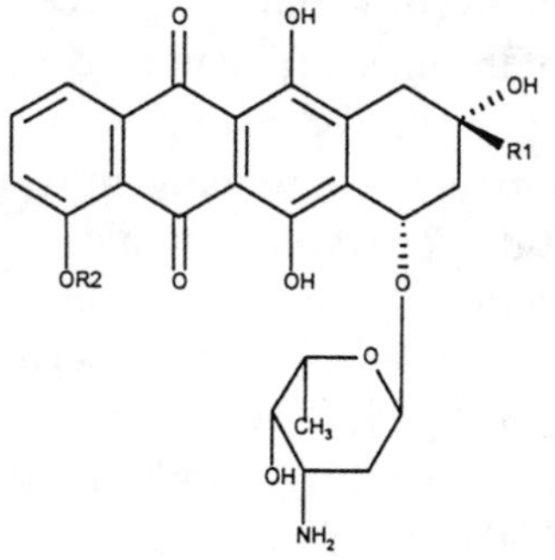

Daunomycin   R1 = COCH$_3$,   R2 = CH$_3$

Adriamycin   R1 = COCH$_2$OH,   R2 = CH$_3$

13 -Dihydrodaunomycin R1 = CHOHCH$_3$,   R2 = CH$_3$

Carminomycin I R1 = COCH$_3$,   R2 = H

Fig. 16.

peuceticus strain is also capable of alkylating carminomycin I to produce daunomycin *(36)*.

Many of these transformations are also carried out on the analogous anthracyclinones—the aglycone portions of these molecules. Others occur on the glycosides, such as the N-acetylation of the daunosamine moiety of dauno-mycin and daunomycinol by *Bacillus subtilis* var. *mycoides (36)*.

Daunomycinone and 13-dihydrodaunomycinone were also converted to glycosylated forms by cultures of *Streptomyces coeruleorubidus (37)*.

6.3.2. Milbemycins

The milbemycins are a group of 16-membered macrolides produced by *Streptomyces hygroscopicus* subsp. *aureolacrimosus*, structurally related to the avermectins, which also have potent antihelminthic and insecticidal activities. As part of a program to prepare new analogs of this family of compounds for further derivatization and as standards of potential animal metabolites, Nakagawa et al. *(38)* tested several hundred strains of actinomycetes, nonfilamentous bacteria, and fungi for the ability to biotransform milbemycin A_4. Organisms were obtained from culture collections and as isolates from soil samples, then cultured on a scale of 20-mL medium in a 100-mL Erlenmeyer flask for 2–3 d, following which milbemycin A_4 was added (5% [w/v] in 1,4-dioxane) to give a final concentration of 0.5 mg/mL. Samples were taken from the cultures at intervals following this, extracted with ethyl acetate, and analyzed for conversion of milbemycin A_4 by TLC with staining with ammonium molybdate. Many strains of actinomycetes and zygomycetes were found to convert the compound, and some of the most efficient converters were selected to carry out larger scale conversions and for testing with other milbemycin analogs. Some of the conversion products of milbemycin A_4 (**Fig. 17**) include 30-hydroxymilbemycin A_4, 26,30-dihydroxymilbemycin A_4 and milbemycin A_4 30-oic acid (all by *Amycolata autotrophica* subsp. *amethystina*) *(38)*, 29-hydroxymilbemycin A_4 *(Syncephalastrum* sp.) *(39)*, 13β-hydroxymilbemycin A_4, 13β,24-dihydroxymilbemycin A_4, 13β,30-dihydroxymilbemycin A_4 *(Cunninghamella echinulata) (40)*, and 13β,29-dihydroxymilbemycin A_4 *(Streptomyces cavourensis) (41)*. Other biotransformations of this compound that have been reported include 13β-hydroxylation and 14,15-epoxidation by *Streptomyces violascens (42)*. Many of these conversions, and others, were also carried out on many of the closely related analogs of this compound resulting in a multiplicity of derivatives from a relatively small number of starting compounds.

Although these strategies of mutasynthesis, precusor-directed biosynthesis, and biotansformation have been discussed separately, one of their main strengths lies in the way in which they can be overlapped and can complement each other. Mutants can provide novel analogs or biosynthetic intermediates, which can be fed in a rational manner to other organisms to provide further chemical modification, or they themselves can be fed other precursors.

7. Combinatorial Biosynthesis

Modification of genetic material can be used on a number of levels to exploit the isolation of a novel natural product. The production of mutants can be used to

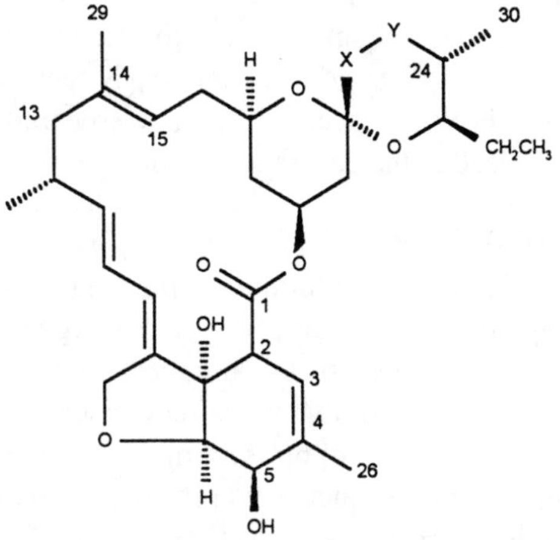

Fig. 17. Milbemycin A$_4$ showing sites of modification.

generate organisms with blocked or altered biosynthetic pathways, which can be used for feeding experiments with precursor analogs (as with the avermectins, 5.3.4). Mutation programs and more precise molecular genetic methods can also be used to improve levels of production of particular metabolites (43).

More recently, however, genetic engineering for the production of secondary metabolites has involved not so much the follow-up and improvement of an initial natural product, but more the creation almost from "scratch" of novel, or "unnatural" natural products, but still using the organism's secondary metabolite apparatus.

The biosynthesis of polyketides, for example, is carried out by polyketide synthases that operate in a production-line mode, each one carrying out one of a series of condensations of regular small building blocks such as acetyl- and malonyl coenzyme A, with subsequent reductions to make the final molecule. The enormous variety of polyketides is essentially the result of different combinations of a relatively small number of reactions with a relatively small number of building blocks, which includes such important secondary metabolites as erythromycin, avermectin, actinorhodin, and rapamycin. It is now becoming possible to shuffle the genes that code for these enzymes in a myriad of ways to produce many different combinations of synthases resulting in a whole new range of polyketides (44–46).

Modification of enzymes involved in the synthesis from universal precursors of other secondary metabolites has also been demonstrated. The sesquiterpene synthases are a large family of enzymes that act by a common mechanism and catalyze the cyclization of farnesyl diphosphate, each to form a distinct sesquiterpene. The active site of the synthase that produces trichodiene, the precursor of the trichothecenes in *Fusarium sporotrichioides*, was modified by site-directed mutagenesis, resulting in altered cyclization products as indicated by the isolation of additional sesquiterpenes not previously seen in this organism *(47)*. In the future, therefore, it is likely that engineering of terpenoid synthases and other classes of enzymes will lead to the generation of many novel metabolites.

8. Combinatorial Synthesis

Combinatorial chemistry has revolutionized the means by which a relatively small number of compounds can be converted into a large number of new compounds. Apart from classical chemistry techniques, the use of natural products as templates and monomers in combinatorial chemistry programs is likely to become one of the major methods for optimizing and maximizing the diversity generated around one natural product. Several libraries that are based around natural products have been created, such as those comprising a set of modified *Rauwolfia* alkaloids *(48)*. The benefits of expending the effort to isolate novel natural products, with their advantages of unpredictable structures, usually in a chiral form, are likely to be greatly enhanced if they can be coupled to the power of combinatorial chemistry to produce a large family of derivatives.

9. Notes

1. This highlights another reason why it is always desirable to account for the total amount of biological activity present in the extract in terms of the level and activity of the metabolite deemed to be responsible. The fact that an isolated compound is active may not mean that it can account for all the observed biological activity of the extract, and it may be that there exists in the extract a more potent minor compound.
2. Such atoms, which are relatively uncommon in biological molecules, often make useful "handles" by which to monitor or follow metabolism of compounds that contain them.
3. As mentioned earlier, this process relies on the fact that the enzymes of secondary metabolism are generally less specific than those of primary metabolism and often accept a relatively wide range of substrates. This may reflect the less immediately important role of secondary metabolism in the organism's survival than the more direct and critical role of primary metabolites. Secondary metabolite biosynthetic systems can afford to be more "relaxed" with regard to substrate specificity as the resultant metabolites may play a more indirect, longer term role (or no role at all) than primary metabolites; indeed, it may even be beneficial to the fitness of the species to have secondary-metabolic machinery with rather broad specificity in order to maximize the number of molecules that may be formed by this process and hence to maximize the possibility of producing a compound to protect the organism from any future challenge.
4. The feed sample can be sterilized by autoclaving or filtration, if it is aqueous. Samples in organic solvents can be regarded as being sterile without treatment.

Although it is preferable to add a sterile solution, in many cases, any contamination is likely to be insignificant as the culture will already have grown substantially and the biosynthesis is likely to occur before growth of the contaminant becomes significant.

5. The HPLC systems used with and without MS were different. The difference in acetonitrile concentration may reflect the fact that as trifluoroacetic acid is a weaker acid than sulfuric acid, as well as the fact that a C18 (ODS) column is generally more retentive than a C6 column, slightly more acetonitrile was required to elute all the compounds in the sample.

6. During the process of generating each of the products, a total of three different HPLC systems was used. A gradient analytical system was employed initially to analyze whole-broth extracts, because these contained a wide range of metabolites of greatly differing polarities and a gradient separation maximized the chances of detecting compounds closely related to the parent molecule. A gradient system could probably have been used for the purification, but once the analog had been detected and its isolation commenced, many of the unwanted components could be fairly simply removed and an isocratic preparative HPLC system developed to resolve the parent and product. The LC-MS system was different again—no gradient was used, but the possible loss of resolution in which this might result is offset by the power of the MS (to which the LC system is coupled). In most cases the molecular weight of the expected compounds is known, and MS is a powerful means of detecting these compounds even if they coelute with other compounds. Chromatography coupled to MS must also take account of the fact that many of the salts and ions commonly used in mobile phases will build up on the MS probe and interfere with the spectrometry. Therefore, only volatile buffer salts and acids can be used; commonly used LC-MS mobile phase components include sodium or ammonium acetate or formate with trifluoroacetic acid, formic acid, or tetrahydrofuran as modifiers.

7. This process does not, of course, have to be confined to natural products—synthetic compounds are just as amenable to this approach and indeed the use of enzymes in organic synthesis is now fairly commonplace.

8. The advantage of using purified enzymes as opposed to whole cells is that enzymes are specific for certain reactions so that, for the production of a specific compound, enzymes might be the method of choice. Also, the reaction mixture is likely to be cleaner, thus facilitating purification. Disadvantages of using enzymes in this context are that they are often unstable outside the cell, often require inconvenient and expensive cofactors, and they tend to be expensive. For the purposes of generating a wide diversity of analogs, whole cells are preferable, as they are capable of a multiplicity of reactions. The use of isolated enzymes as tools of organic chemistry is now widespread and increasing and will not be considered at length here. (For further reading, *see* **refs. *49–51*.**)

9. An additional feature of using microbes to metabolize compounds—be they natural or synthetic—is that many of the biotransformation reactions carried out by microbes are the same as those carried out in humans and animals on xenobiotic

compounds. Thus microbial biotransformation systems can be used as a means of preparing quantities of mammalian metabolites of a drug—metabolites that may be very difficult to generate from animals in any reasonable amount—and can even be used in a limited sense as a method by which to predict the metabolic fate of a drug in an animal *(52)*.

References

1. Grabley, S., Hammann, P., Kluge, H., Wink, J., Kricke, P., and Zeeck, A. (1991) Secondary metabolites by chemical screening 4. Detection, isolation and biological activities of chiral synthons from *Streptomyces*. *J. Antibiot.* **44,** 797–800.
2. Dawson, M. J., Farthing, J. E., Marshall, P. S., Middleton, R. F., O'Neill, M. J., Shuttleworth, A., Stylli, C., Tait, R. M., Taylor, P. M., Wildman, H. G., Buss, A. D. Langley, D., and Hayes, M. V. (1992) The squalestatins, novel inhibitors of squalene synthase produced by a species of *Phoma* I. Taxonomy, fermentation, isolation, physico-chemical properties and biological activity. *J. Antibiot.* **45,** 639–647.
3. Sidebottom, P. J., Highcock, R. M., Lane, S. J., Procopiou, P. A., and Watson, N. S. (1992) The squalestatins, novel inhibitors of squalene synthase produced by a species of *Phoma* II. Structure elucidation. *J. Antibiot.* **45,** 648–658.
4. Blows, W. M., Foster, G., Lane, S. J., Noble, D., Piercey, J. E., Sidebottom, P. J., and Webb, G. (1994) The squalestatins, novel inhibitors of squalene synthase produced by a species of *Phoma* V. Minor metabolites. *J. Antibiot.* **47,** 740–754.
5. Trilli, A. (1990) Kinetics of secondary metabolite production, in *Microbial Growth Dynamics* (Poole, R. K., Bazin, M. J., and Keevil, C. W., eds.), IRL, Oxford, pp. 103–126.
6. Hutter, R. (1982) Design of culture media capable of provoking wide gene expression, in *Bioactive Microbial Products: Search and Discovery* (Bu'Lock, J. D., Nisbet, L. J., and Winstanley, D. J., eds.), Academic, London, pp. 37–50.
7. Furumai, T., Kakinuma, S., Yamamoto, H., Komiyama, N., Suzuki, K., Saitoh, K., and Oki, T. (1993) Biosynthesis of the pradimicin family of antibiotics I. Generation and selection of pradimicin non-producing mutants. *J. Antibiot.* **46,** 412–419.
8. Tsuno, T., Yamamoto, H., Narita, Y., Suzuki, K., Hasegawa, T., Kakinuma, S., Saitoh, K., Furumai, T., and Oki, T. (1993) Biosynthesis of the pradimicin family of antibiotics II. Fermentation, isolation and structure determination of metabolites associated with pradimicins biosynthesis. *J. Antibiot.* **46,** 420–429.
9. Yoshimoto, A., Matsuzawa, Y., Oki, T., Takeuchi, T., and Umezawa, H. (1981) New anthracycline metabolites from mutant strains of *Streptomyces galilaeus* MA144-M1. I. Isolation and characterization of various blocked mutants. *J. Antibiot.* **34,** 951–958.
10. Matsuzawa, Y., Yoshimoto, A., Shibamoto, N., Tobe, H., Oki, T., Naganawa, H., Takeuchi, T., and Umezawa, H. (1981) New anthracycline metabolites from mutant strains of *Streptomyces galilaeus* MA144-M1. II. Structure of 2-hydroxyaklavinone and new aklavinone glycosides. *J. Antibiot.* **34,** 959–964.
11. Tobe, H., Yoshimoto, A., Ishikura, T., Naganawa, H., Takeuchi, T., and Umezawa, H. (1982) New anthracycline metabolites from two blocked mutants of *Streptomyces galilaeus* MA144-M1. *J. Antibiot.* **35,** 1641–1645.

12. Beremand, M. N., VanMiddlesworth, F., Taylor, S., Plattner, R., and Weisleder, D. (1988) Leucine auxotrophy specifically alters the pattern of tricothecene production in a T-2 Toxin-producing strain of *Fusarium sporotrichioides*. *Appl. Env. Microbiol.* **54**, 2759–2766.

13. VanMiddlesworth, F., Desjardins, A., Taylor, S., and Plattner, R. (1986) Trichodiene accumulation by ancymidol treatment of *Gibberella pulicaris*. *J. Chem. Soc. Chem. Comm.* 1156,1157.

14. Jones, C. A., Sidebottom, P. J., Cannell, R. J. P., Noble, D., and Rudd, B. A. M. (1992) The squalestatins, novel inhibitors of squalene synthase produced by a species of *Phoma* III. Biosynthesis. *J. Antibiot.* **45**, 1492–1498.

15. Cannell, R. J. P., Dawson, M. J., Hale, R. S., Hall, R. M., Noble, D. Lynn, S., and Taylor, N. L. (1993) The squalestatins, novel inhibitors of squalene synthase produced by a species of *Phoma* IV. Preparation of fluorinated squalestatins by directed biosynthesis. *J. Antibiot.* **46**, 1381–1389.

16. Cannell, R. J. P., Dawson, M. J., Hale, R. S., Hall, R. M., Noble, D. Lynn, S., and Taylor, N. L. (1994) Production of additional squalestatin analogues by directed biosynthesis. *J. Antibiot.* **47**, 247–249.

17. Thiericke, R. and Rohr, J. (1993) Biological variation of microbial metabolites by precursor-directed biosynthesis. *Nat. Prod. Rep.* **10**, 265–289.

18. Boeck, L. D. and Betzel, R. W. (1990) A54145, a new lipopeptide antibiotic complex: factor control through precursor directed biosynthesis. *J. Antibiot.* **43**, 607–615.

19. Claridge, C., Bush, J. A., Doyle, T. W., Nettleton, D. E., Mosley, J. E., Kimball, D., Kammer, M. F., and Veitch, J. (1986) New mitomycin analogs produced by directed biosynthesis. *J. Antibiot.* **39**, 437–446.

20. Traber, R., Hofmann, H., and Kobel, H. (1989) Cyclosporins–new analogues by precursor directed biosynthesis. *J. Antibiot.* **42**, 591–597.

21. Hensens, O. D., White, R. F., Goegelman, R. T., Inamine, E. S., and Patchett, A. A. (1992) The preparation of [2-deutero-3-fluoro-D-ala[8]]cyclosporin A by directed biosynthesis. *J. Antibiot.* **45**, 133–135.

22. Lawen, A., Traber, R., Geyl, D., Zocher, R., and Kleinkauf, H. (1989) Cell-free biosynthesis of new cyclosporins. *J. Antibiot.* **42**, 1283–1289.

23. Hafner, E. W., Holley, B. W., Holdom, K. S., Lee, S. E., Wax, R. G., Beck, D., McArthur, H. A. I., and Wernau, W. C. (1991) Branched-chain fatty acid requirement for avermectin production by a mutant of *Streptomyces avermitilis* lacking branched-chain 2-oxo acid dehydrogenase activity. *J. Antibiot.* **44**, 349–356.

24. Dutton, C. J., Gibson, S. P., Goudie, A. C., Holdom, K. S., Pacey, M. S., Ruddock, J. C., Bu'Lock, J. D., and Richards, M. K. (1991) Novel avermectins produced by mutational biosynthesis. *J. Antibiot.* **44**, 357–365.

25. Hamill, R. L., Elander, R. P., Mabe, J. A., and Gorman, M. (1970) Metabolism of tryptophan by *Pseudomonas aureofaciens* III. Production of substituted pyrrolnitrins from tryptophan analogues. *Appl. Microbiol.* **19**, 721–725.

26. Kachi, H., Hattori, H., and Sassa, T. (1986) A new antifungal substance, bromomonilicin, and its precursor produced by *Monilinia fructicola*. *J. Antibiot.* **39**, 164–166.

27. Sariaslani, F. S. and Kunz, D. A. (1986) Induction of cytochrome P-450 in *Streptomyces griseus* by soybean flour. *Biochem. Biophys. Res. Comm.* **141**, 405–410.

28. Trower, M. K., Sariaslani, F. S., and F. S. Kitson (1988) Xenobiotic oxidation by cytochrome P-450-enriched extracts of *Streptomyces griseus*. *Biochem. Biophys. Res. Comm.* **157**, 1417–1422.

29. Middleton, R. F., Foster, G., Cannell, R. J. P., Sidebottom, P. J., Taylor, N. L., Noble, D., Todd, M., Dawson M. J., and Lawrence, G. C. (1995) Novel squalestatins produced by biotransformation. *J. Antibiot.* **48**, 311–316.

30. Atta-ur-Rahman, Choudhary, M. I., Ata, A., Alam, M., Farooq, A., Perveen, S., and Shekhani, M. S. (1994) Microbial transformations of 7α-hydroxyfrullanolide. *J. Nat. Prod.* **57**, 1251–1255.

31. Borghi, A., Ferrari, P., Gallo, G. G., Zanol, M., Zerilli, L. F., and Lancini, G. C. (1991) Microbial de-mannosylation and mannosylation of teicoplanin derivatives. *J. Antibiot.* **44**, 1444–1451.

32. Chen , T. S., Doss, G. A., Hsu, A., Hsu, A., Lingham, R. B., White, R. F., and Monaghan, R. L. (1993) Microbial transformation of L-696, 474, a novel cytochalasin as an inhibitor of HIV-1 protease. *J. Nat. Prod.* **56**, 755–761.

33. Marshall, V. P. (1985) Microbial transformation of anthracycline antibiotics and their analogs. *Dev. Ind. Microbiol.* **26**, 129–142.

34. Oki, T., Takatsuki, Y., Tobe, H., Yoshimoto, A., Takeuchi, T., and Umezawa, H. (1981) Microbial conversion of daunomycin, carminomycin I and feudomycin A to adriamycin. *J. Antibiot.* **34**, 1229–1231.

35. Aszalos, A. A., Bachur, N. R., Hamilton, B. K., Langlykke, A., Roller, P. P., Sheikh, M. Y., Sutphin, M. S., Thomas, M. C., Wareheim, D. A., and Wright, L. H. (1977) Microbial reduction of the side-chain carbonyl of daunorubicin and N-acetyl daunorubicin. *J. Antibiot.* **30**, 50–58.

36. Hamilton, B. K., Sutphin, M. S., Thomas, M. C., Wareheim, D. A., and Aszalos, A. A. (1977) Microbial N-acetylation of daunorubicin and daunorubicinol. *J. Antibiot.* **30**, 425–426.

37. Blumauerova, M., Kralovcova, E., Mateju, J., Jizba, J., and Vanek, Z. (1979) Biotransformations of anthracyclinones in *Streptomyces coeruleorubidus* and *Streptomyces galilaeus*. *Folia Microbiol.* **24**, 117–127.

38. Nakagawa, K., Torikata, A., Sato, K., and Tsukamoto, Y. (1990) Microbial conversion of milbemycins: 30-Oxidation of milbemycin A_4 and related compounds by *Amycolata autotrophica* and *Amycolatopsis mediterranei*. *J. Antibiot.* **43**, 1321–1328.

39. Nakagawa, K., Sato, K., Tsukamoto, Y., and Torikata, A. (1992) Microbial conversion of milbemycins: 29-Hydroxylation of milbemycins by genus *Syncephalastrum*. *J. Antibiot.* **45**, 802–805.

40. Nakagawa, K., Miyakoshi, S., Torikata, A., Sato, K., and Tsukamoto, Y. (1991) Microbial conversion of milbemycins: Hydroxylation of milbemycin A_4 and related compounds by *Cunninghamella echinulata* ATCC 9244. *J. Antibiot.* **44**, 232–240.

41. Nakagawa, K., Sato, K., Okazaki, T., and Torikata, A. (1992) Microbial conversion of milbemycins: 13β,29-Dihydroxylation of milbemycins by soil isolate *Streptomyces cavourensis*. *J. Antibiot.* **44**, 803–805.

42. Ramos Tombo, G. M., Ghisalba, O., Schar, H.-P., Frei, B., Maienfisch, P., and O'Sullivan, A. C. (1989) Diastereoselective microbial hydroxylation of milbemycin derivatives. *Agric. Biol. Chem.* **53,** 1531–1535.
43. Baltz, R. H. and Hosted, T. J. (1996) Molecular genetic methods for improving secondary-metabolite production in actinomycetes. *Trends Biotechnol.* **14,** 245–250.
44. Tsoi, C. J. and Khosla, C. (1995) Combinatorial biosynthesis of "unnatural" natural products: The polyketide example. *Chem. Biol.* **2,** 355–362.
45. Khosla, C. and Zawada, R. (1996) Generation of polyketide libraries via combinatorial biosynthesis. *Trends Biotechnol.* **14,** 335–341.
46. Hopwood, D. A. (1993) Genetic engineering of *Streptomyces* to create hybrid antibiotics. *Curr. Opin. Biotechnol.* **4,** 53–537.
47. Cane, D. E. and Xue, Q. (1996) Trichodiene synthase. Enzymatic formation of multiple sesquiterpenes by alteration of the cyclase active site. *J. Am. Chem. Soc.* **118,** 1563,1564.
48. Atuegbu, A. Maclean, D., Nguyen, C., Gordan, E., and Jacobs, J. (1996) Combinatorial modification of natural products: preparation of unencoded and encoded libraries of *Rauwolfia* alkaloids. *Biorg. Med. Chem.* **4,** 1097–1106.
49. Davies H. G., Green, R. H., Kelly, D. R., and Roberts, S. M. (1989) *Biotransformations in Preparative Organic Chemistry: The Use of Isolated Enzymes and Whole Cell Systems in Synthesis.* Academic, London, UK.
50. Faber, K. (1997) *Biotransformations in Organic Chemistry* (3rd ed.), Springer-Verlag, Berlin, Germany.
51. Hanson, J. R. (1995) *An Introduction to Biotransformations in Organic Chemistry,* W. H. Freeman, Oxford, UK.
52. Cannell, R. J. P., Knaggs, A. R., Dawson, M. J., Manchee, G. R., Eddershaw, P. J., Fellows, I., Sutherland, D. R., Bowers, G., and Sidebottom, P. J. (1995) Microbial biotransformation of the angiotensin II antagonist GR117289 by *Streptomyces rimosus* to identify a mammalian metabolite. *Drug Metab. Dispos.* **23,** 724–729.

Index

A

A54145, 441
2-Acetylglaucarubinone, 231, 232
2-Acetylneriifolin, 304, 305
Aclacinomycins, 432, 433
Aconitum forrestii, 237
Actinomadura verrucosospora, 431
Actinorhodin, 318, 319
Adrena sp., 204, 205
Adriamycin, 455
Adsorption chromatography, 15–21,
    112, 113
Affinity chromatography, 19–21
Ajugasterone, 198, 199
Ailanthinone, 231, 232
Alkaloid extraction and detection,
    221, 352, 353, 356, 357
N-Allynorreticuline, 236
Alumina, 121, 139, 140
Amberchrom CG161,CG71, 421
Amberlite, 148–151
3-Amino-1-(2-aminoimidazolyl)-
    prop-1-ene, 381, 382
Ammonium reineckate, 356, 357
Analogs, generating and looking for,
    425–458
Anion exchangers, 146, 147
Aphyllidine, 139, 140
Aplysina fistularis, 397
Aristolen-2-one, 240, 241
Artemesia annua, 212
Artemisinin, 212
Artifacts, 292, 293, 355, 356
Assays, 5–7

    overlay, 7, 240–243
Asterolasia drummondii, 235, 236
Asterolasia trymalioides, 235
Avermectins, 442–444

B

Bacillus cereus, 47
Baljet reagent, 357
Base deactivation, 184, 404
Batzelladines, 385–387
Beauveria nivea, 101, 102, 106, 107,
    441
Benzoanthracenes, 204, 205
Benzopyrenes, 204, 205
Berberis sp., 236
Bial's reagent, 222
Bioassays, 5–7, 233–243
Bioautography,
    direct, 239, 240
    overlay, 240–243, 379
Bio-Gel, 331, 334
Biosynthesis, 431–445
    blocked, 431–434
    directed, 434–445
    enzyme inhibitors, 433, 434
    halogenation, 444, 445
    mutasynthesis, 434, 435
Biotransformation, 445–456
    feeding conditions, 449, 450
    general methods, 446–451
    medium, 450, 451
    organisms for, 447, 448
Bonded phase silica, 115–117, 168–
    170
Boronia coerulescens, 236

Boronia inconspicua, 236
Boronia inornata, 234
Borntrager's reagent, 221
Broadening, peak, 195
Brunsvigia josephinae, 236

C

Calea divaricata, 234
Calystegine, 238
Capacity factor, 23, 34
Capsanthin, 275
Carbapenam carboxylic acids, 191, 192
Carbapenem carboxylic acids, 191, 192
Carbohydrates, detection of, 358
Carminomycin, 455
Cartridge columns, 153, 154, 201
Casearia tremula, 234
Castanospermine, 238
Castanospermum australe, 238
Castilleja rhexifolia, 235
Catalpol, 235
Cation exchangers, 147
CCC, *see* Countercurrent chromatography
Cellex, 148–151
Centrifugal partition chromatography, *see* Countercurrent chromatography
Cephalochromin, 173, 174, 185–187, 195–197
Cephalomannine, 255, 256
Cephalosporin C, 59, 78–80
Cephamycins, 159, 160
Centrifugal TLC, 229–231
Centrifugation, 54, 55
    settling velocity 55
Charge, 9, 10
Chemical detection methods, 219–222, 284–292, 356–358, 426
Chelex, 335
Chiral separations, 203–205

Chloromonicilin, 445
Chloropinselin, 445
Chromatography, general 14–40
    classification, 15–21
    column efficiency 24, 25, 36, 37
    detection, 21
    dispersion, 25, 26
    identification by, 30, 31
    improving separations by, 34–40
    integration, 32, 33
    low-pressure column chromatography, 111–140
        stationary phases, 114–121
        selecting conditions, 122–124
    open-column chromatography, *see* Low-pressure column chromatography
    particle size, 37, 38
    principles of, 21–30
    resolution, 28–30
    selectivity, 27, 28, 38–40
    solvent selection, 34, 35
Cinachyra, 395
Cineromycin B, 237
Cispentacin, 42, 47
Citrus decumana, 237
Clarification of broths, 54
Clerodane diterpenes, 230
Coil planet centrifuge, 248–250, 253, 254
Combinatorial biosynthesis, 318–320, 456–458
Common nonselective bioactive natural products, 285–292, 353–355, 382–385
Cotoneaster acutifolius, 235
Cotonefuran, 235
Countercurrent chromatography, 247–259
    applications, 250–252, 254–257
    instruments, 248–250

method development, 252, 253

CPC, *see* Countercurrent chromatography

CPTLC, *see* Centrifugal TLC

Crambescidins, 385–387

Critical point, 91, 92

Crossflow filtration, 57–59

Croton cuneatus, 299, 300

Cystodites, 391

Crystallization, 265–278
common problems, 270, 271
obtaining crystals, 266–271
selecting a crystal, 271–273
as separation method, 273–276

Cucurbitacins, 304, 305

Cupresol, 234

Cupressus goveniana, 234

Cyclosporin/e, 101, 102, 106, 107, 441, 442

Cytochalasins, 454, 455

D

Databases of natural products, 309–312, 344, 345

Daunomycin, 454–456

Dead-ended filtration, 56, 57

2, 3-Dehydrocephalochromin, 185–187, 195–197

13-Demethylisodysidenin, 400, 401

Dercitins, 391–393

Dercitus, 391

Dereplication, 279–327
bioassay methods, 303–309
confidence levels, 313–315
computational methods, 301–303
mass spectrometry, 294–299
separation methods, 281–284
spectroscopic methods, 293–301

Desalting and sample concentration, 137, 192, 200, 201, 262, 263

Detergent-like natural products, 285, 286

Diaion, 148–151

Diaminopimelic acid, 215

Diatomaceous earths, 56, 57

2-(2',4'-Dibromophenyl)-4,6-dibromophenol, 400, 401

Dihydrogranatirhodin, 319

Dihydrorugosinone, 236

2,9-Dihydroxyaphyllidine, 139, 140

2,8-Dimethyl-1,7-dioxaspiro[5.5]undecane, 204, 205

Dipetalolactone, 235

Diode array detection, 173

Displacement, 195–198

Distribution coefficient, 15, 19, 60, 61

Domoic acid, 339, 340

Doramectin, 443, 444

Dowex, 145, 148–151

Dragendorff's reagent, 221, 356

Dragmacidin, 366

Droplet countercurrent chromatography, 248

Drying, 263–265

Drummondita hassellii, 235

Duolite, 148–151

Dysidea herbacea, 399, 400

E

Ecteinascidin, 397, 398

Ehrlich reagent, 222

Elaiophylin, 283, 284

Eluotropic series, 35, 36

Endcapping, *see* Base deactivation

Epipentenomycin, 42, 46

Eriostemon gardneri, 236

Eriostemon myoporoides, 235, 236

Expanded bed adsorption, 74–84
adsorbents for, 77–81
methods, 81–84

Extraction, *see* Isolation

F

Fatty acids, 290, 353

Fermentation development, 411–417, 430, 431
  experimental design, 414–416
  medium development, 413, 414
  optimization of fermenter conditions, 416, 417
  scale-up, 411–413
  seed stage development, 417
  titer improvement, 413–417
  transfer to liquid medium, 411
Filter aids, 56
Filtration, 56–59
Flash chromatography, 128–130
Flavonoids, detection of, 357
Follow-up of isolation, 425–463
  complete isolation, 427–430
  further isolation, 425–430
Forestine, 237
Fractionation, 4, 5
Friedelanes, 223, 224
Fronting peak, 27
Frullanolides, 454
Fusarium sporotrichioides, 433

G
2-*O*-Galloylpunicallin, 137, 138
Gel filtration, 18, 19
Gel permeation chromatography, 18, 19
Geldanomycin, 283, 284
Gene expression, 430, 431
GLC (gas liquid chromatography), 15
Glucopiericidinols, 42, 44
Gonystylus keithii, 304
Gradient elution, 35, 36, 176, 177
Graminone B, 235
Granaticin, 318, 319
Grease, *see* Artifacts
Gualamycin, 162
Guard columns, 193

H
Halistanol sulfate, 382, 383

Halitoxin, 382, 383
Heat stability, 10
Herbadysidolide, 400, 401
High-performance liquid chromatography, *see* HPLC
High-speed countercurrent chromatography, *see* Countercurrent chromatography
Hippamine, 237
Homalium langifolium, 236
HP20, *see also* Diaion, 120, 192, 421
HPLC, 165–208, 421, 422
  buffers, 178, 179
  column selection, 175, 176
  equipment, 171–175
  fraction collection and work-up, 199–201
  isomer separation,
    enantiomers, 203–205
    positional isomers, 203, 204
  method development, 175–188
  normal phase, 168, 203, 204
  pH effects, 179–183
  recycling HPLC, 198, 199
  scale-up, 193–199
  separation modes, 166–171
  stationary and mobile phases, 167–171
  strongly retained materials, 202, 203
HSCC, *see* Countercurrent chromatography
Hydrophobic resins, 120, 121, 421
Hydrophobicity/hydrophilicity, 9
2-Hydroxyaphyllidine, 139, 140
Hydroxyeutapolide-8-*O*-angellate, 234
7'-Hydroxyseiridin, 236
Hyrtios altum, 395

I
Immunomycin, 76, 135, 136
Imperata cylindrica, 235

'Interfering' natural products, *see* Common nonselective bioactive natural products

Ion-exchange chromatography, 18, 141–164
applications, 158–163
materials, 144–146
methods, 147–158
resin cycle, 155
resin preparation, 154, 155
resin selection, 147–154
theory, 142–144

Ion-pairing/Ion suppression, 18, 177–182, 190–192

Ipsdienol, 204, 205

Isocratic elution, 176, 177

Isolation,
aims of, 2, 3, 5
general strategy, 40, 41
starting, 8–14

J

Jaspamide, 308, 309

K

K_D, *see* Distribution coefficient

Kedde reagent, 357

Kuanoniamines, 391–393

L

Lactones, detection of, 357

LC-IR, 301

Legal reagent, 357

LC-NMR, 299–301

Leonitis ocymifolia, 234

Liebermann-Buchard test, 358

Literature 11, 12, 309–312

Liquid–liquid extraction, *see* Solvent extraction

LH-20, 119, 120, 134, 135, 137, 138

Localization of compound being isolated, 11

Low-pressure column chromatography, 111–140

Lupinus argentus, 139, 140

M

Macroreticular resins, 144, 145

Maculosidine, 236

Marine natural products, 365–408
collection and storage of organisms, 370–375
initial extraction methods, 375–377
invertebrates, 375, 376
macro algae, 376
localization of metabolites, 397–401
method development, 377–379
microbial production of, 396–401
review of literature, 366–369
water-soluble compounds, 381, 382

Mayer reagent, 356

Medium pressure liquid chromatography, *see* MPLC

Milbemycins, 456, 457

Mitomycins, 441, 442

Monilinia fructicola, 445

Mobile phase, 14, 15

Molisch reagent, 358

Morus alba, 238

MPLC, 130–132, 421, 422

N

Nardoa tuberculata, 384

Naringin, 274

Nectria episphaeria, 173, 184–187, 195–197

Neoisostegane, 235

Nature of compound being isolated, 8–11

Niddamycins, 255, 256

Ninhydrin, 221

Nitrocefin, 290, 291

Nocardia, 43

Normal phase, 17, 168
Nuisance compounds, *see* Common
    nonselective bioactive natural
    products
Numbers of natural products
    identified, 312, 313

O

Okadaic acid, 400, 402
Oscillatoria spongeliae, 400
Odyendyea gabonensis, 231
OPTLC, *see* Over-pressure TLC
Overlay assays, *see* TLC, bioassays
Overload, column, 195
Over-pressure TLC, 231, 232
Oxidation/reduction inhibitors, 287–
    289

P

Packing columns, 124–126
    dry packing, 125, 126
    slurry packing, 125
Palau'amine, 161, 162
Panosialins, 290
Papaver somniferum, 236
Paromomycins, 162, 163
Parthenolide, 105, 106
Partisil 40, 192
Partition chromatography, 16, 17,
    113, 114
Partition coefficients, *see* Distribution
    coefficient
Paxilline, 307, 308
Penicillins, 64, 65
Penicillium paxilli, 307
Penicillium sclerotium, 237
Peptide-P951, 398–400
Perlites, 56, 57
Peziza, 46
Phase capacity factor, *see* Capacity
    factor
Phase-transfer catalysts, 190
Phenazine-1-carboxylic acid, 179–183

Phoma sp., 427
Phyllobotryon spathulatum, 223, 224
Phytoecdysteroids, 198, 199
Picea abies, 238
Pigments, 354
Piperine, 274
pKa, 9, 146, 147
Plackett and Burman experimental
    design, 415
Planar chromatography, 209–246
Plants, 343–363
    collection and identification, 344,
        345
    drying and grinding, 345, 346
    general methods of detection, 356–
        358
    general methods of extraction,
        348–353
    initial extraction, 346–356
        aqueous, 351
        maceration, 350, 351
        percolation, 349, 350
        solvents, 347–349
        Soxhlet extraction, 351
Plasticizers, *see* Artifacts
Plate number, *see* theoretical plate
    number
PLC, *see* Planar chromatography
Pneumocandins, 76, 137–139
Polyacridines, 387–393
Polyacrylamide, 117
Polyamines, 383, 384
Polyenes, 308
Polyphenols, *see also* Tannins, 285,
    287, 288, 357
Polystyrene stationary phases, 120,
    121, 136, 137, 145
Pradimicins, 431, 432
Preparative TLC, 223–239
Pristinamycins, 254, 255
Product capture, 53–89

Prostanthera spp., 240
Prostantherol, 240, 241
Pseudomonas aureofaciens, 443, 444
Pseudomonas aeruginosa, 179–182
Pseudonitzschia pungens, 339, 340
Psilocybe mexicana, 212
Psilocybin, 212
Ptilocaulins, 387
Ptilomycalins, 385–387
PTLC, *see* Preparative TLC
Purity, 3, 4, 261, 262
Pyocyanine, 179–183
Pyrrolnitrin, 443, 444

Q

Quantification, 7, 8
Quassinoids, 231, 232
Quinolizidines, 139, 140

R

R_f, 210
Rachelmycin, 137–139
Refractive index, 175
Retention, 22–24
Reverse phase 17, 168–170

S

Saframycin, 397, 398
Salicin, 275
Salkowski reaction, 358
Saponins, 42, 45, 290, 291, 352, 353, 358, 384
Scale-up, 409
    downstream process development, 419–422
        preliminary data, 419
    effect on downstream processing, 417–419
    extracellular products, 420, 421
    intracellular products, 419, 420
    purification, 421
Secondary metabolism, 1, 2
Seiridium sp., 235

Senna multiglandulosa, 237
Sepabeads, 421
Sephadex, 118–120, 146, 148–151, 331, 334, 335
Serjania salzmanniana, 42, 44
Serratia marcescens, 190–192
Sesquicillium sp., 188, 189
SFE, *see* Supercritical fluid extraction
Shermilamine, 392
Shinoda test, 357
Silanes, 116
Silanols, 115, 116, 182–184
Silica, 115–117, 146
Silica column chromatography, general methods, 133, 134
Size exclusion chromatography, 18, 19, 113, 134, 135, 170
Size of natural product, 10, 11
Solanine, 274
Solid–liquid separation, 54–59
    solid–liquid density differences, 55
Solid phase extraction, 12, 13, 68–74, 378
    as dereplication tool, 282, 283
Solvent extraction, 59–68
    of antibiotics, 62
    equipment, 62–64
    methods and examples, 64–68
    solvent selection, 61, 62, 68
Solvent properties, 63, 169
Solvent strength, 34, 35, 212
Solvent selectivity triangle, 38, 39
Sorangium cellulosum, 48
Soraphens, 42, 48
Sorption isotherms, 26, 27
SP200, 120
Spathulenol, 234
Spectral libraries, 173–175, 294
Spirastrella spinispirulifera, 395
Spirocardins, 41–43
Spongia sp., 394

Spongistatins, 393–396
Spongosorites, 365
Squalestatins, *see also* Zaragozic
    acids, 427–430, 437–440, 451–453
Stationary phase, 15
Steganotaenia araliacea, 235
Sternbergia lutea, 237
Sterols, detection of, 358
Streptomyces avermitilis, 442
Streptomyces caeapitosus, 441
Streptomyces djarkartensis, 255
Streptomyces fradiae, 441
Streptomyces galileus, 432
Streptomyces griseoviridis, 237
Streptomyces pristinaespiralis, 254
Streptomyces violaceusniger, 282–284
Styrene divinylbenzene, 120, 121,
    171, 421
Sulfate ester-containing compounds,
    382–385
Supercritical fluid extraction, 91–109
    applications, 103
    method development, 101–103
    sample collection, 97, 98
    sample preparation, 96
    solubility of solids in supercritical
        fluids, 92–94
    systems for, 94–98
Swinholide, 398, 399

T

Tailing, peak, 27, 184
Tannins, 201, 202, 285, 287, 288,
    291, 292, 354, 355
Taricha granulosa, 336, 337
Taxol, 106, 215, 255, 256, 298, 299,
    307, 308
Taxomyces andreanae, 215
Taxus baccata, 298
Taxus brevifolia, 215, 298, 307

Teichaxinella morchella, 382
Teicoplanins, 454
Terminalia chebula, 136
Tetracenomycin, 318, 319
Tetrodotoxins, 336–339
Thalictrum faberi, 237
Thalifaberine, 237
Theonella swinhoei, 398, 399
Theoretical plate number, 24
Thin layer chromatography, *see* TLC
Tinuvin 770, 292, 293
TLC, 209–246
    AMD, *see* Development, forms of,
    applications, 214–216, 233–239
    bioassays, 233–243
    centrifugal TLC, 229–231
    detection, 217–222, 226, 227
        stains/spray, 219–222
        UV, 219
    development, forms of, 217
        tomated multiple development,
            232
    general systems, 218
    modes of separation, 211–214
    preparative plates, 224–226
    principles, 210, 211
    recovery of products from, 227,
        228
    sample application, 226
    scale-up, 223, 224
    two-dimensional, 232, 233
Tocopherols, 203, 204
Topsentin, 365, 366
Toxic natural products, 285, 286
Tricontanol, 292, 293
Tricothecenes, 433
TSK gels, 148–151

U

UV quenching natural products, 288,
    289

Uvaria angolense, 237
Uvarindole, 237

V

Vacuum liquid chromatography, 129, 130
van Deemter equation, 26
Vitexirone, 198, 199
VLC, *see* Vacuum liquid chromatography

W

Wagner reagent, 356
Water-soluble natural products, 329–342

buffers for, 330–332
desalting, 330, 331
general methods, 329–335
heavy metal problems, 333–336

X

XAD, *see also* Amberlite, 120, 192

Z

Zalerion arboricola, 76
Zaluzania grayana, 301, 302
Zaragozic acids, *see also* Squalestatins, 160, 161, 311, 312
Zuelania guidonia, 230, 231